Collins

Collins
Complete
German

HarperCollins Publishers
Westerhill Road
Bishopbriggs
Glasgow
G64 2QT
Great Britain

First Edition 2010

Reprint 10 9 8 7 6 5 4 3 2 1 0

© HarperCollins Publishers 2010

ISBN 978-0-00-732494-1

www.collinslanguage.com

A catalogue record for this book is available
from the British Library

Typeset by Davidson Publishing Solutions,
Glasgow

Printed in Italy by LEGO Spa, Lavis (Trento)

Acknowledgements
We would like to thank those authors and
publishers who kindly gave permission
for copyright material to be used in the
Collins Word Web. We would also like to
thank Times Newspapers Ltd for providing
valuable data.

SERIES EDITOR
Rob Scriven

MANAGING EDITOR
Gaëlle Amiot-Cadey

PROJECT CO-ORDINATOR
Genevieve Gerrard

BASED ON:
Collins Easy Learning German Grammar
Collins Easy Learning German Verbs
Collins Easy Learning German Words

Collins
Complete
German

William Collins' dream of knowledge for all began with the publication of his first book in 1819. A self-educated mill worker, he not only enriched millions of lives, but also founded a flourishing publishing house. Today, staying true to this spirit, Collins books are packed with inspiration, innovation, and practical expertise. They place you at the centre of a world of possibility and give you exactly what you need to explore it.

Language is the key to this exploration, and at the heart of Collins Dictionaries, is language as it is really used. New words, phrases, and meanings spring up every day, and all of them are captured and analysed by the Collins Word Web. Constantly updated, and with over 2.5 billion entries, this living language resource is unique to our dictionaries.

Words are tools for life. And a Collins Dictionary makes them work for you.

Collins. Do more.

Contents

Foreword for language teachers

The *Easy Learning Complete German* is designed to be used with both young and adult learners, as a group reference book to complement your course book during classes, or as a recommended text for self-study and homework/coursework.

The text specifically targets learners from *ab initio* to intermediate or GCSE level, and therefore its structural content and vocabulary have been matched to the relevant specifications up to and including Higher GCSE.

The approach aims to develop knowledge and understanding of grammar and your learners' ability to apply it by:

- defining parts of speech at the start of each major section with examples in English to clarify concepts
- minimizing the use of grammar terminology and providing clear explanations of terms both within the text and in the **Glossary**
- illustrating all points with examples (and their translations) based on topics and contexts which are relevant to beginner and intermediate course content

The text helps you develop positive attitudes to grammar learning in your classes by:

- giving clear, easy-to-follow explanations
- prioritizing content according to relevant specifications for the levels
- sequencing points to reflect course content, e.g. verb tenses
- highlighting useful **Tips** to deal with common difficulties
- summarizing **Key points** at the end of sections to consolidate learning

In addition to fostering success and building a thorough foundation in German grammar, the optional **Grammar Extra** sections will encourage and challenge your learners to further their studies to higher and advanced levels.

The blue pages in the middle section of the book contain **Verb Tables** and a **Verb Index** which students can use as a reference in their work.

Finally the **Vocabulary** section in the last part of the book provides thematic vocabulary lists which can either be used for self-study or as an additional teaching resource.

Introduction for students

Whether you are starting to learn German for the very first time, brushing up on topics you have studied in class, or revising for your GCSE exams, the *Easy Learning Complete German* is here to help. This easy-to-use guide takes you through all the basics you will need to speak and understand modern, everyday German.

Newcomers can sometimes struggle with the technical terms they come across when they start to explore the grammar of a new language. The *Easy Learning Complete German* explains how to get to grips with all the parts of speech you will need to know, using simple language and cutting out jargon.

The text is divided into sections, each dealing with a particular area of grammar. Each section can be studied individually, as numerous cross-references in the text point you to relevant points in other sections of the book for further information.

Every major section begins with an explanation of the area of grammar covered on the following pages. For quick reference, these definitions are also collected together on pages xii–xvi in a glossary of essential grammar terms.

> **What is a verb?**
> A **verb** is a 'doing' word which describes what someone or something does, what someone or something is, or what happens to them, for example, *be*, *sing*, *live*.

Each grammar point in the text is followed by simple examples of real German, complete with English translations, helping you understand the rules. Underlining has been used in examples throughout the text to highlight the grammatical point being explained.

> ➤ If you are talking about a part of your body, you usually use a word like *my* or *his* in English, but in German you usually use the definite article.
>
> | | |
> |---|---|
> | **Er hat sich <u>das</u> Bein gebrochen.** | He's broken his leg. |
> | **Sie hat sich <u>die</u> Hände schon gewaschen.** | She's already washed her hands. |

In German, as with any foreign language, there are certain pitfalls which have to be avoided. **Tips** and **Information** notes throughout the text are useful reminders of the things that often trip learners up.

Key points sum up all the important facts about a particular area of grammar, to save you time when you are revising and help you focus on the main grammatical points.

If you think you would like to continue with your German studies to a higher level, check out the **Grammar Extra** sections. These are intended for advanced students who are interested in knowing a little more about the structures they will come across beyond GCSE.

Grammar Extra!

Some German adjectives are used as feminine nouns. They have feminine adjective endings which change according to the article which comes before them.

eine Deutsche	a German woman
die Abgeordnete	the female MP

⇨ *For more information on **Adjectives which can be used as nouns** and for **Feminine adjective endings**, see pages 50 and 42.*

The blue pages in the middle section of the book contains **Verb Tables**, where 127 important German verbs are conjugated in full. Examples show you how to use these verbs in your own work. You can look up any common verb in the **Verb Index** on pages 462-466 to find either the conjugation of the verb itself, or a cross-reference to a model verb, which will show you the patterns that verb follows.

Finally the **Vocabulary** section at the end of the book is divided into 50 topics, followed by a list of supplementary vocabulary.

Glossary of grammar terms

ABSTRACT NOUN a word used to refer to a quality, idea, feeling or experience, rather than a physical object, for example, *size, reason, happiness*.

ACCUSATIVE CASE the form of nouns, adjectives, pronouns and articles used in German to show the direct object of a verb and after certain prepositions. Compare with **direct object**.

ACTIVE in an active sentence, the subject of the verb is the person or thing that carries out the action described by the verb.

ADJECTIVE a 'describing' word that tells you more about a person or thing, such as their appearance, colour, size or other qualities, for example, *pretty, blue, big*.

ADVERB a word usually used with verbs, adjectives or other adverbs that gives more information about when, where, how or in what circumstances something happens, for example, *quickly, happily, now*.

AGREE (to) to change word endings according to whether you are referring to masculine, feminine, neuter, singular or plural people and things.

AGREEMENT see **agree (to)**.

APOSTROPHE s an ending ('s) added to a noun to show who or what someone or something belongs to, for example, *Danielle's dog, the doctor's husband, the book's cover*.

ARTICLE a word like *the, a* and *an*, which is used in front of a noun. Compare with **definite article** and **indefinite article**.

AUXILIARY VERB a verb such as *be, have* and *do* when used with a main verb to form some tenses, negatives and questions.

BASE FORM the form of the verb without any endings added to it, for example, *walk, have, be, go*. Compare with **infinitive**.

CASE the grammatical function of a noun in a sentence.

CLAUSE a group of words containing a verb.

COMPARATIVE an adjective or adverb with *-er* on the end of it or *more* or *less* in front of it that is used to compare people, things or actions, for example, *slower, less important, more carefully*.

COMPOUND NOUN a word for a living being, thing or idea, which is made up of two or more words, for example, *tin-opener, railway station*.

CONDITIONAL a verb form used to talk about things that would happen or would be true under certain conditions, for example, *I would help you if I could*. It is also used to say what you would like or need, for example, *Could you give me the bill?*

CONJUGATE (to) to give a verb different endings according to whether you are referring to *I, you, they* and so on, and according to whether you are referring to past, present or future, for example, *I have, she had, they will have*.

CONJUGATION a group of verbs which have the same endings as each other or change according to the same pattern.

CONJUNCTION a word such as *and, because* or *but* that links two words or phrases of a similar type or two parts of a sentence, for example, *Diane and I have been friends for years.; I left because I was bored*. Compare with **co-ordinating conjunction** and **subordinating conjunction**.

CO-ORDINATING CONJUNCTION a word such as *and*, *but* or *however* that links two words, phrases or clauses.

CONSONANT a letter of the alphabet which is not a vowel, for example, *b*, *f*, *m*, *s*, *v* etc. Compare with **vowel**.

CONSTRUCTION an arrangement of words together in a phrase or sentence.

DATIVE CASE the form of nouns, adjectives, pronouns and articles used in German to show the indirect object of a verb and after certain verbs and prepositions.

DECLENSION German nouns change according to their gender, case and number. This is called declension.

DEFINITE ARTICLE the word *the*. Compare with **indefinite article**.

DEMONSTRATIVE ADJECTIVE one of the words *this*, *that*, *these* and *those* used with a noun to point out a particular person or thing, for example, <u>*this*</u> *woman*, <u>*that*</u> *dog*.

DEMONSTRATIVE PRONOUN one of the words *this*, *that*, *these* and *those* used instead of a noun to point out people or things, for example, <u>*That*</u> *looks fun*.

DIRECT OBJECT a noun referring to the person or thing affected by the action described by a verb, for example, *She wrote* <u>*her name*</u>.; *I shut* <u>*the window*</u>. Compare with **indirect object**.

DIRECT OBJECT PRONOUN a word such as *me*, *him*, *us* and *them* which is used instead of a noun to stand in for the person or thing most directly affected by the action described by the verb. Compare with **indirect object pronoun**.

ENDING a form added to a verb stem, for example, *geh* → *geht*, and to adjectives and nouns depending on whether they refer to masculine, feminine, neuter, singular or plural things.

FEMININE one of three classifications for the gender of German nouns which determines the form of articles, pronouns and adjectives used with the noun and to refer to it. The other two classifications are **masculine** and **neuter**.

FUTURE a verb tense used to talk about something that will happen or will be true.

GENDER whether a noun, article, pronoun or adjective is feminine, masculine or neuter.

GENITIVE CASE the form of nouns, adjectives, pronouns and articles used in German to show that something belongs to someone and after certain prepositions.

IMPERATIVE the form of a verb used when giving orders and instructions, for example, *Shut the door!*; *Sit down!*; *Don't go!*

IMPERFECT one of the verb tenses used to talk about the past, especially in descriptions, and to say what was happening, for example, *It was sunny at the weekend* or what used to happen, for example, *I used to walk to school*. Compare with **perfect**.

IMPERSONAL VERB one which does not refer to a real person or thing and where the subject is represented by *it*, for example, *It's going to rain*; *It's 10 o'clock*.

INDEFINITE ADJECTIVE one of a small group of adjectives used to talk about people or things in a general way, without saying exactly who or what they are, for example, *several*, *all*, *every*.

INDEFINITE ARTICLE the words *a* and *an*. Compare with **definite article**.

INDEFINITE PRONOUN a small group of pronouns such as *everything*, *nobody* and *something*, which are used to refer to people or things in a general way, without saying exactly who or what they are.

INDIRECT OBJECT a noun or pronoun typically used in English with verbs that take two objects. For example, in *I gave the carrot to the rabbit*, *the rabbit* is the indirect object and *carrot* is the direct object. With some German verbs, what is the direct object in English is treated as an indirect object in, for example, **Ich helfe ihr** → *I'm helping her*. Compare with **direct object**.

INDIRECT OBJECT PRONOUN when a verb has two objects (a direct one and an indirect one), the indirect object pronoun is used instead of a noun to show the person or the thing the action is intended to benefit or harm, for example, *me* in *He gave me a book* and *Can you get me a towel?* Compare with **direct object pronoun**.

INDIRECT SPEECH the words you use to report what someone has said when you aren't using their actual words, for example, *He said that he was going out*.

INFINITIVE the form of the verb with *to* in front of it and without any endings added, for example, *to walk, to have, to be, to go*. Compare with **base form**.

INTERROGATIVE ADJECTIVE a question word used with a noun to ask *who?, what?* or *which?* for example, *Which instruments do you play?*; *Which shoes do you like?*

INTERROGATIVE PRONOUN one of the words *who, whose, whom, what* and *which* when they are used instead of a noun to ask questions, for example, *What's happening?*; *Who's coming?*

MASCULINE one of three classifications for the gender of German nouns which determines the form of articles, pronouns and adjectives used with the noun and to refer to it. The other two classifications are **feminine** and **neuter**.

MIXED VERB a German verb whose stem changes its vowel to form the imperfect tense and the past participle, like strong verbs. Its past participle is formed by adding *–t* to the verb stem, like weak verbs. Compare with **strong verb** and **weak verb**.

MODAL VERBS are used to modify or change other verbs to show such things as *ability, permission* or *necessity*. For example, *he can swim, may I come?* and *he ought to go*.

NEGATIVE a question or statement which contains a word such as *not, never* or *nothing*, and is used to say that something is not happening, or is not true, for example, *I never eat meat*; *Don't you love me?*

NEUTER one of three classifications for the gender of German nouns which determines the form of article, pronouns and adjectives used with the noun and to refer to it. The other two classifications are **masculine** and **feminine**.

NOMINATIVE CASE the basic form of nouns, pronouns, adjectives and articles used in German and the one you find in the dictionary. It is used for the subject of the sentence. Compare with **subject**.

NOUN a 'naming' word for a living being, thing or idea, for example, *woman, desk, happiness, Andrew*.

OBJECT a noun or pronoun which refers to a person or thing that is affected by the action described by the verb. Compare with **direct object**, **indirect object** and **subject**.

OBJECT PRONOUN one of the set of pronouns including *me, him* and *them*, which are used instead of the noun as the object of a verb or preposition. Compare with **subject pronoun**.

ORDINAL NUMBER a number used to indicate where something comes in an order or sequence, for example, *first, fifth, sixteenth*.

PART OF SPEECH one of the categories to which all words are assigned and which describe their forms and how they are used in sentences, for example, *noun, verb, adjective, preposition, pronoun*.

PASSIVE a form of the verb that is used when the subject of the verb is the person or thing that is affected by the action, for example, *we were told*.

PAST PARTICIPLE a verb form, for example, *watched, swum* which is used with an auxiliary verb to form perfect and pluperfect tenses and passives. Some past participles are also used as adjectives, for example, *a broken watch*.

PERFECT one of the verb tenses used to talk about the past, especially about actions that took place and were completed in the past. Compare with **imperfect**.

PERSONAL PRONOUN one of the group of words including *I, you* and *they* which are used to refer to yourself, the people you are talking to, or the people or things you are talking about.

PLUPERFECT one of the verb tenses used to describe something that *had* happened or had been true at a point in the past, for example, *I'd forgotten to finish my homework*.

PLURAL the form of a word which is used to refer to more than one person or thing. Compare with **singular**.

POSSESSIVE ADJECTIVE one of the words *my, your, his, her, its, our* or *their*, used with a noun to show that one person or thing belongs to another.

POSSESSIVE PRONOUN one of the words *mine, yours, hers, his, ours* or *theirs*, used instead of a noun to show that one person or thing belongs to another.

PREPOSITION is a word such as *at, for, with, into* or *from*, which is usually followed by a noun, pronoun or, in English, a word ending in *-ing*. Prepositions show how people and things relate to the rest of the sentence, for example, *She's at home; a tool for cutting grass; It's from David*.

PRESENT a verb form used to talk about what is true at the moment, what happens regularly, and what is happening now, for example, *I'm a student; I travel to college by train; I'm studying languages*.

PRESENT PARTICIPLE a verb form ending in *-ing* which is used in English to form verb tenses, and which may be used as an adjective or a noun, for example, *What are you doing?; the setting sun; Swimming is easy!*

PRONOUN a word which you use instead of a noun, when you do not need or want to name someone or something directly, for example, *it, you, none*.

PROPER NOUN the name of a person, place, organization or thing. Proper nouns are always written with a capital letter, for example, *Kevin, Glasgow, Europe, London Eye*.

QUESTION WORD a word such as *why, where, who, which* or *how* which is used to ask a question.

REFLEXIVE PRONOUN a word ending in *-self* or *-selves*, such as *myself* or *themselves*, which refers back to the subject, for example, *He hurt himself; Take care of yourself*.

REFLEXIVE VERB a verb where the subject and object are the same, and where the action 'reflects back' on the subject. A reflexive verb is used with a reflexive pronoun such as *myself, yourself, herself*, for example, *I washed myself*; *He shaved himself*.

RELATIVE CLAUSE part of the sentence in which the relative pronoun appears.

RELATIVE PRONOUN a word such as *that, who* or *which*, when it is used to link two parts of a sentence together.

SENTENCE a group of words which usually has a verb and a subject. In writing, a sentence has a capital letter at the beginning and a full stop, question mark or exclamation mark at the end.

SINGULAR the form of a word which is used to refer to one person or thing. Compare with **plural**.

STEM the main part of a verb to which endings are added.

STRONG VERB a German verb whose stem changes its vowel to form the imperfect tense and the past participle. Its past participle is not formed by adding –t to the verb stem. Also known as irregular verbs. Compare with **weak verb**.

SUBJECT the noun or pronoun used to refer to the person which does the action described by the verb, for example, *My cat doesn't drink milk*. Compare with **object**.

SUBJECT PRONOUN a word such as *I, he, she* and *they* which carries out the action described by the verb. Pronouns stand in for nouns when it is clear who is being talked about, for example, *My brother isn't here at the moment. He'll be back in an hour*. Compare with **object pronoun**.

SUBJUNCTIVE a verb form used in certain circumstances to express some sort of feeling, or to show doubt about whether something will happen or whether something is true. It is only used occasionally in modern English, for example, *If I were you, I wouldn't bother.*; *So be it*.

SUBORDINATE CLAUSE a clause which begins with a subordinating conjunction such as *because* or *while* and which must be used with a main clause. In German, the verb always goes to the end of the subordinate clause.

SUBORDINATING CONJUNCTION a word such as *when, because* or *while* that links the subordinate clause and the main clause in a sentence. Compare with **subordinate clause**.

SUPERLATIVE an adjective or adverb with -*est* on the end of it or *most* or *least* in front of it that is used to compare people, things or actions, for example, *thinnest, most quickly, least interesting*.

SYLLABLE consonant+vowel units that make up the sounds of a word, for example, ca-the-dral (3 syllables), im-po-ssi-ble (4 syllables).

TENSE the form of a verb which shows whether you are referring to the past, present or future.

VERB a 'doing' word which describes what someone or something does, what someone or something is, or what happens to them, for example, *be, sing, live*.

VOWEL one of the letters *a, e, i, o* or *u*. Compare with **consonant**.

WEAK VERB a German verb whose stem does not change its vowel to form the imperfect tense and the past participle. Its past participle is formed by adding –t to the verb stem. Also known as regular verbs. Compare with **strong verbs**.

Nouns

What is a noun?
A **noun** is a 'naming' word for a living being, thing or idea, for example, *woman*, *happiness*, *Andrew*. German nouns change, according to their <u>gender</u>, <u>case</u> and <u>number</u>. This is called declension.

Using nouns

➤ In German, all nouns are either <u>masculine</u>, <u>feminine</u> or <u>neuter</u>. This is called their <u>gender</u>. In English, we call all things – for example, *table, car, book, apple* – 'it', but in German, even words for things have a gender. It is important to know that the gender of German nouns rarely relates to the sex of the person or thing it refers to. For example, in German, the word for "man" is masculine, but the word for "girl" is neuter and the word for "person" is feminine.

<u>der</u> Mann	man
<u>das</u> Mädchen	girl
<u>die</u> Person	person

> *Tip*
> German nouns are <u>always</u> written with a capital letter.

➤ Whenever you are using a noun, you need to know whether it is masculine, feminine or neuter as this affects the form of other words used with it, such as:

- adjectives that describe it
- articles (such as **der** or **ein**) that go before it
- pronouns (such as **er** or **sie**) that replace it

➪ *For more information on **Adjectives**, **Articles** or **Pronouns**, see pages 40, 25 and 69.*

➤ You can find information about gender by looking the word up in a dictionary – in the *Easy Learning German Dictionary*, for example, you will find the <u>definite article</u> (the word for *the*) in front of the word. When you come across a new noun, always learn the word for *the* that goes with it to help you remember its gender.

- **der** before a noun tells you it is masculine
- **die** before a noun tells you it is feminine
- **das** before a noun tells you it is neuter

➪ *For more information on the **Definite article**, see page 25.*

2 Nouns

➤ We refer to something as <u>singular</u> when we are talking about just one, and as <u>plural</u> when we are talking about more than one. The singular is the form of the noun you will usually find when you look a noun up in the dictionary. As in English, nouns in German change their form in the <u>plural</u>.

> **die Katze** cat → **die Katzen** cats

➤ Adjectives, articles and pronouns are also affected by whether a noun is singular or plural.

> *Tip*
>
> Remember that you have to use the right word for *the*, *a* and so on according to the gender and case of the German noun.

For further explanation of grammatical terms, please see pages xii–xvi.

Gender

➤ In German a noun can be masculine, feminine or neuter. Gender is quite unpredictable – the best thing is simply to learn each noun with its definite article, that is the word for *the* (**der**, **die** or **das**) which goes with it:

<u>der</u> Teppich	carpet
<u>die</u> Zeit	time
<u>das</u> Bild	picture

However, there are some clues which can help you work out or remember the gender of a noun, as explained below.

1 Masculine nouns

➤ Nouns referring to male people and animals are <u>masculine</u>.

<u>der</u> Mann	man
<u>der</u> Löwe	(male) lion

➤ Seasons, months, days of the week, weather and points of the compass are <u>masculine</u>.

<u>der</u> Sommer	summer
<u>der</u> August	August
<u>der</u> Freitag	Friday
<u>der</u> Wind	wind
<u>der</u> Norden	north

➤ Most nouns referring to things that perform an action are also <u>masculine</u>.

<u>der</u> Wecker	alarm clock
<u>der</u> Computer	computer

Grammar Extra!

German nouns taken from other languages and ending in -ant, -ast, -ismus, and -or are <u>masculine</u>:

<u>der</u> Trab<u>ant</u>	satellite
<u>der</u> Ball<u>ast</u>	ballast
<u>der</u> Kapital<u>ismus</u>	capitalism
<u>der</u> Tres<u>or</u>	safe

➤ Nouns with the following endings are <u>masculine</u>.

Masculine Ending	Example	Meaning
-ich	<u>der</u> Tepp<u>ich</u>	carpet
-ig	<u>der</u> Ess<u>ig</u>	vinegar
-ling	<u>der</u> Früh<u>ling</u>	spring

4 Nouns

> **Key points**
> ✔ Nouns referring to male people and animals are masculine.
> ✔ Seasons, months, days of the week, weather and points of the compass are masculine.

2 | Feminine nouns

➤ Most nouns ending in **-e** are <u>feminine</u>.

<u>die</u> **Falte**	crease, wrinkle
<u>die</u> **Brücke**	bridge

ℹ️ Note that male people or animals ending in **-e** are masculine, and, nouns beginning with **Ge-** and ending in **-e** are normally neuter.

<u>der</u> **Löwe**	the lion
<u>das</u> **Getreide**	crop

➤ Nouns with the following endings are <u>feminine</u>.

Feminine Ending	Example	Meaning
-heit	<u>die</u> Schön<u>heit</u>	beauty
-keit	<u>die</u> Sehenswürdig<u>keit</u>	sight
-schaft	<u>die</u> Gewerk<u>schaft</u>	trade union
-ung	<u>die</u> Zeit<u>ung</u>	newspaper
-ei	<u>die</u> Bäcker<u>ei</u>	bakery

Grammar Extra!

German nouns taken from other languages and ending in -anz, -enz, -ie, -ik, -ion, -tät, -ur are <u>feminine</u>, with some exceptions.

die Dist<u>anz</u>	distance	BUT:	<u>der</u> Kr<u>anz</u>	wreath
die Konkurr<u>enz</u>	rivalry			
die Theor<u>ie</u>	theory	BUT:	<u>das</u> Kn<u>ie</u>	knee
die Pan<u>ik</u>	panic	BUT:	<u>der</u> Pazif<u>ik</u>	Pacific
die Un<u>ion</u>	union	BUT:	<u>der</u> Sp<u>ion</u>	spy
die Elektrizi<u>tät</u>	electricity			
die Tempera<u>tur</u>	temperature	BUT:	<u>das</u> Abi<u>tur</u>	A levels

---

For further explanation of grammatical terms, please see pages xii–xvi.

➤ Numbers used in counting, for example one, three, fifty are <u>feminine</u>.

> **Er hat <u>eine</u> Drei gekriegt.**   He got a three.

➤ In German, there are sometimes very different words for male and female, just as in English.

<u>der</u> Mann	man
<u>die</u> Frau	woman
<u>der</u> Vater	father
<u>die</u> Mutter	mother
<u>der</u> Bulle	bull
<u>die</u> Kuh	cow

➤ Many masculine German nouns can be made feminine by adding **-in** in the singular and **-innen** in the plural.

der Lehrer	(male) teacher
die Lehre<u>rin</u>	(female) teacher
Lehrer und Lehre<u>rinnen</u>	(male and female) teachers
der Leser	(male) reader
die Lese<u>rin</u>	(female) reader
unsere Leser und Lese<u>rinnen</u>	our readers

Grammar Extra!

Some German adjectives are used as feminine nouns. They have feminine adjective endings which change according to the article which comes before them.

> **eine Deutsch<u>e</u>**   a German woman
> **die Abgeordnet<u>e</u>**   the female MP

⇨ *For more information on **Adjectives which can be used as nouns** and for **Feminine adjective endings**, see pages 50 and 42.*

Key points

- ✔ Most nouns ending in **-e** are feminine.
- ✔ Many feminine nouns end in: **-heit**, **-keit**, **-schaft**, **-ung**, **-ei**.
- ✔ Masculine German words referring to people can be made feminine by adding **-in** in the singular and **-innen** in the plural.
- ✔ Numbers used in counting are feminine.

6 Nouns

3 Neuter nouns

➤ Most nouns beginning with **Ge-** are <u>neuter</u>.

das Geschirr	crockery, dishes
das Geschöpf	creature
das Getreide	crop

➤ Nouns ending in **-lein** or **-chen** are also neuter. These are called the <u>diminutive form</u> and refer to small persons or objects.

Endings to form the diminutive	Example	Meaning
-lein	<u>das</u> Kind<u>lein</u>	little child
-chen	<u>das</u> Häus<u>chen</u>	little house

> ℹ️ Note that if these words have one of the vowels **a**, **o** or **u**, an umlaut should be added above the vowel. The final **-e** should also be dropped before these endings

der Bach → **Bäch** → <u>das</u> **Bächlein**	(small) stream
die Katze → **Kätz** → <u>das</u> **Kätzchen**	kitten

➤ Fractions are also <u>neuter</u>.

<u>ein</u> Drittel davon	a third of it

➤ Nouns which refer to young humans and animals are <u>neuter</u>.

das Baby	baby
das Kind	child
das Kalb	calf
das Lamm	lamb

> ℹ️ Note that the animals themselves can be any gender.

der Hund	dog
die Schlange	snake
das Vieh	cattle

➤ Infinitives (the "to" form of verbs) used as nouns are <u>neuter</u>.

das Schwimmen	swimming
das Spielen	playing
das Radfahren	cycling

⇨ *For more information on **Infinitives**, see page 134.*

For further explanation of grammatical terms, please see pages xii–xvi.

➤ Nouns with the following endings are <u>neuter</u>.

Neuter Ending	Example	Meaning
-nis	<u>das</u> Ereignis	event
-tum	<u>das</u> Eigentum	property

Grammar Extra!

German nouns taken from other languages and ending in -at, -ett, -fon, -ma, -ment, -um are <u>neuter</u>.

<u>das</u> Reservat	reservation			
<u>das</u> Tablett	tray			
<u>das</u> Telefon	phone			
<u>das</u> Thema	subject, topic			
<u>das</u> Medikament	drug			
<u>das</u> Ultimatum	ultimatum	BUT:	<u>der</u> Reichtum	wealth
<u>das</u> Studium	studies			

Key points

✔ Most nouns beginning with Ge- are neuter.

✔ The diminutive form of nouns is neuter.

✔ Nouns referring to young humans and animals are neuter.

✔ The "to" forms of verbs (called infinitives) used as nouns are neuter.

✔ Nouns ending in -nis or -tum are neuter.

4 Compound nouns

What is a compound noun?
A **compound noun** is a noun made up of two or more words, for example, *tin-opener* and *railway station*.

➤ In German, these words nearly always take their gender from the <u>LAST</u> noun of the compound word.

<u>die</u> Armbanduhr (Armband + <u>die</u> Uhr)	wristwatch
<u>der</u> Tomatensalat (Tomaten + <u>der</u> Salat)	tomato salad
<u>der</u> Fußballspieler (Fußball + <u>der</u> Spieler)	footballer

Grammar Extra!

Some German nouns have more than one gender. A few nouns have two genders and sometimes one of them can only be used in certain regions.

<u>der/das</u> Marzipan	marzipan	(*der Marzipan* is used mostly in Austria)
<u>der/das</u> Keks	biscuit	(*das Keks* is used mostly in Austria)
<u>der/das</u> Kaugummi	chewing gum	

Other nouns have two genders and the meaning of the word changes depending on which gender it has.

<u>der</u> Band	volume, book
<u>das</u> Band	ribbon, band, tape; bond
<u>der</u> See	lake
<u>die</u> See	sea
<u>der</u> Leiter	leader, manager
<u>die</u> Leiter	ladder

➤ In German, abbreviations have the same gender as the word they come from.

<u>die</u> BRD	the Federal Republic of Germany (from <u>die</u> **Bundesrepublik Deutschland**)
<u>die</u> DB	the German Railways (from <u>die</u> **Deutsche Bahn**)
<u>das</u> ZDF	German TV channel (from <u>das</u> **Zweite Deutsche Fernsehen**)

Key points

✔ Compound nouns are nouns made up of two or more words and usually take their gender from the last part of the compound word.

✔ Some German nouns have more than one gender and this can affect their meaning.

✔ German abbreviations have the same gender as the words they come from.

The Cases

➤ In German, there are four grammatical cases – <u>nominative</u>, <u>accusative</u>, <u>genitive</u> and <u>dative</u>. The case you should use depends on the grammatical function of the noun in the sentence.

1 The nominative case

➤ The <u>nominative case</u> is the basic form of the noun and is the one you find in the dictionary.

Case	Masculine	Feminine	Neuter
Nominative	<u>der</u> Wagen <u>ein</u> Wagen	<u>die</u> Dose <u>eine</u> Dose	<u>das</u> Lied <u>ein</u> Lied

➪ *For more information on **Articles**, see page 25.*

➤ The <u>nominative case</u> is used for:

- the subject of the sentence, that is the person, animal or thing 'doing' the action

  <u>Das Mädchen</u> singt.   <u>The girl</u> is singing.

  <u>Die Katze</u> schläft.   <u>The cat</u> is sleeping.

- after the verbs **sein** (meaning *to be*) and **werden** (meaning *to be, to become*)

  Er ist <u>ein</u> guter Lehrer.   He is a good teacher.

  Das wird <u>ein</u> Pullover.   It's going to be a jumper.

2 The accusative case

➤ The article for feminine and neuter nouns in the accusative case has the same form as in the nominative. <u>Der</u> for masculine nouns changes to <u>den</u> and <u>ein</u> to <u>einen</u>.

Case	Masculine	Feminine	Neuter
Nominative	<u>der</u> Wagen <u>ein</u> Wagen	<u>die</u> Dose <u>eine</u> Dose	<u>das</u> Lied <u>ein</u> Lied
Accusative	<u>den</u> Wagen <u>einen</u> Wagen	<u>die</u> Dose <u>eine</u> Dose	<u>das</u> Lied <u>ein</u> Lied

➪ *For more information on **Articles**, see page 25.*

➤ The <u>accusative case</u> is used:

- to show the <u>direct object</u> of a verb. This is the person, animal or thing affected by the action of the verb.

He gave me a book. → *What did he give me?* → a book (=*direct object*)

Can you get me a towel? → *What can you get me?* → a towel (=*direct object*)

Ich sehe den Hund. → *What do I see?* → **den Hund** (=*direct object*)

Er hat ein Lied gesungen. → *What did he sing?* → **ein Lied** (=*direct object*)

- after certain prepositions (words in English such as *at, for, with, into* or *from*) which are always used with the accusative.

Es ist für seine Freundin.	It's for his girlfriend.
Es ist schwierig ohne einen Wagen.	It's difficult without a car.
durch das Rauchen wurde ich krank.	Smoking made me ill.

⇨ *For more information on* **Prepositions followed by the accusative case**, *see page 156.*

- after certain prepositions of place when movement is involved:

an	on, to, at
auf	on, in, to, at
hinter	behind
in	in, into, to
neben	next to, beside
über	over, across, above
unter	under, among
vor	in front of, before
zwischen	between

Stell dein Rad neben mein Auto.	Put your bike next to my car.
Sie legten ein Brett über das Loch.	They put a board over the hole.

[*i*] Note that when there is no movement involved after these prepositions, the dative case is used.

Sie geht in die Stadt. (*accusative*)	She's going into town.
Er war in der Stadt. (*dative*)	He was in town.

⇨ *For more information on* **Prepositions followed by the accusative or the dative case**, *see page 158.*

- in many expressions of time and place which do not have a preposition

Das macht sie jeden Donnerstag.	She does that every Thursday.
Die Schule ist einen Kilometer entfernt.	The school is a kilometre away.

- in some set expressions

Guten Abend!	Good evening!
Vielen Dank!	Thank you very much!

3 The genitive case

➤ **Der** for masculine nouns and **das** for neuter nouns change to **des**. **Ein** changes to **eines**. The endings of <u>masculine</u> and <u>neuter singular</u> nouns also change in the genitive case.

➤ **-s** is added to masculine and neuter nouns ending in **-en**, **-el**, **-er**.

<u>der</u> Wagen car → **des** Wagen**s**

das Rauchen smoking → **des** Rauchen**s**

<u>der</u> Esel donkey → **des** Esel**s**

<u>der</u> Computer computer → **des** Computer**s**

Ich mag die Farbe <u>des</u> Wagens.	I like the colour of the car.
Die Größe <u>des</u> Computers ist nicht wichtig.	The size of the computer isn't important.

➤ **-es** is added to most masculine and neuter nouns of one syllable ending in a consonant.

<u>der</u> Freund friend → **des** Freund**es**

<u>der</u> Mann man → **des** Mann**es**

<u>der</u> Sitz seat → **des** Sitz**es**

<u>der</u> Arzt doctor → des Arzt**es**

<u>der</u> Tisch table → des Tisch**es**

das Schloss castle → **des** Schloss**es**

Die Schwester <u>des</u> Arztes hilft manchmal in der Sprechstunde.	The doctor's sister helps him in the surgery sometimes.
Das Museum befindet sich in der Nähe <u>des</u> Schlosses.	The museum is near the castle.

➤ **Die** changes to **der** and **eine** to **einer** in the genitive. The endings of <u>feminine singular</u> nouns in the genitive case are the same as in the nominative.

die Ärztin (female) doctor → **der** Ärztin

Case	Masculine	Feminine	Neuter
Nominative	<u>der</u> Wagen <u>ein</u> Wagen	<u>die</u> Dose <u>eine</u> Dose	<u>das</u> Lied <u>ein</u> Lied
Accusative	<u>den</u> Wagen <u>einen</u> Wagen	<u>die</u> Dose <u>eine</u> Dose	<u>das</u> Lied <u>ein</u> Lied
Genitive	<u>des</u> Wagen<u>s</u> <u>eines</u> Wagen<u>s</u>	<u>der</u> Dose <u>einer</u> Dose	<u>des</u> Lied<u>s</u> <u>eines</u> Lied<u>s</u>

➡ *For more information on **Articles**, see page 25.*

➤ The genitive case is used:

- to show that something belongs to someone

  Das Auto <u>der</u> Frau war rot.　　　　The woman's car was red.

  Der Hund <u>meiner</u> Mutter ist ganz　My mother's dog is really small.
  klein.

- after certain prepositions which always take the genitive

  <u>Wegen</u> des schlechten Wetters　　We'll have to go home because
  müssen wir nach Hause gehen.　　of the bad weather.

  <u>Trotz</u> ihrer Krankheit geht sie　　She goes for a walk every day,
  jeden Tag spazieren.　　　　　despite her illness.

- in some expressions of time

  <u>eines</u> Tages　　　　　　　　one day

4 | The dative case

➤ **Der** changes to **dem** and **ein** to **einem** in the dative. Singular nouns in the dative have the same form as in the nominative.

  <u>dem</u> Auto　　　　　　　　　to the car
  <u>dem</u> Mädchen　　　　　　　　to the girl

➤ **Die** changes to **der** and **eine** to **einer** in the dative. Singular nouns in the dative have the same form as in the nominative.

Case	Masculine	Feminine	Neuter
Nominative	<u>der</u> Wagen <u>ein</u> Wagen	<u>die</u> Dose <u>eine</u> Dose	<u>das</u> Lied <u>ein</u> Lied
Accusative	<u>den</u> Wagen <u>einen</u> Wagen	<u>die</u> Dose <u>eine</u> Dose	<u>das</u> Lied <u>ein</u> Lied
Genitive	<u>des</u> Wagen<u>s</u> <u>eines</u> Wagen<u>s</u>	<u>der</u> Dose <u>einer</u> Dose	<u>des</u> Lied<u>s</u> <u>eines</u> Lied<u>s</u>
Dative	<u>dem</u> Wagen <u>einem</u> Wagen	<u>der</u> Dose <u>einer</u> Dose	<u>dem</u> Lied <u>einem</u> Lied

⇨　*For more information on **Articles**, see page 25.*

➤ **-e** is added to some nouns in certain set phrases.

  Wir gehen nach Haus<u>e</u>.　　　　We're going home.
  Er hat sich zu Tod<u>e</u> gearbeitet.　He worked himself to death.

Grammar Extra!

-e may also be added to the dative singular of masculine and neuter nouns to make the phrase easier to pronounce

zu welchem Zwecke?　　　　to what purpose?

➤ The dative case is used:

- to show the indirect object of a verb – an indirect object answers the question *who to/for?* or *to/for what?*

  He gave the man the book. → *Who did he give the book to?* → the man (= *noun indirect object*)

  Er gab <u>dem</u> Mann das Buch.

- after certain verbs

  Er hilft <u>seiner</u> Mutter im Haushalt. | He helps his mother with the housework.

➡ *For more information on **Verbs followed by the dative case**, see page 148.*

- after certain prepositions which always take the dative

  Nach <u>dem</u> Essen gingen wir spazieren. | After eating we went for a walk.
  Er kam mit <u>einer</u> Freundin. | He came with a friend.

➡ *For more information on **Prepositions followed by the dative case**, see page 153.*

- after certain prepositions to show position

an	on, to, at
auf	on, in, to, at
hinter	behind
in	in, into, to
neben	next to, beside
über	over, across, above
unter	under, among
vor	in front of, before
zwischen	between

  Ich sitze neben dem Fenster. | I'm sitting next to the window.
  Die Katze lag unter dem Tisch. | The cat lay under the table.

ⓘ Note that when there is some movement involved after these prepositions, the <u>accusative case</u> is used.

Er war <u>in der</u> Stadt. (*dative*)	He was in town.
Sie geht <u>in die</u> Stadt. (*accusative*)	She's going into town.

⇨ *For more information on **Prepositions followed by the accusative or the dative case**, see page 158.*

- in certain expressions

<u>Mir</u> ist kalt.	I'm cold.

- instead of the possessive adjective (*my, your, his, her, its, our* or *their*) to refer to parts of the body and items of clothing

Ich habe <u>mir die</u> Haare gewaschen.	I washed my hair.
Zieh <u>dir die</u> Jacke aus.	Take your jacket off.

⇨ *For more information on **Possessive adjectives**, see page 37.*

➤ Changes to the definite and indefinite articles **der**, **die** or **das** and **ein**, **eine** or **ein** for each case are summarized in the table below, to help make it easier for you to remember them.

Case	Masculine Singular	Feminine Singular	Neuter Singular
Nominative	der	die	das
	ein	eine	ein
Accusative	den	die	das
	einen	eine	ein
Genitive	des	der	des
	eines	einer	eines
Dative	dem	der	dem
	einem	einer	einem

⇨ *For more information on **Articles**, see page 25.*

Key points

✔ In German, there are four grammatical cases – nominative, accusative, genitive and dative.

✔ The case you use depends on the grammatical function of the noun in the sentence.

✔ The nominative case is used to show the subject of a sentence and after the verbs, **sein** and **werden**.

✔ The accusative case is used to show the direct object of a sentence and after certain prepositions.

✔ The genitive case is used to show that something belongs to somebody, and after certain prepositions.

✔ The dative case is used to show the indirect object of a sentence, and after certain prepositions and verbs.

Forming plurals

➤ In English we usually make nouns plural by adding an -s to the end (*garden* → *gardens*; *house* → *houses*), although we do have some nouns which are <u>irregular</u> and do not follow this pattern (*mouse* → *mice*; *child* → *children*).

➤ In German, there are several different ways of making nouns plural.

➤ The definite article changes in the plural, as shown in the table below:

Case	Masculine Singular	Feminine Singular	Neuter Singular	All Genders Plural
Nominative	der	die	das	die
Accusative	den	die	das	die
Genitive	des	der	des	der
Dative	dem	der	dem	den

⇨ *For more information on **Articles**, see page 25.*

> ## Tip
>
> Nouns in the dative plural <u>ALWAYS</u> end in -n, except those nouns which come from other languages. Most of their plural forms end in -s. For example:
>
> **Mit <u>den</u> Auto<u>s</u> hatte sie ständig Probleme.**   The cars caused her constant problems.

1 Feminine plural nouns ending in -n, -en, -nen

➤ Most German <u>feminine nouns</u> form their plural by adding -n, -en or -nen to their singular form.

Case	Singular	Plural
Nominative	die Blume (flower)	die Blume<u>n</u>
	die Frau (woman)	die Frau<u>en</u>
	die Lehrerin (teacher)	die Lehreri<u>nnen</u>
Accusative	die Blume	die Blume<u>n</u>
	die Frau	die Frau<u>en</u>
	die Lehrerin	die Lehreri<u>nnen</u>
Genitive	der Blume	der Blume<u>n</u>
	der Frau	der Frau<u>en</u>
	der Lehrerin	der Lehreri<u>nnen</u>
Dative	der Blume	den Blume<u>n</u>
	der Frau	den Frau<u>en</u>
	der Lehrerin	den Lehreri<u>nnen</u>

Die Blumen waren nicht teuer.	The flowers weren't expensive.
Die Lehrerinnen sind ziemlich jung.	The (female) teachers are quite young.
Das Leben der Frauen in vielen Ländern ist schwierig.	In many countries, women's lives are difficult.
Wo gehst du mit den Blumen hin?	Where are you going with the flowers?

2 Nouns with no ending in the plural

➤ Many nouns have no plural ending – these are mostly <u>masculine</u> or <u>neuter</u> <u>nouns</u> ending in -en, -er or -el.

Case	Singular	Plural
Nominative	der Kuchen (cake) der Lehrer (teacher) der Onkel (uncle)	die Kuchen die Lehrer die Onkel
Accusative	den Kuchen den Lehrer den Onkel	die Kuchen die Lehrer die Onkel
Genitive	des Kuchens des Lehrers des Onkels	der Kuchen der Lehrer der Onkel
Dative	dem Kuchen dem Lehrer dem Onkel	den Kuchen den Lehrern den Onkeln

Die Kuchen sehen lecker aus.	The cakes look delicious.
Die Onkel kommen morgen an.	The uncles are coming tomorrow.
Das war die Schuld der Lehrer.	That was the teachers' fault.
Es gibt ein kleines Problem mit den Kuchen.	There's a slight problem with the cakes.

➤ Some of these nouns also have an umlaut added to the first vowel a, o or u in the plural.

Case	Singular	Plural
Nominative	der Apfel (apple) der Garten (garden)	die Äpfel die Gärten
Accusative	den Apfel den Garten	die Äpfel die Gärten
Genitive	des Apfels des Gartens	der Äpfel der Gärten
Dative	dem Apfel dem Garten	den Äpfeln den Gärten

Die Äpfel sind nicht reif genug.	The apples aren't ripe enough.
Die Gärten waren wunderschön.	The gardens were beautiful.
Schau mal die Größe der Äpfel an!	Look at the size of the apples!
Den Äpfeln fehlt ein bisschen Sonne.	The apples need a bit of sun.

3 | Plural nouns ending in ¨-e

➤ Some masculine nouns add an umlaut above the first vowel **a**, **o** or **u** and an **-e** ending to form the plural. A few feminine nouns with **a** in the stem also follow this pattern. Nouns in this group often have one syllable only.

Case	Singular	Plural
Nominative	der Stuhl (chair) die Angst (fear)	die Stühle die Ängste
Accusative	den Stuhl die Angst	die Stühle die Ängste
Genitive	des Stuhl(e)s der Angst	der Stühle der Ängste
Dative	dem Stuhl der Angst	den Stühlen den Ängsten

Die Stühle sind neu.	The chairs are new.
Die Regierung muss die Ängste der Bevölkerung ernst nehmen.	The government has to take the population's fears seriously.
Die Farbe der Stühle.	The colour of the chairs.
Der Tischler macht den Stühlen neue Beine.	The carpenter is making new legs for the chairs.

4 | Masculine and neuter plural nouns ending in -e, -er or ¨-er

➤ Masculine or neuter nouns often add **-e** or **-er** to form the plural.

Case	Singular	Plural
Nominative	das Geschenk (present) der Tisch (table) das Kind (child)	die Geschenke die Tische die Kinder
Accusative	das Geschenk den Tisch das Kind	die Geschenke die Tische die Kinder
Genitive	des Geschenks des Tisches des Kindes	der Geschenke der Tische der Kinder
Dative	dem Geschenk dem Tisch dem Kind	den Geschenken den Tischen den Kindern

Die Geschenke sind auf dem Tisch.	The presents are on the table.
Ich muss die Kinder abholen.	I have to pick up the children.
Die Auswahl der Tische im Laden war groß.	The shop had a large selection of tables.
Sie geht mit den Kindern spazieren.	She's going for a walk with the children.

➤ Some <u>masculine</u> and <u>neuter nouns</u> add an umlaut above the first vowel a, o or u and an -er ending in the plural.

Case	Singular	Plural
Nominative	das Dach (roof) der Mann (man)	die Dächer die Männer
Accusative	das Dach den Mann	die Dächer die Männer
Genitive	des Dach(e)s des Mannes	der Dächer der Männer
Dative	dem Dach dem Mann	den Dächern den Männern

Die Dächer werden repariert.	The roofs are being repaired.
Man hatte die Männer völlig vergessen.	The men had been completely forgotten.
Was ist die Rolle der Männer in unserer Gesellschaft?	What is the role of men in our society.
Die Frauen sollten den Männern nicht immer recht geben.	Women should not always agree with men.

5 | **Some unusual plurals**

➤ There is another group of German nouns which don't follow any of the rules for forming plurals – you just have to remember them! Here are some of the most common ones. As you will see, many of them are words from other languages, and it is common for such words to form their plural by adding -s:

Singular	Meaning	Plural
das Auto	car	die Autos
das Hotel	hotel	die Hotels
das Restaurant	restaurant	die Restaurants
das Baby	baby	die Babys
das Thema	theme, topic, subject	die Themen
das Drama	drama	die Dramen
das Risiko	risk	die Risiken
der Park	park	die Parks
der Chef	boss, chief, head	die Chefs
die Firma	firm	die Firmen

Die Hotels in der Stadt sind ziemlich teuer.	The hotels in town are quite expensive.
Die Risiken sind sehr hoch.	The risks are very high.
Die Kinder finden die Babys ganz niedlich.	The children think the babies are really cute.
Was hältst du von den Preisen der Autos?	What do you think of the prices of the cars?
Das ist die Stadt mit den vielen Parks.	That's the town with all the parks.

6 Plural versus singular

➤ Some nouns are always plural in English, but singular in German.

eine Brille	glasses, spectacles
eine Schere	scissors
eine Hose	trousers

➤ These nouns are only used in the plural in German to mean more than one pair.

| zwei Hosen | two pairs of trousers |

7 Nouns of measurement and quantity

➤ These nouns, used to describe the quantity or size of something, usually remain singular, even if preceded by a plural number.

| Möchten Sie zwei Stück? | Would you like two? |
| Ich wiege fünfzig Kilo. | I weigh eight stone. |

➤ The substance which they measure follows in the same case as the noun of quantity, and NOT in the genitive case as in English.

Sie hat drei Tassen Kaffee getrunken.	She drank three cups of coffee.
Er wollte zwei Kilo Kartoffeln.	He wanted two kilos of potatoes.
Drei Glas Weißwein, bitte!	Three glasses of white wine, please.

Key points

✔ Most German feminine nouns form their plural by adding -n, -en or -nen to their singular form.

✔ Many nouns have no plural ending – these are mostly masculine or neuter singular nouns ending in -en, -er or -el. Some of these nouns also have an umlaut added to the vowel in the plural.

✔ Some masculine nouns add an umlaut above the first vowel a, o or u and an -e ending to form the plural. A few feminine nouns with a in the stem also follow this pattern.

✔ Masculine and neuter nouns often add -e or -er in the plural, and can sometimes add an umlaut above the first vowel a, o or u.

✔ There are some unusual plural nouns in German which don't follow any pattern.

✔ Some nouns are always plural in English, but singular in German.

✔ Nouns of measurement and quantity usually remain singular even if preceded by a plural number.

✔ The substance which they measure follows in the same case as the noun of quantity.

Weak nouns

➤ As we have seen, German nouns may change, according to their <u>gender</u>, <u>case</u> and <u>number</u>. This is called <u>declension</u>.

➤ Some masculine nouns have a <u>weak declension</u> – this means that they end in -en or, if the word ends in a vowel, in -n, in every case <u>EXCEPT</u> in the nominative singular case.

➤ Weak masculine nouns follow the pattern shown:

Case	Singular	Plural
Nominative	der Junge	die Jungen
Accusative	den Jungen	die Jungen
Genitive	des Jungen	der Jungen
Dative	dem Jungen	den Jungen

➤ Weak masculine nouns include:

- those ending in -og(e) referring to men

  der Psychologe — the psychologist

  Der Psychologe half ihm in seiner Krise. — The psychologist helped him through his crisis.

- those ending in -aph (or -af) or -oph

  der Paragraf — the paragraph
  der Philosoph — the philosopher

  Der Paragraf umfasste 350 Wörter. — The paragraph was 350 words long.

- those ending in -ant

  der Elefant — the elephant
  der Diamant — the diamond

  Der Diamant war sehr viel Geld wert. — The diamond was worth a lot of money.

- those ending in -t referring to men

  der Astronaut — the astronaut
  der Komponist — the composer
  der Architekt — the architect

  Um Astronaut zu werden, muss man jahrelang trainieren. — You have to train for years to become an astronaut.

- some other common masculine nouns:

der Bauer	farmer
der Chirurg	surgeon
der Franzose	Frenchman
der Kollege	colleague
der Mensch	human being
der Ochse	ox
der Spatz	sparrow

Der junge Franzose wollte Schottland besuchen.	The young French guy wanted to visit Scotland.
Ich habe den Franzosen seit einer Woche nicht mehr gesehen.	I haven't seen the French guy for a week.

Grammar Extra!

The noun der Name follows the same pattern as der Junge, except in the genitive singular, where it adds -ns instead of just -n. Der Buchstabe (meaning *letter (of the alphabet)*), der Funke (meaning *spark*) and der Gedanke (meaning *thought*) also follow this pattern.

Case	Singular	Plural
Nominative	der Name	die Namen
Accusative	den Namen	die Namen
Genitive	des Namens	der Namen
Dative	dem Namen	den Namen

Das hängt von der Wichtigkeit des Namens ab.	That depends on how important the name is.

Proper nouns

> **What is a proper noun?**
> A **proper noun** is the name of a person, place, organization or thing. Proper nouns are always written with a capital letter, for example, *Kevin, Glasgow, Europe, London Eye*.

➤ In German, names of people and places only change in the <u>genitive singular</u> when they add **-s**, unless they are preceded by the definite article or a demonstrative adjective (in English, *this, that, these* and *those*).

Annas Buch	Anna's book
Klaras Mantel	Klara's coat
die Werke Goethes	Goethe's works
BUT	
der Untergang <u>der</u> Titanic	the sinking of <u>the</u> Titanic

⇨ *For more information on **Articles** and **Demonstrative adjectives**, see pages 25 and 31.*

Grammar Extra!

Where proper names end in **-s**, **-sch**, **-ss**, **-ß**, **-x**, **-z**, or **-tz**, adding an extra **-s** for the genitive makes them very difficult to pronounce. This is best avoided by using **von** + the dative case.

das Buch von Hans	Hans's book
die Werke von Marx	the works of Marx
die Freundin von Klaus	Klaus's girlfriend

➤ **Herr** (meaning *Mr*) is always declined when it is part of a proper name.

an Herr<u>n</u> Schmidt	to Mr Schmidt
Sehr geehrte Herr<u>en</u>	Dear Sirs

➤ Surnames usually form their plurals by adding **-s**, unless they end in **-s**, **-sch**, **-ss**, **-ß**, **-x**, **-z**, or **-tz**, in which case they add **-ens**. They are often preceded by the definite article.

Die Schmidt<u>s</u> haben uns zum Abendessen eingeladen.	The Schmidts have invited us to dinner.
Die Schultz<u>ens</u> waren nicht zu Hause.	The Schultzes weren't at home.

⇨ *For more information on **Articles**, see page 25.*

Articles

> **What is an article?**
> In English, an **article** is one of the words *the*, *a*, and *an* which is used in front of a noun.

1 | Different types of articles

➤ There are two types of article:

- the <u>definite</u> article: *the* in English. This is used to identify a particular thing or person.

  I'm going to <u>the</u> supermarket.
  That's <u>the</u> woman I was talking to.

- the <u>indefinite</u> article: *a* or *an* in English, *some* or *any* (or no word at all) in the plural. This is used to refer to something unspecific, or something that you do not really know about.

  Is there <u>a</u> supermarket near here?
  I need <u>a</u> day off.

2 | The definite article

➤ In English the definite article *the* always keeps the same form.

   the book
   the books
   with *the* books

➤ In German, however, the definite article has many forms. All German nouns are either <u>masculine</u>, <u>feminine</u> or <u>neuter</u> and, just as in English, they can be either singular or plural. The word you choose for *the* depends on whether the noun it is used with is masculine, feminine or neuter, singular or plural AND it also depends on the case of the noun. This may sound complicated, but it is not too difficult.

<u>Die</u> Frau ging spazieren.	The woman went for a walk.
<u>Der</u> Mann ist geschieden.	The man is divorced.
Sie fährt mit <u>dem</u> Auto in die Stadt.	She travels into town by car.
<u>Die</u> Farbe <u>der</u> Jacke gefällt mir nicht.	I don't like the colour of the jacket.
Ich muss <u>die</u> Kinder abholen.	I have to pick up the children.
Das will ich mit <u>den</u> Behörden besprechen.	I want to discuss that with the authorities.

⇨ *For more information on **Nouns**, see page 1.*

➤ The definite article changes for <u>masculine</u>, <u>feminine</u> and <u>neuter</u> <u>singular</u> nouns.

	Definite Article + Noun	Meaning
Masculine	<u>der</u> Mann	the man
Feminine	<u>die</u> Frau	the woman
Neuter	<u>das</u> Mädchen	the girl

➤ The <u>plural</u> forms of the definite article are the same for all genders.

	Definite Article + Plural Noun	Meaning
Masculine	<u>die</u> Männer	the men
Feminine	<u>die</u> Frauen	the women
Neuter	<u>die</u> Mädchen	the girls

Tip

It is a good idea to learn the <u>article</u> or the <u>gender</u> with the noun when you come across a word for the first time, so that you know whether it is masculine, feminine or neuter. A good dictionary will also give you this information.

➤ The definite article also changes according to the case of the noun in the sentence – nominative, accusative, genitive or dative.

⇨ *For more information on **Cases**, see page 9.*

➤ The forms of the definite article in each case are as follows:

Case	Masculine Singular	Feminine Singular	Neuter Singular	All Genders Plural
Nominative	der	die	das	die
Accusative	den	die	das	die
Genitive	des	der	des	der
Dative	dem	der	dem	den

<u>Der</u> Mann ging ins Haus.	The man went into the house.
<u>Die</u> Frau geht jeden Abend schwimmen.	The woman goes swimming every night.
Sie wollen <u>das</u> Mädchen adoptieren.	They want to adopt the girl.
<u>Die</u> zwei Frauen nebenan wollen ihr Haus renovieren.	The two women next door want to renovate their house.
<u>Der</u> Mann mit <u>der</u> reichen Frau.	The man with the rich wife.
<u>Die</u> Mädchen gehen morgen ins Kino.	The girls are going to the cinema tomorrow.
Ich will nicht nur mit <u>den</u> Männern arbeiten.	I don't just want to work with the men.

Key points

✔ The definite article changes for masculine, feminine and neuter singular nouns.

✔ The plural forms of the definite article are the same for all genders.

✔ The form of the definite article also changes depending on the case of the noun in the sentence.

---

3 Using the definite article

➤ The definite article in German (**der**, **die** or **das**) is used in more or less the same way as we use *the* in English, but it is also used in German in a few places where you might not expect it.

➤ The definite article is used with words like *prices*, *life* and *time* that describe qualities, ideas or experiences (called <u>abstract nouns</u>) rather than something that you can touch with your hand. Usually, *the* is missed out in English with this type of word.

<u>Die</u> Preise sind wirklich hoch.	Prices are really high.
<u>Das</u> Leben ist schön.	Life is wonderful.
<u>Die</u> Zeit vergeht schnell.	Time passes quickly.

i Note that these nouns are sometimes used <u>WITHOUT</u> the article.

Es braucht Mut.	It needs (some) courage.
Gibt es dort Leben?	Is there (any) life there?

➤ You also use the definite article with the genitive case to show that something belongs to someone.

die Jacke <u>der</u> Frau	the woman's jacket

ⓘ Note that you do not usually use the definite article with the genitive case if the noun is a proper name or is being used as a proper name. A proper name is the name of a person, place, organization or thing.

Jans Auto	Jan's car
Muttis Auto	Mummy's car

Occasionally, the definite article IS used with proper names:

- to make the sex of the person or the case clearer

  Er hat es <u>der</u> Frau Kekilli gegeben.   He gave it to Frau Kekilli.

- where an adjective is used before the proper name

  Die <u>alte</u> Frau Schnorr ist gestorben.   Old Frau Schnorr has died.

- in certain informal situations or to emphasize something

  Ich habe heute <u>den</u> Kevin gesehen.   I saw Kevin today.

➤ In German, you have to use the definite article in front of <u>masculine</u> and <u>feminine</u> countries and districts, but you don't need it for neuter ones.

<u>Die</u> Schweiz ist auch schön.	Switzerland is also beautiful.
Deutschland ist sehr schön.	Germany is very beautiful.

Grammar Extra!

You also use the definite article when geographical names are preceded by an adjective.

<u>das</u> heutige Deutschland   today's Germany

➤ The definite article is used with names of seasons.

<u>Der</u> Winter kommt bald.   Soon it will be winter.

➤ You often use the definite article with meals.

Im Hotel wird <u>das</u> Abendessen ab acht Uhr serviert.   Dinner is served from eight o'clock in the hotel.

ⓘ Note that there are certain expressions with meals when you don't use the definite article.

Um acht Uhr ist Frühstück.   Breakfast is at eight o'clock.

➤ You also use the definite article with the names of roads.

> **Sie wohnt jetzt in <u>der</u> Geisener Straße.**　　She lives in Geisener Road now.

➤ The definite article is used with months of the year, except after the prepositions **seit**, **nach** and **vor**.

> **<u>Der</u> Dezember war ziemlich kalt.**　　The December was quite cold.
> **Wir sind seit September hier.**　　We have been here since September.

➪ *For more information on **Prepositions**, see page 153.*

➤ If you're talking about prices and want to say *each*, *per* or *a*, you use the definite article.

> **Die kosten fünf Euro <u>das</u> Pfund.**　　They cost five euros a pound.
> **Ich habe sechs Euro <u>das</u> Stück bezahlt.**　　I paid six euros each.

➤ In certain common expressions the definite article is used.

> **in <u>die</u> Stadt fahren**　　to go into town
> **mit <u>der</u> Post**　　by post
> **mit <u>dem</u> Zug/Bus/Auto**　　by train/bus/car

Grammar Extra!

In German, the definite article can be used instead of <u>a demonstrative adjective</u>.

> **Du willst <u>das</u> Buch lesen!**　　You want to read <u>that</u> book!

➪ *For more information on **Demonstrative adjectives**, see page 31.*

➤ In German, the definite article is left out:

- of certain set expressions

> **von Beruf**　　by profession
> **Nachrichten hören**　　to listen to the news

4 Shortened forms of the definite article

➤ After certain prepositions, the definite article can be shortened, though it is best to avoid using some of these forms in writing:

- **für das → fürs**
  Es ist <u>fürs</u> Baby.   It's for the baby.

- **vor dem → vorm**
  Es liegt vorm Haus.   It's lying in front of the house.

- **um das → ums**
  Es geht ums Geld.   It's a question of money.

➤ The following shortened forms can be used in writing:

- **an dem → am**
  Am 1. Mai fahren wir in die Ferien.   We go on holiday on the 1st of May.

- **in dem → im**
  Das Buch liegt im Haus.   The book's in the house.

- **zu dem → zum**
  Ich muss zum Bahnhof gehen.   I have to go to the station.

- **zu der → zur**
  Sie geht jeden Tag zur Schule.   She goes to school every day.

➡ *For more information on **Shortened forms of prepositions**, see page 165.*

Key points

✔ The definite article is used in German with:

- abstract nouns
- the genitive case to show possession
- proper names, in certain exceptional cases
- masculine and feminine countries and districts
- names of seasons and with months of the year, except after the prepositions **seit**, **nach** and **vor**
- names of roads
- meals and prices

✔ The definite article in German can be used in certain set expressions.

✔ When combined with certain prepositions, the definite article can be shortened.

For further explanation of grammatical terms, please see pages xii–xvi.

5 **Words declined like the definite article**

➤ These words follow the same patterns as the definite article:

	Nominative	Accusative	Genitive	Dative
Plural only	alle	alle	aller	allen
Singular	beides	beides	beides	beiden
Plural	beide	beide	beider	beiden
Singular	dieser, diese, dieses	diesen, diese, dieses	dieses/diesen, dieser, dieses/diesen	diesem, dieser, diesem
Plural	diese	diese	dieser	diesen
Singular	einiger, einige, einiges	einigen, einige, einiges	einiges/einigen, einiger, einiges/einigen	einigem, einiger, einigem
Plural	einige	einige	einiger	einigen
Singular	jeder, jede, jedes	jeden, jede, jedes	jedes/jeden, jeder, jedes/jeden	jedem, jeder, jedem
Plural	jede	jede	jeder	jeden
Singular	jener, jene, jenes	jenen, jene, jenes	jenes/jenen, jener, jenes/jenen	jenem, jener, jenem
Plural	jene	jene	jener	jenen
Singular	mancher, manche, manches	manchen, manche, manches	manches/manchen, mancher, manches/manchen	manchem, mancher, manchem
Plural	manche	manche	mancher	manchen
Singular	solcher, solche, solches	solchen, solche, solches	solches/solchen, solcher, solches/solchen	solchem, solcher, solchem
Plural	solche	solche	solcher	solchen
Singular	welcher, welche, welches	welchen, welche, welches	welches/welchen, welcher, welches/welchen	welchem, welcher, welchem
Plural	welche	welche	welcher	welchen

i Note that **dieser** or **jener** are used to translate the English demonstrative adjectives *this*, *that*, *these* and *those*.

- **alle, aller, allen** (*plural* only)

  Wir haben alle gesehen.

  Die Eltern fuhren mit allen Kindern weg.

  all, all of them

  We saw all of them.

  The parents went off with all their children.

- beide (*plural* only)   both
  Ich habe <u>beide</u> Bücher gelesen.   I've read both books.

- dieser, diese, dieses   this, this one, these
  <u>Dieser</u> junge Mann ist begabt.   This young man is talented.
  <u>Dieses</u> alte Haus ist wirklich schön. This old house is really beautiful.

- einiger, einige, einiges   some, a few, a little
  <u>Einige</u> von uns gingen spazieren.   Some of us went for a walk.
  Wir haben <u>einiges</u> gesehen.   We saw quite a lot of things.

- jeder, jede, jedes   each, each one, every
  <u>Jeder</u> Schüler bekommt ein Zeugnis. Every pupil receives a report.
  Sie kommt <u>jedes</u> Mal zu spät.   She comes late every time.

- jener, jene, jenes   that, that one, those
  <u>Jener</u> Junge hatte seine Brieftasche That boy had lost his wallet.
  verloren.

- mancher, manche, manches   many a, some
  <u>Mancher</u> Mann bleibt gern mit den   Some men like staying at home
  Kindern zu Hause.   with the children.
  <u>Manches</u> Auto fährt schneller als   Some cars can go faster than
  220 km/h.   220 km/h.

- solcher, solche, solches   such, such a
  Ein <u>solches</u> Mountainbike hätte ich I'd really like to have a mountain
  auch gern.   bike like that too.

- welcher, welche, welches   which, which one
  <u>Welche</u> Frau hat die Stelle bekommen? Which woman got the job?

Grammar Extra!

sämtliche and irgendwelcher also follow the same pattern as the definite article:

- sämtliche   all, entire (*usually plural*)
  Sie besitzt Tolkiens <u>sämtliche</u> Werke. She owns the complete works of Tolkien.

- irgendwelcher, -e, -es   some or other
  Sind noch <u>irgendwelche</u> Reste da?   Is there anything left? *or*
                                             Is there still something left?

➤ The words listed above can be used as:

- articles

  <u>Dieser</u> Mann kommt aus Südamerika.   This man comes from South America.
  Sie geht <u>jeden</u> Tag ins Büro.   She goes to the office every day.

For further explanation of grammatical terms, please see pages xii–xvi.

- pronouns – a pronoun is a word you use instead of a noun, when you do not need or want to name someone or something directly, for example, *it*, *you*, *none*.

Willst du <u>diesen</u>?	Do you want this one?
Man kann ja nicht <u>alles</u> wissen.	You can't know everything.
Es gibt <u>manche</u>, die keinen Alkohol mögen.	There are some people who don't like alcohol.

➪ *For more information on **Pronouns**, see page 69.*

Grammar Extra!

einiger and **irgendwelcher** end in **-en** in the genitive before masculine or neuter nouns ending in **-s**.

Er musste wegziehen wegen irgendwel<u>chen</u> Geredes.	He had to move away because of some gossip.

jeder, **welcher**, **mancher** and **solcher** can also do this or can have the usual **-es** ending.

Das Kind solch<u>er</u> Eltern wird Probleme haben.	The child of such parents will have problems.
Trotz jed<u>en</u> Versuchs scheiterten die Verhandlungen.	Despite all attempts, the negotiations failed.

➤ **solcher**, **beide** and **sämtliche** can be used after another article or possessive adjective (in English, one of the words *my*, *your*, *his*, *her*, *its*, *our* or *their*).

Ein <u>solches</u> Rad habe ich früher auch gehabt.	I used to have a bike like that too.
Diese <u>beiden</u> Männer haben es gesehen.	Both of these men have seen it.

➤ Although **beide** generally has plural forms only, there is one singular form, **beides**. While **beide** is more common and can refer to both people and things, **beides** refers only to things. **Beide** is used for two examples of the same thing or person, while **beides** is used for two different examples.

Es gab zwei Bleistifte und er hat <u>beide</u> genommen.	There were two pencils and he took both.

BUT

Es gab einen Bleistift und ein Bild und er hat <u>beides</u> genommen.	There was one pencil and one picture and he took both.

ⓘ Note that **beides** is singular in German, whereas *both* is plural in English.

Beides <u>ist</u> richtig.	Both <u>are</u> correct.

➤ **dies** often replaces the nominative and accusative **dieses** and **diese** when it is used as a pronoun.

Hast du <u>dies</u> schon gelesen?	Have you already read this?
<u>Dies</u> sind meine neuen Sachen.	These are my new things.

⟹ *For more information on **Pronouns**, see page 69.*

➤ **alle** also has a fixed form – **all** – which is used together with other articles or possessive pronouns.

<u>All</u> sein Mut war verschwunden.	All his courage had disappeared.
Was machst du mit <u>all</u> diesem Geld?	What are you doing with all this money?

➤ **ganz** can be used to replace both **alle** and **all** and is declined like an adjective.

Sie ist mit dem ganzen Geld verschwunden.	She disappeared with all the money.

⟹ *For more information on **Adjectives**, see page 40.*

➤ **ganz** must be used:

● in time phrases

Es hat den <u>ganzen</u> Tag geschneit.	It snowed the whole day long.

● when talking about geography

Im <u>ganzen</u> Land gab es keinen besseren Wein.	There wasn't a better wine in the whole country.

● with nouns referring to a collection of people or animals (*collective* <u>nouns</u>)

Die <u>ganze</u> Gesellschaft war auf der Versammlung vertreten.	The entire company was represented at the meeting.

Grammar Extra!

derjenige/diejenige/dasjenige (*the one, those*) is declined in the same way as the definite article (**der**) + a weak adjective.

⟹ *For more information on **Weak adjectives**, see page 42.*

Case	Masculine	Feminine	Neuter
Nominative	<u>der</u>jenige Mann	<u>die</u>jenige Frau	<u>das</u>jenige Kind
Accusative	<u>den</u>jenigen Mann	<u>die</u>jenige Frau	<u>das</u>jenige Kind
Genitive	<u>des</u>jenigen Mann(e)s	<u>der</u>jenigen Frau	<u>des</u>jenigen Kind(e)s
Dative	<u>dem</u>jenigen Mann	<u>der</u>jenigen Frau	<u>dem</u>jenigen Kind

derselbe/dieselbe/dasselbe (*the same, the same one*) is declined in the same way as **derjenige**. However, after prepositions, the shortened forms of the definite article are used for the appropriate parts of **derselbe**.

zur selben (=zu derselben) Zeit	at the same time
im selben (=in demselben) Zimmer	in the same room

⟹ *For more information on **Shortened forms of prepositions**, see page 165.*

For further explanation of grammatical terms, please see pages xii–xvi.

Key points

✔ There is a group of words which are declined like the definite article **der**.

✔ These words can be used as articles or pronouns.

✔ **solcher**, **beide** and **sämtliche** can be used after another article or possessive adjective.

✔ **beide** generally has plural forms only, but there is one singular form, **beides**.

✔ When it is used as a pronoun **dies** often replaces the nominative and accusative **dieses** and **diese**.

✔ **alle** also has a fixed form, **all**.

✔ **ganz** must be used instead of **alle** in certain situations.

---

6 The indefinite article

➤ In English we have the indefinite article *a*, which changes to *an* in front of a word that starts with a vowel. In the plural we say either *some*, *any* or nothing at all.

➤ In German the word you choose for *a* depends on whether the noun it is used with is masculine, feminine or neuter, singular or plural AND it also depends on the case of the noun.

Da ist <u>ein</u> Auto.	There's a car.
Sie hat <u>eine</u> Wohnung.	She has a flat.
Er gab es <u>einem</u> Kind.	He gave it to a child.

➤ It has no plural forms.

Computer sind in letzter Zeit teurer geworden.	Computers have become more expensive recently.

➤ The indefinite article is formed as follows:

Case	Masculine	Feminine	Neuter
Nominative	ein	eine	ein
Accusative	einen	eine	ein
Genitive	eines	einer	eines
Dative	einem	einer	einem

7 Using the indefinite article

➤ The indefinite article is used very much as in English.

Da ist <u>ein</u> Bus.	There's <u>a</u> bus.
Sie hat <u>eine</u> neue Jacke.	She has <u>a</u> new jacket.
Sie gab es <u>einer</u> alten Dame.	She gave it to <u>an</u> old lady.

➤ In certain situations, you do not use the indefinite article:

- when talking about the job someone does

  Sie ist Ärztin.   She's a doctor.

- when talking about someone's nationality or religion

  Sie ist Deutsche.   She's (a) German.

  Er ist Moslem.   He's (a) Muslim.

(i) Note that the indefinite article IS used when an adjective comes before the noun.

     Sie ist _eine_ sehr begabte Journalistin.   She's a very talented journalist.

- in certain fixed expressions

  Es ist Geschmacksache.   It's a question of taste.

  Tatsache ist ...   It's a fact ...

- after **als** (meaning *as a*)

  Als Lehrerin verdiene ich nicht gut.   I don't earn very much as a teacher.

  Als Großmutter darf ich meine Enkel verwöhnen.   As a grandmother, I'm allowed to spoil my grandchildren.

8 The indefinite article in negative sentences

➤ In English we use words like *not* and *never* to indicate that something is not happening or is not true. The sentences that these words are used in are called <u>negative</u> sentences.

     I <u>don't</u> know him.

     I <u>never</u> do my homework on time.

➤ In German, you use a separate negative form of the indefinite article, which is formed exactly like **ein** in the singular, and also has plural forms. It means *no/ not a/not one/not any*.

Case	Masculine Singular	Feminine Singular	Neuter Singular	All Genders Plural
Nominative	kein	keine	kein	keine
Accusative	keinen	keine	kein	keine
Genitive	keines	keiner	keines	keiner
Dative	keinem	keiner	keinem	keinen

Er hatte <u>keine</u> Geschwister.	He had no brothers or sisters.
Ich sehe <u>keinen</u> Unterschied.	I don't see any difference.
Das ist <u>keine</u> richtige Antwort.	That's no answer.
<u>Kein</u> Mensch hat es gesehen.	Not one person has seen it.

Tip

This negative form of the indefinite article is even used when the *positive* form of the phrase has no article.

| Er hatte Angst davor. | He was frightened. |
| Er hatte <u>keine</u> Angst davor. | He wasn't frightened. |

Grammar Extra!

The negative form of the indefinite article is also used in many informal expressions.

Sie hatte <u>kein</u> Geld mehr.	All her money was gone.
Es waren <u>keine</u> drei Monate vergangen, als ...	It was less than three months later that ...
Es hat mich <u>keine</u> zehn Euro gekostet.	It cost me less than ten euros.

If you want to emphasize the **ein** in the sentence, **nicht ein** can be used instead of **kein**.

| <u>Nicht ein</u> Kind hat es singen können. | Not *one* child could sing it. |

⇨ *For more information on **Negatives**, see page 179.*

Key points

✔ The indefinite article is used in German:

- to translate the English *a* and *any* in the singular
- to translate the English *some* or *any* in the plural
- in negative sentences in its separate negative form, **kein**, to translate *not* or *never*

✔ The indefinite article in German is NOT used when:

- talking about someone's job, nationality or religion, unless an adjective is used before the noun
- in certain set expressions or after **als** meaning *as a*

---

9 Words declined like the indefinite article

➤ The following words are <u>possessive adjectives</u>, one of the words *my, your, his, her, its, our* or *their* used with a noun to show that one person or thing belongs to another. They follow the same pattern as the indefinite articles **ein** and **kein**.

mein	my
dein	your (*singular familiar*)
sein	his/its
ihr	her/its
unser	our
euer	your (*plural familiar*)
ihr	their
Ihr	your (*polite singular and plural*)

➤ Possessive adjectives are formed in the following way.

	Nominative	Accusative	Genitive	Dative
Singular	mein, meine, mein	meinen, meine, mein	meines, meiner, meines	meinem, meiner, meinem
Plural	meine	meine	meiner	meinen
Singular	dein, deine, dein	deinen, deine, dein	deines, deiner, deines	deinem, deiner, deinem
Plural	deine	deine	deiner	deinen
Singular	sein, seine, sein	seinen, seine, sein	seines, seiner, seines	seinem, seiner, seinem
Plural	seine	seine	seiner	seinen
Singular	ihr, ihre, ihr	ihren, ihre, ihr	ihres, ihrer, ihres	ihrem, ihrer, ihrem
Plural	ihre	ihre	ihrer	ihren
Singular	unser, unsere, unser	unseren, unsere, unser	unseres, unserer, unseres	unserem, unserer, unserem
Plural	unsere	unsere	unserer	unseren
Singular	euer, eu(e)re, eu(e)res	eu(e)ren, eu(e)re, eu(e)res	eu(e)res, eu(e)rer, eu(e)res	eu(e)rem, eu(e)rer, eu(e)rem
Plural	eu(e)re	eu(e)re	eu(e)rer	eu(e)ren
Singular	ihr, ihre, ihr	ihren, ihre, ihr	ihres, ihrer, ihres	ihrem, ihrer, ihrem
Plural	ihre	ihre	ihrer	ihren
Singular	Ihr, Ihre, Ihr	Ihren, Ihre, Ihr	Ihres, Ihrer, Ihres	Ihrem, Ihrer, Ihrem
Plural	Ihre	Ihre	Ihrer	Ihren

For further explanation of grammatical terms, please see pages xii–xvi.

<u>Mein</u> kleiner Bruder will auch mitkommen.	My little brother wants to come too.
Wo steht <u>dein</u> altes Auto?	Where is your old car?
Er spielt Fußball mit <u>seiner</u> Tante.	He is playing football with his aunt.
Was ist mit <u>ihrem</u> Computer los?	What is wrong with her computer?
<u>Ihre</u> Kinder sind wirklich verwöhnt.	Their children are really spoiled.
Wie geht es <u>Ihrer</u> Schwester?	How is your sister?
Ich will <u>meine</u> Kinder regelmäßig sehen.	I want to see my children regularly.

Grammar Extra!

Possessive adjectives are often followed by other adjectives in German sentences. These adjectives then have the same endings as the indefinite article.

Er liebt sein alt<u>es</u> Auto.	He loves his old car.
Sie hat ihren neu<u>en</u> Computer verkauft.	She sold her new computer.
Wo ist deine rot<u>e</u> Jacke?	Where is your red jacket?

irgendein (meaning *some ... or other*) and its plural form **irgendwelche** also take these endings.

Er ist irgendein bekannt<u>er</u> Schauspieler.	He's some famous actor or other.
Sie ist nur irgendeine alt<u>e</u> Frau.	She's just some old woman or other.
Sie hat irgendein neu<u>es</u> Buch gekauft.	She bought some new book or other.
Ich muss irgendwelche blöd<u>en</u> Touristen herumführen.	I have to show some stupid tourists or other round.

Key point

✔ Possessive adjectives, one of the words *my, your, his, her, its, our* or *their*, are declined like the indefinite articles **ein** and **kein**.

Adjectives

What is an adjective?
An **adjective** is a 'describing' word that tells you more about a person or thing, such as their appearance, colour, size or other qualities, for example, *pretty*, *blue*, *big*.

Using adjectives

➤ Adjectives are words like *clever*, *expensive* and *silly* that tell you more about a noun (a living being, thing or idea). They can also tell you more about a pronoun, such as *he* or *they*. Adjectives are sometimes called 'describing words'. They can be used right next to a noun they are describing, or can be separated from the noun by a verb like *be*, *look*, *feel* and so on.

> a <u>clever</u> girl
> an <u>expensive</u> coat
> a <u>silly</u> idea
> He's just being <u>silly</u>.

⇨ *For more information on **Nouns** and **Pronouns**, see pages 1 and 69.*

➤ In English, the only time an adjective changes its form is when you are making a comparison.

> She's <u>cleverer</u> than her brother.
> That's the <u>silliest</u> idea I ever heard!

➤ In German, however, adjectives usually <u>agree</u> with what they are describing. This means that their endings change depending on whether the person or thing you are referring to is masculine, feminine or neuter, and singular or plural. It also depends on the case of the person or thing you are describing and whether it is preceded by the definite or indefinite article.

Das neue Buch ist da.	The new book has arrived.
Ich wollte es der alten Frau geben.	I wanted to give it to the old woman.
Sie erzählte mir eine langweilige Geschichte.	She told me a boring story.
Die deutschen Traditionen	German traditions

⇨ *For more information on **Cases** and **Articles**, see pages 9 and 25.*

➤ As in English, German adjectives come <u>BEFORE</u> the noun they describe, but <u>AFTER</u> the verb in the sentence. The only time the adjective does not agree with the word it describes is when it comes <u>AFTER</u> the verb.

eine <u>schwarze</u> Katze	a <u>black</u> cat
Das Buch ist <u>neu</u>.	The book is <u>new</u>.

Key points

✔ Most German adjectives change their form according to the case of the noun they are describing and whether the noun is masculine, feminine or neuter, singular or plural.

✔ In German, as in English, adjectives come before the noun they describe, but <u>AFTER</u> the verb in the sentence.

Making adjectives agree

1 The basic rules

➤ In dictionaries, only the basic form of German adjectives is shown. You need to know how to change it to make it agree with the noun or pronoun the adjective describes.

➤ To make an adjective agree with the noun or pronoun it describes, you simply add one of three sets of different endings:

2 The Weak Declension

➤ The endings used after the definite articles **der**, **die** and **das** and other words declined like them are shown below.

Case	Masculine Singular	Feminine Singular	Neuter Singular	All Genders Plural
Nominative	-e	-e	-e	-en
Accusative	-en	-e	-e	-en
Genitive	-en	-en	-en	-en
Dative	-en	-en	-en	-en

➤ The following table shows you how these different endings are added to the adjective **alt**, meaning *old*, when it is used with the definite article.

Case	Masculine Singular	Feminine Singular	Neuter Singular
Nominative	der alte Mann	die alte Frau	das alte Haus
Accusative	den alten Mann	die alte Frau	das alte Haus
Genitive	des alten Mann(e)s	der alten Frau	des alten Hauses
Dative	dem alten Mann	der alten Frau	dem alten Haus

Nominative:

Der alte Mann wohnt nebenan. The old man lives next door.

Accusative:

Ich habe die alte Frau in der Bibliothek gesehen. I saw the old woman in the library.

Genitive:

Die Besitzerin des alten Hauses ist ganz reich. The owner of the old house is very rich.

Dative:

Er hilft dem alten Mann beim Einkaufen. He helps the old man to do his shopping.

For further explanation of grammatical terms, please see pages xii–xvi.

➤ These are the plural endings of adjectives in the weak declension.

Plural	All Genders
Nominative	die alt<u>en</u> Männer/Frauen/Häuser
Accusative	die alt<u>en</u> Männer/Frauen/Häuser
Genitive	der alt<u>en</u> Männer/Frauen/Häuser
Dative	den alt<u>en</u> Männern/Frauen/Häusern

3 The Mixed Declension

➤ The endings used after **ein**, **kein**, **irgendein** and the possessive adjectives are shown below.

i Note that this declension differs from the weak declension only in the three forms underlined below.

Case	Masculine Singular	Feminine Singular	Neuter Singular	All Genders Plural
Nominative	<u>-er</u>	-e	<u>-es</u>	-en
Accusative	-en	-e	<u>-es</u>	-en
Genitive	-en	-en	-en	-en
Dative	-en	-en	-en	-en

➡ For more information on the **Possessive adjectives**, see page 37.

➤ The following table shows you how these different endings are added to the adjective **lang**, meaning *long*.

Case	Masculine Singular	Feminine Singular	Neuter Singular
Nominative	ein langer Weg	eine lange Reise	ein langes Spiel
Accusative	einen langen Weg	eine lange Reise	ein langes Spiel
Genitive	eines langen Weg(e)s	einer langen Reise	eines langen Spiel(e)s
Dative	einem langen Weg	einer langen Reise	einem langen Spiel

Nominative:

Eine lange Reise muss geplant werden.   You have to plan a long trip.

Accusative:

Ich habe einen langen Weg nach   It takes me a long time to get
Hause.   home.

Genitive:

Die vielen Nachteile einer langen   The many disadvantages of a long
Reise ...   journey ...

Dative:

Bei einem langen Spiel kann man   You can get bored with a long
sich langweilen.   game.

➤ These are the plural endings of adjectives when they have a mixed declension.

Plural	All Genders
Nominative	ihre lang**en** Wege/Reisen/Spiele
Accusative	ihre lang**en** Wege/Reisen/Spiele
Genitive	ihrer lang**en** Wege/Reisen/Spiele
Dative	ihren lang**en** Wegen/Reisen/Spielen

4 **The Strong Declension**

➤ The endings used when there is no article before the noun are shown below.

Case	Masculine Singular	Feminine Singular	Neuter Singular	All Genders Plural
Nominative	-er	-e	-es	-e
Accusative	-en	-e	-es	-e
Genitive	-en	-er	-en	-er
Dative	-em	-er	-em	-en

➤ The following table shows you how these different endings are added to the adjective **gut**, meaning *good*.

Case	Masculine Singular	Feminine Singular	Neuter Singular
Nominative	gut**er** Käse	gut**e** Marmelade	gut**es** Bier
Accusative	gut**en** Käse	gut**e** Marmelade	gut**es** Bier
Genitive	gut**en** Käses	gut**er** Marmelade	gut**en** Bier(e)s
Dative	gut**em** Käse	gut**er** Marmelade	gut**em** Bier

For further explanation of grammatical terms, please see pages xii–xvi.

Nominative:

> **Gut<u>es</u> Bier ist sehr wichtig auf**
> **einer Party.**

Good beer is very important at
a party.

Accusative:

> **Wo finde ich gut<u>en</u> Käse?**

Where will I get good cheese?

Genitive:

> **Das ist ein Zeichen gut<u>er</u> Marmelade.**

That is a sign of good jam.

Dative:

> **Zu gut<u>em</u> Käse braucht man auch**
> **Oliven.**

You need olives to go with good
cheese.

➤ These are the plural endings of adjectives when they have a strong declension.

i Note that the plural form of **Käse** is normally **Käsesorten**.

Plural	All Genders
Nominative	gut<u>e</u> Käsesorten/Marmeladen/Biere
Accusative	gut<u>e</u> Käsesorten/Marmeladen/Biere
Genitive	gut<u>er</u> Käsesorten/Marmeladen/Biere
Dative	gut<u>en</u> Käsesorten/Marmeladen/Bieren

i Note that these endings allow the adjective to do the work of the missing article
by showing the case of the noun and whether it is singular or plural, masculine,
feminine or neuter.

➤ The article is omitted more often in German than in English, especially where you
have *preposition + adjective + noun* combinations.

> **Nach kurz<u>er</u> Fahrt kamen wir in**
> **Glasgow an.**

After a short journey we arrived
in Glasgow.

> **Mit gleich<u>em</u> Gehalt wie du würde**
> **ich mir einen Urlaub leisten können.**

I'd be able to afford a holiday on the
same salary as you.

➤ These strong declension endings are also used after any of the following words when the noun they refer to is not preceded by an article.

Word	Meaning
ein bisschen	a little, a bit of
ein wenig	a little
ein paar	a few, a couple
weniger	fewer, less
einige (*plural forms only*)	some
etwas	some, any (*singular*)
mehr	more
lauter	nothing but, sheer, pure
solch	such
was für	what, what kind of
viel	much, many, a lot of
welch ...!	what ...! what a ...!
manch	many a
wenig	little, few, not much
zwei, drei *etc*	two, three *etc*

Morgen hätte ich ein wenig freie Zeit für dich.	I could spare you some time tomorrow.
Sie hat mir ein paar gute Tipps gegeben.	She gave me a few good tips.
Er isst weniger frisches Obst als ich.	He eats less fresh fruit than me.
Heutzutage wollen mehr junge Frauen Ingenieurinnen werden.	Nowadays, more young women want to be engineers.
Solche leckere Schokolade habe ich schon lange nicht mehr gegessen.	I haven't had such good chocolate for a long time.
Wir haben viel kostbare Zeit verschwendet.	We have wasted a lot of valuable time.
Welch herrliches Wetter!	What wonderful weather!

➤ With **wenig** and numbers from **zwei** onwards, adjectives behave as follows:

- Strong, when there is no article:

Es gab damals nur wenig frisch**es** Obst.	There was little fresh fruit at that time.
Zwei klein**e** Jungen kamen die Straße entlang.	Two small boys came along the street.

- Weak, when the definite article comes first:

<u>Das</u> wenige frisch**e** Obst, das es damals gab, war teuer.	The little fresh fruit that was available then, was expensive.
<u>Die</u> zwei klein**en** Jungen, die die Straße entlangkamen.	The two small boys who came along the street.

- Mixed, when a possessive adjective comes first:

<u>Meine</u> zwei klein**en** Jungen sind manchmal frech.	My two small sons are cheeky sometimes.

➤ These strong declension endings also need to be used after possessives where no other word shows the case of the following noun and whether it's masculine, feminine or neuter, singular or plural.

Sebastians alt**es** Buch lag auf dem Tisch.	Sebastian's old book was lying on the table.
Mutters neu**er** Computer sieht toll aus.	Mother's new computer looks great.

Tip

When these various endings are added to adjectives, you have to watch out for some spelling changes.

When endings are added to the adjective **hoch**, meaning *high*, the simple form changes to **hoh**.

Das Gebäude ist hoch.	The building is high.
Das ist ein hohes Gebäude.	That is a high building.

Adjectives ending in **-el** lose the **-e** when endings are added.

Das Zimmer ist dunkel.	The room is dark.
Man sieht nichts in dem dunklen Zimmer.	You can't see anything in the dark room.

Adjectives ending in **-er** often lose the **-e** when endings are added.

Das Auto war teuer.	The car was expensive.
Sie kaufte ein teures Auto.	She bought an expensive car.

> **Key points**
>
> ✔ To make an adjective agree with the noun it is describing, you simply add one of three sets of endings: weak, mixed or strong.
>
> ✔ Strong endings are also used after particular words when not preceded by an article, for example, **ein bisschen**, **ein paar**, **wenig** and after possessive adjectives.

5 **Participles as adjectives**

➤ In English, the present participle is a verb form ending in *-ing*, which may be used as an adjective or a noun. In German, you simply add **-d** to the infinitive of the verb to form the present participle, which may then be used as an adjective with all the usual endings.

Auf dem Tisch stand ein Foto von einem <u>lachenden</u> Kind.	There was a photo of a laughing child on the table.

ℹ Note that the present participles of **sein** and **haben** cannot be used like this.

➤ The past participle of a verb can also be used as an adjective.

Meine Mutter hat meine <u>verlorenen</u> Sachen gefunden.	My mother found my lost things.

⇨ *For more information on **Past participles**, see page 113.*

6 **Adjectives preceded by the dative case**

➤ With many adjectives you use the dative case, for example:

- **ähnlich**   similar to
  Er ist seinem Vater sehr ähnlich.   He's very like his father.

- **bekannt**   familiar to
  Sie kommt mir bekannt vor.   She seems familiar to me.

- **dankbar**   grateful to
  Ich bin dir sehr dankbar.   I'm very grateful to you.

- **fremd**   strange, alien to
  Das ist mir fremd.   That's alien to me.

- **gleich**   all the same to/like
  Es ist mir gleich.   It's all the same to me.

- leicht　　　　easy for
  Du machst es dir wirklich zu leicht.　　You really make things too easy for yourself.

- nah(e)　　　close to
  Unser Haus ist nahe der Universität.　　Our house is near the university.

- peinlich　　　embarrassing for
  Das war ihr aber peinlich.　　She was really embarrassed.

- unbekannt　　unknown to
  Das war mir unbekannt.　　I didn't know that.

Key points

✔ In German, both present and past participles can also be used as adjectives.

✔ With many German adjectives you use the dative case.

Adjectives used as nouns

➤ All adjectives in German, and participles used as adjectives, can also be used as nouns. These are often called <u>adjectival nouns</u>.

➤ Adjectives and participles used as nouns have:

- a capital letter like other nouns

  Der neue Angestellte ist früh angekommen.

  The new employee arrived early.

- weak, strong or mixed endings, depending on which article, if any, comes before them

  Sie ist die neue Angestellte.

  She is the new employee.

  Das Gute daran ist, dass ich mehr verdiene.

  The good thing about it is that I'm earning more.

  Es bleibt beim Alten.

  Things remain as they were.

Key points

✔ Adjectives in German, and participles used as adjectives, can also be used as nouns. These are often called <u>adjectival nouns</u>.

✔ <u>Adjectival nouns</u> begin with a capital letter and take the same endings as normal adjectives.

For further explanation of grammatical terms, please see pages xii–xvi.

Some other points about adjectives

1 Adjectives describing nationality

➤ These are not spelt with a capital letter in German except in public or official names.

Die deutsche Sprache ist schön.	The German language is beautiful.
Das französische Volk war entsetzt.	The people of France were horrified.
BUT:	
Die Deutsche Bahn hat Erfolg.	The German railways are successful.

➤ However, when these adjectives are used as nouns to refer to a language, a capital letter is used.

Sie sprechen kein Englisch.	They don't speak English.

➤ In German, for expressions like *he is English/he is German etc* a noun or adjectival noun is used instead of an adjective.

Er ist Deutscher.	He is German.
Sie ist Deutsche.	She is German.

2 Adjectives taken from place names

➤ These are formed by adding **-er** to names of towns. They never change by adding endings to show case.

Kölner, Frankfurter, Berliner *etc*	from Cologne, Frankfurt, Berlin *etc*
Der Kölner Dom ist wirklich beeindruckend.	Cologne cathedral is really impressive.
Ich möchte ein Frankfurter Würstchen.	I'd like a frankfurter sausage.

➤ Adjectives from **die Schweiz**, meaning Switzerland, and some other regions can also be formed in this way.

Schweizer Käse mag ich gern.	I really like Swiss cheese.

➤ Adjectives like these can be used as nouns denoting the inhabitants of a town, in which case they take the same endings as normal nouns.

Die Sprache des Kölners heißt Kölsch.	People from Cologne speak Kölsch.
Die Entscheidung wurde von den Frankfurtern begrüsst.	People from Frankfurt welcomed the decision.

i Note that the feminine form of such nouns is formed by adding **-in** in the singular and **-innen** in the plural.

Christine, die Londonerin war, wollte nach Glasgow ziehen.	Christine, who was from London, wanted to move to Glasgow.

52 Adjectives

Comparatives of adjectives

> **What is a comparative adjective?**
> A **comparative adjective** in English is one with -er added to it or *more* or *less* in front of it, that is used to compare people or things, for example, *slower, more beautiful*.

➤ In German, to say that something is *easier, more expensive* and so on, you add -er to the simple form of most adjectives.

einfach → einfacher

Das war viel einfacher für dich.	That was much easier for you.

[i] Note that adjectives whose simple form ends in **-en** or **-er** may drop the final -e to form the comparative, as in **teurer**.

teuer → teurer

Diese Jacke ist teurer.	This jacket is more expensive.

➤ To introduce the person or thing you are making the comparison with, use **als** (meaning *than*).

Er ist kleiner als seine Schwester.	He is smaller than his sister.
Diese Frage ist einfacher als die erste.	This question is easier than the first one.

➤ To say that something or someone is *as ... as* something or someone else, you use **so ... wie** or **genauso ... wie**, if you want to make it more emphatic. To say *not as ... as*, you use **nicht so ... wie**.

Sie ist so gut wie ihr Bruder.	She is as good as her brother.
Er war genauso glücklich wie ich.	He was just as happy as I was.
Sie ist nicht so alt wie du.	She is not as old as you.

➤ Here are some examples of commonly used adjectives which have a vowel change in the comparative form:

Adjective	Meaning	Comparative	Meaning
alt	old	älter	older
stark	strong	stärker	stronger
schwach	weak	schwächer	weaker
scharf	sharp	schärfer	sharper
lang	long	länger	longer
kurz	short	kürzer	shorter
warm	warm	wärmer	warmer
kalt	cold	kälter	colder
hart	hard	härter	harder
groß	big	größer	bigger

➤ Adjectives whose simple form ends in **-el** lose the -e before adding the comparative ending **-er**.

eitel → eitler	vain → vainer
Er ist eitler als ich.	He is vainer than me.
dunkel → dunkler	dark → darker
Deine Haare sind dunkler als ihre.	Your hair is darker than hers.

➤ When used before the noun, comparative forms of adjectives take the same weak, strong or mixed endings as their simple forms.

Die jüngere Schwester ist größer als die ältere.	The younger sister is bigger than the older one.
Mein jüngerer Bruder geht jetzt zur Schule.	My younger brother goes to school now.

⇨ For more information on **Making adjectives agree**, see pages 42-48.

Grammar Extra!

➤ With a few adjectives, comparative forms may also be used to translate the idea of -ish or rather ...

Comparative	Meaning
älter	elderly
dünner	thinnish
dicker	fattish
größer	largish
jünger	youngish
kleiner	smallish
kürzer	shortish
neuer	newish

Eine ältere Frau kam die Straße entlang.	An elderly woman was coming along the street.
Er war von jüngerem Aussehen.	He was of youngish appearance.

Key points

✔ In German, to form the comparative you add **-er** to the simple form of most adjectives.

✔ To compare people or things in German, you use so ... wie, genauso ... wie, if you want to make it more emphatic, or nicht so ... wie.

✔ *Than* in comparatives corresponds to **als**.

✔ There is a change in the vowel in many of the simple forms of German adjectives when forming their comparatives.

✔ Adjectives whose simple form ends in **-el**, such as **dunkel**, lose the **-e** before adding the comparative ending **-er**.

For further explanation of grammatical terms, please see pages xii–xvi.

Superlatives of adjectives

> **What is a superlative adjective?**
> A **superlative adjective** in English is one with -*est* on the end of it or *most* or *least* in front of it, that is used to compare people or things, for example, *thinnest*, *most beautiful*.

➤ In German, to say that something or someone is *easiest, youngest, most expensive* and so on, you add -**st** to the simple form of the adjective. As with comparative forms, the vowel in the simple form can change. Superlative forms are generally used with the definite article and take the same weak endings as their simple forms.

Deine Hausaufgaben waren die einfach<u>sten</u>.	Your homework was easiest.
Sie ist die Jüng<u>ste</u> in der Familie.	She is the youngest in the family.
Ich wollte die teuer<u>ste</u> Jacke im Laden kaufen.	I wanted to buy the most expensive jacket in the shop.

➤ Adjectives ending in -**t**, -**tz**, -**z**, -**sch**, -**ss** or -**ß** form the superlative by adding -**est** instead of -**st**.

der/die/das schlechteste	the worst
Das war der schlecht<u>este</u> Film seit Jahren.	That was the worst film in years.
der/die/das schmerzhafteste	the most painful
Das war ihre schmerzhaft<u>este</u> Verletzung.	That was her most painful injury.
der/die/das süßeste	the sweetest
Ich möchte den süß<u>esten</u> Nachtisch.	I would like the sweetest dessert.
der/die/das stolzeste	the proudest
Sie war die stolz<u>este</u> Mutter in der Gegend.	She was the proudest mother in the area.
der/die/das frischeste	the freshest
Für dieses Rezept braucht man das frisch<u>este</u> Obst.	You need the freshest fruit for this recipe.

➤ Adjectives ending in -**eu** and -**au** also add -**est** to form the superlative.

der/die/das neueste	the newest, the latest
Ich brauche die neu<u>este</u> Ausgabe des Wörterbuchs.	I need the latest edition of the dictionary.
der/die/das schlaueste	the cleverest
Sie ist die schlau<u>este</u> Schülerin in der Klasse.	She is the cleverest student in the class.

➤ The English superlative *most*, meaning *very*, can be expressed in German by any of the following words.

Superlative	Meaning
äußerst	extremely
sehr	very
besonders	especially
außerordentlich	exceptionally
höchst	extremely (not used with words of one syllable)
furchtbar	terribly (used only in conversation)
richtig	really/most (used only in conversation)

Sie ist ein äußerst begabter Mensch.	She is a most gifted person.
Das Essen war besonders schlecht.	The food was really dreadful.
Der Wein war furchtbar teuer.	The wine was terribly expensive.
Das sieht richtig komisch aus.	That looks really funny.

Tip

Just as English has some irregular comparative and superlative forms – *better* instead of '*more good*', and *worst* instead of '*most bad*' – German also has a few irregular forms.

Adjective	Meaning	Comparative	Meaning	Superlative	Meaning
gut	good	besser	better	der beste	the best
hoch	high	höher	higher	der höchste	the highest
viel	much/a lot	mehr	more	der meiste	the most
nah	near	näher	nearer	der nächste	the nearest

Ich habe eine bessere Idee.	I have a better idea.
Wo liegt der nächste Bahnhof?	Where is the nearest station?

Key points

✔ Most German superlatives are formed by adding -st to the simple form of the adjective.

✔ Adjectives ending in -t, -tz, -z, -sch, -ss, -ß, -eu or -au, form the superlative by adding -est instead of -st.

✔ Gut, hoch, viel and nah have irregular comparative and superlative forms: gut/besser/der beste, hoch/höher/der höchste, viel/mehr/der meiste, nah/näher/der nächste.

Adverbs

What is an adverb?
An **adverb** is a word usually used with verbs, adjectives or other adverbs that gives more information about when, how, where, or in what circumstances something happens: *quickly, happily, now* are all adverbs.

How adverbs are used

➤ In general, adverbs are used together with:

- verbs (*act <u>quickly</u>, speak <u>strangely</u>, smile <u>cheerfully</u>*)
- adjectives (*<u>rather</u> ill, <u>a lot</u> better, <u>deeply</u> sorry*)
- other adverbs (*<u>really</u> fast, <u>too</u> quickly, <u>very</u> well*)

➤ Adverbs can also relate to the whole sentence; they often tell you what the speaker is thinking or feeling.

<u>Fortunately,</u> Jan had already left.

<u>Actually,</u> I don't think I'll come.

How adverbs are formed

The basic rules

➤ Many English adverbs end in -ly, which is added to the end of the adjective (*quick → quickly; sad → sadly; frequent → frequently*).

➤ In contrast, most German adverbs used to comment on verbs are simply adjectives used as adverbs. And the good news is that unlike adjectives, they do not change by adding different endings.

Habe ich das <u>richtig</u> gehört?	Did I hear that correctly?
Er war <u>schick</u> angezogen.	He was stylishly dressed.

➤ A small number of German adverbs which do not directly comment on the verb are formed by adding **-weise** or **-sweise** to a noun.

58 Adverbs

Noun	Meaning	Adverb	Meaning
das Beispiel	example	beispielsweise	for example
die Beziehung	relation, connection	beziehungsweise	or/or rather/ that is to say
der Schritt	step	schrittweise	step by step
die Zeit	time	zeitweise	at times
der Zwang	compulsion	zwangsweise	compulsorily

Grammar Extra!

Some German adverbs are also formed by adding **-erweise** to an uninflected adjective. These adverbs are mainly used by the person speaking to express an opinion.

Adjective	Meaning	Adverb	Meaning
erstaunlich	astonishing	erstaunlicherweise	astonishingly enough
glücklich	happy, fortunate	glücklicherweise	fortunately
komisch	strange, funny	komischerweise	strangely enough

➤ There is another important group of adverbs which are NOT formed from adjectives or nouns, for example, words like **unten**, **oben** and **leider**.

Das beste Buch lag <u>unten</u> auf dem Stapel.	The best book was at the bottom of the pile.
Die Schlafzimmer sind <u>oben</u>.	The bedrooms are upstairs.
Ich kann <u>leider</u> nicht kommen.	Unfortunately I can't come.

➤ Adverbs of time fit into this category and the following are some common ones:

Adverb of time	Meaning
endlich	finally
heute	today
immer	always
morgen	tomorrow
morgens	in the mornings
sofort	at once

Sie kann erst <u>morgen</u> kommen.	She can't come till tomorrow.
Priska hat <u>immer</u> Hunger.	Priska is always hungry.
Ja, ich mache das <u>sofort</u>.	Yes, I'll do it at once.

For further explanation of grammatical terms, please see pages xii–xvi.

➤ Adverbs often express the idea of 'to what extent', for example, words in English like *extremely* and *especially*. These are sometimes called adverbs of degree. Some common adverbs of this type in German are:

Adverb of degree	Meaning
äußerst	extremely
besonders	especially
beträchtlich	considerably
fast	almost
kaum	hardly, scarcely
ziemlich	fairly

> **Es hat mir nicht <u>besonders</u> gefallen.**   I didn't particularly like it.
> **Ich bin <u>fast</u> fertig.**   I'm almost finished.
> **Er war <u>ziemlich</u> sauer.**   He was quite angry.

Adverbs of place

➤ Adverbs of place are words such as *where?*, *there*, *up*, *nowhere*. German adverbs of place behave very differently from their English counterparts in the following ways:

- Where there is no movement involved and the adverb is simply referring to a location, you use the form of the adverb you find in the dictionary.

<u>Wo</u> ist sie?	Where is she?
Sie sind nicht <u>da</u>.	They're not there.
<u>Hier</u> darf man nicht parken.	You can't park here.

- To show some movement AWAY from the person speaking, you use the adverb **hin**.

Oliver und Andrea geben heute eine Party. Gehen wir <u>hin</u>?	Oliver and Andrea are having a party today. Shall we go?

In German, **hin** is often added to another adverb to create what are called compound adverbs, which show there is some movement involved. In English, we would just use adverbs in this case.

Compound adverb	Meaning
dahin	(to) there
dorthin	there
hierhin	here
irgendwohin	(to) somewhere or other
überallhin	everywhere
wohin?	where (to)?

<u>Wohin</u> fährst du?	Where are you going?
Sie liefen <u>überallhin</u>.	They ran everywhere.

- To show some movement TOWARDS the person speaking, you use the adverb **her**. As with **hin**, this is often added to another adverb.

Compound adverb	Meaning
daher	from there
hierher	here
irgendwoher	from somewhere or other
überallher	from all over
woher?	where from?

<u>Woher</u> kommst du?	Where do you come from?
<u>Woher</u> hast du das?	Where did you get that from?
Das habe ich <u>irgendwoher</u> gekriegt.	I got that from somewhere or other.

For further explanation of grammatical terms, please see pages xii–xvi.

Key points

✔ Many German adverbs are simply adjectives used as adverbs, but they are not declined, unlike adjectives.

✔ In German, some adverbs are formed by adding -weise or -sweise to a noun.

✔ Compound adverbs formed by adding hin or her are often used to show movement away from or towards the person speaking (or writing).

Comparatives and superlatives of adverbs

1 Comparative adverbs

> **What is a comparative adverb?**
> A **comparative adverb** is one which, in English, has *-er* on the end of it or *more* or *less* in front of it, for example, *earlier, later, sooner, more/less frequently*.

➤ Adverbs can be used to make comparisons in German, just as they can in English. The comparative of adverbs is formed in exactly the same way as that of adjectives, that is by adding **-er** to the basic form. **Als** is used for *than*.

Sie läuft schneller als ihr Bruder.	She runs faster than her brother.
Ich sehe ihn seltener als früher.	I see him less often than before.

➤ To make *as … as* or *not as … as* comparisons with adverbs, you use the same phrases as with adjectives.

- **so … wie**   as … as

Er läuft so schnell wie sein Bruder.	He runs as fast as his brother.

- **nicht so … wie**   not as … as

Sie kann nicht so gut schwimmen wie du.	She can't swim as well as you.

➤ The idea of *more and more …* is expressed in German by using **immer** and the comparative form.

Die Männer sprachen immer lauter.	The men were talking louder and louder.

➤ *the more … the more …* is expressed in German by **je … desto …** or **je … umso …**

Je eher, desto besser.	The sooner the better.
Je schneller sie fährt, umso mehr Angst habe ich!	The faster she drives, the more frightened I am!

⇨ *For more information on **Comparative adjectives**, see page 53.*

2 Superlative adverbs

> **What is a superlative adverb?**
> A **superlative adverb** is one which, in English, has *-est* on the end of it or *most* or *least* in front of it, for example, *soonest, fastest, most/least frequently.*

➤ The superlative of adverbs in German is formed in the following way and, unlike adjectives, is not declined:

am + *adverb* + **-sten**

Wer von ihnen arbeitet am schnellsten?	Which of them works fastest?
Er hat es am langsamsten gemacht.	He did it slowest.

➤ Adverbs ending in **-d, -t, -tz, -z, -sch, -ss**, or **-ß** form the superlative by adding **-esten**. This makes pronunciation easier.

Das Erdbeereis war bei den Kindern am beliebtesten.	The strawberry ice cream was the most popular one with the kids.
Am heißesten war es im Südspanien.	It was hottest in southern Spain.

➪ For more information on **Superlative adjectives**, see page 55.

[i] Note that some superlative adverbs are used to show the extent of a quality rather than a comparison. The following adverbs are used in this way:

Adverb	Meaning
bestens	very well
höchstens	at the most/at best
meistens	mostly/most often
spätestens	at the latest
wenigstens	at least

Die Geschäfte gehen bestens.	Business is going very well.
Er kommt meistens zu spät an.	He usually arrives late.
Wenigstens bekomme ich mehr Geld dafür.	At least I'm getting more money for it.

3 **Adverbs with irregular comparatives and superlatives**

➤ A few German adverbs have irregular comparative and superlative forms.

Adverb	Meaning	Comparative	Meaning	Superlative	Meaning
gern	well	lieber	better	am liebsten	best
bald	soon	eher	sooner	am ehesten	soonest
viel	much, a lot	mehr	more	am meisten	most

<u>Am liebsten</u> lese ich Kriminalromane.   I like detective stories best.

Sie hat <u>am meisten</u> gewonnen.   She won the most.

Key points

✔ Comparatives of adverbs are formed in the same way as comparatives of adjectives, adding **-er** to the basic form.

✔ To compare people or things, you use **so … wie**, **ebenso … wie** or **nicht so … wie**.

✔ *Than* in comparatives of adverbs corresponds to **als**.

✔ Superlatives of adverbs are formed by using the formula **am** + *adverb* + **-sten/-esten**.

✔ Unlike adjectives, adverbs do not change their form to agree with the verb, adjective or other adverb they relate to.

Word order with adverbs

➤ In English, adverbs can come in different places in a sentence.

  I'm <u>never</u> coming back.

  See you <u>soon</u>!

  <u>Suddenly</u> the phone rang.

  I'd <u>really</u> like to come.

➤ This is also true of adverbs in German, but as a general rule they are placed close to the word to which they refer.

  ● Adverbs of <u>time</u> often come first in the sentence, but this is not fixed.

    <u>Morgen</u> gehen wir ins Theater OR:

    Wir gehen <u>morgen</u> ins Theater.　　We're going to the theatre tomorrow.

  ● Adverbs of <u>place</u> can be put at the beginning of a sentence to provide emphasis.

    <u>Dort</u> haben sie Fußball gespielt OR:

    Sie haben <u>dort</u> Fußball gespielt　　They played football there.

  ● Adverbs of <u>manner</u> are adverbs which comment on verbs. These are likely to come <u>after</u> the verb to which they refer, but in tenses which are made up of **haben** or **sein** + the past participle of the main verb, they come immediately <u>before</u> the past participle.

Sie spielen <u>gut</u>.	They play well.
Sie haben heute <u>gut</u> gespielt.	They played well today.
Du benimmst dich immer <u>schlecht</u>.	You always behave badly.
Du hast dich <u>schlecht</u> benommen.	You have behaved badly.

➪ *For more information on **Forming the past participle**, see page 114.*

➤ Where there is more than one adverb in a sentence, it's useful to remember the following rule:

  "time, manner, place"

  Wir haben <u>gestern</u> <u>gut</u> <u>dorthin</u> gefunden.　　We found our way there all right yesterday.

  gestern = adverb of time
  gut = adverb of manner
  dorthin = adverb of place

➤ Where there is a pronoun object (a word like *her, it, me* or *them*) in a sentence, it comes before all adverbs.

> **Sie haben es gestern sehr billig gekauft.**
>
> They bought it very cheaply yesterday.
>
> **es** = pronoun object
> **gestern** = adverb of time
> **billig** = adverb of manner

⇨ *For more information on **Pronoun objects**, see page 74.*

Key points

✔ In German, the position of adverbs in a sentence is not fixed, but they generally come close to the words they refer to.

✔ Where there is more than one adverb in a sentence, it is useful to remember the rule: time, manner, place.

✔ Where there is a pronoun object in a sentence, it comes before all adverbs.

Emphasizers

> **What is an emphasizer?**
> An **emphasizer** is a type of word commonly used in both German and English, especially in the spoken language, to emphasize or change the meaning of a sentence.

➤ The following words are the most common emphasizers.

- **aber** is used to add emphasis to a statement

  Das ist <u>aber</u> schön!   Oh, that's pretty!
  Diese Jacke ist <u>aber</u> teuer! This jacket is really expensive!

- **denn** is also used as a conjunction, but here it is used as an adverb to emphasize the meaning.

  Was ist <u>denn</u> hier los? What's going on here then?
  Wo <u>denn</u>?   Where?

> *Tip*
>
> You can't always translate emphasizers directly, especially **denn** and **aber**.

⇨ *For more information on **Conjunctions**, see page 168.*

- **doch** is used in one of three ways:

  As a positive reply to a negative statement or question:

  Hat es dir nicht gefallen? – <u>Doch</u>! Didn't you like it? – Oh yes, I did!

  To strengthen an imperative, that is the form of a verb used when giving instructions:

  Lass ihn <u>doch</u>!   Just leave him.

  To make a question out of a statement:

  Das schaffst du <u>doch</u>? You'll manage it, won't you?

⇨ *For more information on **Imperatives**, see page 105.*

- **mal** can be used in one of two ways:

  With imperatives:

  Komm <u>mal</u> her!   Come here!
  Moment <u>mal</u>, bitte! Just a minute!

In informal language:

<u>Mal</u> sehen.	We'll see.
Hören Sie <u>mal</u> ...	Look here now ...
Er soll es nur <u>mal</u> versuchen!	Just let him try it!

- Ja can also be used in one of two ways.

    To strengthen a statement:

Er sieht <u>ja</u> wie seine Mutter aus.	He looks like his mother.
Das kann <u>ja</u> sein.	That may well be.

    In informal language:

<u>Ja</u> und?	So what?/What then?
Das ist <u>ja</u> lächerlich.	That's ridiculous.
Das ist es <u>ja</u>.	That's just it.

- Schon also has more than one use.

    It is used informally with an imperative:

Mach <u>schon</u>!	Get on with it!

    It is also used in other informal statements:

Da kommt sie <u>schon</u> wieder!	Here she comes again!
<u>Schon</u> gut. Ich habe verstanden.	Okay, I get the message.

Key points

✔ There are lots of little adverbs used in both English and German to emphasize or soften the meaning of a sentence in some way.

✔ The most common of these are **aber**, **denn**, **doch**, **mal**, **ja** and **schon**.

For further explanation of grammatical terms, please see pages xii–xvi.

Pronouns

> **What is a pronoun?**
> A **pronoun** is a word you use instead of a noun, when you do not need or want to name someone or something directly, for example, *it*, *you*, *none*.

➤ There are several different types of pronoun:

- <u>Personal pronouns</u> such as *I*, *you*, *he*, *her* and *they*, which are used to refer to yourself, the person you are talking to, or other people and things. They can be either <u>subject pronouns</u> (*I*, *you*, *he* and so on) or <u>object pronouns</u> (*him*, *her*, *them* and so on).

- <u>Possessive pronouns</u> like *mine* and *yours*, which show who someone or something belongs to.

- <u>Indefinite pronouns</u> like *someone* or *nothing*, which refer to people or things in a general way without saying exactly who or what they are.

- <u>Relative pronouns</u> like *who*, *which* or *that*, which link two parts of a sentence together.

- <u>Demonstrative pronouns</u> like *this* or *those*, which point things or people out.

- <u>Reflexive pronouns</u> – a type of object pronoun that forms part of German reflexive verbs like **sich setzen** (meaning *to sit down*) or **sich waschen** (meaning *to wash*).

⇨ For more information on **Reflexive verbs**, see page 102.

- The pronouns **wer?** (meaning *who?*) and **was?** (meaning *what?*) and their different forms, which are used to ask questions.

➤ Pronouns often stand in for a noun to save repeating it.

> I finished my homework and gave <u>it</u> to my teacher.
> Do you remember Jack? I saw <u>him</u> at the weekend.

➤ Word order with personal pronouns is usually different in German and English.

Personal pronouns: subject

> **What is a subject pronoun?**
> A **subject pronoun** is a word such as *I*, *he*, *she* and *they*. It refers to the person or thing which performs the action expressed by the verb. Pronouns stand in for nouns when it is clear who is being talked about, for example: *My brother isn't here at the moment. He'll be back in an hour.*

1 Using subject pronouns

➤ Here are the German subject pronouns or personal pronouns in the nominative case:

Subject Pronoun (Nominative Case)	Meaning
ich	I
du	you (*familiar*)
er	he/it
sie	she/it
es	it/he/she
man	one
wir	we
ihr	you (*plural*)
sie	they
Sie	you (*polite*)

<u>Ich</u> fahre nächste Woche nach Italien.	I'm going to Italy next week.
<u>Wir</u> wohnen in Frankfurt.	We live in Frankfurt.

⇨ *For more information on the **Nominative case**, see page 9.*

2 du, ihr or Sie?

➤ In English we have only <u>one</u> way of saying *you*. In German, there are <u>three</u> words: **du**, **ihr** and **Sie**. The word you use depends on:

- whether you are talking to one person or more than one person
- whether you are talking to a friend or family member, or someone else

➤ Use the familiar **du** if talking to one person <u>you know well</u>, such as a friend, someone younger than you or a relative

Kommst <u>du</u> mit ins Kino?	Are you coming to the cinema?

➤ Use the formal or polite **Sie** if talking to one person <u>you do not know so well</u>, such as your teacher, your boss or a stranger.

Was haben <u>Sie</u> gesagt?   What did you say?

> ### Tip
>
> If you are in doubt as to which form of *you* to use, it is safest to use **Sie** and you will not offend anybody. However, once a colleague or acquaintance has suggested you call each other **du**, starting to use **Sie** again may be considered insulting.

➤ Use the familiar **ihr** if talking to <u>more than one person you know well</u> or relatives.

Also, was wollt <u>ihr</u> heute Abend essen?   So, what do you want to eat tonight?

➤ Use **Sie** if talking to <u>more than one person you do not know so well</u>.

Wo fahren <u>Sie</u> hin?   Where are you going to?

> ### Tip
>
> Use **Sie** in more formal situations for both the singular and plural *you*.

> ### Tip
>
> All of the subject pronouns only have a capital letter when they begin a sentence, except for the polite form of *you*, **Sie**, which always has a capital letter.

<u>Ich</u> gebe dir das Buch zurück, wenn <u>ich</u> es zu Ende gelesen habe.   I'll give you the book back when I've finished reading it.

<u>Du</u> kannst mich morgen besuchen, wenn <u>du</u> Zeit hast.   You can come and visit me tomorrow, if you have time.

Wir wären Ihnen sehr dankbar, wenn <u>Sie</u> uns telefonisch benachrichtigen würden.   We'd be very grateful if you could phone and let us know.

3 Er/sie/es

➤ In English we generally refer to things (such as *table*, *book*, *car*) only as *it*. In German, **er** (meaning *he*), **sie** (meaning *she*) and **es** (meaning *it*) are used to talk about a thing, as well as about a person or an animal. You use **er** for <u>masculine nouns</u>, **sie** for <u>feminine nouns</u> and **es** for <u>neuter nouns</u>.

Der Tisch ist groß	→	**Er** ist groß
The table is large	→	It is large
Die Jacke ist blau	→	**Sie** ist blau
The jacket is blue	→	It is blue
Das Kind stand auf	→	**Es** stand auf
The child stood up	→	He/she stood up

i Note that English speakers often make the mistake of calling all objects **es**.

➤ The subject pronoun **sie** (meaning *they*) is used in the plural to talk about things, as well as people or animals. Use **sie** for <u>masculine</u>, <u>feminine</u> and <u>neuter nouns</u>.

'Wo sind Michael und Sebastian?' –	'Where are Michael and Sebastian?' –
'**Sie** sind im Garten.'	'They're in the garden.'
'Hast du die Karten gekauft?' –	'Did you buy the tickets?' –
'Nein, <u>sie</u> waren ausverkauft.'	'No, they were sold out.'
'Nimmst du die Hunde mit?' –	'Are you taking the dogs with you?' –
'Nein, die Nachbarin passt auf <u>sie</u> auf.'	'No, the next-door neighbour is looking after them.'

4 Man

➤ This is often used in German in the same way as we use *you* in English to mean people in general.

Wie schreibt <u>man</u> das?	How do you spell that?
Man kann nie wissen.	You never know.

➤ **Man** can also mean *they* used in a vague way.

Man sagt, dass das Wetter immer schlecht ist.	They say the weather is always bad.

Tip

Man is often used to avoid a passive construction in German.

| Man hat das schon oft im Fernsehen gezeigt. | It's already been shown a lot on TV. |

⟱ *For more information on the **Passive**, see page 150.*

The form of the verb you use with man is the same as the er/sie/es form.

⟱ *For more information on **Verbs**, see pages 91-152.*

Key points

✔ The German subject pronouns are: ich, du, er, sie, es, Sie and man in the singular, and wir, ihr, sie and Sie in the plural.

✔ To say *you* in German, use du if you are talking to one person you know well or to someone younger than you; use ihr if you are talking to more than one person you know well and use Sie if you are talking to one or more people you do not know well.

✔ Er/sie/es (masculine/feminine/neuter singular) and sie (masculine or feminine or neuter plural) are used to refer to things, as well as to people or animals.

✔ Man can mean *you*, *they* or people in general. It is often used instead of a passive construction.

Personal pronouns: direct object

> **What is a direct object pronoun?**
> A **direct object pronoun** is a word such as *me*, *him*, *us* and *them* which is used instead of the noun to stand in for the person or thing most directly affected by the action expressed by the verb.

1 Using direct object pronouns

➤ Direct object pronouns stand in for nouns when it is clear who or what is being talked about, and save having to repeat the noun.

> I've lost my glasses. Have you seen <u>them</u>?
> 'Have you met Jo?' – 'Yes, I really like <u>her</u>!'

➤ Here are the German direct object pronouns or personal pronouns in the accusative case:

Direct Object Pronoun (Accusative Case)	Meaning
mich	me
dich	you (*familiar*)
ihn	him/it
sie	her/it
es	it/him/her
einen	one
uns	us
euch	you (*plural*)
sie	them
Sie	you (*polite*)

> Ich lade <u>dich</u> zum Essen ein. I'll invite you for a meal.
> Sie hat <u>ihn</u> letztes Jahr kennengelernt. She met him last year.

2 Word order with direct object pronouns

➤ In tenses consisting of one verb part only, for example the present and the simple past, the direct object pronoun usually comes directly <u>AFTER</u> the verb.

> Sie bringen <u>ihn</u> nach Hause. They'll take him home.

➤ In tenses such as the perfect that are formed with **haben** or **sein** and the past participle, the direct object pronoun comes <u>AFTER</u> the part of the verb that comes from **haben** or **sein** and <u>BEFORE</u> the past participle.

> Er hat <u>mich</u> durchs Fenster gesehen. He saw me through the window.

For further explanation of grammatical terms, please see pages xii–xvi.

➤ When a modal verb like **wollen** (meaning *to want*) or **können** (meaning *to be able to, can*) is followed by another verb in the infinitive (the '*to*' form of the verb), the direct object pronoun comes directly <u>AFTER</u> the modal verb.

> **Wir wollen <u>Sie</u> nicht mehr sehen.**   We don't want to see you anymore.

⇨ *For more information on **Modal verbs**, see page 136.*

*For more information on **Modal verbs**, see page 136.*

Key points

✔ The German direct object pronouns are: **mich**, **dich**, **ihn**, **sie**, **es**, **Sie** and **einen** in the singular, and **uns**, **euch**, **sie** and **Sie** in the plural.

✔ The direct object pronoun usually comes directly after the verb, but in tenses like the perfect comes after the part of the verb that comes from **haben** or **sein** and before the past participle.

✔ When a modal verb such as **wollen** is followed by the infinitive of another verb, the direct object pronoun comes directly after the modal verb.

Personal pronouns: indirect object

> **What is an indirect object pronoun?**
> When a verb has two objects (a <u>direct</u> one and an <u>indirect</u> one), the **indirect object pronoun** is used instead of a noun to show the person or thing the action is intended to benefit or harm, for example, *me* in *He gave me a book; Can you get me a towel?*

1 <u>Using indirect object pronouns</u>

➤ It is important to understand the difference between direct and indirect object pronouns, as they have different forms in German:

- an <u>indirect object</u> answers the question *who to?* or *who for?* and *to what?* or *for what?*

  He gave me a book. → *Who did he give the book to?* → me (=*indirect object pronoun*)

  Can you get me a towel? → *Who can you get a towel for?* → me (=*indirect object pronoun*)

- if something answers the question *what?* or *who?*, then it is the <u>direct object</u> and <u>NOT</u> the indirect object

  He gave me a book → *What did he give me?* → a book (=*direct object*)

  Can you get me a towel? → *What can you get me?* → a towel (=*direct object*)

➤ Here are the German indirect object pronouns in the dative case:

Indirect Object Pronoun (Dative Case)	Meaning
mir	to/for me
dir	to/for you (*familiar*)
ihm	to/for him/it
ihr	to/for her/it
ihm	to/for it/him/her
einem	to/for one
uns	to/for us
euch	to/for you (*plural*)
ihnen	to/for them
Ihnen	to/for you (*polite*)

Er hat <u>mir</u> das geschenkt.	He gave me that as a present.
Sie haben <u>ihnen</u> eine tolle Geschichte erzählt.	They told them a great story.

For further explanation of grammatical terms, please see pages xii–xvi.

2 Word order with indirect object pronouns

➤ Word order for indirect object pronouns is the same as for direct object pronouns. The pronoun usually comes directly after the verb, except with tenses like the perfect and modal verbs such as **wollen**.

Sie bringt <u>mir</u> das Schwimmen bei.	She's teaching me how to swim.
Sie hat es <u>ihm</u> gegeben.	She gave it to him.
Ich will <u>dir</u> etwas sagen.	I want to tell you something.

➤ When you have both a direct object pronoun AND an indirect object pronoun in the same sentence, the direct object pronoun or personal pronoun in the accusative <u>always</u> comes first. A good way of remembering this is to think of the following:

PAD = Pronoun Accusative Dative

Sie haben <u>es</u> <u>ihm</u> verziehen.	They forgave him for it.
Ich bringe <u>es</u> <u>dir</u> schon bei.	I'll teach you.

Key points

✔ The German indirect object pronouns are: **mir, dir, ihm, ihr, ihm, Ihnen** and **einem** in the singular, and **uns, euch, ihnen** and **Ihnen** in the plural.

✔ The indirect object pronoun comes after the verb, except with tenses like the perfect and when used with modal verbs such as **wollen**.

✔ The indirect object pronoun always comes after the direct object pronoun.

Personal pronouns: after prepositions

➤ When a personal pronoun is used after a preposition and refers to a person, the personal pronoun is in the case required by the preposition. For example, the preposition **mit** is always followed by the dative case.

> **Ich bin <u>mit</u> <u>ihm</u> spazieren gegangen.**   I went for a walk with him.

➤ When a thing rather than a person is referred to, **da-** is added at the beginning of the preposition:

> **Manuela hatte ein Messer geholt und wollte <u>damit</u> den Kuchen schneiden.**   Manuela had brought a knife and was about to cut the cake with it.

[i] Note that before a preposition beginning with a vowel, the form **dar-** + preposition is used.

> **Lege es bitte <u>darauf</u>.**   Put it there please.

➤ The following prepositions are affected in this way:

Preposition	Preposition + da or dar
an	<u>dar</u>an
auf	<u>dar</u>auf
aus	<u>dar</u>aus
bei	<u>da</u>bei
durch	<u>da</u>durch
für	<u>da</u>für
in	<u>dar</u>in
mit	<u>da</u>mit
nach	<u>da</u>nach
neben	<u>da</u>neben
über	<u>dar</u>über
unter	<u>dar</u>unter
zwischen	<u>da</u>zwischen

⇨ *For more information on **Prepositions**, see page 153.*

[i] Note that these combined forms are also used after verbs followed by prepositions.

> **sich erinnern an** + accusative case =   to remember
> **Ich erinnere mich nicht <u>daran</u>**   I don't remember (it)

Grammar Extra!

After certain prepositions used to express movement, that is **aus** (meaning *out* or *from*), **auf** (meaning *on*) and **in** (meaning *in* or *into*), combined forms with **hin** and **her** are used to give more emphasis to the action being carried out.

Preposition	hin or her + Preposition
aus	hinaus/heraus
auf	hinauf/herauf
in	hinein/herein

Er ging die Treppe leise <u>hinauf</u>.

He went up the stairs quietly.

Endlich fand sie unser Zelt und kam <u>herein</u>.

She finally found our tent and came inside.

Sie öffnete die Reisetasche und legte die Hose <u>hinein</u>.

She opened the bag and put in her trousers.

Key points

✔ When a personal pronoun referring to a person is used after a preposition, the personal pronoun is in the case required by the preposition.

✔ When a personal pronoun referring to a thing is used after a preposition, the construction **da(r)-** + preposition is used.

Possessive pronouns

> **What is a possessive pronoun?**
>
> In English you can say *This is my car* or *This car is mine*. In the first sentence *my* is a possessive adjective. In the second, *mine* is a possessive pronoun.
>
> A **possessive pronoun** is one of the words *mine, yours, hers, his, ours* or *theirs*, which are used instead of a noun to show that one thing or person belongs to another, for example, *Ask Carol if this pen is hers*.

➤ German possessive pronouns are the same words as the possessive adjectives **mein, dein, sein, ihr, unser, euer, ihr, Ihr**, with the same endings, EXCEPT in the masculine nominative singular, the neuter nominative singular and the neuter accusative singular, as shown below.

	Possessive Adjective	Meaning	Possessive Pronoun	Meaning
Masculine Nominative Singular	Das ist <u>mein</u> Wagen	That is my car	Dieser Wagen ist <u>meiner</u>	That car is mine
Neuter Nominative Singular	Das ist <u>mein</u> Buch	That is my book	Dieses Buch ist <u>meins</u>	That book is mine
Neuter Accusative Singular	Sie hat <u>mein</u> Buch genommen	She has taken my book	Sie hat <u>meins</u> genommen	She has taken mine

➤ Here is the German possessive pronoun **meiner**, meaning *mine*, in all its forms:

Case	Masculine Singular	Feminine Singular	Neuter Singular	All Genders Plural
Nominative	mei<u>ner</u>	mein<u>e</u>	mein<u>(e)s</u>	mein<u>e</u>
Accusative	mein<u>en</u>	mein<u>e</u>	mein<u>(e)s</u>	mein<u>e</u>
Genitive	mein<u>es</u>	mein<u>er</u>	mein<u>es</u>	mein<u>er</u>
Dative	mein<u>em</u>	mein<u>er</u>	mein<u>em</u>	mein<u>en</u>

> *i* Note that the nominative and accusative neuter forms only of all the possessive pronouns are often pronounced without the last **-e**, for example **meins** instead of **meines**.

Der Wagen da drüben ist <u>meiner</u>.	The car over there is mine.
Er ist kleiner als <u>deiner</u>.	It is smaller than yours.
Das ist besser als <u>meins</u>!	That's better than mine!
Das Haus nebenan ist schöner als <u>seins</u>.	The house next door is nicer than his.
Meine Jacke war teurer als <u>ihre</u>.	My jacket was more expensive than hers.

For further explanation of grammatical terms, please see pages xii–xvi.

i Note that **deiner**, meaning *yours (familiar)*, **seiner**, meaning *his/its*, **ihrer**, meaning *hers/its/theirs*, **Ihrer**, meaning *yours (polite)*, **unserer**, meaning *ours* and **euerer**, meaning *yours (plural familiar)* have the same endings as **meiner**.

> *Tip*
>
> **Unserer**, meaning *ours* is often pronounced **unsrer** and **euerer**, meaning *yours (plural familiar)* is often pronounced **eurer**. This pronunciation is occasionally reflected in writing.

Case	Masculine Singular	Feminine Singular	Neuter Singular	All Genders Plural
Nominative	uns(e)rer	uns(e)re	uns(e)res	uns(e)re
Accusative	uns(e)ren	uns(e)re	uns(e)res	uns(e)re
Genitive	uns(e)res	uns(e)rer	uns(e)res	uns(e)rer
Dative	uns(e)rem	uns(e)rer	uns(e)rem	uns(e)ren

Case	Masculine Singular	Feminine Singular	Neuter Singular	All Genders Plural
Nominative	eu(e)rer	eu(e)re	eu(e)res	eu(e)re
Accusative	eu(e)ren	eu(e)re	eu(e)res	eu(e)re
Genitive	eu(e)res	eu(e)rer	eu(e)res	eu(e)rer
Dative	eu(e)rem	eu(e)rer	eu(e)rem	eu(e)ren

War euer Urlaub billiger als <u>unsrer</u>?   Was your holiday cheaper than ours?

i Note the translation of *of mine*, *of yours* etc, where the personal pronoun in the dative is used:

Er ist ein Freund von mir.   He is a friend of mine.

Ich habe eine CD von dir bei mir zu Hause.   I have a CD of yours at home.

Key points

✔ German possessive pronouns have the same form and endings as the possessive adjectives **mein**, **dein**, **sein**, **ihr**, **unser**, **euer**, **ihr**, **Ihr**, except in the masculine nominative singular, the neuter nominative singular and the neuter accusative singular.

✔ The nominative and accusative neuter forms of all the possessive pronouns are often pronounced without the last -e, for example **meins** instead of **meines**.

✔ **Unserer**, meaning *ours* is often pronounced **unsrer** and **euerer**, meaning *yours (plural familiar)* is often pronounced **eurer**. This pronunciation is occasionally reflected in writing.

Indefinite pronouns

> **What is an indefinite pronoun?**
> An **indefinite pronoun** is one of a small group of pronouns such as *everything*, *nobody* and *something* which are used to refer to people or things in a general way without saying exactly who or what they are.

➤ In German, the indefinite pronouns **jemand** (meaning *someone, somebody*) and **niemand** (meaning *no-one, nobody*) are often used in speech without any endings. In written German, the endings are added.

Case	Indefinite Pronoun
Nominative	jemand/niemand
Accusative	jemanden/niemanden
Genitive	jemand(e)s/niemand(e)s
Dative	jemandem/niemandem

Ich habe es jemandem gegeben.	I gave it to someone.
Jemand hat es genommen.	Someone has stolen it.
Sie hat niemanden gesehen.	She didn't see anyone.
Ich bin unterwegs niemandem begegnet.	I didn't meet anyone on the way.

Tip

If you want to express the sense of *somebody or other*, use **irgendjemand** which is declined like **jemand**.

Ich habe es irgendjemandem gegeben.	I gave it to somebody or other.

➤ The indefinite pronoun **keiner** has the same endings as the article **kein**, **keine**, **kein** except in the nominative masculine and nominative and accusative neuter forms, and can be used to refer to people or things. When referring to people it means *nobody*, *not ... anybody* or *none* and when referring to things, it means *not ... any* or *none*.

Case	Masculine Singular	Feminine Singular	Neuter Singular	All Genders Plural
Nominative	keiner	keine	keins	keine
Accusative	keinen	keine	keins	keine
Genitive	keines	keiner	keines	keiner
Dative	keinem	keiner	keinem	keinen

For further explanation of grammatical terms, please see pages xii–xvi.

Ich kenne hier kein<u>en</u>.	I don't know anybody here.
Kein<u>er</u> weiß Bescheid über ihn.	Nobody knows about him.
Das trifft auf kein<u>en</u> zu.	That does not apply to anybody here.
Er wollte ein Stück Schokolade, aber ich hatte kein<u>e</u>.	He wanted a piece of chocolate, but I didn't have any.
„Hast du Geld?" – „Nein, gar kein<u>s</u>."	"Have you got any money?" – "No, none at all."

➤ The indefinite pronoun **einer** (meaning *one*) only has a singular form and can also be used to refer to people or things.

Case	Masculine Singular	Feminine Singular	Neuter Singular
Nominative	einer	eine	ein(e)s
Accusative	einen	eine	ein(e)s
Genitive	eines	einer	eines
Dative	einem	einer	einem

Sie trifft sich mit einem ihrer alten Studienfreunde.	She's meeting one of her old friends from university.

Ich brauche nur einen (e.g. **einen Wagen, einen Pullover** etc) OR:
Ich brauche nur eine (e.g. **eine Blume, eine Tasche** etc) OR:
Ich brauche nur eins (e.g. **ein Buch, ein Notizbuch** etc) I only need one.

Key points

✔ **Jemand** and **niemand** can be used without endings in spoken German but have endings added in written German.

✔ **Keiner** has the same endings as the article **kein, keine, kein** except in the nominative masculine and nominative and accusative neuter forms, and refers to people or things.

✔ **Einer** only has a singular form and refers to people or things.

Reflexive pronouns

> **What is a reflexive pronoun?**
> A **reflexive pronoun** is an object pronoun such as *myself, yourself, himself, herself* and *ourselves* that forms part of German reflexive verbs like **sich waschen** (meaning *to wash*) or **sich setzen** (meaning *to sit down*). A reflexive verb is a verb whose subject and object are the same and whose action is "reflected back" to its subject.

➤ German reflexive pronouns have two forms: accusative (for the direct object pronoun) and dative (for the indirect object pronoun), as follows:

Accusative Form	Dative Form	Meaning
mich	mir	myself
dich	dir	yourself (*familiar*)
sich	sich	himself/herself/itself
uns	uns	ourselves
euch	euch	yourselves (*plural*)
sich	sich	themselves
sich	sich	yourself/yourselves (*polite*)

Er hat <u>sich</u> rasiert.	He had a shave.
Du hast <u>dich</u> gebadet.	You had a bath.
Ich will es <u>mir</u> zuerst überlegen.	I'll have to think about it first.

(i) Note that unlike personal pronouns and possessives, the polite forms have no capital letter.

Setzen Sie <u>sich</u> bitte.	Please take a seat.
Nehmen Sie <u>sich</u> ruhig etwas Zeit.	Take your time.

➤ The reflexive pronoun usually follows the first verb in the sentence, with certain exceptions:

Sie wird <u>sich</u> darüber freuen.	She'll be pleased about that.

● If the subject and verb are swapped round in the sentence, and the subject is a personal pronoun, then the reflexive pronoun must come AFTER the personal pronoun.

Darüber wird sie <u>sich</u> freuen.	She'll be pleased about that.

● If the sentence is made of up two parts or clauses, then the reflexive pronoun comes AFTER the subject in the second clause.

Ich frage mich, ob sie <u>sich</u> darüber freuen wird.	I wonder if she'll be pleased about that.

⇨ For more information on **Word order**, see page 175.
⇨ For more information on **Reflexive verbs**, see page 102.

For further explanation of grammatical terms, please see pages xii–xvi.

➤ Unlike English, reflexive pronouns are also used after prepositions when the pronoun "reflects back" to the subject of the sentence.

Er hatte nicht genug Geld bei <u>sich</u>.	He didn't have enough money on him.
Hatten Sie nicht genug Geld bei <u>sich</u>?	Didn't you have enough money on you?

➤ Another use of reflexive pronouns in German is with transitive verbs where the action is performed for the benefit of the subject, as in the English phrase: I bought *myself* a new hat. The pronoun is not always translated in English.

Ich hole <u>mir</u> einen Kaffee.	I'm going to get (myself) a coffee.
Sie hat <u>sich</u> eine neue Jacke gekauft.	She bought (herself) a new jacket.

➤ Reflexive pronouns are usually used in German where *each other* and *one another* would be used in English.

Wir sind <u>uns</u> letzte Woche begegnet.	We met (each other) last week.

[*i*] Note that **einander**, (meaning *one another, each other*), which does not change in form, may be used instead of a reflexive pronoun in such cases.

Wir kennen <u>uns</u> schon OR	
Wir kennen <u>einander</u> schon.	We already know each other.

➤ After prepositions, **einander** is always used instead of a reflexive pronoun. The preposition and **einander** are then joined to form one word.

Sie redeten <u>miteinander</u>.	They were talking to each other.

➤ In English, pronouns used for emphasis are the same as normal reflexive pronouns, for example, *I did it myself*. In German **selbst** or, in informal spoken language, **selber** are used instead of reflexive pronouns for emphasis. They never change their form and are always stressed, regardless of their position in the sentence:

Ich <u>selbst</u> habe es nicht gelesen, aber ...	I haven't read it *myself*, but ...

Key points

✔ German reflexive pronouns have two forms: accusative for the direct object pronoun and dative for the indirect object pronoun.

✔ Reflexive pronouns are also used after prepositions when the pronoun "reflects back" to the subject of the sentence.

✔ Reflexive pronouns are usually used in German where *each other* or *one another* would be used in English, but **einander** can be used as an alternative and is always used after prepositions.

✔ Selbst or, in informal spoken German, **selber** are used instead of reflexive pronouns for emphasis.

Relative pronouns

> **What is a relative pronoun?**
>
> In English a **relative pronoun** is one of the words *who*, *which* and *that* (and the more formal *whom*). These pronouns are used to introduce information that makes it clear which person or thing is being talked about, for example, *The man* <u>*who*</u> *has just come in is Ann's boyfriend; The vase* <u>*that*</u> *you broke was quite valuable.*
>
> Relative pronouns can also introduce further information about someone or something, for example, *Peter,* <u>*who*</u> *is a brilliant painter, wants to study art; Jane's house,* <u>*which*</u> *was built in 1890, needs a lot of repairs.*

➤ In German the most common relative pronouns **der**, **den**, **dessen**, **dem** etc have the same forms as the definite article, except in the dative plural and genitive singular and plural. They are declined as follows:

Case	Masculine Singular	Feminine Singular	Neuter Singular	All Genders Plural
Nominative	der	die	das	die
Accusative	den	die	das	die
Genitive	dessen	deren	dessen	deren
Dative	dem	der	dem	denen

➤ Relative pronouns must agree in gender and number with the noun to which they refer, but the case they have depends on their function in the relative clause. The relative clause is simply the part of the sentence in which the relative pronoun appears. Relative clauses are <u>ALWAYS</u> separated by commas from the rest of the sentence.

● In the following example, the relative pronoun **den** is in the accusative because it is the direct object in the relative clause.

Der Mann, <u>den</u> ich gestern gesehen habe, kommt aus Zürich.

The man that I saw yesterday comes from Zürich.

● In this second example, the relative pronoun **dessen** is in the genitive because it is used to show that something belongs to someone.

Das Mädchen, <u>dessen</u> Fahrrad gestohlen worden ist.

The girl whose bike was stolen.

Tip

In English we often miss out the object pronouns *who*, *which* and *that*. For example, we can say both *the friends that I see most*, or *the friends I see most*, and *the house which we want to buy*, or *the house we want to buy*. In German you can NEVER miss out the relative pronoun in this way.

Die Frau, mit <u>der</u> ich gestern gesprochen habe, kennt deine Mutter.	The woman I spoke to yesterday knows your mother.

Note that the genitive forms are used in relative clauses in much the same way as in English, but to translate *one of whom*, *some of whom* use the following constructions.

Das Kind, <u>dessen</u> Fahrrad gestohlen worden war, fing an zu weinen.	The child <u>whose</u> bicycle had been stolen started to cry.
Die Kinder, von <u>denen</u> einige schon lesen konnten, ...	The children, some of <u>whom</u> could already read, ...
Meine Freunde, von <u>denen</u> einer ...	My friends, one of <u>whom</u> ...

Grammar Extra!

When a relative clause is introduced by a preposition, the relative pronoun can be replaced by **wo-** or **wor-** if the noun or pronoun it stands for refers to an object or something abstract. The full form of the pronoun plus preposition is much more common.

Das Buch, <u>woraus</u> ich vorgelesen habe, gehört dir.	
OR:	
Das Buch, <u>aus dem</u> ich vorgelesen habe, gehört dir.	The book I read aloud from belongs to you.

➤ In German **wer** and **was** are normally used as interrogative pronouns (meaning *who?* and *what?*) to ask questions. They can also be the subject of a sentence or a relative pronoun. For example, *he who*, *a woman who*, *anyone who*, *those who* etc.

<u>**Wer**</u> **das glaubt, ist verrückt.**	Anyone who believes that is mad.
<u>**Was**</u> **du gestern gekauft hast, steht dir ganz gut.**	The things you bought yesterday really suit you.

(i) Note that **was** is the relative pronoun used in set expressions with certain neuter forms. For example:

alles, was ...	everything which
das, was ...	that which
nichts, was ...	nothing that
vieles, was ...	a lot that
wenig, was ...	little that
Nichts, <u>was</u> er sagte, hat gestimmt.	Nothing that he said was right.
Das, <u>was</u> du jetzt machst, ist unpraktisch.	What you are doing now is impractical.
Mit allem, <u>was</u> du gesagt hast, sind wir einverstanden.	We agree with everything you said.

Key points

✔ The most common relative pronouns **der, den, dessen, dem** etc have the same forms as the definite article, except in the dative plural and genitive singular and plural.

✔ Relative pronouns must agree in gender and number with the noun to which they refer, but take their case from their function in the relative clause.

✔ In German you can <u>NEVER</u> miss out the relative pronoun, unlike in English.

✔ Relative clauses are always separated by commas from the rest of the sentence.

✔ **Wer** and **was** are normally used as interrogative pronouns but can also be the subject of a sentence or a relative pronoun.

Interrogative pronouns

> **What is an interrogative pronoun?**
> This is one of the words *who*, *whose*, *whom*, *what* and *which* when they are used instead of a noun to ask questions, for example, *What*'s *happening?*; *Who*'s *coming?*

1 | Wer? and was?

➤ Wer and **was** only have a singular form.

Case	Persons	Things
Nominative	wer?	was?
Accusative	wen?	was?
Genitive	wessen?	–
Dative	wem?	–

● They can be used in direct questions.

<u>Wer</u> hat es gemacht?	Who did it?
Mit <u>wem</u> bist du gekommen?	Who did you come with?
Wo ist der Kugelschreiber, mit <u>dem</u> du es geschrieben hast?	Where is the pen you wrote it with?

● They can also be used in indirect questions.

Ich weiß nicht, <u>wer</u> es gemacht hat.	I don't know who did it.
Sie wollte wissen, mit <u>wem</u> sie fahren sollte.	She wanted to know who she was to travel with.

2 | Interrogative pronouns with prepositions

➤ When used with prepositions, **was** usually becomes **wo-** and is combined with the preposition to form one word. Where the preposition begins with a vowel, **wor-** is used instead.

<u>Wodurch</u> ist es zerstört worden?	How was it destroyed?
<u>Worauf</u> sollen wir sitzen? Es gibt keine Stühle.	What should we sit on? There aren't any chairs.

3 | **Was für ein?, welcher?**

➤ These are used to mean *what kind of ...?* and *which one?* and are declined like the definite article.

> „Er hat jetzt ein Auto" –   "He has a car now." -
> „<u>Was für eins</u> hat er gekauft?"   "What kind (of one) did he buy?"
> <u>Welches</u> hast du gewollt?   Which one did you want?

⇨ *For more information on* **Words declined like the definite article***, see page 31.*

➤ They can refer to people or things and require the appropriate endings.

> Für <u>welchen</u> (e.g. welchen Job, welchen Whisky etc) hat sie sich entschieden? OR:
> Für <u>welches</u> (e.g. welches Haus, welches Buch etc) hat sie sich entschieden? OR:
> Für <u>welche</u> (e.g. welche Person, welche Jacke etc) hat sie sich entschieden?
> Which one did she choose?

Key points

✔ The interrogative pronouns **wer** and **was** can be used for direct and indirect questions and only have a singular form.

✔ When used with prepositions, **was** becomes **wo-**, or **wor-** when the preposition begins with a vowel.

✔ **Was für ein?** and **welcher?** are used to mean *what kind of ...?* and *which one?*

Verbs

> **What is a verb?**
> A **verb** is a 'doing' word which describes what someone or something does, what someone or something is, or what happens to them, for example, *be, sing, live*.

Weak, strong and mixed verbs

➤ Verbs are usually used with a noun, with a pronoun such as *I, you* or *she,* or with somebody's name. They can relate to the present, the past and the future; this is called their <u>tense</u>.

⇨ *For more information on **Nouns** and **Pronouns**, see pages 1 and 69.*

➤ Verbs are either:
- <u>weak</u>; their forms follow a set pattern. These verbs may also be called <u>regular</u>.
- <u>strong</u> and <u>irregular</u>; their forms change according to different patterns.
  OR
- <u>mixed</u>; their forms follow a mixture of the patterns for weak and strong verbs.

➤ Regular English verbs have a <u>base form</u> (the form of the verb without any endings added to it, for example, *walk*). This is the form you look up in a dictionary. The base form can have *to* in front of it, for example, *to walk*. This is called the <u>infinitive</u>.

➤ German verbs also have an infinitive, which is the form shown in a dictionary; most weak, strong and mixed verbs end in **-en**. For example, **holen** (meaning *to fetch*) is weak, **helfen** (meaning *to help*) is strong and **denken** (meaning *to think*) is mixed. All German verbs belong to one of these groups. We will look at each of these three groups in turn on the next few pages.

➤ English verbs have other forms apart from the base form and infinitive: a form ending in *-s* (*walks*), a form ending in *-ing* (*walking*), and a form ending in *-ed* (*walked*).

➤ German verbs have many more forms than this, which are made up of endings added to a <u>stem</u>. The stem of a verb can usually be worked out from the infinitive and can change, depending on the tense of the verb and who or what you are talking about.

➤ German verb endings also change, depending on who or what you are talking about: **ich** (*I*), **du** (*you* (informal)), **er/sie/es** (*he/she/it*), **Sie** (*you* (formal)) in the singular, or **wir** (*we*), **ihr** (*you* (informal)), **Sie** (*you* (formal)) and **sie** (*they*) in the plural. German verbs also have different forms depending on whether you are referring to the present, future or past.

⇨ *For **Verb Tables**, see middle section.*

Key points

✔ German verbs have different forms depending on what noun or pronoun they are used with, and on their tense.

✔ They are made up of a stem and an ending. The stem is based on the infinitive and can change in form.

✔ All German verbs fit into one of three patterns or conjugations: weak (and regular), strong (and irregular) or mixed (a mixture of the two).

The present tense

> **What is the present tense?**
> The **present tense** is used to talk about what is true at the moment, what happens regularly and what is happening now, for example, I'_m_ a student, I _travel_ to college by train, I'_m studying_ languages.

1 Using the present tense

➤ In English there are two forms of the present tense. One is used to talk about things happening now and the other is used for things that happen all the time. In German, you use the same form for both of these.

- things that are happening now

Es <u>regnet</u>.	It'<u>s</u> raining.
Sie <u>spielen</u> Fußball.	They'<u>re playing</u> football.

- things that happen all the time, or things that you do as a habit

Hier <u>regnet</u> es viel.	It <u>rains</u> a lot here.
Samstags <u>spielen</u> sie Fußball.	They <u>play</u> football on Saturdays.

➤ In German there are three alternative ways of emphasizing that something is happening now:

- present tense + an adverb

  Er kocht <u>gerade</u> das Abendessen.   He's cook<u>ing</u> dinner.

- beim + an infinitive being used as a noun

  Ich bin <u>beim Bügeln</u>.   I am iron<u>ing</u>

- eben/gerade dabei sein zu (meaning _to be in the process of_) + an infinitive

  Sie <u>ist gerade dabei</u>, eine E-Mail zu   She is just writ<u>ing</u> an email.
  schreiben.

➤ In English you can also use the present tense to talk about something that is going to happen in the near future. You can do the same in German.

Morgen <u>spiele</u> ich Tennis.	I'<u>m going</u> to play tennis tomorrow.
Wir <u>nehmen</u> den Zug um zehn Uhr.	We'<u>re getting</u> the ten o'clock train.

> **Tip**
>
> Although English sometimes uses parts of the verb *to be* to form the present tense of other verbs (for example, *I am listening, she's talking*), German <u>NEVER</u> uses the verb **sein** in this way.
>
> When using **seit** or **seitdem** to describe an action which began in the past and is continuing in the present, the present tense is used in German, where in English a verb form with *have* or *has* is used.

Ich <u>wohne</u> <u>seit</u> drei Jahren hier.	I <u>have been living</u> here for three years.
<u>Seit</u> er krank ist, hat er uns nicht besucht.	He <u>hasn't visited</u> us since he's been ill.
<u>Seitdem</u> sie am Gymnasium <u>ist</u>, hat sie kaum mehr Zeit.	Since she's <u>been going</u> to grammar school, she's hardly had any time.

> *i* Note that if the action is finished, the perfect tense is used in German.

<u>Seit</u> seinem Unfall <u>habe</u> ich ihn nur ein einziges Mal <u>gesehen</u>.	I <u>have</u> only <u>seen</u> him once since his accident.

2 Forming the present tense of weak verbs

➤ Nearly all weak verbs in German end in **-en** in their infinitive form. This is the form of the verb you find in the dictionary, for example, **spielen**, **machen**, **holen**. Weak verbs are regular and their changes follow a set pattern or conjugation.

➤ To know which form of the verb to use in German, you need to work out what the stem of the verb is and then add the correct ending. The stem of most verbs in the present tense is formed by chopping the **-en** off the infinitive.

Infinitive	Stem (without -en)
spielen (*to play*)	spiel-
machen (*to make*)	mach-
holen (*to fetch*)	hol-

➤ Where the infinitive of a weak verb ends in **-eln** or **-ern**, only the **-n** is chopped off to form the stem.

Infinitive	Stem (without -n)
wandern (*to hillwalk*)	wander-
segeln (*to sail*)	segel-

➤ Now you know how to find the stem of a verb, you can add the correct ending. Which one you choose will depend on whether you are referring to **ich**, **du**, **er**, **sie**, **es**, **wir**, **ihr**, **Sie** or **sie**.

⇨ *For more information on **Pronouns**, see page 69.*

➤ Here are the present tense endings for weak verbs ending in **-en**:

Pronoun	Ending	Add to Stem, e.g. spiel-	Meanings
ich	-e	ich spiel<u>e</u>	I play I am playing
du	-st	du spiel<u>st</u>	you play you are playing
er sie es	-t	er spiel<u>t</u> sie spiel<u>t</u> es spiel<u>t</u>	he/she/it plays he/she/it is playing
wir	-en	wir spiel<u>en</u>	we play we are playing
ihr	-t	ihr spiel<u>t</u>	you (*plural*) play you are playing
sie	-en	sie spiel<u>en</u>	they play they are playing
Sie		Sie spiel<u>en</u>	you (*polite*) play you are playing

Sie <u>macht</u> ihre Hausaufgaben.	She's doing her homework.
Er <u>holt</u> die Kinder.	He's fetching the children.

ℹ️ Note that you add **-n**, not **-en** to the stem of weak verbs ending in **-ern** and **-eln** to get the **wir**, **sie** and **Sie** forms of the present tense.

Pronoun	Ending	Add to Stem, e.g. wander-	Meanings
wir	-n	wir wander<u>n</u>	we hillwalk we are hillwalking
sie	-n	sie wander<u>n</u>	they hillwalk they are hillwalking
Sie		Sie wander<u>n</u>	you (*polite*) hillwalk you are hillwalking

Sie wander<u>n</u> gern, oder?	You like hillwalking, don't you?
Im Sommer wander<u>n</u> wir fast jedes Wochenende.	In the summer we go hillwalking most weekends.

➤ If the stem of a weak verb ends in **-d** or **-t**, an extra **-e** is added before the usual endings in the **du, er, sie** and **es** and **ihr** parts of the verb to make pronunciation easier.

Pronoun	Ending	Add to Stem, e.g. red-	Meanings
du	-est	du red<u>est</u>	you talk you are talking
er sie es	-et	er red<u>et</u> sie red<u>et</u> es red<u>et</u>	he/she/it talks he/she/it is talking
ihr	-et	ihr red<u>et</u>	you (*plural*) talk you are talking

Du red<u>est</u> doch die ganze Zeit über deine Arbeit! You talk about your work all the time!

Pronoun	Ending	Add to Stem, e.g. arbeit-	Meanings
du	-est	du arbeit<u>est</u>	you work you are working
er sie es	-et	er arbeit<u>et</u> sie arbeit<u>et</u> es arbeit<u>et</u>	he/she/it works he/she/it is working
ihr	-et	ihr arbeit<u>et</u>	you (*plural*) work you are working

Sie arbeit<u>et</u> übers Wochenende. She's working over the weekend.
Ihr arbeit<u>et</u> ganz schön viel. You work a lot.

➤ If the stem of a weak verb ends in **-m** or **-n**, this extra **-e** is added to make pronunciation easier. If the **-m** or **-n** has a consonant in front of it, the **-e** is added, except if the consonant is *l, r* or *h*, for example **lernen**.

Pronoun	Ending	Add to Stem, e.g. atm-	Meanings
du	-est	du atm<u>est</u>	you breathe you are breathing
er sie es	-et	er atm<u>et</u> sie atm<u>et</u> es atm<u>et</u>	he/she/it breathes he/she/it is breathing
ihr	-et	ihr atm<u>et</u>	you (*plural*) breathe you are breathing

Du atm<u>est</u> ganz tief. You're breathing very deeply.

For further explanation of grammatical terms, please see pages xii–xvi.

Pronoun	Ending	Add to Stem, e.g. lern-	Meanings
du	-est	du lern**st**	you learn you are learning
er sie es	-t	er lern**t** sie lern**t** es lern**t**	he/she/it learns he/she/it is learning
ihr	-t	ihr lern**t**	you (*plural*) learn you are learning

Sie lern_t_ alles ganz schnell.   She learns everything very quickly.

Key points

✔ Weak verbs are regular and most of them form their present tense stem by losing the **-en** from the infinitive.

✔ The present tense endings for weak verbs ending in **-en** are:
  -e, -st, -t, -en, -t, -en, -en.

✔ If the stem of a weak verb ends in **-d, -t, -m** or **-n**, an extra **-e** is added before the endings to make pronunciation easier.

---

3 **Forming the present tense of strong verbs**

➤ The present tense of most strong verbs is formed with the same endings that are used for weak verbs.

Pronoun	Ending	Add to Stem, e.g. sing-	Meanings
ich	-e	ich sing**e**	I sing I am singing
du	-st	du sing**st**	you sing you are singing
er sie es	-t	er sing**t** sie sing**t** es sing**t**	he/she/it sings he/she/it is singing
wir	-en	wir sing**en**	we sing we are singing
ihr	-t	ihr sing**t**	you (*plural*) sing you are singing
sie Sie	-en	sie sing**en** Sie sing**en**	they sing they are singing you (*polite*) sing you are singing

Sie sing_en_ in einer Gruppe.   They sing in a band.

➤ However, the vowels in stems of most strong verbs change for the **du** and **er/sie/es** forms. The vowels listed below change as shown in nearly all cases:

long e	→	ie (*see* **sehen**)
short e	→	i (*see* **helfen**)
a	→	ä (*see* **fahren**)
au	→	äu (*see* **laufen**)
o	→	ö (*see* **stoßen**)

● long e → ie

Pronoun	Ending	Add to Stem, e.g. seh-	Meanings
ich	-e	ich sehe	I see I am seeing
du	-st	du siehst	you see you are seeing
er sie es	-t	er sieht sie sieht es sieht	he/she/it sees he/she/it is seeing
wir	-en	wir sehen	we see we are seeing
ihr	-t	ihr seht	you (*plural*) see you are seeing
sie Sie	-en	sie sehen Sie sehen	they see they are seeing you (*polite*) see you are seeing

   Siehst du fern?   Are you watching TV?

● short e → i

Pronoun	Ending	Add to Stem, e.g. helf-	Meanings
ich	-e	ich helfe	I help I am helping
du	-st	du hilfst	you help you are helping
er sie es	-t	er hilft sie hilft es hilft	he/she/it helps he/she/it is helping
wir	-en	wir helfen	we help we are helping
ihr	-t	ihr helft	you (*plural*) help you are helping
sie Sie	-en	sie helfen Sie helfen	they help they are helping you (*polite*) help you are helping

   Heute hilft er beim Kochen.   He's helping with the cooking today.

For further explanation of grammatical terms, please see pages xii–xvi.

● a → ä

Pronoun	Ending	Add to Stem, e.g. fahr-	Meanings
ich	-e	ich fahre	I drive I am driving
du	-st	du fährst	you drive you are driving
er sie es	-t	er fährt sie fährt es fährt	he/she/it drives he/she/it is driving
wir	-en	wir fahren	we drive we are driving
ihr	-t	ihr fahrt	you (plural) drive you are driving
sie Sie	-en	sie fahren Sie fahren	they drive they are driving you (polite) drive you are driving

Am Samstag fährt sie nach Italien.   She's driving to Italy on Saturday.

● au → äu

Pronoun	Ending	Add to Stem, e.g. lauf-	Meanings
ich	-e	ich laufe	I run I am running
du	-st	du läufst	you run you are running
er sie es	-t	er läuft sie läuft es läuft	he/she/it runs he/she/it is running
wir	-en	wir laufen	we run we are running
ihr	-t	ihr lauft	you (plural) run you are running
sie Sie	-en	sie laufen Sie laufen	they run they are running you (polite) run you are running

Er läuft die 100 Meter in Rekordzeit.   He runs the 100 metres in record time.

● o → ö

Pronoun	Ending	Add to Stem, e.g. stoß-	Meanings
ich	-e	ich stoße	I push I am pushing
du	-st	du stößt	you push you are pushing
er sie es	-t	er stößt sie stößt es stößt	he/she/it pushes he/she/it is pushing
wir	-en	wir stoßen	we push we are pushing
ihr	-t	ihr stößt	you (*plural*) push you are pushing
sie Sie	-en	sie stoßen Sie stoßen	they push they are pushing you (*polite*) push you are pushing

Pass auf, dass du nicht an den Tisch stößt.

Watch out that you don't bump into the table.

i Note that strong AND weak verbs whose stem ends in **-s**, **-z**, **-ss** or **-ß** (such as stoßen) add **-t** rather than **-st** to get the du form in the present tense. However, if the stem ends in **-sch**, the normal **-st** is added.

Verb	Stem	Du Form
wachsen	wachs-	wächst
waschen	wasch-	wäschst

Key points

✔ Strong verbs have the same endings in the present tense as weak verbs.

✔ The vowel or vowels of the stem of strong verbs change(s) in the present for the du and er/sie/es forms.

---

4 | Forming the present tense of mixed verbs

➤ There are nine mixed verbs in German. They are very common and are formed according to a mixture of the rules already explained for weak and strong verbs.

For further explanation of grammatical terms, please see pages xii–xvi.

➤ The nine mixed verbs are:

Mixed Verb	Meaning	Mixed Verb	Meaning	Mixed Verb	Meaning
brennen	to burn	kennen	to know	senden	to send
bringen	to bring	nennen	to name	wenden	to turn
denken	to think	rennen	to run	wissen	to know

➤ The present tense of mixed verbs has the same endings as weak verbs and has no vowel or consonant changes in the stem: **ich bringe, du bringst, er/sie/es bringt, wir bringen, ihr bringt, sie bringen, Sie bringen**.

Sie bringt mich nach Hause.	She's bringing me home.
Bringst du mir etwas mit?	Will you bring something for me?

🛈 Note that the present tense of the most important strong, weak and mixed verbs is shown in the Verb Tables.

➪ *For **Verb Tables**, see middle section.*

Key points

✔ There are nine mixed verbs in German.

✔ The present tense of mixed verbs has the same endings as weak verbs and has no vowel or consonant changes in the stem.

Reflexive verbs

> **What is a reflexive verb?**
> A **reflexive verb** is one where the subject and object are the same, and where the action 'reflects back' on the subject. Reflexive verbs are used with a reflexive pronoun such as *myself, yourself* and *herself* in English, for example, *I washed myself; He shaved himself.*

1 Using reflexive verbs

➤ In German, reflexive verbs are much more common than in English, and many are used in everyday German. Reflexive verbs consist of two parts: the reflexive pronoun **sich** (meaning *himself, herself, itself, themselves* or *oneself*) and the infinitive of the verb.

⇨ *For more information on **Reflexive pronouns**, see page 84.*

2 Forming the present tense of reflexive verbs

➤ Reflexive verbs are often used to describe things you do (to yourself) every day or that involve a change of some sort (getting dressed, sitting down, getting excited, being in a hurry).

➤ The reflexive pronoun is either the direct object in the sentence, which means it is in the accusative case, or the indirect object in the sentence, which means it is in the dative case. Only the reflexive pronouns used with the **ich** and **du** forms of the verb have separate accusative and dative forms:

Accusative Form	Dative Form	Meaning
mich	mir	myself
dich	dir	yourself (*familiar*)
sich	sich	himself/herself/itself
uns	uns	ourselves
euch	euch	yourselves (*plural*)
sich	sich	themselves
sich	sich	yourself/yourselves (*polite*)

➤ The present tense forms of a reflexive verb work in just the same way as an ordinary verb, except that the reflexive pronoun is used as well.

➤ Below you will find the present tense of the common reflexive verbs **sich setzen** (meaning *to sit down*) which has its reflexive pronoun in the accusative and **sich erlauben** (meaning *to allow oneself*) which has its reflexive pronoun in the dative.

Reflexive Forms	Meaning
ich setze mich	I sit (myself) down
du setzt dich	you sit (yourself) down
er/sie/es setzt sich	he/she/it sits down
wir setzen uns	we sit down
ihr setzt euch	you (*plural familiar*) sit down
sie setzen sich	they sit down
Sie setzen sich	you (*polite form*) sit down

Ich setze <u>mich</u> neben dich.	I'll sit beside you.
Sie setzen <u>sich</u> aufs Sofa.	They sit down on the sofa.

Reflexive Forms	Meaning
ich erlaube mir	I allow (myself)
du erlaubst dir	you allow (yourself)
er/sie/es erlaubt sich	he/she/it allows himself/herself/itself
wir erlauben uns	we allow ourselves
ihr erlaubt euch	you (plural familiar) allow yourselves
sie erlauben sich	they allow themselves
Sie erlauben sich	you (polite form) allow yourself

Ich erlaube <u>mir</u> jetzt ein Bier.	Now I'm going to allow myself a beer.
Er erlaubt <u>sich</u> ein Stück Kuchen.	He's allowing himself a piece of cake.

➤ Some of the most common German reflexive verbs are listed here:

Reflexive Verb with Reflexive Pronoun in Accusative	Meaning
sich anziehen	to get dressed
sich aufregen	to get excited
sich beeilen	to hurry
sich beschäftigen mit	to be occupied with
sich bewerben um	to apply for
sich erinnern an	to remember
sich freuen auf	to look forward to
sich interessieren für	to be interested in
sich irren	to be wrong
sich melden	to report (for duty etc) *or* to volunteer
sich rasieren	to shave
sich setzen *or* hinsetzen	to sit down
sich trauen	to dare
sich umsehen	to look around

Ich <u>ziehe</u> <u>mich</u> schnell <u>an</u> und dann gehen wir.	I'll get dressed quickly and then we can go.
Wir müssen <u>uns</u> <u>beeilen</u>.	We must hurry.

Reflexive Verb with Reflexive Pronoun in Dative	Meaning
sich abgewöhnen	to give up (something)
sich ansehen	to have a look at
sich einbilden	to imagine (wrongly)
sich erlauben	to allow oneself
sich leisten	to treat oneself
sich nähern	to get close to
sich vornehmen	to plan to do
sich vorstellen	to imagine
sich wünschen	to want

Ich muss mir das Rauchen abgewöhnen.	I must give up smoking.
Sie kann sich ein neues Auto nicht leisten.	She can't afford a new car.
Was wünscht ihr euch zu Weihnachten?	What do you want for Christmas?

[i] Note that a direct object reflexive pronoun changes to an indirect object pronoun if another direct object is present.

Ich wasche <u>mich</u>.	I'm having a wash.
mich = direct object reflexive pronoun	
Ich wasche <u>mir</u> die Hände.	I am washing my hands.
mir = indirect object reflexive pronoun	
die Hände = direct object	

⇨ *For more information on **Pronouns**, see page 69.*

➤ Some German verbs which are not usually reflexive can be made reflexive by adding a reflexive pronoun.

Soll ich es melden?	Should I report it?
Ich habe <u>mich</u> gemeldet.	I volunteered.

⇨ *For more information on word order with **Reflexive pronouns**, see page 84.*

Key points

✔ A reflexive verb is made up of a reflexive pronoun and a verb.

✔ The direct object pronouns in the accusative are **mich, dich, sich, uns, euch, sich, sich**.

✔ The indirect object pronouns in the dative are **mir, dir, sich, uns, euch, sich, sich**.

✔ In the present tense the reflexive pronoun usually comes after the verb.

For further explanation of grammatical terms, please see pages xii–xvi.

The imperative

> **What is the imperative?**
> An **imperative** is a form of the verb used when giving orders and instructions, for example, *Shut the door!; Sit down!; Don't go!*

1 Using the imperative

➤ In German, there are three main forms of the imperative that are used to give instructions or orders to someone. These correspond to the three different ways of saying *you*: **du**, **ihr** and **Sie**. However, it is only in the **Sie** form of the imperative that the pronoun usually appears – in the **du** and **ihr** forms, the pronoun is generally dropped, leaving only the verb.

Hör zu!	Listen!
Hören <u>Sie</u> zu!	Listen!

2 Forming the present tense imperative

➤ Most weak, strong and mixed verbs form the present tense imperative in the following way:

Pronoun	Form of Imperative	Verb Example	Meaning
du (singular)	verb stem (+ **e**)	**hol(e)!**	fetch!
ihr (plural)	verb stem + **t**	**holt!**	fetch!
Sie (polite singular and plural)	verb stem + **en** + **Sie**	**holen Sie!**	fetch!

> Note that the **-e** of the **du** form is often dropped, but NOT where the verb stem ends, for example, in **chn-**, **fn-**, or **tm-**. In such cases, the **-e** is kept to make the imperative easier to pronounce.

	Hör zu!	Listen!
	Hol es!	Fetch it!
BUT:	**Öffn<u>e</u> die Tür!**	Open the door!
	Atme richtig durch!	Take a deep breath!
	Rechne nochmal nach!	Do your sums again!

Grammar Extra!

Weak verbs ending in -**eln** or -**ern** also retain this -**e**, but the other -**e** in the stem itself is often dropped in spoken German.

Verb	Meaning	Imperative	Meaning
wandern	to walk	wand(e)re!	walk!
handeln	to act	hand(e)le!	act!

➤ Any vowel change in the present tense of a strong verb also occurs in the **du** form of its imperative and the -**e** mentioned above is generally not added. However, if this vowel change in the present tense involves adding an umlaut, this umlaut is NOT added to the **du** form of the imperative.

Verb	Meaning	2nd Person Singular	Meaning	2nd Person Singular Imperative	Meaning
nehmen	to take	du nimmst	you take	nimm!	take!
helfen	to help	du hilfst	you help	hilf!	help!
laufen	to run	du läufst	you run	lauf(e)!	run!
stoßen	to push	du stößt	you push	stoß(e)!	push!

3 | Word order with the imperative

➤ An object pronoun is a word like **es** (meaning *it*), **mir** (meaning *me*) or **ihnen** (meaning *them/to them*) that is used instead of a noun as the object of a sentence. In the imperative, the object pronoun comes straight after the verb. However, you can have orders and instructions containing both <u>direct object</u> and <u>indirect object pronouns</u>. In these cases, the direct object pronoun always comes before the indirect object pronoun.

Hol mir das Buch!	Fetch me that book!
Hol es mir!	Fetch me it!
Holt mir das Buch!	Fetch me that book!
Holt es mir!	Fetch me it!
Holen Sie mir das Buch!	Fetch me that book!
Holen Sie es mir!	Fetch me it!

➪ *For more information on **Word order with indirect object pronouns**, see page 77.*

➤ In the imperative form of a reflexive verb such as **sich waschen** (meaning *to wash oneself*) or **sich setzen** (meaning *to sit down*), the reflexive pronoun comes immediately after the verb.

For further explanation of grammatical terms, please see pages xii–xvi.

Reflexive verb	Meaning	Imperative Forms	Meaning
sich setzen	to sit down	setz <u>dich</u>!	sit down!
		setzt <u>euch</u>!	sit down!
		setzen Sie <u>sich</u>!	do sit down!

⇨ *For more information on **Reflexive pronouns**, see page 84.*

➤ In verbs which have separable prefixes, the prefix comes at the end of the imperative.

Verb with Separable Prefix	Meaning	Imperative Example	Meaning
zumachen	to close	Mach die Tür zu!	Close the door!
aufhören	to stop	Hör aber endlich auf!	Do stop it!

⇨ *For more information on **Separable prefixes**, see page 109.*

4 Other points about the imperative

➤ In German, imperatives are usually followed by an exclamation mark, unless they are not being used to give an order or instruction. For example, they can also be used where we might say *Can you...* or *Could you ...* in English.

Lass ihn in Ruhe!	Leave him alone!
Sagen Sie mir bitte, wie spät es ist.	Can you tell me what time it is please?

➤ The verb **sein** (meaning *to be*) is a strong, irregular verb. Its imperative forms are also irregular and the **du**, **Sie** and less common **wir** forms are not the same as the present tense forms of the verb.

Sei ruhig!	be quiet!
Seid ruhig!	be quiet!
Seien Sie ruhig!	be quiet!

Tip

The words **auch**, **nur**, **mal** and **doch** are frequently used with imperatives to change their meanings in different ways, but are often not translated since they have no direct equivalent in English.

Geh doch!	Go on!/Get going!
Sag mal, wo warst du?	Tell me, where were you?
Versuchen Sie es mal!	Give it a try!
Komm schon!	Do come/Please come.
Mach es auch richtig!	Be sure to do it properly.

Grammar Extra!

There are some alternatives to using the imperative in German:

- Infinitives (the *to* form of a verb) are often used instead of the imperative in written instructions or public announcements

Einsteigen!	All aboard!
Zwiebeln abziehen und in Ringe schneiden.	Peel the onions and slice them.

- Nouns, adjectives or adverbs can also be used as imperatives

Ruhe!	Be quiet!/Silence!
Vorsicht!	Careful!/Look out!

  Some of these have become set expressions

Achtung!	Listen!/Attention!
Rauchen verboten!	No smoking.

Key points

✔ The imperative has four forms: **du**, **ihr**, **Sie** and **wir**.

✔ The forms are the same as the **ihr**, **Sie** and **wir** forms of the present tense for most strong, weak and mixed verbs, but the **du** form drops the **-st** present tense ending and sometimes adds an **-e** on the end.

✔ Any vowel change in the stem of a strong verb also occurs in the imperative, except if it involves adding an umlaut.

✔ Object pronouns always go after the verb, with the direct object pronoun coming before the indirect object pronoun.

✔ Reflexive pronouns also come after the verb, while separable verb prefixes come at the end of the imperative sentence.

✔ Sein has irregular imperative forms.

For further explanation of grammatical terms, please see pages xii–xvi.

Verb prefixes in the present tense

> **What is a verb prefix?**
> In English, a **verb prefix** is a word such as *up* or *down* which is used with verbs to create new verbs with an entirely different meaning.
>
> > get → get up → get down
> >
> > put → put up → put down
> >
> > shut → shut up → shut down

➤ In German there is a similar system, but the words are put before the infinitive and joined to it:

> **zu** (meaning *to*) + **geben** (meaning *to give*) = **zugeben** (meaning *to admit*)
>
> **an** (meaning *on, to, by*) + **ziehen** (meaning *to pull*) = **anziehen** (meaning *to put on* or *to attract*)

➤ Prefixes can be found in strong, weak and mixed verbs. Some prefixes are always joined to the verb and never separated from it – these are called inseparable prefixes. However, the majority are separated from the verb in certain tenses and forms, and come at the end of the sentence. They are called separable prefixes.

1 Inseparable prefixes

➤ There are eight inseparable prefixes in German, highlighted in the table of common inseparable verbs below:

Inseparable Verb	Meaning	Inseparable Verb	Meaning	Inseparable Verb	Meaning	Inseparable Verb	Meaning
beschreiben	to describe	enttäuschen	to disappoint	gehören	to belong	verlieren	to lose
empfangen	to receive	erhalten	to preserve	misstrauen	to mistrust	zerlegen	to dismantle

📖 Note that when you pronounce an inseparable verb, the stress is NEVER on the inseparable prefix:

> er*hal*ten
>
> ver*lie*ren
>
> emp*fan*gen
>
> ver*ges*sen

Das muss ich wirklich nicht ver*ges*sen.	I really mustn't forget that.

2 Separable prefixes

➤ There are many separable prefixes in German and some of them are highlighted in the table below which shows a selection of the most common separable verbs:

Separable Verb	Meaning	Separable Verb	Meaning
<u>ab</u>fahren	to leave	<u>mit</u>machen	to join in
<u>an</u>kommen	to arrive	<u>nach</u>geben	to give way/in
<u>auf</u>stehen	to get up	<u>vor</u>ziehen	to prefer
<u>aus</u>gehen	to go out	<u>weg</u>laufen	to run away
<u>ein</u>steigen	to get on	<u>zu</u>schauen	to watch
<u>fest</u>stellen	to establish/see	<u>zurecht</u>kommen	to manage
<u>frei</u>halten	to keep free	<u>zurück</u>kehren	to return
<u>her</u>kommen	to come (here)	<u>zusammen</u>passen	to be well-suited; to go well together
<u>hin</u>legen	to put down		

Der Zug fährt in zehn Minuten <u>ab</u>.	The train is leaving in ten minutes.
Ich stehe jeden Morgen früh <u>auf</u>.	I get up early every morning.
Sie gibt niemals <u>nach</u>.	She'll never give in.

3 | Word order with separable prefixes

➤ In tenses consisting of one verb part only, for example the present and the imperfect, the separable prefix is placed at the end of the main clause.

Der Bus kam immer spät <u>an</u>.	The bus was always late.

⇨ *For more information on **Separable prefixes in the perfect tense**, see page 115.*

➤ In subordinate clauses, the prefix is attached to the verb, which is then placed at the end of the subordinate clause.

Weil der Bus spät <u>an</u>kam, verpasste sie den Zug.	Because the bus arrived late, she missed the train.

⇨ *For more information on **Subordinate clauses**, see page 177.*

➤ In infinitive phrases using **zu**, the **zu** is inserted between the verb and its prefix to form one word.

Um rechtzeitig auf<u>zu</u>stehen, muss ich den Wecker stellen.	In order to get up on time I'll have to set the alarm.

⇨ *For more information on the **Infinitive**, see page 134.*

4 Verb combinations

➤ Below you will see some other types of word which can be combined with verbs. These combinations are mostly written as two separate words and behave like separable verbs:

- Noun + verb combinations

Ski fahren	to ski
Ich <u>fahre</u> gern <u>Ski</u>.	I like skiing
Schlittschuh laufen	to ice-skate
Im Winter kann man <u>Schlittschuh laufen</u>.	You can ice-skate in Winter.

- Infinitive + verb combinations

kennenlernen	to meet or to get to know
Meine Mutter möchte dich <u>kennenlernen</u>.	My mother wants to meet you.
Er <u>lernt</u> sie nie richtig <u>kennen</u>.	He'll never get to know her properly.
sitzen bleiben	to remain seated
<u>Bleiben</u> Sie bitte <u>sitzen</u>.	Please remain seated.
spazieren gehen	to go for a walk
Er <u>geht</u> jeden Tag <u>spazieren</u>.	He goes for a walk every day.

- Other adjective + verb combinations

bekannt machen	to announce
Die Regierung will das morgen <u>bekannt machen</u>.	The government plans to announce it tomorrow.

- Some adverb + verb combinations

kaputt machen	to break
<u>Mach</u> mir bloß mein Fahrrad nicht <u>kaputt</u>!	Don't you dare break my bike!

- Verb combinations with **-seits**

abseitsstehen	to stand apart
Sie <u>steht</u> immer <u>abseits</u> von den anderen.	She always stands apart from the others.

- Prefix combinations with **sein**

auf sein	to be open or to be up
Das Fenster <u>ist auf</u>.	The window is open.
Die Geschäfte <u>sind</u> am Sonntag nicht <u>auf</u>.	The shops are closed on Sundays.
Sie <u>ist</u> noch nicht <u>auf</u>.	She isn't up yet.

zu sein	to be shut
Das Fenster <u>ist</u> <u>zu</u>.	The window is shut.

i Note that **auf** (meaning *open*) is another word for **geöffnet** and **zu** (meaning *shut* or *closed*) is another word for **geschlossen**.

Key points

✔ Prefixes can be found in strong, weak and mixed verbs.

✔ Eight prefixes are inseparable and are never separated from the verb.

✔ Most prefixes are separable and are separated from the verb in certain tenses and forms and come at the end of the sentence.

For further explanation of grammatical terms, please see pages xii–xvi.

The perfect tense

> **What is the perfect tense?**
> The **perfect** is one of the verb tenses used to talk about the past, especially about a single, rather than a repeated action.
>
> Den Nachtisch habe ich schon   I've already eaten dessert.
> gegessen.

1 Using the perfect tense

➤ The German perfect tense is the one generally used to translate an English form such as *I have finished*.

I <u>have</u> finished the book.   **Ich <u>habe</u> das Buch zu Ende <u>gelesen</u>.**

➤ The perfect tense is also sometimes used to translate an English form such as *I gave*.

I gave him my phone number.   **Ich <u>habe</u> ihm meine Nummer
                                      <u>gegeben</u>.**

> *Tip*
>
> When a specific time in the past is referred to, you use the perfect tense in German. In English you use the *-ed* form instead.
>
> **Gestern Abend habe ich einen Krimi   Last night I watched a
> im Fernsehen gesehen.**   thriller on TV.

➤ The perfect tense is used with **seit** or **seitdem** to describe a completed action in the past, whereas the present tense is used to describe an action which started in the past and is still continuing in the present.

<u>Seit</u> dem Unfall <u>habe</u> ich sie nur   I've only seen her once since the
einmal <u>gesehen</u>.   accident.

➪ *For more information on this use of the **Present tense**, see page 94.*

2 Forming the perfect tense

➤ Unlike the present and imperfect tenses, the perfect tense has <u>TWO</u> parts to it:

- the <u>present</u> tense of the irregular weak verb **haben** (meaning *to have*) or the irregular strong verb **sein** (meaning *to be*). They are also known as auxiliary verbs.

- a part of the main verb called the *past participle*, like *given*, *finished* and *done* in English.

➤ In other words, the perfect tense in German is like the form *I have done* in English.

Pronoun	Ending	Present Tense	Meanings
ich	-e	ich hab<u>e</u>	I have
du	-st	du ha<u>st</u>	you have
er sie es	-t	er ha<u>t</u> sie ha<u>t</u> es ha<u>t</u>	he/she/it has
wir	-en	wir hab<u>en</u>	we have
ihr	-t	ihr hab<u>t</u>	you (*plural*) have
sie	-en	sie hab<u>en</u>	they have
Sie		Sie hab<u>en</u>	you (*polite*) have

Pronoun	Ending	Present Tense	Meanings
ich	–	ich bin	I am
du	–	du bist	you are
er sie es	–	er ist sie ist es ist	he/she/it is
wir	–	wir sind	we are
ihr	–	ihr seid	you (*plural*) are
sie	–	sie sind	they are
Sie	–	Sie sind	you (*polite*) are

3 Forming the past participle

➤ To form the past participle of <u>weak</u> verbs, you add **ge-** to the beginning of the verb stem and **-t** to the end.

Infinitive	Take off -en	Add ge- and -t
holen (*to fetch*)	hol-	geholt
machen (*to do*)	mach-	gemacht

i Note that one exception to this rule is weak verbs ending in **-ieren**, which omit the **ge**.

    studieren (*to study*)   **studiert** (*studied*)

➤ To form the past participle of <u>strong</u> verbs, you add **ge-** to the beginning of the verb stem and **-en** to the end. The vowel in the stem may also change.

Infinitive	Take off -en	Add ge- and -en
laufen (*to run*)	lauf-	gelaufen
singen (*to sing*)	sing-	gesungen

For further explanation of grammatical terms, please see pages xii–xvi.

➤ To form the past participle of <u>mixed</u> verbs, you add **ge-** to the beginning of the verb stem and, like <u>weak</u> verbs, **-t** to the end. As with many strong verbs, the stem vowel may also change.

Infinitive	Take off -en	Add ge- and -t
bringen (*to run*)	bring-	gebracht
denken (*to think*)	denk-	gedacht

➤ The perfect tense of <u>separable</u> verbs is also formed in the above way, except that the separable prefix is joined on to the front of the **ge-: ich habe die Flasche aufgemacht, du hast die Flasche aufgemacht** and so on.

➤ With <u>inseparable</u> verbs, the only difference is that past participles are formed without the **ge-: ich habe Kaffee bestellt, du hast Kaffee bestellt** and so on.

⇨ *For more information on **Separable** and **Inseparable verbs**, see page* 109.

---

4 | **Verbs that form their perfect tense with** <u>haben</u>

➤ Most weak, strong and mixed verbs form their perfect tense with **haben**, for example **machen**:

Pronoun	haben	Past Participle	Meaning
ich	habe	gemacht	I did, I have done
du	hast	gemacht	you did, you have done
er sie es	hat	gemacht	he/she/it did, he/she/it has done
wir	haben	gemacht	we did, we have done
ihr	habt	gemacht	you (*plural familiar*) did, you have done
sie	haben	gemacht	they did, they have done
Sie	haben	gemacht	you (*singular/plural formal*) did, you have done

Sie hat ihre Hausaufgaben schon gemacht.	She has already done her homework.
Haben Sie gut geschlafen?	Did you sleep well?
Er hat fleißig gearbeitet.	He has worked hard.

5 haben or sein?

➤ <u>MOST</u> verbs form their perfect tense with **haben**.

Ich **habe** das schon <u>gemacht</u>.	I've already done that.
Wo **haben** Sie früher <u>gearbeitet</u>?	Where did you work before?

➤ With reflexive verbs the reflexive pronoun comes immediately after **haben**.

Ich **habe mich** heute Morgen geduscht.	I had a shower this morning.
Sie **hat sich** nicht daran erinnert.	She didn't remember.

⇨ *For more information on **Reflexive verbs**, see page 102.*

➤ There are two main groups of verbs which form their perfect tense with **sein** instead of **haben**, and most of them are strong verbs:

● verbs which take no direct object and are used mainly to talk about movement or a change of some kind, such as:

gehen	to go
kommen	to come
ankommen	to arrive
abfahren	to leave
aussteigen	to get off
einsteigen	to get on
sterben	to die
sein	to be
werden	to become
bleiben	to remain
begegnen	to meet
gelingen	to succeed
aufstehen	to get up
fallen	to fall

Gestern <u>bin</u> ich ins Kino <u>gegangen</u>.	I went to the cinema yesterday.
Sie <u>ist</u> heute Morgen ganz früh <u>abgefahren</u>.	She left really early this morning.
An welcher Haltestelle <u>sind</u> Sie <u>ausgestiegen</u>?	Which stop did you get off at?

● two verbs which mean *to happen*.

Was **ist geschehen/passiert**?	What happened?

For further explanation of grammatical terms, please see pages xii–xvi.

⇨ Here are the perfect tense forms of a very common strong verb, **gehen**, in full:

Pronoun	sein	Past Participle	Meanings
ich	bin	gegangen	I went, I have gone
du	bist	gegangen	you went, you have gone
er sie es	ist	gegangen	he/she/it went, he/she/it has gone
wir	sind	gegangen	we went, we have gone
ihr	seid	gegangen	you (*plural familiar*) went, you have gone
sie	sind	gegangen	they went, they have gone
Sie	sind	gegangen	you (*singular/plural formal*) went, you have gone

i Note that the perfect tense of the most important strong, weak and mixed verbs is shown in the Verb Tables.

⇨ For **Verb Tables**, *see middle section.*

Key points

✔ The perfect tense describes things that happened and were completed in the past.

✔ The perfect tense is formed with the present tense of **haben** or **sein** and a past participle.

✔ The past participle begins in **ge-** and ends in **-t** for weak verbs, in **ge-** and **-en** for strong verbs often with a stem vowel change, and in **ge-** and **-t** for mixed verbs, with a stem vowel change.

✔ Most verbs take **haben** in the perfect tense. Many strong verbs, especially those referring to movement or change, take **sein**.

The imperfect tense

> **What is the imperfect tense?**
> The **imperfect tense** is one of the verb tenses used to talk about the past, especially in descriptions, and to say what used to happen, for example, *It was sunny at the weekend; I used to walk to school.*

1 Using the imperfect tense

➤ The German imperfect tense is used:

- to describe actions in the past which the speaker feels have no link with the present

Er kam zu spät, um teilnehmen zu können.	He arrived too late to take part.

- to describe what things were like and how people felt in the past

Ich war ganz traurig, als sie wegging.	I was very sad when she left.
Damals gab es ein großes Problem mit Drogen.	There was a big problem with drugs at that time.

- to say what used to happen or what you used to do regularly in the past

Wir machten jeden Tag einen Spaziergang.	We used to go for a walk every day.
Samstags spielte ich Tennis.	I used to play tennis on Saturdays.

[*i*] Note that if you want to talk about an event or action that took place and was completed in the past, you normally use the perfect tense in German conversation. The imperfect tense is normally used in written German.

Was hast du heute gemacht?	What have you done today?

⇨ *For more information on the **Perfect tense**, see page 113.*

➤ When using **seit** or **seitdem** to describe something that had happened or had been true at a point in the past, the imperfect is used in German, where in English a verb form with *had* is used.

Sie war seit ihrer Heirat als Lehrerin beschäftigt.	She had been working as a teacher since her marriage.

⇨ *For more information on the **Pluperfect tense**, see page 127.*

Tip

Remember that you <u>NEVER</u> use the verb **sein** to translate *was* or *were* in forms like *was raining* or *were looking* and so on. You change the German verb ending instead.

2 Forming the imperfect tense of weak verbs

➤ To form the imperfect tense of weak verbs, you use the same stem of the verb as for the present tense. Then you add the correct ending, depending on whether you are referring to **ich**, **du**, **er**, **sie**, **es**, **wir**, **ihr**, **sie** or **Sie**.

Pronoun	Ending	Add to Stem, e.g. spiel-	Meanings
ich	-te	ich spiel<u>te</u>	I played I was playing
du	-test	du spiel<u>test</u>	you played you were playing
er sie es	-te	er spiel<u>te</u> sie spiel<u>te</u> es spiel<u>te</u>	he/she/it played he/she/it played he/she/it were playing
wir	-ten	wir spiel<u>ten</u>	we played we were playing
ihr	-tet	ihr spiel<u>tet</u>	you (*plural*) played you were playing
sie	-ten	sie spiel<u>ten</u>	they played they were playing
Sie		Sie spiel<u>ten</u>	you (*polite*) played you were playing

Sie hol<u>te</u> ihn jeden Tag von der Arbeit ab.	She picked him up from work every day.
Normalerweise mach<u>te</u> ich nach dem Abendessen meine Hausaufgaben.	I usually did my homework after dinner.

➤ As with the present tense, some weak verbs change their spellings slightly when they are used in the imperfect tense.

● If the stem ends in **-d**, **-t**, **-m** or **-n** an extra **-e** is added before the usual imperfect endings to make pronunciation easier.

Pronoun	Ending	Add to Stem, e.g. arbeit-	Meanings
ich	-ete	ich arbeit<u>ete</u>	I worked I was working
du	-etest	du arbeit<u>etest</u>	you worked you were working
er sie es	-ete	er arbeit<u>ete</u> sie arbeit<u>ete</u> es arbeit<u>ete</u>	he/she/it worked he/she/it was working
wir	-eten	wir arbeit<u>eten</u>	we worked we were working
ihr	-etet	ihr arbeit<u>etet</u>	you (*plural*) worked you were working
sie	-eten	sie arbeit<u>eten</u>	they worked they were working
Sie	-eten	Sie arbeit<u>eten</u>	you (*polite*) worked you (*polite*) were working

Sie arbeit<u>ete</u> übers Wochenende.	She was working over the weekend.
Ihr arbeit<u>etet</u> ganz schön viel.	You worked a lot.

- If the **-m** or **-n** has one of the consonants *l*, *r* or *h* in front of it, the **-e** is not added as shown in the **du**, **er**, **sie** and **es**, and **ihr** forms below.

Pronoun	Ending	Add to Stem, e.g. lern-	Meanings
du	-test	du lern<u>test</u>	you learned you were learning
er sie es	-te	er lern<u>te</u> sie lern<u>te</u> es lern<u>te</u>	he/she/it learned he/she/it was learning
ihr	-tet	ihr lern<u>tet</u>	you (*plural*) learned you were learning

Sie lernte alles ganz schnell.	She learned everything very quickly.

3 Forming the imperfect tense of strong verbs

➤ The main difference between strong verbs and weak verbs in the imperfect is that strong verbs have a vowel change and take a different set of endings. For example, let's compare **sagen** and **rufen**:

	Infinitive	Meaning	Present	Imperfect
Weak	sagen	to say	er sagt	er sagte
Strong	rufen	to shout	er ruft	er rief

➤ To form the imperfect tense of strong verbs you add the following endings to the stem, which undergoes a vowel change.

Pronoun	Ending	Add to Stem, e.g. rief-	Meanings
ich	–	ich rief	I shouted I was shouting
du	-st	du riefst	you shouted you were shouting
er sie es	–	er rief sie rief es rief	he/she/it shouted he/she/it were shouting
wir	-en	wir riefen	we shouted we were shouting
ihr	-t	ihr rieft	you (plural) shouted you were shouting
sie	-en	sie riefen	they shouted they were shouting
Sie		Sie riefen	you (polite) shouted you were shouting

Sie rief mich immer freitags an.	She always called me on Friday.
Sie liefen die Straße entlang.	They ran along the street.
Als Kind sangst du viel.	You used to sing a lot as a child.

➤ As in other tenses, the verb **sein** is a very irregular strong verb since the imperfect forms seem to have no relation to the infinitive form of the verb: **ich war, du warst, er/sie/es war, wir waren, ihr wart, sie/Sie waren**.

4 Forming the imperfect tense of mixed verbs

➤ The imperfect tense of mixed verbs is formed by adding the weak verb endings to a stem whose vowel has been changed as for a strong verb.

Pronoun	Ending	Add to Stem, e.g. kann-	Meanings
ich	-te	ich kannte	I knew
du	-test	du kanntest	you knew
er sie es	-te	er kannte sie kannte es kannte	he/she/it knew
wir	-ten	wir kannten	we knew
ihr	-tet	ihr kanntet	you (plural) knew
sie	-ten	sie kannten	they knew
Sie		Sie kannten	you (polite) knew

Er kannte die Stadt nicht.	He didn't know the town.

➤ **Bringen** (meaning *to bring*) and **denken** (meaning *to think*) have a vowel AND a consonant change in their imperfect forms

bringen (*to bring*)	**denken** (*to think*)
ich br**a**ch**te**	ich d**a**ch**te**
du br**a**ch**test**	du d**a**ch**test**
er/sie/es br**a**ch**te**	er/sie/es d**a**ch**te**
wir br**a**ch**ten**	wir d**a**ch**ten**
ihr br**a**ch**tet**	ihr d**a**ch**tet**
sie/Sie br**a**ch**ten**	sie/Sie d**a**ch**ten**

| *i* | Note that the imperfect tense of the most important strong, weak and mixed verbs is shown in the Verb Tables. |

⇨ For **Verb Tables**, see middle section.

Key points

✔ The imperfect tense is generally used for things that happened regularly or for descriptions in the past, especially in written German.

✔ The imperfect of weak verbs is formed using the same stem of the verb as for the present tense + these endings: **-te**, **-test**, **-te**, **-ten**, **-tet**, **-ten**.

✔ If the stem of a weak verb ends in **-d**, **-t**, **-m** or **-n** an extra **-e** is added before the usual imperfect endings to make pronunciation easier. If the **-m** or **-n** has one of the consonants *l*, *r* or *h* in front of it, the **-e** is not added.

✔ The imperfect tense of strong verbs is formed by adding the following endings to the stem, which undergoes a vowel change: **-**, **-st**, **-**, **-en**, **-t**, **-en**.

✔ The imperfect tense of mixed verbs is formed by adding the weak verb endings to a stem whose vowel has been changed as for a strong verb. The verbs **bringen** and **denken** also have a consonant change.

The future tense

What is the future tense?
The **future tense** is a verb tense used to talk about something that will happen or will be true.

1 Using the future tense

➤ In English the future tense is often shown by *will* or its shortened form *'ll*.

What <u>will</u> you do?

The weather <u>will</u> be warm and dry tomorrow.

He'<u>ll</u> be here soon.

I'<u>ll</u> give you a call.

➤ Just as in English, you can use the present tense in German to refer to something that is going to happen in the future.

Wir <u>fahren</u> nächstes Jahr nach Griechenland.	We're going to Greece next year.
Ich <u>nehme</u> den letzten Zug heute Abend.	I'm taking the last train tonight.

➤ The future tense IS used however to:

- emphasize the future

Das <u>werde</u> ich erst nächstes Jahr <u>machen</u> können.	I won't be able to do that until next year.

- express doubt or suppose something about the future

Wenn sie zurückkommt, <u>wird</u> sie mir bestimmt <u>helfen</u>.	I'm sure she'll help me when she returns.

➤ In English we often use *going to* followed by an infinitive to talk about something that will happen in the immediate future. You CANNOT use the German verb **gehen** (meaning *to go*) followed by an infinitive in the same way. Instead, you use either the present or the future tense.

Das <u>wirst</u> du bereuen.	You're going to regret that.
Wenn er sich nicht beeilt, <u>verpasst</u> er den Zug.	He's going to miss the train if he doesn't hurry up.

2 Forming the future tense

➤ The future tense has <u>TWO</u> parts to it and is formed in the same way for all verbs, be they weak, strong or mixed:

- the present tense of the strong verb **werden** (meaning *to become*), which acts as an <u>auxiliary verb</u> like **haben** and **sein** in the perfect tense

Pronoun	Ending	Present Tense	Meanings
ich	-e	ich werde	I become
du	-st	du wirst	you become
er sie es	–	er wird sie wird es wird	he/she/it becomes
wir	-en	wir werden	we become
ihr	-t	ihr werdet	you (*plural*) become
sie	-en	sie werden	they become
Sie	-en	Sie werden	you (*polite*) become

- the infinitive of the main verb, which normally goes at the end of the clause or sentence.

Pronoun	Present Tense of werden	Infinitive of Main Verb	Meanings
ich	werde	holen	I will fetch
du	wirst	holen	you will fetch
er sie es	wird	holen	he/she/it will fetch
wir	werden	holen	we will fetch
ihr	werdet	holen	you (*plural*) will fetch
sie Sie	werden	holen	they will fetch you (*polite*) will fetch

Morgen <u>werde</u> ich mein Fahrrad <u>holen</u>.	I'll fetch my bike tomorrow.
Sie <u>wird</u> dir meine Adresse <u>geben</u>.	She'll give you my address.
Wir <u>werden</u> draußen <u>warten</u>.	We'll wait outside.

i Note that in reflexive verbs, the reflexive pronoun comes after the present tense of **werden**.

Ich <u>werde</u> mich nächste Woche <u>vorbereiten</u>.	I'll prepare next week.

> ### Key points
>
> ✔ You can use a present tense in German to talk about something that will happen or be true in the future, just as in English.
>
> ✔ The future tense is formed from the present tense of **werden** and the infinitive of the main verb.
>
> ✔ You CANNOT use **gehen** with an infinitive to refer to things that will happen in the immediate future.
>
> ✔ The future tense is used to emphasize the future and express doubt or suppose something about the future.

For further explanation of grammatical terms, please see pages xii–xvi.

The conditional

> **What is the conditional?**
> The **conditional** is a verb form used to talk about things that would happen or that would be true under certain conditions, for example, *I would help you if I could*. It is also used to say what you would like or need, for example, *Could you give me the bill?*

1 Using the conditional

➤ You can often recognize a conditional in English by the word *would* or its shortened form *'d*.

   I <u>would</u> be sad if you left.
   If you asked him, he<u>'d</u> help you.

➤ In German, the conditional is also used to express *would*.

Ich <u>würde</u> dir schon <u>helfen</u>, ich habe aber keine Zeit.	I <u>would</u> help you, but I don't have the time.
Was <u>würden</u> Sie an meiner Stelle <u>tun</u>?	What <u>would</u> you do in my position?

2 Forming the conditional

➤ The conditional has <u>TWO</u> parts to it and is formed in the same way for all verbs, be they weak, strong or mixed:

- the **würde** form or subjunctive of the verb **werden** (meaning *to become*)
- the infinitive of the main verb, which normally goes at the end of the clause.

Pronoun	Subjunctive of werden	Infinitive of Main Verb	Meanings
ich	würde	holen	I would fetch
du	würdest	holen	you would fetch
er sie es	würde	holen	he/she/it would fetch
wir	würden	holen	we would fetch
ihr	würdet	holen	you (*plural*) would fetch
sie Sie	würden	holen	they would fetch you (*polite*) would fetch

Das <u>würde</u> ich nie <u>machen</u>.	I would never do that.
<u>Würdest</u> du mir etwas Geld <u>leihen</u>?	Would you lend me some money?
<u>Würden</u> Sie jemals mit dem Rauchen <u>aufhören</u>?	Would you ever stop smoking?

i Note that you have to be careful not to mix up the present tense of **werden**, used to form the future tense, and the subjunctive of **werden**, used to form the conditional. They look similar.

FUTURE USE	CONDITIONAL USE
ich werde	ich würde
du wirst	du würdest
er/sie/es wird	er/sie/es würde
wir werden	wir würden
ihr werdet	ihr würdet
sie/Sie werden	sie/Sie würden

Key points

✔ The conditional tense is formed from the subjunctive or **würde** part of **werden** and the infinitive of the main verb.

✔ The conditional tense is often used with the subjunctive.

The pluperfect tense

> **What is the pluperfect tense?**
> The **pluperfect** is a verb tense which describes something that had happened or had been true at a point in the past, for example, *I'd forgotten* to finish my homework.

1 Using the pluperfect tense

➤ You can often recognize a pluperfect tense in English by a form like *I had arrived, you'd fallen*.

Sie <u>waren</u> schon <u>weggefahren</u>.	They <u>had</u> already <u>left</u>.
Diese Bücher <u>hatten</u> sie schon <u>gelesen</u>.	They <u>had</u> already <u>read</u> these books.
Meine Eltern <u>waren</u> schon ins Bett <u>gegangen</u>.	My parents <u>had gone</u> to bed early.

i Note that when translating *had done/had been doing* in conjunction with **seit/seitdem**, you use the imperfect tense in German.

Sie <u>machte</u> es seit Jahren.	She <u>had been doing</u> it for years.

➪ *For more information on the **Imperfect tense**, see page 118.*

2 Forming the pluperfect tense

➤ Like the perfect tense, the pluperfect tense in German has <u>two</u> parts to it:

- the <u>imperfect</u> tense of the verb **haben** (meaning *to have*) or **sein** (meaning *to be*)
- the past participle.

➤ If a verb takes **haben** in the perfect tense, then it will take **haben** in the pluperfect too. If a verb takes **sein** in the perfect, then it will take **sein** in the pluperfect.

➪ *For more information on the **Imperfect tense** and the **Perfect tense**, see pages 118 and 113.*

3 Verbs taking haben

➤ Here are the pluperfect tense forms of **holen** (meaning *to fetch*) in full.

Pronoun	haben	Past Participle	Meanings
ich	hatte	geholt	I had fetched
du	hattest	geholt	you had fetched
er sie es	hatte	geholt	he/she/it had fetched
wir	hatten	geholt	we had fetched
ihr	hattet	geholt	you (*plural*) had fetched
sie Sie	hatten	geholt	they had fetched you (*polite*) had fetched

Ich <u>hatte</u> schon mit ihm <u>gesprochen</u>.   I had already spoken to him.

4 **Verbs taking sein**

➤ Here are the pluperfect tense forms of **reisen** (meaning *to travel*) in full.

Pronoun	sein	Past Participle	Meanings
ich	war	gereist	I had travelled
du	warst	gereist	you had travelled
er sie es	war	gereist	he/she/it had travelled
wir	waren	gereist	we had travelled
ihr	wart	gereist	you (*plural*) had travelled
sie Sie	waren	gereist	they had travelled you (*polite*) had travelled

Sie war sehr spät angekommen.   She had arrived very late.

Key points

✔ The pluperfect tense describes things that had happened or were true at a point in the past before something else happened.

✔ It is formed with the imperfect tense of **haben** or **sein** and the past participle.

✔ Verbs which take **haben** in the perfect tense will take **haben** in the pluperfect tense and those which take **sein** in the perfect tense will take **sein** in the pluperfect tense.

The subjunctive

> **What is the subjunctive?**
> The **subjunctive** is a verb form that is used in certain circumstances to express some sort of feeling, or to show there is doubt about whether something will happen or whether something is true. It is only used occasionally in modern English, for example, *If I were you, I wouldn't bother; So be it*.

1 | Using the subjunctive

➤ In German, subjunctive forms are used much more frequently than in English, to express uncertainty, speculation or doubt.

> **Es könnte doch wahr sein.**   It could be true.

➤ Subjunctives are also commonly used in <u>indirect speech</u>, also known as <u>reported speech</u>. What a person asks or thinks can be reported <u>directly</u>:

> **Sie sagte: „Er <u>kennt</u> deine Schwester"**   She said, "He <u>knows</u> your sister"
>
> OR <u>indirectly</u>:
>
> **Sie sagte, er <u>kenne</u> meine Schwester.**   She said he <u>knew</u> my sister.

i Note that the change from direct to indirect speech is indicated by a change of tense in English, but is shown by a change to the subjunctive form in German.

Grammar Extra!

➤ There are two ways of introducing indirect speech in German, as in English.

- The conjunction **dass** (meaning *that*) begins the clause containing the indirect speech and the verb goes to the end of the clause.

> **Sie hat uns gesagt, <u>dass</u> sie Italienisch <u>spreche</u>.**   She told us that she spoke Italian.

- **dass** is dropped and normal word order applies in the second clause – the verb comes directly after the subject.

> **Sie hat uns gesagt, sie <u>spreche</u> Italienisch.**   She told us she spoke Italian.

➤ If you want to express a possible situation in English, for example, *I would be happy if you came*, you use *'if'* followed by the appropriate tense of the verb. In German you use the conjunction **wenn** followed by a subjunctive form of the verb.

i Note that the verb <u>ALWAYS</u> goes to the end of a clause beginning with **wenn**.

- **wenn** (meaning *if, whenever*)

  Wenn du <u>käm(e)st *(subjunctive)*</u>, <u>wäre</u> *(subjunctive)* ich froh.

  OR

  Wenn du <u>käm(e)st</u>, würde ich froh sein.   I would be happy if you came.

[i] Note that the main clause can either have a subjunctive form or the conditional tense.

  Wenn es mir nicht <u>gefiele</u>, würde ich
  es nicht bezahlen.

  OR

  Wenn es mir nicht <u>gefiele</u>, <u>bezahlte</u>   If I wasn't happy with it,
  (subjunctive) ich es nicht.   I wouldn't pay for it.

Tip

The imperfect forms of **bezahlen**, and of all weak verbs, are exactly the same as the imperfect subjunctive forms, so it's better to use a conditional tense to avoid confusion.

➤ **wenn ... nur** (meaning *if only*), **selbst wenn** (meaning *even if* or *even though*) and **wie** (meaning *how*) work in the same way as **wenn**. This means that the normal word order is changed and the verb comes at the end of the clause.

- **wenn ... nur**

  <u>Wenn</u> wir <u>nur</u> erfolgreich <u>wären</u>!   If only we were successful!

- **selbst wenn**

  <u>Selbst wenn</u> er etwas <u>wüsste</u>, würde   Even if he knew about it,
  er nichts sagen.   he wouldn't say anything.

- **wie**, expressing uncertainty

  Er wunderte sich, wie es ihr wohl <u>ginge</u>.   He wondered how she was.

➤ Unlike **wenn** and **wie** etc, the word order does not change after **als** (meaning *as if* or *as though*) when it is used in conditional clauses: it is immediately followed by the verb.

  Sie sah aus, <u>als</u> <u>sei</u> sie krank.   She looked as if she were ill.

Tip

It is quite common to hear the subjunctive used when someone is asking you something politely, for example, the person serving you in a shop might ask:

  <u>Wäre</u> da sonst noch etwas?   Will there be anything else?

---

2 Forming the present subjunctive

➤ The three main forms of the subjunctive are the <u>present subjunctive</u>, the <u>imperfect subjunctive</u> and the <u>pluperfect subjunctive</u>.

➤ The present subjunctive of weak, strong and mixed verbs has the same endings:

Pronoun	Present Subjunctive: Weak and Strong Verb Endings
ich	-e
du	-est
er/sie/es	-e
wir	-en
ihr	-et
sie/Sie	-en

- **holen** (weak verb, meaning *to fetch*)

ich hol<u>e</u>	I fetch
du hol<u>est</u>	you fetch

- **fahren** (strong verb, meaning *to drive, to go*)

ich fahr<u>e</u>	I drive, I go
du fahr<u>est</u>	you drive, you go

- **denken** (mixed verb, meaning *to think*)

ich denk<u>e</u>	I think
du denk<u>est</u>	you think

> ### Tip
> The present and the present subjunctive endings are exactly the same for the **ich**, **wir** and **sie/Sie** forms.

3 Forming the imperfect subjunctive

➤ The imperfect subjunctive is very common and is not always used to describe actions in the past. It can, for example, express the future.

> **Wenn ich nur früher kommen könnte!**   If only I could come earlier!

➤ The imperfect tense and the imperfect subjunctive of weak verbs are identical.

Pronoun	Imperfect/Imperfect Subjunctive	Meaning
ich	holte	I fetched
du	holtest	you fetched
er/sie/es	holte	he/she/it fetched
wir	holten	we fetched
ihr	holtet	you (*plural*) fetched
sie/Sie	holten	they/you (*polite*) fetched

➤ The imperfect subjunctive of strong verbs is formed by adding the following endings to the stem of the imperfect. If there is an **a**, **o** or **u** in this stem, an umlaut is also added to it.

Pronoun	Imperfect Subjunctive: Strong Verb Endings
ich	-e
du	-(e)st
er/sie/es	-e
wir	-en
ihr	-(e)t
sie/Sie	-en

ⓘ Note that you add the **-e** to the **du** and **ihr** parts of the verb if it makes pronunciation easier, for example:

    du stießest   you pushed

    ihr stießet   you pushed

Pronoun	Imperfect Subjunctive	Meaning
ich	gäbe	I gave
du	gäb(e)st	you gave
er/sie/es	gäbe	he/she/it gave
wir	gäben	we gave
ihr	gäb(e)t	you (*plural*) gave
sie/Sie	gäben	they/you (*polite*) gave

➤ The imperfect subjunctive forms of the mixed verbs **brennen**, **kennen**, **senden**, **nennen**, **rennen** and **wenden** add weak verb imperfect endings to the stem of the verb, which DOES NOT change the vowel. The imperfect subjunctive forms of the remaining mixed verbs **bringen**, **denken** and **wissen** are also the same as the imperfect with one major difference: not only does the stem vowel change, but an umlaut is also added to the **a** or **u**. However, all of these forms are rare, with the conditional tense being used much more frequently instead.

For further explanation of grammatical terms, please see pages xii–xvi.

Wenn ich du wäre, <u>würde</u> ich
<u>rennen</u>.

INSTEAD OF

Wenn ich du wäre, <u>rennte</u> ich.   If I were you, I would run.

Ich <u>würde</u> so etwas nie <u>denken</u>!

INSTEAD OF

Ich <u>dächte</u> so etwas nie!   I would never think such a thing!

⇨ *For more information on the **Conditional**, see page 125.*

Grammar Extra!

The pluperfect subjunctive is formed from the imperfect subjunctive of haben or sein + the past participle. This subjunctive form is frequently used to translate the English structure 'If I had done something, …'

Wenn ich Geld <u>gehabt hätte</u>,   If I had had money,
<u>wäre</u> ich <u>gereist</u>.   I would have travelled.

Key points

- ✔ In German, subjunctive forms are used much more frequently than in English, to express uncertainty, speculation or doubt.

- ✔ Subjunctive forms are commonly used in indirect speech and in conditional sentences.

- ✔ The present subjunctive of weak, strong and mixed verbs have the same endings.

- ✔ The imperfect tense and the imperfect subjunctive of weak verbs are identical.

- ✔ The imperfect subjunctive of strong verbs is formed by adding the endings -e, -(e)st, -e, -en, -(e)t, -en to the stem of the imperfect and often has an umlaut change.

- ✔ The imperfect subjunctive of mixed verbs is rare and the conditonal form of würde + infinitive is normally used instead.

The infinitive

> **What is the infinitive?**
> The **infinitive** is the 'to' form of the verb, for example, *to go*, and is the form you look up in a dictionary. It is the **-en** form of the verb in German.

Using the infinitive

➤ **zu** is used with the infinitive:

- after other verbs

  Ich versuchte <u>zu</u> kommen.   I tried <u>to come</u>.

- after adjectives

  Es war leicht <u>zu</u> sehen.   It was easy <u>to see</u>.

  Es ist schwierig <u>zu</u> verstehen.   It's hard <u>to understand</u>.

- after nouns

  Ich habe keine Zeit, Sport <u>zu</u> treiben.   I don't have the time <u>to do any sport</u>.

  Ich habe keine Lust, meine Hausaufgaben <u>zu</u> machen.   I don't want <u>to do my homework.</u>

➤ The infinitive is used <u>without</u> **zu** after the following:

- modal verbs, such as **können** (meaning *to be able, can*)

  Sie kann gut schwimmen.   She can swim very well.

⇨ *For more information on **Modal verbs**, see page 136.*

Tip

The English –*ing* form is often translated by the German infinitive, as shown in some of the examples below.

- the verbs **lassen** (meaning *to stop, to leave*), **bleiben** (meaning *to stay*) and **gehen** (meaning *to go*)

  Sie <u>ließen</u> uns <u>warten</u>.   They kept us waiting.

  Sie <u>blieb</u> <u>sitzen</u>.   She remained seated.

  Er <u>ging</u> <u>einkaufen</u>.   He went shopping.

- verbs of perception such as **hören** (meaning *to hear, to listen (to)*) and **sehen** (meaning *to see, to watch*)

  Ich sah ihn kommen.   I saw him coming.

  Er hörte sie singen.   He heard her singing.

For further explanation of grammatical terms, please see pages xii–xvi.

➤ The infinitive can be used to give an order or instruction.

Bitte nicht in diesen Zug <u>einsteigen</u>!   Please don't board this train!

➤ It can also be used as a noun with a capital letter. It is always neuter.

rauchen = to smoke

Sie hat <u>das Rauchen</u> aufgegeben.   She's given up smoking.

Key points

✔ The infinitive is the 'to' form of the verb, the one you look up in a dictionary.

✔ **zu** is used with the infinitive after other verbs, adjectives and nouns.

✔ The infinitive is used WITHOUT **zu** after certain verbs, mostly modal verbs.

✔ The infinitive can be used to give an order or instruction.

✔ It can be used as a noun with a capital letter and is always neuter.

Modal verbs

> **What are modal verbs?**
> **Modal verbs** are used to <u>modify</u> or <u>change</u> other verbs to show such things as *ability*, *permission* or *necessity*. For example, *he <u>can</u> swim*; <u>may</u> I come?; we <u>ought to go</u>.

1 Using modal verbs

➤ In German, the modal verbs are **dürfen, können, mögen, müssen, sollen** and **wollen**.

➤ Modal verbs are different from other verbs in their conjugation, which is shown in the Verb Tables.

⇨ For **Verb Tables**, see middle section.

➤ Here are the main uses of **dürfen**:

- Meaning *to be allowed to* or *may*

  <u>Darfst</u> du mit ins Kino kommen?   Are you allowed to/can you come to the cinema with us?

- Meaning *must not* or *may not*

  Ich <u>darf</u> keine Schokolade essen.   I mustn't eat any chocolate.

- Expressing politeness

  <u>Darf</u> ich?   May I?

➤ Here are the main uses of **können**:

- Meaning *to be able to* or *can*

  Wir <u>können</u> es nicht schaffen.   We can't make it.

- Meaning *would be able to* or *could*

  <u>Könntest</u> du morgen hinfahren?   Could you go there tomorrow?

- As a more common, informal alternative to **dürfen**, with the meaning *to be allowed to* or *can*

  <u>Kann</u> ich/<u>darf</u> ich einen Kaffee haben?   Can I/may I have a coffee?

- Expressing possibility

  Das <u>kann</u> sein.   That may be so.
  Das <u>kann</u> nicht sein.   That can't be true.

➤ Here are the main uses of **mögen**:

- Meaning *to like*, when expressing likes and dislikes

  <u>Magst</u> du Schokolade?   Do you like chocolate?
  Sie <u>mögen</u> es nicht.   They don't like it.

- Meaning *would like to*, when expressing wishes and polite requests

  <u>Möchtest</u> du sie besuchen?   Would you like to visit her?
  <u>Möchten</u> Sie etwas trinken?   Would you like something to drink?

For further explanation of grammatical terms, please see pages xii–xvi.

- Expressing possibility or probability

  Es <u>mag</u> sein, dass es falsch war.   It may well be that it was wrong.

➤ Here are the main uses of **müssen**:

- Meaning *to have to* or *must* or *need to*

  Sie <u>musste</u> jeden Tag um sechs   She had to get up at six o'clock
  aufstehen.   every day.

- Certain common, informal uses

  <u>Muss</u> das sein?   Is that really necessary?
  Den Film <u>muss</u> man gesehen haben.   That film is worth seeing.

[*i*] Note that you can use a negative form of **brauchen** (meaning *to need*) instead of **müssen** for *don't have to* or *need not*

  Das <u>brauchst</u> du nicht zu sagen.   You don't have to say that.

➤ Here are the main uses of **sollen**:

- Meaning *ought to* or *should*

  Das <u>sollten</u> Sie sofort machen.   You ought to do that straight
       away.

  Sie wusste nicht, was sie tun <u>sollte</u>.   She didn't know what to do
       (*what she should do*)

- Meaning *to be (supposed) to* where someone else has asked you to do something

  Du <u>sollst</u> deine Freundin anrufen.   You are to/should phone your
       girlfriend (*she has left a message
       asking you to ring*)

- Meaning *to be said to be*

  Sie <u>soll</u> sehr reich sein.   I've heard she's very rich/
       She is said to be very rich

➤ Here are the main uses of **wollen**:

- Meaning *to want* or *to want to*

  Sie <u>will</u> Lkw-Fahrerin werden.   She wants to be a lorry driver.

- As a common, informal alternative to **mögen**, meaning *to want* or *wish*

  <u>Willst</u> du eins?   Do you want one?
  <u>Willst</u> du/<u>möchtest</u> du etwas trinken?   Do you want/would you like
       something to drink?

- Meaning *to be willing to*

  Er <u>will</u> nichts sagen.   He refuses to say
       anything.

- Expressing something you previously intended to do

  Ich <u>wollte</u> gerade anrufen.   I was just about to phone.

2 Modal verb forms

➤ Modal verbs have unusual present tenses:

dürfen	können	mögen
ich darf	ich kann	ich mag
du darfst	du kannst	du magst
er/sie/es/man darf	er/sie/es/man kann	er/sie/es/man mag
wir dürfen	wir können	wir mögen
ihr dürft	ihr könnt	ihr mögt
sie/Sie dürfen	sie/Sie können	sie/Sie mögen

müssen	sollen	wollen
ich muss	ich soll	ich will
du musst	du sollst	du willst
er/sie/es/man muss	er/sie/es/man soll	er/sie/es/man will
wir müssen	wir sollen	wir wollen
ihr müsst	ihr sollt	ihr wollt
sie/Sie müssen	sie/Sie sollen	sie/Sie wollen

➤ In tenses consisting of one verb part, the infinitive of the verb used with the modal comes at the end of the sentence or clause.

> **Sie <u>kann</u> sehr gut <u>schwimmen</u>.**   She is a very good swimmer.

Grammar Extra!

In sentences with modal verbs where the other verb expresses movement, it can be dropped if there is an adverb or adverbial phrase to show movement instead.

> **Ich <u>muss</u> nach Hause.**   I must go home.
> **Die Kinder <u>sollen jetzt</u> ins Bett.**   The children have to go to bed now.

⇨ *For more information on **Adverbs**, see page 57.*

Key points

✔ Modal verbs are used to <u>modify</u> the meaning of other verbs.

✔ In German, the modal verbs are **dürfen, können, mögen, müssen, sollen** and **wollen**.

✔ Modal verbs are different from other verbs in their conjugation.

For further explanation of grammatical terms, please see pages xii–xvi.

Impersonal verbs

> **What is an impersonal verb?**
> An **impersonal verb** is one that does not relate to a real person or thing and where the subject is represented by *it*, for example, *It's going to rain*; *It's ten o'clock*.

➤ In German, <u>impersonal verbs</u> are used with **es** (meaning it) and the third person singular form of the verb.

Es regnet.	It's raining.
Es gibt ein Problem.	There's a problem.

➤ Here are the most common impersonal verbs. In some of these expressions it is possible to drop the **es**, in which case a personal pronoun such as **mich** or **mir** begins the clause. For example:

Es ist mir egal, ob er mitkommt

OR

Mir ist egal, ob er mitkommt   I don't care if he comes with us.

➪ *For more information on **Personal pronouns**, see page 70.*

➤ These expressions are marked with a * in the list below:

* **es freut mich, dass/zu**   I am glad that/to.
  Es freut mich, dass du gekommen   I'm pleased that you have come.
  bist.

  Es freut mich, Sie in unserer Stadt   I'm pleased to welcome you to
  begrüßen zu dürfen.   our town.

* **es gefällt mir**   I like it.
  Es gefällt mir gar nicht.   I don't like it at all.

* **es geht mir gut/schlecht.**   I'm fine/not too good.

* **es geht nicht.**   it's not possible

* **es geht um**   it's about
  Es geht um die Liebe.   It's about love.

* **es gelingt mir (zu)**   I succeed (in)
  Es ist <u>mir</u> gelungen, ihn zu überzeugen.   I managed to convince him.

* **es handelt sich um**   it's a question of
  Es handelt sich um Zeit und Geld.   It's a question of time and money.

* **es hängt davon ab**   it depends
  Es hängt davon ab, ob ich arbeiten   It depends whether I have to
  muss.   work or not.

- <u>es</u> hat keinen Zweck.　　　　　　　There's no point.

- es ist mir egal (ob)*　　　　　　　it's all the same to me (if)
  <u>Es</u> ist mir egal, ob du kommst　　I don't care if you come or not.
  oder nicht.

- es ist möglich(, dass)　　　　　　it's possible (that)
  <u>Es</u> is doch möglich, dass sie ihr　It's always possible she doesn't
  Handy nicht dabei hat.　　　　　have her mobile with her.

- es ist nötig　　　　　　　　　　it's necessary
  <u>Es</u> wird nicht nötig sein, mir　　It won't be necessary to let me
  Bescheid zu sagen.　　　　　　　know.

- es ist schade(, dass)　　　　　　it's a pity (that)
  <u>Es</u> ist schade, dass sie nicht kommt.　It's a pity (that) she isn't coming.

- es ist mir warm OR es ist mir kalt*　I'm warm OR I'm cold

- es klingelt　　　　　　　　　　someone's ringing the bell OR
  　　　　　　　　　　　　　　　the phone is ringing

  <u>Es</u> hat gerade geklingelt.　　　　The bell just went OR the phone
  　　　　　　　　　　　　　　　just rang.

- es klopft　　　　　　　　　　　someone's knocking (at the door)

- es kommt darauf an(, ob)　　　　it all depends (whether)
  <u>Es</u> kommt darauf an, ob ich　　It all depends whether I have to
  arbeiten muss.　　　　　　　　　work.

- es lohnt sich (nicht)　　　　　　it's (not) worth it
  Ich weiß nicht, ob <u>es</u> sich lohnt oder　I don't know if it's worth it or not.
  nicht.

- es macht nichts　　　　　　　　it doesn't matter

- es macht nichts aus　　　　　　it makes no difference
  Macht <u>es</u> dir etwas aus, wenn wir　Would you mind if we went
  morgen gehen?　　　　　　　　tomorrow?

- es stimmt, dass ...　　　　　　　it's true that ...
  <u>Es</u> stimmt, dass sie keine Zeit hat.　It's true that she doesn't have
  　　　　　　　　　　　　　　　any time.

- es tut mir leid(, dass) ...　　　　I'm sorry(that) ...

- wie geht es (dir)?　　　　　　　How are you?

- Mir wird schlecht*　　　　　　　I feel sick

➤ All weather verbs are impersonal.

Infinitive	Expression	Meaning
donnern und blitzen	es donnert und blitzt	there's thunder and lightning
frieren	es friert	it's freezing
gießen	es gießt	it's pouring
regnen	es regnet	it's raining
schneien	es schneit	it's snowing
sein	es ist warm/kalt	it's cold/warm

Key points

✔ Impersonal verbs are used with **es** (meaning *it*) and the third person singular form of the verb.

✔ All weather verbs are impersonal.

There is/There are

➤ There are two main ways of expressing this in German.

1 Es gibt

- This is always used in the singular form and is followed by a singular or plural object in the accusative case.

  Es gibt zu viele Probleme dabei. — There are too many problems involved.

  Es gibt keinen besseren Wein. — There is no better wine.

- **Es gibt** is used to refer to things of a general nature.

  Es gibt bestimmt Regen. — It's definitely going to rain.

  Wenn wir zu spät kommen, gibt es Ärger. — If we arrive late, there'll be trouble.

- It is often used informally.

  Was gibts (=gibt es) zu essen? — What is there to eat?

  Was gibts? — What's wrong?, What's up?

  So was gibts doch nicht! — That's impossible!

2 Es ist/es sind

- Here, the **es** simply introduces the real subject of the sentence, so if the subject is plural, **es sind** is used. The subject is in the nominative case.

  Es sind kaum Leute da. — There are hardly any people there.

- Where the subject and verb swap places in the clause or sentence, the **es** is dropped.

  Da sind kaum Leute. — There are hardly any people there.

ⓘ Note that **es gibt** is frequently used instead of **es ist/es sind** in the above two examples.

- **Es ist** or **es sind** are used to refer to a temporary situation.

  Es war niemand da. — There was no-one there.

- They are also used to begin a story.

  Es war einmal eine Königin. — Once upon a time there was a Queen ...

Key point

✔ In German there are two main ways of translating *there is/there are*: **es gibt** and **es ist/es sind**.

For further explanation of grammatical terms, please see pages xii–xvi.

Use of "es" as an anticipatory object

➤ The object of many verbs can be a clause beginning with **dass** (meaning *that*) or an infinitive with **zu**.

Er wusste, <u>dass</u> wir pünktlich kommen würden.	He knew that we would come on time.
Sie fing an <u>zu</u> lachen.	She began to laugh.

➤ With some verbs, **es** is often used as the object to anticipate this clause or infinitive phrase.

Er hatte <u>es</u> abgelehnt, mitzukommen.   He refused to come.

➤ When the **dass** clause or infinitive phrase begins the sentence, **es** is not used in the main clause. Instead, it can be replaced by the pronoun **das** (meaning *that*).

<u>Dass</u> es Karla war, <u>das</u> haben wir ihr verschwiegen.

ℹ Note that **dass** is a subordinating conjunction and **das** is a demonstrative pronoun.

⇨ *For more information on **Subordinating conjunctions**, see page 172.*

➤ The following common verbs <u>usually</u> have the **es** object.

- **es ablehnen, zu ...**   to refuse to

- **es aushalten, zu tun/dass ...**   to stand doing

  Ich halte <u>es</u> nicht mehr aus, bei ihnen zu arbeiten.   I can't stand working for them any longer.

- **es ertragen, zu tun/dass ...**   to bear doing

  Ich ertrage <u>es</u> nicht, dass sie mir widerspricht.   I can't bear her contradicting me.

- **es leicht haben, zu ...**   to find it easy to

  Sie hatte <u>es</u> nicht leicht, sie zu überreden.   She didn't have an easy job persuading them.

- **es nötig haben, zu ...**   to need to

  Ich habe <u>es</u> nicht nötig, mit dir darüber zu reden.   I don't have to talk to you about it.

- **es satt haben, zu ...**   to have had enough of (doing)

  Ich habe <u>es</u> satt, englische Verben zu lernen.   I've had enough of learning English verbs.

- **es verstehen, zu ...**   to know how to

  Sie versteht <u>es</u>, Autos zu reparieren.   She knows about repairing cars.

➤ The following common verbs <u>often</u> have the **es** object.

- **es jemandem anhören/ansehen, dass ...**

  to tell by listening to/looking at someone that

  Man hörte <u>es</u> ihm an, dass er kein Deutscher war.

  You could tell by listening to him that he wasn't German.

- **es bereuen, zu tun/dass ...**

  to regret having done/that

  Ich bereue <u>es</u> nicht, dass ich gekommen bin.

  I don't regret coming.

- **es jemandem verbieten, zu ...**

  to forbid someone to

  Ihre Mutter hat <u>es</u> ihr verboten, dort hinzugehen.

  Her mother forbade her to go there.

  es wagen zu ...

  to dare to

  Er wagte <u>es</u> nicht, ein neues Auto zu kaufen.

  He didn't dare buy a new car.

Key points

✔ The object of many verbs can be a clause beginning with **dass** (meaning *that*) or an infinitive with **zu**.

✔ With some verbs, **es** is used as the object to anticipate this clause or infinitive phrase.

✔ When the **dass** clause or infinitive phrase begins the sentence, **es** is not used in the main clause. Instead, it can be replaced by the pronoun **das** (meaning *that*).

For further explanation of grammatical terms, please see pages xii–xvi.

Verbs followed by prepositions

➤ Some English verbs must be followed by prepositions for certain meanings, for example, *to wait for*, *to ask for*. This also happens in German:

sich sehnen <u>nach</u>	to long <u>for</u>
warten <u>auf</u>	to wait <u>for</u>
bitten <u>um</u>	to ask <u>for</u>

> ### Tip
>
> As you can see from the examples above, the preposition that is used in German is not always the same as the one that is used in English. Whenever you learn a new verb, try to learn which preposition is used after it too.
>
> ➤ As in English, using different prepositions with a verb creates completely different meanings.
>
> | | |
> |---|---|
> | bestehen | to pass (a test etc) |
> | bestehen <u>aus</u> | to consist of |
> | bestehen <u>auf</u> | to insist on |
> | sich freuen <u>auf</u> | to look forward to |
> | sich freuen <u>über</u> | to be pleased about |
>
> ⓘ Note that you occasionally need to use a preposition with a German verb whose English equivalent does not have one.
>
> | | |
> |---|---|
> | diskutieren <u>über</u> | to discuss |

➤ Prepositions used with these verbs behave like normal prepositions and affect the case of the following noun in the normal way. For instance, with verbs followed by **für** the accusative case is always used.

sich interessieren **für**	to be interested in
Sie interessiert sich nicht <u>**für den neuen**</u> **Wagen.**	She isn't interested in the new car.

➤ A verb plus preposition is not always followed by a noun or pronoun. It can also be followed by a clause containing another verb. This is often used to translate an *–ing* form in English and is dealt with in one of two ways:

● If the verbs in both parts of the sentence have the same subject, **da-** or **dar-** is added to the beginning of the preposition and the following verb becomes an infinitive used with **zu**.

Ich freue mich sehr <u>**darauf**</u>**, mal wieder mit ihr** <u>**zu**</u> **arbeiten.**	I am looking forward to work<u>ing</u> with her again.

- If the subject is not the same for both verbs, a **dass** (meaning *that*) clause is used.

Ich freue mich sehr <u>darauf</u>, <u>dass</u> du morgen kommst.	I am looking forward to you coming tomorrow.

1 Verbs followed by a preposition + the accusative case

➤ The following list contains the most common verbs followed by a preposition plus the accusative case:

- **sich amüsieren über** — to laugh at, smile about
  Sie haben sich <u>über ihn</u> amüsiert. — They laughed at him.

- **sich ärgern über** — to get annoyed about/with

- **sich bewerben um** — to apply for
  Sie hat sich <u>um die</u> Stelle als Direktorin beworben. — She applied for the position of director.

- **bitten um** — to ask for

- **denken an** — to be thinking of
  <u>Daran</u> habe ich gar nicht mehr gedacht. — I'd forgotten about that.

- **denken über** — to think about, hold an opinion of
  Wie denkt ihr <u>darüber</u>? — What do you think about it?

- **sich erinnern an** — to remember

- **sich freuen auf** — to look forward to

- **sich freuen über** — to be pleased about
  Ich freue mich sehr <u>darüber</u>, dass du gekommen bist. — I'm very glad you came.

- **sich gewöhnen an** — to get used to

- **sich interessieren für** — to be interested in
  Sie interessiert sich sehr <u>für</u> Politik. — She's very interested in politics.

- **kämpfen um** — to fight for

- **sich kümmern um** — to take care of, see to
  Kannst du dich <u>um</u> meine Pflanzen kümmern? — Can you see to my plants?

- **nachdenken über** — to think about
  Er hatte schon lange <u>darüber</u> nachgedacht. — He had been thinking about it for a long time.

- **sich unterhalten über** — to talk about

- **sich verlassen auf** — to rely on, depend on
  Kann sie sich <u>auf</u> ihn verlassen? — Can she rely on him?

- **warten auf** — to wait for

2 Verbs followed by a preposition + the dative case

➤ The following list contains the most common verbs followed by a preposition plus the dative case:

- abhängen von
  Das hängt <u>von</u> der Zeit ab, die uns noch bleibt.

  to depend on
  That depends how much time we have left.

- sich beschäftigen mit
  Sie beschäftigen sich im Moment <u>mit</u> dem neuen Haus.

  to occupy oneself with
  They're busy with their new house at the moment.

- bestehen aus

  to consist of

- leiden an/unter
  Sie hat lange <u>an</u> dieser Krankheit gelitten.

  to suffer from
  She suffered from this illness for a long time.

- riechen nach

  to smell of

- schmecken nach
  Es schmeckt <u>nach</u> Zimt.

  to taste of
  It tastes of cinnamon.

- sich sehnen nach

  to long for

- sterben an
  Sie ist <u>an</u> Krebs gestorben.

  to die of
  She died of cancer.

- teilnehmen an
  Du solltest <u>am</u> Wettbewerb teilnehmen.

  to take part in
  You should take part in the competition.

- träumen von

  to dream of

- sich verabschieden von
  Ich habe mich noch nicht <u>von</u> ihm verabschiedet.

  to say goodbye to
  I haven't said goodbye to him yet.

- sich verstehen mit
  Sie versteht sich ganz gut <u>mit</u> ihr.

  to get along with, get on with
  She gets on really well with her.

Key points

✔ German prepositions after verbs are often not the same as the ones used in English.

✔ Using different prepositions with a verb creates completely different meanings.

✔ German verbs occasionally use prepositions where their English equivalents don't.

✔ Prepositions used with verbs behave like normal prepositions and affect the case of the following noun.

Verbs followed by the dative case

1 Verbs with a direct and indirect object

➤ Some verbs are generally used with a <u>direct object</u> and an <u>indirect object</u>. For example, in the English sentence, *She gave me a book*, the direct object of *gave* is *a book* and would be in the accusative case in German, and *me* (= *to me*) is the indirect object and would be in the dative case in German.

> **Sie gab <u>mir</u> ein Buch.**   She gave me a book.
> direct object = **ein Buch**
> indirect object = **mir**

➤ In German, as in English, this type of verb is usually concerned with giving or telling someone something, or with doing something for someone else.

> **Sie erzählte ihm eine Geschichte.**   She told him a story.
> direct object = **eine Geschichte**
> indirect object = **ihm**

[i] Note that the normal word order after such verbs is for the direct object to follow the indirect, EXCEPT where the direct object is a personal pronoun.

> **Kaufst du <u>mir</u> <u>das Buch</u>?**   Will you buy me the book?
> BUT
> **Kaufst du <u>es mir</u>?**   Will you buy it for me?

⇨ *For more information on **Direct** and **Indirect object pronouns**, see pages 74-77.*

➤ Here are some of the most common examples of verbs which are used with both a direct and an indirect object:

- **anbieten**   to offer
  Sie bot <u>ihr</u> die Arbeitsstelle an.   She offered her the job.

- **bringen**   to bring
  Bringst du <u>mir</u> eins?   Will you bring me one?

- **beweisen**   to prove
  Können Sie es <u>mir</u> beweisen?   Can you prove it to me?

- **fehlen**   to be absent or missing
  Mir fehlt das nötige Geld.   I don't have enough money.

- **geben**   to give
  Gib <u>mir</u> das sofort!   Give me that now!

- **schenken**   to give (as a present)
  Ich schenke <u>ihr</u> einen Computer zum Geburtstag.

  I'm giving her a computer for her birthday.

- **schreiben**   to write
  Schreib <u>ihm</u> mal einen Brief.

  Write him a letter sometime.

- **zeigen**   to show
  Zeig es <u>mir</u>!

  Show me it!

2   Verbs with their object in the dative

➤ Certain verbs in German, such as **helfen** (meaning *to help*) can ONLY be followed by an object in the dative case. In many cases, their English equivalents have a direct object, and you need to learn the most common verbs which are different in this way.

➤ Here are some of the most common ones.

- **begegnen**   to bump into, meet
  Er ist <u>seinem</u> Freund in der Stadt begegnet.

  He bumped into his friend in town.

- **gehören**   to belong to
  <u>Wem</u> gehört dieses Buch?

  Whose book is this?

- **helfen**   to help
  Er wollte <u>ihr</u> nicht helfen.

  He refused to help her.

- **danken**   to thank
  Ich danke <u>dir</u>!

  Thank you!

- **schaden**   to damage
  Rauchen schadet <u>der</u> Gesundheit

  Smoking is bad for your health.

- **schmecken**   to taste
  Das Essen hat <u>ihnen</u> gut geschmeckt.

  They enjoyed the meal.

- **trauen**   to trust
  Ich traue <u>dir</u> nicht.

  I don't trust you.

Key points

✔ Some German verbs are usually used with a direct AND an indirect object.

✔ The indirect object is ALWAYS in the dative case.

✔ The normal word order after such verbs is for the direct object to follow the indirect, EXCEPT where the direct object is a personal pronoun.

✔ Certain German verbs can only be followed by an object in the dative case.

The passive

> **What is the passive?**
> The **passive** is the form of the verb that is used when the subject of the verb is the person or thing that is affected by the action, for example, *I was given, we were told, it had been made.*

1 Using the passive

➤ In a normal, or *active* sentence, the 'subject' of the verb is the person or thing that carries out the action described by the verb. The 'object' of the verb is the person or thing that the verb 'happens' to.

> Ryan (*subject*) hit (*active verb*) me (*object*).

➤ In English, as in German, you can turn an active sentence round to make a passive sentence.

> I (*subject*) was hit (*passive verb*) by Ryan (*agent*).

➤ Very often, however, you cannot identify who is carrying out the action indicated by the verb.

> I was hit in the face.
> The trees will be chopped down.
> I've been chosen to represent the school.

2 Forming the passive

➤ In English we use the verb *to be* with the past participle (*was hit, was given*) to form the passive and the word 'by' usually introduces the agent. In German the passive is formed using **werden** and the past participle, while the agent is introduced by

- **von**, for a person or organisation,
- or **durch**, for a thing.

Das Kind <u>wurde</u> <u>von</u> einem Hund <u>gebissen</u>.	The child was bitten by a dog.
Die Tür <u>wurde</u> <u>durch</u> den Wind <u>geöffnet</u>.	The door was opened by the wind.

⇨ *For more information on the **Past participle**, see page 114.*

➤ Here is the present tense of the verb **sehen** (meaning *to see*) in its passive form.

ich werde gesehen	I am seen
du wirst gesehen	you are seen
er/sie/es wird gesehen	he/she/it is seen
wir werden gesehen	we are seen
ihr werdet gesehen	you (plural) are seen
sie/Sie werden gesehen.	they/you (formal) are seen

Tip

There is/there are can be translated by a verb in the passive tense in German.

Es wird immer viel getrunken auf seiner Party.	There is always a lot of drinking at his party.

➤ You can form other tenses of the passive by changing the tense of the verb **werden**, for example, the imperfect passive.

ich wurde gesehen	I was seen

➪ *For more information on the **Imperfect tense**, see page 118.*

Tip

There is a very important difference between German and English in sentences containing an <u>indirect object</u>. In English we can quite easily turn a normal (active) sentence with an indirect object into a passive sentence.

Active
Someone (*subject*) gave (*active verb*) me (*indirect object*) a book (*direct object*).

Passive
I (*subject*) was given (*passive verb*) a book (*direct object*).

In German, an indirect object can <u>NEVER</u> become the subject of a passive verb. Instead, the indirect object must remain in the dative case, with either the direct object becoming the subject of the passive sentence OR use of an impersonal passive construction.
Ein Buch (*subject*) wurde mir geschenkt.

3 Avoiding the passive

➤ Passives are not as common in German as in English. There are <u>three</u> main ways that German speakers express the same idea.

- by using the pronoun **man** (meaning *they* or *one*) with a normal, active verb.

  <u>Man</u> hatte es mir schon gesagt.   I had already been told.

  (i) Note that **man** is not always translated as *they* or *one*.

  <u>Man</u> hatte es schon verkauft.   It had already been sold.

- by using **sich lassen** plus a verb in the infinitive.

  Das lässt sich machen.   That can be done.

- by using an active tense where the agent of the action is known.

  Susi schenkte ihr ein Auto.   Susi gave her a car.

  INSTEAD OF

  Ihr wurde von Susi ein Auto geschenkt.   She was given a car by Susi.

Key points

✔ The present tense of the passive is formed by using the present tense of **werden** with the past participle.

✔ In German, an indirect object can <u>NEVER</u> become the subject of a passive verb.

✔ You can often avoid a passive construction by using the pronoun **man** or **sich lassen** plus an infinitive or an active tense where the agent is known.

Prepositions

What is a preposition?
A **preposition** is a word such as *at, for, with, into* or *from*, which is usually followed by a noun, pronoun or, in English, a word ending in *-ing*. Prepositions show how people and things relate to the rest of the sentence, for example,
She's at home; a tool for cutting grass; it's from David.

Using prepositions

➤ Prepositions are used in front of nouns and pronouns (such as *me, him, the man* and so on), and show the relationship between the noun or pronoun and the rest of the sentence. Some prepositions can be used before verb forms ending in *-ing* in English.

> I showed my ticket to the inspector.
> Come with me.
> This brush is really good for cleaning shoes.

⇨ *For more information on **Nouns** and **Pronouns**, see pages 1 and 69.*

➤ In English, a preposition does not affect the word or phrase it introduces, for example:

the inspector	to the inspector
me	with me
cleaning shoes	for cleaning shoes

➤ In German, however, the noun following a preposition must be put into the accusative, genitive or dative case.

> *Tip*
> It is important to learn each preposition with the case or cases it governs.

1 Prepositions followed by the dative case

➤ Some of the most common prepositions taking the dative case are:
aus, außer, bei, gegenüber, mit, nach, seit, von, zu

- **aus**   *out of, from*
  Er trinkt **aus** der Flasche.   He is drinking out of the bottle.
  Sie kommt **aus** Essen.   She comes from Essen.

- **außer**   *out of; except*

Der Fahrstuhl war <u>außer</u> Betrieb.	The lift was out of order.
Der Patient ist jetzt <u>außer</u> Gefahr.	The patient is out of danger now.
alle <u>außer</u> mir kamen zu spät.	all except me came too late.

- **bei**   *at the home/shop/work etc of; near*

Feiern wir <u>bei</u> uns?	Shall we celebrate at our house?
<u>Bei</u> uns in Schottland ist das kein Problem.	At home in Scotland that isn't a problem.
Sie ist <u>beim</u> Bäcker.	She is at the baker's.
Er ist noch beim Friseur.	He is still at the hairdresser's.
Er wohnt immer noch <u>bei</u> seinen Eltern.	He still lives with his parents.

[i] Note that **bei** plus the definite article can be shortened to **beim**.

⇨ *For more information on **Shortened forms of prepositions**, see page 165.*

- **gegenüber**   *opposite; towards*

Er wohnt uns <u>gegenüber</u>.	He lives opposite us.
Sie ist mir <u>gegenüber</u> immer sehr freundlich gewesen.	She has always been very friendly towards me.

[i] Note that when used as a preposition, **gegenüber** is placed <u>AFTER</u> a pronoun, but can be placed <u>BEFORE</u> or <u>AFTER</u> a noun.

- **mit**   *with*

Er ging <u>mit</u> seinen Freunden spazieren.	He went for a walk with his friends.

- **nach**   *after; to*

<u>Nach</u> zwei Stunden kam er wieder.	He returned two hours later.
Sie ist <u>nach</u> London gereist.	She went to London.
Ihrer Sprache <u>nach</u> ist sie Süddeutsche.	From the way she talks I would say she is from southern Germany.

[i] Note that when **nach** means *according to*, as in the last example, it can be placed <u>AFTER</u> the noun.

- **seit** *since; for (of time)*

<u>Seit</u> er krank ist, spielt er nicht mehr Fußball.	He's stopped playing football since he became ill.

ⓘ Note that after **seit**, meaning *for*, we use the <u>present tense</u> in German, but the <u>perfect tense</u> in English.

Ich <u>wohne</u> **seit** zwei Jahren in Frankfurt.	<u>I've been living</u> in Frankfurt for two years.
Sie <u>arbeitet</u> **seit** acht Jahren bei uns.	<u>She's been working</u> for us for eight years.

⇨ *For more information on **Tenses**, see page 94.*

- **von** *from; about; by (when used in the passive tense)*

<u>Von</u> Berlin sind wir weiter nach Krakau gefahren.	From Berlin we went on to Krakow.
Ich weiß nichts <u>von</u> ihm.	I know nothing about him.
Sie ist <u>von</u> unseren Argumenten überzeugt worden.	She was convinced by our arguments.

⇨ *For more information on the **Passive**, see page 150.*

ⓘ Note that **von** can be used as a common alternative to the genitive case.

Die Mutter <u>von</u> diesen Mädchen ist Künstlerin.	The mother of these girls is an artist.
Sie ist eine Freundin <u>von</u> Alexander.	She is a friend of Alexander's.

⇨ *For more information on the **Genitive case**, see page 11.*

- **zu** *to; for*

Er ging <u>zum</u> Arzt.	He went to the doctor's.
Wir sind <u>zum</u> Essen eingeladen.	We're invited for dinner.

ⓘ Note that **zu** plus the definite article can be shortened to **zum** or **zur**.

⇨ *For more information on **Shortened forms of prepositions**, see page 165.*

Grammar Extra!

Some of the above prepositions are also used as separable verb prefixes, that is the part at the beginning of a separable German verb.

<u>aus</u>halten	to endure
Ich halte es nicht mehr <u>aus</u>.	I can't stand it any longer.
(jemandem) <u>bei</u>stehen	to stand by (somebody)
Er stand seinem Freund <u>bei</u>.	He stood by his friend.
<u>gegenüber</u>stehen	to have an attitude towards
Er steht ihnen kritisch <u>gegenüber</u>.	He has a critical attitude towards them.
jemanden <u>mit</u>nehmen	to give somebody a lift
Nimmst du mich bitte <u>mit</u>?	Will you give me a lift please?
<u>nach</u>machen	to copy
Sie macht mir alles <u>nach</u>.	She copies everything I do.
<u>zu</u>machen	to shut
Mach die Tür <u>zu</u>!	Shut the door!

➯ For more information on **Separable verbs**, see page 109.

Key points

✔ **gegenüber, aus, bei, mit, nach, seit, von, zu, außer** are the most common prepositions used with the dative case.

✔ Each of them has several different possible meanings, depending on the context they are used in.

✔ **aus, nach, mit, bei** and **zu** can also be used as separable verb prefixes.

---

2 Prepositions followed by the accusative case

➤ The most common prepositions taking the accusative case are:

durch, entlang, für, gegen, ohne, um, wider

Tip

If you want an easy way to remember which prepositions take the accusative case, you could think of the word DOGWUF, which can stand for the prepositions <u>d</u>urch <u>o</u>hne <u>g</u>egen <u>w</u>ider <u>u</u>m <u>f</u>ür.

- durch   *through*

Sie guckte <u>durch</u> das Loch.	She looked through the hole.
<u>Durch</u> Zufall trafen sie sich wieder.	They met again, by chance.

- entlang   *along*

Die Kinder kommen die Straße <u>entlang</u>.	The children are coming along the street.

[i] Note that entlang comes <u>AFTER</u> the noun in this meaning.

- für   *for; to*

Ich habe es <u>für</u> dich getan.	I did it for you.
Das ist <u>für</u> ihn sehr wichtig.	That is very important to him.
Was <u>für</u> eins hat er?	What kind (of one) does he have?
Was <u>für</u> einen Wagen hat sie?	What kind of car does she have?
Was <u>für</u> Äpfel sind das?	What kind of apples are they?

- gegen   *against; around*

Stelle es <u>gegen</u> die Wand.	Put it against the wall.
Haben Sie etwas <u>gegen</u> Heuschnupfen?	Have you got something for hayfever?
Wir sind <u>gegen</u> vier angekommen.	We arrived at around four o'clock.

- ohne   *without*

<u>Ohne</u> sie gehts nicht.	It won't work without her.

- um   *(a)round, round about; at (with time); by (with quantity)*

Der Bahnhof liegt <u>um</u> die Ecke.	The station is round the corner.
Es fängt <u>um</u> neun Uhr an.	It begins at nine.
Es ist <u>um</u> zehn Euro billiger.	It is cheaper by ten euros.

[i] Note that um is used after certain verbs.

Sie baten <u>um</u> ein bisschen mehr Zeit.	They asked for a bit more time.
Es handelt sich <u>um</u> dein Benehmen.	It's a question of your behaviour.

⇨ *For more information on **Verbs followed by prepositions**, see page 145.*

- wider   *contrary to, against*

Das geht mir <u>wider</u> die Natur.	That's against my nature.

Grammar Extra!

Some of the above prepositions are also used as separable verb prefixes, that is the part at the beginning of a separable German verb.

<u>durch</u>machen

Sie hat viel <u>durch</u>gemacht in ihrem Leben.	She's been through a lot in her life.

<u>entlang</u>gehen

Wir gingen die Straße <u>entlang</u>.	We went along the street.

um and wider are also used as separable or inseparable verb prefixes (<u>variable</u> verb prefixes), depending on the verb and meaning.

<u>um</u>armen	*inseparable*	to embrace
Er hat sie <u>um</u>armt.		He gave her a hug.
<u>um</u>fallen	*separable*	to fall over
Sie ist <u>um</u>gefallen.		She fell over.
<u>wider</u>sprechen	*inseparable*	to go against
Das hat meinen Wünschen <u>wider</u>sprochen.		That went against my wishes.
(sich) <u>wider</u>spiegeln	*separable*	to reflect
Der Baum spiegelt sich im Wasser <u>wider</u>.		The tree is reflected in the water.

➪ *For more information on **Separable verbs** and **Inseparable verbs**, see pages 109 and 110.*

Key points

✔ durch, entlang, für, gegen, ohne, um, and wider are the most common prepositions used with the accusative case.

✔ Most of them have several different possible meanings, depending on the context they are used in.

✔ durch, entlang and gegen can also be used as separable verb prefixes.

✔ um and wider can also be used as variable verbal prefixes.

---

3 Prepositions followed by the accusative or the dative case

➤ There are a number of prepositions which can be followed by the accusative or the dative case. You use:

● the accusative case when there is some movement towards a different place

● the dative case when a location is described rather than movement, or when there is movement within the same place

➤ The most common prepositions in this category are:

an, auf, hinter, in, neben, über, unter, vor, zwischen

➤ You use **an**:

- with the <u>accusative</u> case

Die Lehrerin schrieb das Wort <u>an die</u> Tafel.	The teacher wrote the word on the board.
Ich habe einen Brief <u>an meine</u> Mutter geschrieben.	I wrote a letter to my mother.
Ich ziehe im Sommer <u>an die</u> Küste.	In the summer I move to the coast.

- with the <u>dative</u> case

Das Wort stand <u>an der</u> Tafel.	The word was written on the blackboard.
Wir treffen uns <u>am</u> Bahnhof.	We're meeting at the station.

> [*i*] Note that **an** plus the definite article can be shortened to **am**.

⇨ *For more information on **Shortened forms of prepositions**, see page 165.*

➤ You use **auf**:

- with the <u>accusative</u> case

Stell die Suppe bitte <u>auf den</u> Tisch.	Put the soup on the table please.
Wir fahren morgen <u>aufs</u> Land.	We're going to the country tomorrow.
Er warf einen Blick <u>auf das</u> Buch.	He glanced at the book.

> [*i*] Note that **auf** plus the definite article can be shortened to **aufs**.

⇨ *For more information on **Shortened forms of prepositions**, see page 165.*

- with the <u>dative</u> case

Die Suppe steht <u>auf dem</u> Tisch.	The soup's on the table.
<u>Auf dem</u> Land ist die Luft besser.	The air is better in the country.

➤ You use **hinter**:

- with the <u>accusative</u> case

Stell dich <u>hinter deinen</u> Bruder.	Stand behind your brother.

- with the <u>dative</u> case

Sie saß <u>hinter mir</u>.	She was sitting behind me.

➤ You use **in**:

- with the <u>accusative</u> case

  Sie ging <u>ins</u> Zimmer.   She entered the room.
  Er wollte nicht <u>in die</u> Schule gehen.   He didn't want to go to school.

- with the <u>dative</u> case

  Was hast du heute <u>in der</u> Schule   What did you do at school
  gemacht?   today?
  <u>Im</u> Zimmer warteten viele   A lot of people were waiting
  Leute auf ihn.   for him in the room.

[*i*] Note that **in** plus the definite article can be shortened to **im** or **ins**.

⇨ *For more information on **Shortened forms of prepositions**, see page 165.*

➤ You use **neben**:

- with the <u>accusative</u> case

  Stell dein Rad <u>neben meines</u>.   Put your bike next to mine.

- with the <u>dative</u> case

  Dein Rad steht <u>neben meinem</u>.   Your bike's next to mine.

➤ You use **über**:

- with the <u>accusative</u> case

  Zieh den Pullover <u>über deinen</u>   Pull the jumper over your head!
  Kopf!
  Sie ging quer <u>über das</u> Feld.   She went across the field.
  Flugzeuge dürfen nicht <u>über</u>   Planes are not allowed to fly over
  dieses Gebiet fliegen.   this area.

- with the <u>dative</u> case

  Die Lampe soll <u>über dem</u> Tisch   The lamp should hang over the
  hängen.   table.

[*i*] Note that when **über** means *about*, it is always followed by the accusative case,
NOT the dative.

  Wir haben viel <u>über sie</u> gesprochen.   We talked about her a lot.

➤ You use **unter**:

- with the <u>accusative</u> case

  Sie stellte sich <u>unter den</u> Baum.   She (came and) stood under
                                                       the tree.

- with the <u>dative</u> case

  Sie lebte dort <u>unter</u> Freunden. | She lived there among friends.

➤ You use **vor**:

- with the <u>accusative</u> case

  Stell den Stuhl <u>vor das</u> Fenster. | Put the chair in front of the window.

- with the <u>dative</u> case

  Auf dem Foto stand sie <u>vor dem</u> Haus. | In the photo she was standing in front of the house.
  Ich war <u>vor ihm</u> da. | I was there before him.
  <u>Vor dem</u> Krankenhaus links abbiegen. | Turn left at the hospital.

➤ You use **zwischen**:

- with the <u>accusative</u> case

  Er legte es <u>zwischen die</u> beiden Teller. | He put it between the two plates.

- with the <u>dative</u> case

  Das Dorf liegt <u>zwischen den</u> Bergen. | The village lies between the mountains.

➤ Each of these prepositions can also be used with verbs and are then called <u>prepositional objects</u>.

  abhängen <u>von</u> + *dative* | to depend on
  Das hängt <u>von</u> dir ab. | That depends on you.

  schmecken <u>nach</u> + *dative* | to taste of
  Der Nachtisch schmeckt <u>nach</u> Zimt. | The dessert tastes of cinnamon.

➤ When **auf** or **an** is used in this way, the case used depends on the verb – it's much easier to learn such examples together with the case which follows them.

  sich verlassen <u>auf</u> + *accusative* | to depend on
  Ich verlasse mich <u>auf</u> dich. | I'm depending on you.

  bestehen <u>auf</u> + *dative* | to insist on
  Wir bestehen <u>auf</u> sofortiger Bezahlung. | We insist on immediate payment.

  glauben <u>an</u> + *accusative* | to believe in
  Sie glaubt <u>an</u> ihre Schwester. | She believes in her sister.

  leiden <u>an</u> + *dative* | to suffer from
  Er leidet <u>an</u> einer tödlichen Krankheit. | He is suffering from a terminal illness.

sich freuen <u>auf</u> + *accusative*	to look forward to
Ich freue mich <u>auf</u> die Sommerferien.	I'm looking forward to the summer holidays.
warten <u>auf</u> + *accusative*	to wait for
Er wartet jeden morgen <u>auf</u> den Bus.	Every morning he waits for the bus.

⇨ *For more information on **Verbs with prepositional objects**, see page 145.*

Grammar Extra!

Some of the above prepositions are also used as separable or inseparable verb prefixes.

<u>an</u>rechnen	*separable*	to charge for
Das wird Ihnen später <u>an</u>gerechnet.		You'll be charged for that later.
<u>auf</u>setzen	*separable*	to put on
Er setzte sich die Mütze <u>auf</u>.		He put his cap on.
<u>über</u>queren	*inseparable*	to cross
Sie hat die Straße <u>über</u>quert.		She crossed the street.

⇨ *For more information on **Separable verbs** and **Inseparable verbs**, see pages 109 and 110.*

Key points

✔ **an**, **auf**, **hinter**, **in**, **neben**, **über**, **unter**, **vor** and **zwischen** are the most common prepositions which can be followed by the accusative or dative case.

✔ Most of them have several different possible meanings, depending on the context they are used in.

✔ Each of them can also be prepositional objects of certain verbs.

✔ Many of them can also be used as verb prefixes.

---

4 Prepositions followed by the genitive case

➤ The following are some of the more common prepositions which take the genitive case:

außerhalb, infolge, innerhalb, statt, trotz, um ... willen, während, wegen

---

- **außerhalb**   *outside*

  Es liegt <u>außerhalb</u> <u>der</u> Stadt.   It's outside the town.

- **infolge**   *as a result of*

  <u>Infolge</u> des starken Regens kam   As a result of the heavy rain,
  es zu Überschwemmungen.   there were floods.

- **innerhalb**   *within, inside*

  Ich schaffe das nicht <u>innerhalb</u>   I won't manage that within the
  der gesetzten Frist.   deadline.

- **statt**   *instead of*

  <u>Statt</u> nach Hause zu gehen, sind   Instead of going home, we went
  wir noch in die Stadt gegangen.   into town.

  Sie kam <u>statt</u> ihres Bruders.   She came instead of her brother.

- **trotz**   *in spite of*

  <u>Trotz</u> ihrer Krankheit ging sie   In spite of her illness, she went
  jeden Tag spazieren.   for a walk every day.

- **um ... willen**   *for ... sake, because of ...*

  Ich komme <u>um</u> deine<u>twillen</u>.   I'm coming for your sake.

  Tun Sie das bitte <u>um</u> meiner   Please do it, for my mother's sake.
  Mutter <u>willen</u>.

- **während**   *during*

  Was hast du <u>während</u> der Ferien   What did you do during the
  gemacht?   holidays?

- **wegen**   *because of, on account of*

  <u>Wegen</u> des schlechten Wetters   The event was cancelled because
  wurde die Veranstaltung abgesagt.   of bad weather.

[i] Note that **statt, trotz, während** and **wegen** can also be followed by the dative case.

Statt <u>dem</u> Abendessen musste   Instead of having dinner, I had
ich arbeiten.   to work.

Trotz <u>allem</u> will ich weiterstudieren.   In spite of everything, I want to
     continue studying.

Während <u>dem</u> Vortrag schlief er ein.   He fell asleep during the lecture.

Wegen <u>mir</u> musste sie früh nach   She had to go home early because
Hause.   of me.

Grammar Extra!

There are some other prepositions which take the genitive case:

- beiderseits   *on both sides of*
  <u>Beiderseits</u> des Flusses gibt es ein Ufer.   On both sides of the river there is a river bank.

- diesseits   *on this side of*
  <u>Diesseits</u> der Grenze spricht man Polnisch und Deutsch.   On this side of the border Polish and German are spoken.

- ... halber
  <u>Vorsichtshalber</u> nehme ich heute meinen Regenschirm mit.   To be on the safe side I'm taking an umbrella today.
  <u>Sicherheitshalber</u> verschließt er die Tür.   For safety's sake he locks the door.

- hinsichtlich   *with regard to*
  <u>Hinsichtlich</u> Ihrer Beschwerde habe ich Ihren Brief an die zuständigen Behörden geschickt.   With regards to your complaint, I have passed on your letter to the relevant authorities.

- jenseits   *on the other side of*
  Das Dorf liegt 2 km <u>jenseits</u> der Grenze.   The village is 2km on the other side of the border.

Grammar Extra!

Special forms of the possessive and relative pronouns are used with **wegen**:

- meinetwegen
  Hat er sich <u>meinetwegen</u> so aufgeregt?   Did he get so upset on my account?

- deinetwegen
  Ich ging nicht <u>deinetwegen</u> nach Hause.   I didn't go home because of you.

- seinetwegen
  Ihr müsst <u>seinetwegen</u> nicht auf euren Urlaub verzichten.   You don't have to do without your holiday for his sake.

- ihretwegen
  Wir sind <u>ihretwegen</u> früher gegangen.   We went earlier because of them.

- unsertwegen
  Sie musste <u>unsertwegen</u> Strafe zahlen.   She had to pay a fine because of us.

- euretwegen
  <u>Euretwegen</u> durfte er nicht mitspielen.   Because of you he wasn't allowed to play.

- Ihretwegen
  Sollte es <u>Ihretwegen</u> Probleme geben, dann gehen wir alle nach Hause.   Should you cause any problems, then we'll all go home.

⇨ *For more information on **Possessive pronouns** and **Relative pronouns**, see pages 80 and 86.*

For further explanation of grammatical terms, please see pages xii–xvi.

Key points

✔ außerhalb, beiderseits, diesseits, ... halber, hinsichtlich, infolge, innerhalb, jenseits, statt, trotz, um ... willen, während and wegen are the most common prepositions which take the genitive case.

✔ statt, trotz, während and wegen can also take the dative case.

✔ Special forms of possessive and relative pronouns are used with wegen.

---

5 **Shortened forms of prepositions**

➤ After many German prepositions, a shortened or <u>contracted</u> form of the definite article can be merged with the preposition to make one word.

auf + das	→	aufs
bei + dem	→	beim
zu + der	→	zur

⇨ *For more information on the **Definite article**, see page 25.*

➤ This can be done with all of the following prepositions:

Preposition	+ das	+ den	+ dem	+ der
an	ans		am	
auf	aufs			
bei			beim	
durch	durchs			
für	fürs			
hinter	hinters	hintern	hinterm	
in	ins		im	
über	übers	übern	überm	
um	ums			
unter	unters	untern	unterm	
vor	vors		vorm	
von			vom	
zu			zum	zur

Er ging <u>ans</u> Fenster.	He went to the window.
Wir waren gestern <u>am</u> Meer.	We were at the seaside yesterday.
Er ist <u>beim</u> Friseur.	He's at the hairdresser's.
Wir gehen heute Abend <u>ins</u> Kino.	We're going to the cinema tonight.
Im Sommer lese ich gern <u>im</u> Garten.	In the summer I like reading in the garden.
Es ging immer <u>ums</u> Thema Geld.	It was always about the subject of money.
Der Hund lief <u>unters</u> Auto.	The dog ran under the car.
Der Ball rollte <u>untern</u> Tisch.	The ball rolled under the table.
Die Katze lag <u>unterm</u> Schreibtisch.	The cat lay under the desk.
Er erzählte <u>vom</u> Urlaub.	He talked about his holiday.
Sie fährt <u>zum</u> Bahnhof.	She drives to the station.
Er geht <u>zur</u> Schule.	He goes to school.

➤ The following shortened forms are normally only used in informal, spoken German:

- aufs

Wir fahren morgen <u>aufs</u> Land.	We're going to the country tomorrow.

- durchs

Sie flog <u>durchs</u> Abitur.	She failed her 'A' Levels.

- fürs

Das ist <u>fürs</u> neue Haus.	That's for the new house.

- hinters, hintern, hinterm

Er lief <u>hinters</u> Auto.	He ran behind the car.
Stell es <u>hintern</u> Tisch.	Put it behind the table.
Es liegt <u>hinterm</u> Sofa.	It's behind the couch.

- übers, übern, überm

Sie legten ein Brett <u>übers</u> Loch.	They put a board over the hole.
Man muss das <u>übern</u> Kopf ziehen.	You have to pull it over your head.
<u>Überm</u> Tisch hängt eine Lampe.	There's a lamp hanging over the table.

- unters, untern, unterm

Die Katze ging <u>unters</u> Bett.	The cat went under the bed.
Der Ball rollte <u>untern</u> Tisch.	The ball rolled under the table.
Der Hund liegt <u>unterm</u> Tisch.	The dog is lying under the table.

- vors, vorm

Stell den Stuhl <u>vors</u> Fenster.	Put the chair in front of the window.
Er stand <u>vorm</u> Spiegel.	He stood in front of the mirror.

i Note that if you want to stress the article in a sentence, shortened forms are <u>NOT</u> used.

<u>In dem</u> Anzug kann ich mich nicht sehen lassen!	I can't go out in that suit!

➤ Shortened forms of prepositions can also be used:

- with personal pronouns representing inanimate objects, that is objects which are not living things

Sie war <u>damit</u> zufrieden.	She was satisfied with that.
Er hat es <u>darauf</u> angelegt, dass er die beste Note kriegen würde.	He was determined to get the best grade.

⇨ *For more information on **Personal pronouns**, see page 70.*

Key points

✔ It is often possible to combine the definite article and a preposition to create a shortened form.

✔ Some of these shortened forms should only be used in spoken German.

Conjunctions

What is a conjunction?
A **conjunction** is a linking word such as *and, but, if* and *because*, that links two words or phrases of a similar type, for example, *Diane and I have been friends for years*. Conjunctions also link two clauses, for example, *I left because I was bored*. In German there are two types of conjunctions, called **co-ordinating conjunctions** and **subordinating conjunctions**.

Co-ordinating conjunctions

➤ **aber, denn, oder, sondern** and **und** are the most important co-ordinating conjunctions.

- **aber** but

  Wir wollten ins Kino, <u>aber</u> wir hatten kein Geld.

  We wanted to go to the cinema, <u>but</u> we had no money.

i Note that you can't use **aber** after a negative to mean *not … but …*: you must use **sondern**.

- **aber** however

  Ich wollte nach Hause, er <u>aber</u> wollte nicht mit.

  I wanted to go home; however, he wouldn't come.

i Note that when **aber** means 'however', it comes between the subject and verb in the clause.

- **denn** because, since

  Wir wollten heute fahren, <u>denn</u> montags ist weniger Verkehr.

  We wanted to travel today because there is less traffic on Mondays.

- **oder** or

  Sie hatte noch nie Whisky <u>oder</u> Schnaps getrunken.

  She had never drunk whisky or schnapps.

  Willst du eins <u>oder</u> hast du vielleicht keinen Hunger?

  Do you want one or aren't you hungry?

- **sondern** but

  Es kostet nicht zwanzig, <u>sondern</u> fünfzig Euro.

  It doesn't cost twenty euros, but fifty.

- **und** and

  Susi und Oliver

  Susi and Oliver

  Er ging in die Stadt <u>und</u> kaufte sich ein neues Hemd.

  He went into town and bought himself a new shirt.

For further explanation of grammatical terms, please see pages xii–xvi.

➤ If you use a co-ordinating conjunction, you do not put the verb at the end of the clause beginning with the conjunction.

Wir wollten ins Theater, <u>aber</u> <u>wir</u> <u>hatten</u> kein Geld.	We wanted to go to the theatre but we had no money.

wir = subject
hatten = verb

Co-ordinating conjunctions with two parts

➤ German, like English, also has conjunctions which have more than one part. Here are the most common ones:

- **sowohl ... als (auch)** both ... and

  The verb is plural, whether the individual subjects are singular or plural.

<u>Sowohl</u> sein Vater <u>als auch</u> seine Mutter haben sich darüber gefreut.	Both his father and mother were pleased about it.
<u>Sowohl</u> unser Lehrkörper <u>als auch</u> unsere Schüler haben teilgenommen.	Both our staff and pupils took part.

- **weder ... noch** neither ... nor

  With this conjunction, the verb is plural unless both subjects are singular, as shown below.

<u>Weder</u> die Lehrer <u>noch</u> die Schüler haben recht.	Neither the teachers nor the pupils are right.
<u>Weder</u> du <u>noch</u> ich würde es schaffen.	Neither you nor I would be able to do it.

  When **weder ... noch** is used to link clauses, the subject and verb are swapped round in <u>BOTH</u> clauses.

<u>Weder</u> mag ich ihn <u>noch</u> respektiere ich ihn.	I neither like nor respect him.

- **nicht nur ... sondern auch** not only ... but also

  The verb agrees in number with the subject nearest to it.

<u>Nicht nur</u> sie, <u>sondern auch</u> ich habe es gehört.	They weren't the only ones to hear it – I heard it too.

  When **nicht nur ... sondern auch** is used to link clauses, the subject and verb are only swapped round in the first clause, not the second, BUT if **nicht nur** does not begin the clause, word order is normal.

<u>Nicht nur</u> ist sie geschickt, <u>sondern auch</u> intelligent.	

  OR

Sie ist <u>nicht nur</u> geschickt, <u>sondern auch</u> intelligent.	She is not only skilful but also intelligent.

- **entweder ... oder** either ... or

  The verb agrees in number with the subject nearest to it. When **entweder ... oder** is used to link clauses, the subject and verb are only swapped round in the first clause, not the second.

<u>Entweder</u> du <u>oder</u> Karla muss es getan haben.	It must have been either you or Karla.
<u>Entweder</u> komme ich vorbei, <u>oder</u> ich rufe dich an.	I'll either drop in or I'll give you a ring.

Key points

✔ A conjunction is a word that links two words or clauses of a similar type, or two parts of a sentence.

✔ **Aber**, **denn**, **oder**, **sondern** and **und** are the most important co-ordinating conjunctions.

✔ Single-word co-ordinating conjunctions do not change the order of the subject and the verb in the clause.

Subordinating conjunctions

➤ The subordinate clause is always separated from the main clause by a comma. It is called a subordinate clause because it cannot stand on its own without the other clause in the sentence and is linked to this by a subordinating conjunction.

Sie ist zu Fuß gekommen, <u>weil</u> der Bus zu teuer <u>ist</u>.	She came on foot because the bus is too dear.
MAIN CLAUSE	= Sie ist zu Fuß gekommen
SUBORDINATE CLAUSE	= weil der Bus zu teuer ist

ⓘ Note that the verb comes at the end of the subordinate clause.

➤ als, da, damit, dass, ob, obwohl, während, wenn, weil, um ... zu, and ohne ... zu are some of the most important subordinating conjunctions.

- als (when)

Es regnete, <u>als</u> ich in Glasgow ankam.	It was raining when I arrived in Glasgow.

- da (as, since)

<u>Da</u> du nicht kommen willst, gehe ich allein.	Since you don't want to come, I'll go on my own.

- damit so (that)

Ich sage dir das, <u>damit</u> du es weißt.	I'm telling you so that you know.

- dass that

Ich weiß, <u>dass</u> du besser in Mathe bist als ich.	I know (that) you're better at maths than me.

- ob if, whether

Sie fragt, <u>ob</u> du auch kommst.	She wants to know if you're coming too.

- obwohl although

Sie blieb lange auf, <u>obwohl</u> sie müde war.	She stayed up late although she was tired.

- während while

Sie sah fern, <u>während</u> sie ihre Hausaufgaben machte.	She was watching TV while she was doing her homework.

- wenn when, whenever/if

<u>Wenn</u> ich nach Hause komme, dusche ich erst mal.	When I get home, the first thing I'm going to do is have a shower.
<u>Wenn</u> er anruft, sag mir Bescheid.	If he calls, tell me.

For further explanation of grammatical terms, please see pages xii–xvi.

> **Tip**
>
> If translating *when* in a sentence which describes a single, completed action in the past, you use **als**, NOT **wenn**. You use **wenn** for single, momentary actions in the present or future.

- weil because

  Morgen komme ich nicht, <u>weil</u> ich keine Zeit habe.

  I'm not coming tomorrow because I don't have the time.

- um ... zu in order to ...

  <u>Um</u> früh auf<u>zu</u>stehen, musste sie den Wecker stellen.

  In order to get up early, she had to set the alarm.

[i] Note that **zu** is inserted between a separable verb and its prefix.

⇨ *For more information on **Separable verbs**, see page 109.*

- ohne ... zu without ...

  Er verließ das Haus, <u>ohne</u> ein Wort <u>zu</u> sagen.

  He left the house without saying a word.

[i] Note that **um ... zu** and **ohne ... zu** are always used with infinitive constructions.

[i] Note that with the subordinating conjunctions **als**, **da**, **damit**, **dass**, **ob**, **obwohl**, **während**, **wenn**, **weil**, **um ... zu**, and **ohne ... zu**, the subordinate clause can come <u>BEFORE</u> the main clause, as seen in the example with **da**. When this happens, the verb and subject of the main clause swap places.

⇨ *For more information on the **Infinitive**, see page 134.*

➤ In tenses which only have one verb part, such as the present and imperfect, the verb comes last in the subordinate clause.

  <u>Wenn</u> er mich <u>sah</u>, lief er davon.

  Whenever he saw me, he ran away.

➤ In tenses which have two verb parts, such as the perfect tense, it is the form of **haben**, **sein** or **werden** which comes last in the subordinate clause, after the past participle.

  Sie will nicht ausgehen, <u>weil</u> sie noch nichts <u>gegessen</u> hat.

  She doesn't want to go out because she hasn't eaten anything yet.

⇨ *For more information on the **Perfect** and **Imperfect tenses**, see pages 113 and 118.*

➤ Any modal verb, for example **mögen** (meaning *to like*) and **können** (meaning *can, to be able to*), used in a subordinate clause is placed last in the clause.

  Sie wusste nicht, <u>ob</u> sie kommen <u>konnte</u>.

  She didn't know if she could come.

⇨ *For more information on **Modal verbs**, see page 136.*

Key points

✔ Subordinating conjunctions link the main clause and subordinating clause in a sentence.

✔ After subordinating conjunctions, verbs go to the end of the clause.

✔ Als, da, damit, dass, ob, obwohl, während, wenn, weil, um ... zu, and ohne ... zu are some of the most important subordinating conjunctions.

✔ The subordinate clause can come before the main clause. When this happens, the verb and subject of the main clause swap places.

✔ In tenses which only have one verb part, the verb comes last in the subordinate clause. In tenses which have two verb parts, haben, sein or werden comes last in the subordinate clause, after the past participle.

Word order

➤ Here is a ready-reference guide to the key points of German word order.

1 Main clauses

➤ In a main clause the subject comes first and is followed by the verb, as in English.

Seine Mutter *(subject)* **trinkt** *(verb)* **Whisky.**	His mother *(subject)* drinks *(verb)* whisky.

➤ In tenses with more than one verb element, such as the perfect tense and the passive, the part of **haben**, **sein** or **werden** comes after the subject, and the past participle or infinitive goes to the end of the clause.

Sie <u>hat</u> mir nichts <u>gesagt</u>.	She told me nothing.
Er <u>ist</u> spät <u>angekommen</u>.	He arrived late.
Es <u>wurde</u> für ihn <u>gekauft</u>.	It was bought for him.

➤ A direct object usually follows an indirect object, except where the direct object is a personal pronoun.

Ich gab dem Mann *(indirect object)* **das Geld** *(direct object)*.	I gave the man the money.
Ich gab ihm *(indirect object)* **das Geld** *(direct object)*.	I gave him the money.
BUT	
Ich gab es *(direct object)* **ihm** *(indirect object)*.	I gave it to him.

i Note that the indirect object can also be placed last for emphasis, providing it is NOT a pronoun.

Er gab das Geld seiner Schwester.	He gave the money to his sister. *(not his brother)*

⇨ *For more information on **Direct** and **Indirect objects**, see pages 9 and 13.*

⇨ *For more information on **Using direct** and **Indirect object pronouns**, see pages 74 and 76.*

➤ As a general rule, adverbs are placed next to the words to which they refer.

● Adverbs of <u>time</u> often come first in the clause, but this is not fixed.

<u>Gestern</u> gingen wir ins Theater	
OR	
Wir gingen <u>gestern</u> ins Theater	We went to the theatre yesterday.

● Adverbs of <u>place</u> can also come first in the clause when you want to emphasize something.

<u>Dort</u> haben sie Fußball gespielt.	That's where they played football.

- Adverbs of <u>manner</u> comment on verbs and so are likely to come immediately after the verb they refer to.

  Sie spielen <u>gut</u> Fußball.　　　　They play football well.

- Where there is more than one adverb, a useful rule of thumb is: "TIME, MANNER, PLACE"

  Wir haben <u>gestern</u> <u>gut</u> <u>hierhin</u> gefunden.　　We found our way here all right yesterday.

  gestern = adverb of time
  gut = adverb of manner
  hierhin = adverb of place

- If there is a pronoun object (a word like *her, it, me* or *them*) in the clause, it comes before all adverbs.

  Sie haben <u>es</u> gestern sehr billig gekauft.　　They bought it very cheaply yesterday.

➤ The normal word order in a main clause is subject followed by verb. The subject can be replaced as the first element by any of the words and phrases below. In such cases, the verb is the second element in the clause.

- an adverb

  <u>Gestern</u> sind wir ins Theater gegangen.　　We went to the theatre yesterday.

- a direct or indirect object

  <u>Seinen Freunden</u> wollte er es nicht zeigen.　　He wouldn't show it to his friends.

- an infinitive phrase

  <u>Ihren Freunden zu helfen</u>, hat sie nicht versucht.　　She didn't try to help her friends.

- another noun or pronoun

  <u>Deine Schwester</u> war es.　　It was your sister.
  <u>Sie</u> war es.　　It was her.

- a past participle

  <u>Geraucht</u> hatte er nie.　　He had never, ever smoked.

- a phrase with a preposition

  <u>In diesem Haus</u> bin ich auf die Welt gekommen.　　I was born in this house.

- a clause which acts as the object of the verb

  <u>Was mit ihm los war</u>, haben wir nie herausgefunden.　　We never found out what was wrong with him.

For further explanation of grammatical terms, please see pages xii–xvi.

- a subordinate clause

  Nachdem ich ihn gesehen hatte, ging ich nach Hause.

  I went home after seeing him.

2 Subordinate clauses

➤ A subordinate clause may be introduced by a relative pronoun (a word such as **der**, **die** or **dessen**) or a subordinating conjunction (a word such as **da**, **als** or **ob**).

  Die Kinder, die wir gesehen haben … The children whom we saw …

  Da sie nicht schwimmen wollte, ist sie nicht mitgekommen.

  As she didn't want to swim, she didn't come.

➤ The subject follows the conjunction or relative pronoun.

  Ich weiß nicht, ob er kommt. I don't know if he's coming.

➤ The main verb ALMOST ALWAYS goes to the end of a subordinate clause.

  Als ich nach Hause kam, war ich ganz müde.

  When I came home I was really tired.

Grammar Extra!

The exceptions to this are:

- A clause which normally begins with **wenn**, but from which it can be left out.

  Findest du mein Handy, so ruf mich bitte an.

  INSTEAD OF

  Wenn du mein Handy findest, ruf mich bitte an.

  If you find my mobile, please give me a call.

- Indirect speech without the conjunction **dass** (meaning that).

  Sie meint, sie werde es innerhalb einer Stunde schaffen.

  INSTEAD OF

  Sie meint, dass sie es innerhalb einer Stunde schaffen wird.

  She thinks (that) she will manage it inside an hour.

➤ The rules applying to the order of articles, nouns, adjectives, adverbs, direct and indirect objects are the same in subordinate clauses as in main clauses, EXCEPT that all these words are placed between the subject of the clause and the relevant verb part.

MAIN CLAUSE:

Sie ist <u>gestern mit ihrer Mutter in die Stadt</u> gefahren.

She went into town with her mother yesterday.

SUBORDINATE CLAUSE:

<u>Da</u> sie <u>gestern mit ihrer Mutter in die Stadt</u> gefahren ist.

Since she went into town with her mother yesterday.

> *Tip*
>
> The rule "time, manner, place" applies equally to subordinate clauses, EXCEPT that the verb goes to the end.
>
> ⇨ *For more information on **Subordinate clauses**, see page 193.*

➤ Word order in the imperative, in direct and indirect speech and in verbs with separable prefixes is covered in the relevant chapters:

⇨ *For more information on the **Imperative**, see page 105.*

⇨ *For more information on **Direct** and **Indirect speech**, see page 129.*

⇨ *For more information on **Verbs with separable prefixes**, see page 109.*

Negatives

What is a negative?
A **negative** question or statement is one which contains a word such as *not*,
never or *nothing* and is used to say that something is not happening, is not true
or is absent.

1 Using negatives

➤ In English we use words like *not*, *no*, *nothing* and *never* to show a negative.

I'm <u>not</u> very pleased.
Dan <u>never</u> rang me.
Nothing <u>ever</u> happens here!
There's <u>no</u> milk left.

➤ In German, if you want to make something negative, you generally add **nicht**
(meaning *not*) or **nie** (meaning *never*) next to the phrase or word referred to.

Ich will <u>nicht</u> mitgehen.	I <u>don't</u> want to come.
Sie fährt <u>nie</u> mit ans Meer.	She <u>never</u> comes with us to the seaside.

➤ Here is a list of the other common German negatives:

- **nein** (meaning *no*)

  <u>Nein</u>, ich habe keine Zeit.   No, I don't have any time.

- **nichts** (meaning *nothing*)

  Sie hat <u>nichts</u> damit zu tun.   She has nothing to do with it.

- **nicht mehr** (meaning *not ... any more, no longer*)

Ich rauche <u>nicht mehr</u>.	I don't smoke any more/ I no longer smoke.
Sie geht <u>nicht mehr</u> hin.	She doesn't go any more.

[i] Note that **nicht** and **mehr** always appear next to each other.

kein (meaning *none*)

<u>Keiner</u> meiner Freunde wollte kommen.	None of my friends wanted to come.
Wo ist die Milch? – Es ist <u>keine</u> mehr da.	Where is the milk? – There is none left.

Tip

Nicht applies to verbs. Remember that when you want to make a
negative statement about a noun, you must use **kein**. If you want to say
I don't drink milk any more, you would say **Ich trinke <u>keine</u> Milch <u>mehr</u>**.

⇨ *For more information on the **Indefinite article in negative sentences** and on **Indefinite pronouns**, see pages 36 and 82.*

- niemand (meaning *nobody* or *no one*)

  Es war niemand im Büro.   There was nobody in the office.

⇨ *For more information on **Indefinite pronouns**, see page 82.*

- nirgendwo or nirgends (meaning *nowhere, not … anywhere*)

  <u>Nirgends</u> sonst gibt es so schöne   Nowhere else will you find such
  Blumen.   beautiful flowers.

  Hier gibts <u>nirgendwo</u> ein   There isn't a swimming pool
  Schwimmbad.   anywhere here.

- weder noch (meaning *neither of two things*)

  Karotten oder Erbsen? –   Carrots or peas? –
  <u>Weder noch</u>, danke.   Neither, thanks.

- weder … noch (meaning *neither … nor*)

  Weder Sabina <u>noch</u> Oliver kommen   Neither Sabina nor Oliver are
  zur Party.   coming to the party.

⇨ *For more information on **Co-ordinating conjunctions with two parts**, see page 170.*

- … auch nicht (meaning *neither have I, nor does he, nor are we* etc)

  Ich mag ihn nicht. – Ich <u>auch</u> <u>nicht</u>!   I don't like him. – Neither do I!
  Er war noch nie im Spanien. –   He's never been to Spain. –
  Sie <u>auch</u> <u>nicht</u>!   Neither has she!

2 Word order with negatives

➤ In a sentence with only one verb part, such as the present tense, **nicht** and **nie** usually come directly after the verb. However, in direct questions, the negative word comes after the subject.

  Du arbeitest <u>nicht</u>.   You're not working.
  BUT
  Arbeitest du <u>nicht</u>?   Aren't you working?

➤ In a sentence with two verb parts, such as the perfect tense and the passive, the part of **haben**, **sein** or **werden** comes after the subject and the negative word usually comes directly before the past participle or infinitive. The position of the negative doesn't change in direct questions.

  Sie haben es <u>nicht</u> gemacht.   You haven't done it.
  Haben Sie es <u>nicht</u> gemacht?   Haven't you done it?

For further explanation of grammatical terms, please see pages xii–xvi.

➤ You can change the emphasis in a sentence by moving the position of the negative. For example, **nie** can be placed at the start of the sentence. The subject and verb then swap positions.

Nie waren sie glücklicher gewesen.	They had <u>never</u> been happier.
Nie im Leben hatte er so etwas gesehen.	<u>Never</u> in his life had he seen such a thing.

➤ **nicht** comes at the end of a negative imperative, except if the verb is separable, in which case it comes before the separable prefix.

Iss das <u>nicht</u>!	Don't eat that!
Setzen Sie sich <u>nicht</u>!	Don't sit down!
BUT	
Geh <u>nicht</u> weg!	Don't go away!

➤ **nicht** + the indefinite article **ein** is usually replaced by forms of **kein**.

Gibt es <u>keine</u> Plätzchen?	Aren't there any biscuits?
<u>Kein</u> einziger Student hatte die Arbeit gemacht.	Not a single student had done the work.

⇨ *For more information on the **Indefinite article**, see page 35.*

➤ To contradict a negative statement, **doch** is used instead of **ja**, to mean *yes*.

Du kommst nicht mit. – <u>Doch</u>, ich komme mit.	You're not coming. – Yes I am.
Das ist nicht wahr. – <u>Doch</u>!	That isn't true! – Yes it is!

➤ **nicht ... sondern** (meaning *not ... but*) is used to correct a wrong idea or false impression.

<u>Nicht</u> Susi, <u>sondern</u> ihr Bruder war es.	It wasn't Susi, it was her brother.

Key points

✔ A statement is usually made negative by adding **nicht** (meaning *not*) or **nie** (meaning *never*).

✔ The most common German negatives are: **nicht, nein, nie, nichts, nicht mehr, kein, niemand, nirgends** or **nirgendwo, weder noch, weder ... noch** and **... auch nicht**.

✔ **Nicht** comes at the end of a negative imperative, except if the verb is separable, in which case it comes before the separable prefix.

✔ **Nicht** + the indefinite article **ein** is usually replaced by forms of **kein**.

✔ To contradict a negative statement, **doch** is used instead of **ja**, to mean *yes*.

✔ **Nicht ... sondern** (meaning *not ... but*) is used to correct a wrong idea or false impression.

Questions

> **What is a question?**
> A **question** is a sentence which is used to ask someone about something and which in English normally has the verb in front of the subject. Question words such as *why*, *where*, *who*, *which* or *how* are also used to ask a question.

How to ask a question in German

1 The basic rules

➤ There are three ways of asking direct questions in German:

- by changing round the order of words in a sentence
- by adding **nicht**, **nicht wahr**, **oder** or **doch** (meaning *isn't it*) to a sentence
- by using a question word

2 Asking a question by changing word order

➤ Many questions are formed in German by simply changing the normal word order of a sentence. You swap round the subject and verb, and add a question mark.

Magst *(verb)* **du** *(subject)* **ihn?**	Do you like him?
Gehst *(verb)* **du** *(subject)* **ins Kino?**	Do you go to the cinema? OR Are you going to the cinema?

➤ In tenses with more than one verb, such as the perfect tense and the passive, the part of **haben**, **sein** or **werden** comes <u>BEFORE</u> the subject, and the past participle or infinitive goes to the end of the clause.

Haben Sie es gesehen?	Did you see it?

3 Asking a question by adding nicht, nicht wahr, oder or doch

➤ A statement can be made into a question by adding **nicht**, **nicht wahr**, **oder** or **doch**, in the same way as *isn't it, won't you* etc is added in English. You'd normally expect the answer to such questions to be a simple *yes* or *no*.

Das stimmt, <u>nicht wahr</u>?	That's true, isn't it?
Das Essen ist fertig, <u>nicht</u>?	The food's ready, isn't it?
Sie machen das, <u>oder</u>?	They'll do it, won't they?
Das schaffst du <u>doch</u>?	You'll manage, won't you?

➤ When a question is put in the negative, **doch** can be used to answer it more positively than **ja**.

Glaubst du mir nicht? – Doch!	Don't you believe me? – Yes, I do!

For further explanation of grammatical terms, please see pages xii–xvi.

4 | Asking a question by using a question word

➤ A question word is a word like *when* or *how* that is used to ask for information. In German, these words are a mixture of interrogative adverbs, pronouns and adjectives. Listed below are the most common question words:

wie? (*how?*)	**wo?** (*where?*)	**wem?** (*whom?*)
was? (*what?*)	**welcher?** (*which?*)	**wessen?** (*whose?*)
wann? (*when?*)	**wer?** (*who?*)	**warum?** (*why?*)

i Note that **wer** means *who*, NOT *where*.

➤ When questions are formed with interrogative adverbs like **wann**, **wo**, **wie** and **warum**, normal word order changes and the subject and verb swap places.

<u>Wann</u> ist er gekommen?	When did he come?
<u>Wo</u> willst du hin?	Where are you off to?
<u>Wie</u> haben Sie das gemacht?	How did you do that?
<u>Warum</u> ist sie so spät aufgestanden?	Why did she get up so late?

Tip

Remember to use **woher** and **wohin** when direction is involved.

<u>Woher</u> kommst du?	Where do you come from?
<u>Wohin</u> fahren Sie?	Where are you going?

➤ When questions are formed with interrogative pronouns and adjectives, word order is normal if the interrogative pronoun or adjective is the subject of the verb at the beginning of the clause.

<u>Wer</u> (*subject*) hat (*verb*) das gemacht?	Who did that?

➤ If the interrogative pronoun or adjective is NOT the subject of the verb at the beginning of the clause, the subject and verb swap places.

<u>Wem</u> hast (*verb*) du (*subject*) es geschenkt?	Who did you give it to?

⇨ *For more information on **Interrogative pronouns** and **Adjectives**, see pages 89 and 31.*

i Note that in indirect questions, that is questions following verbs of *asking* and *wondering*, the verb comes at the end of the question.

Sie fragte, ob du mitkommen wolltest.	She asked if you wanted to come.

> **Key points**
>
> ✔ There are three basic ways of asking direct questions in German: changing the word order; adding **nicht**, **nicht wahr**, **oder** or **doch**; and using a question word.
>
> ✔ When a question is put in the negative, **doch** can be used to answer it more positively than **ja**.
>
> ✔ The most common question words are the interrogative adverbs **wann**, **wo**, **wie** and **warum**, the interrogative pronouns **was**, **wer**, **wem** and **wessen**, and the interrogative adjective **welcher**.

Numbers

0	null
1	eins
2	zwei
3	drei
4	vier
5	fünf
6	sechs
7	sieben
8	acht
9	neun
10	zehn
11	elf
12	zwölf
13	dreizehn
14	vierzehn
15	fünfzehn
16	sechzehn
17	siebzehn
18	achtzehn
19	neunzehn
20	zwanzig
21	einundzwanzig
22	zweiundzwanzig
30	dreißig
40	vierzig
50	fünfzig
60	sechzig
70	siebzig
80	achtzig
90	neunzig
a hundred	hundert
one hundred	einhundert
101	hunderteins
102	hundertzwei
121	hunderteinundzwanzig
200	zweihundert
a thousand	tausend
one thousand	eintausend
1001	tausendeins
2000	zweitausend
100,000	hunderttausend
1,000,000	eine Million

i Note that **zwo** often replaces **zwei** in speech, to distinguish it clearly from **drei**.

> ## Tip
> In German, spaces or full stops are used with large numbers where English uses a comma. Decimals are written with a comma instead of a full stop.

1,000,000	**1.000.000** *or* **1 000 000**
7.5 *(seven point five)*	7,5 (sieben Komma fünf)

1st	1.	der erste
2nd	2.	der zweite
3rd	3.	der dritte
4th	4.	der vierte
5th	5.	der fünfte
6th	6.	der sechste
7th	7.	der siebte
8th	8.	der achte
9th	9.	der neunte
10th	10.	der zehnte
11th	11.	der elfte
12th	12.	der zwölfte
13th	13.	der dreizehnte
14th	14.	der vierzehnte
15th	15.	der fünfzehnte
16th	16.	der sechzehnte
17th	17.	der siebzehnte
18th	18.	der achtzehnte
19th	19.	der neunzehnte
20th	20.	der zwanzigste
21st	21.	der einundzwanzigste
22nd	22.	der zweiundzwanzigste
30th	30.	der dreißigste
40th	40.	der vierzigste
50th	50.	der fünfzigste
60th	60.	der sechzigste
70th	70.	der siebzigste
80th	80.	der achtzigste
90th	90.	der neunzigste
100th	100.	der hunderste
101st	101.	der hunderterste
102nd	102.	der hundertzweite
121st	121.	der hunderteinundzwanzigste
200th	200.	der zweihundertste

1000th	1000.	der tausendste
1001st	1001.	der tausenderste
2000th	2000.	der zweitausendste
100,000th	100 000.	der hunderttausendste
1,000,000th	1 000 000.	der millionste

Tip

When these numbers are used as nouns, they are written with a capital letter.

Sie ist die Zehnte.		She's the tenth.
half	$\frac{1}{2}$	halb
third	$\frac{1}{3}$	das Drittel
two thirds	$\frac{2}{3}$	zwei Drittel
quarter	$\frac{1}{4}$	das Viertel
three quarters	$\frac{3}{4}$	drei Viertel
one and a half	$1\frac{1}{2}$	anderthalb, eineinhalb
two and a half	$2\frac{1}{2}$	zweieinhalb

BEISPIELE	EXAMPLES
Sie hat zwei Autos.	She has two cars.
Er ist zwanzig Jahre alt.	He is twenty years old.
Sie wohnt im dritten Stock.	She lives on the third floor.
Er hat am 31. August Geburtstag.	His birthday is on the 31st of August.
Ich brauche anderthalb Stunden, um nach Hause zu kommen.	I need an hour and a half *or* one and a half hours to get home.
Sie aß zwei Drittel von dem Kuchen.	She ate two thirds of the cake.

i Note that ordinal numbers (**erste**, **zweite**, and so on) are declined according to the number, case and gender of the noun.

Ich habe gerade mein <u>erstes</u> Auto gekauft.	I've just bought my first car.
Sie kam zum <u>zweiten</u> Mal mit Verspätung an.	She arrived late for the second time.

⇨ *For more information on **Nouns**, see page 1.*

DIE ZEIT	THE TIME
Wie spät ist es? *or*	What time is it?
Wie viel Uhr ist es?	
Es ist ...	It's ...
Mitternacht *or* **null Uhr** *or* **vierundzwanzig Uhr** *or* **zwölf Uhr**	midnight *or* twelve o'clock
zehn (Minuten) nach zwölf *or* **null Uhr zehn**	ten (minutes) past twelve
Viertel nach zwölf *or* **null Uhr fünfzehn**	quarter past twelve
halb eins *or* **null Uhr dreißig**	half past twelve
zwanzig (Minuten) vor eins *or* **null Uhr vierzig**	twenty (minutes) to one
Viertel vor eins *or* **drei viertel eins** *or* **null Uhr fünfundvierzig**	quarter to one
ein Uhr	one o'clock
zehn (Minuten) nach eins *or* **ein Uhr zehn**	ten (minutes) past one
Viertel nach eins *or* **ein Uhr fünfzehn**	quarter past one
halb zwei *or* **ein Uhr dreißig**	half past one
zwanzig (Minuten) vor zwei *or* **ein Uhr vierzig**	twenty (minutes) to two
Viertel vor zwei *or* **drei viertel zwei** *or* **ein Uhr fünfundvierzig**	quarter to two
zehn (Minuten) vor zwei *or* **ein Uhr fünfzig**	ten (minutes) to two
zwölf Uhr	twelve o'clock (midday)
halb eins *or* **zwölf Uhr dreißig**	half past twelve
ein Uhr *or* **dreizehn Uhr**	one o'clock
halb fünf *or* **sechzehn Uhr dreißig**	half past four
zehn Uhr *or* **zweiundzwanzig Uhr** *or* **zwoundzwanzig Uhr**	ten o'clock

Um wie viel Uhr?	At what time?
Wann?	**When?**
morgen um halb drei	tomorrow at half past two
um drei Uhr (nachmittags)	at three (pm)
kurz vor zehn Uhr	just before ten o'clock
gegen vier Uhr (nachmittags)	around four o'clock (in the afternoon)
erst um halb neun	not until half past-eight
ab neun Uhr	from nine o'clock onwards
morgen früh	tomorrow morning
morgen Abend	tomorrow evening

For further explanation of grammatical terms, please see pages xii–xvi.

DAS DATUM	THE DATE
WOCHENTAGE	**DAYS OF THE WEEK**

Montag	Monday
Dienstag	Tuesday
Mittwoch	Wednesday
Donnerstag	Thursday
Freitag	Friday
Samstag	Saturday
Sonntag	Sunday

Wann?	**When?**
Montag	(on) Monday
montags	(on) Mondays
jeden Montag	every Monday
letzten Dienstag	last Tuesday
nächsten Freitag	next Friday
Samstag in einer Woche *or* in acht Tagen	a week on Saturday
Samstag in zwei Wochen	two weeks on Saturday

MONATE	**MONTHS**
Januar	January
Februar	February
März	March
April	April
Mai	May
Juni	June
Juli	July
August	August
September	September
Oktober	October
November	November
Dezember	December

Wann?	**When?**
im Dezember	in December
im April	in April
nächsten Januar	next January
letzten August	last August
Anfang/Ende September	at the beginning/ end of September

| Der Wievielte is heute? | What's the date today? |
| Welches Datum haben wir heute? | |

Heute ist ...
    der zwanzigste März
    der Zwanzigste

It's ...
    the twentieth of March
    the twentieth

Heute haben wir ...
    den zwanzigsten März
    den Zwanzigsten

It's ...
    the twentieth of March
    the twentieth

Am Wievielten findet es statt?
    am ersten April ...
    am Ersten ...
    (am) Montag, den ersten April or
    Montag, den 1. April

When does it take place?
    ... on the first of April
    ... on the first
    on Monday, the first of April or
    April 1st

JAHRESZEITEN

im Winter
im Sommer
im Herbst
im Frühling

SEASONS

in winter
in summer
in autumn
in spring

NÜTZLICHE VOKABELN

Wann?
    heute
    heute Morgen
    heute Nachmittag
    heute Abend
    (im Jahr(e)) 2005

USEFUL VOCABULARY

When?
    today
    this morning
    this afternoon
    this evening
    in 2005

Wie oft?
    jeden Tag
    alle zwei Tage
    einmal in der Woche/pro Woche
    zweimal pro Woche
    einmal im Monat/pro Monat

How often?
    every day
    every other day
    once a week
    twice a week
    once a month

Wann ist das passiert?	**When did it happen?**
am Morgen/Vormittag	in the morning
morgens/vormittags	in the mornings
am Abend	in the evening
abends	in the evenings
gestern	yesterday
gestern Abend	yesterday evening
vorgestern	the day before yesterday
vor einer Woche	a week ago
vor zwei Wochen	two weeks ago
letztes Jahr	last year

Wann passiert das?	**When is it going to happen?**
morgen	tomorrow
morgen früh	tomorrow morning
übermorgen	the day after tomorrow
in zwei Tagen	in two days
in einer Woche	in a week
in vierzehn Tagen/zwei Wochen	in two weeks
nächsten Monat	next month
nächstes Jahr	next year

i Note that to talk about the year in which something happens, you don't use **in** in German.

Das findet 2006 statt.	That's taking place in 2006.
Sie wurde 1990 geboren.	She was born in 1990.
Ich ging 1991 für ein Jahr nach Deutschland.	I went to Germany for a year in 1991.

Some common difficulties

General problems

➤ You can't always translate German into English and English into German word for word. While occasionally it is possible to do this, often it is not. For example:

- Sentences which contain a verb and preposition in English might <u>NOT</u> contain a preposition in German.

Jemanden/etwas ansehen	to look at somebody/something
Jemandem/etwas zuhören	to listen to somebody/something

- However, many sentences which contain a verb and preposition in German <u>DO</u> contain a preposition in English.

sich interessiern <u>für</u>	to be interested <u>in</u>
denken <u>über</u>	to think <u>about</u>

➤ Remember that German prepositions are of two types:

- Some are only ever used with one case, such as **gegen** (accusative), **bei** (dative) and **außerhalb** (genitive). For all of these it is useful to learn the preposition and its case by heart.

- The second type are used either with the accusative or the dative, according to whether movement from one place to another is involved or not. The translation of the same preposition from the last group can change according to the case being used.

Sie schrieb einen Brief <u>an</u> ihren Bruder.	She wrote a letter <u>to</u> her brother.
Wir treffen uns <u>am</u> Bahnhof.	We're meeting <u>at</u> the station.

⇨ *For more information on **Prepositions**, see page 153.*

➤ A word which is plural in English may not be in German.

eine Brille	glasses, spectacles
eine Schere	scissors
eine Hose	trousers

[i] Note that they are only used in the plural in German to mean more than one pair, for example, **zwei Hosen** = two pairs of trousers.

⇨ *For more information on **Nouns**, see page 1.*

➤ In English, you use 's to show who or what something belongs to; in German you generally either use the genitive case or **von** + the dative case.

> **Das Auto meiner Schwester**
> OR
> **Das Auto von meiner Schwester**   My sister's car

⇨ *For more information on the **Genitive case**, see page 11.*

➤ German punctuation differs from English in several ways.

- Decimal places are always shown by a comma, NOT a full stop.

  3,4 (drei Komma vier)   3.4 (three point four)

- Large numbers are separated by means of a space or a full stop, NOT a comma.

  20 000
  OR: **20.000 (zwanzigtausend)**   20,000 (twenty thousand)

- Subordinate clauses are always separated from the rest of the sentence by a comma.

  Er bleibt gesund, obwohl er zu viel trinkt.   He stays healthy, even though he drinks too much.

⇨ *For more information on **Subordinate clauses**, see page 177.*

- When two main clauses are linked by **und** (meaning *and*) or **oder** (meaning *or*), no comma is required.

  Wir gehen ins Kino oder wir bleiben zu Hause.   We'll go to the cinema or stay at home.

Specific problems

1 Nouns with capital letters

➤ Unlike English, <u>ALL</u> German nouns start with a capital letter, not just proper names.

der Tisch	the table
die Politikerin	the politician
die Königin	the Queen

(i) Note that this also applies to verbs being used as nouns.

Sie hat ihr <u>Können</u> bewiesen.	She has proved her ability.

2 Three forms of you

➤ In English we have only <u>one</u> way of saying *you*. In German, there are <u>three</u> words: **du**, **ihr** and **Sie**. You use:

● the familiar **du** if talking to one person <u>you know well</u>, such as a friend, someone younger than you or a relative.

Kommst <u>du</u> mit ins Kino?	Are you coming to the cinema?

● the familiar **ihr** if talking to more than one person <u>you know well</u>.

Also, was wollt ihr heute Abend machen?	So, what do you want to do tonight?

● the formal or polite **Sie** if talking to one or more people <u>you do not know so well</u>, such as your teacher, your boss or a stranger.

Was haben <u>Sie</u> gemacht?	What did you do?

3 -ing

➤ Although English sometimes uses parts of the verb *to be* to form the present tense of other verbs (for example, *I <u>am</u> listening*, *she'<u>s</u> talking*), German <u>NEVER</u> uses the verb **sein** in this way. Instead, it uses the normal present tense of the verb.

Ich <u>spiele</u> Tennis.	I <u>play</u> tennis
	OR:
	I <u>am playing</u> tennis

4 | To be

➤ The verb *to be* is generally translated by **sein**.

Es ist spät.	It's late.
Das ist nicht möglich.	That's not possible.

➤ When you are talking about the physical position of something you can use **liegen**. You may also come across **sich befinden** in more formal contexts.

Wo liegt/befindet sich der Bahnhof? Where's the station?

➤ In certain set phrases which describe how you are feeling or a state you are in, the verb **haben** is used.

Hunger haben	to be hungry
Durst haben	to be thirsty
Angst haben	to be afraid
unrecht haben	to be wrong
recht haben	to be right

[*i*] Note that to say *I etc am hot* or *I etc am cold*, you use a personal pronoun in the dative case followed by **sein**.

Mir ist heiß	I am hot
NOT	
Ich bin heiß	
Ihr is kalt	She is cold
NOT	
Sie ist kalt	

➤ When talking about your health, use the following forms of the verb **gehen**.

Wie geht es dir/Ihnen?	How are you?
Es geht mir gut	
OR	
Mir geht es gut.	I'm fine.

5 | It

➤ There are three ways of saying *it* in German: **er**, **sie** and **es**. These correspond to the three different genders, masculine, feminine and neuter.

Wo ist der Wagen? – Er steht da drüben.	Where is the car? – It's over There.
Ich finde meine Uhr nicht. Hast du sie gesehen?	I can't find my watch. Have you seen it?
Was hältst du von meinem Haus? – Es ist ganz schön.	What do you think of my house? – It's really nice.

⇨ *For more information on **Gender**, see page 3.*

6 | Date and time

➤ When talking about a particular day or date, use the preposition **an** + the dative case in the following constructions:

Ich fahre <u>am Montag</u> nach Hause.	I'm going home <u>on Monday</u>.
Sie wurde <u>am Dienstag, den 1. April</u> aus dem Krankenhaus entlassen.	She was discharged from hospital <u>on Tuesday, the 1st of April</u>.
Meine Nichte hat <u>am 6. September</u> Geburtstag.	My niece's birthday is <u>on the 6th of September</u>.

➤ When stating the time of a particular event, use the preposition **um** + the accusative case in the following construction.

Ich bin <u>um 9 Uhr</u> aufgestanden.	I got up <u>at 9 o'clock</u>.
Der Zug ist <u>um 22.30 Uhr</u> abgefahren.	The train left <u>at 22.30 hours</u>.

➪ *For more information on **Prepositions**, see pages 153.*

7 | There is, there are

➤ Both *there is* and *there are* are translated by **es gibt**.

Hier <u>gibt es</u> ein schönes Freibad.	<u>There's</u> a lovely open-air pool here.
In Stuttgart <u>gibt es</u> viele Parks.	<u>There are</u> lots of parks in Stuttgart.

8 | The imperfect of modal verbs

➤ Modal verbs never have an umlaut in the imperfect tense.

können (can, to be able)	**konnte**
müssen (must, to have to)	**musste**
mögen (to like)	**mochte**
dürfen (to be allowed to)	**durfte**
sollen (to ought to)	**sollte**
wollen (to want)	**wollte**

➪ *For more information on **Modal verbs**, see page 136.*

9 Er/sie/es parts of strong verbs in the imperfect

➤ You do <u>NOT</u> add a –t to the **er/sie/es** parts of the imperfect tense of strong verbs.

Er/sie/es ging	He/she/it went
NOT	
Er/sie/es gingt	
Er/sie/es sang	He/she/it sang
NOT	
Er/sie/es sangt	

➪ *For more information on the **Imperfect tense**, see page 118.*

10 Inseparable verbs in the perfect tense

➤ Inseparable verbs have no **ge-** added to beginning of the past participle in the perfect tense. For example:

Das habe ich schon <u>be</u>zahlt.	I've already paid for that.
Er hat sich endlich <u>ent</u>schlossen.	He's finally decided.

➪ *For more information on **Inseparable verbs**, see page 109.*

11 Can, to be able

➤ If you want to say *could*, meaning *was able*, you use **konnte**, the imperfect form of **können**, you do <u>NOT</u> use the conditional form **könnte**.

Sie <u>konnte</u> nicht kommen.	She couldn't make it.
Er <u>konnte</u> das einfach nicht.	He just wasn't able to do it.

Alphabet

➤ The German alphabet is pronounced differently from the way it is pronounced in English. Use the list below to help you sound out the letters.

A, a	[aː]	(ah)	
B, b	[beː]	(bay)	
C, c	[tseː]	(tsay)	
D, d	[deː]	(day)	
E, e	[eː]	(ay)	
F, f	[ɛf]	(ef)	
G, g	[geː]	(gay)	
H, h	[haː]	(hah)	
I, i	[iː]	(ee)	
J, j	[jɔt]	(yot)	
K, k	[kaː]	(kah)	
L, l	[ɛl]	(el)	
M, m	[ɛm]	(em)	
N, n	[ɛn]	(en)	
O, o	[oː]	(oh)	
P, p	[peː]	(pay)	
Q, q	[kuː]	(koo)	
R, r	[ɛr]	(air)	
S, s	[ɛs]	(es)	
T, t	[teː]	(tay)	
U, u	[uː]	(oo)	
V, v	[fau]	(fow)	
W, w	[veː]	(vay)	
X, x	[ɪks]	(ix)	
Y, y	[ʏpsilɔn]	(üpsilon)	like 'ü' in 'über'
Z, z	[tsɛt]	(tset)	

For further explanation of grammatical terms, please see pages xii–xvi.

Main Index

Verb Tables

VERB TABLES

Introduction

The **Verb Tables** in the following section contain 127 tables of German verbs (strong, weak and mixed) in alphabetical order. Each table shows you the following forms: **Present, Present Subjunctive, Perfect, Imperfect, Future, Conditional, Pluperfect, Pluperfect Subjunctive, Imperative** and the **Present** and **Past Participles**. For more information on these tenses and how they are formed you should look at the section on Verbs in the grammar section on pages 91–152.

In order to help you use the verbs shown in Verb Tables correctly, there are also a number of example phrases at the bottom of each page to show the verb as it is used in context.

In German there are **weak** verbs (their forms follow regular patterns), **strong** verbs (their forms follow irregular patterns) and **mixed** verbs (their forms follow a mixture of regular and irregular patterns). Two of the weak verbs in these tables are holen (to fetch) and machen (to do, to make). All weak, strong and mixed verbs are shown in full.

The **Verb Index** at the end of this section contains over 1000 verbs, each of which is cross-referred to one of the verbs given in the Verb Tables. The table shows the patterns that the verb listed in the index follows.

annehmen (to accept) strong, separable, *formed with* haben

PRESENT

ich	**nehme an**
du	**nimmst an**
er/sie/es	**nimmt an**
wir	**nehmen an**
ihr	**nehmt an**
sie/Sie	**nehmen an**

PRESENT SUBJUNCTIVE

ich	**nehme an**
du	**nehmest an**
er/sie/es	**nehme an**
wir	**nehmen an**
ihr	**nehmet an**
sie/Sie	**nehmen an**

PERFECT

ich	**habe angenommen**
du	**hast angenommen**
er/sie/es	**hat angenommen**
wir	**haben angenommen**
ihr	**habt angenommen**
sie/Sie	**haben angenommen**

IMPERFECT

ich	**nahm an**
du	**nahmst an**
er/sie/es	**nahm an**
wir	**nahmen an**
ihr	**nahmt an**
sie/Sie	**nahmen an**

PRESENT PARTICIPLE

annehmend

PAST PARTICIPLE

angenommen

EXAMPLE PHRASES

Ich **nehme an**, dass er heute nicht mehr kommt. I assume that he isn't coming today.

Er sagt, er **nehme an**, ich sei einverstanden. He says he assumes I would agree.

Ich **habe** die neue Stelle **angenommen**. I have accepted the new job.

Wir **nahmen an**, dass die Beweise ausreichen würden. We assumed the evidence to be sufficient.

ich = I du = you er = he/it sie = she/it es = it/he/she wir = we ihr = you sie = they Sie = you *(polite)*

annehmen

FUTURE

ich	**werde annehmen**
du	**wirst annehmen**
er/sie/es	**wird annehmen**
wir	**werden annehmen**
ihr	**werdet annehmen**
sie/Sie	**werden annehmen**

CONDITIONAL

ich	**würde annehmen**
du	**würdest annehmen**
er/sie/es	**würde annehmen**
wir	**würden annehmen**
ihr	**würdet annehmen**
sie/Sie	**würden annehmen**

PLUPERFECT

ich	**hatte angenommen**
du	**hattest angenommen**
er/sie/es	**hatte angenommen**
wir	**hatten angenommen**
ihr	**hattet angenommen**
sie/Sie	**hatten angenommen**

PLUPERFECT SUBJUNCTIVE

ich	**hätte angenommen**
du	**hättest angenommen**
er/sie/es	**hätte angenommen**
wir	**hätten angenommen**
ihr	**hättet angenommen**
sie/Sie	**hätten angenommen**

IMPERATIVE

nimm an!/nehmen wir an!/nehmt an!/nehmen Sie an!

EXAMPLE PHRASES

Ihr **werdet annehmen**, dass ich verrückt bin. You will think that I am mad.

Ich **würde** Ihr Angebot gern **annehmen**. I would be pleased to accept your offer.

Sie **hatte angenommen**, dass sie zu der Party gehen darf. She had assumed that she was allowed to go to the party.

Ich **hätte angenommen**, dass in dieser Stadt mehr los ist. I would have thought there was more going on in this town.

ich = I du = you er = he/it sie = she/it es = it/he/she wir = we ihr = you sie = they Sie = you *(polite)*

arbeiten (to work)

weak, *formed with* **haben**

PRESENT

ich	**arbeite**
du	**arbeitest**
er/sie/es	**arbeitet**
wir	**arbeiten**
ihr	**arbeitet**
sie/Sie	**arbeiten**

PRESENT SUBJUNCTIVE

ich	**arbeite**
du	**arbeitest**
er/sie/es	**arbeite**
wir	**arbeiten**
ihr	**arbeitet**
sie/Sie	**arbeiten**

PERFECT

ich	**habe gearbeitet**
du	**hast gearbeitet**
er/sie/es	**hat gearbeitet**
wir	**haben gearbeitet**
ihr	**habt gearbeitet**
sie/Sie	**haben gearbeitet**

IMPERFECT

ich	**arbeitete**
du	**arbeitetest**
er/sie/es	**arbeitete**
wir	**arbeiteten**
ihr	**arbeitetet**
sie/Sie	**arbeiteten**

PRESENT PARTICIPLE

arbeitend

PAST PARTICIPLE

gearbeitet

EXAMPLE PHRASES

Er **arbeitet** seit einem Jahr bei der Computerfirma. He has been working for the computer firm for a year.

Sie sagt, sie **arbeite** 50 Stunden in der Woche. She says she works 50 hours a week.

Er **hat** früher als Elektriker **gearbeitet**. He used to work as an electrician.

Sie **arbeitete** wochenlang an dem Projekt. She worked for weeks on the project.

ich = I **du** = you **er** = he/it **sie** = she/it **es** = it/he/she **wir** = we **ihr** = you **sie** = they **Sie** = you (polite)

arbeiten

FUTURE

ich	**werde arbeiten**
du	**wirst arbeiten**
er/sie/es	**wird arbeiten**
wir	**werden arbeiten**
ihr	**werdet arbeiten**
sie/Sie	**werden arbeiten**

CONDITIONAL

ich	**würde arbeiten**
du	**würdest arbeiten**
er/sie/es	**würde arbeiten**
wir	**würden arbeiten**
ihr	**würdet arbeiten**
sie/Sie	**würden arbeiten**

PLUPERFECT

ich	**hatte gearbeitet**
du	**hattest gearbeitet**
er/sie/es	**hatte gearbeitet**
wir	**hatten gearbeitet**
ihr	**hattet gearbeitet**
sie/Sie	**hatten gearbeitet**

PLUPERFECT SUBJUNCTIVE

ich	**hätte gearbeitet**
du	**hättest gearbeitet**
er/sie/es	**hätte gearbeitet**
wir	**hätten gearbeitet**
ihr	**hättet gearbeitet**
sie/Sie	**hätten gearbeite**

IMPERATIVE

arbeite!/arbeiten wir!/arbeitet!/arbeiten Sie!

EXAMPLE PHRASES

Wie lange **wirst** du daran **arbeiten**? How long will you be working on it?

Ich **würde** nicht gern sonntags **arbeiten**. I wouldn't like to work on Sundays.

Wir **hatten** alle hart **gearbeitet**. We had all worked hard.

Ich **hätte** lieber in einer Kneipe **gearbeitet**. I would rather have worked in a pub.

ich = I **du** = you **er** = he/it **sie** = she/it **es** = it/he/she **wir** = we **ihr** = you **sie** = they **Sie** = you (*polite*)

atmen (to breathe)

weak, *formed with* **haben**

PRESENT

ich	**atme**
du	**atmest**
er/sie/es	**atmet**
wir	**atmen**
ihr	**atmet**
sie/Sie	**atmen**

PRESENT SUBJUNCTIVE

ich	**atme**
du	**atmest**
er/sie/es	**atme**
wir	**atmen**
ihr	**atmet**
sie/Sie	**atmen**

PERFECT

ich	**habe geatmet**
du	**hast geatmet**
er/sie/es	**hat geatmet**
wir	**haben geatmet**
ihr	**habt geatmet**
sie/Sie	**haben geatmet**

IMPERFECT

ich	**atmete**
du	**atmetest**
er/sie/es	**atmete**
wir	**atmeten**
ihr	**atmetet**
sie/Sie	**atmeten**

PRESENT PARTICIPLE

atmend

PAST PARTICIPLE

geatmet

EXAMPLE PHRASES

Sie **atmet** jetzt wieder etwas freier. She is now breathing a bit more freely again.

Er sagt, die Luft, die er **atme**, sei verschmutzt. He says the air he is breathing is polluted.

Er **hat** ganz normal **geatmet**. He breathed normally.

Wir **atmeten** tief ein und aus. We took deep breaths.

ich = I **du** = you **er** = he/it **sie** = she/it **es** = it/he/she **wir** = we **ihr** = you **sie** = they **Sie** = you (*polite*)

atmen

FUTURE

ich	**werde atmen**
du	**wirst atmen**
er/sie/es	**wird atmen**
wir	**werden atmen**
ihr	**werdet atmen**
sie/Sie	**werden atmen**

CONDITIONAL

ich	**würde atmen**
du	**würdest atmen**
er/sie/es	**würde atmen**
wir	**würden atmen**
ihr	**würdet atmen**
sie/Sie	**würden atmen**

PLUPERFECT

ich	**hatte geatmet**
du	**hattest geatmet**
er/sie/es	**hatte geatmet**
wir	**hatten geatmet**
ihr	**hattet geatmet**
sie/Sie	**hatten geatmet**

PLUPERFECT SUBJUNCTIVE

ich	**hätte geatmet**
du	**hättest geatmet**
er/sie/es	**hätte geatmet**
wir	**hätten geatmet**
ihr	**hättet geatmet**
sie/Sie	**hätten geatmet**

IMPERATIVE

atme!/atmen wir!/atmet!/atmen Sie!

EXAMPLE PHRASES

Dort **werden** wir frischere Luft **atmen**. We'll breathe fresher air there.

Mit einem Inhalator **würde** er besser **atmen**. An inhaler would improve his breathing.

Wir **hatten** seit Tagen keine Frischluft **geatmet**. We hadn't breathed fresh air for days.

Ich **hätte** lieber Landluft **geatmet**. I would have preferred to breathe country air.

ich = I **du** = you **er** = he/it **sie** = she/it **es** = it/he/she **wir** = we **ihr** = you **sie** = they **Sie** = you (*polite*)

ausreichen (to be enough)

weak, separable,
formed with haben

PRESENT

ich	**reiche aus**
du	**reichst aus**
er/sie/es	**reicht aus**
wir	**reichen aus**
ihr	**reicht aus**
sie/Sie	**reichen aus**

PRESENT SUBJUNCTIVE

ich	**reiche aus**
du	**reichest aus**
er/sie/es	**reiche aus**
wir	**reichen aus**
ihr	**reichet aus**
sie/Sie	**reichen aus**

PERFECT

ich	**habe ausgereicht**
du	**hast ausgereicht**
er/sie/es	**hat ausgereicht**
wir	**haben ausgereicht**
ihr	**habt ausgereicht**
sie/Sie	**haben ausgereicht**

IMPERFECT

ich	**reichte aus**
du	**reichtest aus**
er/sie/es	**reichte aus**
wir	**reichten aus**
ihr	**reichtet aus**
sie/Sie	**reichten aus**

PRESENT PARTICIPLE

ausreichend

PAST PARTICIPLE

ausgereicht

EXAMPLE PHRASES

Reicht dir das **aus**? Is that enough for you?

Er meint, das Geld **reiche** nicht **aus**. He thinks the money isn't enough.

Die Vorräte **haben** nicht **ausgereicht**. There weren't enough provisions.

Die Zeit **reichte** nie **aus**. There was never enough time.

---

ich = I **du** = you **er** = he/it **sie** = she/it **es** = it/he/she **wir** = we **ihr** = you **sie** = they **Sie** = you *(polite)*

ausreichen

FUTURE

ich	werde ausreichen
du	wirst ausreichen
er/sie/es	wird ausreichen
wir	werden ausreichen
ihr	werdet ausreichen
sie/Sie	werden ausreichen

CONDITIONAL

ich	würde ausreichen
du	würdest ausreichen
er/sie/es	würde ausreichen
wir	würden ausreichen
ihr	würdet ausreichen
sie/Sie	würden ausreichen

PLUPERFECT

ich	hatte ausgereicht
du	hattest ausgereicht
er/sie/es	hatte ausgereicht
wir	hatten ausgereicht
ihr	hattet ausgereicht
sie/Sie	hatten ausgereicht

PLUPERFECT SUBJUNCTIVE

ich	hätte ausgereicht
du	hättest ausgereicht
er/sie/es	hätte ausgereicht
wir	hätten ausgereicht
ihr	hättet ausgereicht
sie/Sie	hätten ausgereicht

IMPERATIVE

reiche(e) aus!/reichen wir aus!/reicht aus!/reichen Sie aus!

EXAMPLE PHRASES

Das **wird** uns nicht **ausreichen**. That won't be enough for us.

Es **würde** uns **ausreichen**, wenn Sie 50 Euro zahlen. It would be sufficient if you paid us 50 euros.

Eine halbe Stunde **hatte ausgereicht**. Half an hour had been sufficient.

Das Essen **hätte** für 60 Personen **ausgereicht**. The food would have been enough for 60 people.

ich = I **du** = you **er** = he/it **sie** = she/it **es** = it/he/she **wir** = we **ihr** = you **sie** = they **Sie** = you (*polite*)

befehlen (to command)

strong, inseparable,
formed with haben

PRESENT

ich	**befehle**
du	**befiehlst**
er/sie/es	**befiehlt**
wir	**befehlen**
ihr	**befehlt**
sie/Sie	**befehlen**

PRESENT SUBJUNCTIVE

ich	**befehle**
du	**befehlest**
er/sie/es	**befehle**
wir	**befehlen**
ihr	**befehlet**
sie/Sie	**befehlen**

PERFECT

ich	**habe befohlen**
du	**hast befohlen**
er/sie/es	**hat befohlen**
wir	**haben befohlen**
ihr	**habt befohlen**
sie/Sie	**haben befohlen**

IMPERFECT

ich	**befahl**
du	**befahlst**
er/sie/es	**befahl**
wir	**befahlen**
ihr	**befahlt**
sie/Sie	**befahlen**

PRESENT PARTICIPLE

befehlend

PAST PARTICIPLE

befohlen

EXAMPLE PHRASES

Er **befiehlt** gern. He likes giving orders.

Er sagt, er **befehle** ihm, hier zu bleiben. He says he is ordering him to stay.

Er **hat** uns Stillschweigen **befohlen**. He has ordered us to be silent.

Er **befahl**, den Mann zu erschießen. He ordered the man to be shot.

ich = I **du** = you **er** = he/it **sie** = she/it **es** = it/he/she **wir** = we **ihr** = you **sie** = they **Sie** = you *(polite)*

befehlen

FUTURE

ich	**werde befehlen**
du	**wirst befehlen**
er/sie/es	**wird befehlen**
wir	**werden befehlen**
ihr	**werdet befehlen**
sie/Sie	**werden befehlen**

CONDITIONAL

ich	**würde befehlen**
du	**würdest befehlen**
er/sie/es	**würde befehlen**
wir	**würden befehlen**
ihr	**würdet befehlen**
sie/Sie	**würden befehlen**

PLUPERFECT

ich	**hatte befohlen**
du	**hattest befohlen**
er/sie/es	**hatte befohlen**
wir	**hatten befohlen**
ihr	**hattet befohlen**
sie/Sie	**hatten befohlen**

PLUPERFECT SUBJUNCTIVE

ich	**hätte befohlen**
du	**hättest befohlen**
er/sie/es	**hätte befohlen**
wir	**hätten befohlen**
ihr	**hättet befohlen**
sie/Sie	**hätten befohlen**

IMPERATIVE

befiehl!/befehlen wir!/befehlt!/befehlen Sie!

EXAMPLE PHRASES

Ich **werde** ihn zu mir **befehlen.** I will summon him to me.

Sie **würde** gern allen Leuten **befehlen.** She would like to give orders to everybody.

Der General **hatte** den Rückzug **befohlen.** The general had ordered his troops to retreat.

Er blieb stehen, als **hätte** jemand es ihm **befohlen.** He stopped as if someone had ordered him to.

ich = I du = you er = he/it sie = she/it es = it/he/she wir = we ihr = you sie = they Sie = you (*polite*)

beginnen (to begin)   strong, inseparable, *formed with* haben

PRESENT

ich	**beginne**
du	**beginnst**
er/sie/es	**beginnt**
wir	**beginnen**
ihr	**beginnt**
sie/Sie	**beginnen**

PRESENT SUBJUNCTIVE

ich	**beginne**
du	**beginnest**
er/sie/es	**beginne**
wir	**beginnen**
ihr	**beginnet**
sie/Sie	**beginnen**

PERFECT

ich	**habe begonnen**
du	**hast begonnen**
er/sie/es	**hat begonnen**
wir	**haben begonnen**
ihr	**habt begonnen**
sie/Sie	**haben begonnen**

IMPERFECT

ich	**begann**
du	**begannst**
er/sie/es	**begann**
wir	**begannen**
ihr	**begannt**
sie/Sie	**begannen**

PRESENT PARTICIPLE

beginnend

PAST PARTICIPLE

begonnen

EXAMPLE PHRASES

Die Vorstellung **beginnt** gleich. The performance is about to begin.

Sie sagt, sie **beginne** jeden Tag mit einem Gebet. She says she starts each day with a prayer.

Er **hat** als Lehrling **begonnen**. He started off as an apprentice.

Sie **begann** mit der Arbeit. She started working.

beginnen

FUTURE

ich	**werde beginnen**
du	**wirst beginnen**
er/sie/es	**wird beginnen**
wir	**werden beginnen**
ihr	**werdet beginnen**
sie/Sie	**werden beginnen**

CONDITIONAL

ich	**würde beginnen**
du	**würdest beginnen**
er/sie/es	**würde beginnen**
wir	**würden beginnen**
ihr	**würdet beginnen**
sie/Sie	**würden beginnen**

PLUPERFECT

ich	**hatte begonnen**
du	**hattest begonnen**
er/sie/es	**hatte begonnen**
wir	**hatten begonnen**
ihr	**hattet begonnen**
sie/Sie	**hatten begonnen**

PLUPERFECT SUBJUNCTIVE

ich	**hätte begonnen**
du	**hättest begonnen**
er/sie/es	**hätte begonnen**
wir	**hätten begonnen**
ihr	**hättet begonnen**
sie/Sie	**hätten begonnen**

IMPERATIVE

beginn(e)!/beginnen wir!/beginnt!/beginnen Sie!

EXAMPLE PHRASES

Wann **werdet** ihr endlich damit **beginnen**? When will you get started on it?

Wir **würden** nicht ohne dich **beginnen**. We wouldn't start without you.

Wir **hatten** gerade **begonnen**, als er kam. We had just got started when he came.

Wenn du gestern **begonnen hättest**, wärest du jetzt fertig. If you had started yesterday, you would be finished now.

ich = I **du** = you **er** = he/it **sie** = she/it **es** = it/he/she **wir** = we **ihr** = you **sie** = they **Sie** = you (*polite*)

beißen (to bite)

strong, *formed with* **haben**

PRESENT

ich	**beiße**
du	**beißt**
er/sie/es	**beißt**
wir	**beißen**
ihr	**beißt**
sie/Sie	**beißen**

PRESENT SUBJUNCTIVE

ich	**beiße**
du	**beißest**
er/sie/es	**beiße**
wir	**beißen**
ihr	**beißet**
sie/Sie	**beißen**

PERFECT

ich	**habe gebissen**
du	**hast gebissen**
er/sie/es	**hat gebissen**
wir	**haben gebissen**
ihr	**habt gebissen**
sie/Sie	**haben gebissen**

IMPERFECT

ich	**biss**
du	**bissest**
er/sie/es	**biss**
wir	**bissen**
ihr	**bisst**
sie/Sie	**bissen**

PRESENT PARTICIPLE

beißend

PAST PARTICIPLE

gebissen

EXAMPLE PHRASES

Rosa **beißt** sich mit Orange. Pink clashes with orange.

Er versichert uns, sein Hund **beiße** nicht. He assures us his dog doesn't bite.

Der Hund **hat** mich **gebissen**. The dog bit me.

Sie **biss** in den Apfel. She bit into the apple.

beißen

FUTURE

ich	**werde beißen**
du	**wirst beißen**
er/sie/es	**wird beißen**
wir	**werden beißen**
ihr	**werdet beißen**
sie/Sie	**werden beißen**

CONDITIONAL

ich	**würde beißen**
du	**würdest beißen**
er/sie/es	**würde beißen**
wir	**würden beißen**
ihr	**würdet beißen**
sie/Sie	**würden beißen**

PLUPERFECT

ich	**hatte gebissen**
du	**hattest gebissen**
er/sie/es	**hatte gebissen**
wir	**hatten gebissen**
ihr	**hattet gebissen**
sie/Sie	**hatten gebissen**

PLUPERFECT SUBJUNCTIVE

ich	**hätte gebissen**
du	**hättest gebissen**
er/sie/es	**hätte gebissen**
wir	**hätten gebissen**
ihr	**hättet gebissen**
sie/Sie	**hätten gebissen**

IMPERATIVE

beiß(e)!/beißen wir!/beißt!/beißen Sie!

EXAMPLE PHRASES

Er **wird** dich schon nicht **beißen!** He won't bite you!

Ich wette, die Katze **würde** dich **beißen.** I bet the cat would bite you.

Der Hund **hatte** den Einbrecher **gebissen.** The dog had bitten the burglar.

Die Katze **hätte** mich fast **gebissen.** The cat almost bit me.

ich = I **du** = you **er** = he/it **sie** = she/it **es** = it/he/she **wir** = we **ihr** = you **sie** = they **Sie** = you (*polite*)

bestellen (to order)

weak, inseparable, *formed with* haben

PRESENT

ich	bestelle
du	bestellst
er/sie/es	bestellt
wir	bestellen
ihr	bestellt
sie/Sie	bestellen

PRESENT SUBJUNCTIVE

ich	bestelle
du	bestellest
er/sie/es	bestelle
wir	bestellen
ihr	bestellet
sie/Sie	bestellen

PERFECT

ich	habe bestellt
du	hast bestellt
er/sie/es	hat bestellt
wir	haben bestellt
ihr	habt bestellt
sie/Sie	haben bestellt

IMPERFECT

ich	bestellte
du	bestelltest
er/sie/es	bestellte
wir	bestellten
ihr	bestelltet
sie/Sie	bestellten

PRESENT PARTICIPLE

bestellend

PAST PARTICIPLE

bestellt

EXAMPLE PHRASES

Ich **bestelle** uns schon mal ein Bier. I'll go and order a beer for us.

Er sagt, er **bestelle** alles im Internet. He says he orders everything on the Internet.

Haben Sie schon **bestellt**? Have you ordered yet?

Wir **bestellten** einen Tisch für zwei. We reserved a table for two.

---

ich = I **du** = you **er** = he/it **sie** = she/it **es** = it/he/she **wir** = we **ihr** = you **sie** = they **Sie** = you (*polite*)

bestellen

FUTURE

ich	**werde bestellen**
du	**wirst bestellen**
er/sie/es	**wird bestellen**
wir	**werden bestellen**
ihr	**werdet bestellen**
sie/Sie	**werden bestellen**

CONDITIONAL

ich	**würde bestellen**
du	**würdest bestellen**
er/sie/es	**würde bestellen**
wir	**würden bestellen**
ihr	**würdet bestellen**
sie/Sie	**würden bestellen**

PLUPERFECT

ich	**hatte bestellt**
du	**hattest bestellt**
er/sie/es	**hatte bestellt**
wir	**hatten bestellt**
ihr	**hattet bestellt**
sie/Sie	**hatten bestellt**

PLUPERFECT SUBJUNCTIVE

ich	**hätte bestellt**
du	**hättest bestellt**
er/sie/es	**hätte bestellt**
wir	**hätten bestellt**
ihr	**hättet bestellt**
sie/Sie	**hätten bestellt**

IMPERATIVE

bestelle(e)!/bestellen wir!/bestellt!/bestellen Sie!

EXAMPLE PHRASES

Dort **werde** ich nicht mehr **bestellen**. I won't be ordering anything from there anymore.

Ich **würde** die Karten gern im Voraus **bestellen**. I'd like to book the tickets in advance.

Ich **hatte** das Essen für 12 Uhr **bestellt**. I had ordered the meal for 12 o'clock.

Wir **hätten** gern noch mehr **bestellt**. We would have liked to have ordered more.

ich = I **du** = you **er** = he/it **sie** = she/it **es** = it/he/she **wir** = we **ihr** = you **sie** = they **Sie** = you (*polite*)

biegen (to bend/to turn)   strong, *formed with* haben/sein*

PRESENT

ich	**biege**
du	**biegst**
er/sie/es	**biegt**
wir	**biegen**
ihr	**biegt**
sie/Sie	**biegen**

PRESENT SUBJUNCTIVE

ich	**biege**
du	**biegest**
er/sie/es	**biege**
wir	**biegen**
ihr	**bieget**
sie/Sie	**biegen**

PERFECT

ich	**habe gebogen**
du	**hast gebogen**
er/sie/es	**hat gebogen**
wir	**haben gebogen**
ihr	**habt gebogen**
sie/Sie	**haben gebogen**

IMPERFECT

ich	**bog**
du	**bogst**
er/sie/es	**bog**
wir	**bogen**
ihr	**bogt**
sie/Sie	**bogen**

PRESENT PARTICIPLE

biegend

PAST PARTICIPLE

gebogen

When biegen is used with no direct object, it is formed with sein.

EXAMPLE PHRASES

Die Bäume **biegen** sich im Wind. The trees are bending in the wind.

Er sagt, er **biege** gleich in die Hauptstraße. He says he'll turn into the main road soon.

Er **hat** den Löffel **gebogen**. He bent the spoon.

Ein Auto **bog** um die Kurve. A car came round the corner.

ich = I **du** = you **er** = he/it **sie** = she/it **es** = it/he/she **wir** = we **ihr** = you **sie** = they **Sie** = you (*polite*)

biegen

FUTURE

ich	**werde biegen**
du	**wirst biegen**
er/sie/es	**wird biegen**
wir	**werden biegen**
ihr	**werdet biegen**
sie/Sie	**werden biegen**

CONDITIONAL

ich	**würde biegen**
du	**würdest biegen**
er/sie/es	**würde biegen**
wir	**würden biegen**
ihr	**würdet biegen**
sie/Sie	**würden biegen**

PLUPERFECT

ich	**hatte gebogen**
du	**hattest gebogen**
er/sie/es	**hatte gebogen**
wir	**hatten gebogen**
ihr	**hattet gebogen**
sie/Sie	**hatten gebogen**

PLUPERFECT SUBJUNCTIVE

ich	**hätte gebogen**
du	**hättest gebogen**
er/sie/es	**hätte gebogen**
wir	**hätten gebogen**
ihr	**hättet gebogen**
sie/Sie	**hätten gebogen**

IMPERATIVE

bieg(e)!/biegen wir!/biegt!/biegen Sie!

EXAMPLE PHRASES

Ich **werde** die Stäbe gerade **biegen**. I'll straighten the bars.

Ich **würde** nicht in diese Straße **biegen**. I wouldn't turn into that street.

Wir **hatten** uns vor Lachen **gebogen**. We had doubled up with laughter.

Er **wäre** in die Seitenstraße **gebogen**. He would have turned into the side street.

ich = I du = you er = he/it sie = she/it es = it/he/she wir = we ihr = you sie = they Sie = you (polite)

bieten (to offer)

strong, *formed with* haben

PRESENT

ich	**biete**
du	**bietest**
er/sie/es	**bietet**
wir	**bieten**
ihr	**bietet**
sie/Sie	**bieten**

PRESENT SUBJUNCTIVE

ich	**biete**
du	**bietest**
er/sie/es	**biete**
wir	**bieten**
ihr	**bietet**
sie/Sie	**bieten**

PERFECT

ich	**habe geboten**
du	**hast geboten**
er/sie/es	**hat geboten**
wir	**haben geboten**
ihr	**habt geboten**
sie/Sie	**haben geboten**

IMPERFECT

ich	**bot**
du	**bot(e)st**
er/sie/es	**bot**
wir	**boten**
ihr	**botet**
sie/Sie	**boten**

PRESENT PARTICIPLE

bietend

PAST PARTICIPLE

geboten

EXAMPLE PHRASES

Diese Stadt **bietet** mir nichts. This town has nothing to offer me.

Er sagt, er **biete** mir 5000 Euro für mein Auto. He says he's offering me 5000 euros for my car.

Für das Bild **haben** sie 2000 Euro **geboten**. They have made a bid of 2000 euros for the painting.

Er **bot** ihm die Hand. He held out his hand to him.

ich = I du = you er = he/it sie = she/it es = it/he/she wir = we ihr = you sie = they Sie = you (*polite*)

bieten

FUTURE

ich	**werde bieten**
du	**wirst bieten**
er/sie/es	**wird bieten**
wir	**werden bieten**
ihr	**werdet bieten**
sie/Sie	**werden bieten**

CONDITIONAL

ich	**würde bieten**
du	**würdest bieten**
er/sie/es	**würde bieten**
wir	**würden bieten**
ihr	**würdet bieten**
sie/Sie	**würden bieten**

PLUPERFECT

ich	**hatte geboten**
du	**hattest geboten**
er/sie/es	**hatte geboten**
wir	**hatten geboten**
ihr	**hattet geboten**
sie/Sie	**hatten geboten**

PLUPERFECT SUBJUNCTIVE

ich	**hätte geboten**
du	**hättest geboten**
er/sie/es	**hätte geboten**
wir	**hätten geboten**
ihr	**hättet geboten**
sie/Sie	**hätten geboten**

IMPERATIVE

biet(e)!/bieten wir!/bietet!/bieten Sie!

EXAMPLE PHRASES

Was **werden** sie uns **bieten**? What will they offer us?

Wir **würden** ihm gern mehr **bieten**. We would like to offer him more.

Sie **hatten** ihr eine Million für das Haus **geboten**. They had offered her one million for the house.

Ich **hätte** ihr gern noch mehr **geboten**. I would have liked to offer her even more.

ich = I **du** = you **er** = he/it **sie** = she/it **es** = it/he/she **wir** = we **ihr** = you **sie** = they **Sie** = you (*polite*)

binden (to tie)

strong, *formed with* haben

PRESENT

ich	binde
du	bindest
er/sie/es	bindet
wir	binden
ihr	bindet
sie/Sie	binden

PRESENT SUBJUNCTIVE

ich	binde
du	bindest
er/sie/es	binde
wir	binden
ihr	bindet
sie/Sie	binden

PERFECT

ich	habe gebunden
du	hast gebunden
er/sie/es	hat gebunden
wir	haben gebunden
ihr	habt gebunden
sie/Sie	haben gebunden

IMPERFECT

ich	band
du	band(e)st
er/sie/es	band
wir	banden
ihr	bandet
sie/Sie	banden

PRESENT PARTICIPLE

bindend

PAST PARTICIPLE

gebunden

EXAMPLE PHRASES

Er **bindet** sich die Schuhe. **He is tying his shoelaces.**

Sie sagt, sie **binde** sich nicht gern. **She says she doesn't like getting involved.**

Sie **hat** die Haare zu einem Pferdeschwanz **gebunden**. **She has tied her hair back into a ponytail.**

Sie **band** ihm die Hände auf den Rücken. **She tied his hands behind his back.**

---

ich = I du = you er = he/it sie = she/it es = it/he/she wir = we ihr = you sie = they Sie = you *(polite)*

binden

FUTURE

ich	**werde binden**
du	**wirst binden**
er/sie/es	**wird binden**
wir	**werden binden**
ihr	**werdet binden**
sie/Sie	**werden binden**

CONDITIONAL

ich	**würde binden**
du	**würdest binden**
er/sie/es	**würde binden**
wir	**würden binden**
ihr	**würdet binden**
sie/Sie	**würden binden**

PLUPERFECT

ich	**hatte gebunden**
du	**hattest gebunden**
er/sie/es	**hatte gebunden**
wir	**hatten gebunden**
ihr	**hattet gebunden**
sie/Sie	**hatten gebunden**

PLUPERFECT SUBJUNCTIVE

ich	**hätte gebunden**
du	**hättest gebunden**
er/sie/es	**hätte gebunden**
wir	**hätten gebunden**
ihr	**hättet gebunden**
sie/Sie	**hätten gebunden**

IMPERATIVE

bind(e)!/binden wir!/bindet!/binden Sie!

EXAMPLE PHRASES

Ich **werde** diese Blumen zu einem Strauß **binden**. I'll make these flowers into a bunch.

Ich **würde** sie nie an mich **binden**. I would never want to tie her to me.

Mich **hatte** nichts an diese Stadt **gebunden**. I had no special ties to keep me in this town.

Wenn ich sie geheiratet hätte, **hätte** ich mich zu früh **gebunden**. If I had married her, I would have committed myself too early.

ich = I du = you er = he/it sie = she/it es = it/he/she wir = we ihr = you sie = they Sie = you *(polite)*

bitten (to request)

strong, *formed with* haben

PRESENT

ich	**bitte**
du	**bittest**
er/sie/es	**bittet**
wir	**bitten**
ihr	**bittet**
sie/Sie	**bitten**

PRESENT SUBJUNCTIVE

ich	**bitte**
du	**bittest**
er/sie/es	**bitte**
wir	**bitten**
ihr	**bittet**
sie/Sie	**bitten**

PERFECT

ich	**habe gebeten**
du	**hast gebeten**
er/sie/es	**hat gebeten**
wir	**haben gebeten**
ihr	**habt gebeten**
sie/Sie	**haben gebeten**

IMPERFECT

ich	**bat**
du	**bat(e)st**
er/sie/es	**bat**
wir	**baten**
ihr	**batet**
sie/Sie	**baten**

PRESENT PARTICIPLE

bittend

PAST PARTICIPLE

gebeten

EXAMPLE PHRASES

Ich **bitte** Sie, uns in Ruhe zu lassen. **I'm asking you to leave us alone.**

Er sagt, er **bitte** uns darum, seinem Plan zuzustimmen. **He says he's asking us to agree to his plan.**

Man **hat** die Bevölkerung um Mithilfe **gebeten**. **The public was asked for assistance.**

Sie **bat** ihn um Hilfe. **She asked him for help.**

ich = I **du** = you **er** = he/it **sie** = she/it **es** = it/he/she **wir** = we **ihr** = you **sie** = they **Sie** = you (*polite*)

bitten

FUTURE

ich	**werde bitten**
du	**wirst bitten**
er/sie/es	**wird bitten**
wir	**werden bitten**
ihr	**werdet bitten**
sie/Sie	**werden bitten**

CONDITIONAL

ich	**würde bitten**
du	**würdest bitten**
er/sie/es	**würde bitten**
wir	**würden bitten**
ihr	**würdet bitten**
sie/Sie	**würden bitten**

PLUPERFECT

ich	**hatte gebeten**
du	**hattest gebeten**
er/sie/es	**hatte gebeten**
wir	**hatten gebeten**
ihr	**hattet gebeten**
sie/Sie	**hatten gebeten**

PLUPERFECT SUBJUNCTIVE

ich	**hätte gebeten**
du	**hättest gebeten**
er/sie/es	**hätte gebeten**
wir	**hätten gebeten**
ihr	**hättet gebeten**
sie/Sie	**hätten gebeten**

IMPERATIVE

bitt(e)!/bitten wir!/bittet!/bitten Sie!

EXAMPLE PHRASES

Wir **werden** ihn nicht länger darum **bitten**. We won't ask him for it any longer.

Ich **würde** Sie **bitten**, still zu sein. I would ask you to keep quiet.

Ihr **hattet** uns **gebeten**, euch zu besuchen. You had asked us to visit you.

Sie selbst **hätte** niemals um Hilfe **gebeten**. She would never have asked for help herself.

ich = I **du** = you **er** = he/it **sie** = she/it **es** = it/he/she **wir** = we **ihr** = you **sie** = they **Sie** = you (*polite*)

bleiben (to remain)

strong, *formed with* sein

PRESENT

ich	bleibe
du	bleibst
er/sie/es	bleibt
wir	bleiben
ihr	bleibt
sie/Sie	bleiben

PRESENT SUBJUNCTIVE

ich	bleibe
du	bleibest
er/sie/es	bleibe
wir	bleiben
ihr	bleibet
sie/Sie	bleiben

PERFECT

ich	bin geblieben
du	bist geblieben
er/sie/es	ist geblieben
wir	sind geblieben
ihr	seid geblieben
sie/Sie	sind geblieben

IMPERFECT

ich	blieb
du	bliebst
er/sie/es	blieb
wir	blieben
ihr	bliebt
sie/Sie	blieben

PRESENT PARTICIPLE

bleibend

PAST PARTICIPLE

geblieben

EXAMPLE PHRASES

Hoffentlich **bleibt** das Wetter schön. **I hope the weather stays fine.**

Er meint, er **bleibe** bei seiner Meinung. **He thinks he will stick to his opinion.**

Vom Kuchen **ist** nur noch ein Stück **geblieben**. **There's only one piece of cake left.**

Dieses Erlebnis **blieb** in meiner Erinnerung. **This experience stayed with me.**

ich = I du = you er = he/it sie = she/it es = it/he/she wir = we ihr = you sie = they Sie = you (*polite*)

bleiben

FUTURE

ich	**werde bleiben**
du	**wirst bleiben**
er/sie/es	**wird bleiben**
wir	**werden bleiben**
ihr	**werdet bleiben**
sie/Sie	**werden bleiben**

CONDITIONAL

ich	**würde bleiben**
du	**würdest bleiben**
er/sie/es	**würde bleiben**
wir	**würden bleiben**
ihr	**würdet bleiben**
sie/Sie	**würden bleiben**

PLUPERFECT

ich	**war geblieben**
du	**warst geblieben**
er/sie/es	**war geblieben**
wir	**waren geblieben**
ihr	**wart geblieben**
sie/Sie	**waren geblieben**

PLUPERFECT SUBJUNCTIVE

ich	**wäre geblieben**
du	**wär(e)st geblieben**
er/sie/es	**wäre geblieben**
wir	**wären geblieben**
ihr	**wär(e)t geblieben**
sie/Sie	**wären geblieben**

IMPERATIVE

bleib(e)!/bleiben wir!/bleibt!/bleiben Sie!

EXAMPLE PHRASES

Wir **werden** nicht länger als eine Stunde **bleiben**. We won't stay longer than an hour.

Ich **würde** gern noch in der Stadt **bleiben**. I would like to stay in town.

Das Verbrechen **war** unbestraft **geblieben**. The crime had remained unpunished.

Wir **wären** gern Freunde **geblieben**. We would have liked to stay friends.

ich = I **du** = you **er** = he/it **sie** = she/it **es** = it/he/she **wir** = we **ihr** = you **sie** = they **Sie** = you (*polite*)

brechen (to break)

strong, *formed with* **haben/sein***

PRESENT

ich	**breche**
du	**brichst**
er/sie/es	**bricht**
wir	**brechen**
ihr	**brecht**
sie/Sie	**brechen**

PRESENT SUBJUNCTIVE

ich	**breche**
du	**brechest**
er/sie/es	**breche**
wir	**brechen**
ihr	**brechet**
sie/Sie	**brechen**

PERFECT

ich	**habe gebrochen**
du	**hast gebrochen**
er/sie/es	**hat gebrochen**
wir	**haben gebrochen**
ihr	**habt gebrochen**
sie/Sie	**haben gebrochen**

IMPERFECT

ich	**brach**
du	**brachst**
er/sie/es	**brach**
wir	**brachen**
ihr	**bracht**
sie/Sie	**brachen**

PRESENT PARTICIPLE

brechend

PAST PARTICIPLE

gebrochen

*When brechen is used with no direct object, it is formed with sein.

EXAMPLE PHRASES

Mir **bricht** das Herz. It's breaking my heart.

Sie sagt, das **breche** die Abmachung. She says it meant breaking the agreement.

Sie **hat** ihr Versprechen **gebrochen**. She broke her promise.

Der Sturz **brach** ihm fast den Arm. The fall almost broke his arm.

ich = I **du** = you **er** = he/it **sie** = she/it **es** = it/he/she **wir** = we **ihr** = you **sie** = they **Sie** = you (*polite*)

brechen

FUTURE

ich	**werde brechen**
du	**wirst brechen**
er/sie/es	**wird brechen**
wir	**werden brechen**
ihr	**werdet brechen**
sie/Sie	**werden brechen**

CONDITIONAL

ich	**würde brechen**
du	**würdest brechen**
er/sie/es	**würde brechen**
wir	**würden brechen**
ihr	**würdet brechen**
sie/Sie	**würden brechen**

PLUPERFECT

ich	**hatte gebrochen**
du	**hattest gebrochen**
er/sie/es	**hatte gebrochen**
wir	**hatten gebrochen**
ihr	**hattet gebrochen**
sie/Sie	**hatten gebrochen**

PLUPERFECT SUBJUNCTIVE

ich	**hätte gebrochen**
du	**hättest gebrochen**
er/sie/es	**hätte gebrochen**
wir	**hätten gebrochen**
ihr	**hättet gebrochen**
sie/Sie	**hätten gebrochen**

IMPERATIVE

brich!/brechen wir!/brecht!/brechen Sie!

EXAMPLE PHRASES

Wir **werden** ihren Widerstand **brechen**. We will break their resistance.

Ich **würde** ihm nie die Treue **brechen**. I would never break his trust.

Wir **hatten** mit der Tradition **gebrochen**. We had broken with tradition.

Er **hätte** diesen Rekord gern **gebrochen**. He would have liked to break that record.

---

ich = I **du** = you **er** = he/it **sie** = she/it **es** = it/he/she **wir** = we **ihr** = you **sie** = they **Sie** = you (*polite*)

brennen (to burn)

mixed, *formed with* haben

PRESENT

ich	brenne
du	brennst
er/sie/es	brennt
wir	brennen
ihr	brennt
sie/Sie	brennen

PRESENT SUBJUNCTIVE

ich	brenne
du	brennest
er/sie/es	brenne
wir	brennen
ihr	brennet
sie/Sie	brennen

PERFECT

ich	habe gebrannt
du	hast gebrannt
er/sie/es	hat gebrannt
wir	haben gebrannt
ihr	habt gebrannt
sie/Sie	haben gebrannt

IMPERFECT

ich	brannte
du	branntest
er/sie/es	brannte
wir	brannten
ihr	branntet
sie/Sie	brannten

PRESENT PARTICIPLE

brennend

PAST PARTICIPLE

gebrannt

EXAMPLE PHRASES

Das Streichholz **brennt** nicht. **The match won't light.**

Sie sagt, das Problem **brenne** ihr auf der Seele. **She says the problem is preying on her mind.**

Im Zimmer **hat** noch Licht **gebrannt**. **The light was still on in the room.**

Das ganze Haus **brannte**. **The entire house was on fire.**

---

ich = I **du** = you **er** = he/it **sie** = she/it **es** = it/he/she **wir** = we **ihr** = you **sie** = they **Sie** = you *(polite)*

brennen

FUTURE

ich	**werde brennen**
du	**wirst brennen**
er/sie/es	**wird brennen**
wir	**werden brennen**
ihr	**werdet brennen**
sie/Sie	**werden brennen**

CONDITIONAL

ich	**würde brennen**
du	**würdest brennen**
er/sie/es	**würde brennen**
wir	**würden brennen**
ihr	**würdet brennen**
sie/Sie	**würden brennen**

PLUPERFECT

ich	**hatte gebrannt**
du	**hattest gebrannt**
er/sie/es	**hatte gebrannt**
wir	**hatten gebrannt**
ihr	**hattet gebrannt**
sie/Sie	**hatten gebrannt**

PLUPERFECT SUBJUNCTIVE

ich	**hätte gebrannt**
du	**hättest gebrannt**
er/sie/es	**hätte gebrannt**
wir	**hätten gebrannt**
ihr	**hättet gebrannt**
sie/Sie	**hätten gebrannt**

IMPERATIVE

brenn(e)!/brennen wir!/brennet!/brennen Sie!

EXAMPLE PHRASES

Wir **werden** diese CD zuerst **brennen**. We'll burn this CD first.

Er **würde** darauf **brennen**, das zu tun. He would be dying to do it.

Die Zigarette **hatte** ein Loch in ihr Kleid **gebrannt**. The cigarette had burned a hole in her dress.

Fast **hätte** die ganze Stadt **gebrannt**. The whole town had almost been on fire.

ich = I **du** = you **er** = he/it **sie** = she/it **es** = it/he/she **wir** = we **ihr** = you **sie** = they **Sie** = you (*polite*)

bringen (to bring)

mixed, *formed with* haben

PRESENT

ich	bringe
du	bringst
er/sie/es	bringt
wir	bringen
ihr	bringt
sie/Sie	bringen

PRESENT SUBJUNCTIVE

ich	bringe
du	bringest
er/sie/es	bringe
wir	bringen
ihr	bringet
sie/Sie	bringen

PERFECT

ich	habe gebracht
du	hast gebracht
er/sie/es	hat gebracht
wir	haben gebracht
ihr	habt gebracht
sie/Sie	haben gebracht

IMPERFECT

ich	brachte
du	brachtest
er/sie/es	brachte
wir	brachten
ihr	brachtet
sie/Sie	brachten

PRESENT PARTICIPLE

bringend

PAST PARTICIPLE

gebracht

EXAMPLE PHRASES

Bringst du mich zum Flughafen? Can you take me to the airport?

Sie beschwert sich, er **bringe** ihr nie Geschenke. She is complaining he never brings her presents.

Max **hat** mir Blumen **gebracht**. Max brought me flowers.

Das **brachte** mich auf eine Idee. It gave me an idea.

ich = I **du** = you **er** = he/it **sie** = she/it **es** = it/he/she **wir** = we **ihr** = you **sie** = they **Sie** = you (*polite*)

bringen

FUTURE

ich	**werde bringen**
du	**wirst bringen**
er/sie/es	**wird bringen**
wir	**werden bringen**
ihr	**werdet bringen**
sie/Sie	**werden bringen**

CONDITIONAL

ich	**würde bringen**
du	**würdest bringen**
er/sie/es	**würde bringen**
wir	**würden bringen**
ihr	**würdet bringen**
sie/Sie	**würden bringen**

PLUPERFECT

ich	**hatte gebracht**
du	**hattest gebracht**
er/sie/es	**hatte gebracht**
wir	**hatten gebracht**
ihr	**hattet gebracht**
sie/Sie	**hatten gebracht**

PLUPERFECT SUBJUNCTIVE

ich	**hätte gebracht**
du	**hättest gebracht**
er/sie/es	**hätte gebracht**
wir	**hätten gebracht**
ihr	**hättet gebracht**
sie/Sie	**hätten gebracht**

IMPERATIVE

bring(e)!/bringen wir!/bringt!/bringen Sie!

EXAMPLE PHRASES

Das **wird** dich noch ins Gefängnis **bringen**. You'll end up in prison if you do that.

Ich **würde** die Kinder gern ins Bett **bringen**. I would like to put the children to bed.

Er **hatte** sie fast zum Weinen **gebracht**. He had almost made her cry.

Ich **hätte** das gern hinter mich **gebracht**. I would like to get it over and done with.

ich = I du = you er = he/it sie = she/it es = it/he/she wir = we ihr = you sie = they Sie = you (polite)

denken (to think)

mixed, *formed with* haben

PRESENT

ich	denke
du	denkst
er/sie/es	denkt
wir	denken
ihr	denkt
sie/Sie	denken

PRESENT SUBJUNCTIVE

ich	denke
du	denkest
er/sie/es	denke
wir	denken
ihr	denket
sie/Sie	denken

PERFECT

ich	habe gedacht
du	hast gedacht
er/sie/es	hat gedacht
wir	haben gedacht
ihr	habt gedacht
sie/Sie	haben gedacht

IMPERFECT

ich	dachte
du	dachtest
er/sie/es	dachte
wir	dachten
ihr	dachtet
sie/Sie	dachten

PRESENT PARTICIPLE

denkend

PAST PARTICIPLE

gedacht

EXAMPLE PHRASES

Wie **denken** Sie darüber? **What do you think about it?**

Er sagt, er **denke** nicht daran, das zu tun. **He says there is no way he will do it.**

Er **hat** an sie **gedacht**. **He thought of her.**

Es war das Erste, woran ich **dachte**. **It was the first thing I thought of.**

---

ich = I du = you er = he/it sie = she/it es = it/he/she wir = we ihr = you sie = they Sie = you (*polite*)

denken

FUTURE

ich	**werde denken**
du	**wirst denken**
er/sie/es	**wird denken**
wir	**werden denken**
ihr	**werdet denken**
sie/Sie	**werden denken**

CONDITIONAL

ich	**würde denken**
du	**würdest denken**
er/sie/es	**würde denken**
wir	**würden denken**
ihr	**würdet denken**
sie/Sie	**würden denken**

PLUPERFECT

ich	**hatte gedacht**
du	**hattest gedacht**
er/sie/es	**hatte gedacht**
wir	**hatten gedacht**
ihr	**hattet gedacht**
sie/Sie	**hatten gedacht**

PLUPERFECT SUBJUNCTIVE

ich	**hätte gedacht**
du	**hättest gedacht**
er/sie/es	**hätte gedacht**
wir	**hätten gedacht**
ihr	**hättet gedacht**
sie/Sie	**hätten gedacht**

IMPERATIVE

denk(e)!/denken wir!/denkt!/denken Sie!

EXAMPLE PHRASES

Ich **werde** versuchen, nicht daran zu **denken**. I'll try not to think of it.

Ich **würde** nie schlecht von ihm **denken**. I would never think badly of him.

So **hatte** ich mir das nicht **gedacht**. That's not what I had thought of.

Ich **hätte** nicht **gedacht**, dass er kommt. I wouldn't have thought that he'd come.

ich = I **du** = you **er** = he/it **sie** = she/it **es** = it/he/she **wir** = we **ihr** = you **sie** = they **Sie** = you (*polite*)

durchsetzen (to enforce)

weak, separable,
formed with **haben**

PRESENT

ich	**setze durch**
du	**setzt durch**
er/sie/es	**setzt durch**
wir	**setzen durch**
ihr	**setzt durch**
sie/Sie	**setzen durch**

PRESENT SUBJUNCTIVE

ich	**setze durch**
du	**setzest durch**
er/sie/es	**setze durch**
wir	**setzen durch**
ihr	**setzet durch**
sie/Sie	**setzen durch**

PERFECT

ich	**habe durchgesetzt**
du	**hast durchgesetzt**
er/sie/es	**hat durchgesetzt**
wir	**haben durchgesetzt**
ihr	**habt durchgesetzt**
sie/Sie	**haben durchgesetzt**

IMPERFECT

ich	**setzte durch**
du	**setztest durch**
er/sie/es	**setzte durch**
wir	**setzten durch**
ihr	**setztet durch**
sie/Sie	**setzten durch**

PRESENT PARTICIPLE

durchsetzend

PAST PARTICIPLE

durchgesetzt

EXAMPLE PHRASES

Sie **setzt** immer ihren Willen **durch**. She always gets her own way.

Er meint, er **setze** sich damit nicht durch. He thinks he won't be successful with it.

Ich **habe** mich mit meinem Vorschlag **durchgesetzt**. They accepted my suggestion.

Er **setzte** sich mit seinem Plan **durch**. He was successful with his plan.

ich = I **du** = you **er** = he/it **sie** = she/it **es** = it/he/she **wir** = we **ihr** = you **sie** = they **Sie** = you *(polite)*

durchsetzen

FUTURE

ich	**werde durchsetzen**
du	**wirst durchsetzen**
er/sie/es	**wird durchsetzen**
wir	**werden durchsetzen**
ihr	**werdet durchsetzen**
sie/Sie	**werden durchsetzen**

CONDITIONAL

ich	**würde durchsetzen**
du	**würdest durchsetzen**
er/sie/es	**würde durchsetzen**
wir	**würden durchsetzen**
ihr	**würdet durchsetzen**
sie/Sie	**würden durchsetzen**

PLUPERFECT

ich	**hatte durchgesetzt**
du	**hattest durchgesetzt**
er/sie/es	**hatte durchgesetzt**
wir	**hatten durchgesetzt**
ihr	**hattet durchgesetzt**
sie/Sie	**hatten durchgesetzt**

PLUPERFECT SUBJUNCTIVE

ich	**hätte durchgesetzt**
du	**hättest durchgesetzt**
er/sie/es	**hätte durchgesetzt**
wir	**hätten durchgesetzt**
ihr	**hättet durchgesetzt**
sie/Sie	**hätten durchgesetztt**

IMPERATIVE

setz(e) durch!/setzen wir durch!/setzt durch!/setzen Sie durch!

EXAMPLE PHRASES

Ich **werde** mich gegen ihn **durchsetzen**. I will assert myself against him.

Ich **würde** dieses Ziel gern bald **durchsetzen**. I would like to achieve this aim soon.

Er **hatte** sich im Leben **durchgesetzt**. He had made his way in life.

Diese Idee **hätte** sich früher nicht **durchgesetzt**. This idea wouldn't have been accepted in the past.

ich = I **du** = you **er** = he/it **sie** = she/it **es** = it/he/she **wir** = we **ihr** = you **sie** = they **Sie** = you (*polite*)

dürfen (to be allowed to)

modal, *formed with* haben

PRESENT

ich	**darf**
du	**darfst**
er/sie/es	**darf**
wir	**dürfen**
ihr	**dürft**
sie/Sie	**dürfen**

PRESENT SUBJUNCTIVE

ich	**dürfe**
du	**dürfest**
er/sie/es	**dürfe**
wir	**dürfen**
ihr	**dürfet**
sie/Sie	**dürfen**

PERFECT

ich	**habe gedurft/dürfen**
du	**hast gedurft/dürfen**
er/sie/es	**hat gedurft/dürfen**
wir	**haben gedurft/dürfen**
ihr	**habt gedurft/dürfen**
sie/Sie	**haben gedurft/dürfen**

IMPERFECT

ich	**durfte**
du	**durftest**
er/sie/es	**durfte**
wir	**durften**
ihr	**durftet**
sie/Sie	**durften**

PRESENT PARTICIPLE

dürfend

PAST PARTICIPLE

gedurft/dürfen*

This form is used when combined with another infinitive.

EXAMPLE PHRASES

Darf ich ins Kino? **Can I go to the cinema?**

Er meint, er **dürfe** das nicht. **He thinks he isn't allowed to.**

Er **hat** nicht **gedurft**. **I wasn't allowed to.**

Wir **durften** nicht ausgehen. **We weren't allowed to go out.**

dürfen

FUTURE

ich	**werde dürfen**
du	**wirst dürfen**
er/sie/es	**wird dürfen**
wir	**werden dürfen**
ihr	**werdet dürfen**
sie/Sie	**werden dürfen**

CONDITIONAL

ich	**würde dürfen**
du	**würdest dürfen**
er/sie/es	**würde dürfen**
wir	**würden dürfen**
ihr	**würdet dürfen**
sie/Sie	**würden dürfen**

PLUPERFECT

ich	**hatte gedurft/dürfen**
du	**hattest gedurft/dürfen**
er/sie/es	**hatte gedurft/dürfen**
wir	**hatten gedurft/dürfen**
ihr	**hattet gedurft/dürfen**
sie/Sie	**hatten gedurft/dürfen**

PLUPERFECT SUBJUNCTIVE

ich	**hätte gedurft/dürfen**
du	**hättest gedurft/dürfen**
er/sie/es	**hätte gedurft/dürfen**
wir	**hätten gedurft/dürfen**
ihr	**hättet gedurft/dürfen**
sie/Sie	**hätten gedurft/dürfen**

EXAMPLE PHRASES

Dort **werden** wir nicht rauchen **dürfen**. We won't be allowed to smoke there.

Das **würde** ich zu Hause nicht **dürfen**. I wouldn't be allowed to do that at home.

Die Katze **hatte** nie ins Haus **gedurft**. The cat had never been allowed in the house.

Das **hätte** ich als Kind nicht **gedurft**. I wouldn't have been allowed to do that as a child.

ich = I du = you er = he/it sie = she/it es = it/he/she wir = we ihr = you sie = they Sie = you (*polite*)

empfehlen (to recommend)

strong, inseparable,
formed with **haben**

PRESENT		PRESENT SUBJUNCTIVE	
ich	**empfehle**	ich	**empfehle**
du	**empfiehlst**	du	**empfehlest**
er/sie/es	**empfiehlt**	er/sie/es	**empfehle**
wir	**empfehlen**	wir	**empfehlen**
ihr	**empfehlt**	ihr	**empfehlet**
sie/Sie	**empfehlen**	sie/Sie	**empfehlen**

PERFECT		IMPERFECT	
ich	**habe empfohlen**	ich	**empfahl**
du	**hast empfohlen**	du	**empfahlst**
er/sie/es	**hat empfohlen**	er/sie/es	**empfahl**
wir	**haben empfohlen**	wir	**empfahlen**
ihr	**habt empfohlen**	ihr	**empfahlt**
sie/Sie	**haben empfohlen**	sie/Sie	**empfahlen**

PRESENT PARTICIPLE	PAST PARTICIPLE
empfehlend	empfohlen

EXAMPLE PHRASES

Was **empfiehlst** du mir zu tun? What would you recommend I do?

Er meint, er **empfehle** mir Vorsicht. He says he would recommend caution.

Man **hat** uns **empfohlen**, nach Ägypten zu reisen. They recommended we
travel to Egypt.

Sie **empfahl** uns, eine Diät zu machen. She recommended that we go on
a diet.

ich = I **du** = you **er** = he/it **sie** = she/it **es** = it/he/she **wir** = we **ihr** = you **sie** = they **Sie** = you *(polite)*

empfehlen

FUTURE

ich	**werde empfehlen**
du	**wirst empfehlen**
er/sie/es	**wird empfehlen**
wir	**werden empfehlen**
ihr	**werdet empfehlen**
sie/Sie	**werden empfehlen**

CONDITIONAL

ich	**würde empfehlen**
du	**würdest empfehlen**
er/sie/es	**würde empfehlen**
wir	**würden empfehlen**
ihr	**würdet empfehlen**
sie/Sie	**würden empfehlen**

PLUPERFECT

ich	**hatte empfohlen**
du	**hattest empfohlen**
er/sie/es	**hatte empfohlen**
wir	**hatten empfohlen**
ihr	**hattet empfohlen**
sie/Sie	**hatten empfohlen**

PLUPERFECT SUBJUNCTIVE

ich	**hätte empfohlen**
du	**hättest empfohlen**
er/sie/es	**hätte empfohlen**
wir	**hätten empfohlen**
ihr	**hättet empfohlen**
sie/Sie	**hätten empfohlen**

IMPERATIVE

empfiehl!/empfehlen wir!/empfehlt!/empfehlen Sie!

EXAMPLE PHRASES

Ich **werde** ihm **empfehlen**, das Land zu verlassen. I will recommend that
he leaves the country.

Ich **würde** Ihnen **empfehlen**, zu gehen. I would advise you to go.

Sie **hatten** uns dieses Restaurant **empfohlen**. They had recommended this
restaurant to us.

Ich **hätte** Ihnen mehr Geduld **empfohlen**. I would have recommended you
to be more patient.

ich = I **du** = you **er** = he/it **sie** = she/it **es** = it/he/she **wir** = we **ihr** = you **sie** = they **Sie** = you (polite)

entdecken (to discover)

weak, inseparable,
formed with haben

PRESENT

ich	entdecke
du	entdeckst
er/sie/es	entdeckt
wir	entdecken
ihr	entdeckt
sie/Sie	entdecken

PRESENT SUBJUNCTIVE

ich	entdecke
du	entdeckest
er/sie/es	entdecke
wir	entdecken
ihr	entdecket
sie/Sie	entdecken

PERFECT

ich	habe entdeckt
du	hast entdeckt
er/sie/es	hat entdeckt
wir	haben entdeckt
ihr	habt entdeckt
sie/Sie	haben entdeckt

IMPERFECT

ich	entdeckte
du	entdecktest
er/sie/es	entdeckte
wir	entdeckten
ihr	entdecktet
sie/Sie	entdeckten

PRESENT PARTICIPLE

entdeckend

PAST PARTICIPLE

entdeckt

EXAMPLE PHRASES

Ich **entdecke** im Park oft neue Insekten. **I often discover new insects in
the park.**

Sie sagt, sie **entdecke** ihr Interesse an Musik. **She says she's discovering
an interest in music.**

Kolumbus **hat** Amerika **entdeckt**. **Columbus discovered America.**

Er **entdeckte** sie in der Menge. **He spotted her in the crowd.**

ich = I **du** = you **er** = he/it **sie** = she/it **es** = it/he/she **wir** = we **ihr** = you **sie** = they **Sie** = you *(polite)*

entdecken

FUTURE

ich	**werde entdecken**
du	**wirst entdecken**
er/sie/es	**wird entdecken**
wir	**werden entdecken**
ihr	**werdet entdecken**
sie/Sie	**werden entdecken**

CONDITIONAL

ich	**würde entdecken**
du	**würdest entdecken**
er/sie/es	**würde entdecken**
wir	**würden entdecken**
ihr	**würdet entdecken**
sie/Sie	**würden entdecken**

PLUPERFECT

ich	**hatte entdeckt**
du	**hattest entdeckt**
er/sie/es	**hatte entdeckt**
wir	**hatten entdeckt**
ihr	**hattet entdeckt**
sie/Sie	**hatten entdeckt**

PLUPERFECT SUBJUNCTIVE

ich	**hätte entdeckt**
du	**hättest entdeckt**
er/sie/es	**hätte entdeckt**
wir	**hätten entdeckt**
ihr	**hättet entdeckt**
sie/Sie	**hätten entdeckt**

IMPERATIVE

entdeck(e)!/entdecken wir!/entdeckt!/entdecken Sie!

EXAMPLE PHRASES

Ich hoffe, er **wird** meine Fehler nicht **entdecken**. I hope he won't spot my mistakes.

Ich **würde** gern die spanische Küche **entdecken**. I'd like to discover Spanish cooking.

Die Raumfahrer **hatten** einen neuen Planeten **entdeckt**. The astronauts had discovered a new planet.

Fast **hätte** sie uns **entdeckt**. She almost spotted us.

ich = I du = you er = he/it sie = she/it es = it/he/she wir = we ihr = you sie = they Sie = you (polite)

erschrecken* (to be startled)
strong, inseparable, formed with **sein**

PRESENT

ich	**erschrecke**
du	**erschrickst**
er/sie/es	**erschrickt**
wir	**erschrecken**
ihr	**erschreckt**
sie/Sie	**erschrecken**

PRESENT SUBJUNCTIVE

ich	**erschrecke**
du	**erschreckest**
er/sie/es	**erschrecke**
wir	**erschrecken**
ihr	**erschrecket**
sie/Sie	**erschrecken**

PERFECT

ich	**bin erschrocken**
du	**bist erschrocken**
er/sie/es	**ist erschrocken**
wir	**sind erschrocken**
ihr	**seid erschrocken**
sie/Sie	**sind erschrocken**

IMPERFECT

ich	**erschrak**
du	**erschrakst**
er/sie/es	**erschrak**
wir	**erschraken**
ihr	**erschrakt**
sie/Sie	**erschraken**

PRESENT PARTICIPLE

erschreckend

PAST PARTICIPLE

erschrocken

°Weak when means to frighten.

EXAMPLE PHRASES

Diese Vorstellung **erschreckt** mich. This prospect scares me.

Sie sagt, sie **erschrecke** leicht. She says she's easily frightened.

Ich **bin** schon bei dem Gedanken **erschrocken**. The mere thought frightened me.

Ich **erschrak**, wie schlecht er aussah. It gave me a shock to see how bad he looked.

---

ich = I du = you er = he/it sie = she/it es = it/he/she wir = we ihr = you sie = they Sie = you (polite)

erschrecken

FUTURE

ich	**werde erschrecken**
du	**wirst erschrecken**
er/sie/es	**wird erschrecken**
wir	**werden erschrecken**
ihr	**werdet erschrecken**
sie/Sie	**werden erschrecken**

CONDITIONAL

ich	**würde erschrecken**
du	**würdest erschrecken**
er/sie/es	**würde erschrecken**
wir	**würden erschrecken**
ihr	**würdet erschrecken**
sie/Sie	**würden erschrecken**

PLUPERFECT

ich	**war erschrocken**
du	**warst erschrocken**
er/sie/es	**war erschrocken**
wir	**waren erschrocken**
ihr	**wart erschrocken**
sie/Sie	**waren erschrocken**

PLUPERFECT SUBJUNCTIVE

ich	**wäre erschrocken**
du	**wär(e)st erschrocken**
er/sie/es	**wäre erschrocken**
wir	**wären erschrocken**
ihr	**wär(e)t erschrocken**
sie/Sie	**wären erschrocken**

IMPERATIVE

erschrick!/erschrecken wir!/erschreckt!/erschrecken Sie!

EXAMPLE PHRASES

Du **wirst erschrecken**, wenn ich dir das Ergebnis sage. You'll get a shock when I tell you the result.

Er **würde erschrecken**, wenn er das wüsste. He would get a shock if he knew.

Sie **war** bei dem Knall **erschrocken**. The bang had startled her.

Sie **wären** sicher **erschrocken**, wenn sie uns so gesehen hätten. They would certainly have got a shock if they had seen us like this.

---

ich = I **du** = you **er** = he/it **sie** = she/it **es** = it/he/she **wir** = we **ihr** = you **sie** = they **Sie** = you (polite)

erzählen (to tell)

weak, inseparable, *formed with* haben

PRESENT

ich erzähle
du erzählst
er/sie/es erzählt
wir erzählen
ihr erzählt
sie/Sie erzählen

PRESENT SUBJUNCTIVE

ich erzähle
du erzählest
er/sie/es erzähle
wir erzählen
ihr erzählet
sie/Sie erzählen

PERFECT

ich habe erzählt
du hast erzählt
er/sie/es hat erzählt
wir haben erzählt
ihr habt erzählt
sie/Sie haben erzählt

IMPERFECT

ich erzählte
du erzähltest
er/sie/es erzählte
wir erzählten
ihr erzähltet
sie/Sie erzählten

PRESENT PARTICIPLE

erzählend

PAST PARTICIPLE

erzählt

EXAMPLE PHRASES

Man **erzählt** sich, dass er Millionär ist. **People say that he is a millionaire.**

Er denkt, sie **erzähle** nur Lügen. He thinks all she tells is lies.

Er **hat** mir **erzählt**, dass er schon oft in dieser Pizzeria war. He told me that he has often been to this pizzeria.

Sie **erzählte** uns ihren Traum. She told us about her dream.

erzählen

FUTURE

ich	**werde erzählen**
du	**wirst erzählen**
er/sie/es	**wird erzählen**
wir	**werden erzählen**
ihr	**werdet erzählen**
sie/Sie	**werden erzählen**

CONDITIONAL

ich	**würde erzählen**
du	**würdest erzählen**
er/sie/es	**würde erzählen**
wir	**würden erzählen**
ihr	**würdet erzählen**
sie/Sie	**würden erzählen**

PLUPERFECT

ich	**hatte erzählt**
du	**hattest erzählt**
er/sie/es	**hatte erzählt**
wir	**hatten erzählt**
ihr	**hattet erzählt**
sie/Sie	**hatten erzählt**

PLUPERFECT SUBJUNCTIVE

ich	**hätte erzählt**
du	**hättest erzählt**
er/sie/es	**hätte erzählt**
wir	**hätten erzählt**
ihr	**hättet erzählt**
sie/Sie	**hätten erzählt**

IMPERATIVE

erzähl(et)!/erzählen wir!/erzählt!/erzählen Sie!

EXAMPLE PHRASES

Ihm **werde** ich was **erzählen**! I'll give him a piece of my mind!

Er **würde** mir immer alles **erzählen**. He would always tell me everything.

Sie **hatte** uns die ganze Geschichte **erzählt**. She had told us the whole story.

Es **wäre** besser, wenn wir es ihm **erzählt hätten**. It would have been better
   if we had told him.

ich = I du = you er = he/it sie = she/it es = it/he/she wir = we ihr = you sie = they Sie = you (*polite*)

essen (to eat)

strong, *formed with* haben

PRESENT

ich	**esse**
du	**isst**
er/sie/es	**isst**
wir	**essen**
ihr	**esst**
sie/Sie	**essen**

PRESENT SUBJUNCTIVE

ich	**esse**
du	**essest**
er/sie/es	**esse**
wir	**essen**
ihr	**esset**
sie/Sie	**essen**

PERFECT

ich	**habe gegessen**
du	**hast gegessen**
er/sie/es	**hat gegessen**
wir	**haben gegessen**
ihr	**habt gegessen**
sie/Sie	**haben gegessen**

IMPERFECT

ich	**aß**
du	**aßest**
er/sie/es	**aß**
wir	**aßen**
ihr	**aßt**
sie/Sie	**aßen**

PRESENT PARTICIPLE

essend

PAST PARTICIPLE

gegessen

EXAMPLE PHRASES

Ich **esse** kein Fleisch. I don't eat meat.

Er sagt, er **esse** kein Fleisch. He says he doesn't eat meat.

Wir **haben** nichts **gegessen**. We haven't had anything to eat.

Ich **aß** den ganzen Kuchen. I ate the whole cake.

ich = I **du** = you **er** = he/it **sie** = she/it **es** = it/he/she **wir** = we **ihr** = you **sie** = they **Sie** = you *(polite)*

essen

FUTURE

ich	**werde essen**
du	**wirst essen**
er/sie/es	**wird essen**
wir	**werden essen**
ihr	**werdet essen**
sie/Sie	**werden essen**

CONDITIONAL

ich	**würde essen**
du	**würdest essen**
er/sie/es	**würde essen**
wir	**würden essen**
ihr	**würdet essen**
sie/Sie	**würden essen**

PLUPERFECT

ich	**hatte gegessen**
du	**hattest gegessen**
er/sie/es	**hatte gegessen**
wir	**hatten gegessen**
ihr	**hattet gegessen**
sie/Sie	**hatten gegessen**

PLUPERFECT SUBJUNCTIVE

ich	**hätte gegessen**
du	**hättest gegessen**
er/sie/es	**hätte gegessen**
wir	**hätten gegessen**
ihr	**hättet gegessen**
sie/Sie	**hätten gegessen**

IMPERATIVE

iss!/essen wir!/esst!/essen Sie!

EXAMPLE PHRASES

Wirst du deinen Teller leer **essen**? Will you clear your plate?

Das **würde** nicht mal mein Hund **essen**. Not even my dog would eat that.

Wir **hatten** gerade **gegessen**, als sie kam. We had just finished our meal when she came.

Wenn ich das gewusst hätte, **hätten** wir früher **gegessen**. If I had known that, we would have eaten earlier.

ich = I du = you er = he/it sie = she/it es = it/he/she wir = we ihr = you sie = they Sie = you (polite)

fahren (to drive/to go) strong, *formed with* haben/sein*

PRESENT

ich	**fahre**
du	**fährst**
er/sie/es	**fährt**
wir	**fahren**
ihr	**fahrt**
sie/Sie	**fahren**

PRESENT SUBJUNCTIVE

ich	**fahre**
du	**fahrest**
er/sie/es	**fahre**
wir	**fahren**
ihr	**fahret**
sie/Sie	**fahren**

PERFECT

ich	**bin gefahren**
du	**bist gefahren**
er/sie/es	**ist gefahren**
wir	**sind gefahren**
ihr	**seid gefahren**
sie/Sie	**sind gefahren**

IMPERFECT

ich	**fuhr**
du	**fuhrst**
er/sie/es	**fuhr**
wir	**fuhren**
ihr	**fuhrt**
sie/Sie	**fuhren**

PRESENT PARTICIPLE
fahrend

PAST PARTICIPLE
gefahren

When fahren is used with a direct object, it is formed with haben.

EXAMPLE PHRASES

In Deutschland **fährt** man rechts. In Germany they drive on the right.

Er sagt, er **fahre** nicht gern nach England. He says he doesn't like going to England.

Ich **bin** mit der Familie nach Spanien **gefahren**. I went to Spain with my family.

Sie **fuhren** mit dem Bus in die Schule. They went to school by bus.

ich = I **du** = you **er** = he/it **sie** = she/it **es** = it/he/she **wir** = we **ihr** = you **sie** = they **Sie** = you *(polite)*

fahren

FUTURE

ich	**werde fahren**
du	**wirst fahren**
er/sie/es	**wird fahren**
wir	**werden fahren**
ihr	**werdet fahren**
sie/Sie	**werden fahren**

CONDITIONAL

ich	**würde fahren**
du	**würdest fahren**
er/sie/es	**würde fahren**
wir	**würden fahren**
ihr	**würdet fahren**
sie/Sie	**würden fahren**

PLUPERFECT

ich	**war gefahren**
du	**warst gefahren**
er/sie/es	**war gefahren**
wir	**waren gefahren**
ihr	**wart gefahren**
sie/Sie	**waren gefahren**

PLUPERFECT SUBJUNCTIVE

ich	**wäre gefahren**
du	**wär(e)st gefahren**
er/sie/es	**wäre gefahren**
wir	**wären gefahren**
ihr	**wär(e)t gefahren**
sie/Sie	**wären gefahren**

IMPERATIVE

fahr(e)!/fahren wir!/fahrt!/fahren Sie!

EXAMPLE PHRASES

Ihr **werdet** morgen nach Köln **fahren**. You'll be going to Cologne tomorrow.

Wir **würden** gern in die Berge **fahren**. We would like to go to the mountains.

Wir **waren** fünf Stunden lang **gefahren**. We had been driving for five hours.

Sie **wäre** lieber mit ihm **gefahren**. She would have preferred to go with him.

---

ich = I **du** = you **er** = he/it **sie** = she/it **es** = it/he/she **wir** = we **ihr** = you **sie** = they **Sie** = you (*polite*)

fallen (to fall)

strong, *formed with* sein

PRESENT

ich	**falle**
du	**fällst**
er/sie/es	**fällt**
wir	**fallen**
ihr	**fallt**
sie/Sie	**fallen**

PRESENT SUBJUNCTIVE

ich	**falle**
du	**fallest**
er/sie/es	**falle**
wir	**fallen**
ihr	**fallet**
sie/Sie	**fallen**

PERFECT

ich	**bin gefallen**
du	**bist gefallen**
er/sie/es	**ist gefallen**
wir	**sind gefallen**
ihr	**seid gefallen**
sie/Sie	**sind gefallen**

IMPERFECT

ich	**fiel**
du	**fielst**
er/sie/es	**fiel**
wir	**fielen**
ihr	**fielt**
sie/Sie	**fielen**

PRESENT PARTICIPLE

fallend

PAST PARTICIPLE

gefallen

EXAMPLE PHRASES

Die Aktien **fallen** im Kurs. Share prices are falling.

Er meint, der Euro **falle** im Wert. He thinks the euro is going down in value.

Ich **bin** durch die Prüfung **gefallen**. I failed my exam.

Er **fiel** vom Fahrrad. He fell off his bike.

---

ich = I **du** = you **er** = he/it **sie** = she/it **es** = it/he/she **wir** = we **ihr** = you **sie** = they **Sie** = you (*polite*)

fallen

FUTURE

ich	**werde fallen**
du	**wirst fallen**
er/sie/es	**wird fallen**
wir	**werden fallen**
ihr	**werdet fallen**
sie/Sie	**werden fallen**

CONDITIONAL

ich	**würde fallen**
du	**würdest fallen**
er/sie/es	**würde fallen**
wir	**würden fallen**
ihr	**würdet fallen**
sie/Sie	**würden fallen**

PLUPERFECT

ich	**war gefallen**
du	**warst gefallen**
er/sie/es	**war gefallen**
wir	**waren gefallen**
ihr	**wart gefallen**
sie/Sie	**waren gefallen**

PLUPERFECT SUBJUNCTIVE

ich	**wäre gefallen**
du	**wär(e)st gefallen**
er/sie/es	**wäre gefallen**
wir	**wären gefallen**
ihr	**wär(e)t gefallen**
sie/Sie	**wären gefallen**

IMPERATIVE

fall(e)!/fallen wir!/fallt!/fallen Sie!

EXAMPLE PHRASES

Ihr **werdet** noch **fallen** und euch wehtun. You'll end up falling and hurting yourselves.

Ich **würde** Ihnen nicht gern ins Wort **fallen**. I wouldn't like to interrupt you.

Die Entscheidung **war** gestern **gefallen**. The decision had been made yesterday.

Sie **wäre** fast aus dem Fenster **gefallen**. She almost fell out of the window.

ich = I **du** = you **er** = he/it **sie** = she/it **es** = it/he/she **wir** = we **ihr** = you **sie** = they **Sie** = you (*polite*)

fangen (to catch)

strong, *formed with* haben

PRESENT

ich	**fange**
du	**fängst**
er/sie/es	**fängt**
wir	**fangen**
ihr	**fangt**
sie/Sie	**fangen**

PRESENT SUBJUNCTIVE

ich	**fange**
du	**fangest**
er/sie/es	**fange**
wir	**fangen**
ihr	**fanget**
sie/Sie	**fangen**

PERFECT

ich	**habe gefangen**
du	**hast gefangen**
er/sie/es	**hat gefangen**
wir	**haben gefangen**
ihr	**habt gefangen**
sie/Sie	**haben gefangen**

IMPERFECT

ich	**fing**
du	**fingst**
er/sie/es	**fing**
wir	**fingen**
ihr	**fingt**
sie/Sie	**fingen**

PRESENT PARTICIPLE

fangend

PAST PARTICIPLE

gefangen

EXAMPLE PHRASES

Die Katze **fängt** die Maus. The cat catches the mouse.

Er sagt, seine Katze **fange** keine Mäuse. He says his cat doesn't catch mice.

Die Polizei **hat** die Verbrecher **gefangen**. The police caught the criminals.

Ich **fing** den Ball. I caught the ball.

---

ich = I   du = you   er = he/it   sie = she/it   es = it/he/she   wir = we   ihr = you   sie = they   Sie = you (*polite*)

fangen

FUTURE

ich	**werde fangen**
du	**wirst fangen**
er/sie/es	**wird fangen**
wir	**werden fangen**
ihr	**werdet fangen**
sie/Sie	**werden fangen**

CONDITIONAL

ich	**würde fangen**
du	**würdest fangen**
er/sie/es	**würde fangen**
wir	**würden fangen**
ihr	**würdet fangen**
sie/Sie	**würden fangen**

PLUPERFECT

ich	**hatte gefangen**
du	**hattest gefangen**
er/sie/es	**hatte gefangen**
wir	**hatten gefangen**
ihr	**hattet gefangen**
sie/Sie	**hatten gefangen**

PLUPERFECT SUBJUNCTIVE

ich	**hätte gefangen**
du	**hättest gefangen**
er/sie/es	**hätte gefangen**
wir	**hätten gefangen**
ihr	**hättet gefangen**
sie/Sie	**hätten gefangen**

IMPERATIVE

fang(e)!/fangen wir!/fangt!/fangen Sie!

EXAMPLE PHRASES

In diesem Fluss **werden** wir nichts **fangen**. We won't catch anything in this river.

Ich **würde** gern Fische **fangen**. I would like to catch fish.

Er **hatte** sich wieder **gefangen**. He had managed to steady himself.

Hättest du den Fisch **gefangen**? Would you have caught the fish?

ich = I du = you er = he/it sie = she/it es = it/he/she wir = we ihr = you sie = they Sie = you (*polite*)

finden (to find)

strong, *formed with* **haben**

PRESENT

ich	**finde**
du	**findest**
er/sie/es	**findet**
wir	**finden**
ihr	**findet**
sie/Sie	**finden**

PRESENT SUBJUNCTIVE

ich	**finde**
du	**findest**
er/sie/es	**finde**
wir	**finden**
ihr	**findet**
sie/Sie	**finden**

PERFECT

ich	**habe gefunden**
du	**hast gefunden**
er/sie/es	**hat gefunden**
wir	**haben gefunden**
ihr	**habt gefunden**
sie/Sie	**haben gefunden**

IMPERFECT

ich	**fand**
du	**fand(e)st**
er/sie/es	**fand**
wir	**fanden**
ihr	**fandet**
sie/Sie	**fanden**

PRESENT PARTICIPLE

findend

PAST PARTICIPLE

gefunden

EXAMPLE PHRASES

Ich **finde**, sie ist eine gute Lehrerin. I think she's a good teacher.

Sie sagt, sie **finde** ihn attraktiv. She says she finds him attractive.

Hast du deine Brieftasche **gefunden**? Have you found your wallet?

Er **fand** den Mut, sie zu fragen. He found the courage to ask her.

---

ich = I **du** = you **er** = he/it **sie** = she/it **es** = it/he/she **wir** = we **ihr** = you **sie** = they **Sie** = you (*polite*)

finden

FUTURE

ich	**werde finden**
du	**wirst finden**
er/sie/es	**wird finden**
wir	**werden finden**
ihr	**werdet finden**
sie/Sie	**werden finden**

CONDITIONAL

ich	**würde finden**
du	**würdest finden**
er/sie/es	**würde finden**
wir	**würden finden**
ihr	**würdet finden**
sie/Sie	**würden finden**

PLUPERFECT

ich	**hatte gefunden**
du	**hattest gefunden**
er/sie/es	**hatte gefunden**
wir	**hatten gefunden**
ihr	**hattet gefunden**
sie/Sie	**hatten gefunden**

PLUPERFECT SUBJUNCTIVE

ich	**hätte gefunden**
du	**hättest gefunden**
er/sie/es	**hätte gefunden**
wir	**hätten gefunden**
ihr	**hättet gefunden**
sie/Sie	**hätten gefunden**

IMPERATIVE

find(e)!/finden wir!/findet!/finden Sie!

EXAMPLE PHRASES

Wir **werden** dieses Dorf nie **finden**. We'll never find that village.

6000 Euro **würde** ich zu teuer **finden**. I would find 6000 euros too expensive.

Wir **hatten** nicht nach Hause **gefunden**. We hadn't been able to find our way home.

Dazu **hätte** ich nicht den Mut **gefunden**. I wouldn't have had the courage for it.

ich = I **du** = you **er** = he/it **sie** = she/it **es** = it/he/she **wir** = we **ihr** = you **sie** = they **Sie** = you *(polite)*

fliegen (to fly)

strong, *formed with* haben/sein*

PRESENT

ich	**fliege**
du	**fliegst**
er/sie/es	**fliegen**
wir	**fliegen**
ihr	**fliegt**
sie/Sie	**fliegen**

PRESENT SUBJUNCTIVE

ich	**fliege**
du	**fliegest**
er/sie/es	**fliege**
wir	**fliegen**
ihr	**flieget**
sie/Sie	**fliegen**

PERFECT

ich	**habe geflogen**
du	**hast geflogen**
er/sie/es	**hat geflogen**
wir	**haben geflogen**
ihr	**habt geflogen**
sie/Sie	**haben geflogen**

IMPERFECT

ich	**flog**
du	**flogst**
er/sie/es	**flog**
wir	**flogen**
ihr	**flogt**
sie/Sie	**flogen**

PRESENT PARTICIPLE

fliegend

PAST PARTICIPLE

geflogen

When fliegen is used with no direct object, it is formed with sein.

EXAMPLE PHRASES

Die Zeit **fliegt**. Time flies.

Sie sagt, sie **fliege** nicht gern. She says she doesn't like flying.

Hast du das Flugzeug selbst **geflogen**? Did you fly the plane yourself?

Wir **flogen** zusammen nach Spanien. We flew to Spain together.

ich = I **du** = you **er** = he/it **sie** = she/it **es** = it/he/she **wir** = we **ihr** = you **sie** = they **Sie** = you *(polite)*

fliegen

FUTURE

ich	**werde fliegen**
du	**wirst fliegen**
er/sie/es	**wird fliegen**
wir	**werden fliegen**
ihr	**werdet fliegen**
sie/Sie	**werden fliegen**

CONDITIONAL

ich	**würde fliegen**
du	**würdest fliegen**
er/sie/es	**würde fliegen**
wir	**würden fliegen**
ihr	**würdet fliegen**
sie/Sie	**würden fliegen**

PLUPERFECT

ich	**hatte geflogen**
du	**hattest geflogen**
er/sie/es	**hatte geflogen**
wir	**hatten geflogen**
ihr	**hattet geflogen**
sie/Sie	**hatten geflogen**

PLUPERFECT SUBJUNCTIVE

ich	**hätte geflogen**
du	**hättest geflogen**
er/sie/es	**hätte geflogen**
wir	**hätten geflogen**
ihr	**hättet geflogen**
sie/Sie	**hätten geflogen**

IMPERATIVE

flieg(e)!/fliegen wir!/fliegt!/fliegen Sie!

EXAMPLE PHRASES

Wir **werden** morgen in Urlaub **fliegen**. We'll fly on holiday tomorrow.

Es war, als **würde** ich **fliegen**. It was as if I was flying.

Wir **waren** drei Stunden lang **geflogen**. We had been flying for three hours.

Ich **wäre** lieber nach Teneriffa **geflogen**. I would have preferred to fly to
  Tenerife.

ich = I **du** = you **er** = he/it **sie** = she/it **es** = it/he/she **wir** = we **ihr** = you **sie** = they **Sie** = you (*polite*)

fliehen (to flee)

strong, *formed with* haben/sein*

PRESENT

ich	fliehe
du	fliehst
er/sie/es	flieht
wir	fliehen
ihr	flieht
sie/Sie	fliehen

PRESENT SUBJUNCTIVE

ich	fliehe
du	fliehest
er/sie/es	fliehe
wir	fliehen
ihr	fliehet
sie/Sie	fliehen

PERFECT

ich	bin geflohen
du	bist geflohen
er/sie/es	ist geflohen
wir	sind geflohen
ihr	seid geflohen
sie/Sie	sind geflohen

IMPERFECT

ich	floh
du	flohst
er/sie/es	floh
wir	flohen
ihr	floht
sie/Sie	flohen

PRESENT PARTICIPLE

fliehend

PAST PARTICIPLE

geflohen

*When *fliehen* is used with a direct object, it is formed with *haben*.

EXAMPLE PHRASES

Warum **fliehst** du vor mir? Why are you running away from me?

Er glaubt, sie **fliehe** seine Gesellschaft. He thinks she is shunning his company.

Sie **sind** aus Afghanistan **geflohen**. They are refugees from Afghanistan.

Sie **floh** vor der Polizei. She fled from the police.

ich = I **du** = you **er** = he/it **sie** = she/it **es** = it/he/she **wir** = we **ihr** = you **sie** = they **Sie** = you (polite)

fliehen

FUTURE

ich	**werde fliehen**
du	**wirst fliehen**
er/sie/es	**wird fliehen**
wir	**werden fliehen**
ihr	**werdet fliehen**
sie/Sie	**werden fliehen**

CONDITIONAL

ich	**würde fliehen**
du	**würdest fliehen**
er/sie/es	**würde fliehen**
wir	**würden fliehen**
ihr	**würdet fliehen**
sie/Sie	**würden fliehen**

PLUPERFECT

ich	**war geflohen**
du	**warst geflohen**
er/sie/es	**war geflohen**
wir	**waren geflohen**
ihr	**wart geflohen**
sie/Sie	**waren geflohen**

PLUPERFECT SUBJUNCTIVE

ich	**wäre geflohen**
du	**wär(e)st geflohen**
er/sie/es	**wäre geflohen**
wir	**wären geflohen**
ihr	**wär(e)t geflohen**
sie/Sie	**wären geflohen**

IMPERATIVE

flieh(e)!/fliehen wir!/flieht!/fliehen Sie!

EXAMPLE PHRASES

Wenn die Gefahr zu groß wird, **wird** sie **fliehen**. If the danger becomes too great she will flee.

Wenn er könnte, **würde** er aus dem Gefängnis **fliehen**. If he could he would escape from prison.

Sie **waren** vor dem Krieg **geflohen**. They had fled from the war.

Wenn er **geflohen wäre**, würde er noch leben. If he had escaped he would still be alive.

ich = I **du** = you **er** = he/it **sie** = she/it **es** = it/he/she **wir** = we **ihr** = you **sie** = they **Sie** = you (*polite*)

fließen (to flow)

strong, formed with **sein**

PRESENT

ich	**fließe**
du	**fließt**
er/sie/es	**fließt**
wir	**fließen**
ihr	**fließt**
sie/Sie	**fließen**

PRESENT SUBJUNCTIVE

ich	**fließe**
du	**fließest**
er/sie/es	**fließe**
wir	**fließen**
ihr	**fließet**
sie/Sie	**fließen**

PERFECT

ich	**bin geflossen**
du	**bist geflossen**
er/sie/es	**ist geflossen**
wir	**sind geflossen**
ihr	**seid geflossen**
sie/Sie	**sind geflossen**

IMPERFECT

ich	**floss**
du	**flossest**
er/sie/es	**floss**
wir	**flossen**
ihr	**flosst**
sie/Sie	**flossen**

PRESENT PARTICIPLE

fließend

PAST PARTICIPLE

geflossen

EXAMPLE PHRASES

Welcher Fluss **fließt** durch Hamburg? **Which river flows through Hamburg?**

Er meint, das Wasser **fließe** zu langsam. **He thinks the water is flowing too slowly.**

Es **ist** genug Blut **geflossen**. **Enough blood has been spilled.**

Die Tränen **flossen** in Strömen. **There were floods of tears.**

---

ich = I du = you er = he/it sie = she/it es = it/he/she wir = we ihr = you sie = they Sie = you *(polite)*

fließen

FUTURE

ich	**werde fließen**
du	**wirst fließen**
er/sie/es	**wird fließen**
wir	**werden fließen**
ihr	**werdet fließen**
sie/Sie	**werden fließen**

CONDITIONAL

ich	**würde fließen**
du	**würdest fließen**
er/sie/es	**würde fließen**
wir	**würden fließen**
ihr	**würdet fließen**
sie/Sie	**würden fließen**

PLUPERFECT

ich	**war geflossen**
du	**warst geflossen**
er/sie/es	**war geflossen**
wir	**waren geflossen**
ihr	**wart geflossen**
sie/Sie	**waren geflossen**

PLUPERFECT SUBJUNCTIVE

ich	**wäre geflossen**
du	**wär(e)st geflossen**
er/sie/es	**wäre geflossen**
wir	**wären geflossen**
ihr	**wär(e)t geflossen**
sie/Sie	**wären geflossen**

IMPERATIVE

fließ(e)!/fließen wir!/fließt!/fließen Sie!

EXAMPLE PHRASES

Wohin **wird** dieses Geld **fließen**? Where will this money go?

Wenn sie wegginge, **würden** viele Tränen **fließen**. If she left there would be many tears.

Der Schweiß **war** ihm von der Stirn **geflossen**. Sweat had been pouring off his forehead.

Wenn er das gesagt hätte, **wäre** Blut **geflossen**. If he had said that there would have been bloodshed.

ich = I du = you er = he/it sie = she/it es = it/he/she wir = we ihr = you sie = they Sie = you *(polite)*

frieren (to freeze)

strong, *formed with* **haben/sein***

PRESENT

ich	**friere**
du	**frierst**
er/sie/es	**friert**
wir	**frieren**
ihr	**friert**
sie/Sie	**frieren**

PRESENT SUBJUNCTIVE

ich	**friere**
du	**frierest**
er/sie/es	**friere**
wir	**frieren**
ihr	**frieret**
sie/Sie	**frieren**

PERFECT

ich	**habe gefroren**
du	**hast gefroren**
er/sie/es	**hat gefroren**
wir	**haben gefroren**
ihr	**habt gefroren**
sie/Sie	**haben gefroren**

IMPERFECT

ich	**fror**
du	**frorst**
er/sie/es	**fror**
wir	**froren**
ihr	**frort**
sie/Sie	**froren**

PRESENT PARTICIPLE

frierend

PAST PARTICIPLE

gefroren

When the meaning is to freeze over, *frieren is formed with sein.*

EXAMPLE PHRASES

Ich **friere**. I'm freezing.

Sie sagt, es **friere** sie. She says she's cold.

Letzte Nacht **hat** es **gefroren**. It was frosty last night.

Er **fror** stark. He was very cold.

frieren

FUTURE

ich	**werde frieren**
du	**wirst frieren**
er/sie/es	**wird frieren**
wir	**werden frieren**
ihr	**werdet frieren**
sie/Sie	**werden frieren**

CONDITIONAL

ich	**würde frieren**
du	**würdest frieren**
er/sie/es	**würde frieren**
wir	**würden frieren**
ihr	**würdet frieren**
sie/Sie	**würden frieren**

PLUPERFECT

ich	**hatte gefroren**
du	**hattest gefroren**
er/sie/es	**hatte gefroren**
wir	**hatten gefroren**
ihr	**hattet gefroren**
sie/Sie	**hatten gefroren**

PLUPERFECT SUBJUNCTIVE

ich	**hätte gefroren**
du	**hättest gefroren**
er/sie/es	**hätte gefroren**
wir	**hätten gefroren**
ihr	**hättet gefroren**
sie/Sie	**hätten gefroren**

IMPERATIVE

frier(e)!/frieren wir!/friert!/frieren Sie!

EXAMPLE PHRASES

Heute Nacht **wird** es bestimmt **frieren**. I'm sure temperatures will be below
   freezing tonight.

Ohne meinen Wintermantel **würde** ich **frieren**. I would be cold without my
   winter coat.

Ohne seinen Pullover **hatte** er sehr **gefroren**. He had been very cold without
   his jumper.

Bei minus zehn Grad **wäre** der ganze See **gefroren**. At minus ten degrees the
   whole lake would have frozen over.

ich = I **du** = you **er** = he/it **sie** = she/it **es** = it/he/she **wir** = we **ihr** = you **sie** = they **Sie** = you (*polite*)

geben (to give)

strong, *formed with* haben

PRESENT

ich	gebe
du	gibst
er/sie/es	gibt
wir	geben
ihr	gebt
sie/Sie	geben

PRESENT SUBJUNCTIVE

ich	gebe
du	gebest
er/sie/es	gebe
wir	geben
ihr	gebet
sie/Sie	geben

PERFECT

ich	habe gegeben
du	hast gegeben
er/sie/es	hat gegeben
wir	haben gegeben
ihr	habt gegeben
sie/Sie	haben gegeben

IMPERFECT

ich	gab
du	gabst
er/sie/es	gab
wir	gaben
ihr	gabt
sie/Sie	gaben

PRESENT PARTICIPLE

gebend

PAST PARTICIPLE

gegeben

EXAMPLE PHRASES

Was **gibt** es im Kino? What's on at the cinema?

Er sagt, er **gebe** Bettlern kein Geld. He says he won't give money to beggars.

Das **hat** mir wieder Selbstvertrauen **gegeben**. This has given me new self-confidence.

Er **gab** mir das Geld für die Bücher. He gave me the money for the books.

ich = I du = you er = he/it sie = she/it es = it/he/she wir = we ihr = you sie = they Sie = you (polite)

geben

FUTURE

ich	**werde geben**
du	**wirst geben**
er/sie/es	**wird geben**
wir	**werden geben**
ihr	**werdet geben**
sie/Sie	**werden geben**

CONDITIONAL

ich	**würde geben**
du	**würdest geben**
er/sie/es	**würde geben**
wir	**würden geben**
ihr	**würdet geben**
sie/Sie	**würden geben**

PLUPERFECT

ich	**hatte gegeben**
du	**hattest gegeben**
er/sie/es	**hatte gegeben**
wir	**hatten gegeben**
ihr	**hattet gegeben**
sie/Sie	**hatten gegeben**

PLUPERFECT SUBJUNCTIVE

ich	**hätte gegeben**
du	**hättest gegeben**
er/sie/es	**hätte gegeben**
wir	**hätten gegeben**
ihr	**hättet gegeben**
sie/Sie	**hätten gegeben**

IMPERATIVE

gib!/geben wir!/gebt!/geben Sie!

EXAMPLE PHRASES

Das **wird** sich schon **geben**. That'll sort itself out.

Wir **würden** alles darum **geben**, ins Finale zu kommen. We would give anything to reach the finals.

Ich **hatte** das Buch seiner Mutter **gegeben**. I had given the book to his mother.

Wir **hätten** alles darum **gegeben**, ihn wiederzusehen. We would have given anything to see him again.

ich = I **du** = you **er** = he/it **sie** = she/it **es** = it/he/she **wir** = we **ihr** = you **sie** = they **Sie** = you (*polite*)

gehen (to go)

strong, *formed with* **sein**

PRESENT

ich	**gehe**
du	**gehst**
er/sie/es	**geht**
wir	**gehen**
ihr	**geht**
sie/Sie	**gehen**

PRESENT SUBJUNCTIVE

ich	**gehe**
du	**gehest**
er/sie/es	**gehe**
wir	**gehen**
ihr	**gehet**
sie/Sie	**gehen**

PERFECT

ich	**bin gegangen**
du	**bist gegangen**
er/sie/es	**ist gegangen**
wir	**sind gegangen**
ihr	**seid gegangen**
sie/Sie	**sind gegangen**

IMPERFECT

ich	**ging**
du	**gingst**
er/sie/es	**ging**
wir	**gingen**
ihr	**gingt**
sie/Sie	**gingen**

PRESENT PARTICIPLE

gehend

PAST PARTICIPLE

gegangen

EXAMPLE PHRASES

Wie **geht** es dir? How are you?

Er meint, das **ginge** zu weit. He thinks that would go too far.

Wir **sind** gestern schwimmen **gegangen**. We went swimming yesterday.

Die Kinder **gingen** ins Haus. The children went into the house.

gehen

FUTURE

ich	**werde gehen**
du	**wirst gehen**
er/sie/es	**wird gehen**
wir	**werden gehen**
ihr	**werdet gehen**
sie/Sie	**werden gehen**

CONDITIONAL

ich	**würde gehen**
du	**würdest gehen**
er/sie/es	**würde gehen**
wir	**würden gehen**
ihr	**würdet gehen**
sie/Sie	**würden gehen**

PLUPERFECT

ich	**war gegangen**
du	**warst gegangen**
er/sie/es	**war gegangen**
wir	**waren gegangen**
ihr	**wart gegangen**
sie/Sie	**waren gegangen**

PLUPERFECT SUBJUNCTIVE

ich	**wäre gegangen**
du	**wär(e)st gegangen**
er/sie/es	**wäre gegangen**
wir	**wären gegangen**
ihr	**wär(e)t gegangen**
sie/Sie	**wären gegangen**

IMPERATIVE

geh(e)!/gehen wir!/geht!/gehen Sie!

EXAMPLE PHRASES

Dabei **wird** es um sehr viel Geld **gehen**. A lot of money will be at stake here.

In diesen Kleidern **würde** ich nicht ins Theater **gehen**. I wouldn't go to the theatre in these clothes.

Wir **waren** durch den Wald **gegangen**. We had gone through the wood.

Ohne Schirm **wäre** ich nicht aus dem Haus **gegangen**. I wouldn't have left the house without an umbrella.

ich = I **du** = you **er** = he/it **sie** = she/it **es** = it/he/she **wir** = we **ihr** = you **sie** = they **Sie** = you (*polite*)

gehorchen (to obey) — weak, inseparable, *formed with* haben

PRESENT
- ich **gehorche**
- du **gehorchst**
- er/sie/es **gehorcht**
- wir **gehorchen**
- ihr **gehorcht**
- sie/Sie **gehorchen**

PRESENT SUBJUNCTIVE
- ich **gehorche**
- du **gehorchest**
- er/sie/es **gehorche**
- wir **gehorchen**
- ihr **gehorchet**
- sie/Sie **gehorchen**

PERFECT
- ich **habe gehorcht**
- du **hast gehorcht**
- er/sie/es **hat gehorcht**
- wir **haben gehorcht**
- ihr **habt gehorcht**
- sie/Sie **haben gehorcht**

IMPERFECT
- ich **gehorchte**
- du **gehorchtest**
- er/sie/es **gehorchte**
- wir **gehorchten**
- ihr **gehorchtet**
- sie/Sie **gehorchten**

PRESENT PARTICIPLE
gehorchend

PAST PARTICIPLE
gehorcht

EXAMPLE PHRASES

Der Hund **gehorcht** mir nicht. That dog is disobedient.

Er sagt, sein Sohn **gehorche** ihm nicht. He says his son is disobedient.

Meine Schwester **hat** meinen Eltern überhaupt nicht **gehorcht**. My sister didn't obey my parents at all.

Er **gehorchte** seiner Mutter. He obeyed his mother.

ich = I du = you er = he/it sie = she/it es = it/he/she wir = we ihr = you sie = they Sie = you (*polite*)

gehorchen

FUTURE

ich	**werde gehorchen**
du	**wirst gehorchen**
er/sie/es	**wird gehorchen**
wir	**werden gehorchen**
ihr	**werdet gehorchen**
sie/Sie	**werden gehorchen**

CONDITIONAL

ich	**würde gehorchen**
du	**würdest gehorchen**
er/sie/es	**würde gehorchen**
wir	**würden gehorchen**
ihr	**würdet gehorchen**
sie/Sie	**würden gehorchen**

PLUPERFECT

ich	**hatte gehorcht**
du	**hattest gehorcht**
er/sie/es	**hatte gehorcht**
wir	**hatten gehorcht**
ihr	**hattet gehorcht**
sie/Sie	**hatten gehorcht**

PLUPERFECT SUBJUNCTIVE

ich	**hätte gehorcht**
du	**hättest gehorcht**
er/sie/es	**hätte gehorcht**
wir	**hätten gehorcht**
ihr	**hättet gehorcht**
sie/Sie	**hätten gehorcht**

IMPERATIVE

gehorch(e)!/gehorchen wir!/gehorcht!/gehorchen Sie!

EXAMPLE PHRASES

Ich hoffe, das Auto **wird** mir heute **gehorchen**. I hope the car will behave today.

Wenn ich strenger mit ihm wäre, **würde** er mir besser **gehorchen**. If I was stricter with him he would be more obedient.

Ich **hatte** meinem Vater immer **gehorcht**. I had always obeyed my father.

Ich **hätte** meinem Chef in dieser Frage nicht **gehorcht**. I would have gone against my boss in this matter.

ich = I **du** = you **er** = he/it **sie** = she/it **es** = it/he/she **wir** = we **ihr** = you **sie** = they **Sie** = you (*polite*)

genießen (to enjoy)   strong, inseparable, *formed with* **haben**

PRESENT

ich	**genieße**
du	**genießt**
er/sie/es	**genießt**
wir	**genießen**
ihr	**genießt**
sie/Sie	**genießen**

PRESENT SUBJUNCTIVE

ich	**genieße**
du	**genießest**
er/sie/es	**genieße**
wir	**genießen**
ihr	**genießet**
sie/Sie	**genießen**

PERFECT

ich	**habe genossen**
du	**hast genossen**
er/sie/es	**hat genossen**
wir	**haben genossen**
ihr	**habt genossen**
sie/Sie	**haben genossen**

IMPERFECT

ich	**genoss**
du	**genossest**
er/sie/es	**genoss**
wir	**genossen**
ihr	**genosst**
sie/Sie	**genossen**

PRESENT PARTICIPLE

genießend

PAST PARTICIPLE

genossen

EXAMPLE PHRASES

Ich **genieße** meine Freizeit. I'm enjoying my spare time.

Sie sagt, sie **genieße** das Leben. She says she's enjoying life.

Wir **haben** die Ferien **genossen**. We enjoyed our holidays.

Er **genoss** ein Glas Wein. He enjoyed a glass of wine.

genießen

FUTURE

ich	**werde genießen**
du	**wirst genießen**
er/sie/es	**wird genießen**
wir	**werden genießen**
ihr	**werdet genießen**
sie/Sie	**werden genießen**

CONDITIONAL

ich	**würde genießen**
du	**würdest genießen**
er/sie/es	**würde genießen**
wir	**würden genießen**
ihr	**würdet genießen**
sie/Sie	**würden genießen**

PLUPERFECT

ich	**hatte genossen**
du	**hattest genossen**
er/sie/es	**hatte genossen**
wir	**hatten genossen**
ihr	**hattet genossen**
sie/Sie	**hatten genossen**

PLUPERFECT SUBJUNCTIVE

ich	**hätte genossen**
du	**hättest genossen**
er/sie/es	**hätte genossen**
wir	**hätten genossen**
ihr	**hättet genossen**
sie/Sie	**hätten genossen**

IMPERATIVE

genieß(e)!/genießen wir!/genießt!/genießen Sie!

EXAMPLE PHRASES

Diese Prüfung **werde** ich nicht **genießen**. I won't enjoy this test.

Ich **würde** mein Leben gern **genießen**. I'd like to enjoy my life.

Ich **hatte** das Wochenende in Paris **genossen**. I had enjoyed the weekend in Paris.

Ich **hätte** den Urlaub besser **genossen**, wenn du dabei gewesen wärst.
   I would have enjoyed the holiday more if you had been with me.

ich = I **du** = you **er** = he/it **sie** = she/it **es** = it/he/she **wir** = we **ihr** = you **sie** = they **Sie** = you (*polite*)

gewinnen (to win) strong, inseparable, *formed with* haben

PRESENT

ich	gewinne
du	gewinnst
er/sie/es	gewinnt
wir	gewinnen
ihr	gewinnt
sie/Sie	gewinnen

PRESENT SUBJUNCTIVE

ich	gewinne
du	gewinnest
er/sie/es	gewinne
wir	gewinnen
ihr	gewinnet
sie/Sie	gewinnen

PERFECT

ich	habe gewonnen
du	hast gewonnen
er/sie/es	hat gewonnen
wir	haben gewonnen
ihr	habt gewonnen
sie/Sie	haben gewonnen

IMPERFECT

ich	gewann
du	gewannst
er/sie/es	gewann
wir	gewannen
ihr	gewannt
sie/Sie	gewannen

PRESENT PARTICIPLE

gewinnend

PAST PARTICIPLE

gewonnen

EXAMPLE PHRASES

Er **gewinnt** immer beim Kartenspielen. **He always wins at cards.**

Er sagt, seine Mannschaft **gewinne** alle Spiele. **He says his team wins all the matches.**

Er **hat** den ersten Preis **gewonnen**. **He won first prize.**

Das Flugzeug **gewann** an Höhe. **The plane gained in altitude.**

gewinnen

FUTURE

ich	**werde gewinnen**
du	**wirst gewinnen**
er/sie/es	**wird gewinnen**
wir	**werden gewinnen**
ihr	**werdet gewinnen**
sie/Sie	**werden gewinnen**

CONDITIONAL

ich	**würde gewinnen**
du	**würdest gewinnen**
er/sie/es	**würde gewinnen**
wir	**würden gewinnen**
ihr	**würdet gewinnen**
sie/Sie	**würden gewinnen**

PLUPERFECT

ich	**hatte gewonnen**
du	**hattest gewonnen**
er/sie/es	**hatte gewonnen**
wir	**hatten gewonnen**
ihr	**hattet gewonnen**
sie/Sie	**hatten gewonnen**

PLUPERFECT SUBJUNCTIVE

ich	**hätte gewonnen**
du	**hättest gewonnen**
er/sie/es	**hätte gewonnen**
wir	**hätten gewonnen**
ihr	**hättet gewonnen**
sie/Sie	**hätten gewonnen**

IMPERATIVE

gewinn(e)!/gewinnen wir!/gewinnt!/gewinnen Sie!

EXAMPLE PHRASES

Gegen ihn **werden** wir niemals **gewinnen**. We'll never win against him.

Am liebsten **würde** ich im Lotto **gewinnen**. What I'd love most is to win the lottery.

Ich **hatte** ihn zum Freund **gewonnen**. I had won him as a friend.

Hättest du **gewonnen**, wärest du jetzt reich. If you had won you would be rich now.

ich = I du = you er = he/it sie = she/it es = it/he/she wir = we ihr = you sie = they Sie = you *(polite)*

gießen (to pour)

strong, *formed with* haben

PRESENT

ich	**gieße**
du	**gießt**
er/sie/es	**gießt**
wir	**gießen**
ihr	**gießt**
sie/Sie	**gießen**

PRESENT SUBJUNCTIVE

ich	**gieße**
du	**gießest**
er/sie/es	**gieße**
wir	**gießen**
ihr	**gießet**
sie/Sie	**gießen**

PERFECT

ich	**habe gegossen**
du	**hast gegossen**
er/sie/es	**hat gegossen**
wir	**haben gegossen**
ihr	**habt gegossen**
sie/Sie	**haben gegossen**

IMPERFECT

ich	**goss**
du	**gossest**
er/sie/es	**goss**
wir	**gossen**
ihr	**gosst**
sie/Sie	**gossen**

PRESENT PARTICIPLE

gießend

PAST PARTICIPLE

gegossen

EXAMPLE PHRASES

Sie **gießt** den Garten. She is watering the garden.

Sie sagt, es **gieße** draußen. She says it's pouring outside.

Ich **habe** das Glas voll **gegossen**. I filled the glass up.

Er **goss** mir Wasser über den Kopf. He poured water over my head.

gießen

FUTURE

ich	**werde gießen**
du	**wirst gießen**
er/sie/es	**wird gießen**
wir	**werden gießen**
ihr	**werdet gießen**
sie/Sie	**werden gießen**

CONDITIONAL

ich	**würde gießen**
du	**würdest gießen**
er/sie/es	**würde gießen**
wir	**würden gießen**
ihr	**würdet gießen**
sie/Sie	**würden gießen**

PLUPERFECT

ich	**hatte gegossen**
du	**hattest gegossen**
er/sie/es	**hatte gegossen**
wir	**hatten gegossen**
ihr	**hattet gegossen**
sie/Sie	**hatten gegossen**

PLUPERFECT SUBJUNCTIVE

ich	**hätte gegossen**
du	**hättest gegossen**
er/sie/es	**hätte gegossen**
wir	**hätten gegossen**
ihr	**hättet gegossen**
sie/Sie	**hätten gegossen**

IMPERATIVE
gieß(e)!/gießen wir!/gießt!/gießen Sie!

EXAMPLE PHRASES

Ich **werde** gleich die Rosen **gießen**. I'll water the roses in a moment.

An deiner Stelle **würde** ich die Blumen nicht so oft **gießen**. If I were you I wouldn't water the flowers so often.

Dienstag **hatte** es in Strömen **gegossen**. On Tuesday it had been bucketing down.

Ich **hätte** besser die Pflanzen **gegossen**. I should have watered the plants.

ich = I **du** = you **er** = he/it **sie** = she/it **es** = it/he/she **wir** = we **ihr** = you **sie** = they **Sie** = you *(polite)*

graben (to dig)

strong, *formed with* haben

PRESENT

ich	grabe
du	gräbst
er/sie/es	gräbt
wir	graben
ihr	grabt
sie/Sie	graben

PRESENT SUBJUNCTIVE

ich	grabe
du	grabest
er/sie/es	grabe
wir	graben
ihr	grabet
sie/Sie	graben

PERFECT

ich	habe gegraben
du	hast gegraben
er/sie/es	hat gegraben
wir	haben gegraben
ihr	habt gegraben
sie/Sie	haben gegraben

IMPERFECT

ich	grub
du	grubst
er/sie/es	grub
wir	gruben
ihr	grubt
sie/Sie	gruben

PRESENT PARTICIPLE

grabend

PAST PARTICIPLE

gegraben

EXAMPLE PHRASES

Er **gräbt** ein Loch. **He is digging a hole.**

Er sagt, er **grabe** in Alaska nach Gold. **He says he digs for gold in Alaska.**

Der Fluss **hat** sich in den Fels **gegraben**. **The river has eaten its way into the rock.**

Der Archäologe **grub** nach antiken Schätzen. **The archaeologist was digging for antique treasures.**

ich = I **du** = you **er** = he/it **sie** = she/it **es** = it/he/she **wir** = we **ihr** = you **sie** = they **Sie** = you *(polite)*

graben

FUTURE

ich	**werde graben**
du	**wirst graben**
er/sie/es	**wird graben**
wir	**werden graben**
ihr	**werdet graben**
sie/Sie	**werden graben**

CONDITIONAL

ich	**würde graben**
du	**würdest graben**
er/sie/es	**würde graben**
wir	**würden graben**
ihr	**würdet graben**
sie/Sie	**würden graben**

PLUPERFECT

ich	**hatte gegraben**
du	**hattest gegraben**
er/sie/es	**hatte gegraben**
wir	**hatten gegraben**
ihr	**hattet gegraben**
sie/Sie	**hatten gegraben**

PLUPERFECT SUBJUNCTIVE

ich	**hätte gegraben**
du	**hättest gegraben**
er/sie/es	**hätte gegraben**
wir	**hätten gegraben**
ihr	**hättet gegraben**
sie/Sie	**hätten gegraben**

IMPERATIVE

grab(e)!/graben wir!/grabt!/graben Sie!

EXAMPLE PHRASES

Wir **werden** uns durch diese Probleme **graben**. We'll work our way through these problems.

Ich **würde** nicht in seiner Vergangenheit **graben**. I wouldn't dig around in his past.

Das **hatte** sich mir ins Gedächtnis **gegraben**. It had imprinted itself on my memory.

Wir **hätten** gern ein tieferes Loch **gegraben**. We would have liked to dig a deeper hole.

ich = I du = you er = he/it sie = she/it es = it/he/she wir = we ihr = you sie = they Sie = you (polite)

greifen (to take hold of, seize)

strong, *formed with* **haben**

PRESENT

ich	**greife**
du	**greifst**
er/sie/es	**greift**
wir	**greifen**
ihr	**greift**
sie/Sie	**greifen**

PRESENT SUBJUNCTIVE

ich	**greife**
du	**greifest**
er/sie/es	**greife**
wir	**greifen**
ihr	**greifet**
sie/Sie	**greifen**

PERFECT

ich	**habe gegriffen**
du	**hast gegriffen**
er/sie/es	**hat gegriffen**
wir	**haben gegriffen**
ihr	**habt gegriffen**
sie/Sie	**haben gegriffen**

IMPERFECT

ich	**griff**
du	**griffst**
er/sie/es	**griff**
wir	**griffen**
ihr	**grifft**
sie/Sie	**griffen**

PRESENT PARTICIPLE

griefend

PAST PARTICIPLE

gegriffen

EXAMPLE PHRASES

Die Geschichte **greift** ans Herz. The story pulls at one's heartstrings.

Sie sagt, sie **greife** nicht gern zu diesen Mitteln. She says she doesn't like to resort to these measures.

Er **hat** zum Äußersten **gegriffen**. He has resorted to extremes.

Er **griff** das Buch. He grabbed the book.

ich = I **du** = you **er** = he/it **sie** = she/it **es** = it/he/she **wir** = we **ihr** = you **sie** = they **Sie** = you (*polite*)

greifen

FUTURE

ich	**werde greifen**
du	**wirst greifen**
er/sie/es	**wird greifen**
wir	**werden greifen**
ihr	**werdet greifen**
sie/Sie	**werden greifen**

CONDITIONAL

ich	**würde greifen**
du	**würdest greifen**
er/sie/es	**würde greifen**
wir	**würden greifen**
ihr	**würdet greifen**
sie/Sie	**würden greifen**

PLUPERFECT

ich	**hatte gegriffen**
du	**hattest gegriffen**
er/sie/es	**hatte gegriffen**
wir	**hatten gegriffen**
ihr	**hattet gegriffen**
sie/Sie	**hatten gegriffen**

PLUPERFECT SUBJUNCTIVE

ich	**hätte gegriffen**
du	**hättest gegriffen**
er/sie/es	**hätte gegriffen**
wir	**hätten gegriffen**
ihr	**hättet gegriffen**
sie/Sie	**hätten gegriffen**

IMPERATIVE

greif(e)!/greifen wir!/greift!/greifen Sie!

EXAMPLE PHRASES

Der Staat **wird** uns tief in die Tasche **greifen**. The state will be asking us to dig deep.

Wenn ich könnte, **würde** ich nach den Sternen **greifen**. If I could I would reach for the stars.

Er **hatte** wieder zur Flasche **gegriffen**. He had taken to the bottle again.

In dieser Situation **hätte** ich zur Pistole **gegriffen**. In that situation I would have reached for my gun.

ich = I **du** = you **er** = he/it **sie** = she/it **es** = it/he/she **wir** = we **ihr** = you **sie** = they **Sie** = you *(polite)*

grüßen (to greet)

weak, *formed with* haben

PRESENT

ich	grüße
du	grüßt
er/sie/es	grüßt
wir	grüßen
ihr	grüßt
sie/Sie	grüßen

PRESENT SUBJUNCTIVE

ich	grüße
du	grüßest
er/sie/es	grüße
wir	grüßen
ihr	grüßet
sie/Sie	grüßen

PERFECT

ich	habe gegrüßt
du	hast gegrüßt
er/sie/es	hat gegrüßt
wir	haben gegrüßt
ihr	habt gegrüßt
sie/Sie	haben gegrüßt

IMPERFECT

ich	grüßte
du	grüßtest
er/sie/es	grüßte
wir	grüßten
ihr	grüßtet
sie/Sie	grüßten

PRESENT PARTICIPLE

grüßend

PAST PARTICIPLE

gegrüßt

EXAMPLE PHRASES

Unsere Nachbarin **grüßt** uns jeden Morgen. **Our neighbour greets us every morning.**

Er sagt, er **grüße** sie nicht einmal. **He says he doesn't even say hello to her.**

Er **hat** mich nicht **gegrüßt**. **He didn't say hello to me.**

Sie **grüßte** mich mit einem Lächeln. **She greeted me with a smile.**

ich = I **du** = you **er** = he/it **sie** = she/it **es** = it/he/she **wir** = we **ihr** = you **sie** = they **Sie** = you *(polite)*

grüßen

FUTURE

ich	**werde grüßen**
du	**wirst grüßen**
er/sie/es	**wird grüßen**
wir	**werden grüßen**
ihr	**werdet grüßen**
sie/Sie	**werden grüßen**

CONDITIONAL

ich	**würde grüßen**
du	**würdest grüßen**
er/sie/es	**würde grüßen**
wir	**würden grüßen**
ihr	**würdet grüßen**
sie/Sie	**würden grüßen**

PLUPERFECT

ich	**hatte gegrüßt**
du	**hattest gegrüßt**
er/sie/es	**hatte gegrüßt**
wir	**hatten gegrüßt**
ihr	**hattet gegrüßt**
sie/Sie	**hatten gegrüßt**

PLUPERFECT SUBJUNCTIVE

ich	**hätte gegrüßt**
du	**hättest gegrüßt**
er/sie/es	**hätte gegrüßt**
wir	**hätten gegrüßt**
ihr	**hättet gegrüßt**
sie/Sie	**hätten gegrüßt**

IMPERATIVE

grüß(e)!/grüßen wir!/grüßt!/grüßen Sie!

EXAMPLE PHRASES

In Österreich **werden** uns die Berge **grüßen**. In Austria we will be greeted
by the mountains.

Solche Nachbarn **würde** ich nicht **grüßen**. I wouldn't say hello to neighbours
like that.

Er **hatte** mich auf der Straße **gegrüßt**. He had greeted me in the street.

Sie **hätte** dich gegrüßt, wenn sie dich erkannt hätte. She would have said hello
if she had recognized you.

ich = I du = you er = he/it sie = she/it es = it/he/she wir = we ihr = you sie = they Sie = you *(polite)*

haben (to have)

strong, formed with haben

PRESENT

ich	**habe**
du	**hast**
er/sie/es	**hat**
wir	**haben**
ihr	**habt**
sie/Sie	**haben**

PRESENT SUBJUNCTIVE

ich	**habe**
du	**habest**
er/sie/es	**habe**
wir	**haben**
ihr	**habet**
sie/Sie	**haben**

PERFECT

ich	**habe gehabt**
du	**hast gehabt**
er/sie/es	**hat gehabt**
wir	**haben gehabt**
ihr	**habt gehabt**
sie/Sie	**haben gehabt**

IMPERFECT

ich	**hatte**
du	**hattest**
er/sie/es	**hatte**
wir	**hatten**
ihr	**hattet**
sie/Sie	**hatten**

PRESENT PARTICIPLE

habend

PAST PARTICIPLE

gehabt

EXAMPLE PHRASES

Hast du eine Schwester? Have you got a sister?

Er sagt, er **habe** keine Zeit. He says he has no time

Sie **hat** letzte Woche Geburtstag **gehabt**. Her birthday was last week.

Er **hatte** Hunger. He was hungry.

haben

FUTURE

ich	**werde haben**
du	**wirst haben**
er/sie/es	**wird haben**
wir	**werden haben**
ihr	**werdet haben**
sie/Sie	**werden haben**

CONDITIONAL

ich	**würde haben**
du	**würdest haben**
er/sie/es	**würde haben**
wir	**würden haben**
ihr	**würdet haben**
sie/Sie	**würden haben**

PLUPERFECT

ich	**hatte gehabt**
du	**hattest gehabt**
er/sie/es	**hatte gehabt**
wir	**hatten gehabt**
ihr	**hattet gehabt**
sie/Sie	**hatten gehabt**

PLUPERFECT SUBJUNCTIVE

ich	**hätte gehabt**
du	**hättest gehabt**
er/sie/es	**hätte gehabt**
wir	**hätten gehabt**
ihr	**hättet gehabt**
sie/Sie	**hätten gehabt**

IMPERATIVE

hab(e)!/haben wir!/habt!/haben Sie!

EXAMPLE PHRASES

Diese Gelegenheit **werden** wir nie wieder **haben**. We'll never have this opportunity again.

Ich **würde** gern viel Geld **haben**. I'd like to have a lot of money.

Davor **hatten** wir immer Angst **gehabt**. We had always been afraid of that.

Er **hätte** sie gern zur Freundin **gehabt**. He would have liked her to be his girlfriend.

ich = I **du** = you **er** = he/it **sie** = she/it **es** = it/he/she **wir** = we **ihr** = you **sie** = they **Sie** = you (*polite*)

halten (to hold)

strong, *formed with* haben

PRESENT

ich	halte
du	hältst
er/sie/es	hält
wir	halten
ihr	haltet
sie/Sie	halten

PRESENT SUBJUNCTIVE

ich	halte
du	haltest
er/sie/es	halte
wir	halten
ihr	haltet
sie/Sie	halten

PERFECT

ich	habe gehalten
du	hast gehalten
er/sie/es	hat gehalten
wir	haben gehalten
ihr	habt gehalten
sie/Sie	haben gehalten

IMPERFECT

ich	hielt
du	hielt(e)st
er/sie/es	hielt
wir	hielten
ihr	hieltet
sie/Sie	hielten

PRESENT PARTICIPLE

haltend

PAST PARTICIPLE

gehalten

EXAMPLE PHRASES

Hältst du das mal für mich? **Can you hold that for me?**

Sie sagt, sie **halte** nicht viel von diesem Vorschlag. **She says she doesn't think much of this suggestion.**

Ich **habe** sie für deine Mutter **gehalten**. **I took her for your mother.**

Der Bus **hielt** vor dem Rathaus. **The bus stopped in front of the town hall.**

ich = I du = you er = he/it sie = she/it es = it/he/she wir = we ihr = you sie = they Sie = you *(polite)*

halten

FUTURE

ich	**werde halten**
du	**wirst halten**
er/sie/es	**wird halten**
wir	**werden halten**
ihr	**werdet halten**
sie/Sie	**werden halten**

CONDITIONAL

ich	**würde halten**
du	**würdest halten**
er/sie/es	**würde halten**
wir	**würden halten**
ihr	**würdet halten**
sie/Sie	**würden halten**

PLUPERFECT

ich	**hatte gehalten**
du	**hattest gehalten**
er/sie/es	**hatte gehalten**
wir	**hatten gehalten**
ihr	**hattet gehalten**
sie/Sie	**hatten gehalten**

PLUPERFECT SUBJUNCTIVE

ich	**hätte gehalten**
du	**hättest gehalten**
er/sie/es	**hätte gehalten**
wir	**hätten gehalten**
ihr	**hättet gehalten**
sie/Sie	**hätten gehalten**

IMPERATIVE

halt(e)!/halten wir!/haltet!/halten Sie!

EXAMPLE PHRASES

Sie **werden** das Land besetzt **halten**. They will keep the country under occupation.

Ich **würde** mich an diese Methode **halten**. I would stick with that method.

Ich **hatte** ihn für ehrlicher **gehalten**. I had thought him to be more honest.

Das **hätte** ich nie für möglich **gehalten**. I would never have thought it possible.

ich = I **du** = you **er** = he/it **sie** = she/it **es** = it/he/she **wir** = we **ihr** = you **sie** = they **Sie** = you (*polite*)

handeln (to trade; to act)

weak, *formed with* **haben**

PRESENT

ich	**handle**
du	**handelst**
er/sie/es	**handelt**
wir	**handeln**
ihr	**handelt**
sie/Sie	**handeln**

PRESENT SUBJUNCTIVE

ich	**handle**
du	**handlest**
er/sie/es	**handle**
wir	**handlen**
ihr	**handlet**
sie/Sie	**handlen**

PERFECT

ich	**habe gehandelt**
du	**hast gehandelt**
er/sie/es	**hat gehandelt**
wir	**haben gehandelt**
ihr	**habt gehandelt**
sie/Sie	**haben gehandelt**

IMPERFECT

ich	**handelte**
du	**handeltest**
er/sie/es	**handelte**
wir	**handelten**
ihr	**handeltet**
sie/Sie	**handelten**

PRESENT PARTICIPLE

handelnd

PAST PARTICIPLE

gehandelt

EXAMPLE PHRASES

Die Geschichte **handelt** von einem alten Mann. The story is about an old man.

Er sagt, der Roman **handle** von einem Bankraub. He says the novel is about a bank robbery.

Er **hat** früher in Gebrauchtwagen **gehandelt**. He used to deal in used cars.

Die Polizei **handelte** schnell. The police acted quickly.

---

ich = I du = you er = he/it sie = she/it es = it/he/she wir = we ihr = you sie = they Sie = you (polite)

handeln

FUTURE

ich	**werde handeln**
du	**wirst handeln**
er/sie/es	**wird handeln**
wir	**werden handeln**
ihr	**werdet handeln**
sie/Sie	**werden handeln**

CONDITIONAL

ich	**würde handeln**
du	**würdest handeln**
er/sie/es	**würde handeln**
wir	**würden handeln**
ihr	**würdet handeln**
sie/Sie	**würden handeln**

PLUPERFECT

ich	**hatte gehandelt**
du	**hattest gehandelt**
er/sie/es	**hatte gehandelt**
wir	**hatten gehandelt**
ihr	**hattet gehandelt**
sie/Sie	**hatten gehandelt**

PLUPERFECT SUBJUNCTIVE

ich	**hätte gehandelt**
du	**hättest gehandelt**
er/sie/es	**hätte gehandelt**
wir	**hätten gehandelt**
ihr	**hättet gehandelt**
sie/Sie	**hätten gehandelt**

IMPERATIVE

handle!/handeln wir!/handelt!/handeln Sie!

EXAMPLE PHRASES

Wir **werden** sofort **handeln**. We will act at once.

Er **würde** nie mit Drogen **handeln**. He would never deal in drugs.

Es **hatte** sich ums Überleben **gehandelt**. It had been a question of survival.

Ich **hätte** gern mit ihm über den Preis **gehandelt**. I would have liked to bargain with him over the price.

ich = I **du** = you **er** = he/it **sie** = she/it **es** = it/he/she **wir** = we **ihr** = you **sie** = they **Sie** = you (*polite*)

hängen* (to hang)

strong, *formed with* haben

PRESENT

ich	**hänge**
du	**hängst**
er/sie/es	**hängt**
wir	**hängen**
ihr	**hängt**
sie/Sie	**hängen**

PRESENT SUBJUNCTIVE

ich	**hänge**
du	**hängest**
er/sie/es	**hänge**
wir	**hängen**
ihr	**hänget**
sie/Sie	**hängen**

PERFECT

ich	**habe gehangen**
du	**hast gehangen**
er/sie/es	**hat gehangen**
wir	**haben gehangen**
ihr	**habt gehangen**
sie/Sie	**haben gehangen**

IMPERFECT

ich	**hing**
du	**hingst**
er/sie/es	**hing**
wir	**hingen**
ihr	**hingt**
sie/Sie	**hingen**

PRESENT PARTICIPLE

hängend

PAST PARTICIPLE

gehangen

Conjugated as a weak verb when it has a direct object.

EXAMPLE PHRASES

Er **hängt** an seinem Beruf. He loves his job.

Sie sagt, sie **hänge** sehr an ihm. She says she's very attached to him.

Sie **hat** schon immer an ihrem Vater **gehangen**. She has always been attached to her father.

Das Bild **hing** an der Wand. The picture was hanging on the wall.

ich = I du = you er = he/it sie = she/it es = it/he/she wir = we ihr = you sie = they Sie = you (polite)

hängen

FUTURE

ich	**werde hängen**
du	**wirst hängen**
er/sie/es	**wird hängen**
wir	**werden hängen**
ihr	**werdet hängen**
sie/Sie	**werden hängen**

CONDITIONAL

ich	**würde hängen**
du	**würdest hängen**
er/sie/es	**würde hängen**
wir	**würden hängen**
ihr	**würdet hängen**
sie/Sie	**würden hängen**

PLUPERFECT

ich	**hatte gehangen**
du	**hattest gehangen**
er/sie/es	**hatte gehangen**
wir	**hatten gehangen**
ihr	**hattet gehangen**
sie/Sie	**hatten gehangen**

PLUPERFECT SUBJUNCTIVE

ich	**hätte gehangen**
du	**hättest gehangen**
er/sie/es	**hätte gehangen**
wir	**hätten gehangen**
ihr	**hättet gehange**
sie/Sie	**hätten gehangen**

IMPERATIVE

häng(e)!/hängen wir!/hängt!/hängen Sie!

EXAMPLE PHRASES

Wir **werden** die Wäsche auf die Leine **hängen**. We'll hang the washing on the line.

Daran **würde** viel Arbeit **hängen**. A lot of work would be involved in it.

Ihre Blicke **hatten** an ihm **gehangen**. Her eyes had been fixed on him.

Wenn das Bild dort **gehangen hätte**, hätte ich es gesehen. If the picture had been hanging there, I would have seen it.

ich = I du = you er = he/it sie = she/it es = it/he/she wir = we ihr = you sie = they Sie = you (*polite*)

heben (to lift)

strong, *formed with* haben

PRESENT

ich	**hebe**
du	**hebst**
er/sie/es	**hebt**
wir	**heben**
ihr	**hebt**
sie/Sie	**heben**

PRESENT SUBJUNCTIVE

ich	**hebe**
du	**hebest**
er/sie/es	**hebe**
wir	**heben**
ihr	**hebet**
sie/Sie	**heben**

PERFECT

ich	**habe gehoben**
du	**hast gehoben**
er/sie/es	**hat gehoben**
wir	**haben gehoben**
ihr	**habt gehoben**
sie/Sie	**haben gehoben**

IMPERFECT

ich	**hob**
du	**hobst**
er/sie/es	**hob**
wir	**hoben**
ihr	**hobt**
sie/Sie	**hoben**

PRESENT PARTICIPLE

hebend

PAST PARTICIPLE

gehoben

EXAMPLE PHRASES

Ich **hebe** die Hand. I raise my hand.

Sie sagt, das **hebe** ihre Stimmung. She says it cheers her up.

Wir **haben** diesen Schatz zusammen **gehoben**. We raised the treasure together.

Er **hob** das Kind auf die Mauer. He lifted the child onto the wall.

---

ich = I **du** = you **er** = he/it **sie** = she/it **es** = it/he/she **wir** = we **ihr** = you **sie** = they **Sie** = you (*polite*)

heben

FUTURE

ich	**werde heben**
du	**wirst heben**
er/sie/es	**wird heben**
wir	**werden heben**
ihr	**werdet heben**
sie/Sie	**werden heben**

CONDITIONAL

ich	**würde heben**
du	**würdest heben**
er/sie/es	**würde heben**
wir	**würden heben**
ihr	**würdet heben**
sie/Sie	**würden heben**

PLUPERFECT

ich	**hatte gehoben**
du	**hattest gehoben**
er/sie/es	**hatte gehoben**
wir	**hatten gehoben**
ihr	**hattet gehoben**
sie/Sie	**hatten gehoben**

PLUPERFECT SUBJUNCTIVE

ich	**hätte gehoben**
du	**hättest gehoben**
er/sie/es	**hätte gehoben**
wir	**hätten gehoben**
ihr	**hättet gehoben**
sie/Sie	**hätten gehoben**

IMPERATIVE

heb(e)!/heben wir!/hebt!/heben Sie!

EXAMPLE PHRASES

Wirst du endlich die Füße **heben**? Will you pick up your feet?

Das **würde** meinen Mut **heben**. It would boost my morale.

Er **hatte** den Ball ins Tor **gehoben**. He had lobbed the ball into the goal.

Das **hätte** unseren Wohlstand **gehoben**. It would have improved our prosperity.

ich = I **du** = you **er** = he/it **sie** = she/it **es** = it/he/she **wir** = we **ihr** = you **sie** = they **Sie** = you (polite)

heizen (to heat)

weak, *formed with* haben

PRESENT

ich	**heize**
du	**heizt**
er/sie/es	**heizt**
wir	**heizen**
ihr	**heizt**
sie/Sie	**heizen**

PRESENT SUBJUNCTIVE

ich	**heize**
du	**heizest**
er/sie/es	**heize**
wir	**heizen**
ihr	**heizet**
sie/Sie	**heizen**

PERFECT

ich	**habe geheizt**
du	**hast geheizt**
er/sie/es	**hat geheizt**
wir	**haben geheizt**
ihr	**habt geheizt**
sie/Sie	**haben geheizt**

IMPERFECT

ich	**heizte**
du	**heiztest**
er/sie/es	**heizte**
wir	**heizten**
ihr	**heiztet**
sie/Sie	**heizten**

PRESENT PARTICIPLE

heizend

PAST PARTICIPLE

geheizt

EXAMPLE PHRASES

Der Ofen **heizt** gut. The stove gives off a good heat.

Er sagt, er **heize** am liebsten mit Strom. He says he prefers electric heating.

Wir **haben** mit Holz geheizt. We used wood for heating.

Das Zimmer **heizte** sich nur schlecht. The room was hard to heat.

---

ich = I **du** = you **er** = he/it **sie** = she/it **es** = it/he/she **wir** = we **ihr** = you **sie** = they **Sie** = you (*polite*)

heizen

FUTURE

ich	**werde heizen**
du	**wirst heizen**
er/sie/es	**wird heizen**
wir	**werden heizen**
ihr	**werdet heizen**
sie/Sie	**werden heizen**

CONDITIONAL

ich	**würde heizen**
du	**würdest heizen**
er/sie/es	**würde heizen**
wir	**würden heizen**
ihr	**würdet heizen**
sie/Sie	**würden heizen**

PLUPERFECT

ich	**hatte geheizt**
du	**hattest geheizt**
er/sie/es	**hatte geheizt**
wir	**hatten geheizt**
ihr	**hattet geheizt**
sie/Sie	**hatten geheizt**

PLUPERFECT SUBJUNCTIVE

ich	**hätte geheizt**
du	**hättest geheizt**
er/sie/es	**hätte geheizt**
wir	**hätten geheizt**
ihr	**hättet geheizt**
sie/Sie	**hätten geheizt**

IMPERATIVE

heiz(e)!/heizen wir!/heizt!/heizen Sie!

EXAMPLE PHRASES

Ab Oktober **werden** wir **heizen**. We'll put the heating on in October.

An Ihrer Stelle **würde** ich das Haus besser **heizen**. If I were you, I would heat the house better.

Er **hatte** den Backofen **geheizt**. He had heated the oven.

Ein Gasofen **hätte** den Raum besser **geheizt**. A gas fire would have heated the room better.

ich = I du = you er = he/it sie = she/it es = it/he/she wir = we ihr = you sie = they Sie = you (*polite*)

helfen (to help)

strong, + dative, *formed with* **haben**

PRESENT

ich	**helfe**
du	**hilfst**
er/sie/es	**hilft**
wir	**helfen**
ihr	**helft**
sie/Sie	**helfen**

PRESENT SUBJUNCTIVE

ich	**helfe**
du	**helfest**
er/sie/es	**helfe**
wir	**helfen**
ihr	**helfet**
sie/Sie	**helfen**

PERFECT

ich	**habe geholfen**
du	**hast geholfen**
er/sie/es	**hat geholfen**
wir	**haben geholfen**
ihr	**habt geholfen**
sie/Sie	**haben geholfen**

IMPERFECT

ich	**half**
du	**halfst**
er/sie/es	**half**
wir	**halfen**
ihr	**halft**
sie/Sie	**halfen**

PRESENT PARTICIPLE

helfend

PAST PARTICIPLE

geholfen

EXAMPLE PHRASES

Diese Arznei **hilft** gegen Kopfschmerzen. This medicine is good for headaches.

Sie sagt, sie **helfe** gern anderen. She says she likes to help others.

Er **hat** mir dabei **geholfen**. He helped me with it.

Sein Vorschlag **half** mir wenig. His suggestion was not much help to me.

---

ich = I **du** = you **er** = he/it **sie** = she/it **es** = it/he/she **wir** = we **ihr** = you **sie** = they **Sie** = you (*polite*)

helfen

FUTURE

ich	**werde helfen**
du	**wirst helfen**
er/sie/es	**wird helfen**
wir	**werden helfen**
ihr	**werdet helfen**
sie/Sie	**werden helfen**

CONDITIONAL

ich	**würde helfen**
du	**würdest helfen**
er/sie/es	**würde helfen**
wir	**würden helfen**
ihr	**würdet helfen**
sie/Sie	**würden helfen**

PLUPERFECT

ich	**hatte geholfen**
du	**hattest geholfen**
er/sie/es	**hatte geholfen**
wir	**hatten geholfen**
ihr	**hattet geholfen**
sie/Sie	**hatten geholfen**

PLUPERFECT SUBJUNCTIVE

ich	**hätte geholfen**
du	**hättest geholfen**
er/sie/es	**hätte geholfen**
wir	**hätten geholfen**
ihr	**hättet geholfen**
sie/Sie	**hätten geholfen**

IMPERATIVE

hilf!/helfen wir!/helft!/helfen Sie!

EXAMPLE PHRASES

Er **wird** mir **helfen**, den Aufsatz zu schreiben. He will help me write the essay.

Ich weiß, das Sie mir gern **helfen würden**. I know you would like to help me.

Sie **hatte** mir aus einer schwierigen Lage **geholfen**. She had helped me out of a difficult situation.

Das Geld **hätte** ihm auch nicht **geholfen**. The money wouldn't have helped him either.

ich = I **du** = you **er** = he/it **sie** = she/it **es** = it/he/she **wir** = we **ihr** = you **sie** = they **Sie** = you (*polite*)

holen (to fetch)

weak, *formed with* haben

PRESENT

ich	hole
du	holst
er/sie/es	holt
wir	holen
ihr	holt
sie/Sie	holen

PRESENT SUBJUNCTIVE

ich	hole
du	holest
er/sie/es	hole
wir	holen
ihr	holet
sie/Sie	holen

PERFECT

ich	habe geholt
du	hast geholt
er/sie/es	hat geholt
wir	haben geholt
ihr	habt geholt
sie/Sie	haben geholt

IMPERFECT

ich	holte
du	holtest
er/sie/es	holte
wir	holten
ihr	holtet
sie/Sie	holten

PRESENT PARTICIPLE

holend

PAST PARTICIPLE

geholt

EXAMPLE PHRASES

Er **holt** jeden Tag frische Milch vom Supermarkt. **He gets fresh milk from the supermarket every day.**

Er sagt, er **hole** gleich die Polizei. **He says he was about to call the police.**

Ich **habe** mir eine Erkältung **geholt**. **I caught a cold.**

Ich **holte** ihn ans Telefon. **I got him to come to the phone.**

ich = I du = you er = he/it sie = she/it es = it/he/she wir = we ihr = you sie = they Sie = you *(polite)*

holen

FUTURE

ich	**werde holen**
du	**wirst holen**
er/sie/es	**wird holen**
wir	**werden holen**
ihr	**werdet holen**
sie/Sie	**werden holen**

CONDITIONAL

ich	**würde holen**
du	**würdest holen**
er/sie/es	**würde holen**
wir	**würden holen**
ihr	**würdet holen**
sie/Sie	**würden holen**

PLUPERFECT

ich	**hatte geholt**
du	**hattest geholt**
er/sie/es	**hatte geholt**
wir	**hatten geholt**
ihr	**hattet geholt**
sie/Sie	**hatten geholt**

PLUPERFECT SUBJUNCTIVE

ich	**hätte geholt**
du	**hättest geholt**
er/sie/es	**hätte geholt**
wir	**hätten geholt**
ihr	**hättet geholt**
sie/Sie	**hätten gehol**

IMPERATIVE

hol(e)!/holen wir!/holt!/holen Sie!

EXAMPLE PHRASES

Du **wirst** dir da draußen noch den Tod **holen**. You'll end up catching your death out there!

Ich **würde** mir gern die neue CD **holen**. I'd like to go and get the new CD.

Er **hatte** ihn aus dem Bett **geholt**. He had got him out of bed.

Wenn ich nicht gekommen wäre, **hätte** sie Hilfe **geholt**. If I hadn't come she would have called for help.

ich = I **du** = you **er** = he/it **sie** = she/it **es** = it/he/she **wir** = we **ihr** = you **sie** = they **Sie** = you (*polite*)

kennen (to know) *(be acquainted with)*   mixed, *formed with* haben

PRESENT

ich	**kenne**
du	**kennst**
er/sie/es	**kennt**
wir	**kennen**
ihr	**kennt**
sie/Sie	**kennen**

PRESENT SUBJUNCTIVE

ich	**kenne**
du	**kennest**
er/sie/es	**kenne**
wir	**kennen**
ihr	**kennet**
sie/Sie	**kennen**

PERFECT

ich	**habe gekannt**
du	**hast gekannt**
er/sie/es	**hat gekannt**
wir	**haben gekannt**
ihr	**habt gekannt**
sie/Sie	**haben gekannt**

IMPERFECT

ich	**kannte**
du	**kanntest**
er/sie/es	**kannte**
wir	**kannten**
ihr	**kanntet**
sie/Sie	**kannten**

PRESENT PARTICIPLE

kennend

PAST PARTICIPLE

gekannt

EXAMPLE PHRASES

Ich **kenne** ihn nicht. I don't know him.

Er sagt, er **kenne** diese Sängerin nicht. He says he doesn't know this singer.

Er **hat** kein Erbarmen **gekannt**. He knew no mercy.

Kanntest du mich noch? Did you remember me?

ich = I du = you er = he/it sie = she/it es = it/he/she wir = we ihr = you sie = they Sie = you *(polite)*

kennen

FUTURE

ich	**werde kennen**
du	**wirst kennen**
er/sie/es	**wird kennen**
wir	**werden kennen**
ihr	**werdet kennen**
sie/Sie	**werden kennen**

CONDITIONAL

ich	**würde kennen**
du	**würdest kennen**
er/sie/es	**würde kennen**
wir	**würden kennen**
ihr	**würdet kennen**
sie/Sie	**würden kennen**

PLUPERFECT

ich	**hatte gekannt**
du	**hattest gekannt**
er/sie/es	**hatte gekannt**
wir	**hatten gekannt**
ihr	**hattet gekannt**
sie/Sie	**hatten gekannt**

PLUPERFECT SUBJUNCTIVE

ich	**hätte gekannt**
du	**hättest gekannt**
er/sie/es	**hätte gekannt**
wir	**hätten gekannt**
ihr	**hättet gekannt**
sie/Sie	**hätten gekannt**

IMPERATIVE

kenn(e)!/kennen wir!/kennt!/kennen Sie!

EXAMPLE PHRASES

Wenn du älter bist, **wirst** du den Unterschied **kennen**. When you're older you'll know the difference.

Er sprach von ihr, als **würde** er sie **kennen**. He spoke of her as if he knew her.

Damals **hatte** ich ihn noch nicht **gekannt**. I hadn't known him then.

Ich **hätte** mich vor Wut nicht mehr **gekannt**. I would have been beside myself with anger.

ich = I **du** = you **er** = he/it **sie** = she/it **es** = it/he/she **wir** = we **ihr** = you **sie** = they **Sie** = you (*polite*)

klingen (to sound)

strong, *formed with* haben

PRESENT

ich	klinge
du	klingst
er/sie/es	klingt
wir	klingen
ihr	klingt
sie/Sie	klingen

PRESENT SUBJUNCTIVE

ich	klinge
du	klingest
er/sie/es	klinge
wir	klingen
ihr	klinget
sie/Sie	klingen

PERFECT

ich	habe geklungen
du	hast geklungen
er/sie/es	hat geklungen
wir	haben geklungen
ihr	habt geklungen
sie/Sie	haben geklungen

IMPERFECT

ich	klang
du	klangst
er/sie/es	klang
wir	klangen
ihr	klangt
sie/Sie	klangen

PRESENT PARTICIPLE

klingend geklungen

PAST PARTICIPLE

EXAMPLE PHRASES

Du **klingst** deprimiert. You sound depressed.

Sie meinte, das **klinge** nach Neid. She thinks this sounds like envy.

Die Glocke **hat** hell **geklungen**. The bell had a clear ring.

Das Klavier **klang** verstimmt. The piano sounded out of tune.

---

ich = I du = you er = he/it sie = she/it es = it/he/she wir = we ihr = you sie = they Sie = you (polite)

klingen

FUTURE

ich	**werde klingen**
du	**wirst klingen**
er/sie/es	**wird klingen**
wir	**werden klingen**
ihr	**werdet klingen**
sie/Sie	**werden klingen**

CONDITIONAL

ich	**würde klingen**
du	**würdest klingen**
er/sie/es	**würde klingen**
wir	**würden klingen**
ihr	**würdet klingen**
sie/Sie	**würden klingen**

PLUPERFECT

ich	**hatte geklungen**
du	**hattest geklungen**
er/sie/es	**hatte geklungen**
wir	**hatten geklungen**
ihr	**hattet geklungen**
sie/Sie	**hatten geklungen**

PLUPERFECT SUBJUNCTIVE

ich	**hätte geklungen**
du	**hättest geklungen**
er/sie/es	**hätte geklungen**
wir	**hätten geklungen**
ihr	**hättet geklungen**
sie/Sie	**hätten geklungen**

IMPERATIVE

kling(e)!/klingen wir!/klingt!/klingen Sie!

EXAMPLE PHRASES

Morgen **werden** bei uns die Gläser **klingen**. Tomorrow we'll hear the sound
 of clinking glasses.

Das **würde** nicht richtig **klingen**. It wouldn't sound right.

Es **hatte** mir wie Musik in den Ohren **geklungen**. It had been music to my ears.

Das **hätte** so **geklungen**, als ob ich ihn beleidigen wollte. It would have
 sounded as if I wanted to insult him.

ich = I **du** = you **er** = he/it **sie** = she/it **es** = it/he/she **wir** = we **ihr** = you **sie** = they **Sie** = you (*polite*)

kommen (to come)

strong, *formed with* **sein**

PRESENT

ich	**komme**
du	**kommst**
er/sie/es	**kommt**
wir	**kommen**
ihr	**kommt**
sie/Sie	**kommen**

PRESENT SUBJUNCTIVE

ich	**komme**
du	**kommest**
er/sie/es	**komme**
wir	**kommen**
ihr	**kommet**
sie/Sie	**kommen**

PERFECT

ich	**bin gekommen**
du	**bist gekommen**
er/sie/es	**ist gekommen**
wir	**sind gekommen**
ihr	**seid gekommen**
sie/Sie	**sind gekommen**

IMPERFECT

ich	**kam**
du	**kamst**
er/sie/es	**kam**
wir	**kamen**
ihr	**kamt**
sie/Sie	**kamen**

PRESENT PARTICIPLE

kommend

PAST PARTICIPLE

gekommen

EXAMPLE PHRASES

Ich **komme** zu deiner Party. I'm coming to your party.

Sie meint, das **komme** nicht in Frage. She thinks it's out of the question.

Aus welcher Richtung **bist** du **gekommen**? Which direction did you come from?

Er **kam** die Straße entlang. He was coming along the street.

---

ich = I **du** = you **er** = he/it **sie** = she/it **es** = it/he/she **wir** = we **ihr** = you **sie** = they **Sie** = you (*polite*)

kommen

FUTURE

ich	**werde kommen**
du	**wirst kommen**
er/sie/es	**wird kommen**
wir	**werden kommen**
ihr	**werdet kommen**
sie/Sie	**werden kommen**

CONDITIONAL

ich	**würde kommen**
du	**würdest kommen**
er/sie/es	**würde kommen**
wir	**würden kommen**
ihr	**würdet kommen**
sie/Sie	**würden kommen**

PLUPERFECT

ich	**war gekommen**
du	**warst gekommen**
er/sie/es	**war gekommen**
wir	**waren gekommen**
ihr	**wart gekommen**
sie/Sie	**waren gekommen**

PLUPERFECT SUBJUNCTIVE

ich	**wäre gekommen**
du	**wär(e)st gekommen**
er/sie/es	**wäre gekommen**
wir	**wären gekommen**
ihr	**wär(e)t gekommen**
sie/Sie	**wären gekommen**

IMPERATIVE

komm(e)!/kommen wir!/kommt!/kommen Sie!

EXAMPLE PHRASES

Gleich **wird** die Grenze **kommen**. We'll soon be at the border.

Ich **würde** lieber etwas später **kommen**. I'd prefer to come a bit later.

Sie **war** zuerst an die Reihe **gekommen**. It had been her turn first.

Er **wäre** fast ums Leben **gekommen**. He would almost have lost his life.

---

ich = I **du** = you **er** = he/it **sie** = she/it **es** = it/he/she **wir** = we **ihr** = you **sie** = they **Sie** = you (polite)

können (to be able to)

modal, *formed with* haben

PRESENT

ich	**kann**
du	**kannst**
er/sie/es	**kann**
wir	**können**
ihr	**könnt**
sie/Sie	**können**

PRESENT SUBJUNCTIVE

ich	**könne**
du	**könnest**
er/sie/es	**könne**
wir	**können**
ihr	**könnet**
sie/Sie	**können**

PERFECT

ich	**habe gekonnt/können**
du	**hast gekonnt/können**
er/sie/es	**hat gekonnt/können**
wir	**haben gekonnt/können**
ihr	**habt gekonnt/können**
sie/Sie	**haben gekonnt/können**

IMPERFECT

ich	**konnte**
du	**konntest**
er/sie/es	**konnte**
wir	**konnten**
ihr	**konntet**
sie/Sie	**konnten**

PRESENT PARTICIPLE

könnend

PAST PARTICIPLE

gekonnt/können°

°This form is used when combined with another infinitive.

EXAMPLE PHRASES

Er **kann** gut schwimmen. He can swim well.

Sie sagt, ich **könne** jetzt noch nicht gehen. She says I can't leave yet.

Damals **habe** ich noch kein Deutsch **gekonnt**. I couldn't speak German then.

Sie **konnte** kein Wort Englisch. She couldn't speak a word of English.

---

ich = I du = you er = he/it sie = she/it es = it/he/she wir = we ihr = you sie = they Sie = you (polite)

können

FUTURE

ich	**werde können**
du	**wirst können**
er/sie/es	**wird können**
wir	**werden können**
ihr	**werdet können**
sie/Sie	**werden können**

CONDITIONAL

ich	**würde können**
du	**würdest können**
er/sie/es	**würde können**
wir	**würden können**
ihr	**würdet können**
sie/Sie	**würden können**

PLUPERFECT

ich	**hatte gekonnt/können**
du	**hattest gekonnt/können**
er/sie/es	**hatte gekonnt/können**
wir	**hatten gekonnt/können**
ihr	**hattet gekonnt/können**
sie/Sie	**hatten gekonnt/können**

PLUPERFECT SUBJUNCTIVE

ich	**hätte gekonnt/können**
du	**hättest gekonnt/können**
er/sie/es	**hätte gekonnt/können**
wir	**hätten gekonnt/können**
ihr	**hättet gekonnt/können**
sie/Sie	**hätten gekonnt/können**

EXAMPLE PHRASES

Morgen **werde** ich nicht kommen **können**. I won't be able to come tomorrow.

Ohne dich **würde** ich das nicht **können**. I wouldn't be able to do it without you.

Ich **habe** diese Übung nicht **gekonnt**. I wasn't able to do this exercise.

Das **hätte** ich dir gleich sagen **können**. I could have told you that straight away.

ich = I **du** = you **er** = he/it **sie** = she/it **es** = it/he/she **wir** = we **ihr** = you **sie** = they **Sie** = you (polite)

laden (to load; to invite)

strong, *formed with* haben

PRESENT

ich	**lade**
du	**lädst**
er/sie/es	**lädt**
wir	**laden**
ihr	**ladet**
sie/Sie	**laden**

PRESENT SUBJUNCTIVE

ich	**lade**
du	**ladest**
er/sie/es	**lade**
wir	**laden**
ihr	**ladet**
sie/Sie	**laden**

PERFECT

ich	**habe geladen**
du	**hast geladen**
er/sie/es	**hat geladen**
wir	**haben geladen**
ihr	**habt geladen**
sie/Sie	**haben geladen**

IMPERFECT

ich	**lud**
du	**lud(e)st**
er/sie/es	**lud**
wir	**luden**
ihr	**ludet**
sie/Sie	**luden**

PRESENT PARTICIPLE

ladend

PAST PARTICIPLE

geladen

EXAMPLE PHRASES

Der Computer **lädt** das Programm. The computer is loading the program.

Er sagt, er **lade** gerade den Lastwagen. He says he is loading the truck.

Das Schiff **hat** Autos **geladen**. The ship has a cargo of cars.

Er **lud** die Waffe. He loaded the weapon.

laden

FUTURE

ich	**werde laden**
du	**wirst laden**
er/sie/es	**wird laden**
wir	**werden laden**
ihr	**werdet laden**
sie/Sie	**werden laden**

CONDITIONAL

ich	**würde laden**
du	**würdest laden**
er/sie/es	**würde laden**
wir	**würden laden**
ihr	**würdet laden**
sie/Sie	**würden laden**

PLUPERFECT

ich	**hatte geladen**
du	**hattest geladen**
er/sie/es	**hatte geladen**
wir	**hatten geladen**
ihr	**hattet geladen**
sie/Sie	**hatten geladen**

PLUPERFECT SUBJUNCTIVE

ich	**hätte geladen**
du	**hättest geladen**
er/sie/es	**hätte geladen**
wir	**hätten geladen**
ihr	**hättet geladen**
sie/Sie	**hätten geladen**

IMPERATIVE

lad(e)!/laden wir!/ladet!/laden Sie!

EXAMPLE PHRASES

Dieses Problem **werde** ich nicht auf mich **laden**. I won't take that problem on.

Damit **würdest** du Schuld auf dich **laden**. You would take on a burden of guilt.

Wir **hatten** das Gepäck ins Auto **geladen**. We had loaded the luggage into the car.

Ich **hätte** gern noch mehr Gäste **geladen**. I would have liked to invite more guests.

ich = I **du** = you **er** = he/it **sie** = she/it **es** = it/he/she **wir** = we **ihr** = you **sie** = they **Sie** = you (*polite*)

lassen (to leave; to allow)

strong, *formed with* haben

PRESENT

ich	lasse
du	lässt
er/sie/es	lässt
wir	lassen
ihr	lasst
sie/Sie	lassen

PRESENT SUBJUNCTIVE

ich	lasse
du	lassest
er/sie/es	lasse
wir	lassen
ihr	lasset
sie/Sie	lassen

PERFECT

ich	habe gelassen
du	hast gelassen
er/sie/es	hat gelassen
wir	haben gelassen
ihr	habt gelassen
sie/Sie	haben gelassen

IMPERFECT

ich	ließ
du	ließest
er/sie/es	ließ
wir	ließen
ihr	ließt
sie/Sie	ließen

PRESENT PARTICIPLE

lassend

PAST PARTICIPLE

gelassen/lassen

EXAMPLE PHRASES

Ich **lasse** den Hund nicht auf das Sofa. I won't let the dog on the sofa.

Er sagt, er **lasse** sich das nicht bieten. He says he won't stand for it.

Sie **haben** ihn allein im Auto **gelassen**. They left him alone in the car.

Sie **ließ** uns warten. She kept us waiting.

---

ich = I **du** = you **er** = he/it **sie** = she/it **es** = it/he/she **wir** = we **ihr** = you **sie** = they **Sie** = you (polite)

lassen

FUTURE

ich	**werde lasssen**
du	**wirst lassen**
er/sie/es	**wird lassen**
wir	**werden lassen**
ihr	**werdet lassen**
sie/Sie	**werden lassen**

CONDITIONAL

ich	**würde lassen**
du	**würdest lassen**
er/sie/es	**würde lassen**
wir	**würden lassen**
ihr	**würdet lassen**
sie/Sie	**würden lassen**

PLUPERFECT

ich	**hatte gelassen**
du	**hattest gelassen**
er/sie/es	**hatte gelassen**
wir	**hatten gelassen**
ihr	**hattet gelassen**
sie/Sie	**hatten gelassen**

PLUPERFECT SUBJUNCTIVE

ich	**hätte gelassen**
du	**hättest gelassen**
er/sie/es	**hätte gelassen**
wir	**hätten gelassen**
ihr	**hättet gelassen**
sie/Sie	**hätten gelassen**

IMPERATIVE

lass!/lassen wir!/lasst!/lassen Sie!

EXAMPLE PHRASES

Wir **werden** uns dazu nicht zwingen **lassen**. We won't be forced into it.

Ich **würde** das Baby nie allein **lassen**. I would never leave the baby alone.

Sie **hatte** mich nicht fernsehen **lassen**. She hadn't allowed me to watch TV.

Ich **hätte** die Tasche besser im Auto **gelassen**. It would have been better if I had left the bag in the car.

ich = I du = you er = he/it sie = she/it es = it/he/she wir = we ihr = you sie = they Sie = you (*polite*)

laufen (to run)

strong, *formed with* **sein**

PRESENT

ich	laufe
du	läufst
er/sie/es	läuft
wir	laufen
ihr	lauft
sie/Sie	laufen

PRESENT SUBJUNCTIVE

ich	laufe
du	laufest
er/sie/es	laufe
wir	laufen
ihr	laufet
sie/Sie	laufen

PERFECT

ich	bin gelaufen
du	bist gelaufen
er/sie/es	ist gelaufen
wir	sind gelaufen
ihr	seid gelaufen
sie/Sie	sind gelaufen

IMPERFECT

ich	lief
du	liefst
er/sie/es	lief
wir	liefen
ihr	lieft
sie/Sie	liefen

PRESENT PARTICIPLE
laufend

PAST PARTICIPLE
gelaufen

EXAMPLE PHRASES

Sie **läuft** ständig zur Polizei. She's always running to the police.

Er sagt, ihm **laufe** die Nase. He says he's got a runny nose.

Das Schiff **ist** auf Grund **gelaufen**. The ship ran aground.

Er **lief** so schnell er konnte. He ran as fast as he could.

ich = I **du** = you **er** = he/it **sie** = she/it **es** = it/he/she **wir** = we **ihr** = you **sie** = they **Sie** = you (polite)

laufen

FUTURE

ich	**werde laufen**
du	**wirst laufen**
er/sie/es	**wird laufen**
wir	**werden laufen**
ihr	**werdet laufen**
sie/Sie	**werden laufen**

CONDITIONAL

ich	**würde laufen**
du	**würdest laufen**
er/sie/es	**würde laufen**
wir	**würden laufen**
ihr	**würdet laufen**
sie/Sie	**würden laufen**

PLUPERFECT

ich	**war gelaufen**
du	**warst gelaufen**
er/sie/es	**war gelaufen**
wir	**waren gelaufen**
ihr	**wart gelaufen**
sie/Sie	**waren gelaufen**

PLUPERFECT SUBJUNCTIVE

ich	**wäre gelaufen**
du	**wär(e)st gelaufen**
er/sie/es	**wäre gelaufen**
wir	**wären gelaufen**
ihr	**wär(e)t gelaufen**
sie/Sie	**wären gelaufen**

IMPERATIVE

lauf(e)!/laufen wir!/lauft!/laufen Sie!

EXAMPLE PHRASES

Wird er einen neuen Rekord **laufen**? Will he run a new record time?

Mit guter Planung **würde** alles besser **laufen**. With good planning everything would improve.

Ich **war** noch nie 10.000 Meter **gelaufen**. I had never run 10,000 metres.

Er **wäre** fast am schnellsten **gelaufen**. He would almost have been the fastest runner.

ich = I **du** = you **er** = he/it **sie** = she/it **es** = it/he/she **wir** = we **ihr** = you **sie** = they **Sie** = you (*polite*)

leiden (to suffer)

strong, *formed with* haben

PRESENT

ich	leide
du	leidest
er/sie/es	leidet
wir	leiden
ihr	leidet
sie/Sie	leiden

PRESENT SUBJUNCTIVE

ich	leide
du	leidest
er/sie/es	leide
wir	leiden
ihr	leidet
sie/Sie	leiden

PERFECT

ich	habe gelitten
du	hast gelitten
er/sie/es	hat gelitten
wir	haben gelitten
ihr	habt gelitten
sie/Sie	haben gelitten

IMPERFECT

ich	litt
du	litt(e)st
er/sie/es	litt
wir	litten
ihr	littet
sie/Sie	litten

PRESENT PARTICIPLE

leidend

PAST PARTICIPLE

gelitten

EXAMPLE PHRASES

Wir **leiden** sehr unter der Hitze. **We're suffering badly from the heat.**

Sie sagt, sie **leide** an Rückenschmerzen. **She says she's suffering from backache.**

Wir **haben** unter dieser Regierung **gelitten**. **We have suffered under his government.**

Sie **litt** an Asthma. **She suffered from asthma.**

---

ich = I **du** = you **er** = he/it **sie** = she/it **es** = it/he/she **wir** = we **ihr** = you **sie** = they **Sie** = you (polite)

leiden

FUTURE

ich	**werde leiden**
du	**wirst leiden**
er/sie/es	**wird leiden**
wir	**werden leiden**
ihr	**werdet leiden**
sie/Sie	**werden leiden**

CONDITIONAL

ich	**würde leiden**
du	**würdest leiden**
er/sie/es	**würde leiden**
wir	**würden leiden**
ihr	**würdet leiden**
sie/Sie	**würden leiden**

PLUPERFECT

ich	**hatte gelitten**
du	**hattest gelitten**
er/sie/es	**hatte gelitten**
wir	**hatten gelitten**
ihr	**hattet gelitten**
sie/Sie	**hatten gelitten**

PLUPERFECT SUBJUNCTIVE

ich	**hätte gelitten**
du	**hättest gelitten**
er/sie/es	**hätte gelitten**
wir	**hätten gelitten**
ihr	**hättet gelitten**
sie/Sie	**hätten gelitten**

IMPERATIVE
leid(e)!/leiden wir!/leidet!/leiden Sie!

EXAMPLE PHRASES

Darunter **werden** wir noch lange **leiden**. We'll be suffering the consequences for a long time.

Ohne dich **würde** ich unter Einsamkeit **leiden**. I would be lonely without you.

Er **hatte** seit Jahren an dieser Krankheit **gelitten**. He had been suffering from this illness for years.

Ohne seine Hilfe **hätte** ich Hunger **gelitten**. Without his help I would have suffered from hunger.

ich = I **du** = you **er** = he/it **sie** = she/it **es** = it/he/she **wir** = we **ihr** = you **sie** = they **Sie** = you (*polite*)

leihen (to lend)

strong, *formed with* haben

PRESENT

ich	**leihe**
du	**leihst**
er/sie/es	**leiht**
wir	**leihen**
ihr	**leiht**
sie/Sie	**leihen**

PRESENT SUBJUNCTIVE

ich	**leihe**
du	**leihest**
er/sie/es	**leihe**
wir	**leihen**
ihr	**leihet**
sie/Sie	**leihen**

PERFECT

ich	**habe geliehen**
du	**hast geliehen**
er/sie/es	**hat geliehen**
wir	**haben geliehen**
ihr	**habt geliehen**
sie/Sie	**haben geliehen**

IMPERFECT

ich	**lieh**
du	**liehst**
er/sie/es	**lieh**
wir	**liehen**
ihr	**lieht**
sie/Sie	**liehen**

PRESENT PARTICIPLE

leihend

PAST PARTICIPLE

geliehen

EXAMPLE PHRASES

Ich **leihe** ihm mein Auto. I lend him my car.

Er sagt, er **leihe** nie jemandem Geld. He says he never lends money to anyone.

Ich **habe** das Fahrrad von meiner Schwester **geliehen**. I have borrowed my sister's bike.

Ich **lieh** mir ein Auto. I hired a car.

leihen

FUTURE

ich	**werde leihen**
du	**wirst leihen**
er/sie/es	**wird leihen**
wir	**werden leihen**
ihr	**werdet leihen**
sie/Sie	**werden leihen**

CONDITIONAL

ich	**würde leihen**
du	**würdest leihen**
er/sie/es	**würde leihen**
wir	**würden leihen**
ihr	**würdet leihen**
sie/Sie	**würden leihen**

PLUPERFECT

ich	**hatte geliehen**
du	**hattest geliehen**
er/sie/es	**hatte geliehen**
wir	**hatten geliehen**
ihr	**hattet geliehen**
sie/Sie	**hatten geliehen**

PLUPERFECT SUBJUNCTIVE

ich	**hätte geliehen**
du	**hättest geliehen**
er/sie/es	**hätte geliehen**
wir	**hätten geliehen**
ihr	**hättet geliehen**
sie/Sie	**hätten geliehen**

IMPERATIVE

leih(e)!/leihen wir!/leiht!/leihen Sie!

EXAMPLE PHRASES

Ich **werde** dir das Geld **leihen**. I'll lend you the money.

Wenn dein Laptop kaputt ist, **würde** ich dir meinen **leihen**. If your laptop
   is broken I would lend you mine.

Er **hatte** mir 50 Euro **geliehen**. He had lent me 50 euros

Wenn ich ihn gefragt hätte, **hätte** er mir 50 Euro **geliehen**. He would have
   lent me 50 euros if I had asked him.

ich = I **du** = you **er** = he/it **sie** = she/it **es** = it/he/she **wir** = we **ihr** = you **sie** = they **Sie** = you (*polite*)

lesen (to read)

strong, *formed with* haben

PRESENT

ich	lese
du	liest
er/sie/es	liest
wir	lesen
ihr	lest
sie/Sie	lesen

PRESENT SUBJUNCTIVE

ich	lese
du	lesest
er/sie/es	lese
wir	lesen
ihr	leset
sie/Sie	lesen

PERFECT

ich	habe gelesen
du	hast gelesen
er/sie/es	hat gelesen
wir	haben gelesen
ihr	habt gelesen
sie/Sie	haben gelesen

IMPERFECT

ich	las
du	lasest
er/sie/es	las
wir	lasen
ihr	last
sie/Sie	lasen

PRESENT PARTICIPLE

lesend

PAST PARTICIPLE

gelesen

EXAMPLE PHRASES

Dieses Buch **liest** sich gut. This book is a good read.

Er sagt, er **lese** jeden Tag zwei Zeitungen. He says he reads two newspapers every day.

Das **habe** ich in der Zeitung **gelesen**. I read it in the newspaper.

Sie **las** sich in den Schlaf. She read herself to sleep.

ich = I du = you er = he/it sie = she/it es = it/he/she wir = we ihr = you sie = they Sie = you (*polite*)

lesen

FUTURE

ich	**werde lesen**
du	**wirst lesen**
er/sie/es	**wird lesen**
wir	**werden lesen**
ihr	**werdet lesen**
sie/Sie	**werden lesen**

CONDITIONAL

ich	**würde lesen**
du	**würdest lesen**
er/sie/es	**würde lesen**
wir	**würden lesen**
ihr	**würdet lesen**
sie/Sie	**würden lesen**

PLUPERFECT

ich	**hatte gelesen**
du	**hattest gelesen**
er/sie/es	**hatte gelesen**
wir	**hatten gelesen**
ihr	**hattet gelesen**
sie/Sie	**hatten gelesen**

PLUPERFECT SUBJUNCTIVE

ich	**hätte gelesen**
du	**hättest gelesen**
er/sie/es	**hätte gelesen**
wir	**hätten gelesen**
ihr	**hättet gelesen**
sie/Sie	**hätten gelesen**

IMPERATIVE

lies!/lesen wir!/lest!/lesen Sie!

EXAMPLE PHRASES

Morgen **werde** ich Harry Potter **lesen**. I'll read Harry Potter tomorrow.

Wenn ich könnte, **würde** ich jeden Tag ein Buch **lesen**. If I could I'd read
a book every day.

Ich **hatte** den Artikel noch nicht **gelesen**. I hadn't read the article yet.

Wenn ich mehr **gelesen hätte**, wäre ich klüger. If I had read more, I'd be more
intelligent.

ich = I **du** = you **er** = he/it **sie** = she/it **es** = it/he/she **wir** = we **ihr** = you **sie** = they **Sie** = you (polite)

liegen (to lie)

strong, *formed with* **haben**

PRESENT

ich	**liege**
du	**liegst**
er/sie/es	**liegt**
wir	**liegen**
ihr	**liegt**
sie/Sie	**liegen**

PRESENT SUBJUNCTIVE

ich	**liege**
du	**liegest**
er/sie/es	**liege**
wir	**liegen**
ihr	**lieget**
sie/Sie	**liegen**

PERFECT

ich	**habe gelegen**
du	**hast gelegen**
er/sie/es	**hat gelegen**
wir	**haben gelegen**
ihr	**habt gelegen**
sie/Sie	**haben gelegen**

IMPERFECT

ich	**lag**
du	**lagst**
er/sie/es	**lag**
wir	**lagen**
ihr	**lagt**
sie/Sie	**lagen**

PRESENT PARTICIPLE

liegend gelegen

PAST PARTICIPLE

EXAMPLE PHRASES

Köln **liegt** am Rhein. Cologne is on the Rhine.

Er sagt, es **liege** nicht an ihm. He says it isn't because of him.

Es **hat** daran **gelegen**, dass ich krank war. It was because I was ill.

Wir **lagen** den ganzen Tag am Strand. We lay on the beach all day.

ich = I **du** = you **er** = he/it **sie** = she/it **es** = it/he/she **wir** = we **ihr** = you **sie** = they **Sie** = you (*polite*)

liegen

FUTURE

ich	**werde liegen**
du	**wirst liegen**
er/sie/es	**wird liegen**
wir	**werden liegen**
ihr	**werdet liegen**
sie/Sie	**werden liegen**

CONDITIONAL

ich	**würde liegen**
du	**würdest liegen**
er/sie/es	**würde liegen**
wir	**würden liegen**
ihr	**würdet liegen**
sie/Sie	**würden liegen**

PLUPERFECT

ich	**hatte gelegen**
du	**hattest gelegen**
er/sie/es	**hatte gelegen**
wir	**hatten gelegen**
ihr	**hattet gelegen**
sie/Sie	**hatten gelegen**

PLUPERFECT SUBJUNCTIVE

ich	**hätte gelegen**
du	**hättest gelegen**
er/sie/es	**hätte gelegen**
wir	**hätten gelegen**
ihr	**hättet gelegen**
sie/Sie	**hätten gelegen**

IMPERATIVE

lieg(e)!/liegen wir!/liegt!/liegen Sie!

EXAMPLE PHRASES

Das **wird** am Wetter **liegen**. It'll be because of the weather.

Auf diesem Bett **würde** ich nicht gern **liegen**. I wouldn't like to lie on this bed.

Das Schiff **hatte** vor Anker **gelegen**. The ship had been lying at anchor.

Daran **hätte** mir viel **gelegen**. It would have mattered a lot to me.

lügen (to (tell a) lie)

strong, *formed with* **haben**

PRESENT

ich	**lüge**
du	**lügst**
er/sie/es	**lügt**
wir	**lügen**
ihr	**lügt**
sie/Sie	**lügen**

PRESENT SUBJUNCTIVE

ich	**lüge**
du	**lügest**
er/sie/es	**lüge**
wir	**lügen**
ihr	**lüget**
sie/Sie	**lügen**

PERFECT

ich	**habe gelogen**
du	**hast gelogen**
er/sie/es	**hat gelogen**
wir	**haben gelogen**
ihr	**habt gelogen**
sie/Sie	**haben gelogen**

IMPERFECT

ich	**log**
du	**logst**
er/sie/es	**log**
wir	**logen**
ihr	**logt**
sie/Sie	**logen**

PRESENT PARTICIPLE

lügend

PAST PARTICIPLE

gelogen

EXAMPLE PHRASES

Du **lügst**! You're a liar!

Sie behauptet, sie **lüge** nie. She says she never lies.

Er **hat gelogen**! He told a lie!

Er **log** ständig. He was always telling lies.

lügen

FUTURE

ich	**werde lügen**
du	**wirst lügen**
er/sie/es	**wird lügen**
wir	**werden lügen**
ihr	**werdet lügen**
sie/Sie	**werden lügen**

CONDITIONAL

ich	**würde lügen**
du	**würdest lügen**
er/sie/es	**würde lügen**
wir	**würden lügen**
ihr	**würdet lügen**
sie/Sie	**würden lügen**

PLUPERFECT

ich	**hatte gelogen**
du	**hattest gelogen**
er/sie/es	**hatte gelogen**
wir	**hatten gelogen**
ihr	**hattet gelogen**
sie/Sie	**hatten gelogen**

PLUPERFECT SUBJUNCTIVE

ich	**hätte gelogen**
du	**hättest gelogen**
er/sie/es	**hätte gelogen**
wir	**hätten gelogen**
ihr	**hättet gelogen**
sie/Sie	**hätten gelogen**

IMPERATIVE

lüg(e)!/lügen wir!/lügt!/lügen Sie!

EXAMPLE PHRASES

Er **wird** doch wieder nur **lügen**! He'll only tell lies again!

Ich **würde lügen**, wenn ich das sagen würde. I would be lying if I said that.

Ich **hatte** noch nie im Leben **gelogen**. I had never told a lie in my life.

Sie **hätte gelogen**, um ihren Freund zu schützen. She would have lied to protect her boyfriend.

ich = I **du** = you **er** = he/it **sie** = she/it **es** = it/he/she **wir** = we **ihr** = you **sie** = they **Sie** = you (*polite*)

machen (to do *or* to make)   weak, *formed with* haben

PRESENT

ich	**mache**
du	**machst**
er/sie/es	**macht**
wir	**machen**
ihr	**macht**
sie/Sie	**machen**

PRESENT SUBJUNCTIVE

ich	**mache**
du	**machest**
er/sie/es	**mache**
wir	**machen**
ihr	**machet**
sie/Sie	**machen**

PERFECT

ich	**habe gemacht**
du	**hast gemacht**
er/sie/es	**hat gemacht**
wir	**haben gemacht**
ihr	**habt gemacht**
sie/Sie	**haben gemacht**

IMPERFECT

ich	**machte**
du	**machtest**
er/sie/es	**machte**
wir	**machten**
ihr	**machtet**
sie/Sie	**machten**

PRESENT PARTICIPLE

machend

PAST PARTICIPLE

gemacht

EXAMPLE PHRASES

Was **machst** du? What are you doing?

Sie sagt, sie **mache** sich wegen ihm Sorgen. She says she's worried about him.

Ich **habe** die Betten **gemacht**. I made the beds.

Er **machte** es sich im Wohnzimmer bequem. He made himself comfortable in the lounge.

ich = I **du** = you **er** = he/it **sie** = she/it **es** = it/he/she **wir** = we **ihr** = you **sie** = they **Sie** = you (*polite*)

machen

FUTURE

ich	**werde machen**
du	**wirst machen**
er/sie/es	**wird machen**
wir	**werden machen**
ihr	**werdet machen**
sie/Sie	**werden machen**

CONDITIONAL

ich	**würde machen**
du	**würdest machen**
er/sie/es	**würde machen**
wir	**würden machen**
ihr	**würdet machen**
sie/Sie	**würden machen**

PLUPERFECT

ich	**hatte gemacht**
du	**hattest gemacht**
er/sie/es	**hatte gemacht**
wir	**hatten gemacht**
ihr	**hattet gemacht**
sie/Sie	**hatten gemacht**

PLUPERFECT SUBJUNCTIVE

ich	**hätte gemacht**
du	**hättest gemacht**
er/sie/es	**hätte gemacht**
wir	**hätten gemacht**
ihr	**hättet gemacht**
sie/Sie	**hätten gemacht**

IMPERATIVE

mach!/macht!/machen Sie!

EXAMPLE PHRASES

Ich **werde** es morgen **machen**. I'll do it tomorrow.

Ich **würde** es mir nicht so schwer **machen**. I wouldn't make things so difficult for myself.

So etwas **hatte** ich noch nie **gemacht**. I had never done something like that.

Das **hätte** ich an Ihrer Stelle nicht **gemacht**. I wouldn't have done this if I were you.

ich = I **du** = you **er** = he/it **sie** = she/it **es** = it/he/she **wir** = we **ihr** = you **sie** = they **Sie** = you (*polite*)

messen (to measure)

strong, *formed with* haben

PRESENT

ich	messe
du	misst
er/sie/es	misst
wir	messen
ihr	messt
sie/Sie	messen

PRESENT SUBJUNCTIVE

ich	messe
du	messest
er/sie/es	messe
wir	messen
ihr	messet
sie/Sie	messen

PERFECT

ich	habe gemessen
du	hast gemessen
er/sie/es	hat gemessen
wir	haben gemessen
ihr	habt gemessen
sie/Sie	haben gemessen

IMPERFECT

ich	maß
du	maßest
er/sie/es	maß
wir	maßen
ihr	maßt
sie/Sie	maßen

PRESENT PARTICIPLE

messend

PAST PARTICIPLE

gemessen

EXAMPLE PHRASES

Ich **messe** 1,80 Meter. I'm 1 metre 80.

Er sagt, dieses Instrument **messe** die Temperatur. He says this instrument measures the temperature.

Der Arzt **hat** meinen Blutdruck **gemessen**. The doctor took my blood pressure.

Während ich lief, **maß** er die Zeit. He timed me while I ran.

messen

FUTURE

ich	**werde messen**
du	**wirst messen**
er/sie/es	**wird messen**
wir	**werden messen**
ihr	**werdet messen**
sie/Sie	**werden messen**

CONDITIONAL

ich	**würde messen**
du	**würdest messen**
er/sie/es	**würde messen**
wir	**würden messen**
ihr	**würdet messen**
sie/Sie	**würden messen**

PLUPERFECT

ich	**hatte gemessen**
du	**hattest gemessen**
er/sie/es	**hatte gemessen**
wir	**hatten gemessen**
ihr	**hattet gemessen**
sie/Sie	**hatten gemessen**

PLUPERFECT SUBJUNCTIVE

ich	**hätte gemessen**
du	**hättest gemessen**
er/sie/es	**hätte gemessen**
wir	**hätten gemessen**
ihr	**hättet gemessen**
sie/Sie	**hätten gemessen**

IMPERATIVE
miss!/messen wir!/messt!/messen Sie!

EXAMPLE PHRASES

Wir **werden** unsere Kräfte mit ihnen **messen**. We'll measure our strengths against theirs.

Wie **würdest** du die Entfernung **messen**? How would you gauge the distance?

Er **hatte** ihn mit den Blicken **gemessen**. He had looked him up and down.

Ich dachte, jemand **hätte** die Zeit **gemessen**. I thought somebody had timed it.

---

ich = I **du** = you **er** = he/it **sie** = she/it **es** = it/he/she **wir** = we **ihr** = you **sie** = they **Sie** = you (*polite*)

misstrauen (to mistrust)

weak, inseparable, formed with haben

PRESENT

ich	misstraue
du	misstraust
er/sie/es	misstraut
wir	misstrauen
ihr	misstraut
sie/Sie	misstrauen

PRESENT SUBJUNCTIVE

ich	misstraue
du	misstrauest
er/sie/es	misstraue
wir	misstrauen
ihr	misstrauet
sie/Sie	misstrauen

PERFECT

ich	habe misstraut
du	hast misstraut
er/sie/es	hat misstraut
wir	haben misstraut
ihr	habt misstraut
sie/Sie	haben misstraut

IMPERFECT

ich	misstraute
du	misstrautest
er/sie/es	misstraute
wir	misstrauten
ihr	misstrautet
sie/Sie	misstrauten

PRESENT PARTICIPLE

misstrauend

PAST PARTICIPLE

misstraut

EXAMPLE PHRASES

Warum **misstraut** ihr uns? Why don't you trust us?

Er sagt, er **misstraue** allen Politikern. He says he mistrusts all politicians.

Ich **habe** ihr von Anfang an **misstraut**. I didn't trust her from the start.

Sie **misstraute** ihrem Gedächtnis. She didn't trust her memory.

ich = I **du** = you **er** = he/it **sie** = she/it **es** = it/he/she **wir** = we **ihr** = you **sie** = they **Sie** = you (*polite*)

misstrauen

FUTURE

ich	**werde misstrauen**
du	**wirst misstrauen**
er/sie/es	**wird misstrauen**
wir	**werden misstrauen**
ihr	**werdet misstrauen**
sie/Sie	**werden misstrauen**

CONDITIONAL

ich	**würde misstrauen**
du	**würdest misstrauen**
er/sie/es	**würde misstrauen**
wir	**würden misstrauen**
ihr	**würdet misstrauen**
sie/Sie	**würden misstrauen**

PLUPERFECT

ich	**hatte misstraut**
du	**hattest misstraut**
er/sie/es	**hatte misstraut**
wir	**hatten misstraut**
ihr	**hattet misstraut**
sie/Sie	**hatten misstraut**

PLUPERFECT SUBJUNCTIVE

ich	**hätte misstraut**
du	**hättest misstraut**
er/sie/es	**hätte misstraut**
wir	**hätten misstraut**
ihr	**hättet misstraut**
sie/Sie	**hätten misstraut**

IMPERATIVE

misstrau(e)!/misstrauen wir!/misstraut!/misstrauen Sie!

EXAMPLE PHRASES

Von jetzt an **werde** ich Ihnen nicht mehr **misstrauen**. From now on I will trust you.

Ich **würde** seinen Ratschlägen **misstrauen**. I would not trust his advice.

Sie **hatte** seinen Versprechungen **misstraut**. She had not trusted his promises.

Wenn er nicht so nett gewesen wäre, **hätte** ich ihm **misstraut**. If he hadn't been so nice, I wouldn't have trusted him.

ich = I **du** = you **er** = he/it **sie** = she/it **es** = it/he/she **wir** = we **ihr** = you **sie** = they **Sie** = you (polite)

mögen (to like)

modal, formed with **haben**

PRESENT

ich	**mag**
du	**magst**
er/sie/es	**mag**
wir	**mögen**
ihr	**mögt**
sie/Sie	**mögen**

PRESENT SUBJUNCTIVE

ich	**möge**
du	**mögest**
er/sie/es	**möge**
wir	**mögen**
ihr	**möget**
sie/Sie	**mögen**

PERFECT

ich	**habe gemocht/mögen**
du	**hast gemocht/mögen**
er/sie/es	**hat gemocht/mögen**
wir	**haben gemocht/mögen**
ihr	**habt gemocht/mögen**
sie/Sie	**haben gemocht/mögen**

IMPERFECT

ich	**mochte**
du	**mochtest**
er/sie/es	**mochte**
wir	**mochten**
ihr	**mochtet**
sie/Sie	**mochten**

PRESENT PARTICIPLE

mögend

PAST PARTICIPLE

gemocht/mögen*

This form is used when combined with another infinitive.

EXAMPLE PHRASES

Ich **mag** gern Vanilleeis. I like vanilla ice cream.

Er sagt, er **möge** jetzt nicht mit mir reden. He says he doesn't want to talk to me right now.

Ich **habe** ihn noch nie **gemocht**. I never liked him.

Er **mochte** sie nicht danach fragen. He didn't want to ask her about it.

ich = I **du** = you **er** = he/it **sie** = she/it **es** = it/he/she **wir** = we **ihr** = you **sie** = they **Sie** = you (*polite*)

mögen

FUTURE

ich	**werde mögen**
du	**wirst mögen**
er/sie/es	**wird mögen**
wir	**werden mögen**
ihr	**werdet mögen**
sie/Sie	**werden mögen**

CONDITIONAL

ich	**würde mögen**
du	**würdest mögen**
er/sie/es	**würde mögen**
wir	**würden mögen**
ihr	**würdet mögen**
sie/Sie	**würden mögen**

PLUPERFECT

ich	**hatte gemocht/mögen**
du	**hattest gemocht/mögen**
er/sie/es	**hatte gemocht/mögen**
wir	**hatten gemocht/mögen**
ihr	**hattet gemocht/mögen**
sie/Sie	**hatten gemocht/mögen**

PLUPERFECT SUBJUNCTIVE

ich	**hätte gemocht/mögen**
du	**hättest gemocht/mögen**
er/sie/es	**hätte gemocht/mögen**
wir	**hätten gemocht/mögen**
ihr	**hättet gemocht/mögen**
sie/Sie	**hätten gemocht/mögen**

EXAMPLE PHRASES

Ich bin gespannt, ob ich den Film **mögen werde**. I wonder if I'm going to like the film.

Ich **würde** ihn lieber **mögen**, wenn er größer wäre. I would like him more if he was taller.

Sie **hatte** Katzen noch nie **gemocht**. She had never liked cats.

Ich weiß nicht, ob er dieses Buch **gemocht hätte**. I don't know if he would have liked this book.

ich = I **du** = you **er** = he/it **sie** = she/it **es** = it/he/she **wir** = we **ihr** = you **sie** = they **Sie** = you (*polite*)

müssen (to have to)

modal, *formed with* **haben**

PRESENT

ich	**muss**
du	**musst**
er/sie/es	**muss**
wir	**müssen**
ihr	**müsst**
sie/Sie	**müssen**

PRESENT SUBJUNCTIVE

ich	**müsse**
du	**müssest**
er/sie/es	**müsse**
wir	**müssen**
ihr	**müsset**
sie/Sie	**müssen**

PERFECT

ich	**habe gemusst/müssen**
du	**hast gemusst/müssen**
er/sie/es	**hat gemusst/müssen**
wir	**haben gemusst/müssen**
ihr	**habt gemusst/müssen**
sie/Sie	**haben gemusst/müssen**

IMPERFECT

ich	**musste**
du	**musstest**
er/sie/es	**musste**
wir	**mussten**
ihr	**musstet**
sie/Sie	**mussten**

PRESENT PARTICIPLE

müssend

PAST PARTICIPLE

gemusst/müssen*

This form is used when combined with another infinitive.

EXAMPLE PHRASES

Ich **muss** auf die Toilette. I must go to the toilet.

Er meint, er **müsse** jetzt gehen. He thinks he'll have to leave now.

Sie **hat** abwaschen **müssen**. She had to wash up.

Wir **mussten** jeden Abend unsere Hausaufgaben machen. We had to do our
  homework every night.

müssen

FUTURE

ich	**werde müssen**
du	**wirst müssen**
er/sie/es	**wird müssen**
wir	**werden müssen**
ihr	**werdet müssen**
sie/Sie	**werden müssen**

CONDITIONAL

ich	**würde müssen**
du	**würdest müssen**
er/sie/es	**würde müssen**
wir	**würden müssen**
ihr	**würdet müssen**
sie/Sie	**würden müssen**

PLUPERFECT

ich	**hatte gemusst/müssen**
du	**hattest gemusst/müssen**
er/sie/es	**hatte gemusst/müssen**
wir	**hatten gemusst/müssen**
ihr	**hattet gemusst/müssen**
sie/Sie	**hatten gemusst/müssen**

PLUPERFECT SUBJUNCTIVE

ich	**hätte gemusst/müssen**
du	**hättest gemusst/müssen**
er/sie/es	**hätte gemusst/müssen**
wir	**hätten gemusst/müssen**
ihr	**hättet gemusst/müssen**
sie/Sie	**hätten gemusst/müssen**

EXAMPLE PHRASES

Morgen **werden** wir nicht in die Schule **müssen**. We won't have to go to school tomorrow.

Dann **würde** er mich heiraten **müssen**. Then he would have to marry me.

Sylvia **hatte** ins Krankenhaus **gemusst**. Sylvia had had to go into hospital.

Nach diesem Foul **hätte** er eigentlich vom Platz **gemusst**. After that foul he should really have been sent off.

nehmen (to take)

strong, *formed with* **haben**

PRESENT

ich	**nehme**
du	**nimmst**
er/sie/es	**nimmt**
wir	**nehmen**
ihr	**nehmt**
sie/Sie	**nehmen**

PRESENT SUBJUNCTIVE

ich	**nehme**
du	**nehmest**
er/sie/es	**nehme**
wir	**nehmen**
ihr	**nehmet**
sie/Sie	**nehmen**

PERFECT

ich	**habe genommen**
du	**hast genommen**
er/sie/es	**hat genommen**
wir	**haben genommen**
ihr	**habt genommen**
sie/Sie	**haben genommen**

IMPERFECT

ich	**nahm**
du	**nahmst**
er/sie/es	**nahm**
wir	**nahmen**
ihr	**nahmt**
sie/Sie	**nahmen**

PRESENT PARTICIPLE

nehmend

PAST PARTICIPLE

genommen

EXAMPLE PHRASES

Wie viel **nimmst** du dafür? How much do you want for it?

Sie sagt, sie **nehme** keine Drogen. She says she doesn't take any drugs.

Hast du den Bus in die Stadt **genommen**? Did you take the bus into town?

Er **nahm** sich vom Brot. He helped himself to bread.

nehmen

FUTURE

ich	**werde nehmen**
du	**wirst nehmen**
er/sie/es	**wird nehmen**
wir	**werden nehmen**
ihr	**werdet nehmen**
sie/Sie	**werden nehmen**

CONDITIONAL

ich	**würde nehmen**
du	**würdest nehmen**
er/sie/es	**würde nehmen**
wir	**würden nehmen**
ihr	**würdet nehmen**
sie/Sie	**würden nehmen**

PLUPERFECT

ich	**hatte genommen**
du	**hattest genommen**
er/sie/es	**hatte genommen**
wir	**hatten genommen**
ihr	**hattet genommen**
sie/Sie	**hatten genommen**

PLUPERFECT SUBJUNCTIVE

ich	**hätte genommen**
du	**hättest genommen**
er/sie/es	**hätte genommen**
wir	**hätten genommen**
ihr	**hättet genommen**
sie/Sie	**hätten genommen**

IMPERATIVE

nimm/nehmen wir!/nehmt!/nehmen Sie!

EXAMPLE PHRASES

Wir **werden** den Bus in die Stadt **nehmen**. We'll take the bus into town.

Ich **würde** gern noch vom Brot **nehmen**. I'd like to take some more bread.

Er **hatte** seine Medizin nicht **genommen**. He hadn't taken his medicine.

An Ihrer Stelle **hätte** ich ihn nicht ernst **genommen**. If I were you I wouldn't have taken him seriously.

ich = I **du** = you **er** = he/it **sie** = she/it **es** = it/he/she **wir** = we **ihr** = you **sie** = they **Sie** = you (*polite*)

nennen (to name)

mixed, *formed with* **haben**

PRESENT

ich	**nenne**
du	**nennst**
er/sie/es	**nennt**
wir	**nennen**
ihr	**nennt**
sie/Sie	**nennen**

PRESENT SUBJUNCTIVE

ich	**nenne**
du	**nennest**
er/sie/es	**nenne**
wir	**nennen**
ihr	**nennet**
sie/Sie	**nennen**

PERFECT

ich	**habe genannt**
du	**hast genannt**
er/sie/es	**hat genannt**
wir	**haben genannt**
ihr	**habt genannt**
sie/Sie	**haben genannt**

IMPERFECT

ich	**nannte**
du	**nanntest**
er/sie/es	**nannte**
wir	**nannten**
ihr	**nanntet**
sie/Sie	**nannten**

PRESENT PARTICIPLE

nennend

PAST PARTICIPLE

gennant

EXAMPLE PHRASES

Das **nenne** ich Mut! That's what I call courage!

Er sagt, er **nenne** ihn 'Franzi'. He says he calls him 'Franzi'.

Er **hat** ihn nach seinem Vater **genannt**. He named him after his father.

Sie **nannte** mir den Namen ihres Arztes. She told me the name of her doctor.

---

ich = I **du** = you **er** = he/it **sie** = she/it **es** = it/he/she **wir** = we **ihr** = you **sie** = they **Sie** = you (*polite*)

nennen

FUTURE

ich	**werde nennen**
du	**wirst nennen**
er/sie/es	**wird nennen**
wir	**werden nennen**
ihr	**werdet nennen**
sie/Sie	**werden nennen**

CONDITIONAL

ich	**würde nennen**
du	**würdest nennen**
er/sie/es	**würde nennen**
wir	**würden nennen**
ihr	**würdet nennen**
sie/Sie	**würden nennen**

PLUPERFECT

ich	**hätte gennant**
du	**hättest gennant**
er/sie/es	**hätte gennant**
wir	**hätten gennant**
ihr	**hättet gennant**
sie/Sie	**hätten gennant**

PLUPERFECT SUBJUNCTIVE

ich	**hätte gennant**
du	**hättest gennant**
er/sie/es	**hätte gennant**
wir	**hätten gennant**
ihr	**hättet gennant**
sie/Sie	**hätten gennant**

IMPERATIVE

nenn(e)!/nennen wir!/nennt!/nennen Sie!

EXAMPLE PHRASES

Werden Sie mir seinen Namen **nennen**? Are you going to tell me his name?

Ich **würde** sie nicht gerade freundlich **nennen**. I wouldn't exactly say she's
friendly.

Er **hatte** der Polizei alle Komplizen **genannt**. He had named all his accomplices
to the police.

Ich **hätte** Ihnen gern noch mehr Gründe **genannt**. I would have liked to give
you more reasons.

ich = I **du** = you **er** = he/it **sie** = she/it **es** = it/he/she **wir** = we **ihr** = you **sie** = they **Sie** = you (polite)

raten (to guess; to advise)

strong, *formed with* haben

PRESENT

ich	**rate**
du	**rätst**
er/sie/es	**rät**
wir	**raten**
ihr	**ratet**
sie/Sie	**raten**

PRESENT SUBJUNCTIVE

ich	**rate**
du	**ratest**
er/sie/es	**rate**
wir	**raten**
ihr	**ratet**
sie/Sie	**raten**

PERFECT

ich	**habe geraten**
du	**hast geraten**
er/sie/es	**hat geraten**
wir	**haben geraten**
ihr	**habt geraten**
sie/Sie	**haben geraten**

IMPERFECT

ich	**riet**
du	**riet(e)st**
er/sie/es	**riet**
wir	**rieten**
ihr	**rietet**
sie/Sie	**rieten**

PRESENT PARTICIPLE

ratend

PAST PARTICIPLE

geraten

EXAMPLE PHRASES

Ich **rate** dir, zu gehen. I advise you to go.

Sie sagt, sie **rate** ihm, die Stadt zu verlassen. She says she's advising him to leave town.

Ich **habe** das nur so **geraten**. I was only guessing.

Er **riet** mir, einen Astrologen aufzusuchen. He advised me to consult an astrologer.

---

ich = I **du** = you **er** = he/it **sie** = she/it **es** = it/he/she **wir** = we **ihr** = you **sie** = they **Sie** = you *(polite)*

raten

FUTURE

ich	**werde raten**
du	**wirst raten**
er/sie/es	**wird raten**
wir	**werden raten**
ihr	**werdet raten**
sie/Sie	**werden raten**

CONDITIONAL

ich	**würde raten**
du	**würdest raten**
er/sie/es	**würde raten**
wir	**würden raten**
ihr	**würdet raten**
sie/Sie	**würden raten**

PLUPERFECT

ich	**hatte geraten**
du	**hattest geraten**
er/sie/es	**hatte geraten**
wir	**hatten geraten**
ihr	**hattet geraten**
sie/Sie	**hatten geraten**

PLUPERFECT SUBJUNCTIVE

ich	**hätte geraten**
du	**hättest geraten**
er/sie/es	**hätte geraten**
wir	**hätten geraten**
ihr	**hättet geraten**
sie/Sie	**hätten geraten**

IMPERATIVE

rat(e)!/raten wir!/ratet!/raten Sie!

EXAMPLE PHRASES

Das **wirst** du nie **raten**! You'll never guess!

Das **würde** ich dir nicht **raten**. I wouldn't recommend it.

Er **hatte** mir zu einer Auslandsreise **geraten**. He had advised me to travel abroad.

Ich **hätte** nie **geraten**, dass sie deine Schwester ist. I would never have guessed that she's your sister.

ich = I du = you er = he/it sie = she/it es = it/he/she wir = we ihr = you sie = they Sie = you (*polite*)

rechnen (to calculate)

weak, formed with **haben**

PRESENT

ich	**rechne**
du	**rechnest**
er/sie/es	**rechnet**
wir	**rechnen**
ihr	**rechnet**
sie/Sie	**rechnen**

PRESENT SUBJUNCTIVE

ich	**rechne**
du	**rechnest**
er/sie/es	**rechne**
wir	**rechnen**
ihr	**rechnet**
sie/Sie	**rechnen**

PERFECT

ich	**habe gerechnet**
du	**hast gerechnet**
er/sie/es	**hat gerechnet**
wir	**haben gerechnet**
ihr	**habt gerechnet**
sie/Sie	**haben gerechnet**

IMPERFECT

ich	**rechnete**
du	**rechnetest**
er/sie/es	**rechnete**
wir	**rechneten**
ihr	**rechnetet**
sie/Sie	**rechneten**

PRESENT PARTICIPLE

rechnend

PAST PARTICIPLE

gerechnet

EXAMPLE PHRASES

Wir **rechnen** auf dich. We are counting on you.

Sie sagt, sie **rechne** damit, dass es regnet. She says she expects it to rain.

Damit **habe** ich nicht **gerechnet**. I wasn't expecting that.

Man **rechnete** ihn zu den besten Spielern. He was regarded as one of the
    top players.

ich = I **du** = you **er** = he/it **sie** = she/it **es** = it/he/she **wir** = we **ihr** = you **sie** = they **Sie** = you (*polite*)

rechnen

FUTURE

ich **werde rechnen**
du **wirst rechnen**
er/sie/es **wird rechnen**
wir **werden rechnen**
ihr **werdet rechnen**
sie/Sie **werden rechnen**

CONDITIONAL

ich **würde rechnen**
du **würdest rechnen**
er/sie/es **würde rechnen**
wir **würden rechnen**
ihr **würdet rechnen**
sie/Sie **würden rechnen**

PLUPERFECT

ich **hatte gerechnet**
du **hattest gerechnet**
er/sie/es **hatte gerechnet**
wir **hatten gerechnet**
ihr **hattet gerechnet**
sie/Sie **hatten gerechnet**

PLUPERFECT SUBJUNCTIVE

ich **hätte gerechnet**
du **hättest gerechnet**
er/sie/es **hätte gerechnet**
wir **hätten gerechnet**
ihr **hättet gerechnet**
sie/Sie **hätten gerechnet**

IMPERATIVE
rechne!/rechnen wir!/rechnet!/rechnen Sie!

EXAMPLE PHRASES

Ich **werde** mal schnell **rechnen**, wie viel das wird. I'll work out quickly how much that's going to be.

Ich **würde** jetzt nicht mehr mit ihm **rechnen**. I wouldn't reckon on him coming now.

Da **hattest** du falsch **gerechnet**! You had got that wrong!

Ich **hätte** nie damit **gerechnet**, dass er gewinnt. I would never have expected him to win.

ich = I **du** = you **er** = he/it **sie** = she/it **es** = it/he/she **wir** = we **ihr** = you **sie** = they **Sie** = you (polite)

reden (to talk)

weak, formed with **haben**

PRESENT

ich	**rede**
du	**redest**
er/sie/es	**redet**
wir	**reden**
ihr	**redet**
sie/Sie	**reden**

PRESENT SUBJUNCTIVE

ich	**rede**
du	**redest**
er/sie/es	**rede**
wir	**reden**
ihr	**redet**
sie/Sie	**reden**

PERFECT

ich	**habe geredet**
du	**hast geredet**
er/sie/es	**hat geredet**
wir	**haben geredet**
ihr	**habt geredet**
sie/Sie	**haben geredet**

IMPERFECT

ich	**redete**
du	**redetest**
er/sie/es	**redete**
wir	**redeten**
ihr	**redetet**
sie/Sie	**redeten**

PRESENT PARTICIPLE
redend

PAST PARTICIPLE
geredet

EXAMPLE PHRASES

Wir **reden** besser erst darüber. We should talk about it first.

Er meint, ich **rede** Unsinn. He thinks I'm talking nonsense.

Sie **hat** ununterbrochen **geredet**. She was talking the whole time.

Er **redete** ständig von seinem Hund. He kept talking about his dog.

ich = I du = you er = he/it sie = she/it es = it/he/she wir = we ihr = you sie = they Sie = you (*polite*)

reden

FUTURE

ich	**werde reden**
du	**wirst reden**
er/sie/es	**wird reden**
wir	**werden reden**
ihr	**werdet reden**
sie/Sie	**werden reden**

CONDITIONAL

ich	**würde reden**
du	**würdest reden**
er/sie/es	**würde reden**
wir	**würden reden**
ihr	**würdet reden**
sie/Sie	**würden reden**

PLUPERFECT

ich	**hatte geredet**
du	**hattest geredet**
er/sie/es	**hatte geredet**
wir	**hatten geredet**
ihr	**hattet geredet**
sie/Sie	**hatten geredet**

PLUPERFECT SUBJUNCTIVE

ich	**hätte geredet**
du	**hättest geredet**
er/sie/es	**hätte geredet**
wir	**hätten geredet**
ihr	**hättet geredet**
sie/Sie	**hätten geredet**

IMPERATIVE

red(e)!/reden wir!/redet!/reden Sie!

EXAMPLE PHRASES

Ich **werde** mit deinem Vater **reden**. I'll speak to your father.

Er **würde** am liebsten nicht mehr darüber **reden**. He would prefer not to talk about it anymore.

Er **hatte** davon **geredet**, ins Ausland zu ziehen. He had been talking about moving abroad.

Ich wünschte, ich **hätte** mit ihm **geredet**. I wished I had talked to him.

ich = I **du** = you **er** = he/it **sie** = she/it **es** = it/he/she **wir** = we **ihr** = you **sie** = they **Sie** = you (polite)

reißen (to tear)

strong, *formed with* **haben/sein***

PRESENT

ich	**reiße**
du	**reißt**
er/sie/es	**reißt**
wir	**reißen**
ihr	**reißt**
sie/Sie	**reißen**

PRESENT SUBJUNCTIVE

ich	**reiße**
du	**reißest**
er/sie/es	**reiße**
wir	**reißen**
ihr	**reißet**
sie/Sie	**reißen**

PERFECT

ich	**habe gerissen**
du	**hast gerissen**
er/sie/es	**hat gerissen**
wir	**haben gerissen**
ihr	**habt gerissen**
sie/Sie	**haben gerissen**

IMPERFECT

ich	**riss**
du	**rissest**
er/sie/es	**riss**
wir	**rissen**
ihr	**risst**
sie/Sie	**rissen**

PRESENT PARTICIPLE

reißend

PAST PARTICIPLE

gerissen

When reißen is used with no direct object, it is formed with sein.

EXAMPLE PHRASES

Das Seil **reißt**. The rope is breaking.

Er sagt, ihm **reiße** bald die Geduld. He says his patience will soon be at an end.

Er **hat** mir den Geldbeutel aus der Hand **gerissen**. He snatched my purse from my hand.

Sie **riss** ihn zu Boden. She dragged him to the floor.

reißen

FUTURE

ich	**werde reißen**
du	**wirst reißen**
er/sie/es	**wird reißen**
wir	**werden reißen**
ihr	**werdet reißen**
sie/Sie	**werden reißen**

CONDITIONAL

ich	**würde reißen**
du	**würdest reißen**
er/sie/es	**würde reißen**
wir	**würden reißen**
ihr	**würdet reißen**
sie/Sie	**würden reißen**

PLUPERFECT

ich	**hatte gerissen**
du	**hattest gerissen**
er/sie/es	**hatte gerissen**
wir	**hatten gerissen**
ihr	**hattet gerissen**
sie/Sie	**hatten gerissen**

PLUPERFECT SUBJUNCTIVE

ich	**hätte gerissen**
du	**hättest gerissen**
er/sie/es	**hätte gerissen**
wir	**hätten gerissen**
ihr	**hättet gerissen**
sie/Sie	**hätten gerissen**

IMPERATIVE

reiß(e)!/reißen wir!/reißt!/reißen Sie!

EXAMPLE PHRASES

Die Kunden **werden** sich um die Sonderangebote **reißen**. The customers will be scrambling for the special offers.

Ich **würde** ihn nicht gern aus seinen Gedanken **reißen**. I wouldn't like to interrupt his thoughts.

Er **hatte** uns alle ins Verderben **gerissen**. He had ruined all of us.

Die Lawine **hätte** ihn in den Tod **gerissen**. The avalanche would have swept him to his death.

ich = I du = you er = he/it sie = she/it es = it/he/she wir = we ihr = you sie = they Sie = you (*polite*)

rennen (to run)

mixed, *formed with* **sein**

PRESENT

ich	**renne**
du	**rennst**
er/sie/es	**rennt**
wir	**rennen**
ihr	**rennt**
sie/Sie	**rennen**

PRESENT SUBJUNCTIVE

ich	**renne**
du	**rennest**
er/sie/es	**renne**
wir	**rennen**
ihr	**rennet**
sie/Sie	**rennen**

PERFECT

ich	**bin gerannt**
du	**bist gerannt**
er/sie/es	**ist gerannt**
wir	**sind gerannt**
ihr	**seid gerannt**
sie/Sie	**sind gerannt**

IMPERFECT

ich	**rannte**
du	**ranntest**
er/sie/es	**rannte**
wir	**rannten**
ihr	**ranntet**
sie/Sie	**rannten**

PRESENT PARTICIPLE

rennend

PAST PARTICIPLE

gerannt

EXAMPLE PHRASES

Er **rennt** dauernd zum Chef. He keeps running to the boss.

Sie denkt, ich **renne** ins Unglück. She thinks I'm rushing into disaster.

Ich **bin** mit dem Kopf gegen die Wand **gerannt**. I bumped my head against the wall.

Sie **rannte** schnell weg. She ran away fast.

ich = I **du** = you **er** = he/it **sie** = she/it **es** = it/he/she **wir** = we **ihr** = you **sie** = they **Sie** = you (*polite*)

rennen

FUTURE

ich	**werde rennen**
du	**wirst rennen**
er/sie/es	**wird rennen**
wir	**werden rennen**
ihr	**werdet rennen**
sie/Sie	**werden rennen**

CONDITIONAL

ich	**würde rennen**
du	**würdest rennen**
er/sie/es	**würde rennen**
wir	**würden rennen**
ihr	**würdet rennen**
sie/Sie	**würden rennen**

PLUPERFECT

ich	**war gerannt**
du	**warst gerannt**
er/sie/es	**war gerannt**
wir	**waren gerannt**
ihr	**wart gerannt**
sie/Sie	**waren gerannt**

PLUPERFECT SUBJUNCTIVE

ich	**wäre gerannt**
du	**wär(e)st gerannt**
er/sie/es	**wäre gerannt**
wir	**wären gerannt**
ihr	**wär(e)t gerannt**
sie/Sie	**wären gerannt**

IMPERATIVE

renn(e)!/rennen wir!/rennt!/rennen Sie

EXAMPLE PHRASES

Ich **werde** die 100 Meter nicht **rennen**. I won't run the 100 metres.

Bei Kopfschmerzen **würde** er sofort zum Arzt **rennen**. If he had a headache he would rush straight to the doctor.

Ich **war** so **gerannt**, dass mir die Luft wegblieb. I had been running so much that I was out of breath.

Wenn wir nicht **gerannt wären**, hätten wir den Zug verpasst. If we hadn't run we'd have missed the train.

ich = I **du** = you **er** = he/it **sie** = she/it **es** = it/he/she **wir** = we **ihr** = you **sie** = they **Sie** = you (*polite*)

riechen (to smell)

strong, *formed with* haben

PRESENT

ich	**rieche**
du	**riechst**
er/sie/es	**riecht**
wir	**riechen**
ihr	**riecht**
sie/Sie	**riechen**

PRESENT SUBJUNCTIVE

ich	**rieche**
du	**riechest**
er/sie/es	**rieche**
wir	**riechen**
ihr	**riechet**
sie/Sie	**riechen**

PERFECT

ich	**habe gerochen**
du	**hast gerochen**
er/sie/es	**hat gerochen**
wir	**haben gerochen**
ihr	**habt gerochen**
sie/Sie	**haben gerochen**

IMPERFECT

ich	**roch**
du	**rochst**
er/sie/es	**roch**
wir	**rochen**
ihr	**rocht**
sie/Sie	**rochen**

PRESENT PARTICIPLE

riechend

PAST PARTICIPLE

gerochen

EXAMPLE PHRASES

Ich **rieche** Gas. I can smell gas.

Sie sagt, sie **rieche** nichts. She says she can't smell anything.

Sie **hat** an der Rose **gerochen**. She smelled the rose.

In der Küche **roch** es angebrannt. There was a smell of burning in the kitchen.

---

riechen

FUTURE

ich	**werde riechen**
du	**wirst riechen**
er/sie/es	**wird riechen**
wir	**werden riechen**
ihr	**werdet riechen**
sie/Sie	**werden riechen**

CONDITIONAL

ich	**würde riechen**
du	**würdest riechen**
er/sie/es	**würde riechen**
wir	**würden riechen**
ihr	**würdet riechen**
sie/Sie	**würden riechen**

PLUPERFECT

ich	**hatte gerochen**
du	**hattest gerochen**
er/sie/es	**hatte gerochen**
wir	**hatten gerochen**
ihr	**hattet gerochen**
sie/Sie	**hatten gerochen**

PLUPERFECT SUBJUNCTIVE

ich	**hätte gerochen**
du	**hättest gerochen**
er/sie/es	**hätte gerochen**
wir	**hätten gerochen**
ihr	**hättet gerochen**
sie/Sie	**hätten gerochen**

IMPERATIVE

riech(e)!/riechen wir!/riecht!/riechen Sie!

EXAMPLE PHRASES

Endlich **werde** ich wieder Landluft **riechen**. At last I'll smell country air again.

Wenn ich nicht geduscht hätte, **würde** ich nach Schweiß **riechen**. If I hadn't taken a shower I would smell of sweat.

In der Garage **hatte** es nach Benzin **gerochen**. There had been a smell of petrol in the garage.

Das **hätte** fast nach Betrug **gerochen**. It almost smacked of deceit.

ich = I **du** = you **er** = he/it **sie** = she/it **es** = it/he/she **wir** = we **ihr** = you **sie** = they **Sie** = you *(polite)*

rufen (to shout, call)

strong, *formed with* haben

PRESENT

ich	**rufe**
du	**rufst**
er/sie/es	**ruft**
wir	**rufen**
ihr	**ruft**
sie/Sie	**rufen**

PRESENT SUBJUNCTIVE

ich	**rufe**
du	**rufest**
er/sie/es	**rufe**
wir	**rufen**
ihr	**rufet**
sie/Sie	**rufen**

PERFECT

ich	**habe gerufen**
du	**hast gerufen**
er/sie/es	**hat gerufen**
wir	**haben gerufen**
ihr	**habt gerufen**
sie/Sie	**haben gerufen**

IMPERFECT

ich	**rief**
du	**riefst**
er/sie/es	**rief**
wir	**riefen**
ihr	**rieft**
sie/Sie	**riefen**

PRESENT PARTICIPLE

rufend

PAST PARTICIPLE

gerufen

EXAMPLE PHRASES

Sie **ruft** um Hilfe. She is shouting for help.

Er meint, er **rufe** besser ein Taxi. He thinks it's best to call a taxi.

Ich **habe** dir ein Taxi **gerufen**. I called you a taxi.

Er **rief** seine Schwester zu sich. He sent for his sister.

rufen

FUTURE

ich	**werde rufen**
du	**wirst rufen**
er/sie/es	**wird rufen**
wir	**werden rufen**
ihr	**werdet rufen**
sie/Sie	**werden rufen**

CONDITIONAL

ich	**würde rufen**
du	**würdest rufen**
er/sie/es	**würde rufen**
wir	**würden rufen**
ihr	**würdet rufen**
sie/Sie	**würden rufen**

PLUPERFECT

ich	**hatte gerufen**
du	**hattest gerufen**
er/sie/es	**hatte gerufen**
wir	**hatten gerufen**
ihr	**hattet gerufen**
sie/Sie	**hatten gerufen**

PLUPERFECT SUBJUNCTIVE

ich	**hätte gerufen**
du	**hättest gerufen**
er/sie/es	**hätte gerufen**
wir	**hätten gerufen**
ihr	**hättet gerufen**
sie/Sie	**hätten gerufen**

IMPERATIVE

ruf(e)!/rufen wir!/ruft!/rufen Sie!

EXAMPLE PHRASES

Ich **werde** ihn **rufen**, damit er hereinkommt. I'll call him so that he comes in.

Im Notfall **würden** wir den Arzt **rufen**. In an emergency we would call the doctor.

Hattest du die Polizei **gerufen**? Had you called the police?

Sie **hätte** einen Krankenwagen **gerufen**, aber sie hatte kein Handy. She would have called an ambulance, but she didn't have a mobile.

ich = I **du** = you **er** = he/it **sie** = she/it **es** = it/he/she **wir** = we **ihr** = you **sie** = they **Sie** = you *(polite)*

schaffen* (to create)

strong, *formed with* haben

PRESENT

ich	schaffe
du	schaffst
er/sie/es	schafft
wir	schaffen
ihr	schafft
sie/Sie	schaffen

PRESENT SUBJUNCTIVE

ich	schaffe
du	schaffest
er/sie/es	schaffe
wir	schaffen
ihr	schaffet
sie/Sie	schaffen

PERFECT

ich	habe geschaffen
du	hast geschaffen
er/sie/es	hat geschaffen
wir	haben geschaffen
ihr	habt geschaffen
sie/Sie	haben geschaffen

IMPERFECT

ich	schuf
du	schufst
er/sie/es	schuf
wir	schufen
ihr	schuft
sie/Sie	schufen

PRESENT PARTICIPLE

schaffend

PAST PARTICIPLE

geschaffen

*Weak when means to manage.

EXAMPLE PHRASES

Du **schaffst** dir nur Probleme. You're only creating problems for yourself.

Er sagt, das **schaffe** er heute nicht. He says he won't manage it today.

Die Regierung **hat** 20.000 Arbeitsplätze **geschaffen**. The government has created 20,000 jobs.

Gott **schuf** Himmel und Erde. God created heaven and earth.

schaffen

FUTURE

ich	**werde schaffen**
du	**wirst schaffen**
er/sie/es	**wird schaffen**
wir	**werden schaffen**
ihr	**werdet schaffen**
sie/Sie	**werden schaffen**

CONDITIONAL

ich	**würde schaffen**
du	**würdest schaffen**
er/sie/es	**würde schaffen**
wir	**würden schaffen**
ihr	**würdet schaffen**
sie/Sie	**würden schaffen**

PLUPERFECT

ich	**hatte geschaffen**
du	**hattest geschaffen**
er/sie/es	**hatte geschaffen**
wir	**hatten geschaffen**
ihr	**hattet geschaffen**
sie/Sie	**hatten geschaffen**

PLUPERFECT SUBJUNCTIVE

ich	**hätte geschaffen**
du	**hättest geschaffen**
er/sie/es	**hätte geschaffen**
wir	**hätten geschaffen**
ihr	**hättet geschaffen**
sie/Sie	**hätten geschaffen**

IMPERATIVE

schaff(e)!/schaffen wir!/schafft!/schaffen Sie!

EXAMPLE PHRASES

Diese Medizin **wird** Linderung **schaffen**. This medicine will bring relief.

Das **würde** endlich Klarheit **schaffen**. This would finally provide clarification.

Diese Politik **hatte** eine neue Situation **geschaffen**. This policy had created a new situation.

Er **hätte** doch nur Ärger **geschaffen**. He would only have caused trouble.

ich = I **du** = you **er** = he/it **sie** = she/it **es** = it/he/she **wir** = we **ihr** = you **sie** = they **Sie** = you (*polite*)

scheinen (to shine; to seem) strong, *formed with* haben

PRESENT

ich	scheine
du	scheinst
er/sie/es	scheint
wir	scheinen
ihr	scheint
sie/Sie	scheinen

PRESENT SUBJUNCTIVE

ich	scheine
du	scheinest
er/sie/es	scheine
wir	scheinen
ihr	scheinet
sie/Sie	scheinen

PERFECT

ich	habe geschienen
du	hast geschienen
er/sie/es	hat geschienen
wir	haben geschienen
ihr	habt geschienen
sie/Sie	haben geschienen

IMPERFECT

ich	schien
du	schienst
er/sie/es	schien
wir	schienen
ihr	schient
sie/Sie	schienen

PRESENT PARTICIPLE

scheinend

PAST PARTICIPLE

geschienen

EXAMPLE PHRASES

Es **scheint**, als ob du recht hast. It appears as if you're right.

Er meint, das **scheine** uns nicht zu interessieren. He thinks we don't seem to be interested.

Gestern **hat** die Sonne nicht **geschienen**. The sun wasn't shining yesterday.

Sie **schienen** glücklich zu sein. They seemed to be happy.

---

ich = I **du** = you **er** = he/it **sie** = she/it **es** = it/he/she **wir** = we **ihr** = you **sie** = they **Sie** = you (*polite*)

scheinen

FUTURE

ich	**werde scheinen**
du	**wirst scheinen**
er/sie/es	**wird scheinen**
wir	**werden scheinen**
ihr	**werdet scheinen**
sie/Sie	**werden scheinen**

CONDITIONAL

ich	**würde scheinen**
du	**würdest scheinen**
er/sie/es	**würde scheinen**
wir	**würden scheinen**
ihr	**würdet scheinen**
sie/Sie	**würden scheinen**

PLUPERFECT

ich	**hatte geschienen**
du	**hattest geschienen**
er/sie/es	**hatte geschienen**
wir	**hatten geschienen**
ihr	**hattet geschienen**
sie/Sie	**hatten geschienen**

PLUPERFECT SUBJUNCTIVE

ich	**hätte geschienen**
du	**hättest geschienen**
er/sie/es	**hätte geschienen**
wir	**hätten geschienen**
ihr	**hättet geschienen**
sie/Sie	**hätten geschienen**

IMPERATIVE

schein(e)!/scheinen wir!/scheint!/scheinen Sie!

EXAMPLE PHRASES

In Italien **wird** bestimmt die Sonne **scheinen**. I'm sure the sun will be shining in Italy.

Es **würde scheinen**, als ob wir das Spiel verlieren. It would seem we'll be losing the match.

Die Sonne **hatte** den ganzen Tag nicht **geschienen**. There had been no sunshine all day.

Wenn doch nur die Sonne **geschienen hätte**! If only the sun had been shining!

ich = I **du** = you **er** = he/it **sie** = she/it **es** = it/he/she **wir** = we **ihr** = you **sie** = they **Sie** = you (*polite*)

schießen (to shoot)

strong, *formed with* **haben**

PRESENT

ich	**schieße**
du	**schießt**
er/sie/es	**schießt**
wir	**schießen**
ihr	**schießt**
sie/Sie	**schießen**

PRESENT SUBJUNCTIVE

ich	**schieße**
du	**schießest**
er/sie/es	**schieße**
wir	**schießen**
ihr	**schießet**
sie/Sie	**schießen**

PERFECT

ich	**habe geschossen**
du	**hast geschossen**
er/sie/es	**hat geschossen**
wir	**haben geschossen**
ihr	**habt geschossen**
sie/Sie	**haben geschossen**

IMPERFECT

ich	**schoss**
du	**schossest**
er/sie/es	**schoss**
wir	**schossen**
ihr	**schosst**
sie/Sie	**schossen**

PRESENT PARTICIPLE

schießend

PAST PARTICIPLE

geschossen

EXAMPLE PHRASES

Sie **schießen** auf uns. They are shooting at us.

Er sagt, er **schieße** nie auf Menschen. He says he never shoots at people.

Er **hat** ein Kaninchen **geschossen**. He shot a rabbit.

Sie **schoss** den Ball ins Tor. She kicked the ball into the goal.

schießen

FUTURE

ich	**werde schießen**
du	**wirst schießen**
er/sie/es	**wird schießen**
wir	**werden schießen**
ihr	**werdet schießen**
sie/Sie	**werden schießen**

CONDITIONAL

ich	**würde schießen**
du	**würdest schießen**
er/sie/es	**würde schießen**
wir	**würden schießen**
ihr	**würdet schießen**
sie/Sie	**würden schießen**

PLUPERFECT

ich	**hatte geschossen**
du	**hattest geschossen**
er/sie/es	**hatte geschossen**
wir	**hatten geschossen**
ihr	**hattet geschossen**
sie/Sie	**hatten geschossen**

PLUPERFECT SUBJUNCTIVE

ich	**hätte geschossen**
du	**hättest geschossen**
er/sie/es	**hätte geschossen**
wir	**hätten geschossen**
ihr	**hättet geschossen**
sie/Sie	**hätten geschossen**

IMPERATIVE

schieß(e)!/schießen wir!/schießt!/schießen Sie!

EXAMPLE PHRASES

Wir **werden** dort ein paar Bilder **schießen**. We'll shoot a few pictures there.

Er **würde** niemals auf einen Polizisten **schießen**. He would never shoot at a
policeman.

Sie **hatte** ihn zum Krüppel **geschossen**. She had shot and crippled him.

Wenn ich **geschossen hätte**, wäre ich verhaftet worden. If I had fired a shot
I would have been arrested.

ich = I **du** = you **er** = he/it **sie** = she/it **es** = it/he/she **wir** = we **ihr** = you **sie** = they **Sie** = you (*polite*)

schlafen (to sleep)

strong, *formed with* **haben**

PRESENT

ich	**schlafe**
du	**schläfst**
er/sie/es	**schläft**
wir	**schlafen**
ihr	**schlaft**
sie/Sie	**schlafen**

PRESENT SUBJUNCTIVE

ich	**schlafe**
du	**schlafest**
er/sie/es	**schlafe**
wir	**schlafen**
ihr	**schlafet**
sie/Sie	**schlafen**

PERFECT

ich	**habe geschlafen**
du	**hast geschlafen**
er/sie/es	**hat geschlafen**
wir	**haben geschlafen**
ihr	**habt geschlafen**
sie/Sie	**haben geschlafen**

IMPERFECT

ich	**schlief**
du	**schliefst**
er/sie/es	**schlief**
wir	**schliefen**
ihr	**schlieft**
sie/Sie	**schliefen**

PRESENT PARTICIPLE
schlafend

PAST PARTICIPLE
geschlafen

EXAMPLE PHRASES

Sie **schläft** immer noch. She's still asleep.

Er sagt, sie **schlafe** immer noch. He says she's still asleep.

Hast du gut **geschlafen**? Did you sleep well?

Er **schlief** während des Unterrichts. He slept during lessons.

ich = I **du** = you **er** = he/it **sie** = she/it **es** = it/he/she **wir** = we **ihr** = you **sie** = they **Sie** = you *(polite)*

schlafen

FUTURE

ich	**werde schlafen**
du	**wirst schlafen**
er/sie/es	**wird schlafen**
wir	**werden schlafen**
ihr	**werdet schlafen**
sie/Sie	**werden schlafen**

CONDITIONAL

ich	**würde schlafen**
du	**würdest schlafen**
er/sie/es	**würde schlafen**
wir	**würden schlafen**
ihr	**würdet schlafen**
sie/Sie	**würden schlafen**

PLUPERFECT

ich	**hatte geschlafen**
du	**hattest geschlafen**
er/sie/es	**hatte geschlafen**
wir	**hatten geschlafen**
ihr	**hattet geschlafen**
sie/Sie	**hatten geschlafen**

PLUPERFECT SUBJUNCTIVE

ich	**hätte geschlafen**
du	**hättest geschlafen**
er/sie/es	**hätte geschlafen**
wir	**hätten geschlafen**
ihr	**hättet geschlafen**
sie/Sie	**hätten geschlafen**

IMPERATIVE

schlaf(e)!/schlafen wir!/schlaft!/schlafen Sie!

EXAMPLE PHRASES

Heute Nacht **wirst** du bestimmt gut **schlafen**. I'm sure you'll sleep well tonight.

Mit einer Schlaftablette **würde** ich besser **schlafen**. I would sleep better if I took a sleeping pill.

Ich **hatte** drei Tage lang nicht **geschlafen**. I hadn't slept for three days.

Ohne den Lärm **hätte** ich besser **geschlafen**. Without the noise I'd have slept better.

ich = I du = you er = he/it sie = she/it es = it/he/she wir = we ihr = you sie = they Sie = you (*polite*)

schlagen (to hit)

strong, *formed with* **haben**

PRESENT

ich	**schlage**
du	**schlägst**
er/sie/es	**schlägt**
wir	**schlagen**
ihr	**schlagt**
sie/Sie	**schlagen**

PRESENT SUBJUNCTIVE

ich	**schlage**
du	**schlagest**
er/sie/es	**schlage**
wir	**schlagen**
ihr	**schlaget**
sie/Sie	**schlagen**

PERFECT

ich	**habe geschlagen**
du	**hast geschlagen**
er/sie/es	**hat geschlagen**
wir	**haben geschlagen**
ihr	**habt geschlagen**
sie/Sie	**haben geschlagen**

IMPERFECT

ich	**schlug**
du	**schlugst**
er/sie/es	**schlug**
wir	**schlugen**
ihr	**schlugt**
sie/Sie	**schlugen**

PRESENT PARTICIPLE

schlagend

PAST PARTICIPLE

geschlagen

EXAMPLE PHRASES

Mein Herz **schlägt** schneller. My heart is beating faster.

Er glaubt, sein Nachbar **schlage** seine Kinder. He believes his neighbour beats his children.

England **hat** Deutschland **geschlagen**. England beat Germany.

Ihr Herz **schlug** schneller. Her heart beat faster.

---

ich = I **du** = you **er** = he/it **sie** = she/it **es** = it/he/she **wir** = we **ihr** = you **sie** = they **Sie** = you (*polite*)

schlagen

FUTURE

ich	**werde schlagen**
du	**wirst schlagen**
er/sie/es	**wird schlagen**
wir	**werden schlagen**
ihr	**werdet schlagen**
sie/Sie	**werden schlagen**

CONDITIONAL

ich	**würde schlagen**
du	**würdest schlagen**
er/sie/es	**würde schlagen**
wir	**würden schlagen**
ihr	**würdet schlagen**
sie/Sie	**würden schlagen**

PLUPERFECT

ich	**hatte geschlagen**
du	**hattest geschlagen**
er/sie/es	**hatte geschlagen**
wir	**hatten geschlagen**
ihr	**hattet geschlagen**
sie/Sie	**hatten geschlagen**

PLUPERFECT SUBJUNCTIVE

ich	**hätte geschlagen**
du	**hättest geschlagen**
er/sie/es	**hätte geschlagen**
wir	**hätten geschlagen**
ihr	**hättet geschlagen**
sie/Sie	**hätten geschlagen**

IMPERATIVE

schlag(e)!/schlagen wir!/schlagt!/schlagen Sie!

EXAMPLE PHRASES

Wir **werden** alle unsere Gegner **schlagen**. We will beat all our opponents.

Ich **würde** mich nicht mit ihm **schlagen**. I wouldn't fight with him.

Die Uhr **hatte** zehn **geschlagen**. The clock had struck ten.

Mit etwas Glück **hätten** wir sie **geschlagen**. With a little luck we would have beaten them.

ich = I **du** = you **er** = he/it **sie** = she/it **es** = it/he/she **wir** = we **ihr** = you **sie** = they **Sie** = you (*polite*)

schließen (to close)

strong, *formed with* haben

PRESENT

ich	schließe
du	schließt
er/sie/es	schließt
wir	schließen
ihr	schließt
sie/Sie	schließen

PRESENT SUBJUNCTIVE

ich	schließe
du	schließest
er/sie/es	schließe
wir	schließen
ihr	schließet
sie/Sie	schließen

PERFECT

ich	habe geschlossen
du	hast geschlossen
er/sie/es	hat geschlossen
wir	haben geschlossen
ihr	habt geschlossen
sie/Sie	haben geschlossen

IMPERFECT

ich	schloss
du	schlossest
er/sie/es	schloss
wir	schlossen
ihr	schlosst
sie/Sie	schlossen

PRESENT PARTICIPLE

schließend

PAST PARTICIPLE

geschlossen

EXAMPLE PHRASES

Ich **schließe** die Tür. I shut the door.
Sie sagt, die Tür **schließe** nicht. She says the door won't shut.
Er **hat** den Betrieb **geschlossen**. He shut the company down.
Sie **schloss** die Augen. She shut her eyes.

---

ich = I **du** = you **er** = he/it **sie** = she/it **es** = it/he/she **wir** = we **ihr** = you **sie** = they **Sie** = you (*polite*)

schließen

FUTURE

ich	**werde schließen**
du	**wirst schließen**
er/sie/es	**wird schließen**
wir	**werden schließen**
ihr	**werdet schließen**
sie/Sie	**werden schließen**

CONDITIONAL

ich	**würde schließen**
du	**würdest schließen**
er/sie/es	**würde schließen**
wir	**würden schließen**
ihr	**würdet schließen**
sie/Sie	**würden schließen**

PLUPERFECT

ich	**hatte geschlossen**
du	**hattest geschlossen**
er/sie/es	**hatte geschlossen**
wir	**hatten geschlossen**
ihr	**hattet geschlossen**
sie/Sie	**hatten geschlossen**

PLUPERFECT SUBJUNCTIVE

ich	**hätte geschlossen**
du	**hättest geschlossen**
er/sie/es	**hätte geschlossen**
wir	**hätten geschlossen**
ihr	**hättet geschlossen**
sie/Sie	**hätten geschlossen**

IMPERATIVE

schließ(e)!/schließen wir!/schließt!/schließen Sie!

EXAMPLE PHRASES

Sie **wird** ihn bestimmt in ihr Herz **schließen**. I'm sure she will take him to her heart.

Ich **würde** daraus **schließen**, dass er schuldig ist. From this I would conclude that he is guilty.

Der Laden **hatte** bereits **geschlossen**. The shop had already closed.

Mit ihm **hätte** ich keinen Vertrag **geschlossen**. I would not have entered into a contract with him.

ich = I du = you er = he/it sie = she/it es = it/he/she wir = we ihr = you sie = they Sie = you (polite)

schneiden (to cut)

strong, *formed with* haben

PRESENT

ich	schneide
du	schneidest
er/sie/es	schneidet
wir	schneiden
ihr	schneidet
sie/Sie	schneiden

PRESENT SUBJUNCTIVE

ich	schneide
du	schneidest
er/sie/es	schneide
wir	schneiden
ihr	schneidet
sie/Sie	schneiden

PERFECT

ich	habe geschnitten
du	hast geschnitten
er/sie/es	hat geschnitten
wir	haben geschnitten
ihr	habt geschnitten
sie/Sie	haben geschnitten

IMPERFECT

ich	schnitt
du	schnittst
er/sie/es	schnitt
wir	schnitten
ihr	schnittet
sie/Sie	schnitten

PRESENT PARTICIPLE

schneidend

PAST PARTICIPLE

geschnitten

EXAMPLE PHRASES

Sie **schneidet** ihm die Haare. She cuts his hair.

Er sagt, das Messer **schneide** nicht gut. He says the knife isn't cutting well.

Ich **habe** mir in den Finger **geschnitten**. I've cut my finger.

Sie **schnitt** die Tomaten in Scheiben. She sliced the tomatoes.

ich = I **du** = you **er** = he/it **sie** = she/it **es** = it/he/she **wir** = we **ihr** = you **sie** = they **Sie** = you (polite)

schneiden

FUTURE

ich	**werde schneiden**
du	**wirst schneiden**
er/sie/es	**wird schneiden**
wir	**werden schneiden**
ihr	**werdet schneiden**
sie/Sie	**werden schneiden**

CONDITIONAL

ich	**würde schneiden**
du	**würdest schneiden**
er/sie/es	**würde schneiden**
wir	**würden schneiden**
ihr	**würdet schneiden**
sie/Sie	**würden schneiden**

PLUPERFECT

ich	**hatte geschnitten**
du	**hattest geschnitten**
er/sie/es	**hatte geschnitten**
wir	**hatten geschnitten**
ihr	**hattet geschnitten**
sie/Sie	**hatten geschnitten**

PLUPERFECT SUBJUNCTIVE

ich	**hätte geschnitten**
du	**hättest geschnitten**
er/sie/es	**hätte geschnitten**
wir	**hätten geschnitten**
ihr	**hättet geschnitten**
sie/Sie	**hätten geschnitten**

IMPERATIVE

schneid(e)!/schneiden wir!/schneidet!/schneiden Sie!

EXAMPLE PHRASES

Ich **werde** das Brot in Scheiben **schneiden**. I'll slice the bread.

Ich **würde** ihm gern die Haare **schneiden**. I would like to cut his hair.

Sie **hatte** den Kuchen in Stücke **geschnitten**. She had cut the cake into pieces.

Wenn er nicht so vorsichtig gewesen wäre, **hätte** er sich **geschnitten**.
    If he hadn't been so careful he would have cut himself.

ich = I **du** = you **er** = he/it **sie** = she/it **es** = it/he/she **wir** = we **ihr** = you **sie** = they **Sie** = you (*polite*)

schreiben (to write)

strong, formed with haben

PRESENT

ich	schreibe
du	schreibst
er/sie/es	schreibt
wir	schreiben
ihr	schreibt
sie/Sie	schreiben

PRESENT SUBJUNCTIVE

ich	schreibe
du	schreibest
er/sie/es	schreibe
wir	schreiben
ihr	schreibet
sie/Sie	schreiben

PERFECT

ich	habe geschrieben
du	hast geschrieben
er/sie/es	hat geschrieben
wir	haben geschrieben
ihr	habt geschrieben
sie/Sie	haben geschrieben

IMPERFECT

ich	schrieb
du	schriebst
er/sie/es	schrieb
wir	schrieben
ihr	schriebt
sie/Sie	schrieben

PRESENT PARTICIPLE

schreibend

PAST PARTICIPLE

geschrieben

EXAMPLE PHRASES

Wie **schreibst** du deinen Namen? How do you spell your name?

Er sagt, er **schreibe** nicht gern Briefe. He says he doesn't like writing letters.

Sie **hat** mir einen Brief **geschrieben**. She wrote me a letter.

Er **schrieb** das Wort an die Tafel. He wrote the word on the blackboard.

---

ich = I du = you er = he/it sie = she/it es = it/he/she wir = we ihr = you sie = they Sie = you (*polite*)

schreiben

FUTURE

ich	**werde schreiben**
du	**wirst schreiben**
er/sie/es	**wird schreiben**
wir	**werden schreiben**
ihr	**werdet schreiben**
sie/Sie	**werden schreiben**

CONDITIONAL

ich	**würde schreiben**
du	**würdest schreiben**
er/sie/es	**würde schreiben**
wir	**würden schreiben**
ihr	**würdet schreiben**
sie/Sie	**würden schreiben**

PLUPERFECT

ich	**hatte geschrieben**
du	**hattest geschrieben**
er/sie/es	**hatte geschrieben**
wir	**hatten geschrieben**
ihr	**hattet geschrieben**
sie/Sie	**hatten geschrieben**

PLUPERFECT SUBJUNCTIVE

ich	**hätte geschrieben**
du	**hättest geschrieben**
er/sie/es	**hätte geschrieben**
wir	**hätten geschrieben**
ihr	**hättet geschrieben**
sie/Sie	**hätten geschrieben**

IMPERATIVE

schreib(e)!/schreiben wir!/schreibt!/schreiben Sie!

EXAMPLE PHRASES

Ich **werde** Ihnen aus dem Urlaub **schreiben**. I'll write to you when I'm on holiday.

Ich **würde** dir gern öfter **schreiben**. I'd like to write to you more often.

Er **hatte** bereits drei Romane **geschrieben**. He had already written three novels.

Ich **hätte** euch **geschrieben**, aber ich hatte keine Zeit. I would have written to you, but I had no time.

ich = I **du** = you **er** = he/it **sie** = she/it **es** = it/he/she **wir** = we **ihr** = you **sie** = they **Sie** = you (polite)

schreien (to shout)

strong, *formed with* haben

PRESENT

ich	schreie
du	schreist
er/sie/es	schreit
wir	schreien
ihr	schreit
sie/Sie	schreien

PRESENT SUBJUNCTIVE

ich	schreie
du	schreiest
er/sie/es	schreie
wir	schreien
ihr	schreiet
sie/Sie	schreien

PERFECT

ich	habe geschrien
du	hast geschrien
er/sie/es	hat geschrien
wir	haben geschrien
ihr	habt geschrien
sie/Sie	haben geschrien

IMPERFECT

ich	schrie
du	schriest
er/sie/es	schrie
wir	schrieen
ihr	schriet
sie/Sie	schrieen

PRESENT PARTICIPLE

schreiend

PAST PARTICIPLE

geschrie(e)n

EXAMPLE PHRASES

Er **schreit** dauernd. He shouts all the time.

Sie sagt, er **schreie** zu laut. She says he's shouting too loud.

Wir **haben geschrien**, er hat uns aber nicht gehört. We shouted but he didn't hear us.

Sie **schrie** vor Schmerzen. She screamed with pain.

ich = I **du** = you **er** = he/it **sie** = she/it **es** = it/he/she **wir** = we **ihr** = you **sie** = they **Sie** = you (*polite*)

schreien

FUTURE

ich	**werde schreien**
du	**wirst schreien**
er/sie/es	**wird schreien**
wir	**werden schreien**
ihr	**werdet schreien**
sie/Sie	**werden schreien**

CONDITIONAL

ich	**würde schreien**
du	**würdest schreien**
er/sie/es	**würde schreien**
wir	**würden schreien**
ihr	**würdet schreien**
sie/Sie	**würden schreien**

PLUPERFECT

ich	**hatte geschrien**
du	**hattest geschrien**
er/sie/es	**hatte geschrien**
wir	**hatten geschrien**
ihr	**hattet geschrien**
sie/Sie	**hatten geschrien**

PLUPERFECT SUBJUNCTIVE

ich	**hätte geschrien**
du	**hättest geschrien**
er/sie/es	**hätte geschrien**
wir	**hätten geschrien**
ihr	**hättet geschrien**
sie/Sie	**hätten geschrien**

IMPERATIVE

schrei(e)!/schreien wir!/schreit!/schreien Sie!

EXAMPLE PHRASES

Wenn Sie uns bedrohen, **werden** wir **schreien**. If you threaten us, we will scream.

Ich **würde** so laut **schreien**, dass er mich hört. I would shout loud enough for him to hear me.

Sie **hatte** vor Schmerzen **geschrien**. She had been screaming with pain.

Wir **hätten** fast vor Lachen **geschrien**. We had almost been screaming with laughter.

ich = I du = you er = he/it sie = she/it es = it/he/she wir = we ihr = you sie = they Sie = you *(polite)*

schweigen (to be silent)

strong, *formed with* **haben**

PRESENT

ich	**schweige**
du	**schweigst**
er/sie/es	**schweigt**
wir	**schweigen**
ihr	**schweigt**
sie/Sie	**schweigen**

PRESENT SUBJUNCTIVE

ich	**schweige**
du	**schweigest**
er/sie/es	**schweige**
wir	**schweigen**
ihr	**schweiget**
sie/Sie	**schweigen**

PERFECT

ich	**habe geschwiegen**
du	**hast geschwiegen**
er/sie/es	**hat geschwiegen**
wir	**haben geschwiegen**
ihr	**habt geschwiegen**
sie/Sie	**haben geschwiegen**

IMPERFECT

ich	**schwieg**
du	**schwiegst**
er/sie/es	**schwieg**
wir	**schwiegen**
ihr	**schwiegt**
sie/Sie	**schwiegen**

PRESENT PARTICIPLE

schweigend

PAST PARTICIPLE

geschwiegen

EXAMPLE PHRASES

Seit gestern **schweigen** die Waffen. Yesterday the guns fell silent.

Er meint, er **schweige** lieber darüber. He thinks he'd rather say nothing about it.

Sie **hat geschwiegen** wie ein Grab. She has kept completely quiet.

Plötzlich **schwieg** er. Suddenly he went silent.

ich = I **du** = you **er** = he/it **sie** = she/it **es** = it/he/she **wir** = we **ihr** = you **sie** = they **Sie** = you (*polite*)

schweigen

FUTURE

ich	**werde schweigen**
du	**wirst schweigen**
er/sie/es	**wird schweigen**
wir	**werden schweigen**
ihr	**werdet schweigen**
sie/Sie	**werden schweigen**

CONDITIONAL

ich	**würde schweigen**
du	**würdest schweigen**
er/sie/es	**würde schweigen**
wir	**würden schweigen**
ihr	**würdet schweigen**
sie/Sie	**würden schweigen**

PLUPERFECT

ich	**hatte geschwiegen**
du	**hattest geschwiegen**
er/sie/es	**hatte geschwiegen**
wir	**hatten geschwiegen**
ihr	**hattet geschwiegen**
sie/Sie	**hatten geschwiegen**

PLUPERFECT SUBJUNCTIVE

ich	**hätte geschwiegen**
du	**hättest geschwiegen**
er/sie/es	**hätte geschwiegen**
wir	**hätten geschwiegen**
ihr	**hättet geschwiegen**
sie/Sie	**hätten geschwiegen**

IMPERATIVE

schweig(e)!/schweigen wir!/schweigt!/schweigen Sie!

EXAMPLE PHRASES

Wir **werden** nicht länger **schweigen**. We won't keep quiet anymore.

Würdest du **schweigen**, wenn ich dich darum bitte? Would you keep quiet
   if I asked you to?

Er **hatte** zu lange **geschwiegen**. He had remained silent for too long.

Wenn die Sache nicht so wichtig gewesen wäre, **hätte** ich **geschwiegen**.
   I would have kept quiet if the matter hadn't been so important.

ich = I **du** = you **er** = he/it **sie** = she/it **es** = it/he/she **wir** = we **ihr** = you **sie** = they **Sie** = you (*polite*)

schwimmen (to swim)

strong, *formed with* **sein**

PRESENT

ich	**schwimme**
du	**schwimmst**
er/sie/es	**schwimmt**
wir	**schwimmen**
ihr	**schwimmt**
sie/Sie	**schwimmen**

PRESENT SUBJUNCTIVE

ich	**schwimme**
du	**schwimmest**
er/sie/es	**schwimme**
wir	**schwimmen**
ihr	**schwimmet**
sie/Sie	**schwimmen**

PERFECT

ich	**bin geschwommen**
du	**bist geschwommen**
er/sie/es	**ist geschwommen**
wir	**sind geschwommen**
ihr	**seid geschwommen**
sie/Sie	**sind geschwommen**

IMPERFECT

ich	**schwamm**
du	**schwammst**
er/sie/es	**schwamm**
wir	**schwammen**
ihr	**schwammt**
sie/Sie	**schwammen**

PRESENT PARTICIPLE

schwimmend

PAST PARTICIPLE

geschwommen

EXAMPLE PHRASES

Sie **schwimmt gern** im Meer. She likes swimming in the sea.

Er meint, sie **schwimme** im Geld. He thinks she's rolling in money.

Er **ist** über den Fluss **geschwommen**. He swam across the river.

Wir **schwammen** in der Nordsee. We were swimming in the North Sea.

ich = I **du** = you **er** = he/it **sie** = she/it **es** = it/he/she **wir** = we **ihr** = you **sie** = they **Sie** = you (*polite*)

schwimmen

FUTURE

ich	**werde schwimmen**
du	**wirst schwimmen**
er/sie/es	**wird schwimmen**
wir	**werden schwimmen**
ihr	**werdet schwimmen**
sie/Sie	**werden schwimmen**

CONDITIONAL

ich	**würde schwimmen**
du	**würdest schwimmen**
er/sie/es	**würde schwimmen**
wir	**würden schwimmen**
ihr	**würdet schwimmen**
sie/Sie	**würden schwimmen**

PLUPERFECT

ich	**war geschwommen**
du	**warst geschwommen**
er/sie/es	**war geschwommen**
wir	**waren geschwommen**
ihr	**wart geschwommen**
sie/Sie	**waren geschwommen**

PLUPERFECT SUBJUNCTIVE

ich	**wäre geschwommen**
du	**wär(e)st geschwommen**
er/sie/es	**wäre geschwommen**
wir	**wären geschwommen**
ihr	**wär(e)t geschwommen**
sie/Sie	**wären geschwommen**

IMPERATIVE

schwimm(e)!/schwimmen wir!/schwimmt!/schwimmen Sie!

EXAMPLE PHRASES

Wenn sie das hört, **wird** sie in Tränen **schwimmen**. When she hears this,
   she will be in floods of tears.

Ich **würde** gern öfter **schwimmen**. I'd like to swim more often.

Er **war** einen neuen Rekord **geschwommen**. He had swum a new record time.

Wir **wären geschwommen**, wenn das Wasser nicht so kalt gewesen wäre.
   We would have swum if the water hadn't been so cold.

ich = I **du** = you **er** = he/it **sie** = she/it **es** = it/he/she **wir** = we **ihr** = you **sie** = they **Sie** = you (*polite*)

sehen (to see)

strong, *formed with* haben

PRESENT

ich	**sehe**
du	**siehst**
er/sie/es	**sieht**
wir	**sehen**
ihr	**seht**
sie/Sie	**sehen**

PRESENT SUBJUNCTIVE

ich	**sehe**
du	**sehest**
er/sie/es	**sehe**
wir	**sehen**
ihr	**sehet**
sie/Sie	**sehen**

PERFECT

ich	**habe gesehen**
du	**hast gesehen**
er/sie/es	**hat gesehen**
wir	**haben gesehen**
ihr	**habt gesehen**
sie/Sie	**haben gesehen**

IMPERFECT

ich	**sah**
du	**sahst**
er/sie/es	**sah**
wir	**sahen**
ihr	**saht**
sie/Sie	**sahen**

PRESENT PARTICIPLE

sehend

PAST PARTICIPLE

gesehen

EXAMPLE PHRASES

Mein Vater **sieht** schlecht. My father has bad eyesight.

Er sagt, er **sehe** das ganz anders. He says he sees this quite differently.

Ich **habe** diesen Film noch nicht **gesehen**. I haven't seen this film yet.

Er **sah** auf die Uhr. He looked at his watch.

ich = I **du** = you **er** = he/it **sie** = she/it **es** = it/he/she **wir** = we **ihr** = you **sie** = they **Sie** = you (*polite*)

sehen

FUTURE

ich	**werde sehen**
du	**wirst sehen**
er/sie/es	**wird sehen**
wir	**werden sehen**
ihr	**werdet sehen**
sie/Sie	**werden sehen**

CONDITIONAL

ich	**würde sehen**
du	**würdest sehen**
er/sie/es	**würde sehen**
wir	**würden sehen**
ihr	**würdet sehen**
sie/Sie	**würden sehen**

PLUPERFECT

ich	**hatte gesehen**
du	**hattest gesehen**
er/sie/es	**hatte gesehen**
wir	**hatten gesehen**
ihr	**hattet gesehen**
sie/Sie	**hatten gesehen**

PLUPERFECT SUBJUNCTIVE

ich	**hätte gesehen**
du	**hättest gesehen**
er/sie/es	**hätte gesehen**
wir	**hätten gesehen**
ihr	**hättet gesehen**
sie/Sie	**hätten gesehen**

IMPERATIVE

sieh(e)!/sehen wir!/seht!/sehen Sie!

EXAMPLE PHRASES

Wir **werden sehen**, wie sich die Dinge entwickeln. We'll see how things develop.

Das **würde** ich ganz anders **sehen**. That's not how I would see it.

Wir **hatten** ihn seit zwei Jahren nicht mehr **gesehen**. We hadn't seen him for two years.

Ich **hätte** es lieber **gesehen**, wenn du dich entschuldigt hättest. I would have preferred it if you had apologized.

ich = I **du** = you **er** = he/it **sie** = she/it **es** = it/he/she **wir** = we **ihr** = you **sie** = they **Sie** = you (*polite*)

sein (to be)

strong, *formed with* sein

PRESENT

ich	**bin**
du	**bist**
er/sie/es	**ist**
wir	**sind**
ihr	**seid**
sie/Sie	**sind**

PRESENT SUBJUNCTIVE

ich	**sei**
du	**sei(e)st**
er/sie/es	**sei**
wir	**seien**
ihr	**seiet**
sie/Sie	**seien**

PERFECT

ich	**bin gewesen**
du	**bist gewesen**
er/sie/es	**ist gewesen**
wir	**sind gewesen**
ihr	**seid gewesen**
sie/Sie	**sind gewesen**

IMPERFECT

ich	**war**
du	**warst**
er/sie/es	**war**
wir	**waren**
ihr	**wart**
sie/Sie	**waren**

PRESENT PARTICIPLE

seiend

PAST PARTICIPLE

gewesen

EXAMPLE PHRASES

Er **ist** zehn Jahre. He's ten years old.

Ich **bin** seit einem Jahr nicht mehr dort **gewesen**. I haven't been there for
a year.

Wir **waren** gestern im Theater. We were at the theatre yesterday.

ich = I **du** = you **er** = he/it **sie** = she/it **es** = it/he/she **wir** = we **ihr** = you **sie** = they **Sie** = you (*polite*)

sein

FUTURE

ich	**werde sein**
du	**wirst sein**
er/sie/es	**wird sein**
wir	**werden sein**
ihr	**werdet sein**
sie/Sie	**werden sein**

CONDITIONAL

ich	**würde sein**
du	**würdest sein**
er/sie/es	**würde sein**
wir	**würden sein**
ihr	**würdet sein**
sie/Sie	**würden sein**

PLUPERFECT

ich	**war gewesen**
du	**warst gewesen**
er/sie/es	**war gewesen**
wir	**waren gewesen**
ihr	**wart gewesen**
sie/Sie	**waren gewesen**

PLUPERFECT SUBJUNCTIVE

ich	**wäre gewesen**
du	**wär(e)st gewesen**
er/sie/es	**wäre gewesen**
wir	**wären gewesen**
ihr	**wär(e)t gewesen**
sie/Sie	**wären gewesen**

IMPERATIVE

sei!/seien wir!/seid!/seien Sie!

EXAMPLE PHRASES

Morgen **werde** ich in Berlin **sein**. I'll be in Berlin tomorrow.

Ich **würde** gern so **sein** wie du. I would like to be like you.

Sie **war** uns eine gute Mutter **gewesen**. She had been a good mother to us.

Wenn du nicht **gewesen wär(e)st**, wäre ich jetzt tot. If it hadn't been for you
  I would be dead now.

---

ich = I **du** = you **er** = he/it **sie** = she/it **es** = it/he/she **wir** = we **ihr** = you **sie** = they **Sie** = you *(polite)*

senden* (to send)

mixed, *formed with* haben

PRESENT

ich	**sende**
du	**sendest**
er/sie/es	**sendet**
wir	**senden**
ihr	**sendet**
sie/Sie	**senden**

PRESENT SUBJUNCTIVE

ich	**sende**
du	**sendest**
er/sie/es	**sende**
wir	**senden**
ihr	**sendet**
sie/Sie	**senden**

PERFECT

ich	**habe gesandt**
du	**hast gesandt**
er/sie/es	**hat gesandt**
wir	**haben gesandt**
ihr	**habt gesandt**
sie/Sie	**haben gesandt**

IMPERFECT

ich	**sandte**
du	**sandtest**
er/sie/es	**sandte**
wir	**sandten**
ihr	**sandtet**
sie/Sie	**sandten**

PRESENT PARTICIPLE

sendend

PAST PARTICIPLE

gesandt

Weak when means to broadcast.

EXAMPLE PHRASES

Sie **sendet** viele Grüße. She sends best regards.

Er sagt, er **sende** seine besten Wünsche. He says he sends best wishes.

Sie **haben** mir den neuesten Katalog **gesandt**. They sent me their latest catalogue.

Er **sandte** nach mir. He sent for me.

ich = I **du** = you **er** = he/it **sie** = she/it **es** = it/he/she **wir** = we **ihr** = you **sie** = they **Sie** = you (*polite*)

senden

FUTURE

ich	**werde senden**
du	**wirst senden**
er/sie/es	**wird senden**
wir	**werden senden**
ihr	**werdet senden**
sie/Sie	**werden senden**

CONDITIONAL

ich	**würde senden**
du	**würdest senden**
er/sie/es	**würde senden**
wir	**würden senden**
ihr	**würdet senden**
sie/Sie	**würden senden**

PLUPERFECT

ich	**hatte gesandt**
du	**hattest gesandt**
er/sie/es	**hatte gesandt**
wir	**hatten gesandt**
ihr	**hattet gesandt**
sie/Sie	**hatten gesandt**

PLUPERFECT SUBJUNCTIVE

ich	**hätte gesandt**
du	**hättest gesandt**
er/sie/es	**hätte gesandt**
wir	**hätten gesandt**
ihr	**hättet gesandt**
sie/Sie	**hätten gesandt**

IMPERATIVE

send(e)!/senden wir!/sendet!/senden Sie!

EXAMPLE PHRASES

Ich **werde** ihr einen Brief **senden**. I'll send her a letter.

Ich **würde** den Brief lieber als Einschreiben **senden**. I would prefer to send the letter recorded delivery.

Er **hatte** das Paket per Kurier **gesandt**. He had sent the parcel by courier.

Sie **hätte** dir besser ein Foto von ihr **gesandt**. It would have been better if she had sent you a photograph of her.

ich = I   du = you   er = he/it   sie = she/it   es = it/he/she   wir = we   ihr = you   sie = they   Sie = you (*polite*)

singen (to sing)

strong, *formed with* haben

PRESENT

ich	**singe**
du	**singst**
er/sie/es	**singt**
wir	**singen**
ihr	**singt**
sie/Sie	**singen**

PRESENT SUBJUNCTIVE

ich	**singe**
du	**singest**
er/sie/es	**singe**
wir	**singen**
ihr	**singet**
sie/Sie	**singen**

PERFECT

ich	**habe gesungen**
du	**hast gesungen**
er/sie/es	**hat gesungen**
wir	**haben gesungen**
ihr	**habt gesungen**
sie/Sie	**haben gesungen**

IMPERFECT

ich	**sang**
du	**sangst**
er/sie/es	**sang**
wir	**sangen**
ihr	**sangt**
sie/Sie	**sangen**

PRESENT PARTICIPLE

singend

PAST PARTICIPLE

gesungen

EXAMPLE PHRASES

Er **singt** nicht gut. **He's a bad singer.**

Sie meint, er **singe** nicht gut. **She thinks he's a bad singer.**

Ich **habe** dieses Lied früher oft **gesungen.** I used to sing this song a lot.

Sie **sang** das Kind in den Schlaf. **She sang the child to sleep.**

ich = I **du** = you **er** = he/it **sie** = she/it **es** = it/he/she **wir** = we **ihr** = you **sie** = they **Sie** = you (*polite*)

singen

FUTURE

ich	**werde singen**
du	**wirst singen**
er/sie/es	**wird singen**
wir	**werden singen**
ihr	**werdet singen**
sie/Sie	**werden singen**

CONDITIONAL

ich	**würde singen**
du	**würdest singen**
er/sie/es	**würde singen**
wir	**würden singen**
ihr	**würdet singen**
sie/Sie	**würden singen**

PLUPERFECT

ich	**hatte gesungen**
du	**hattest gesungen**
er/sie/es	**hatte gesungen**
wir	**hatten gesungen**
ihr	**hattet gesungen**
sie/Sie	**hatten gesungen**

PLUPERFECT SUBJUNCTIVE

ich	**hätte gesungen**
du	**hättest gesungen**
er/sie/es	**hätte gesungen**
wir	**hätten gesungen**
ihr	**hättet gesungen**
sie/Sie	**hätten gesungen**

IMPERATIVE

sing(e)!/singen wir!/singt!/singen Sie!

EXAMPLE PHRASES

Wir **werden** jetzt die Nationalhymne **singen**. We will sing the national anthem now.

Ich **würde** jetzt gern ein Lied **singen**. I'd like to sing a song now.

Sie **hatte** das Kind in den Schlaf **gesungen**. She had sung the child to sleep.

Er **hätte** dieses Lied so gern **gesungen**. He would have loved to sing this song.

ich = I du = you **er** = he/it **sie** = she/it **es** = it/he/she **wir** = we **ihr** = you **sie** = they **Sie** = you (polite)

sinken (to sink)

strong, *formed with* **sein**

PRESENT

ich	**sinke**
du	**sinkst**
er/sie/es	**sinkt**
wir	**sinken**
ihr	**sinkt**
sie/Sie	**sinken**

PRESENT SUBJUNCTIVE

ich	**sinke**
du	**sinkest**
er/sie/es	**sinke**
wir	**sinken**
ihr	**sinket**
sie/Sie	**sinken**

PERFECT

ich	**bin gesunken**
du	**bist gesunken**
er/sie/es	**ist gesunken**
wir	**sind gesunken**
ihr	**seid gesunken**
sie/Sie	**sind gesunken**

IMPERFECT

ich	**sank**
du	**sankst**
er/sie/es	**sank**
wir	**sanken**
ihr	**sankt**
sie/Sie	**sanken**

PRESENT PARTICIPLE

sinkend

PAST PARTICIPLE

gesunken

EXAMPLE PHRASES

Die Preise für Handys **sinken**. Prices of mobile phones are falling.

Sie sagt, sie **sinke** gleich in Ohnmacht. She says she's about to faint.

Wann **ist** die Titanic **gesunken**? When did the Titanic sink?

Er **sank** zu Boden. He sank to the ground.

sinken

FUTURE

ich	**werde sinken**
du	**wirst sinken**
er/sie/es	**wird sinken**
wir	**werden sinken**
ihr	**werdet sinken**
sie/Sie	**werden sinken**

CONDITIONAL

ich	**würde sinken**
du	**würdest sinken**
er/sie/es	**würde sinken**
wir	**würden sinken**
ihr	**würdet sinken**
sie/Sie	**würden sinken**

PLUPERFECT

ich	**war gesunken**
du	**warst gesunken**
er/sie/es	**war gesunken**
wir	**waren gesunken**
ihr	**wart gesunken**
sie/Sie	**waren gesunken**

PLUPERFECT SUBJUNCTIVE

ich	**wäre gesunken**
du	**wär(e)st gesunken**
er/sie/es	**wäre gesunken**
wir	**wären gesunken**
ihr	**wär(e)t gesunken**
sie/Sie	**wären gesunken**

IMPERATIVE

sink(e)!/sinken wir!/sinkt!/sinken Sie!

EXAMPLE PHRASES

Preise und Löhne **werden** deutlich **sinken**. Prices and wages will go down considerably.

Man dachte, dieses Schiff **würde** niemals **sinken**. It was thought this ship would never sink.

Sie **war** in meiner Achtung **gesunken**. She had gone down in my estimation.

Mir **wäre** die Hoffnung **gesunken**. I would have lost courage.

---

ich = I du = you er = he/it sie = she/it es = it/he/she wir = we ihr = you sie = they Sie = you (*polite*)

sitzen (to sit)

strong, *formed with* haben

PRESENT

ich	**sitze**
du	**sitzt**
er/sie/es	**sitzt**
wir	**sitzen**
ihr	**sitzt**
sie/Sie	**sitzen**

PRESENT SUBJUNCTIVE

ich	**sitze**
du	**sitzest**
er/sie/es	**sitze**
wir	**sitzen**
ihr	**sitzet**
sie/Sie	**sitzen**

PERFECT

ich	**habe gesessen**
du	**hast gesessen**
er/sie/es	**hat gesessen**
wir	**haben gesessen**
ihr	**habt gesessen**
sie/Sie	**haben gesessen**

IMPERFECT

ich	**saß**
du	**saßest**
er/sie/es	**saß**
wir	**saßen**
ihr	**saßt**
sie/Sie	**saßen**

PRESENT PARTICIPLE

sitzend gesessen

PAST PARTICIPLE

EXAMPLE PHRASES

Deine Krawatte **sitzt** nicht richtig. Your tie isn't straight.

Sie sagt, sie **sitze** schon seit Stunden hier. She says she's been sitting here
   for hours.

Ich **habe** zwei Jahre über dieser Arbeit **gesessen**. I've spent two years on this
   piece of work.

Er **saß** auf meinem Stuhl. He was sitting on my chair.

ich = I **du** = you **er** = he/it **sie** = she/it **es** = it/he/she **wir** = we **ihr** = you **sie** = they **Sie** = you (*polite*)

sitzen

FUTURE

ich **werde sitzen**

du **wirst sitzen**

er/sie/es **wird sitzen**

wir **werden sitzen**

ihr **werdet sitzen**

sie/Sie **werden sitzen**

CONDITIONAL

ich **würde sitzen**

du **würdest sitzen**

er/sie/es **würde sitzen**

wir **würden sitzen**

ihr **würdet sitzen**

sie/Sie **würden sitzen**

PLUPERFECT

ich **hatte gesessen**

du **hattest gesessen**

er/sie/es **hatte gesessen**

wir **hatten gesessen**

ihr **hattet gesessen**

sie/Sie **hatten gesessen**

PLUPERFECT SUBJUNCTIVE

ich **hätte gesessen**

du **hättest gesessen**

er/sie/es **hätte gesessen**

wir **hätten gesessen**

ihr **hättet gesessen**

sie/Sie **hätten gesessen**

IMPERATIVE

sitz(e)!/sitzen wir!/sitzt!/sitzen Sie!

EXAMPLE PHRASES

Wo **wird** der Präsident **sitzen**? Where will the president be sitting?

Wir **würden** gern in der ersten Reihe **sitzen**. We'd like to sit in the front row.

Wir **hatten** dort sehr bequem **gesessen**. We had been sitting very comfortably
there.

Sie **hätten** lieber draußen **gesessen**. They would have preferred to sit outside.

---

ich = I **du** = you **er** = he/it **sie** = she/it **es** = it/he/she **wir** = we **ihr** = you **sie** = they **Sie** = you (*polite*)

sollen (to be to)

modal, *formed with* haben

PRESENT

ich	**soll**
du	**sollst**
er/sie/es	**soll**
wir	**sollen**
ihr	**sollt**
sie/Sie	**sollen**

PRESENT SUBJUNCTIVE

ich	**solle**
du	**sollest**
er/sie/es	**solle**
wir	**sollen**
ihr	**sollet**
sie/Sie	**sollen**

PERFECT

ich	**habe gesollt/sollen**
du	**hast gesollt/sollen**
er/sie/es	**hat gesollt/sollen**
wir	**haben gesollt/sollen**
ihr	**habt gesollt/sollen**
sie/Sie	**haben gesollt/sollen**

IMPERFECT

ich	**sollte**
du	**solltest**
er/sie/es	**sollte**
wir	**sollten**
ihr	**solltet**
sie/Sie	**sollten**

PRESENT PARTICIPLE

sollend

PAST PARTICIPLE

gesollt/sollen*

*This form is used when combined with another infinitive.

EXAMPLE PHRASES

Ich **soll** um 5 Uhr dort sein. I'm supposed to be there at 5 o'clock.

Er sagt, ich **solle** ihm nicht böse sein. He says I shouldn't be cross with him.

Das **hast** du nicht **gesollt**. You shouldn't have done that.

Ich **sollte** draußen bleiben. I was supposed to stay outside.

ich = I **du** = you **er** = he/it **sie** = she/it **es** = it/he/she **wir** = we **ihr** = you **sie** = they **Sie** = you (*polite*)

sollen

FUTURE

ich	**werde sollen**
du	**wirst sollen**
er/sie/es	**wird sollen**
wir	**werden sollen**
ihr	**werdet sollen**
sie/Sie	**werden sollen**

CONDITIONAL

ich	**würde sollen**
du	**würdest sollen**
er/sie/es	**würde sollen**
wir	**würden sollen**
ihr	**würdet sollen**
sie/Sie	**würden sollen**

PLUPERFECT

ich	**hatte gesollt/sollen**
du	**hattest gesollt/sollen**
er/sie/es	**hatte gesollt/sollen**
wir	**hatten gesollt/sollen**
ihr	**hattet gesollt/sollen**
sie/Sie	**hatten gesollt/sollen**

PLUPERFECT SUBJUNCTIVE

ich	**hätte gesollt/sollen**
du	**hättest gesollt/sollen**
er/sie/es	**hätte gesollt/sollen**
wir	**hätten gesollt/sollen**
ihr	**hättet gesollt/sollen**
sie/Sie	**hätten gesollt/sollen**

EXAMPLE PHRASES

Das Gebäude **hatte** ein Museum werden **sollen**. The building had been meant
to become a museum

Das **hättest** du nicht tun **sollen**. You shouldn't have done that.

ich = I **du** = you **er** = he/it **sie** = she/it **es** = it/he/she **wir** = we **ihr** = you **sie** = they **Sie** = you (*polite*)

sprechen (to speak)

strong, *formed with* haben

PRESENT

ich	**spreche**
du	**sprichst**
er/sie/es	**spricht**
wir	**sprechen**
ihr	**sprecht**
sie/Sie	**sprechen**

PRESENT SUBJUNCTIVE

ich	**spreche**
du	**sprechest**
er/sie/es	**spreche**
wir	**sprechen**
ihr	**sprechet**
sie/Sie	**sprechen**

PERFECT

ich	**habe gesprochen**
du	**hast gesprochen**
er/sie/es	**hat gesprochen**
wir	**haben gesprochen**
ihr	**habt gesprochen**
sie/Sie	**haben gesprochen**

IMPERFECT

ich	**sprach**
du	**sprachst**
er/sie/es	**sprach**
wir	**sprachen**
ihr	**spracht**
sie/Sie	**sprachen**

PRESENT PARTICIPLE

sprechend

PAST PARTICIPLE

gesprochen

EXAMPLE PHRASES

Er **spricht** kein Italienisch. He doesn't speak Italian.

Sie sagt, sie **spreche** aus Erfahrung. She says she's speaking from experience.

Hast du mit ihr **gesprochen**? Have you spoken to her?

Er **sprach** nur gebrochen Deutsch. He only spoke broken German.

ich = I **du** = you **er** = he/it **sie** = she/it **es** = it/he/she **wir** = we **ihr** = you **sie** = they **Sie** = you (*polite*)

sprechen

FUTURE

ich	**werde** sprechen
du	**wirst** sprechen
er/sie/es	**wird** sprechen
wir	**werden** sprechen
ihr	**werdet** sprechen
sie/Sie	**werden** sprechen

CONDITIONAL

ich	**würde** sprechen
du	**würdest** sprechen
er/sie/es	**würde** sprechen
wir	**würden** sprechen
ihr	**würdet** sprechen
sie/Sie	**würden** sprechen

PLUPERFECT

ich	**hatte** gesprochen
du	**hattest** gesprochen
er/sie/es	**hatte** gesprochen
wir	**hatten** gesprochen
ihr	**hattet** gesprochen
sie/Sie	**hatten** gesprochen

PLUPERFECT SUBJUNCTIVE

ich	**hätte** gesprochen
du	**hättest** gesprochen
er/sie/es	**hätte** gesprochen
wir	**hätten** gesprochen
ihr	**hättet** gesprochen
sie/Sie	**hätten** gesprochen

IMPERATIVE

sprich!/sprechen wir!/sprecht!/sprechen Sie!

EXAMPLE PHRASES

Ich **werde** mit ihm darüber **sprechen**. I'll speak to him about it.

Ich **würde** dich gern privat **sprechen**. I would like to speak to you privately.

Er **hatte** davon **gesprochen**, einen Computer zu kaufen. He had been talking about buying a computer.

Ich **hätte** gern länger mit Ihnen darüber **gesprochen**. I would have liked to have spoken to you about it for longer.

ich = I du = you er = he/it sie = she/it es = it/he/she wir = we ihr = you sie = they Sie = you *(polite)*

springen (to jump)

strong, *formed with* sein

PRESENT

ich	**springe**
du	**springst**
er/sie/es	**springt**
wir	**springen**
ihr	**springt**
sie/Sie	**springen**

PRESENT SUBJUNCTIVE

ich	**springe**
du	**springest**
er/sie/es	**springe**
wir	**springen**
ihr	**springet**
sie/Sie	**springen**

PERFECT

ich	**bin gesprungen**
du	**bist gesprungen**
er/sie/es	**ist gesprungen**
wir	**sind gesprungen**
ihr	**seid gesprungen**
sie/Sie	**sind gesprungen**

IMPERFECT

ich	**sprang**
du	**sprangst**
er/sie/es	**sprang**
wir	**sprangen**
ihr	**sprangt**
sie/Sie	**sprangen**

PRESENT PARTICIPLE

springend

PAST PARTICIPLE

gesprungen

EXAMPLE PHRASES

Die Katze **springt** auf den Tisch. **The cat jumps on the table.**

Sie sagt, sie **springe** gern vom Sprungbrett. **She says she likes jumping from the springboard.**

Der Zug **ist** aus dem Gleis **gesprungen**. **The train came off the rails.**

Er **sprang** über den Zaun. **He jumped over the fence.**

---

ich = I **du** = you **er** = he/it **sie** = she/it **es** = it/he/she **wir** = we **ihr** = you **sie** = they **Sie** = you *(polite)*

springen

FUTURE

ich	**werde springen**
du	**wirst springen**
er/sie/es	**wird springen**
wir	**werden springen**
ihr	**werdet springen**
sie/Sie	**werden springen**

CONDITIONAL

ich	**würde springen**
du	**würdest springen**
er/sie/es	**würde springen**
wir	**würden springen**
ihr	**würdet springen**
sie/Sie	**würden springen**

PLUPERFECT

ich	**war gesprungen**
du	**warst gesprungen**
er/sie/es	**war gesprungen**
wir	**waren gesprungen**
ihr	**wart gesprungen**
sie/Sie	**waren gesprungen**

PLUPERFECT SUBJUNCTIVE

ich	**wäre gesprungen**
du	**wär(e)st gesprungen**
er/sie/es	**wäre gesprungen**
wir	**wären gesprungen**
ihr	**wär(e)t gesprungen**
sie/Sie	**wären gesprungen**

IMPERATIVE

spring(e)!/springen wir!/springt!/springen Sie!

EXAMPLE PHRASES

Er **wird** bestimmt einen neuen Rekord **springen**. He's sure to make a record jump.

Ich **würde** ihm am liebsten an die Kehle **springen**. I could strangle him.

Er **war** zwei Meter hoch **gesprungen**. He had jumped two metres high.

Ich **wäre** nicht vom fahrenden Zug **gesprungen**. I wouldn't have jumped off the moving train.

---

ich = I du = you er = he/it sie = she/it es = it/he/she wir = we ihr = you sie = they Sie = you *(polite)*

stechen (to sting, to prick)

strong, *formed with* haben

PRESENT

ich	**steche**
du	**stichst**
er/sie/es	**sticht**
wir	**stechen**
ihr	**stecht**
sie/Sie	**stechen**

PRESENT SUBJUNCTIVE

ich	**steche**
du	**stechest**
er/sie/es	**steche**
wir	**stechen**
ihr	**stechet**
sie/Sie	**stechen**

PERFECT

ich	**habe gestochen**
du	**hast gestochen**
er/sie/es	**hat gestochen**
wir	**haben gestochen**
ihr	**habt gestochen**
sie/Sie	**haben gestochen**

IMPERFECT

ich	**stach**
du	**stachst**
er/sie/es	**stach**
wir	**stachen**
ihr	**stacht**
sie/Sie	**stachen**

PRESENT PARTICIPLE

stechend

PAST PARTICIPLE

gestochen

EXAMPLE PHRASES

Libellen **stechen** nicht. Dragonflies don't sting.

Er sagt, es **steche** ihm im Rücken. He says he has a sharp pain in his back.

Eine Mücke **hat** mich **gestochen**. A midge bit me.

Die Sonne **stach** uns in die Augen. The sun hurt our eyes.

stechen

FUTURE

ich	**werde stechen**
du	**wirst stechen**
er/sie/es	**wird stechen**
wir	**werden stechen**
ihr	**werdet stechen**
sie/Sie	**werden stechen**

CONDITIONAL

ich	**würde stechen**
du	**würdest stechen**
er/sie/es	**würde stechen**
wir	**würden stechen**
ihr	**würdet stechen**
sie/Sie	**würden stechen**

PLUPERFECT

ich	**hatte gestochen**
du	**hattest gestochen**
er/sie/es	**hatte gestochen**
wir	**hatten gestochen**
ihr	**hattet gestochen**
sie/Sie	**hatten gestochen**

PLUPERFECT SUBJUNCTIVE

ich	**hätte gestochen**
du	**hättest gestochen**
er/sie/es	**hätte gestochen**
wir	**hätten gestochen**
ihr	**hättet gestochen**
sie/Sie	**hätten gestochen**

IMPERATIVE

stich!/stechen wir!/stecht!/stechen Sie!

EXAMPLE PHRASES

Morgen **werden** wir in See **stechen**. We'll put to sea tomorrow.

Die Wespe **würde** dich nur **stechen**, wenn sie Angst hätte. The wasp would only sting you if it was scared.

Der Geruch **hatte** mir in die Nase **gestochen**. The smell had made my nose sting.

Fast **hätte** eine Biene sie **gestochen**. A bee had almost stung her.

ich = I **du** = you **er** = he/it **sie** = she/it **es** = it/he/she **wir** = we **ihr** = you **sie** = they **Sie** = you *(polite)*

stehen (to stand)

strong, *formed with* haben

PRESENT

ich	stehe
du	stehst
er/sie/es	steht
wir	stehen
ihr	steht
sie/Sie	stehen

PRESENT SUBJUNCTIVE

ich	stehe
du	stehest
er/sie/es	stehe
wir	stehen
ihr	stehet
sie/Sie	stehen

PERFECT

ich	habe gestanden
du	hast gestanden
er/sie/es	hat gestanden
wir	haben gestanden
ihr	habt gestanden
sie/Sie	haben gestanden

IMPERFECT

ich	stand
du	stand(e)st
er/sie/es	stand
wir	standen
ihr	standet
sie/Sie	standen

PRESENT PARTICIPLE

stehend

PAST PARTICIPLE

gestanden

EXAMPLE PHRASES

Die Vase **steht** auf dem Tisch. **The vase is on the table.**

Er sagt, das Buch **stehe** auf der Leseliste. **He says the book is on the reading list.**

Es **hat** in der Zeitung **gestanden**. **It was in the newspaper.**

Wir **standen** an der Bushaltestelle. **We stood at the bus stop.**

---

ich = I   du = you   er = he/it   sie = she/it   es = it/he/she   wir = we   ihr = you   sie = they   Sie = you (polite)

stehen

FUTURE

ich	**werde stehen**
du	**wirst stehen**
er/sie/es	**wird stehen**
wir	**werden stehen**
ihr	**werdet stehen**
sie/Sie	**werden stehen**

CONDITIONAL

ich	**würde stehen**
du	**würdest stehen**
er/sie/es	**würde stehen**
wir	**würden stehen**
ihr	**würdet stehen**
sie/Sie	**würden stehen**

PLUPERFECT

ich	**hatte gestanden**
du	**hattest gestanden**
er/sie/es	**hatte gestanden**
wir	**hatten gestanden**
ihr	**hattet gestanden**
sie/Sie	**hatten gestanden**

PLUPERFECT SUBJUNCTIVE

ich	**hätte gestanden**
du	**hättest gestanden**
er/sie/es	**hätte gestanden**
wir	**hätten gestanden**
ihr	**hättet gestanden**
sie/Sie	**hätten gestanden**

IMPERATIVE
steh(e)!/stehen wir!/steht!/stehen Sie!

EXAMPLE PHRASES

Das neue Modell **wird** bald zur Verfügung **stehen**. The new model will be available soon.

Dieses Kleid **würde** dir gut **stehen**. This dress would suit you.

Ich **hatte** lange im Regen **gestanden**. I had been standing in the rain for a long time.

Diese Farbe **hätte** mir gar nicht **gestanden**. This colour wouldn't have suited me at all.

ich = I **du** = you **er** = he/it **sie** = she/it **es** = it/he/she **wir** = we **ihr** = you **sie** = they **Sie** = you (*polite*)

stehlen (to steal)

strong, *formed with* haben

PRESENT

ich	stehle
du	stiehlst
er/sie/es	stiehlt
wir	stehlen
ihr	stehlt
sie/Sie	stehlen

PRESENT SUBJUNCTIVE

ich	stehle
du	stehlest
er/sie/es	stehle
wir	stehlen
ihr	stehlet
sie/Sie	stehlen

PERFECT

ich	habe gestohlen
du	hast gestohlen
er/sie/es	hat gestohlen
wir	haben gestohlen
ihr	habt gestohlen
sie/Sie	haben gestohlen

IMPERFECT

ich	stahl
du	stahlst
er/sie/es	stahl
wir	stahlen
ihr	stahlt
sie/Sie	stahlen

PRESENT PARTICIPLE

stehlend

PAST PARTICIPLE

gestohlen

EXAMPLE PHRASES

Du **stiehlst** uns doch nur die Zeit. You're just wasting our time.

Er sagt, er **stehle** nicht gern von Freunden. He says he doesn't like stealing from friends.

Er **hat** das ganze Geld **gestohlen**. He stole all the money.

Er **stahl** sich aus dem Haus. He stole out of the house.

stehlen

FUTURE

ich	**werde stehlen**
du	**wirst stehlen**
er/sie/es	**wird stehlen**
wir	**werden stehlen**
ihr	**werdet stehlen**
sie/Sie	**werden stehlen**

CONDITIONAL

ich	**würde stehlen**
du	**würdest stehlen**
er/sie/es	**würde stehlen**
wir	**würden stehlen**
ihr	**würdet stehlen**
sie/Sie	**würden stehlen**

PLUPERFECT

ich	**hatte gestohlen**
du	**hattest gestohlen**
er/sie/es	**hatte gestohlen**
wir	**hatten gestohlen**
ihr	**hattet gestohlen**
sie/Sie	**hatten gestohlen**

PLUPERFECT SUBJUNCTIVE

ich	**hätte gestohlen**
du	**hättest gestohlen**
er/sie/es	**hätte gestohlen**
wir	**hätten gestohlen**
ihr	**hättet gestohlen**
sie/Sie	**hätten gestohlen**

IMPERATIVE

stiehl!/stehlen wir!/stehlt!/stehlen Sie!

EXAMPLE PHRASES

Ich **werde** mich nicht aus der Verantwortung **stehlen**. I won't evade my responsibility.

Ich **würde** euch nichts **stehlen**. I wouldn't steal anything from you.

Die Einbrecher **hatten** ihren ganzen Schmuck **gestohlen**. The burglars had stolen all her jewellery.

Er **hätte** fast alle meine CDs **gestohlen**. He almost stole all my CDs.

ich = I **du** = you **er** = he/it **sie** = she/it **es** = it/he/she **wir** = we **ihr** = you **sie** = they **Sie** = you (*polite*)

steigen (to climb) *Himalaya / Alps* strong, formed with sein

PRESENT		**PRESENT SUBJUNCTIVE**	
ich	steige	ich	steige
du	steigst	du	steigest
er/sie/es	steigt	er/sie/es	steige
wir	steigen	wir	steigen
ihr	steigt	ihr	steiget
sie/Sie	steigen	sie/Sie	steigen

PERFECT		**IMPERFECT**	
ich	bin gestiegen	ich	stieg
du	bist gestiegen	du	stiegst
er/sie/es	ist gestiegen	er/sie/es	stieg
wir	sind gestiegen	wir	stiegen
ihr	seid gestiegen	ihr	stiegt
sie/Sie	sind gestiegen	sie/Sie	stiegen

PRESENT PARTICIPLE	**PAST PARTICIPLE**
steigend	gestiegen

EXAMPLE PHRASES

Die Passagiere **steigen** aus dem Flugzeug. The passengers are getting off
the plane.

Sie sagt, ihr Gehalt **steige** jedes Jahr. She says her salary increases every year.

Sie **ist** auf die Leiter **gestiegen**. She climbed up the ladder.

Die Temperatur **stieg** auf 28 Grad. The temperature rose to 28 degrees.

ich = I **du** = you **er** = he/it **sie** = she/it **es** = it/he/she **wir** = we **ihr** = you **sie** = they **Sie** = you *(polite)*

steigen

FUTURE

ich	**werde steigen**
du	**wirst steigen**
er/sie/es	**wird steigen**
wir	**werden steigen**
ihr	**werdet steigen**
sie/Sie	**werden steigen**

CONDITIONAL

ich	**würde steigen**
du	**würdest steigen**
er/sie/es	**würde steigen**
wir	**würden steigen**
ihr	**würdet steigen**
sie/Sie	**würden steigen**

PLUPERFECT

ich	**war gestiegen**
du	**warst gestiegen**
er/sie/es	**war gestiegen**
wir	**waren gestiegen**
ihr	**wart gestiegen**
sie/Sie	**waren gestiegen**

PLUPERFECT SUBJUNCTIVE

ich	**wäre gestiegen**
du	**wär(e)st gestiegen**
er/sie/es	**wäre gestiegen**
wir	**wären gestiegen**
ihr	**wär(e)t gestiegen**
sie/Sie	**wären gestiegen**

IMPERATIVE

steig(e)!/steigen wir!/steigt!/steigen Sie!

EXAMPLE PHRASES

Wir **werden** morgen aufs Matterhorn **steigen**. We'll climb the Matterhorn tomorrow.

Ich **würde** nie in ein Flugzeug **steigen**. I would never go on a plane.

Meine Stimmung **war gestiegen**. My mood had improved.

Wenn er dir geholfen hätte, **wäre** er in meiner Achtung **gestiegen**. If he had helped you he would have risen in my estimation.

ich = I du = you er = he/it sie = she/it es = it/he/she wir = we ihr = you sie = they Sie = you (polite)

sterben (to die)

strong, *formed with* **sein**

PRESENT		PRESENT SUBJUNCTIVE	
ich	**sterbe**	ich	**sterbe**
du	**stirbst**	du	**sterbest**
er/sie/es	**stirbt**	er/sie/es	**sterbe**
wir	**sterben**	wir	**sterben**
ihr	**sterbt**	ihr	**sterbet**
sie/Sie	**sterben**	sie/Sie	**sterben**

PERFECT		IMPERFECT	
ich	**bin gestorben**	ich	**starb**
du	**bist gestorben**	du	**starbst**
er/sie/es	**ist gestorben**	er/sie/es	**starb**
wir	**sind gestorben**	wir	**starben**
ihr	**seid gestorben**	ihr	**starbt**
sie/Sie	**sind gestorben**	sie/Sie	**starben**

PRESENT PARTICIPLE	PAST PARTICIPLE
sterbend	gestorben

EXAMPLE PHRASES

Ich **sterbe** hier vor Langeweile. I'm dying of boredom here.

Sie sagt, sie **sterbe** vor Angst. She says she's frightened to death.

Shakespeare **ist** 1616 **gestorben**. Shakespeare died in 1616.

Er **starb** eines natürlichen Todes. He died a natural death.

sterben

FUTURE

ich	**werde sterben**
du	**wirst sterben**
er/sie/es	**wird sterben**
wir	**werden sterben**
ihr	**werdet sterben**
sie/Sie	**werden sterben**

CONDITIONAL

ich	**würde sterben**
du	**würdest sterben**
er/sie/es	**würde sterben**
wir	**würden sterben**
ihr	**würdet sterben**
sie/Sie	**würden sterben**

PLUPERFECT

ich	**war gestorben**
du	**warst gestorben**
er/sie/es	**war gestorben**
wir	**waren gestorben**
ihr	**wart gestorben**
sie/Sie	**waren gestorben**

PLUPERFECT SUBJUNCTIVE

ich	**wäre gestorben**
du	**wär(e)st gestorben**
er/sie/es	**wäre gestorben**
wir	**wären gestorben**
ihr	**wär(e)t gestorben**
sie/Sie	**wären gestorben**

IMPERATIVE

stirb!/sterben wir!/sterbt!/sterben Sie!

EXAMPLE PHRASES

Daran **wirst** du nicht **sterben**! It won't kill you!

Ich **würde** lieber **sterben**, als ihn zu heiraten. I would rather die than marry him.

Er **war** für mich **gestorben**. He might as well have been dead as far as I was concerned.

Sie **wäre** fast an ihrer Krankheit **gestorben**. She nearly died of her illness.

ich = I **du** = you **er** = he/it **sie** = she/it **es** = it/he/she **wir** = we **ihr** = you **sie** = they **Sie** = you (polite)

stoßen (to push)

strong, formed with haben

PRESENT

ich	**stoße**
du	**stößt**
er/sie/es	**stößt**
wir	**stoßen**
ihr	**stoßt**
sie/Sie	**stoßen**

PRESENT SUBJUNCTIVE

ich	**stoße**
du	**stoßest**
er/sie/es	**stoße**
wir	**stoßen**
ihr	**stoßet**
sie/Sie	**stoßen**

PERFECT

ich	**habe gestoßen**
du	**hast gestoßen**
er/sie/es	**hat gestoßen**
wir	**haben gestoßen**
ihr	**habt gestoßen**
sie/Sie	**haben gestoßen**

IMPERFECT

ich	**stieß**
du	**stießest**
er/sie/es	**stieß**
wir	**stießen**
ihr	**stießt**
sie/Sie	**stießen**

PRESENT PARTICIPLE

stoßend

PAST PARTICIPLE

gestoßen

EXAMPLE PHRASES

Unser Vorschlag **stößt** auf Ablehnung. **Our proposal is meeting with disapproval.**

Sie sagt, sie **stoße** sich an seinem Benehmen. **She says she's taking exception to his behaviour.**

Ich **habe** mir den Kopf **gestoßen**. I bumped my head.

Er **stieß** den Ball mit dem Kopf ins Tor. **He headed the ball into the goal.**

---

ich = I du = you er = he/it sie = she/it es = it/he/she wir = we ihr = you sie = they Sie = you (polite)

stoßen

FUTURE

ich	**werde stoßen**
du	**wirst stoßen**
er/sie/es	**wird stoßen**
wir	**werden stoßen**
ihr	**werdet stoßen**
sie/Sie	**werden stoßen**

CONDITIONAL

ich	**würde stoßen**
du	**würdest stoßen**
er/sie/es	**würde stoßen**
wir	**würden stoßen**
ihr	**würdet stoßen**
sie/Sie	**würden stoßen**

PLUPERFECT

ich	**hatte gestoßen**
du	**hattest gestoßen**
er/sie/es	**hatte gestoßen**
wir	**hatten gestoßen**
ihr	**hattet gestoßen**
sie/Sie	**hatten gestoßen**

PLUPERFECT SUBJUNCTIVE

ich	**hätte gestoßen**
du	**hättest gestoßen**
er/sie/es	**hätte gestoßen**
wir	**hätten gestoßen**
ihr	**hättet gestoßen**
sie/Sie	**hätten gestoßen**

IMPERATIVE

stoß(e)!/stoßen wir!/stoßt!/stoßen Sie!

EXAMPLE PHRASES

Sie **werden** dort auf Erdöl **stoßen**. They'll strike oil there.

Ich bin sicher, seine Ideen **würden** auf großes Interesse **stoßen**. I'm sure a lot of people would be interested in his ideas.

Er **hatte** sie von der Treppe **gestoßen**. He had pushed her down the stairs.

Sie liebte ihn und **hätte** ihn nie von sich **gestoßen**. She loved him and would never have cast him aside.

ich = I **du** = you **er** = he/it **sie** = she/it **es** = it/he/she **wir** = we **ihr** = you **sie** = they **Sie** = you (*polite*)

streiten (to quarrel)

strong, *formed with* haben

PRESENT

ich	**streite**
du	**streitest**
er/sie/es	**streitet**
wir	**streiten**
ihr	**streitet**
sie/Sie	**streiten**

PRESENT SUBJUNCTIVE

ich	**streite**
du	**streitest**
er/sie/es	**streite**
wir	**streiten**
ihr	**streitet**
sie/Sie	**streiten**

PERFECT

ich	**habe gestritten**
du	**hast gestritten**
er/sie/es	**hat gestritten**
wir	**haben gestritten**
ihr	**habt gestritten**
sie/Sie	**haben gestritten**

IMPERFECT

ich	**stritt**
du	**stritt(e)st**
er/sie/es	**stritt**
wir	**stritten**
ihr	**strittet**
sie/Sie	**stritten**

PRESENT PARTICIPLE

streitend

PAST PARTICIPLE

gestritten

EXAMPLE PHRASES

Sie **streiten** sich ständig. They argue constantly.

Er sagt, er **streite** sich deswegen nicht mit uns. He says he doesn't want to fall out with us over this.

Habt ihr euch schon wieder **gestritten**? Have you been fighting again?

Sie **stritten** mit Fäusten. They fought with their fists.

---

ich = I **du** = you **er** = he/it **sie** = she/it **es** = it/he/she **wir** = we **ihr** = you **sie** = they **Sie** = you (*polite*)

streiten

FUTURE

ich	**werde streiten**
du	**wirst streiten**
er/sie/es	**wird streiten**
wir	**werden streiten**
ihr	**werdet streiten**
sie/Sie	**werden streiten**

CONDITIONAL

ich	**würde streiten**
du	**würdest streiten**
er/sie/es	**würde streiten**
wir	**würden streiten**
ihr	**würdet streiten**
sie/Sie	**würden streiten**

PLUPERFECT

ich	**hatte gestritten**
du	**hattest gestritten**
er/sie/es	**hatte gestritten**
wir	**hatten gestritten**
ihr	**hattet gestritten**
sie/Sie	**hatten gestritten**

PLUPERFECT SUBJUNCTIVE

ich	**hätte gestritten**
du	**hättest gestritten**
er/sie/es	**hätte gestritten**
wir	**hätten gestritten**
ihr	**hättet gestritten**
sie/Sie	**hätten gestritten**

IMPERATIVE

streit(e)!/streiten wir!/streitet!/streiten Sie!

EXAMPLE PHRASES

Darüber **werden** wir uns noch **streiten**. We'll end up arguing about this.

Ich **würde** mich nie mit meiner Frau **streiten**. I would never quarrel with my wife.

Sie **hatten** darum **gestritten**, wer gewonnen hatte. They had argued about who had won.

Ich **hätte** nicht mit dir **gestritten**, wenn du nicht angefangen hättest. I wouldn't have argued with you if you hadn't started it.

ich = I **du** = you **er** = he/it **sie** = she/it **es** = it/he/she **wir** = we **ihr** = you **sie** = they **Sie** = you (polite)

studieren (to study)

strong, *formed with* haben

PRESENT

ich	**studiere**
du	**studierst**
er/sie/es	**studiert**
wir	**studieren**
ihr	**studiert**
sie/Sie	**studieren**

PRESENT SUBJUNCTIVE

ich	**studiere**
du	**studierest**
er/sie/es	**studiere**
wir	**studieren**
ihr	**studieret**
sie/Sie	**studieren**

PERFECT

ich	**habe studiert**
du	**hast studiert**
er/sie/es	**hat studiert**
wir	**haben studiert**
ihr	**habt studiert**
sie/Sie	**haben studiert**

IMPERFECT

ich	**studierte**
du	**studiertest**
er/sie/es	**studierte**
wir	**studierten**
ihr	**studiertet**
sie/Sie	**studierten**

PRESENT PARTICIPLE

studierend

PAST PARTICIPLE

studiert

EXAMPLE PHRASES

Mein Bruder **studiert** Deutsch. My brother is studying German.

Er sagt, er **studiere** in München. He says he's studying in Munich.

Sie **hat** in Köln **studiert**. She was a student at Cologne University.

Er **studierte** den Text gründlich. He studied the text carefully.

---

ich = I du = you er = he/it sie = she/it es = it/he/she wir = we ihr = you sie = they Sie = you *(polite)*

studieren

FUTURE

ich	**werde studieren**
du	**wirst studieren**
er/sie/es	**wird studieren**
wir	**werden studieren**
ihr	**werdet studieren**
sie/Sie	**werden studieren**

CONDITIONAL

ich	**würde studieren**
du	**würdest studieren**
er/sie/es	**würde studieren**
wir	**würden studieren**
ihr	**würdet studieren**
sie/Sie	**würden studieren**

PLUPERFECT

ich	**hatte studiert**
du	**hattest studiert**
er/sie/es	**hatte studiert**
wir	**hatten studiert**
ihr	**hattet studiert**
sie/Sie	**hatten studiert**

PLUPERFECT SUBJUNCTIVE

ich	**hätte studiert**
du	**hättest studiert**
er/sie/es	**hätte studiert**
wir	**hätten studiert**
ihr	**hättet studiert**
sie/Sie	**hätten studiert**

IMPERATIVE

studiere!/studieren wir!/studiert!/studieren Sie!

EXAMPLE PHRASES

Sie würde gern Biologie **studieren**. She would like to study biology.
Sie **hatte** vier Jahre lang **studiert**. She had been a student for four years.
Wir **hätten** besser Sprachen **studiert**. It would have been better if we had
  studied languages.

ich = I du = you er = he/it sie = she/it es = it/he/she wir = we ihr = you sie = they Sie = you (polite)

tragen (to wear, to carry)

strong, *formed with* haben

PRESENT

ich	**trage**
du	**trägst**
er/sie/es	**trägt**
wir	**tragen**
ihr	**tragt**
sie/Sie	**tragen**

PRESENT SUBJUNCTIVE

ich	**trage**
du	**tragest**
er/sie/es	**trage**
wir	**tragen**
ihr	**traget**
sie/Sie	**tragen**

PERFECT

ich	**habe getragen**
du	**hast getragen**
er/sie/es	**hat getragen**
wir	**haben getragen**
ihr	**habt getragen**
sie/Sie	**haben getragen**

IMPERFECT

ich	**trug**
du	**trugst**
er/sie/es	**trug**
wir	**trugen**
ihr	**trugt**
sie/Sie	**trugen**

PRESENT PARTICIPLE

tragend

PAST PARTICIPLE

getragen

EXAMPLE PHRASES

Du **trägst** die ganze Verantwortung dafür. You bear the full responsibility for it.

Er sagt, er **trage** nie neue Kleider. He says he never wears new clothes.

Der Apfelbaum **hat** viele Früchte **getragen**. The apple tree has produced a good crop of fruit.

Ich **trug** ihren Koffer zum Bahnhof. I carried her case to the station.

ich = I du = you er = he/it sie = she/it es = it/he/she wir = we ihr = you sie = they Sie = you (polite)

tragen

FUTURE

ich	**werde tragen**
du	**wirst tragen**
er/sie/es	**wird tragen**
wir	**werden tragen**
ihr	**werdet tragen**
sie/Sie	**werden tragen**

CONDITIONAL

ich	**würde tragen**
du	**würdest tragen**
er/sie/es	**würde tragen**
wir	**würden tragen**
ihr	**würdet tragen**
sie/Sie	**würden tragen**

PLUPERFECT

ich	**hatte getragen**
du	**hattest getragen**
er/sie/es	**hatte getragen**
wir	**hatten getragen**
ihr	**hattet getragen**
sie/Sie	**hatten getragen**

PLUPERFECT SUBJUNCTIVE

ich	**hätte getragen**
du	**hättest getragen**
er/sie/es	**hätte getragen**
wir	**hätten getragen**
ihr	**hättet getragen**
sie/Sie	**hätten getragen**

IMPERATIVE

trag(e)!/tragen wir!/tragt!/tragen Sie!

EXAMPLE PHRASES

Du **wirst** die Verantwortung dafür **tragen**. You will bear the responsibility for it.

Ich **würde** meine Haare gern länger **tragen**. I'd like to wear my hair longer.

Wir **hatten** alle Kosten selbst **getragen**. We had borne all the cost ourselves.

Du **hättest** besser einen Anzug **getragen**. It would have been better if you had worn a suit.

ich = I du = you er = he/it sie = she/it es = it/he/she wir = we ihr = you sie = they Sie = you (*polite*)

treffen (to meet)

strong, *formed with* haben

PRESENT

ich	**treffe**
du	**triffst**
er/sie/es	**trifft**
wir	**treffen**
ihr	**trefft**
sie/Sie	**treffen**

PRESENT SUBJUNCTIVE

ich	**treffe**
du	**treffest**
er/sie/es	**treffe**
wir	**treffen**
ihr	**treffet**
sie/Sie	**treffen**

PERFECT

ich	**habe getroffen**
du	**hast getroffen**
er/sie/es	**hat getroffen**
wir	**haben getroffen**
ihr	**habt getroffen**
sie/Sie	**haben getroffen**

IMPERFECT

ich	**traf**
du	**trafst**
er/sie/es	**traf**
wir	**trafen**
ihr	**traft**
sie/Sie	**trafen**

PRESENT PARTICIPLE

treffend

PAST PARTICIPLE

getroffen

EXAMPLE PHRASES

Sie **trifft** sich zweimal pro Woche mit ihm. She meets with him twice a week.

Er sagt, er **treffe** sie jeden Tag. He says he meets her every day.

Du **hast** das Ziel gut **getroffen**. You hit the target well.

Der Ball **traf** ihn am Kopf. The ball hit him on the head.

ich = I **du** = you **er** = he/it **sie** = she/it **es** = it/he/she **wir** = we **ihr** = you **sie** = they **Sie** = you (*polite*)

treffen

FUTURE

ich	**werde treffen**
du	**wirst treffen**
er/sie/es	**wird treffen**
wir	**werden treffen**
ihr	**werdet treffen**
sie/Sie	**werden treffen**

CONDITIONAL

ich	**würde treffen**
du	**würdest treffen**
er/sie/es	**würde treffen**
wir	**würden treffen**
ihr	**würdet treffen**
sie/Sie	**würden treffen**

PLUPERFECT

ich	**hatte getroffen**
du	**hattest getroffen**
er/sie/es	**hatte getroffen**
wir	**hatten getroffen**
ihr	**hattet getroffen**
sie/Sie	**hatten getroffen**

PLUPERFECT SUBJUNCTIVE

ich	**hätte getroffen**
du	**hättest getroffen**
er/sie/es	**hätte getroffen**
wir	**hätten getroffen**
ihr	**hättet getroffen**
sie/Sie	**hätten getroffen**

IMPERATIVE

triff!/treffen wir!/trefft!/treffen Sie!

EXAMPLE PHRASES

Wir **werden** uns am Bahnhof **treffen**. We'll meet at the station.

Ich **würde** dich gern öfter **treffen**. I'd like to meet with you more often.

Ich **hatte** ihn noch nie im Leben **getroffen**. I had never met him in my life.

Mich **hätte** fast der Schlag **getroffen**! I was completely flabbergasted!

---

ich = I **du** = you **er** = he/it **sie** = she/it **es** = it/he/she **wir** = we **ihr** = you **sie** = they **Sie** = you (*polite*)

treiben (to drive)

strong, *formed with* haben

PRESENT

ich	**treibe**
du	**treibst**
er/sie/es	**treibt**
wir	**treiben**
ihr	**treibt**
sie/Sie	**treiben**

PRESENT SUBJUNCTIVE

ich	**treibe**
du	**treibest**
er/sie/es	**treibe**
wir	**treiben**
ihr	**treibet**
sie/Sie	**treiben**

PERFECT

ich	**habe getrieben**
du	**hast getrieben**
er/sie/es	**hat getrieben**
wir	**haben getrieben**
ihr	**habt getrieben**
sie/Sie	**haben getrieben**

IMPERFECT

ich	**trieb**
du	**triebst**
er/sie/es	**trieb**
wir	**trieben**
ihr	**triebt**
sie/Sie	**trieben**

PRESENT PARTICIPLE

treibend

PAST PARTICIPLE

getrieben

EXAMPLE PHRASES

Er **treibt** uns zu sehr. He pushes us too hard.

Er sagt, er **treibe** viel Sport. He says he does a lot of sport.

Sie **hat** uns zur Eile **getrieben**. She made us hurry up.

Sie **trieben** die Kühe auf das Feld. They drove the cows into the field.

ich = I du = you **er** = he/it **sie** = she/it **es** = it/he/she **wir** = we **ihr** = you **sie** = they **Sie** = you (*polite*)

treiben

FUTURE

ich	**werde treiben**
du	**wirst treiben**
er/sie/es	**wird treiben**
wir	**werden treiben**
ihr	**werdet treiben**
sie/Sie	**werden treiben**

CONDITIONAL

ich	**würde treiben**
du	**würdest treiben**
er/sie/es	**würde treiben**
wir	**würden treiben**
ihr	**würdet treiben**
sie/Sie	**würden treiben**

PLUPERFECT

ich	**hatte getrieben**
du	**hattest getrieben**
er/sie/es	**hatte getrieben**
wir	**hatten getrieben**
ihr	**hattet getrieben**
sie/Sie	**hatten getrieben**

PLUPERFECT SUBJUNCTIVE

ich	**hätte getrieben**
du	**hättest getrieben**
er/sie/es	**hätte getrieben**
wir	**hätten getrieben**
ihr	**hättet getrieben**
sie/Sie	**hätten getrieben**

IMPERATIVE

treib(e)!/treiben wir!/treibt!/treiben Sie!

EXAMPLE PHRASES

Du **wirst** mich noch zur Verzweiflung **treiben**. You'll drive me to despair.

Du **würdest** doch nur Unsinn **treiben**. All you would do is fool around.

Die Inflation **hatte** die Preise in die Höhe **getrieben**. Inflation had driven prices up.

Er **hätte** sie fast in den Selbstmord **getrieben**. He would almost have driven her to suicide.

ich = I **du** = you **er** = he/it **sie** = she/it **es** = it/he/she **wir** = we **ihr** = you **sie** = they **Sie** = you (polite)

treten (to kick/to step)

strong, *formed with* haben/sein*

PRESENT

ich	**trete**
du	**trittst**
er/sie/es	**tritt**
wir	**treten**
ihr	**tretet**
sie/Sie	**treten**

PRESENT SUBJUNCTIVE

ich	**trete**
du	**tretest**
er/sie/es	**trete**
wir	**treten**
ihr	**tretet**
sie/Sie	**treten**

PERFECT

ich	**habe getreten**
du	**hast getreten**
er/sie/es	**hat getreten**
wir	**haben getreten**
ihr	**habt getreten**
sie/Sie	**haben getreten**

IMPERFECT

ich	**trat**
du	**trat(e)st**
er/sie/es	**trat**
wir	**traten**
ihr	**tratet**
sie/Sie	**traten**

PRESENT PARTICIPLE

tretend

PAST PARTICIPLE

getreten

*When *treten* is used with no direct object, it is formed with *sein*.

EXAMPLE PHRASES

Pass auf, wohin du **trittst**! Watch your step!

Er sagt, er **trete** in den Streik. He says he is going on strike.

Er **hat** mich **getreten**. He kicked me.

Sie **trat** auf die Bremse. She stepped on the brakes.

treten

FUTURE

ich	**werde treten**
du	**wirst treten**
er/sie/es	**wird treten**
wir	**werden treten**
ihr	**werdet treten**
sie/Sie	**werden treten**

CONDITIONAL

ich	**würde treten**
du	**würdest treten**
er/sie/es	**würde treten**
wir	**würden treten**
ihr	**würdet treten**
sie/Sie	**würden treten**

PLUPERFECT

ich	**hatte getreten**
du	**hattest getreten**
er/sie/es	**hatte getreten**
wir	**hatten getreten**
ihr	**hattet getreten**
sie/Sie	**hatten getreten**

PLUPERFECT SUBJUNCTIVE

ich	**hätte getreten**
du	**hättest getreten**
er/sie/es	**hätte getreten**
wir	**hätten getreten**
ihr	**hättet getreten**
sie/Sie	**hätten getreten**

IMPERATIVE

tritt!/treten wir!/tretet!/treten Sie!

EXAMPLE PHRASES

Wir **werden** mit ihnen in Verbindung **treten**. We'll get in touch with them.

Bei starkem Regen **würde** der Fluss über die Ufer **treten**. The river would burst its banks if there is a lot of rain.

Die Tränen **waren** ihr in die Augen **getreten**. Her eyes started to fill with tears.

Er **hätte** mir fast auf den Fuß **getreten**. He had almost stepped on my foot.

ich = I **du** = you **er** = he/it **sie** = she/it **es** = it/he/she **wir** = we **ihr** = you **sie** = they **Sie** = you (polite)

trinken (to drink)

strong, *formed with* haben

PRESENT

ich	**trinke**
du	**trinkst**
er/sie/es	**trinkt**
wir	**trinken**
ihr	**trinkt**
sie/Sie	**trinken**

PRESENT SUBJUNCTIVE

ich	**trinke**
du	**trinkest**
er/sie/es	**trinke**
wir	**trinken**
ihr	**trinket**
sie/Sie	**trinken**

PERFECT

ich	**habe getrunken**
du	**hast getrunken**
er/sie/es	**hat getrunken**
wir	**haben getrunken**
ihr	**habt getrunken**
sie/Sie	**haben getrunken**

IMPERFECT

ich	**trank**
du	**trankst**
er/sie/es	**trank**
wir	**tranken**
ihr	**trankt**
sie/Sie	**tranken**

PRESENT PARTICIPLE

trinkend

PAST PARTICIPLE

getrunken

EXAMPLE PHRASES

Was **trinkst** du? What would you like to drink?

Er sagt, er **trinke** abends nur Wodka. He says he only drinks vodka in the evening.

Ich **habe** zu viel **getrunken**. I've had too much to drink.

Er **trank** die ganze Flasche leer. He drank the whole bottle.

ich = I du = you er = he/it sie = she/it es = it/he/she wir = we ihr = you sie = they Sie = you (polite)

trinken

FUTURE

ich	**werde trinken**
du	**wirst trinken**
er/sie/es	**wird trinken**
wir	**werden trinken**
ihr	**werdet trinken**
sie/Sie	**werden trinken**

CONDITIONAL

ich	**würde trinken**
du	**würdest trinken**
er/sie/es	**würde trinken**
wir	**würden trinken**
ihr	**würdet trinken**
sie/Sie	**würden trinken**

PLUPERFECT

ich	**hatte getrunken**
du	**hattest getrunken**
er/sie/es	**hatte getrunken**
wir	**hatten getrunken**
ihr	**hattet getrunken**
sie/Sie	**hatten getrunken**

PLUPERFECT SUBJUNCTIVE

ich	**hätte getrunken**
du	**hättest getrunken**
er/sie/es	**hätte getrunken**
wir	**hätten getrunken**
ihr	**hättet getrunken**
sie/Sie	**hätten getrunken**

IMPERATIVE

trink(e)!/trinken wir!/trinkt!/trinken Sie!

EXAMPLE PHRASES

Ab morgen **werde** ich keinen Alkohol mehr **trinken**. From tomorrow I won't drink any alcohol.

Ich **würde** gern ein Bier mit Ihnen **trinken**. I'd like to have a beer with you.

Wir **hatten** auf sein Wohl **getrunken**. We had drunk his health.

Er **hätte** gern noch mehr **getrunken**. He would have drunk even more.

ich = I   **du** = you   **er** = he/it   **sie** = she/it   **es** = it/he/she   **wir** = we   **ihr** = you   **sie** = they   **Sie** = you (polite)

tun (to do)

strong, *formed with* haben

PRESENT

ich	**tue**
du	**tust**
er/sie/es	**tut**
wir	**tun**
ihr	**tut**
sie/Sie	**tun**

PRESENT SUBJUNCTIVE

ich	**tue**
du	**tuest**
er/sie/es	**tue**
wir	**tuen**
ihr	**tuet**
sie/Sie	**tuen**

PERFECT

ich	**habe getan**
du	**hast getan**
er/sie/es	**hat getan**
wir	**haben getan**
ihr	**habt getan**
sie/Sie	**haben getan**

IMPERFECT

ich	**tat**
du	**tat(e)st**
er/sie/es	**tat**
wir	**taten**
ihr	**tatet**
sie/Sie	**taten**

PRESENT PARTICIPLE

tuend

PAST PARTICIPLE

getan

EXAMPLE PHRASES

So etwas **tut** man nicht! That's just not done!

Sie sagt, ihr Hund **tue** dir nichts. She says her dog won't hurt you.

Er **hat** den ganzen Tag nichts **getan**. He hasn't done anything all day.

Sie **tat**, als ob sie schliefe. She pretended to be sleeping.

---

ich = I du = you er = he/it sie = she/it es = it/he/she wir = we ihr = you sie = they Sie = you (polite)

tun

FUTURE

ich	**werde tun**
du	**wirst tun**
er/sie/es	**wird tun**
wir	**werden tun**
ihr	**werdet tun**
sie/Sie	**werden tun**

CONDITIONAL

ich	**würde tun**
du	**würdest tun**
er/sie/es	**würde tun**
wir	**würden tun**
ihr	**würdet tun**
sie/Sie	**würden tun**

PLUPERFECT

ich	**hatte getan**
du	**hattest getan**
er/sie/es	**hatte getan**
wir	**hatten getan**
ihr	**hattet getan**
sie/Sie	**hatten getan**

PLUPERFECT SUBJUNCTIVE

ich	**hätte getan**
du	**hättest getan**
er/sie/es	**hätte getan**
wir	**hätten getan**
ihr	**hättet getan**
sie/Sie	**hätten getan**

IMPERATIVE

tu(e)!/tun wir!/tut!/tun Sie!

EXAMPLE PHRASES

Ich **werde** das auf keinen Fall **tun**. There is no way I'll do that.

Würdest du mir einen Gefallen **tun**? Would you do me a favour?

Das **hatte** er nur für sie **getan**. He had done it only for her.

Ich **hätte** es **getan**, wenn du mich darum gebeten hättest. I would have done it if you had asked me.

ich = I du = you er = he/it sie = she/it es = it/he/she wir = we ihr = you sie = they Sie = you (*polite*)

sich überlegen (to consider)
weak, inseparable, reflexive, formed with **haben**

PRESENT

ich	**überlege mir**
du	**überlegst dir**
er/sie/es	**überlegt sich**
wir	**überlegen uns**
ihr	**überlegt euch**
sie/Sie	**überlegen sich**

PRESENT SUBJUNCTIVE

ich	**überlege mir**
du	**überlegest dir**
er/sie/es	**überlege sich**
wir	**überlegen uns**
ihr	**überleget euch**
sie/Sie	**überlegen sich**

PERFECT

ich	**habe mir überlegt**
du	**hast dir überlegt**
er/sie/es	**hat sich überlegt**
wir	**haben uns überlegt**
ihr	**habt euch überlegt**
sie/Sie	**haben sich überlegt**

IMPERFECT

ich	**überlegt mir**
du	**überlegtest dir**
er/sie/es	**überlegte sich**
wir	**überlegten uns**
ihr	**überlegtet euch**
sie/Sie	**überlegten sich**

PRESENT PARTICIPLE

überlegend

PAST PARTICIPLE

überlegt

EXAMPLE PHRASES

Ich **überlege** es **mir**. I'll think about it.

Er meint, er **überlege** es **sich** noch einmal. He thinks he's going to reconsider it.

Ich **habe mir** schon **überlegt**, was ich machen werde. I've already thought about what I'm going to do.

Er **überlegte sich** einen schlauen Plan. He thought of a clever plan.

ich = I **du** = you **er** = he/it **sie** = she/it **es** = it/he/she **wir** = we **ihr** = you **sie** = they **Sie** = you (*polite*)

sich überlegen

FUTURE

ich	werde mir überlegen
du	wirst dir überlegen
er/sie/es	wird sich überlegen
wir	werden uns überlegen
ihr	werdet euch überlegen
sie/Sie	werden sich überlegen

CONDITIONAL

ich	würde mir überlegen
du	würdest dir überlegen
er/sie/es	würde sich überlegen
wir	würden uns überlegen
ihr	würdet euch überlegen
sie/Sie	würden sich überlegen

PLUPERFECT

ich	hatte mir überlegt
du	hattest dir überlegt
er/sie/es	hatte sich überlegt
wir	hatten uns überlegt
ihr	hattet euch überlegt
sie/Sie	hatten sich überlegt

PLUPERFECT SUBJUNCTIVE

ich	hätte mir überlegt
du	hättest dir überlegt
er/sie/es	hätte sich überlegt
wir	hätten uns überlegt
ihr	hättet euch überlegt
sie/Sie	hätten sich überlegt

IMPERATIVE

überleg(e)dir!/überlegen wir uns!/überlegt euch!/überlegen Sie sich!

EXAMPLE PHRASES

Das **werde** ich **mir überlegen**. I'll have a think about it.

Würden Sie es **sich** noch einmal **überlegen**? Would you reconsider?

Er **hatte sich überlegt**, dass er viel Zeit sparen konnte. He had come to the conclusion that he could save a lot of time.

Das **hätte** sie **sich** besser früher **überlegt**. She should have thought of that earlier.

---

ich = I **du** = you **er** = he/it **sie** = she/it **es** = it/he/she **wir** = we **ihr** = you **sie** = they **Sie** = you (*polite*)

vergessen (to forget)   strong, inseparable, *formed with* haben

PRESENT		**PRESENT SUBJUNCTIVE**	
ich	**vergesse**	ich	**vergesse**
du	**vergisst**	du	**vergessest**
er/sie/es	**vergisst**	er/sie/es	**vergesse**
wir	**vergessen**	wir	**vergessen**
ihr	**vergesst**	ihr	**vergesset**
sie/Sie	**vergessen**	sie/Sie	**vergessen**

PERFECT		**IMPERFECT**	
ich	**habe vergessen**	ich	**vergaß**
du	**hast vergessen**	du	**vergaßest**
er/sie/es	**hat vergessen**	er/sie/es	**vergaß**
wir	**haben vergessen**	wir	**vergaßen**
ihr	**habt vergessen**	ihr	**vergaßt**
sie/Sie	**haben vergessen**	sie/Sie	**vergaßen**

PRESENT PARTICIPLE

vergessend

PAST PARTICIPLE

vergessen

EXAMPLE PHRASES

Sie **vergisst** ständig ihre Bücher. **She always forgets to bring her books.**

Er sagt, er **vergesse** nie ein Gesicht. **He says he never forgets a face.**

Ich **habe** seinen Namen **vergessen**. **I've forgotten his name.**

Sie **vergaß**, die Blumen zu gießen. **She forgot to water the flowers.**

ich = I **du** = you **er** = he/it **sie** = she/it **es** = it/he/she **wir** = we **ihr** = you **sie** = they **Sie** = you (*polite*)

vergessen

FUTURE

ich	**werde vergessen**
du	**wirst vergessen**
er/sie/es	**wird vergessen**
wir	**werden vergessen**
ihr	**werdet vergessen**
sie/Sie	**werden vergessen**

CONDITIONAL

ich	**würde vergessen**
du	**würdest vergessen**
er/sie/es	**würde vergessen**
wir	**würden vergessen**
ihr	**würdet vergessen**
sie/Sie	**würden vergessen**

PLUPERFECT

ich	**hatte vergessen**
du	**hattest vergessen**
er/sie/es	**hatte vergessen**
wir	**hatten vergessen**
ihr	**hattet vergessen**
sie/Sie	**hatten vergessen**

PLUPERFECT SUBJUNCTIVE

ich	**hätte vergessen**
du	**hättest vergessen**
er/sie/es	**hätte vergessen**
wir	**hätten vergessen**
ihr	**hättet vergessen**
sie/Sie	**hätten vergessen**

IMPERATIVE

vergiss!/vergessen wir!/vergesst!/vergessen Sie!

EXAMPLE PHRASES

Das **werde** ich dir nie **vergessen**. I'll never forget that.

Dieses Examen **würde** ich am liebsten **vergessen**. I'd rather forget this exam.

Ich **hatte vergessen**, die Post abzuholen. I had forgotten to collect the mail.

Fast **hättest** du **vergessen**, mir das Geld zu geben. You had almost forgotten
to give me the money.

ich = I **du** = you **er** = he/it **sie** = she/it **es** = it/he/she **wir** = we **ihr** = you **sie** = they **Sie** = you (*polite*)

verlangen (to demand) weak, inseparable, *formed with* haben

PRESENT

ich	**verlange**
du	**verlangst**
er/sie/es	**verlangt**
wir	**verlangen**
ihr	**verlangt**
sie/Sie	**verlangen**

PRESENT SUBJUNCTIVE

ich	**verlange**
du	**verlangest**
er/sie/es	**verlange**
wir	**verlangen**
ihr	**verlanget**
sie/Sie	**verlangen**

PERFECT

ich	**habe verlangt**
du	**hast verlangt**
er/sie/es	**hat verlangt**
wir	**haben verlangt**
ihr	**habt verlangt**
sie/Sie	**haben verlangt**

IMPERFECT

ich	**verlangte**
du	**verlangtest**
er/sie/es	**verlangte**
wir	**verlangten**
ihr	**verlangtet**
sie/Sie	**verlangten**

PRESENT PARTICIPLE

verlangend

PAST PARTICIPLE

verlangt

EXAMPLE PHRASES

Unsere Lehrerin **verlangt** wirklich sehr viel von uns. Our teacher demands
an awful lot of us.

Er sagt, er **verlange** 5000 Euro für das Auto. He says he wants 5000 euros
for the car.

Wie viel **hat** er dafür **verlangt**? How much did he want for it?

Sie **verlangten**, dass man sie anhört. They demanded to be heard.

ich = I **du** = you **er** = he/it **sie** = she/it **es** = it/he/she **wir** = we **ihr** = you **sie** = they **Sie** = you (*polite*)

verlangen

FUTURE

ich	**werde verlangen**
du	**wirst verlangen**
er/sie/es	**wird verlangen**
wir	**werden verlangen**
ihr	**werdet verlangen**
sie/Sie	**werden verlangen**

CONDITIONAL

ich	**würde verlangen**
du	**würdest verlangen**
er/sie/es	**würde verlangen**
wir	**würden verlangen**
ihr	**würdet verlangen**
sie/Sie	**würden verlangen**

PLUPERFECT

ich	**hatte verlangt**
du	**hattest verlangt**
er/sie/es	**hatte verlangt**
wir	**hatten verlangt**
ihr	**hattet verlangt**
sie/Sie	**hatten verlangt**

PLUPERFECT SUBJUNCTIVE

ich	**hätte verlangt**
du	**hättest verlangt**
er/sie/es	**hätte verlangt**
wir	**hätten verlangt**
ihr	**hättet verlangt**
sie/Sie	**hätten verlangt**

IMPERATIVE

verlang(e)!/verlangen wir!/verlangt!/verlangen Sie!

EXAMPLE PHRASES

Die Kunden **werden** eine Preissenkung **verlangen**. The customers will demand a price cut.

Das **würde** ich nicht von dir **verlangen**. I wouldn't ask that of you.

Er **hatte** zu viel von mir **verlangt**. He had demanded too much of me.

Er **hätte verlangt**, meinen Pass zu sehen. He would have demanded to see my passport.

---

ich = I **du** = you **er** = he/it **sie** = she/it **es** = it/he/she **wir** = we **ihr** = you **sie** = they **Sie** = you (*polite*)

verlieren (to lose)

strong, inseparable, *formed with* haben

PRESENT

ich	**verliere**
du	**verlierst**
er/sie/es	**verliert**
wir	**verlieren**
ihr	**verliert**
sie/Sie	**verlieren**

PRESENT SUBJUNCTIVE

ich	**verliere**
du	**verlierest**
er/sie/es	**verliere**
wir	**verlieren**
ihr	**verlieret**
sie/Sie	**verlieren**

PERFECT

ich	**habe verloren**
du	**hast verloren**
er/sie/es	**hat verloren**
wir	**haben verloren**
ihr	**habt verloren**
sie/Sie	**haben verloren**

IMPERFECT

ich	**verlor**
du	**verlorst**
er/sie/es	**verlor**
wir	**verloren**
ihr	**verlort**
sie/Sie	**verloren**

PRESENT PARTICIPLE

verlierend

PAST PARTICIPLE

verloren

EXAMPLE PHRASES

Wenn du **verlierst**, musst du mir 10 Euro zahlen. If you lose, you'll have to pay
   me 10 euros.

Er sage, er **verliere** oft die Geduld. He says he often loses his patience.

Wir **haben** drei Spiele hintereinander **verloren**. We lost three matches in a row.

Er **verlor** kein Wort darüber. He didn't say a word about it.

ich = I **du** = you **er** = he/it **sie** = she/it **es** = it/he/she **wir** = we **ihr** = you **sie** = they **Sie** = you (*polite*)

verlieren

FUTURE

ich	**werde verlieren**
du	**wirst verlieren**
er/sie/es	**wird verlieren**
wir	**werden verlieren**
ihr	**werdet verlieren**
sie/Sie	**werden verlieren**

CONDITIONAL

ich	**würde verlieren**
du	**würdest verlieren**
er/sie/es	**würde verlieren**
wir	**würden verlieren**
ihr	**würdet verlieren**
sie/Sie	**würden verlieren**

PLUPERFECT

ich	**hatte verloren**
du	**hattest verloren**
er/sie/es	**hatte verloren**
wir	**hatten verloren**
ihr	**hattet verloren**
sie/Sie	**hatten verloren**

PLUPERFECT SUBJUNCTIVE

ich	**hätte verloren**
du	**hättest verloren**
er/sie/es	**hätte verloren**
wir	**hätten verloren**
ihr	**hättet verloren**
sie/Sie	**hätten verloren**

IMPERATIVE

verlier(e)!/verlieren wir!/verliert!/verlieren Sie!

EXAMPLE PHRASES

Ich **werde** kein Wort über sie **verlieren**. I won't say a word about them.

In diesem Kaufhaus **würde** ich mich **verlieren**. I would get lost in this department store.

Sie **hatte** die Wette **verloren**. She had lost the bet.

Borussia **hätte** fast das Spiel **verloren**. Borussia would nearly have lost the match.

ich = I **du** = you **er** = he/it **sie** = she/it **es** = it/he/she **wir** = we **ihr** = you **sie** = they **Sie** = you (*polite*)

verschwinden (to disappear)

strong, inseparable,
formed with **sein**

PRESENT

ich	**verschwinde**
du	**verschwindest**
er/sie/es	**verschwindet**
wir	**verschwinden**
ihr	**verschwindet**
sie/Sie	**verschwinden**

PRESENT SUBJUNCTIVE

ich	**verschwinde**
du	**verschwindest**
er/sie/es	**verschwinde**
wir	**verschwinden**
ihr	**verschwindet**
sie/Sie	**verschwinden**

PERFECT

ich	**bin verschwunden**
du	**bist verschwunden**
er/sie/es	**ist verschwunden**
wir	**sind verschwunden**
ihr	**seid verschwunden**
sie/Sie	**sind verschwunden**

IMPERFECT

ich	**verschwand**
du	**verschwand(e)st**
er/sie/es	**verschwand**
wir	**verschwanden**
ihr	**verschwandet**
sie/Sie	**verschwanden**

PRESENT PARTICIPLE

verschwindend

PAST PARTICIPLE

verschwunden

EXAMPLE PHRASES

Du **verschwindest** immer wochenlang. You keep disappearing for weeks on end.

Er meint, diese Tradition **verschwinde** langsam. He thinks this tradition is disappearing slowly.

Er **ist** seit Sonntag **verschwunden**. He has been missing since Sunday.

Sie **verschwanden** in der Dunkelheit. They disappeared into the darkness.

ich = I **du** = you **er** = he/it **sie** = she/it **es** = it/he/she **wir** = we **ihr** = you **sie** = they **Sie** = you (*polite*)

verschwinden

FUTURE

ich	**werde verschwinden**
du	**wirst verschwinden**
er/sie/es	**wird verschwinden**
wir	**werden verschwinden**
ihr	**werdet verschwinden**
sie/Sie	**werden verschwinden**

CONDITIONAL

ich	**würde verschwinden**
du	**würdest verschwinden**
er/sie/es	**würde verschwinden**
wir	**würden verschwinden**
ihr	**würdet verschwinden**
sie/Sie	**würden verschwinden**

PLUPERFECT

ich	**war verschwunden**
du	**warst verschwunden**
er/sie/es	**war verschwunden**
wir	**waren verschwunden**
ihr	**wart verschwunden**
sie/Sie	**waren verschwunden**

PLUPERFECT SUBJUNCTIVE

ich	**wäre verschwunden**
du	**wär(e)st verschwunden**
er/sie/es	**wäre verschwunden**
wir	**wären verschwunden**
ihr	**wär(e)t verschwunden**
sie/Sie	**wären verschwunden**

IMPERATIVE

verschwind(e)!/verschwinden wir!/verschwindet!/verschwinden Sie!

EXAMPLE PHRASES

Unsere Sorgen **werden** bald **verschwinden**. Our worries will soon disappear.

Ich wollte, diese Leute **würden verschwinden**. I wish these people would
disappear.

Nach dem Erdbeben **war** die Stadt von der Landkarte **verschwunden**.
After the earthquake the town had disappeared off the map.

Sie **wäre** gern aus seinem Leben **verschwunden**. She would have liked to
disappear from his life.

ich = I **du** = you **er** = he/it **sie** = she/it **es** = it/he/she **wir** = we **ihr** = you **sie** = they **Sie** = you *(polite)*

verzeihen (to pardon)   strong, inseparable, *formed with* haben

PRESENT	
ich	**verzeihe**
du	**verzeihst**
er/sie/es	**verzeiht**
wir	**verzeihen**
ihr	**verzeiht**
sie/Sie	**verzeihen**

PRESENT SUBJUNCTIVE	
ich	**verzeihe**
du	**verzeihest**
er/sie/es	**verzeihe**
wir	**verzeihen**
ihr	**verzeihet**
sie/Sie	**verzeihen**

PERFECT	
ich	**habe verziehen**
du	**hast verziehen**
er/sie/es	**hat verziehen**
wir	**haben verziehen**
ihr	**habt verziehen**
sie/Sie	**haben verziehen**

IMPERFECT	
ich	**verzieh**
du	**verziehst**
er/sie/es	**verzieh**
wir	**verziehen**
ihr	**verzieht**
sie/Sie	**verziehen**

PRESENT PARTICIPLE
verzeihend

PAST PARTICIPLE
verziehen

EXAMPLE PHRASES

Ich **verzeihe** dir. I forgive you.

Er **hat** mir nie **verziehen**, dass ich ihn geschlagen habe. He has never forgiven me for hitting him.

Sie war verärgert, aber sie **verzieh** mir. She was angry but she forgave me.

verzeihen

FUTURE

ich	**werde verzeihen**
du	**wirst verzeihen**
er/sie/es	**wird verzeihen**
wir	**werden verzeihen**
ihr	**werdet verzeihen**
sie/Sie	**werden verzeihen**

CONDITIONAL

ich	**würde verzeihen**
du	**würdest verzeihen**
er/sie/es	**würde verzeihen**
wir	**würden verzeihen**
ihr	**würdet verzeihen**
sie/Sie	**würden verzeihen**

PLUPERFECT

ich	**hatte verziehen**
du	**hattest verziehen**
er/sie/es	**hatte verziehen**
wir	**hatten verziehen**
ihr	**hattet verziehen**
sie/Sie	**hatten verziehen**

PLUPERFECT SUBJUNCTIVE

ich	**hätte verziehen**
du	**hättest verziehen**
er/sie/es	**hätte verziehen**
wir	**hätten verziehen**
ihr	**hättet verziehen**
sie/Sie	**hätten verziehen**

IMPERATIVE

verzeih(e)!/verzeihen wir!/verzeiht!/verzeihen Sie!

EXAMPLE PHRASES

Das **wird** sie mir nicht **verzeihen**. She won't forgive me for that.

Diese Lüge **würde** ich ihm nicht **verzeihen**. I wouldn't forgive him for this lie.

Er **hatte** ihr diese Affäre niemals **verziehen**. He had never forgiven her for this affair.

Ich **hätte** ihm **verziehen**, wenn er mich gebeten hätte. I would have forgiven him if he had asked me.

ich = I **du** = you **er** = he/it **sie** = she/it **es** = it/he/she **wir** = we **ihr** = you **sie** = they **Sie** = you (*polite*)

wachsen (to grow)

strong, *formed with* **sein**

PRESENT	**PRESENT SUBJUNCTIVE**
ich **wachse**	ich **wachse**
du **wächst**	du **wachsest**
er/sie/es **wächst**	er/sie/es **wachse**
wir **wachsen**	wir **wachsen**
ihr **wachst**	ihr **wachset**
sie/Sie **wachsen**	sie/Sie **wachsen**

PERFECT	**IMPERFECT**
ich **bin gewachsen**	ich **wuchs**
du **bist gewachsen**	du **wuchsest**
er/sie/es **ist gewachsen**	er/sie/es **wuchs**
wir **sind gewachsen**	wir **wuchsen**
ihr **seid gewachsen**	ihr **wuchst**
sie/Sie **sind gewachsen**	sie/Sie **wuchsen**

PRESENT PARTICIPLE	**PAST PARTICIPLE**
wachsend	gewachsen

EXAMPLE PHRASES

Der Baum **wächst** nicht mehr. The tree has stopped growing.

Sie meint, ihr Sohn **wachse** zu schnell. She thinks her son is growing too fast.

Ich **bin** im letzten Jahr 10 Zentimeter **gewachsen**. I've grown 10 centimetres in the past year.

Ihm **wuchs** ein Bart. He grew a beard.

---

ich = I **du** = you **er** = he/it **sie** = she/it **es** = it/he/she **wir** = we **ihr** = you **sie** = they **Sie** = you (*polite*)

wachsen

FUTURE

ich	**werde wachsen**
du	**wirst wachsen**
er/sie/es	**wird wachsen**
wir	**werden wachsen**
ihr	**werdet wachsen**
sie/Sie	**werden wachsen**

CONDITIONAL

ich	**würde wachsen**
du	**würdest wachsen**
er/sie/es	**würde wachsen**
wir	**würden wachsen**
ihr	**würdet wachsen**
sie/Sie	**würden wachsen**

PLUPERFECT

ich	**war gewachsen**
du	**warst gewachsen**
er/sie/es	**war gewachsen**
wir	**waren gewachsen**
ihr	**wart gewachsen**
sie/Sie	**waren gewachsen**

PLUPERFECT SUBJUNCTIVE

ich	**wäre gewachsen**
du	**wär(e)st gewachsen**
er/sie/es	**wäre gewachsen**
wir	**wären gewachsen**
ihr	**wär(e)t gewachsen**
sie/Sie	**wären gewachsen**

IMPERATIVE

wachs(e)!/wachsen wir!/wachst!/wachsen Sie!

EXAMPLE PHRASES

Meine Probleme **werden** weiter **wachsen**. My problems will keep on growing.

Ohne Sonne **würde** hier nichts **wachsen**. Nothing would grow here without sunlight.

Die Preise **waren** drastisch **gewachsen**. Prices had risen dramatically.

Ohne dieses Spray **wäre** das Unkraut weiter **gewachsen**. Without this spray the weeds would have kept on growing.

ich = I **du** = you **er** = he/it **sie** = she/it **es** = it/he/she **wir** = we **ihr** = you **sie** = they **Sie** = you (*polite*)

wandern (to roam)

weak, formed with sein

PRESENT

ich	**wand(e)re**
du	**wanderst**
er/sie/es	**wandert**
wir	**wandern**
ihr	**wandert**
sie/Sie	**wandern**

PRESENT SUBJUNCTIVE

ich	**wand(e)re**
du	**wandrest**
er/sie/es	**wand(e)re**
wir	**wandern**
ihr	**wandert**
sie/Sie	**wandern**

PERFECT

ich	**bin gewandert**
du	**bist gewandert**
er/sie/es	**ist gewandert**
wir	**sind gewandert**
ihr	**seid gewandert**
sie/Sie	**sind gewandert**

IMPERFECT

ich	**wanderte**
du	**wandertest**
er/sie/es	**wanderte**
wir	**wanderten**
ihr	**wandertet**
sie/Sie	**wanderten**

PRESENT PARTICIPLE

wandernd

PAST PARTICIPLE

gewandert

EXAMPLE PHRASES

Im Schwarzwald **wandert** man gut. The Black Forest is good for walking.

Er sagt, er **wand(e)re** gern. He says he loves hiking.

Wir **sind** am Wochenende **gewandert**. We went walking at the weekend.

Seine Gedanken **wanderten** zurück in die Vergangenheit. His thoughts strayed back to the past.

ich = I **du** = you **er** = he/it **sie** = she/it **es** = it/he/she **wir** = we **ihr** = you **sie** = they **Sie** = you *(polite)*

wandern

FUTURE

ich	**werde wandern**
du	**wirst wandern**
er/sie/es	**wird wandern**
wir	**werden wandern**
ihr	**werdet wandern**
sie/Sie	**werden wandern**

CONDITIONAL

ich	**würde wandern**
du	**würdest wandern**
er/sie/es	**würde wandern**
wir	**würden wandern**
ihr	**würdet wandern**
sie/Sie	**würden wandern**

PLUPERFECT

ich	**war gewandert**
du	**warst gewandert**
er/sie/es	**war gewandert**
wir	**waren gewandert**
ihr	**wart gewandert**
sie/Sie	**waren gewandert**

PLUPERFECT SUBJUNCTIVE

ich	**wäre gewandert**
du	**wär(e)st gewandert**
er/sie/es	**wäre gewandert**
wir	**wären gewandert**
ihr	**wär(e)t gewandert**
sie/Sie	**wären gewandert**

IMPERATIVE

wandre!/wandern wir!/wandert!/wandern Sie!

EXAMPLE PHRASES

Im Urlaub **werden** wir jeden Tag **wandern**. On our holiday we'll go hiking every day.

Ich **würde** lieber im Schnee **wandern**. I'd prefer to go walking in the snow.

Dieses Dokument **war** in den Papierkorb **gewandert**. This document had ended up in the wastepaper bin.

Ich **wäre** gern mit ihm **gewandert**. I would have liked to go hiking with him.

ich = I du = you er = he/it sie = she/it es = it/he/she wir = we ihr = you sie = they Sie = you *(polite)*

waschen (to wash)

strong, *formed with* haben

PRESENT

ich	**wasche**
du	**wäschst**
er/sie/es	**wäscht**
wir	**waschen**
ihr	**wascht**
sie/Sie	**waschen**

PRESENT SUBJUNCTIVE

ich	**wasche**
du	**waschest**
er/sie/es	**wasche**
wir	**waschen**
ihr	**waschet**
sie/Sie	**waschen**

PERFECT

ich	**habe gewaschen**
du	**hast gewaschen**
er/sie/es	**hat gewaschen**
wir	**haben gewaschen**
ihr	**habt gewaschen**
sie/Sie	**haben gewaschen**

IMPERFECT

ich	**wusch**
du	**wuschest**
er/sie/es	**wusch**
wir	**wuschen**
ihr	**wuscht**
sie/Sie	**wuschen**

PRESENT PARTICIPLE

waschend

PAST PARTICIPLE

gewaschen

EXAMPLE PHRASES

Sie **wäscht** jeden Tag. She does the washing every day.

Er sagt, er **wasche** immer im Waschsalon. He says he always does his washing at the laundrette.

Ich **habe** mir die Hände **gewaschen**. I washed my hands.

Die Katze **wusch** sich in der Sonne. The cat was washing itself in the sunshine.

ich = I **du** = you **er** = he/it **sie** = she/it **es** = it/he/she **wir** = we **ihr** = you **sie** = they **Sie** = you (*polite*)

waschen

FUTURE

ich	**werde waschen**
du	**wirde waschen**
er/sie/es	**wird waschen**
wir	**werden waschen**
ihr	**werdet waschen**
sie/Sie	**werden waschen**

CONDITIONAL

ich	**würde waschen**
du	**würdest waschen**
er/sie/es	**würde waschen**
wir	**würden waschen**
ihr	**würdet waschen**
sie/Sie	**würden waschen**

PLUPERFECT

ich	**hatte gewaschen**
du	**hattest gewaschen**
er/sie/es	**hatte gewaschen**
wir	**hatten gewaschen**
ihr	**hattet gewaschen**
sie/Sie	**hatten gewaschen**

PLUPERFECT SUBJUNCTIVE

ich	**hätte gewaschen**
du	**hättest gewaschen**
er/sie/es	**hätte gewaschen**
wir	**hätten gewaschen**
ihr	**hättet gewaschen**
sie/Sie	**hätten gewaschen**

IMPERATIVE

wasche(e)!/waschen wir!/wascht!/waschen Sie!

EXAMPLE PHRASES

Ich **werde** mir jetzt die Haare **waschen**. I'll go and wash my hair now.

Sonntags **würde** ich keine Wäsche **waschen**. I wouldn't do my washing on Sundays.

Sie **hatte** das Auto schon **gewaschen**. She had already washed the car.

Wenn du mich gebeten hättest, **hätte** ich dein Auto **gewaschen**. If you had asked me, I would have washed your car.

ich = I **du** = you **er** = he/it **sie** = she/it **es** = it/he/she **wir** = we **ihr** = you **sie** = they **Sie** = you (*polite*)

werben (to recruit, to advertise) strong, *formed with* haben

PRESENT

ich	**werbe**
du	**wirbst**
er/sie/es	**wirbt**
wir	**werben**
ihr	**werbt**
sie/Sie	**werben**

PRESENT SUBJUNCTIVE

ich	**werbe**
du	**werbest**
er/sie/es	**werbe**
wir	**werben**
ihr	**werbet**
sie/Sie	**werben**

PERFECT

ich	**habe geworben**
du	**hast geworben**
er/sie/es	**hat geworben**
wir	**haben geworben**
ihr	**habt geworben**
sie/Sie	**haben geworben**

IMPERFECT

ich	**warb**
du	**warbst**
er/sie/es	**warb**
wir	**warben**
ihr	**warbt**
sie/Sie	**warben**

PRESENT PARTICIPLE

werbend

PAST PARTICIPLE

geworben

EXAMPLE PHRASES

Die Partei **wirbt** zur Zeit Mitglieder. The party is currently recruiting members.

Er sagt, er **werbe** um jede Stimme. He says he is campaigning for every vote.

Unsere Firma hat um neue Kunden **geworben**. Our company has tried to attract new customers.

Die Partei **warb** für ihren Kandidaten. The party promoted its candidate.

werben

FUTURE

ich	**werde werben**
du	**wirst werben**
er/sie/es	**wird werben**
wir	**werden werben**
ihr	**werdet werben**
sie/Sie	**werden werben**

CONDITIONAL

ich	**würde werben**
du	**würdest werben**
er/sie/es	**würde werben**
wir	**würden werben**
ihr	**würdet werben**
sie/Sie	**würden werben**

PLUPERFECT

ich	**hatte geworben**
du	**hattest geworben**
er/sie/es	**hatte geworben**
wir	**hatten geworben**
ihr	**hattet geworben**
sie/Sie	**hatten geworben**

PLUPERFECT SUBJUNCTIVE

ich	**hätte geworben**
du	**hättest geworben**
er/sie/es	**hätte geworben**
wir	**hätten geworben**
ihr	**hättet geworben**
sie/Sie	**hätten geworben**

IMPERATIVE

wirb!/**werben wir!**/**werbt!**/**werben Sie!**

EXAMPLE PHRASES

Wir **werden** für unser neues Produkt **werben**. We will advertise our new product.

Wenn wir mehr Geld hätten, **würden** wir mehr **werben**. If we had more money we would do more advertising.

Wir **hatten** 500 neue Mitglieder **geworben**. We had recruited 500 new members.

Wir **hätten** gern noch mehr Mitglieder **geworben**. We would have liked to recruit even more members.

ich = I du = you er = he/it sie = she/it es = it/he/she wir = we ihr = you sie = they Sie = you (*polite*)

werden (to become)

strong, *formed with* **sein**

PRESENT

ich	**werde**
du	**wirst**
er/sie/es	**wird**
wir	**werden**
ihr	**werdet**
sie/Sie	**werden**

PRESENT SUBJUNCTIVE

ich	**werde**
du	**werdest**
er/sie/es	**werde**
wir	**werden**
ihr	**werdet**
sie/Sie	**werden**

PERFECT

ich	**bin geworden**
du	**bist geworden**
er/sie/es	**ist geworden**
wir	**sind geworden**
ihr	**seid geworden**
sie/Sie	**sind geworden**

IMPERFECT

ich	**wurde**
du	**wurdest**
er/sie/es	**wurde**
wir	**wurden**
ihr	**wurdet**
sie/Sie	**wurden**

PRESENT PARTICIPLE

werdendgeworden

PAST PARTICIPLE

EXAMPLE PHRASES

Mit **wird** schlecht. I feel ill.

Er meint, aus mir **werde** nie etwas. He thinks I'll never amount to anything.

Der Kuchen **ist** gut **geworden**. The cake turned out well.

Er **wurde** im Mai 40 Jahre. He turned 40 in May.

ich = I **du** = you **er** = he/it **sie** = she/it **es** = it/he/she **wir** = we **ihr** = you **sie** = they **Sie** = you (*polite*)

werden

FUTURE

ich	**werde werden**
du	**wirst werden**
er/sie/es	**wird werden**
wir	**werden werden**
ihr	**werdet werden**
sie/Sie	**werden werden**

CONDITIONAL

ich	**würde werden**
du	**würdest werden**
er/sie/es	**würde werden**
wir	**würden werden**
ihr	**würdet werden**
sie/Sie	**würden werden**

PLUPERFECT

ich	**war geworden**
du	**warst geworden**
er/sie/es	**war geworden**
wir	**waren geworden**
ihr	**wart geworden**
sie/Sie	**waren geworden**

PLUPERFECT SUBJUNCTIVE

ich	**wäre geworden**
du	**wär(e)st geworden**
er/sie/es	**wäre geworden**
wir	**wären geworden**
ihr	**wär(e)t geworden**
sie/Sie	**wären geworden**

IMPERATIVE

werde!/werden wir!/werdet!/werden Sie!

EXAMPLE PHRASES

Ich **werde** Lehrerin **werden**. I'll become a teacher.

Er **würde** gern Lehrer **werden**. He would like to become a teacher.

Aus ihm **war** ein großer Komponist **geworden**. He had become a great composer.

Es **wäre** fast noch einmal Winter **geworden**. It seemed that winter had almost returned.

ich = I **du** = you **er** = he/it **sie** = she/it **es** = it/he/she **wir** = we **ihr** = you **sie** = they **Sie** = you (polite)

werfen (to throw)

strong, *formed with* haben

PRESENT

ich	**werfe**
du	**wirfst**
er/sie/es	**wirft**
wir	**werfen**
ihr	**werft**
sie/Sie	**werfen**

PRESENT SUBJUNCTIVE

ich	**werfe**
du	**werfest**
er/sie/es	**werfe**
wir	**werfen**
ihr	**werfet**
sie/Sie	**werfen**

PERFECT

ich	**habe geworfen**
du	**hast geworfen**
er/sie/es	**hat geworfen**
wir	**haben geworfen**
ihr	**habt geworfen**
sie/Sie	**haben geworfen**

IMPERFECT

ich	**warf**
du	**warfst**
er/sie/es	**warf**
wir	**warfen**
ihr	**warft**
sie/Sie	**warfen**

PRESENT PARTICIPLE

werfend

PAST PARTICIPLE

geworfen

EXAMPLE PHRASES

Sie **wirft** mit Geld um sich. She is throwing her money around.

Er drohte ihm, er **werfe** ihn aus dem Haus. He threatened to throw him out of the house.

Der Chef **hat** ihn aus der Firma **geworfen**. The boss has kicked him out of the company.

Die Sonne **warf** ihre Strahlen auf den See. The sun cast its rays on the lake.

ich = I **du** = you **er** = he/it **sie** = she/it **es** = it/he/she **wir** = we **ihr** = you **sie** = they **Sie** = you (*polite*)

werfen

FUTURE

ich	**werde werfen**
du	**wirst werfen**
er/sie/es	**wird werfen**
wir	**werden werfen**
ihr	**werdet werfen**
sie/Sie	**werden werfen**

CONDITIONAL

ich	**würde werfen**
du	**würdest werfen**
er/sie/es	**würde werfen**
wir	**würden werfen**
ihr	**würdet werfen**
sie/Sie	**würden werfen**

PLUPERFECT

ich	**hatte geworfen**
du	**hattest geworfen**
er/sie/es	**hatte geworfen**
wir	**hatten geworfen**
ihr	**hattet geworfen**
sie/Sie	**hatten geworfen**

PLUPERFECT SUBJUNCTIVE

ich	**hätte geworfen**
du	**hättest geworfen**
er/sie/es	**hätte geworfen**
wir	**hätten geworfen**
ihr	**hättet geworfen**
sie/Sie	**hätten geworfen**

IMPERATIVE

wirf!/werfen wir!/werft!/werfen Sie!

EXAMPLE PHRASES

Er **wird** bestimmt einen neuen Rekord **werfen**. He will definitely throw a
new record.

Am liebsten **würde** ich das Handtuch **werfen**. I feel like throwing in the towel.

Er **hatte** den Ball über den Zaun **geworfen**. He had thrown the ball over
the fence.

Ich **hätte** ihn ins Gefängnis **geworfen**. I would have thrown him into prison.

ich = I **du** = you **er** = he/it **sie** = she/it **es** = it/he/she **wir** = we **ihr** = you **sie** = they **Sie** = you (*polite*)

wiegen (to weigh)

strong, *formed with* **haben**

PRESENT

ich	**wiege**
du	**wiegst**
er/sie/es	**wiegt**
wir	**wiegen**
ihr	**wiegt**
sie/Sie	**wiegen**

PRESENT SUBJUNCTIVE

ich	**wiege**
du	**wiegest**
er/sie/es	**wiege**
wir	**wiegen**
ihr	**wieget**
sie/Sie	**wiegen**

PERFECT

ich	**habe gewogen**
du	**hast gewogen**
er/sie/es	**hat gewogen**
wir	**haben gewogen**
ihr	**habt gewogen**
sie/Sie	**haben gewogen**

IMPERFECT

ich	**wog**
du	**wogst**
er/sie/es	**wog**
wir	**wogen**
ihr	**wogt**
sie/Sie	**wogen**

PRESENT PARTICIPLE

wiegend

PAST PARTICIPLE

gewogen

EXAMPLE PHRASES

Ich **wiege** 60 Kilo. I weigh 60 kilos.

Er meint, er **wiege** zu viel. He thinks he is too heavy.

Ich **habe** mich heute früh **gewogen**. I weighed myself this morning.

Ich **wog** die Zutaten. I weighed the ingredients.

wiegen

FUTURE

ich	**werde wiegen**
du	**wirst wiegen**
er/sie/es	**wird wiegen**
wir	**werden wiegen**
ihr	**werdet wiegen**
sie/Sie	**werden wiegen**

CONDITIONAL

ich	**würde wiegen**
du	**würdest wiegen**
er/sie/es	**würde wiegen**
wir	**würden wiegen**
ihr	**würdet wiegen**
sie/Sie	**würden wiegen**

PLUPERFECT

ich	**hatte gewogen**
du	**hattest gewogen**
er/sie/es	**hatte gewogen**
wir	**hatten gewogen**
ihr	**hattet gewogen**
sie/Sie	**hatten gewogen**

PLUPERFECT SUBJUNCTIVE

ich	**hätte gewogen**
du	**hättest gewogen**
er/sie/es	**hätte gewogen**
wir	**hätten gewogen**
ihr	**hättet gewogen**
sie/Sie	**hätten gewogen**

IMPERATIVE

wieg(e)!/wiegen wir!/wiegt!/wiegen Sie!

EXAMPLE PHRASES

Dieses Argument **wird** schwer **wiegen**. This argument will carry a lot of weight.

Ich **würde** gern weniger **wiegen**. I would rather weigh less.

Ich **hatte** das Fleisch schon **gewogen**. I had already weighed the meat.

Ohne die Diät **hättest** du bald zu viel **gewogen**. Without the diet you would soon have been overweight.

---

ich = I **du** = you **er** = he/it **sie** = she/it **es** = it/he/she **wir** = we **ihr** = you **sie** = they **Sie** = you (*polite*)

wissen (to know)

mixed, *formed with* haben

PRESENT

ich	**weiß**
du	**weißt**
er/sie/es	**weiß**
wir	**wissen**
ihr	**wisst**
sie/Sie	**wissen**

PRESENT SUBJUNCTIVE

ich	**wisse**
du	**wissest**
er/sie/es	**wisse**
wir	**wissen**
ihr	**wisset**
sie/Sie	**wissen**

PERFECT

ich	**habe gewusst**
du	**hast gewusst**
er/sie/es	**hat gewusst**
wir	**haben gewusst**
ihr	**habt gewusst**
sie/Sie	**haben gewusst**

IMPERFECT

ich	**wusste**
du	**wusstest**
er/sie/es	**wusste**
wir	**wussten**
ihr	**wusstet**
sie/Sie	**wussten**

PRESENT PARTICIPLE

wissend

PAST PARTICIPLE

gewusst

EXAMPLE PHRASES

Ich **weiß** nicht. I don't know.

Sie meint, sie **wisse** über alles Bescheid. She thinks she knows about everything.

Er **hat** nichts davon **gewusst**. He didn't know anything about it.

Sie **wussten**, wo das Kino war. They knew where the cinema was.

ich = I **du** = you **er** = he/it **sie** = she/it **es** = it/he/she **wir** = we **ihr** = you **sie** = they **Sie** = you (*polite*)

wissen

FUTURE

ich	werde wissen
du	wirst wissen
er/sie/es	wird wissen
wir	werden wissen
ihr	werdet wissen
sie/Sie	werden wissen

CONDITIONAL

ich	würde wissen
du	würdest wissen
er/sie/es	würde wissen
wir	würden wissen
ihr	würdet wissen
sie/Sie	würden wissen

PLUPERFECT

ich	hatte gewusst
du	hattest gewusst
er/sie/es	hatte gewusst
wir	hatten gewusst
ihr	hattet gewusst
sie/Sie	hatten gewusst

PLUPERFECT SUBJUNCTIVE

ich	hätte gewusst
du	hättest gewusst
er/sie/es	hätte gewusst
wir	hätten gewusst
ihr	hättet gewusst
sie/Sie	hätten gewusst

IMPERATIVE

wisse!/wissen wir!/wisset!/wissen Sie!

EXAMPLE PHRASES

Morgen **werden** wir **wissen**, wer gewonnen hat. **Tomorrow we'll know who has won.**

Ich **würde** gern **wissen**, warum du mich belogen hast. **I would like to know why you lied to me.**

Er **hatte** von dem Verbrechen **gewusst**. **He had known about the crime.**

Ich **hätte** nicht **gewusst**, was ich ohne dich gemacht hätte. **I wouldn't have known what I would have done without you.**

ich = I du = you er = he/it sie = she/it es = it/he/she wir = we ihr = you sie = they Sie = you *(polite)*

wollen (to want)

modal, *formed with* **haben**

PRESENT

ich	**will**
du	**willst**
er/sie/es	**will**
wir	**wollen**
ihr	**wollt**
sie/Sie	**wollen**

PRESENT SUBJUNCTIVE

ich	**wolle**
du	**wollest**
er/sie/es	**wolle**
wir	**wollen**
ihr	**wollet**
sie/Sie	**wollen**

PERFECT

ich	**habe gewollt/wollen**
du	**hast gewollt/wollen**
er/sie/es	**hat gewollt/wollen**
wir	**haben gewollt/wollen**
ihr	**habt gewollt/wollen**
sie/Sie	**haben gewollt/wollen**

IMPERFECT

ich	**wollte**
du	**wolltest**
er/sie/es	**wollte**
wir	**wolten**
ihr	**wolltet**
sie/Sie	**wollten**

PRESENT PARTICIPLE

wollend

PAST PARTICIPLE

gewollt/wollen*

*This form is used when combined with another infinitive.

EXAMPLE PHRASES

Er **will** nach London gehen. He wants to go to London.

Sie sagt, sie **wolle** ihn nie mehr sehen. She says she doesn't want to see him ever again.

Das **habe** ich nicht **gewollt**. I didn't want this to happen.

Sie **wollten** nur mehr Geld. All they wanted was more money.

wollen

FUTURE

ich	**werde wollen**
du	**wirst wollen**
er/sie/es	**wird wollen**
wir	**werden wollen**
ihr	**werdet wollen**
sie/Sie	**werden wollen**

CONDITIONAL

ich	**würde wollen**
du	**würdest wollen**
er/sie/es	**würde wollen**
wir	**würden wollen**
ihr	**würdet wollen**
sie/Sie	**würden wollen**

PLUPERFECT

ich	**hatte gewollt/wollen**
du	**hattest gewollt/wollen**
er/sie/es	**hatte gewollt/wollen**
wir	**hatten gewollt/wollen**
ihr	**hattet gewollt/wollen**
sie/Sie	**hatten gewollt/wollen**

PLUPERFECT SUBJUNCTIVE

ich	**hätte gewollt/wollen**
du	**hättest gewollt/wollen**
er/sie/es	**hätte gewollt/wollen**
wir	**hätten gewollt/wollen**
ihr	**hättet gewollt/wollen**
sie/Sie	**hätten gewollt/wollen**

IMPERATIVE

wolle!/wollen wir!/wollt!/wollen Sie!

EXAMPLE PHRASES

Das **wirst** du doch nicht im Ernst **wollen**! You cannot seriously want that!

Wir **würden** nicht **wollen**, dass das passiert. We wouldn't want that to happen.

Ich **hatte** doch gar nichts von ihm **gewollt**. I hadn't wanted anything from him.

Hätte ich es **gewollt**, wäre es auch geschehen. If I had wanted it, it would have happened.

ich = I   **du** = you   **er** = he/it   **sie** = she/it   **es** = it/he/she   **wir** = we   **ihr** = you   **sie** = they   **Sie** = you (*polite*)

zerstören (to destroy)   weak, inseparable, *formed with* haben

PRESENT		**PRESENT SUBJUNCTIVE**	
ich	zerstöre	ich	zerstöre
du	zerstörst	du	zerstörest
er/sie/es	zerstört	er/sie/es	zerstöre
wir	zerstören	wir	zerstören
ihr	zerstört	ihr	zerstöret
sie/Sie	zerstören	sie/Sie	zerstören

PERFECT		**IMPERFECT**	
ich	habe zerstört	ich	zerstörte
du	hast zerstört	du	zerstörtest
er/sie/es	hat zerstört	er/sie/es	zerstörte
wir	haben zerstört	wir	zerstörten
ihr	habt zerstört	ihr	zerstörtet
sie/Sie	haben zerstört	sie/Sie	zerstörten

PRESENT PARTICIPLE
zerstörend

PAST PARTICIPLE
zerstört

EXAMPLE PHRASES

Die ganzen Abgase **zerstören** die Ozonschicht. **All the fumes are destroying the ozone layer.**

Er meint, sie **zerstöre** ihre Gesundheit. He thinks she is wrecking her health.

Er hat ihr Selbstvertrauen **zerstört**. He has destroyed her self-confidence.

Er **zerstörte** ihre Ehe. He wrecked their marriage.

---

ich = I   **du** = you   **er** = he/it   **sie** = she/it   **es** = it/he/she   **wir** = we   **ihr** = you   **sie** = they   **Sie** = you (*polite*)

zerstören

FUTURE

ich	**werde zerstören**
du	**wirst zerstören**
er/sie/es	**wird zerstören**
wir	**werden zerstören**
ihr	**werdet zerstören**
sie/Sie	**werden zerstören**

CONDITIONAL

ich	**würde zerstören**
du	**würdest zerstören**
er/sie/es	**würde zerstören**
wir	**würden zerstören**
ihr	**würdet zerstören**
sie/Sie	**würden zerstören**

PLUPERFECT

ich	**hatte zerstört**
du	**hattest zerstört**
er/sie/es	**hatte zerstört**
wir	**hatten zerstört**
ihr	**hattet zerstört**
sie/Sie	**hatten zerstört**

PLUPERFECT SUBJUNCTIVE

ich	**hätte zerstört**
du	**hättest zerstört**
er/sie/es	**hätte zerstört**
wir	**hätten zerstört**
ihr	**hättet zerstört**
sie/Sie	**hätten zerstört**

IMPERATIVE

zerstör(e)!/zerstören wir!/zerstört!/zerstören Sie!

EXAMPLE PHRASES

Diese Waffen **werden** noch die Welt **zerstören**. These weapons will end up destroying the world.

Das **würde** unsere Freundschaft **zerstören**. It would destroy our friendship.

Eine Bombe **hatte** das Gebäude **zerstört**. A bomb had wrecked the building.

Dieses Ereignis **hätte** fast mein Leben **zerstört**. This event nearly ruined my life.

ich = I **du** = you **er** = he/it **sie** = she/it **es** = it/he/she **wir** = we **ihr** = you **sie** = they **Sie** = you (*polite*)

ziehen (to go/to pull)

strong, *formed with* **sein/haben***

PRESENT

ich	**ziehe**
du	**ziehst**
er/sie/es	**zieht**
wir	**ziehen**
ihr	**zieht**
sie/Sie	**ziehen**

PRESENT SUBJUNCTIVE

ich	**ziehe**
du	**ziehest**
er/sie/es	**ziehe**
wir	**ziehen**
ihr	**ziehet**
sie/Sie	**ziehen**

PERFECT

ich	**bin/habe gezogen**
du	**bist/hast gezogen**
er/sie/es	**ist/hat gezogen**
wir	**sind/haben gezogen**
ihr	**seid/habt gezogen**
sie/Sie	**sind/haben gezogen**

IMPERFECT

ich	**zog**
du	**zogst**
er/sie/es	**zog**
wir	**zogen**
ihr	**zogt**
sie/Sie	**zogen**

PRESENT PARTICIPLE

ziehend

PAST PARTICIPLE

gezogen

*When *ziehen* is used with a direct object, it is formed with *haben*.

EXAMPLE PHRASES

In diesem Zimmer **zieht** es. There's a draught in this room.

Er sagt, er **ziehe** bald nach Hamburg. He says he's going to move to Hamburg soon.

Seine Familie **ist** nach München **gezogen**. His family has moved to Munich.

Sie **zog** mich am Ärmel. She pulled at my sleeve.

ich = I **du** = you **er** = he/it **sie** = she/it **es** = it/he/she **wir** = we **ihr** = you **sie** = they **Sie** = you (polite)

ziehen

FUTURE

ich	**werde ziehen**
du	**wirst ziehen**
er/sie/es	**wird ziehen**
wir	**werden ziehen**
ihr	**werdet ziehen**
sie/Sie	**werden ziehen**

CONDITIONAL

ich	**würde ziehen**
du	**würdest ziehen**
er/sie/es	**würde ziehen**
wir	**würden ziehen**
ihr	**würdet ziehen**
sie/Sie	**würden ziehen**

PLUPERFECT

ich	**war/hatte gezogen**
du	**warst/hattest gezogen**
er/sie/es	**war/hatte gezogen**
wir	**waren/hatten gezogen**
ihr	**wart/hattet gezogen**
sie/Sie	**waren/hatten gezogen**

PLUPERFECT SUBJUNCTIVE

ich	**wäre/hätte gezogen**
du	**wär(e)st/hättest gezogen**
er/sie/es	**wäre/hätte gezogen**
wir	**wären/hätten gezogen**
ihr	**wär(e)t/hättet gezogen**
sie/Sie	**wären/hätten gezogen**

IMPERATIVE

zieh(e)!/ziehen wir!/zieht!/ziehen Sie

EXAMPLE PHRASES

Du **wirst** seinen Hass auf dich **ziehen**. You will incur his hatred.

Ich **würde** nie nach Bayern **ziehen**. I would never move to Bavaria.

Sie **waren** zuversichtlich in den Krieg **gezogen**. They had felt confident about going to war.

Das **hätte** schlimme Folgen nach sich **gezogen**. It would have had terrible consequences.

ich = I du = you er = he/it sie = she/it es = it/he/she wir = we ihr = you sie = they Sie = you (*polite*)

zwingen (to force)

strong, formed with haben

PRESENT

ich	zwinge
du	zwingst
er/sie/es	zwingt
wir	zwingen
ihr	zwingt
sie/Sie	zwingen

PRESENT SUBJUNCTIVE

ich	zwinge
du	zwingest
er/sie/es	zwinge
wir	zwingen
ihr	zwinget
sie/Sie	zwingen

PERFECT

ich	habe gezwungen
du	hast gezwungen
er/sie/es	hat gezwungen
wir	haben gezwungen
ihr	habt gezwungen
sie/Sie	haben gezwungen

IMPERFECT

ich	zwang
du	zwangst
er/sie/es	zwang
wir	zwangen
ihr	zwangt
sie/Sie	zwangen

PRESENT PARTICIPLE

zwingend

PAST PARTICIPLE

gezwungen

EXAMPLE PHRASES

Ich **zwinge** mich dazu. I force myself to do it.

Sie sagt, sie **zwinge** mich nicht. She says she's not forcing me.

Er **hat** ihn **gezwungen**, das zu tun. He forced him to do it.

Sie **zwangen** uns, den Vertrag zu unterschreiben. They forced us to sign the contract.

---

ich = I **du** = you **er** = he/it **sie** = she/it **es** = it/he/she **wir** = we **ihr** = you **sie** = they **Sie** = you (*polite*)

zwingen

FUTURE

ich	**werde zwingen**
du	**wirst zwingen**
er/sie/es	**wird zwingen**
wir	**werden zwingen**
ihr	**werdet zwingen**
sie/Sie	**werden zwingen**

CONDITIONAL

ich	**würde zwingen**
du	**würdest zwingen**
er/sie/es	**würde zwingen**
wir	**würden zwingen**
ihr	**würdet zwingen**
sie/Sie	**würden zwingen**

PLUPERFECT

ich	**hatte gezwungen**
du	**hattest gezwungen**
er/sie/es	**hatte gezwungen**
wir	**hatten gezwungen**
ihr	**hattet gezwungen**
sie/Sie	**hatten gezwungen**

PLUPERFECT SUBJUNCTIVE

ich	**hätte gezwungen**
du	**hättest gezwungen**
er/sie/es	**hätte gezwungen**
wir	**hätten gezwungen**
ihr	**hättet gezwungen**
sie/Sie	**hätten gezwungen**

IMPERATIVE

zwing(e)!/zwingen wir!/zwingt!/zwingen Sie

EXAMPLE PHRASES

Wir werden ihn zum Handeln **zwingen**. We will force him into action.

Ich **würde** ihn **zwingen**, sich zu entschuldigen. I would force him to apologize.

Man **hatte** ihn zum Rücktritt **gezwungen**. He had been forced to resign.

Wenn du mich gezwungen hättest, **hätte** ich **unterschrieben**. If you had forced me I would have signed.

How to use the Verb Index

The verbs in bold are the model verbs which you will find in the verb tables. All the other verbs follow one of these patterns, so the number next to each verb indicates which pattern fits this particular verb. For example, **begleiten** (*to accompany*) follows the same pattern as **arbeiten** (*to work*), number 210 in the verb tables.

All the verbs are in alphabetical order. For reflexive verbs like **sich setzen** (*to sit down*) look under **setzen**, not under **sich**.

With the exception of reflexive verbs which are always formed with **haben**, most verbs have the same auxiliary (**sein** or **haben**) as their model verb. If this is different, it is shown in the Verb Index. Certain verbs can be formed with both **haben** or **sein** and there is a note about this at the relevant verb tables.

Some verbs in the Verb Index have a dividing line through them to show that the verb is separable, for example, **durch|setzen**.

*For more information on **separable** and **inseparable** verbs, see pages 91–152.*

ab|brechen	234	ab|ziehen	252	an|ordnen	346	auf|haben	290
ab|fahren	256	achten	210	an|probieren	412	auf|halten	292
ab|fliegen	264	addieren	412	an|rufen	356	auf|hängen	296
ab|fragen	214	adressieren	412	an|schalten	210	auf|heitern *(haben)*	440
ab|geben	272	ähneln +*dat*	294	an|schauen	214	auf|hören	214
ab|gewöhnen	304	amüsieren *sich acc*	412	an|schreien	168	auf|klären	214
ab|hängen	296	an|bauen	214	an|sehen	380	auf|lassen	316
ab|holen	214	an|bieten	226	an|sprechen	394	auf|lösen *(sich acc)*	214
ab|kürzen	300	an|brechen	234	an|starren	214	auf|machen	214
ab|laufen	318	an|brennen	236	an|stecken	214	auf|muntern *(haben)*	440
ab|lehnen	214	ändern *(sich acc)*		an|stellen	214	auf|nehmen	340
ab|lenken	214	(*haben*)	440	an|strengen *(sich acc)*	214	auf|passen	288
ab|liefern *(haben)*	440	an|deuten	210	antworten	210	auf|räumen	214
ab|machen	214	an|fahren	256	an|zeigen	214	aufrecht|erhalten	292
ab|nehmen	340	an|fangen	260	an|ziehen	252	auf|regen	214
abonnieren	412	an|fassen	288	an|zünden	348	auf|schreiben	372
ab|reisen *(sein)*	214	an|geben	272	**arbeiten**	**210**	auf|sehen	380
ab|sagen +*dat*	214	an|gehen	274	ärgern *(haben)*	440	auf|setzen	300
ab|schaffen	214	angeln	294	**atmen**	**212**	auf|stehen	400
ab|schicken	214	an|gewöhnen	304	auf|bauen	214	auf|steigen	404
ab|schneiden	370	an|haben	290	auf|bewahren	304	auf|stellen	214
ab|schreiben	372	an|halten	292	auf|bleiben	232	auf|tauchen	214
ab|schrecken	214	an|hören	214	auf|brechen	234	auf|tauen	214
ab|setzen *(sich acc)*	300	an|kommen	310	auf|essen	254	auf|teilen	214
ab|stellen	214	an|kreuzen	300	auf|fallen +*dat*	258	auf|treten	420
ab|stürzen *(sein)*	300	an|kündigen	214	auf|fangen	260	auf|wachen	214
ab|trocknen	346	an|machen	214	auf|führen	214	auf|wachsen	438
ab|waschen	442	an|melden	348	auf|geben	272	auf|wecken	214
ab|werten	210	**an|nehmen**	**208**	auf|gehen	274	auf|zählen	214

Verb Index

Vocabulary

contents

This section is divided into 50 topics, arranged in alphabetical order. This thematic approach enables you to learn related words and phrases together, so that you can become confident in using particular vocabulary in context.

Vocabulary within each topic is divided into nouns and useful phrases which are aimed at helping you to express yourself in idiomatic German. Vocabulary within each topic is graded to help you prioritize your learning. Essential words include the basic words you will need to be able to communicate effectively, important words help expand your knowledge, and useful words provide additional vocabulary which will enable you to express yourself more fully.

Nouns are grouped by gender, which makes it easier to remember if they are masculine ("der") nouns, feminine ("die") nouns and neuter ("das") nouns. In addition, all plural forms are shown, with the exception of feminine nouns ending in –in (these regularly become –innen in the plural) and those forms, of whatever gender, which have the same form in both singular and plural.

Nouns which have been derived from adjectives follow the style:

Alte(r), -n   old man/woman

This means that the noun ending depends on whether the article is definite or indefinite, masculine or feminine, singular or plural. For example:

der Alte	*masculine singular (definite article)*
ein Alter	*masculine singular (indefinite article)*
die Alte	*feminine singular (definite article)*
eine Alte	*feminine singular (indefinite article)*
die Alten	*masculine and feminine singular (definite article)*
Alte	*masculine and feminine singular (no article)*

At the end of the book you will find a list of supplementary vocabulary, grouped according to part of speech – adjective, verb, noun and so on. This is vocabulary which you will come across in many everyday situations.

Finally, there is an English index which lists all the essential and important nouns given under the topic headings for quick reference.

ABBREVIATIONS

acc	accusative
adj	adjective
adv	adverb
conj	conjunction
dat	dative
etw	etwas (meaning *something*)
f	feminine
gen	genitive
jdm	jemandem (meaning *somebody – dative case*)
jdn	jemanden (meaning *somebody – accusative case*)
m	masculine
n	noun
nt	neuter
pl	plural
prep	preposition
sb	somebody
sth	something

ESSENTIAL WORDS (masculine)

der	Ausgang, ̈e	way out, exit
der	Ausstieg, -e	exit
der	Check-in, -s	check-in
der	Eingang, ̈e	entrance
der	Fahrgast, ̈e	passenger
der	Fahrkartenschalter	ticket office
der	Fahrplan, ̈e	timetable
die	Ferien (pl)	holiday
der	Flug, ̈e	flight
der	Fluggast, ̈e	airline passenger
der	Flughafen, ̈	airport
der	Flugplan, ̈e	flight schedule
der	Flugplatz, ̈e	airfield; airport
der	Flugpreis, -e	(air) fare
der	Flugschein, -e	(plane) ticket
der	Gepäckträger	porter
der	Gepäckwagen	luggage trolley
der	Geschäftsmann, -leute	businessman
der	Koffer	case, suitcase
der	Kofferkuli, -s	luggage trolley
der	Notausgang, ̈e	emergency exit
der	Pass, ̈e	passport
der	Passagier, -e	passenger
der	Personalausweis, -e	identity card
der	Reisende(r), -n	traveller
der	Reisepass, ̈e	passport
der	Sicherheitsbereich, -e	security area
der	Steward, -s	steward
der	Tourist, -en	tourist
der	Urlaub	holiday(s)
der	Urlauber	holidaymaker
der	Zoll	customs; duty
der	Zuschlag, ̈e	extra charge

ESSENTIAL WORDS (feminine)

die	Ankunft, ⁐e	arrival
die	Auskunft, ⁐e	information; information desk
die	(einfache) Fahrkarte, -n	(single) ticket
die	Gepäckausgabe	baggage reclaim
die	Maschine, -n	plane
die	Personenkontrolle, -n	checkpoint (for passengers)
die	Reservierung, -en	booking, reservation
die	Richtung, -en	direction
die	Rückfahrkarte, -n	return (ticket)
die	Sicherheitskontrolle, -n	security check
die	Stewardess, -en	air hostess
die	Tasche, -n	bag
die	Toilette, -n	toilet
die	Touristin	tourist
die	Uhr, -en	clock; time
die	Urlauberin	holiday-maker

ESSENTIAL WORDS (neuter)

das	Fliegen	flying
das	Flugzeug, -e	plane, aeroplane
das	Fundbüro, -s	lost property office
das	Gepäck	luggage
das	Passagierflugzeug, -e	airliner
das	Schließfach, ⁐er	left luggage locker
das	Taxi, -s	taxi
das	Ticket, -s	(plane) ticket

USEFUL PHRASES

einen Flugschein or ein Ticket lösen to buy a (plane) ticket
einen Rückflug buchen to book a return flight
hin und zurück nach Köln a return to Cologne
ich packe I pack; ich packe aus I unpack
das Gepäck durchleuchten to scan the luggage
einchecken to check in; fliegen to fly; wir fliegen ab we fly off
erreichen to catch; verpassen to miss

IMPORTANT WORDS *(masculine)*

der	**Abflug, ⸚e**	takeoff, departure
der	**Duty-free-Shop, -s**	duty-free shop
der	**Jumbojet, -s**	jumbo jet
der	**Kontrollturm, ⸚e**	control tower
der	**Metalldetektor, -en**	metal detector
der	**Pilot, -en**	pilot
der	**Sicherheitsbeamte(r), -n**	security officer
der	**Sicherheitsgurt, -e**	seat belt
der	**Start, -s**	takeoff
der	**Terminal, -s**	(air) terminal
der	**Terrorist, -en**	terrorist
der	**Zollbeamte(r), -n**	customs officer

IMPORTANT WORDS *(feminine)*

die	**Autovermietung, -en**	car hire
die	**Bordkarte, -n**	boarding card
die	**Landung, -en**	landing
die	**Sicherheitsbeamtin**	security officer
die	**Startbahn, -en**	runway
die	**Terroristin**	terrorist
die	**Verbindung, -en**	connection
die	**Verspätung, -en**	delay
die	**Zollkontrolle**	customs control *or* check

IMPORTANT WORDS *(neuter)*

das	**Abfluggate, -s**	departure gate
das	**E-Ticket, -s**	e-ticket
das	**Flugticket, -s**	ticket
das	**Handgepäck**	hand luggage
das	**Reisebüro, -s**	travel agent's
das	**Reiseziel, -e**	destination

USEFUL PHRASES

starten to take off; **beim Start** during the takeoff
an Bord on board; **luftkrank** airsick
ein Flugzeug entführen to hijack a plane
landen to land; **verspätet** delayed, late

USEFUL WORDS *(masculine)*

der	**Anhänger**	label, tag
der	**Aufkleber**	sticker, label
der	**Babyraum, ̈-e**	mother and baby room
der	**Fluglotse, -n**	air traffic controller
der	**Flugsteig, -e**	gate

USEFUL WORDS *(feminine)*

die	**Besatzung, -en**	crew
die	**Besucherterrasse, -n**	spectator terrace
die	**Bombe, -n**	bomb
die	**Gepäckermittlung**	lost luggage office
die	**Landebahn, -en**	runway
die	**Rollbahn, -en**	runway
die	**Rolltreppe, -n**	escalator
die	**Schallmauer**	sound barrier
die	**Turbulenz**	turbulence
die	**Wechselstube, -n**	bureau de change
die	**Zwischenlandung, -en**	stopover

USEFUL WORDS *(neuter)*

das	**Bodenpersonal**	ground staff
das	**Durchleuchtungsgerät, -e**	scanner
das	**Düsenflugzeug, -e**	jet plane
das	**Restaurant, -s**	restaurant

USEFUL PHRASES

einen Zuschlag zahlen to pay a supplement
zuschlagpflichtig subject to an extra charge
gültig valid
erhältlich available
durch den Zoll gehen to go through customs
verzollen to pay duty on
haben Sie etwas zu verzollen? do you have anything to declare?
nichts zu verzollen nothing to declare
zollfrei duty-free

ESSENTIAL WORDS *(masculine)*

der	**Elefant, -en**	elephant
der	**Fisch, -e**	fish
der	**Hals, ̈e**	neck; throat
der	**Hund, -e**	dog
der	**Tiergarten, ̈**	zoo, zoological park
der	**Versuch, -e**	experiment
der	**Zoo, -s**	zoo

IMPORTANT WORDS *(masculine)*

der	**Affe, -n**	monkey
der	**Bär, -en**	bear
der	**Bock, ̈e**	buck, ram
der	**Hamster**	hamster
der	**Huf, -e**	hoof
der	**Löwe, -n**	lion
der	**Schwanz, ̈e**	tail
der	**Tiger**	tiger
der	**Wolf, ̈e**	wolf

ESSENTIAL WORDS *(feminine)*

die	**Katze, -n**	cat
die	**Tierhandlung, -en**	pet shop

IMPORTANT WORDS *(feminine)*

die	**Giraffe, -n**	giraffe
die	**Hundehütte, -n**	kennel
die	**Kuh, ̈e**	cow
die	**Löwin**	lioness
die	**Maus, Mäuse**	mouse
die	**Ratte, -n**	rat
die	**Schlange, -n**	snake
die	**Tigerin**	tigress

USEFUL PHRASES

laufen to run; hüpfen to hop
springen to jump; kriechen to slither, crawl

ESSENTIAL WORDS *(neuter)*

das	**Bein**, -e	leg
das	**Haar**, -e	hair
das	**Haustier**, -e	pet
die	**Jungen** *(pl)*	young
das	**Ohr**, -en	ear
das	**Tier**, -e	animal

IMPORTANT WORDS *(neuter)*

das	**Horn**, ̈-er	horn
das	**Kamel**, -e	camel
das	**Känguru**, -s	kangaroo
das	**Kaninchen**	rabbit
das	**Krokodil**, -e	crocodile
das	**Pferd**, -e	horse
das	**Pony**, -s	pony
das	**Rhinozeros**, -se	rhinoceros
das	**Schaf**, -e	sheep
das	**Schwein**, -e	pig
das	**Zebra**, -s	zebra

USEFUL PHRASES

wir haben keine Haustiere **we don't have any pets**
zahm **tame**; wild **wild**; gehorsam **obedient**
füttern **to feed**; fressen **to eat**
trinken **to drink**
schlafen **to sleep**
bellen **to bark**; miauen **to miaow**
knurren **to growl**; schnurren **to purr**
beißen **to bite**; kratzen **to scratch**
ich habe Angst vor Hunden **I'm afraid of dogs**

USEFUL WORDS *(masculine)*

der	**Beutel**	pouch *(of kangaroo)*
der	**Bulle, -n**	bull
der	**Eisbär, -en**	polar bear
der	**Esel**	donkey
der	**Frosch, ⸚e**	frog
der	**Fuchs, ⸚e**	fox
der	**Hase, -n**	hare
der	**Hirsch, -e**	stag
der	**Höcker**	hump *(of camel)*
der	**Igel**	hedgehog
der	**Kater**	tomcat
der	**Maulwurf, ⸚e**	mole
der	**Ochse, -n**	ox
der	**Panzer**	shell *(of tortoise)*
der	**Pelz, -e**	fur
der	**Rüssel**	snout *(of pig)*; trunk *(of elephant)*
der	**Seehund, -e**	seal
der	**Stachel, -n**	spine *(of hedgehog)*
der	**Stier, -e**	bull
der	**Stoßzahn, ⸚e**	tusk
der	**Streifen**	stripe *(of zebra)*
der	**Wal(fisch), -e**	whale
der	**Ziegenbock, ⸚e**	billy goat

USEFUL PHRASES

jagen **to hunt; to shoot**
zu Pferd **on horseback**
reiten gehen **to go riding**
auf die Fuchsjagd gehen **to go fox-hunting**
„Vorsicht, bissiger Hund" **"beware of the dog"**
der Hund wedelt mit dem Schwanz **the dog wags its tail**
die Katze streicheln **to stroke the cat**

USEFUL WORDS (feminine)

die	Falle, -n	trap
die	Fledermaus, -mäuse	bat
die	Heuschrecke, -n	grasshopper
die	Kralle, -n	claw; talon
die	Kröte, -n	toad
die	Mähne, -n	mane
die	Natter, -n	adder
die	Pfote, -n	paw (*small*)
die	Pranke, -n	paw (*large*)
die	Ringelnatter, -n	grass snake
die	Robbe, -n	seal
die	Schildkröte, -n	tortoise
die	Schnauze, -n	snout, muzzle
die	Tatze, -n	paw
die	Ziege, -n	goat, nanny goat

USEFUL WORDS (neuter)

das	Eichhörnchen	squirrel
das	Fell, -e	coat, fur
das	Geweih	antlers (*pl*)
das	Hufeisen	horseshoe
das	Maul, Mäuler	mouth
das	Maultier, -e	mule
das	Meerschweinchen	guinea pig
das	Merkmal, -e	characteristic
das	Nashorn, ̈-er	rhinoceros
das	Nilpferd, -e	hippopotamus
das	Reh, -e	roe deer

USEFUL PHRASES

ein Tier freilassen to set an animal free
ein Löwe ist aus dem Zoo entlaufen a lion has escaped from the zoo
in eine Falle gehen to be caught in a trap

ESSENTIAL + IMPORTANT WORDS *(masculine)*

der	Gang, ¨e	gear
der	Gepäckträger	luggage carrier
der	Motorradfahrer	motorcyclist
der	Radfahrer	cyclist
der	Rad(fahr)weg, -e	cycle track *or* path
der	Radsport	cycling
der	Reifen	tyre
der	Sattel, ¨	saddle, seat

ESSENTIAL + IMPORTANT WORDS *(feminine)*

die	Achtung	attention
die	Bahn, -en	road, way; (cycle) lane
die	Bremse, -n	brake
die	Ecke, -n	corner
die	Fahrradlampe, -n	cycle lamp
die	Gefahr, -en	danger, risk
die	Geschwindigkeit, -en	speed
die	Hauptstraße, -n	main street, main road
die	Kette, -n	chain
die	Klingel, -n	bell
die	Lampe, -n	lamp
die	Nebenstraße, -n	side street
die	Pumpe, -n	pump
die	Radfahrerin	cyclist
die	Reifenpanne, -n	puncture
die	Reparatur, -en	repair; repairing

USEFUL PHRASES

mit dem (Fahr)rad fahren **to cycle**
mit dem Rad in die Stadt fahren **to cycle into town**
er kam mit dem Rad **he came on his bike, he came by bike**
„Radfahren verboten" **"cycling prohibited"**
Radsport betreiben **to go in for cycling**
aufsteigen **to get on**; absteigen **to get off**
bergauf **uphill**; bergab **downhill**
klingeln **to ring one's bell**; schalten **to change gear**

ESSENTIAL WORDS *(neuter)*

das	Fahrrad, -̈er	bicycle
das	Hinterrad, -̈er	back wheel
das	Motorrad, -̈er	motorbike, motorcycle
das	Pedal, -e	pedal
das	Rad, -̈er	wheel; bike
das	Radfahren	cycling
das	Vorderrad, -̈er	front wheel

USEFUL WORDS *(masculine)*

der	Dynamo, -s	dynamo
der	Helm, -e	helmet
der	Korb, -̈e	pannier; basket
der	Rückstrahler	reflector

USEFUL WORDS *(feminine)*

die	Lenkstange, -n	handlebars
die	Satteltasche, -n	saddlebag, pannier
die	Speiche, -n	spoke
die	Steigung, -en	gradient
die	Straßenverkehrsordnung	Highway Code

USEFUL WORDS *(neuter)*

das	Flickzeug, -e	puncture repair kit
das	Katzenauge, -n	rear light; reflector; cat's eye
das	Moped, -s	moped
das	Mountainbike, -s	mountain bike
das	Schutzblech, -e	mudguard

USEFUL PHRASES

bremsen **to brake;** reparieren **to repair**
einen Platten haben **to have a flat tyre**
geplatzt **burst;** kaputt **broken, done**
das Loch flicken **to mend the puncture**
die Reifen aufpumpen **to blow up the tyres**
glänzend **shiny;** rostig **rusty;** Leucht- **fluorescent**

ESSENTIAL + IMPORTANT WORDS *(masculine)*

der	Flamingo, -s	flamingo
der	Hahn, ⁝e	cock
der	Himmel	sky
der	Käfig, -e	cage
der	Kanarienvogel, ⁝	canary
der	Kuckuck, -e	cuckoo
der	Pinguin, -e	penguin
der	Schwan, ⁝e	swan
der	Storch, ⁝e	stork
der	Truthahn, ⁝e	turkey
der	Vogel, ⁝	bird
der	Wellensittich, -e	budgie, budgerigar

ESSENTIAL + IMPORTANT WORDS *(feminine)*

die	Ente, -n	duck
die	Feder, -n	feather
die	Gans, ⁝e	goose
die	Henne, -n	hen
die	Luft	air
die	Nachtigall, -en	nightingale

ESSENTIAL + IMPORTANT WORDS *(neuter)*

das	Huhn, ⁝er	hen, fowl
das	Nest, -er	nest
das	Rotkehlchen	robin (redbreast)
das *or* der	(Vogel)bauer	birdcage

USEFUL PHRASES
fliegen to fly; abfliegen to fly away
ein Nest bauen to build a nest; nisten to nest
Eier legen to lay eggs
singen to sing
pfeifen to whistle
zwitschern to twitter
Lärm machen to make a noise

USEFUL WORDS *(masculine)*

der	Adler	eagle
der	Eisvogel, ̈	kingfisher
der	Falke, -n	falcon
der	Fasan, -e(n)	pheasant
der	Fink, -en	finch
der	Flügel	wing
der	Geier	vulture
der	Habicht, -e	hawk
der	Hirtenstar, -s	mynah bird
der	Papagei, -en	parrot
der	Pfau, -en	peacock
der	Puter	turkey(-cock)
der	Rabe, -n	raven
der	Schnabel, ̈	beak, bill
der	Sittich, -e	parakeet
der	Spatz, -en	sparrow
der	Specht, -e	woodpecker
der	Sperling, -e	sparrow
der	Star, -e	starling
der	Strauß, -e	ostrich
der	Zaunkönig, -e	wren

USEFUL WORDS *(feminine)*

die	Amsel, -n	blackbird
die	Blaumeise, -n	bluetit
die	Dohle, -n	jackdaw
die	Drossel, -n	thrush
die	Elster, -n	magpie
die	Eule, -n	owl
die	Krähe, -n	crow
die	Lerche, -n	lark
die	Möwe, -n	seagull
die	Saatkrähe, -n	rook
die	Schwalbe, -n	swallow
die	Taube, -n	dove; pigeon

ESSENTIAL WORDS (*masculine*)

der	**Arm, -e**	arm
der	**Bauch, Bäuche**	stomach
der	**Finger**	finger
der	**Fuß, ¨-e**	foot
der	**Hals, ¨-e**	neck, throat
der	**Kopf, ¨-e**	head
der	**Magen, -** *or* **¨-**	stomach
der	**Mund, ¨-er**	mouth
der	**Rücken**	back
der	**Zahn, ¨-e**	tooth

ESSENTIAL WORDS (*feminine*)

die	**Bewegung, -en**	movement, motion
die	**Hand, ¨-e**	hand
die	**Nase, -n**	nose
die	**Seite, -n**	side

ESSENTIAL WORDS (*neuter*)

das	**Auge, -n**	eye
das	**Bein, -e**	leg
das	**Fleisch**	flesh
das	**Gesicht, -er**	face
das	**Haar, -e**	hair
das	**Ohr, -en**	ear

USEFUL PHRASES

ich habe mir den Arm/das Bein gebrochen I've broken my arm/leg
mein Arm/Bein tut weh my arm/leg hurts
zu Fuß on foot; barfuß gehen to go *or* walk barefoot
von Kopf bis Fuß from head to foot, from top to toe
den Kopf schütteln to shake one's head
mit den Kopf nicken to nod one's head
jdm die Hand geben to shake hands with sb
(mit der Hand) winken to wave
auf etwas zeigen to point to something

IMPORTANT WORDS (masculine)

der	**Atem**	breath
der	**Daumen**	thumb
der	**Körper**	body
der	**Körperteil, -e**	part of the body
der	**Zeigefinger**	forefinger, index finger

IMPORTANT WORDS (feminine)

die	**Lippe, -n**	lip
die	**Schulter, -n**	shoulder
die	**Stimme, -n**	voice
die	**Zunge, -n**	tongue

IMPORTANT WORDS (neuter)

das	**Blut**	blood
das	**Herz, -en**	heart
das	**Knie**	knee

USEFUL PHRASES

sehen **to see**; hören **to hear**
fühlen **to feel**; riechen **to smell**
tasten **to touch**; schmecken **to taste**
sich die Nase putzen **to blow one's nose**
jdm auf die Schulter klopfen **to tap sb on the shoulder**
sein Herz klopfte **his heart was beating**
die linke/rechte Körperseite **the left-hand/right-hand side of the body**
neben mir **at my side**
eine leise/laute Stimme haben **to have a soft/loud voice**
leise/laut sprechen **to speak softly/loudly**
ich lasse mir die Haare schneiden **I'm having my hair cut**
auf den Knien **on one's knees**
stehen **to stand**; sitzen **to sit**
sich legen **to lie down**; knien **to kneel (down)**
bewegen **to move** (part of the body)
sich bewegen **to move**

USEFUL WORDS *(masculine)*

der	**Ell(en)bogen**	elbow
der	**(Fuß)knöchel**	ankle
der	**Hintern**	bottom
der	**Kiefer**	jaw
der	**Knöchel**	knuckle; ankle
der	**Knochen**	bone
der	**Muskel, -n**	muscle
der	**Nacken**	nape of the neck
der	**Nagel, ̈**	nail
der	**Nerv, -en**	nerve
der	**Schenkel**	thigh

USEFUL WORDS *(neuter)*

das	**(Augen)lid, -er**	eyelid
das	**Blutgefäß, -e**	blood vessel
das	**Fußgelenk, -e**	ankle
das	**Gehirn, -e**	brain
das	**Gelenk, -e**	joint
das	**Genick, -e**	nape of the neck
das	**Glied, -er**	limb
das	**Handgelenk, -e**	wrist
das	**Kinn, -e**	chin
die	**Maße** *(pl)*	measurements
das	**Rückgrat, -e**	spine
das	**Skelett, -e**	skeleton

USEFUL PHRASES

ich habe mir den Knöchel verstaucht I've sprained my ankle
biegen to bend; strecken to stretch
stürzen to fall; verletzen, verwunden to injure
müde tired
fit fit; unfit unfit
ich ruhe mich aus I'm resting or having a rest
taub deaf; blind blind; stumm dumb
körperbehindert physically handicapped
geistig behindert mentally handicapped

USEFUL WORDS *(feminine)*

die	**Ader, -n**	vein
die	**Arterie, -n**	artery
die	**Augenbraue, -n**	eyebrow
die	**(Augen)wimper, -n**	eyelash
die	**Brust, ̈-e**	breast; chest
die	**Faust, Fäuste**	fist
die	**Ferse, -n**	heel
die	**Figur, -en**	figure
die	**Form, -en**	shape, figure
die	**Fußsohle, -n**	sole of the foot
die	**Gestalt, -en**	figure, form, shape
die	**Geste, -n**	gesture
die	**Haut**	skin
die	**Hüfte, -n**	hip
die	**Kehle, -n**	throat
die	**Leber, -n**	liver
die	**Lunge, -n**	lung
die	**Niere, -n**	kidney
die	**Pupille, -n**	pupil *(of eye)*
die	**Rippe, -n**	rib
die	**Schläfe, -n**	temple
die	**Schlagader, -n**	artery
die	**Stirn, -en**	forehead
die	**Taille, -n**	waist
die	**Wade, -n**	calf *(of leg)*
die	**Wange, -n**	neck
die	**Zehe, -n**	toe
die	**große Zehe, -n -n**	big toe

USEFUL PHRASES

Brustumfang *(m)* bust *or* chest measurement
Hüftweite *(f)* hip measurement
Taillenweite *(f)* waist measurement

THE SEASONS

der	**Frühling**	spring
der	**Sommer**	summer
der	**Herbst**	autumn
der	**Winter**	winter

im Frühling/Sommer/Herbst/Winter in spring/summer/autumn/winter

THE MONTHS

Januar	January	**Juli**	July
Februar	February	**August**	August
März	March	**September**	September
April	April	**Oktober**	October
Mai	May	**November**	November
Juni	June	**Dezember**	December

im September *etc* in September *etc*
der erste April **April Fools' Day**
der Erste Mai **May Day**
der fünfte November (*Tag der Pulververschwörung in England*) Guy Fawkes
  Night

THE DAYS OF THE WEEK

Montag	Monday
Dienstag	Tuesday
Mittwoch	Wednesday
Donnerstag	Thursday
Freitag	Friday
Samstag } **Sonnabend**	Saturday
Sonntag	Sunday

USEFUL PHRASES
freitags *etc* on Fridays *etc*
am Freitag *etc* on Friday *etc*
nächsten/letzten Freitag *etc* next/last Friday *etc*
am nächsten Freitag *etc* the following Friday *etc*

THE CALENDAR

Advent (m) Advent
der Adventskranz Advent wreath
Allerheiligen (nt) All Saints' Day
der Abend vor Allerheiligen Hallowe'en
Allerseelen (nt) All Souls' Day
Aschermittwoch (m) Ash Wednesday
Dreikönigfest (nt) Epiphany, Twelfth Night
Faschingszeit (f) the Fasching festival, carnival time
Fastenzeit (f) Lent
Fastnacht (f) Shrove Tuesday
Heiliger Abend, Heiligabend (m) Christmas Eve
Karfreitag (m) Good Friday
Neujahr (nt) New Year
Neujahrstag (m) New Year's Day
Ostern (nt) Easter
Ostersonntag (m) Easter Sunday
Palmsonntag (m) Palm Sunday
Passahfest (nt) (Feast of the) Passover
Pfingsten (nt) Whitsun
Pfingstmontag (m) Whit Monday
Silvester, Sylvester (nt) New Year's Eve, Hogmanay
Silvesterabend (m) New Year's Eve, Hogmanay
Valentinstag (m) St Valentine's Day
der Valentinsgruß Valentine card
Weihnachten (nt) Christmas
Weihnachtsabend (m) Christmas Eve
Weihnachtstag (m) Christmas Day
zweiter Weihnachtstag (m) Boxing Day
die Weihnachtskarte Christmas card

USEFUL PHRASES

zu Weihnachten/Ostern/Pfingsten at Christmas/Easter/Whitsun

SPECIAL EVENTS

die	**Beerdigung, -en**	funeral, burial
die	**Bescherung, -en**	distribution of Christmas presents
der	**Feiertag, -e**	holiday
das	**Festival, -s**	festival
der	**Festtag, -e**	holiday
das	**Feuerwerk, -e**	firework display
der	**Feuerwerkskörper**	firework
der	**Friedhof, -̈e**	cemetery, graveyard
der	**Geburstag, -e**	birthday
das	**Geschenk, -e**	present
die	**Heirat, -en**	marriage
der	**Hochzeitstag, -e**	wedding day
die	**Jahreszeit, -en**	season
der	**Kalender**	calendar
das	**Konfetti**	confetti
der	**Wochentag, -e**	weekday
der	**Tanz, -̈e** *or* **Tanzabend**	dance
die	**Taufe, -n**	christening, baptism
der	**Tod, -e**	death
der	**Werktag, -e**	working day
der	**Zirkus, -se**	circus

USEFUL PHRASES

seinen Geburtstag feiern **to celebrate one's birthday**
der Silvestertanz **New Year's Eve dance**
prosit Neujahr! **happy New Year!**
jdm ein Geschenk machen **to give somebody a present**
ein Feuerwerk abbrennen **to set off fireworks**
ihr dritter Hochzeitstag **their third (wedding) anniversary**
beglückwünschen (zu) **to congratulate (on)**
wünschen **to wish**
(herzlich) willkommen! **you are (very) welcome!**
in Trauer **in mourning**
den Wievielten haben wir heute? **what is today's date?**

SPECIAL EVENTS

die	**Blaskapelle, -n**	brass band
das	**Fest, -e**	fête, feast (day)
die	**Flitterwochen** (pl)	honeymoon (time)
das	**Folksongfestival**	folk music festival
die	**Geburt, -en**	birth
die	**Hochzeit, -en**	wedding
die	**Hochzeitsreise, -n**	honeymoon (journey)
der	**Jahrmarkt, ̈e**	fair
die	**Kirchweih, -en**	fair
die	**Kirmes, -sen**	funfair
die	**Messe, -n**	(commercial) fair
der	**Namenstag, -e**	saint's day
die	**Party, -s**	party
der	**Ruhestand**	retirement
der	**Rummelplatz, ̈e**	fairground
die	**Trauung, -en**	wedding ceremony
die	**Verabredung, -en**	date (with sb)
die	**Verlobung, -en**	engagement
das	**Volksfest**	funfair
die	**Zeremonie, -n**	ceremony

USEFUL PHRASES

auf eine or zu einer Hochzeit gehen to go to a wedding
silberne/goldene/diamantene Hochzeit silver/golden/diamond wedding
in den Ruhestand gehen to retire, go into retirement
die Stadt mit Blumen ausschmücken to decorate the town with flowers
die ganze Stadt war beflaggt there were flags out all over town
gute Vorsätze fassen to make good resolutions
beerdigen to bury

ESSENTIAL WORDS (masculine)

der	**Camper**	camper (*person*)
der	**Campingplatz, ⸚e**	camp site
der	**Löffel**	spoon
der	**Rucksack, ⸚e**	backpack, rucksack
der	**Schlafsack, ⸚e**	sleeping bag
der	**Teller**	plate
der	**Urlaub**	holiday(s)
der	**Wohnwagen**	caravan
der	**Zuschlag, ⸚e**	extra charge

ESSENTIAL WORDS (feminine)

die	**Anmeldung, -en**	registration
die	**Camperin**	camper (*person*)
die	**Dusche, -n**	shower
die	**Gabel, -n**	fork
die	**Landkarte, -n**	map
die	**Luft, ⸚e**	air
die	**Nacht, ⸚e**	night
die	**Sache, -n**	thing
die	**Tasse, -n**	cup
die	**Toilette, -n**	toilet
die	**Übernachtung, -en**	overnight stay
die	**Waschmaschine, -n**	washing machine

ESSENTIAL WORDS (neuter)

das	**Camping**	camping
das	**Essen**	food; meal
das	**Glas, ⸚er**	glass
das	**Messer**	knife
das	**(Trink)wasser**	(drinking) water
das	**Zelt, -e**	tent

USEFUL PHRASES

Camping machen to go camping
ein Zelt aufbauen *or* aufschlagen to pitch a tent
ein Zelt abbauen to take down a tent
„Zelten verboten!" "no camping"

IMPORTANT + USEFUL WORDS *(masculine)*

der	**Aufenthalt, -e**	stay
der	**Campingkocher**	camping stove
der	**Dosenöffner**	tin-opener
der	**Feuerlöscher**	fire extinguisher
der	**Klappstuhl, ̈e**	folding chair
der	**Klapptisch, -e**	folding table
der	**Korkenzieher**	corkscrew
der	**Liegestuhl, ̈e**	deck chair
der	**Mülleimer**	dustbin
der	**Rasierapparat, -e**	razor
der	**Schatten**	shade; shadow
der	**Waschraum, -räume**	washroom
der	**Zeltboden, ̈**	ground sheet
der	**Zimmernachweis, -e**	accommodation office

IMPORTANT + USEFUL WORDS *(feminine)*

die	**Büchse, -n**	tin, can; box
die	**Luftmatratze, -n**	lilo, air bed
die	**Nachtruhe**	lights-out
die	**Ruhe**	peace; rest
die	**Taschenlampe, -n**	torch
die	**Unterkunft, ̈e**	accommodation
die	**Veranstaltung, -en**	organization
die	**Wäsche**	washing (*things*)
die	**Wäscherei, -en**	laundry (*place*)

IMPORTANT + USEFUL WORDS *(neuter)*

das	**Campinggas**	camping gas
das	**Fahrzeug, -e**	vehicle
das	**Geschirr**	dishes, crockery; pots and pans
das	**Lagerfeuer**	campfire
das	**Streichholz, ̈er**	match
das	**Waschpulver**	washing powder, detergent
das	**Wohnmobil, -e**	camper, motor caravan

ESSENTIAL WORDS *(masculine)*

der	Arbeiter	worker, labourer
	Arbeitslose(r), -n	unemployed man/woman
der	Arzt, ⁻e	doctor
der	Briefträger	postman
der	Chef, -s	boss, head
der	Geschäftsmann, -leute	businessman
der	Job, -s	(spare time) job
der	Koch, ⁻e	cook
der	Krankenpfleger	nurse
der	Last(kraft)wagenfahrer; der LKW-Fahrer	lorry driver
der	Lehrer	teacher
der	Polizist, -en	policeman
der	Taxifahrer	taxi driver
der	Techniker	technician
der	Teilzeitjob, -s	part-time job
der	Zahnarzt, ⁻e	dentist

ESSENTIAL WORDS *(feminine)*

die	Arbeit, -en	work; job
die	Arbeiterin	worker
die	Ärztin	doctor
die	Bank, -en	bank
die	Bezahlung, -en	payment
die	Chefin	boss
die	Empfangsdame, -n	receptionist
die	Fabrik, -en	factory
die	Geschäftsfrau, -en	businesswoman
die	Geschäftsreise, -n	business trip
die	Industrie, -n	industry
die	Köchin	cook
die	Krankenschwester, -n	nurse
die	Lehrerin	teacher
die	Polizistin	policewoman
die	Zahnärztin	dentist

ESSENTIAL WORDS *(neuter)*

das	**Büro, -s**	office
das	**Geschäft, -e**	business, trade; shop
das	**Job-Center, -s**	job centre

USEFUL PHRASES

arbeiten to work; bei X arbeiten to work at X's
interessant interesting; langweilig boring
mit der Arbeit anfangen, zu arbeiten beginnen to start work,
  get down to work
berufstätig sein to be employed
arbeitslos sein to be out of work, be unemployed
arbeitslos werden to be made redundant
Arbeitslosengeld beziehen to be on the dole
seine Stelle verlieren to lose one's job
entlassen to dismiss
entlassen werden to be sacked, get the sack
jobben to do odd jobs
eine Stelle suchen to look for a job
„Stellenangebote" "situations vacant"
fest permanent; vorübergehend temporary
ganztags full-time; halbtags part-time
sich um eine Stelle bewerben to apply for a job
eine Stelle antreten to start a new job
verdienen to earn
500 Pfund in der Woche verdienen to earn £500 per week
sparen für (+ acc) to save up for
was sind Sie von Beruf? what is your job?
ich bin Elektriker (von Beruf) I am an electrician (to trade)
ehrgeizig ambitious
selbstständig self-employed
ich möchte Sekretärin werden I'd like to be a secretary
sein eigenes Geschäft haben to have one's own shop or business
eine Geschäftsreise machen to go away on business
streiken to strike, be on strike

IMPORTANT WORDS (*masculine*)

	Angestellte(r), -n	employee
der	Apotheker	chemist
der	Arbeitgeber	employer
der	Arbeitslohn, ̈-e	wages, pay
der	Arbeitnehmer	employee
der	Architekt, -en	architect
der	Arzthelfer	doctor's receptionist
der	Astronaut, -en	astronaut
der	Bankkaufmann, -leute	bank clerk
der	Bäcker	baker
	Beamte(r), -n	official
der	Beruf, -e	profession, occupation
der	Betrieb, -e	firm, concern
der	Bibliothekar, -e	librarian
	Büroangestellte(r), -n	office worker, clerk
der	Elektriker	electrician
der	Feuerwehrmann, -männer	fireman
der	Fotograf, -en	photographer
der	Friseur, -e	hairdresser
der	Geschäftsführer	executive; manager
der	Informatiker	computer scientist
der	Ingenieur, -e	engineer
der	Journalist, -en	journalist
der	Kfz-Mechaniker	motor mechanic
der	Lehrling, -e	apprentice, trainee
der	Lohn, ̈-e	wages, pay
der	Maler	painter
der	Pilot, -en	pilot
der	Politiker	politician
der	Präsident, -en	president
der	Premierminister	prime minister, premier
der	Priester	priest
der	Reporter	reporter
der	Sekretär, -e	secretary
der	Star, -s	star
der	Tierarzt, ̈-e	veterinary surgeon, vet
der	Verkäufer	salesman, shop assistant
der	Webdesigner	Web designer

IMPORTANT WORDS *(feminine)*

die	Arbeitnehmerin	employee
die	Architektin	architect
die	Arzthelferin	doctor's receptionist
die	Astronautin	astronaut
die	Bäckerin	baker
die	Bankkauffrau, -en	bank clerk
die	Beamtin	official
die	Berufsberatung	careers *or* vocational guidance
die	Bewerbung	application
die	Bibliothekarin	librarian
die	Firma, Firmen	firm, company
die	Friseuse, -n	hairdresser
die	Geschäftsführerin	executive; manageress
die	Gesellschaft, -en	company
die	Informatikerin	computer scientist
die	Journalistin	journalist
die	Kfz-Mechanikerin	motor mechanic
die	Lehrzeit, -en	apprenticeship
die	Politikerin	politician
die	Putzfrau, -en	cleaner, cleaning woman
die	Sekretärin	secretary
die	Stelle, -n	job, post
die	Tagesmutter, ¨	child minder
die	Tierärztin	veterinary surgeon, vet
die	Verkäuferin	salesgirl, shop assistant
die	Webdesignerin	Web designer
die	Zukunft	future

IMPORTANT WORDS *(neuter)*

das	Einkommen	income
das	Gehalt, ¨er	salary
das	Handwerk, -e	trade; craft
das	Kindermädchen	nanny
das	Model, -s	model

USEFUL WORDS (*masculine*)

	Abgeordnete(r), -n	M.P., member of parliament
der	Augenoptiker	optician
der	Autor, -en	author
der	Bauunternehmer	builder, building contractor
der	Bergarbeiter	miner
der	Betriebsleiter	managing director
der	Chirurg, -en	surgeon
der	Dichter	poet
der	Dolmetscher	interpreter
der	Florist, -en	florist
der	Forscher	researcher
der	Gewerkschaftler	trade unionist
der	Handel	commerce
der	Hausmeister	caretaker; janitor
der	Hotelfachmann, -leute	hotel manager
der	Kameramann, -männer	cameraman
der	Klempner	plumber
der	König, -e	king
der	Künstler	artist
der	Matrose, -n	sailor
der	Modeschöpfer	fashion designer
der	Mönch, -e	monk
der	Pfarrer	minister, clergyman
der	Produzent, -en	manufacturer; (film) producer
der	Rechtsanwalt, -̈e	lawyer, solicitor
der	Redakteur, -e	editor
der	Schneider	tailor
der	Schriftsteller	writer
der	Soldat, -en	soldier
der	Tischler	joiner, carpenter
der	Verleger	publisher
der	Vertreter	representative, rep
	Vorsitzende(r), -n	chairman/-woman
der	Winzer	wine grower, vineyard owner
der	Wirtschaftsprüfer	chartered accountant
der	Wissenschaftler	scientist

USEFUL WORDS *(feminine)*

die	**Absicht, -en**	intention, aim
die	**Augenoptikerin**	optician
die	**Ausbildung**	training, education
die	**Autorin**	author
die	**Chirurgin**	surgeon
die	**Dichterin**	poet
die	**Dolmetscherin**	interpreter
die	**Floristin**	florist
die	**Forscherin**	researcher
die	**Gewerkschaft, -en**	trade union
die	**Hotelfachfrau, -en**	hotel manageress
die	**Jobvermittlung, -en**	employment agency
die	**Kamerafrau, -en**	camerawoman
die	**Königin**	queen
die	**Künstlerin**	artist
die	**Laufbahn, -en**	career
die	**Leiterin**	leader, manager
die	**Lohnerhöhung, -en**	wage increase
die	**Modeschöpferin**	fashion designer
die	**Nonne, -n**	nun
die	**Platzanweiserin**	usherette
die	**Rechtsanwältin**	lawyer, solicitor
die	**Redakteurin**	editor
die	**Schneiderin**	dressmaker
die	**Schriftstellerin**	writer
die	**Soldatin**	soldier
die	**Sprechstundenhilfe, -n**	(medical) receptionist
die	**Stenotypistin**	shorthand typist
die	**Stewardess, -en**	flight attendant
die	**Verwaltung, -en**	administration
die	**Wissenschaftlerin**	scientist

ESSENTIAL WORDS *(masculine)*

der (Auto)fahrer	motorist, driver
der Diesel	diesel (oil)
der Führerschein, -e	driving licence
der Kilometer	kilometre
der Koffer	suitcase
der Lastkraftwagen (LKW)	lorry, truck
der Lastwagenfahrer	lorry driver
der Liter	litre
der Parkplatz, ̈e	parking space; car park
der Passagier, -e	passenger
der Personenkraftwagen (PKW)	private car
der Polizist, -en	policeman
der Rasthof, ̈e	service station
der Rastplatz, ̈e	lay-by
der Reifen	tyre
der Reifendruck	tyre pressure
der (Sport)wagen	(sports) car
der Weg, -e	road, way
der Wohnwagen	caravan

ESSENTIAL WORDS *(neuter)*

das Auto, -s	car
das Benzin, -e	petrol
das Dieselöl	diesel (oil)
das Gepäck	luggage
das Mietauto, -s	hired car
das Normalbenzin	2-star (petrol)
das Öl, -e	oil
das Parkhaus, -häuser	(covered) multistorey car park
das Parken	parking
das Rad, ̈er	wheel
das Selbsttanken	self-service petrol
das Straßenschild, -er	road sign
das Super	4-star (petrol)
das Wasser	water

ESSENTIAL WORDS (feminine)

die	Achtung	attention
die	Ampel, -n	traffic lights
die	Ausfahrt, -en	exit; drive; slip road
die	Autobahn, -en	motorway
die	(Auto)fahrerin	motorist, driver
die	Bahn, -en	road, way; lane
die	Batterie, -n	battery
die	Ecke, -n	corner
die	Einbahnstraße, -n	one-way street
die	Fahrt, -en	journey; trip; drive
die	Garage, -n	garage
die	Hauptstraße, -n	main road, main street
die	grüne Versicherungskarte, -n, -n	green card
die	Landkarte, -n	map
die	Maschine, -n	engine
die	Meile, -n	mile
die	Polizei	police
die	Polizistin	policewoman
die	Raststätte, -n	service area
die	Reise, -n	journey
die	Reparatur, -en	repair; repairing
die	(Reparatur)werkstatt, ⏦en	garage, workshop
die	Richtung, -en	direction
die	Selbstbedienung (SB)	self-service
die	Straße, -n	street, road
die	Straßenkarte, -n	road map, plan
die	Straßenverkehrsordnung	Highway Code
die	Tankstelle, -n	petrol station, filling station, service station
die	Umleitung, -en	diversion
die	Verkehrsampel, -n	traffic lights
die	Vorfahrt	right of way
die	Vorsicht	caution, care
die	Warnung, -en	warning
die	Werkstatt, ⏦en	garage, workshop

IMPORTANT WORDS (*masculine*)

der Abstand, ⸚e	distance
der Blinker	indicator
der Chauffeur, -e	chauffeur
der Dachgepäckträger	roof rack
der Fahrlehrer	driving instructor
der Fahrschüler	learner driver
der Fußgänger	pedestrian
der Gang, ⸚e	gear
der Kofferraum, -räume	boot
der Mechaniker	mechanic; engineer
der Motorschaden, -schäden	engine trouble
der Parkschein, -e	parking permit
der Rückspiegel	rear-view *or* driving mirror
der Scheinwerfer	headlight, headlamp
der Sicherheitsgurt, -e	seat belt
der Stau, -e	(traffic) jam
der Tramper	hitch-hiker
der Umweg, -e	detour
der Unfall, ⸚e	accident
der Verkehr	traffic
der Verkehrspolizist, -en	traffic warden
der Verkehrsunfall, ⸚e	road accident
Verletzte(r), -n	casualty
der Zusammenstoß, ⸚e	collision, crash

IMPORTANT WORDS (*neuter*)

das Autobahndreieck, -e	motorway junction
das Autobahnkreuz, -e	motorway intersection
das Fahrzeug, -e	vehicle
das Firmenauto, -s	company car
das Navigationssystem, -e	(satellite) navigation system
das Parkverbot, -e	parking ban
das Reserverad, ⸚er	spare wheel
das Trampen	hitch-hiking
das Wohngebiet, -e	built-up area

IMPORTANT WORDS *(feminine)*

die	Autoschlange, -n	line of cars
die	Autowäsche, -n	car wash
die	Bremse, -n	brake
die	Fahrlehrerin	driving instructress
die	Fahrprüfung, -en	driving test
die	Fahrschule, -n	driving school
die	Fahrschülerin	learner driver
die	Fahrstunde, -n	driving lesson
die	Gebühr, -en	toll
die	Gefahr, -en	danger, risk
die	Geldstrafe, -n	fine
die	Geschwindigkeit, -en	speed
die	Grenze, -n	border, frontier
die	Hauptverkehrszeit, -en	rush hour
die	Kreuzung, -en	crossroads
die	Kurve, -n	bend, corner
die	Notbremsung, -en	emergency stop
die	Panne, -n	breakdown
die	Parkuhr, -en	parking meter
die	Querstraße, -n	junction, intersection
die	Reifenpanne, -n	puncture
die	(Reise)route, -n	route, itinerary
die	Ringstraße, -n	ring road
die	Tiefgarage, -n	underground garage
die	Verkehrspolizistin	traffic warden
die	Versicherung, -en	insurance
die	Windschutzscheibe, -n	windscreen

USEFUL PHRASES

fahren to drive; abfahren to leave, set off
einsteigen to get in; aussteigen to get out
sich anschnallen to put on one's seat belt
(voll) tanken to fill up (with petrol)
reisen to travel
hinten in the back; vorn(e) in the front

USEFUL WORDS (*masculine*)

der	Abschleppdienst	breakdown service
der	Abschleppwagen	breakdown van
der	Anhänger	trailer
der	Anlasser	starter
der	Durchgangsverkehr	through traffic
der	Fußgängerüberweg, -e	pedestrian crossing
der	Katalysator, -en	catalytic converter
der	Kreisverkehr, -e	roundabout
der	Leerlauf	neutral (gear)
der	Scheibenwischer	windscreen wiper
der	Strafzettel	(parking) ticket
der	Tachometer	speedometer
der	Verkehrsrowdy, -s	road hog
der	Wagenheber	jack

USEFUL WORDS (*neuter*)

das	Armaturenbrett, -er	dashboard
das	Ersatzreifen	spare tyre
das	Ersatzteil, -e	spare part
das	Getriebe	gearbox
das	Kat-Auto, -s	car with a catalytic converter
das	polizeiliche Kennzeichen	registration number
das	Lenkrad, ¨-er	steering wheel
das	Nummernschild, -er	number plate
das	Steuerrad, ¨-er	steering wheel
das	Verdeck, -e	hood
das	Verkehrsdelikt, -e	traffic offence
das	Warndreieck, -e	warning triangle

USEFUL PHRASES

gute Reise! have a good trip!
bremsen to brake; schalten to change gear
hupen to sound *or* toot the horn
überholen to overtake; sich einordnen to get into lane
abbiegen to turn off; halten to stop
abstellen to park, to switch off; abschleppen to tow away
parken to park; abschließen to lock; ankommen to arrive

USEFUL WORDS *(feminine)*

die	**Abzweigung, -en**	junction
die	**Auffahrt, -en**	slip road
die	**Autovermietung, -en**	car hire
die	**Beleuchtung, -en**	lights *(pl)*
die	**Biegung, -en**	bend, curve
die	**Gasse, -n**	alley, lane, back street
die	**Geschwindigkeits-**	speed limit, speed
	begrenzung, -en	restriction
die	**Hupe, -n**	horn, hooter
die	**Karosserie, -n**	bodywork, body
die	**Kupplung, -en**	clutch
die	**Marke, -n**	make *(of car)*
die	**(Motor)haube, -n**	bonnet
die	**Politesse, -n**	traffic warden
die	**Stoßstange, -n**	bumper
die	**(Versicherungs)police, -n**	insurance policy

USEFUL PHRASES

schnell fast; **langsam** slowly
gefährlich dangerous; **kaputt** broken, done
sperren to block; **prüfen** to check
Abstand halten to keep one's distance
in ein Auto fahren to bump into a car
das Auto reparieren lassen to have the car repaired
100 Kilometer in der Stunde machen to do 100 kilometres an hour
beschleunigen, Gas geben to accelerate
die Ampel überfahren to go through the lights at red
mir ist das Benzin ausgegangen I've run out of petrol
verbleit leaded; **unverbleit, bleifrei** unleaded
sich verfahren to get lost, take the wrong road
sich zurechtfinden to find one's way
trampen, per Anhalter fahren to hitch-hike
„Anlieger frei" "residents only"
„Parken verboten" "no parking"; **„freihalten"** "keep clear"
„Vorfahrt achten" "give way"

ESSENTIAL WORDS *(masculine)*

der	**Anorak, -s**	anorak
der	**Badeanzug, ⸚e**	swimming *or* bathing costume
der	**Gürtel**	belt
der	**Handschuh, -e**	glove
der	**Kleiderschrank, ⸚e**	wardrobe
der	**Knopf, ⸚e**	button
der	**Mantel, ⸚e**	coat, overcoat
der	**Pullover; der Pulli, -s**	pullover, jumper, jersey
der	**Pyjama, -s**	(pair of) pyjamas
der	**Regenmantel, ⸚**	raincoat
der	**Rock, ⸚e**	skirt
der	**Schlips, -e**	tie
der	**Schuh, -e**	shoe
der	**(Spazier)stock, ⸚e**	walking stick
der	**Umkleideraum, -räume**	changing room

USEFUL PHRASES

ich ziehe mich an **I get dressed, I put on my clothes**
ich ziehe mich aus **I get undressed, I take off my clothes**
ich ziehe mich um **I get changed, I change my clothes**
tragen **to wear**
Hosen/einen Mantel tragen **to wear trousers/a coat**
seine Schuhe/seinen Mantel anziehen **to put on one's shoes/coat**
seine Schuhe/seinen Mantel ausziehen **to take off one's shoes/coat**
einen Hut tragen **to wear a hat**
sich (dat) den Hut aufsetzen **to put on one's hat**
den Hut abnehmen **to take off one's hat**
darf ich dieses Kleid anprobieren? **may I try on this dress?**
das steht Ihnen (gut) **that suits you**
passen **to fit**; groß **big**; klein **small**
das passt mir nicht **that doesn't fit me**; passend **matching**
waschen **to wash**; bügeln **to iron**
chemisch reinigen **to dryclean**

ESSENTIAL WORDS *(feminine)*

die	**Badehose, -n**	swimming *or* bathing trunks
die	**Bluse, -n**	blouse
die	**Brille, -n**	(pair of) glasses
die	**Größe, -n**	size
die	**Handtasche, -n**	handbag
die	**Hose, -n**	(pair of) trousers
die	**Jacke, -n**	jacket
die	**Jeans** *(pl)*	jeans
die	**Kleidung**	clothing
die	**Krawatte, -n**	tie
die	**Lederhose, -n**	(pair of) leather shorts *or* trousers
die	**Mode, -n**	fashion
die	**Sandale, -n**	sandal
die	**Socke, -n**	sock
die	**Tasche, -n**	pocket; bag

ESSENTIAL WORDS *(neuter)*

das	**Abendkleid, -er**	evening dress *(woman's)*
das	**Band, ¨er**	ribbon
das	**Hemd, -en**	shirt
das	**Kleid, -er**	dress
die	**Kleider** *(pl)*	clothes, clothing
das	**Nachthemd, -en**	nightdress; nightshirt
das	**Taschentuch, ¨er**	handkerchief
das	**T-Shirt, -s**	T-shirt, tee-shirt

USEFUL PHRASES

bunt coloured; kariert checked; gestreift striped
in Mode in fashion
modisch fashionable; unmodisch out of fashion
altmodisch old-fashioned; sehr schick very smart
Brustumfang *(m)* bust *or* chest measurement
Hüftweite *(f)* hip measurement
Kragenweite *(f)* collar size; Schuhgröße *(f)* shoe size
Taillenweite *(f)* waist measurement

IMPORTANT WORDS *(masculine)*

der Anzug, ⁀e	suit
der BH, -s (Büstenhalter)	bra
der Hausschuh, -e	slipper
der Hut, ⁀e	hat
der Overall, -s	(set of) overalls
der Schal, -e *or* -s	scarf
der Schlafanzug, ⁀e	(pair of) pyjamas
der Schleier	veil
der Stiefel	boot
der Strumpf, ⁀e	stocking, (long) sock
der Trainingsanzug, ⁀e	tracksuit
der Turban, -e	turban
die Turnschuhe *(pl)*	trainers, training shoes
der Unterrock, ⁀e	underskirt, petticoat

IMPORTANT WORDS *(feminine)*

die Fliege, -n	bow tie
die Freizeitkleidung	casual clothes
die Herrenkonfektion	menswear
die Modenschau, -en	fashion show
die Mütze, -n	cap
die Schultertasche, -n	shoulder bag
die Strumpfhose, -n	(pair of) tights
die Uniform, -en	uniform
die Unterhose, -n	(under)pants *(pl)*
die Unterwäsche	underwear
die Wäsche, -n	washing; (under)clothes

IMPORTANT WORDS *(neuter)*

das Blouson, -s	bomber jacket
das Jackett, -s *or* -e	jacket
das Kostüm, -e	(lady's) suit
die Shorts *(pl)*	shorts
das Sweatshirt, -s	sweatshirt
das Unterhemd, -en	vest

USEFUL WORDS (*masculine*)

der **Ärmel**	sleeve
der **Gesellschaftsanzug, ⸚e**	evening dress (*man's*)
der **Hosenanzug, ⸚e**	trouser suit
der **Hosenrock, ⸚e**	culottes
der **Hosenträger**	braces (*pl*)
der **Jogginganzug, ⸚e**	jogging suit
der **Kragen**	collar
die **Lumpen** (*pl*)	rags
der **Morgenrock, ⸚e**	dressing gown
der **Reißverschluss, ⸚e**	zip
der **Rollkragen**	polo neck
der **Schnürsenkel**	shoelace
der **Smoking, -s**	dinner jacket

USEFUL WORDS (*feminine*)

die **Falte, -n**	pleat
die **Kappe, -n**	cap, hood
die **Kragenweite, -n**	collar size
die **Latzhose, -n**	dungarees
die **Markenkleidung**	branded clothes (*pl*)
die **Melone, -n**	bowler hat
die **Schürze, -n**	apron
die **Strickjacke, -n**	cardigan
die **Tracht, -en**	costume, dress
die **Weste, -n**	waistcoat
die **Wolljacke, -n**	cardigan

USEFUL WORDS (*neuter*)

das **Hochzeitskleid, -er**	wedding dress
das **Kopftuch, ⸚er**	headscarf, headsquare
das **Zubehör**	accessories (*pl*)

USEFUL PHRASES

sich verkleiden **to disguise oneself**; maskiert **masked**
maßgeschneidert **made to measure**
von der Stange **off the peg**

beige	beige, fawn
blau	blue
braun	brown
gelb	yellow
golden	golden
grau	grey
grün	green
lila	purple
orange	orange
pink	shocking pink
rehbraun	fawn
rosa	pink
rot	red
schwarz	black
silbern	silver
veilchenblau	violet
violett	violet, purple
weiß	white
dunkelblau	dark blue
hellblau	light blue, pale blue
bläulich	bluish
himmelblau	sky blue
königsblau	royal blue
marineblau	navy blue

USEFUL PHRASES

das Blau steht ihr blue suits her
etwas blau anstreichen to paint something blue
die Farbe wechseln to change colour
bunte/dunkle Farben bright/dark colours
das Farbfernsehen colour television

SOME COLOURFUL PHRASES

was für eine Farbe hat es? **what colour is it?**
blau vor Kälte **blue with cold**
eine Fahrt ins Blaue **a mystery tour**
ein blaues Auge **a black eye**
sie hat blaue Augen **she has blue eyes**
braun werden **to go** or **turn brown** (*people, leaves*)
gelb vor Neid **green with envy**
grün und blau **black and blue**
die grüne Versicherungskarte **green card** (*for motor insurance*)
die Grünen **the Green party**
Rotkäppchen **Little Red Riding Hood**
in den roten Zahlen **in the red, in debt**
in den schwarzen Zahlen **in the black**
ein Schwarzer **a black man**
eine Schwarze **a black woman**
ein schwarzes Brett **a notice board**
ein Weißer **a white man**
eine Weiße **a white woman**
das Weiße Haus **the White House**
schneeweiß **as white as snow**
leichenblass **as white as a sheet**

ESSENTIAL + IMPORTANT WORDS *(masculine)*

der	Bildschirm, -e	monitor, screen
der	Computer	computer
der	Cursor	cursor
der	Drucker	printer
der	Monitor, -e	monitor
der	PC, -s	PC, personal computer
der	Programmierer	(computer) programmer
der	Speicher	memory
der	Virus, Viren	virus

ESSENTIAL + IMPORTANT WORDS *(feminine)*

die	CD-ROM, -s	CD-ROM
die	Datei, -en	file
die	Diskette, -n	disk; floppy disk
die	E-Mail, -s	e-mail
die	Festplatte, -n	hard disk
die	Hardware	hardware
die	Maus, Mäuse	mouse
die	Sicherheitskopie, -n	backup (copy)
die	Software	software
die	Tastatur, -en	keyboard
die	Taste, -n	key

ESSENTIAL + IMPORTANT WORDS *(neuter)*

das	Betriebssystem, -e	operating system
das	Breitband	broadband
die	Daten *(pl)*	data
das	Fenster	window
das	Internet	Internet
das	Laufwerk, -e	drive
das	Menü, -s	menu
das	Modem, -s	modem
das	Passwort, -wörter	password
das	Popup-Menü, -s	pop-up menu
das	Programm, -e	program

USEFUL WORDS (*masculine*)

der	Ausdruck, -e	printout
der	Benutzer	user
der	Browser	browser
der	Chip, -s	chip
der	Hacker	hacker
der	Heimcomputer	home computer
der	Informatiker	computer scientist
der	Joystick, -s	joystick
der	Laserdrucker	laser printer
der	Ordner	folder
der	Papierkorb, ⸚e	trash, recycle bin
der	Programmierer	(computer) programmer
der	Provider	provider
der	Rechner	computer; calculator
der	Schrägstrich, -e	slash
der	Seitenwechsel	page break
der	Server	server
der	Spamfilter	spam filter
der	Tintenstrahldrucker	ink-jet (printer)
der	Zeilenabstand, ⸚e	line spacing

USEFUL WORDS (*feminine*)

die	Anwendung, -en	application
die	Datenbank, -en	database
die	Eingabetaste, -n	enter key
die	E-Mail-Adresse, -n	e-mail address
die	Funktion, -en	function
die	Hilfefunktion, -en	help function
die	Homepage, -s	homepage

USEFUL PHRASES

spielen to play; sich amüsieren to have fun
ein Programm schreiben to write a program
den Computer programmieren to program the computer
den Cursor bewegen to move the cursor; klicken to click
bearbeiten to edit; einfügen to insert; to paste
formatieren to format; kopieren to copy; löschen to delete

USEFUL WORDS *(feminine continued)*

die	**Informatik**	computer science, computing
die	**Internetauktion, -en**	Internet auction
die	**Leertaste, -n**	space bar
die	**Löschtaste, -n**	delete key
die	**Mausmatte, -n**	mouse pad
die	**Rechtschreibprüfung,-en**	spellchecker
die	**Schaltfläche, -n**	button
die	**Schnittstelle, -n**	interface
die	**Schriftart, -en**	font
die	**Sicherungskopie, -n**	back-up (copy)
die	**Suchmaschine, -n**	search engine
die	**Tabellenkalkulation, -en**	spreadsheet (program)
die	**Textverarbeitung, -en**	word processor
die	**Webadresse, -n**	Web address
die	**Webseite, -n**	Web page

USEFUL WORDS *(neuter)*

das	**Bildschirmgerät, -e**	VDU, visual display unit
das	**CD-ROM-Laufwerk, -e**	CD-ROM drive
das	**Computerspiel, -e**	computer game
das	**Diskettenlaufwerk, -e**	disk drive
das	**Dokument, -e**	document
das	**DVD-Laufwerk, -e**	DVD drive
das	**Interface, -s**	interface
das	**Notebook, -s**	notebook (computer)
das	**Programmieren**	(computer) programming
das	**RAM**	RAM (*random access memory*)
das	**ROM**	ROM (*read only memory*)
das	**Symbol, -e**	icon
das	**Virensuchprogramm, -e**	virus checker
das	**Zeichen**	character

USEFUL PHRASES

die Daten speichern **to store the data**; die Daten sichern **to save the data**
im Internet surfen **to surf the Internet**; ausdrucken **to print out**; mailen **to e-mail**
elektronisch **electronic**; fett **bold**; kursiv **italic**; mager **roman**; tragbar **portable**
linksbündig **left adjusted**; rechtsbündig **right adjusted**

COUNTRIES

All countries are neuter unless marked otherwise. Where an article is shown, the noun is used with the article.

	Afrika	Africa
	Asien	Asia
	Australien	Australia
	Belgien	Belgium
	Brasilien	Brazil
	Bulgarien	Bulgaria
die	Bundesrepublik Deutschland (BRD)	Germany
	China	China
	Dänemark	Denmark
	Deutschland	Germany
	England	England
	Europa	Europe
die	Europäische Union (EU)	the European Union (EU)
	Finnland	Finland
	Frankreich	France
	Großbritannien	Great Britain
	Griechenland	Greece
	Holland	Holland
	Indien	India
der	Irak	Iraq
der	Iran	Iran
	Irland	Ireland
	Italien	Italy
	Japan	Japan
	Kanada	Canada
	Korea	Korea
	Luxemburg	Luxembourg
	Mexiko	Mexico
	Neuseeland	New Zealand
die	Niederlande (pl)	the Netherlands
	Nordirland	Northern Ireland
	Norwegen	Norway
	Österreich	Austria

COUNTRIES (continued)

Pakistan	Pakistan
Polen	Poland
Portugal	Portugal
Rumänien	Romania
Russland	Russia
Saudi-Arabien	Saudi Arabia
Schottland	Scotland
Schweden	Sweden
die Schweiz	Switzerland
Skandinavien	Scandinavia
Spanien	Spain
Südafrika	South Africa
Südamerika	South America
die Tschechische Republik	the Czech Republic
die Türkei	Turkey
Ungarn	Hungary
das Vereinigte Königreich	the United Kingdom
die Vereinigten Staaten	the United States
(mpl) (von Amerika)	(of America)
Vietnam	Vietnam
Wales	Wales

USEFUL PHRASES

in die Niederlande/in die Schweiz fahren to go to the Netherlands/
  to Switzerland
nach Deutschland fahren to go to Germany
ein Land, (pl) Länder country
die Entwicklungsländer (pl) developing countries
ins Ausland fahren or gehen to go or travel abroad
im Ausland sein to be abroad
ein Ausländer, eine Ausländerin a foreigner
die Hauptstadt capital
ich bin in Deutschland geboren I was born in Germany

NATIONALITIES (*masculine*)

ein	Afrikaner	an African
ein	Amerikaner	an American
ein	Araber	an Arab
ein	Asiat, -en	an Asian
ein	Australier	an Australian
ein	Belgier	a Belgian
ein	Brasilianer	a Brazilian
ein	Brite, -n	a Briton (*pl* the British)
ein	Chinese, -n	a Chinese
ein	Däne, -n	a Dane
ein	Deutscher, -n	a German
ein	Engländer	an Englishman
ein	Europäer	a European
ein	Finne, -n	a Finn
ein	Franzose, -n	a Frenchman
ein	Grieche, -n	a Greek
ein	Holländer	a Dutchman
ein	Inder	an Indian
ein	Iraker	an Iraqi
ein	Iraner	an Iranian
ein	Ire	an Irishman
ein	Italiener	an Italian
ein	Japaner	a Japanese
ein	Kanadier	a Canadian
ein	Luxemburger	a native of Luxemburg
ein	Mexikaner	a Mexican
ein	Neuseeländer	a New Zealander
ein	Niederländer	a Dutchman
ein	Norweger	a Norwegian
ein	Österreicher	an Austrian
ein	Pole, -n	a Pole
ein	Portugiese, -n	a Portuguese
ein	Rumäne, -n	a Romanian
ein	Russe, -n	a Russian
ein	Schotte, -n	a Scotsman, a Scot
ein	Schwede, -n	a Swede
ein	Schweizer	a Swiss
ein	Spanier	a Spaniard

NATIONALITIES *(masculine continued)*

ein	**Türke, -n**	a Turk
ein	**Ungar, -n**	a Hungarian
ein	**Vietnamese, -n**	a Vietnamese
ein	**Waliser**	a Welshman

The forms given above and on the following two pages are the noun forms. The corresponding adjectives begin with a small letter and end in **-isch**.

Most can be formed by changing **-er(in)** or **-ier(in)** to **-isch**.

The main exceptions are as follows: **deutsch** (German), **englisch** (English), **französisch** (French), **schweizerisch** (Swiss).

NATIONALITIES *(feminine)*

eine	**Afrikanerin**	an African (girl *or* woman)
eine	**Amerikanerin**	an American (girl *or* woman)
eine	**Araberin**	an Arabian (girl *or* woman)
eine	**Asiatin**	an Asian (girl *or* woman)
eine	**Australierin**	an Australian (girl *or* woman)
eine	**Belgierin**	a Belgian (girl *or* woman)
eine	**Brasilianerin**	a Brazilian (girl *or* woman)
eine	**Britin**	a Briton, a British girl *or* woman
eine	**Chinesin**	a Chinese (girl *or* woman)
eine	**Dänin**	a Dane, a Danish girl *or* woman
eine	**Deutsche**	a German (girl *or* woman)
eine	**Engländerin**	an Englishwoman, an English girl
eine	**Europäerin**	a European (girl *or* woman)
eine	**Finnin**	a Finn, a Finnish girl *or* woman
eine	**Französin**	a Frenchwoman, a French girl
eine	**Griechin**	a Greek, a Greek girl *or* woman
eine	**Holländerin**	a Dutchwoman, a Dutch girl
eine	**Inderin**	an Indian (girl *or* woman)
eine	**Irakerin**	an Iraqi (girl *or* woman)
eine	**Iranerin**	an Iranian (girl *or* woman)
eine	**Irin**	an Irishwoman, an Irish girl
eine	**Italienerin**	an Italian (girl *or* woman)

NATIONALITIES *(feminine continued)*

eine	**Japanerin**	a Japanese (girl *or* woman)
eine	**Kanadierin**	a Canadian (girl *or* woman)
eine	**Luxemburgerin**	a native of Luxemburg
eine	**Mexikanerin**	a Mexican (girl *or* woman)
eine	**Neuseeländerin**	a New Zealander, a New Zealand girl *or* woman
eine	**Niederländerin**	a Dutchwoman, a Dutch girl
eine	**Norwegerin**	a Norwegian (girl *or* woman)
eine	**Österreicherin**	an Austrian (girl *or* woman)
eine	**Polin**	a Pole, a Polish girl *or* woman
eine	**Portugiesin**	a Portuguese (girl *or* woman)
eine	**Rumänin**	a Rumanian (girl *or* woman)
eine	**Russin**	a Russian (girl *or* woman)
eine	**Schottin**	a Scotswoman, a Scots girl
eine	**Schwedin**	a Swede, a Swedish girl *or* woman
eine	**Schweizerin**	a Swiss girl *or* woman
eine	**Spanierin**	a Spaniard, a Spanish girl *or* woman
eine	**Türkin**	a Turkish girl *or* woman
eine	**Ungarin**	a Hungarian (girl *or* woman)
eine	**Vietnamesin**	a Vietnamese (girl *or* woman)
eine	**Waliserin**	a Welshwoman, a Welsh girl

USEFUL PHRASES

die Staatsangehörigkeit **nationality**
die Religion **religion**
die Muttersprache **native language**

ESSENTIAL WORDS *(masculine)*

der	Bauernhof, ⁻e	farmyard, farm
der	Baum, Bäume	tree
der	Berg, -e	mountain, hill
der	Fluss, ⁻e	river
der	Gasthof, ⁻e	inn
der	Grund	ground
der	Hügel	hill
der	Lärm	noise
der	Markt, ⁻e	market
der	See, -n	lake
der	Stein, -e	stone, rock
der	Stock, ⁻e	cane, stick
der	Turm, ⁻e	tower; (church) steeple
der	Wald, ⁻er	wood, forest

ESSENTIAL WORDS *(neuter)*

das	Dorf, ⁻er	village
das	Feld, -er	field
das	Gasthaus, -häuser	inn
das	Land, ⁻er	land; country
das	Picknick, -e *or* -s	picnic
das	Schloss, ⁻er	castle
das	Tal, ⁻er	valley
das	Wirtshaus, -häuser	inn

USEFUL PHRASES

aufs Land gehen **to go into the country**
auf dem Lande wohnen **to live in the country**
auf dem Bauernhof **on the farm**
ein Picknick machen **to go for a picnic**
im Freien **in the open air**

ESSENTIAL WORDS *(feminine)*

die	**Blume, -n**	flower
die	**Brücke, -n**	bridge
die	**Burg, -en**	castle
die	**Höhle, -n**	cave, hole
die	**Jugendherberge, -n**	youth hostel
die	**Kirche, -n**	church
die	**Landschaft, -en**	countryside, scenery
die	**Landstraße, -n**	country road
die	**Luft**	air
die	**Straße, -n**	road, street
die	**Wiese, -n**	meadow

USEFUL PHRASES

hügelig **hilly**; flach **flat**; steil **steep**

ruhig **peaceful**

fruchtbar **fertile**; schlecht **bad, poor**

kultivieren, anbauen **to cultivate, grow**

fließen **to flow**

bummeln **to wander, stroll**

überqueren **to cross**

jagen **to hunt; to shoot**

in einer Jugendherberge übernachten **to spend the night in a youth hostel**

sich auf den Weg machen **to set out, set off**

der Weg zum Dorf **the way to the village**

in der Ferne **in the distance**

IMPORTANT WORDS *(masculine)*

der	Bach, ̈-e	stream, brook
der	Bauer, -n	farmer; peasant
der	Boden, ̈-	ground, earth
der	Forst, -e	forest
der	Friede(n)	peace
der	Gipfel	(mountain) top
der	Gummistiefel	wellington (boot)
der	Spazierstock, ̈-e	walking stick
der	Stiefel	boot
der	Strom, ̈-e	river
der	Tourist, -en	tourist
der	Wasserfall, ̈-e	waterfall
der	Weg, -e	path, way, road

IMPORTANT WORDS *(feminine)*

die	Bäuerin	lady farmer; farmer's wife; peasant
die	Bauersfrau, -en	farmer's wife
die	Erde, -n	earth, soil
die	Gegend, -en	district, area
die	Heide, -n	heath; heather
die	Landwirtschaft	agriculture, farming
die	Talsperre, -n	dam

IMPORTANT WORDS *(neuter)*

das	Bauernhaus, -häuser	farmhouse
das	Fernglas, ̈-er	(pair of) binoculars
das	Flachland	lowlands *(pl)*
das	Gebiet, -e	area
das	Gebirge	mountain chain
das	Heideland	heath
das	Heu	hay
das	Korn	corn, grain
das	Tor, -e	gate
das	Ufer	(river) bank

USEFUL WORDS (masculine)

der	Acker, ⸚	field
der	Bewohner	inhabitant
der	Dorfbewohner	villager
der	Erdboden, ⸚	ground
der	Jäger	hunter
der	Landwirt, -e	farmer
der	Pfad, -e	path
der	Schlamm	mud
der	Sumpf, ⸚e	marsh
der	Teich, -e	pond
der	Wegweiser	signpost
der	Weiher	pond, lake
der	Weiler	hamlet
der	Weinberg, -e	vineyard
der	Wipfel	treetop

USEFUL WORDS (feminine)

die	Ebene, -n	plain
die	Ernte, -n	harvest, crop
die	Falle, -n	trap
die	Gemeinde, -n	community
die	Hecke, -n	hedge
die	Jagd, -en	hunt; hunting
die	Quelle, -n	spring; source
die	Spitze, -n	tip, peak, point
die	(Wind)mühle, -n	(wind)mill

USEFUL WORDS (neuter)

das	Geräusch, -e	noise, sound
das	Getreide	grain, cereal crop
das	Grundstück, -e	estate; plot of land
das	Heidekraut	heather
das	Loch, ⸚er	hole

ESSENTIAL WORDS (masculine)

der	Ausländer	foreigner
der	Bart, -̈e	beard
der	Herr, -en	gentleman
der	Junge, -n	boy
der	Mann, -̈er	man
der	Mensch, -en	human being; man; person
der	Schnurrbart, -̈e	moustache

ESSENTIAL WORDS (feminine)

die	Ähnlichkeit, -en (mit)	similarity (to)
die	Auge, -n	eye
die	Ausländerin	foreigner
die	Bewegung, -en	movement, motion
die	Brille, -n	(pair of) glasses
die	Dame, -n	lady
die	Frau, -en	woman
die	Gesichtsfarbe, -n	complexion
die	Größe, -n	height; size
die	Hautfarbe, -n	skin colour
die	Person, -en	person
die	Schönheit	beauty

ESSENTIAL WORDS (neuter)

das	Alter	age
das	Aussehen	appearance
das	Haar, -e	hair
das	Mädchen	girl

USEFUL PHRASES

ich heiße Wolfgang my name is Wolfgang
wie heißen Sie? what is your name?
jung young; alt old
wie alt sind Sie? how old are you?, what age are you?
ich bin 16 (Jahre alt) I am 16 (years old)
mittleren Alters middle-aged

USEFUL PHRASES

bärtig **bearded**; schnurrbärtig **with a moustache**

glatt rasiert **clean-shaven**

er sieht wie sein Vater aus/wie seine Mutter aus **he looks like his father/his mother**

er ist seinem Vater/seiner Mutter ähnlich **he resembles his father/ his mother**

erkennen **to recognize**

gut/schlecht aussehen **to look well/poorly**

müde/zornig/komisch aussehen **to look tired/angry/funny**

ein gut aussehender Mann **a handsome** or **good-looking man**

eine schöne Frau **a beautiful woman**

groß **tall, big**; klein **short, small**; lang **long**; kurz **short**

ein Mann von mittlerer Größe **a man of medium height**

sie ist 1 Meter 70 groß **she is 1 metre 70 tall**

weiß **white**; schwarz **black**; gemischtrassig **of mixed ethnic origins**

grüne/blaue/braune Augen haben **to have green/blue/brown eyes**

Kontaktlinsen/eine Brille tragen **to wear contact lenses/glasses**

er hat blonde/dunkle/schwarze/rote/graue Haare **he has blond** or **fair/dark/black/red/grey hair**

rothaarig **red-haired**

eine Glatze bekommen **to be going bald**

lockiges/welliges/glattes Haar **curly/wavy/straight hair**

sich benehmen **to behave (oneself)**

weinen **to cry**; lachen **to laugh**; lächeln **to smile**

vor Freude lachen/weinen **to laugh/cry with joy**

eine gute Figur haben **to have a nice figure**

wie viel wiegst du? **what do you weigh?**

die Gewohnheit haben, etw zu tun **to have a habit of doing sth**

(nicht) in der Laune or in der Stimmung für etw (acc) sein **(not) to be in the mood for sth**

gut/schlecht gelaunt **in a good/bad mood**

auf jdn böse sein **to be angry with sb**

ärgern **to annoy**

IMPORTANT WORDS (*masculine*)

der **Charakter**	character
der **Gang, ⸚e**	walk, gait
der **Mangel, ⸚**	defect, fault
der **Zorn**	anger

IMPORTANT WORDS (*feminine*)

die **Figur, -en**	figure
die **Freude, -n**	joy, delight
die **Geste, -n**	gesture
die **Kontaktlinsen** (*pl*)	contact lenses
die **Natur, -en**	nature
die **Rasse, -n**	race
die **Schüchternheit**	shyness

IMPORTANT WORDS (*neuter*)

das **Gewicht, -e**	weight
das **Wesen**	character, personality

USEFUL WORDS (*masculine*)

der **Afrikaner**	African (man)
der **Asiat, -en**	Asian (man)
der **Ausdruck, ⸚e**	expression
der **Faulenzer**	lazybones
der **Gesichtszug, ⸚e**	(facial) feature
der **Körperbau**	build
der **Leberfleck, -e**	mole
der **Muslim, -e**	Muslim (man)
der **Pickel**	spot, pimple
der **Pony, -s**	fringe
der **Riese, -n**	giant
der **Schönheitsfleck, -e**	beauty spot
der **Schweiß**	sweat, perspiration
der **Teint, -s**	complexion
der **Turban, -e**	turban
der **Zug, ⸚e**	feature

USEFUL WORDS *(feminine)*

die	Afrikanerin	African (woman)
die	Ängstlichkeit	nervousness
die	Asiatin	Asian (woman)
die	Dauerwelle, -n	perm
die	Eigenschaft, -en	quality, attribute
die	Falte, -n	wrinkle
die	Faulenzerin	lazybones
die	Frisur, -en	hairstyle
die	Gestalt, -en	figure
die	Gewohnheit, -en	habit
die	Glatze, -n	bald head
die	Hässlichkeit	ugliness
die	Laune, -n	mood, humour, temper
die	Locke, -n	curl
die	Muslimin	Muslim (woman)
die	Narbe, -n	scar
die	Runzel, -n	wrinkle
die	Sommersprosse, -n	freckle
die	Stimmung, -en	mood, frame of mind
die	Träne, -n	tear
die	Wut	fury, rage

USEFUL WORDS *(neuter)*

das	Benehmen	behaviour
das	Doppelkinn, -e	double chin
das	Gebiss, -e	false teeth
das	Gefühl, -e	feeling
das	Gewissen	conscience
das	Grübchen	dimple
das	Kopftuch, ¨er	headscarf
das	(Lebe)wesen	creature
das	Selbstvertrauen	self-confidence

ähnlich (+ *dat*)	similar (to), like
ängstlich	nervous, worried
auffallend	striking
blass	pale
blind	blind
böse	angry; evil
bucklig	hunch-backed
dick	fat
dumm	stupid
dunkel	dark
dünn	thin
Durchschnitts-	average
ehrlich	honest
einsam	lonely
enttäuscht	disappointed
ernst	serious
frech (zu + *dat*)	cheeky (to)
freundlich (zu + *dat*)	friendly (to), kind (to)
froh, fröhlich	glad, happy
gebräunt	tanned
geduldig	patient
geschickt	skilful, clever
glücklich	happy
grausam	cruel
groß	tall; big
gutmütig	good-natured
hässlich	ugly
hell	fair (*skin*); light
homosexuell	homosexual
hübsch	pretty
intelligent	intelligent
klein	small
klug	clever
komisch	funny
kräftig	strong
kurz	short
kurzsichtig/weitsichtig	short-sighted/long-sighted
lächerlich	ridiculous
lahm	lame

lang	long
lesbisch	lesbian
mager	skinny, thin, lean
mürrisch	sullen
nachlässig	careless
nackt	bare, naked
nervös	nervous
nett	neat; nice
neugierig	curious, nosy
pickelig	spotty
reizend	charming
rund	round
schlank	slender
schön	beautiful
schüchtern	shy
schwach	weak
schwarz	black
seltsam	strange
sorgfältig	careful, painstaking
stark	strong
stolz (auf + *acc*)	proud (of)
streng	hard, harsh; strict
sympathisch	nice, likeable
tapfer	brave
taub	deaf
traurig	sad
unartig	naughty
ungeschickt	clumsy, awkward
vernünftig	sensible
verrückt	crazy, mad
verschieden	different
vorsichtig	careful, cautious
weise	wise
weiß	white
winzig	tiny
zornig	angry
zufrieden (mit + *dat*)	pleased (with)

ESSENTIAL WORDS (*masculine*)

der	Bleistift, -e	pencil
der	Computer	computer
der	Direktor, -en	principal, headmaster
die	Ferien *(pl)*	holidays
der	Fernseher	television
der	Filzstift, -e	felt-tip pen
der	Freund, -e	friend
der	Informatikunterricht	computer studies
der	Kindergarten, ̈	nursery school
der	Klassenlehrer	form teacher
der	Kugelschreiber	ballpoint pen
der	Kuli, -s	Biro®, ballpoint pen
der	Lehrer	(school)teacher
der	Preis, -e	prize
der	Prüfer	examiner
der	Rechner	calculator; computer
der	Schreibtisch, -e	desk
der	Schulanfang	beginning of term
der	Schüler	schoolboy, pupil, student
der	Schulfreund, -e	schoolfriend
der	Schulhof, ̈e	playground
der	Schulkamerad, -en	schoolfriend
der	Speisesaal, -säle	dining hall
der	Spielplatz, ̈e	playground
der	Stundenplan, ̈e	timetable
der	Taschenrechner	pocket calculator
der	Test, -s	test
der	Unterricht, -e	instruction; *(pl)* lessons
der	Versuch, -e	experiment

ESSENTIAL WORDS *(feminine)*

die	Abschlussprüfung	final exam
die	Antwort, -en	answer
die	Arbeit, -en	work; test
die	Aufgabe, -n	exercise, task
die	Bibliothek, -en	library
die	Biologie	biology
die	Chemie	chemistry
die	Direktorin	headmistress (*of secondary school*)
die	Erdkunde	geography
die	Frage, -n	question
die	Freundin	friend
die	Gemeinschaftskunde	social studies
die	Geografie	geography
die	Gesamtschule, -n	comprehensive school
die	Geschichte, -n	history; story
die	Grundschule, -n	primary school
die	Gruppe, -n	group
die	Handarbeit	handicrafts; needlework
die	Hauptschule, -n	secondary school
die	Hausaufgabe, -n	homework
die	Karte, -n	map; card
die	Klasse, -n	class, form
die	Klassenarbeit, -en	test
die	Klassenfahrt, -en	(class) trip, outing
die	Klassenlehrerin	form teacher
die	Kreide	chalk
die	Kunst	art
die	Lehrerin	(school)teacher
die	Mappe, -n	briefcase; folder
die	Mathematik; die Mathe	mathematics, maths
die	Mittagspause, -n	lunch break
die	Musik	music
die	Pause, -n	break, interval
die	Physik	physics

USEFUL PHRASES

die Schule besuchen to attend school
in der Schule at school
ich gehe in die Schule I'm going to school
arbeiten to work
aufpassen to pay attention; zuhören to listen
lernen to learn; studieren to study; vergessen to forget
lesen to read; schreiben to write; sprechen to speak
sprichst du Deutsch? do you speak German?
seit wie vielen Jahren lernen Sie Deutsch? how many years have you been
    learning German?
ich lerne seit 3 Jahren Deutsch I've been learning German for 3 years
lehren, unterrichten to teach
ich möchte Lehrer werden I'd like to be a teacher
der Französischlehrer the French teacher (*teacher of French*)
eine Prüfung machen to sit an exam
das Abitur machen to sit one's A-levels (*approx*)
wiederholen to repeat; to revise
mündlich oral; schriftlich written
eine Prüfung bestehen/nicht bestehen to pass/fail an exam
den ersten Preis gewinnen to win first prize
durchfallen to fail
sitzen bleiben to repeat a year
Fortschritte machen to make progress
versetzen to move *or* put up
die Schule verlassen to leave school
klug clever; intelligent intelligent; dumm stupid
fragen to ask; antworten to answer, reply
jdm eine Frage stellen to ask sb a question
eine Frage beantworten to answer a question

ESSENTIAL WORDS *(feminine continued)*

die	Prüfung, -en	exam, examination
die	Realschule, -n	secondary school
die	(höhere) Schule, (-n) -n	(secondary) school
die	Schülerin	schoolgirl, pupil; student
die	Schulfreundin *or*	schoolfriend
	die Schulkameradin	
die	Schultasche, -n	satchel, school bag
die	Schuluniform, -en	school uniform
die	Seite, -n	page
die	Sozialkunde	social studies
die	Tafel, -n	blackboard
die	Technik	technology
die	Tinte	ink
die	Turnhalle, -n	gym, gymnasium
die	Universität, -en; die Uni	university

ESSENTIAL WORDS *(neuter)*

das	Buch, ¨er	book
das	Deutsch	German
das	Englisch	English
das	Examen, - *or* Examina	exam, examination
das	Französisch	French
das	Gymnasium, -ien	grammar school
das	Klassenzimmer	classroom, schoolroom
das	Lineal, -e	ruler
das	Papier, -e	paper
das	(Schul)fach, ¨er	(school) subject
das	(Schul)heft, -e	exercise book
das	Semester	term (2 *per year*)
das	Technisches Zeichnen Spanisch	technical drawing Spanish
das	Trimester	term (3 *per year*)
das	Turnen	P.E.; gymnastics
das	Werken	handicrafts
das	Wörterbuch, ¨er	dictionary

IMPORTANT WORDS *(masculine)*

der	Austausch, -e	exchange
der	Buchstabe, -n	letter of alphabet
der	Erfolg, -e	success
der	Ethikunterricht	ethics
der	Fehler	mistake, error; fault
der	Hochschüler	college student
der	Klassenkamerad, -en	classmate
der	Klassensprecher	form prefect
der	Kurs, -e	course
der	Mitschüler	classmate, schoolmate
der	Radiergummi, -s	rubber, eraser
der	Rektor, -en	headmaster *(primary)*; rector
der	Schlafsaal, -säle	dormitory
der	Schülerlotse, -n	*pupil who helps with school crossing patrol*
der	Student, -en	student
der	Zettel	piece of paper; note; form

IMPORTANT WORDS *(neuter)*

das	Abitur	German school-leaving certificate/exam
das	Bestehen	pass *(in exam)*
das	Blatt, ¨er	sheet *(of paper)*
das	Diplom, -e	diploma
das	Ergebnis, -se	result *(of exam)*
das	Italienisch	Italian
das	Klassenbuch, ¨er	class register
das	Latein	Latin
das	Lehrerzimmer	staff room
das	Pflichtfach, ¨er	compulsory subject
das	Rechnen	arithmetic
das	(Schul)zeugnis, -se	(school) report
das	(Sprach)labor, -e	(language) lab
das	Vokabular	vocabulary
das	Wahlfach, ¨er	option, optional subject
das	Zeichnen	drawing *(subject)*

IMPORTANT WORDS *(feminine)*

die	Algebra	algebra
die	Aula, Aulen *or* -s	assembly hall
die	Berufsschule, -n	vocational *or* trade school
die	Fach(hoch)schule, -n	technical college
die	Fremdsprache, -n	foreign language
die	Ganztagsschule, -n	all-day school *or* schooling
die	Garderobe, -n	cloakroom
die	gemischte Schule, -n -n	mixed school, co-ed
die	Geometrie	geometry
die	Grammatik	grammar
die	Halbtagsschule, -n	half-day school
die	Hochschule, -n	college; university
die	Klassenkameradin	classmate
die	Lehre	teaching
die	Leistung, -en	achievement
die	Methode, -n	method
die	Mitschülerin	classmate, schoolmate
die	mittlere Reife	intermediate school-leaving certificate/exam
die	Nachhilfe	private coaching *or* tuition
die	Naturwissenschaft, -en	natural history
die	Note, -n	mark, grade
die	Oberstufe, -n	upper school
die	Reihe, -n	row (*of seats etc*)
die	Rektorin	headmistress (*primary*)
die	Religion	religion
die	Schülermitverwaltung, -en (SMV)	school *or* student council
die	Sprache, -n	language
die	neueren Sprachen *(pl)*	modern languages
die	Strafarbeit, -en	punishment exercise
die	Studentin	student
die	Technische Hochschule, -n -n	technical college
die	Übersetzung, -en	translation
die	Übung, -en	practice; exercise
die	Zeichnung, -en	drawing (*piece of work*)

USEFUL WORDS *(masculine)*

die	**Abwesenden** *(pl)*	absentees
die	**Anwesenden** *(pl)*	those present
der	**Aufsatz, ̈e**	composition, essay
der	**Aufsichtsschüler**	prefect
der	**Bericht, -e**	report
der	**Bleistiftspitzer**	pencil sharpener
der	**Drehbleistift, -e**	propelling pencil
der	**Federhalter**	(fountain) pen
die	**Fortschritte** *(pl)*	progress
der	**Füllfederhalter;** der **Füller**	fountain pen
der	**Gang, ̈e**	corridor
der	**Gesang**	singing
der	**Internatsschüler**	boarder
der	**Irrtum, ̈er**	error
der	**Klecks, -e**	blot, stain
der	**Religionsunterricht**	religious education
der	**Satz, ̈e**	sentence
der	**Tageslichtprojektor, -en**	overhead projector
der	**Tagesschüler**	day-boy
der	**Vortrag, ̈e**	talk, lecture

USEFUL PHRASES
schwierig **difficult**; einfach **easy**
interessant **interesting**; langweilig **boring**
faul **lazy**; fleißig **hard-working**; streng **strict**
mein Lieblingsfach **my favourite subject**
letztes Jahr habe ich einen Austausch gemacht **I did an exchange last year**
schulfrei haben **to have a day off**
hitzefrei haben **to have a day off because of very hot weather**

USEFUL WORDS *(feminine)*

die	Aktentasche, -n	briefcase
die	Aufsichtsschülerin	prefect
die	Dichtung	poetry
die	Doppelstunde, -n	double period
die	Erziehung	education, schooling
die	Handelsschule, -n	commercial college
die	Hauswirtschaft	home economics
die	Internatsschülerin	boarder
die	Kantine, -n	canteen
die	Lektion, -en	lesson, unit
die	Lektüre, -n	reading
die	Pädagogische Hochschule, -n -n (PH)	College of Education
die	Preisverleihung, -en	prize-giving
die	Rechtschreibung	spelling
die	Regel, -n	rule
die	Tagesschülerin	day-girl
die	Vorlesung, -en	lecture

USEFUL WORDS *(neuter)*

das	Benehmen	behaviour, conduct
das	Diktat, -e	dictation
das	Griechisch	Greek
das	Internat, -e	boarding school
das	Nachsitzen	detention
das	Notizbuch, ¨er	jotter; notebook
das	Pult, -e	desk
das	Russisch	Russian
das	Studenten(wohn)heim, -e	students' hall of residence
das	Tonbandgerät, -e	tape recorder

USEFUL PHRASES

abschreiben **to copy**
die Schule schwänzen **to skip school**
bestrafen **to punish**; loben **to praise**
jdn nachsitzen lassen **to keep sb in (after school)**

ESSENTIAL WORDS *(masculine)*

der	Abfall, ̈-e	waste
der	Baum, Bäume	tree
der	Berg, -e	hill, mountain
der	Energieverbrauch	energy consumption
der	Fisch, -e	fish
der	Fluss, ̈-e	river
der	Müll	rubbish, refuse
der	Regen	rain
der	saure Regen	acid rain
der	Schadstoff, -e	harmful substance
der	See, -n	lake
der	Smog	smog
der	Umweltschutz	conservation
der	Strand, ̈-e	beach
der	Wald, ̈-er	forest, wood

ESSENTIAL WORDS *(feminine)*

die	Atmosphäre	atmosphere
die	Blume, -n	flower
die	Fabrik, -en	factory
die	Flasche, -n	bottle
die	Frage, -n	question
die	globale Erwärmung	global warming
die	Insel, -n	island
die	Krise, -n	crisis
die	Luft	air
die	Ozonschicht	ozone layer
die	See, -n	sea
die	Temperatur, -en	temperature
die	Welt	world
die	Windenergie	wind energy
die	Windfarm, -en	wind farm
die	Zeit, -en	time
die	Zeitschrift, -en	magazine
die	Zeitung, -en	newspaper

ESSENTIAL WORDS *(neuter)*

das	**Auto, -s**	car
das	**Benzin**	petrol
das	**Essen**	food
das	**Gas, -e**	gas
das	**Gemüse**	vegetables
das	**Glas**	glass
das	**Land, ̈er**	country
das	**Meer, -e**	ocean; sea
das	**Obst**	fruit
das	**Ozonloch, ̈er**	hole in the ozone layer
das	**Schwermetall, -e**	heavy metal
das	**Tier, -e**	animal
das	**Treibgas, -e**	propellant
das	**Waldsterben**	dying of the forests
das	**Wasser**	water
das	**Wetter**	weather

USEFUL PHRASES

eine Weltreise machen **to go round the world**
das höchste/größte/schönste ... der Welt **the highest/biggest/ most beautiful ... in the world**
in der Zukunft **in future**
aussterben **to become extinct**
verschmutzen **to pollute**
zerstören **to destroy**
verunreinigen **to contaminate**
etw verbieten **to ban sth**
retten **to save**
wieder aufbereiten **to reprocess**
wieder verwerten, recyceln **to recycle**
biologisch abbaubar **biodegradable**
umweltfreundlich **environment-friendly**
umweltschädlich **harmful to the environment**
grün **green;** ökologisch **ecological**
organisch **organic;** bleifrei **unleaded**

IMPORTANT WORDS (masculine)

die	**Grünen** (pl)	the Greens
der	**Kanal, Kanäle**	canal
der	**Mond**	moon
der	**Müllabladeplatz, ⁀e**	rubbish tip or dump
der	**Planet, -en**	planet
die	**tropischen Regenwälder** (pl)	tropical rainforests
der	**Strom, ⁀e**	river

IMPORTANT WORDS (feminine)

die	**Chemikalien** (pl)	chemicals
die	**Erde**	the earth
die	**Gegend, -en**	region, area
die	**Hitze**	heat
die	**Katastrophe, -n**	catastrophe
die	**Kernkraft**	nuclear power
die	**Küste, -n**	coast
die	**Lösung, -en**	solution
die	**Pflanze, -n**	plant
die	**Solaranlage, -n**	solar power plant
die	**Sprühdose, -n**	aerosol
die	**Wiederverwertung**	recycling, reprocessing
die	**Zukunft**	future

IMPORTANT WORDS (neuter)

das	**Aluminium**	aluminium
das	**Deodorant -s or -e**	deodorant
das	**Gebiet, -e**	area
das	**Kernkraftwerk, -e**	nuclear power station
das	**Klima, -s or -te**	climate
das	**Ökosystem**	ecosystem
das	**Produkt, -e**	product; (pl) produce
das	**Recycling**	recycling
das	**Spülmittel**	washing-up liquid
das	**Waschmittel**	detergent
das	**Waschpulver**	washing powder

USEFUL WORDS (masculine)

die	**Bodenschätze** (pl)	mineral resources
der	**Bohrturm, ⸚e**	drilling or oil rig
der	**Brennstoff, -e**	fuel (for heating)
der	**Dieselkraftstoff**	diesel oil
der	**Elektrosmog**	electromagnetic radiation
der	**FCKW, -s**	CFC
der	**Ökologe, -n**	ecologist
der	**Ozean, -e**	ocean
der	**Recyclinghof, ⸚e**	recycling plant
der	**Schaden, ⸚**	damage, harm
der	**Treibhauseffekt**	greenhouse effect
der	**Treibstoff, -e**	fuel (for vehicles)
der	**Umweltschützer**	conservationist, environmentalist

USEFUL WORDS (feminine)

die	**Lärmbelästigung**	noise pollution
die	**Luftverschmutzung**	air pollution
die	**Mülldeponie, -n**	waste disposal site
die	**Ökologin**	ecologist
die	**Steuer, -n**	tax
die	**Umwelt**	environment
die	**(Umwelt)verschmutzung**	(environmental) pollution
die	**Wiederaufarbeitungsanlage, -n**	reprocessing plant
die	**Windkraft**	wind power
die	**Wüste, -n**	desert

USEFUL WORDS (neuter)

das	**Abgas**	exhaust fumes
die	**Abwässer** (pl)	sewage
das	**Altpapier**	waste paper
das	**Erdbeben**	earthquake
das	**Loch, ⸚er**	hole
das	**Weltall**	universe

ESSENTIAL WORDS *(masculine)*

	Alte(r), -n	old man/woman
der	Babysitter	babysitter
der	Bruder, ᐧᐧ	brother
die	Eltern *(pl)*	parents
	Erwachsene(r), -n	grown-up, adult
der	Familienname, -n	surname
der	Freund, -e	friend
die	Geschwister *(pl)*	brothers and sisters
die	Großeltern *(pl)*	grandparents
der	Großvater, ᐧᐧ	grandfather
der	Junge, -n	boy
die	Leute *(pl)*	people
der	Mädchenname, -n	maiden name
der	Mann, ᐧᐧer	man; husband
der	junge Mann, -n ᐧᐧer	youth, young man
der	Mensch, -en	human being, person
der	Name, -n	name
der	Onkel	uncle
der	Opa, -s; der Opi, -s	grandpa
der	Sohn, ᐧᐧe	son
der	Vater, ᐧᐧ	father
der	Vati, -s	dad, daddy
der	Vorname, -n	first name, Christian name
der	Zwilling, -e	twin
der	Zwillingsbruder, ᐧᐧ	twin brother

USEFUL PHRASES

ich heiße Karl **my name is Karl**
ich bin 17 (Jahre alt) **I am 17 (years old)**
ich bin 1986 geboren **I was born in 1986**
wie heißt du? – wie alt bist du? **what's your name? – how old are you?**
männlich **male**; weiblich **female**
kennen **to know**; kennen lernen **to get to know**
vorstellen **to introduce**; erinnern (an + *acc*) **to remind (of)**
unsere Familie stammt aus Polen **our family comes from Poland**
wir wohnen jetzt in Österreich **we live in Austria now**

ESSENTIAL WORDS *(feminine)*

die	**Dame, -n**	lady
die	**Familie, -n**	family
die	**Frau, -en**	woman; wife
die	**Freundin**	friend
die	**Großmutter, ∺**	grandmother
die	**Hausfrau, -en**	housewife
die	**Mutter, ∺**	mother
die	**Mutti, -s**	mum, mummy
die	**Oma, -s; die Omi, -s**	granny
die	**Person, -en**	person
die	**Schwester, -n**	sister
die	**Tante, -n**	aunt
die	**Tochter, ∺**	daughter
die	**Zwillingsschwester, -n**	twin sister

ESSENTIAL WORDS *(neuter)*

das	**Alter**	age; old age
das	**Baby, -s**	baby
das	**Einzelkind, -er**	only child
das	**Fräulein**	young lady
das	**Kind, -er**	child
das	**Mädchen**	(young) girl
das	**Paar, -e**	couple

USEFUL PHRASES

verlobt **engaged**; verheiratet **married**
ledig **single**; geschieden **divorced**
meine Eltern leben getrennt **my parents are separated**
sich verloben **to get engaged**; sich verheiraten **to get married**
sich scheiden lassen **to get divorced**
älter/jünger als ich **older/younger than me**
die ganze Familie **the whole family**
bei uns **at our place, at our house**
mein Großvater ist 1990 gestorben **my grandfather died in 1990**
tot **dead**; streiten **to quarrel**; sich vertragen **to get along**

IMPORTANT WORDS *(masculine)*

der	Austauschpartner	partner (*in an exchange*)
	Bekannte(r), -n	acquaintance
der	Cousin, -s	cousin
der	Ehemann, ⸚er	married man; husband
der	Enkel	grandson; (*pl*) grandchildren
	Jugendliche(r), -n	teenager, young person
der	Nachbar, -n	neighbour
der	Nachname, -n	surname
der	Neffe, -n	nephew
der	Rentner	(old age) pensioner
der	Schwiegersohn, ⸚e	son-in-law
der	Schwiegervater, ⸚	father-in-law
	Verlobte(r), -n	fiancé/fiancée
	Verwandte(r), -n	relation, relative
der	Vetter, -n	cousin
der	Witwer	widower

IMPORTANT WORDS *(feminine)*

die	Cousine, -n	cousin
die	Ehefrau, -en	married woman; wife
die	Enkelin	granddaughter
die	Jugend	youth (*stage of life*)
die	Kusine, -n	cousin
die	Nachbarin	neighbour
die	Nichte, -n	niece
die	Rentnerin	(old age) pensioner
die	Schwiegermutter, ⸚	mother-in-law
die	Schwiegertochter, ⸚	daughter-in-law
die	Witwe, -n	widow

IMPORTANT WORDS *(neuter)*

das	Aupairmädchen	au pair
das	Ehepaar, -e	married couple
das	Enkelkind, -er	grandchild
das	Kindermädchen	nanny

USEFUL WORDS *(masculine)*

der	Bräutigam, -e	bridegroom
die	Drillinge *(pl)*	triplets
der	Elternteil, -e	parent
der	Geburtsort, -e	place of birth
der	Junggeselle, -n	bachelor
die	Jungverheirateten *(pl)*	newly-weds
der	Pate, -n	godfather
der	Rufname, -n	first name, usual name
der	Säugling, -e	baby, infant
der	Schwager, :	brother-in-law
der	Spitzname, -n	nickname
der	Stiefbruder, :	stepbrother
der	Stiefvater, :	stepfather
der	Vorfahr, -en	ancestor
der	Vormund, -e *or* :er	guardian
der	Zuname, -n	surname

USEFUL WORDS *(feminine)*

die	Braut, Bräute	bride
die	Hochzeit, -en	wedding
die	alte Jungfer, -n -n	spinster, old maid
die	Junggesellin	unmarried woman
die	Patin	godmother
die	Schwägerin	sister-in-law
die	Stiefmutter, :	stepmother
die	Stiefschwester, -n	stepsister
die	Waise, -n	orphan

USEFUL WORDS *(neuter)*

das	Geburtsdatum, -daten	date of birth
das	Greisenalter	(extreme) old age
das	Waisenhaus, -häuser	orphanage
das	Weib, -er	woman *(old-fashioned or pejorative)*

ESSENTIAL WORDS (masculine)

der	**Bauer, -n**	farmer; peasant, countryman
der	**Bauernhof, ⸚e**	farm, farmyard
der	**Hahn, ⸚e**	cock, rooster
der	**Hügel**	hill
der	**Hund, -e**	dog
der	**Landarbeiter**	farm labourer
der	**Markt, ⸚e**	market
der	**Wald, ⸚er**	wood, forest

ESSENTIAL WORDS (feminine)

die	**Bäuerin**	lady farmer; farmer's wife; peasant
die	**Bauersfrau, -en**	farmer's wife
die	**Ente, -n**	duck
die	**Erde**	earth, soil
die	**Gans, ⸚e**	goose
die	**Henne, -n**	hen
die	**(Heu)gabel, -n**	pitchfork
die	**Katze, -n**	cat
die	**Wiese, -n**	meadow

ESSENTIAL WORDS (neuter)

das	**Dorf, ⸚er**	village
das	**Feld, -er**	field
das	**Kalb, ⸚er**	calf
das	**Land, ⸚er**	land; country
das	**Tier, -e**	animal

USEFUL PHRASES

auf einem Bauernhof wohnen to live on a farm
Ferien auf dem Bauernhof farm holidays
der Bauer sorgt für die Tiere the farmer looks after the animals
die Felder pflügen to plough the fields
die Ernte einbringen to bring in the harvest or the crops
zur Erntezeit at harvest-time

IMPORTANT WORDS *(masculine)*

der	Bach, ⸚e	stream, brook
der	Boden, ⸚	ground, earth; floor; loft
der	Bulle, -n	bull
der	Lieferwagen	van
der	Ochse, -n	ox
der	Ökobauer, -n	organic farmer
der	Puter	turkey(-cock)
der	Traktor, -en	tractor
der	Weizen	wheat
der	Zaun, Zäune	fence

IMPORTANT WORDS *(feminine)*

die	Feldmaus, -mäuse	fieldmouse
die	Heide, -n	heath
die	Herde, -n	herd; flock
die	Kuh, ⸚e	cow
die	Landschaft, -en	countryside, scenery
die	Landwirtschaft	agriculture, farming
die	Milchkanne, -n	milk churn
die	Ökobäuerin	organic farmer
die	Pute, -n	turkey(-hen)

IMPORTANT WORDS *(neuter)*

das	Bauernhaus, -häuser	farmhouse
das	Gebäude	building
das	Heu	hay
das	Huhn, ⸚er	chicken, hen; *(pl)* poultry
das	Hühnerhaus, -häuser	henhouse
das	Korn, ⸚er	corn, grain
das	Lamm, ⸚er	lamb
das	Pferd, -e	horse
das	Schaf, -e	sheep
das	Schwein, -e	pig
das	Stroh	straw

USEFUL WORDS (*masculine*)

der	**Acker,** ⁻	field
der	**Brunnen**	well
der	**Dünger**	dung, manure; fertilizer
der	**Eimer**	bucket, pail
der	**Esel**	donkey
der	**Graben,** ⁻	ditch
der	**Hafer**	oats (*pl*)
der	**Hase, -n**	hare
der	**Haufen**	heap, pile
der	**Heuboden,** ⁻	hayloft
der	**Karren**	cart
der	**Kuhstall,** ⁻e	cowshed, byre
der	**Landwirt, -e**	farmer
der	**Mähdrescher**	combine harvester
der	**Mais**	maize
der	**Pferdestall,** ⁻e	stable
der	**Pflug,** ⁻e	plough
der	**Roggen**	rye
der	**Schäfer**	shepherd
der	**Schäferhund, -e**	sheepdog, German shepherd
der	**Schlamm**	mud
der	**Schuppen**	shed
der	**Stall,** ⁻e	stable; sty; (hen)house
der	**Stapel**	pile
der	**Staub**	dust
der	**Stier, -e**	bull
der	**Teich, -e**	pond
der	**Truthahn,** ⁻e	turkey(-cock)
der	**Widder**	ram

USEFUL WORDS *(feminine)*

die	**Ernte, -n**	harvest, crop
die	**Erntezeit, -en**	harvest (time)
die	**Furche, -n**	furrow
die	**Garbe, -n**	sheaf
die	**Gerste**	barley
die	**Kleie**	bran
die	**Leiter, -n**	ladder
die	**Scheune, -n**	barn
die	**Vogelscheuche, -n**	scarecrow
die	**Weide, -n**	pasture
die	**(Wind)mühle, -n**	(wind)mill
die	**Ziege, -n**	goat

USEFUL WORDS *(neuter)*

das	**Gatter**	gate; railing
das	**Geflügel**	poultry
das	**Geschirr, -e**	harness
das	**Getreide**	cereals, grain
das	**Küken**	chicken, chick
das	**(Rind)vieh**	cattle *(pl)*, livestock
das	**Zugpferd, -e**	carthorse

USEFUL PHRASES

genmanipulierte Lebensmittel **genetically modified food**
organisch **organic**
Eier aus Freilandhaltung **free-range eggs**
aus biologischem Anbau **organically grown**

ESSENTIAL + IMPORTANT WORDS *(masculine)*

der **Fisch**, -e	fish
der **Goldfisch**, -e	goldfish
der **Schwanz**, -̈e	tail

USEFUL WORDS *(masculine)*

der **Aal**, -e	eel
der **Floh**, -̈e	flea
der **Flügel**	wing
der **Frosch**, -̈e	frog
der **Hai(fisch)**, -e	shark
der **Hecht**, -e	pike
der **Hering**, -e	herring
der **Hummer**	lobster
der **Kabeljau**, -e *or* -s	cod
der **Käfer**	beetle
der **Krebs**, -e	crab; crayfish
der **Lachs**, -e	salmon
der **Maikäfer**	cockchafer
der **Marienkäfer**	ladybird
der **Nachtfalter**	moth
der **Schellfisch**, -e	haddock
der **Schmetterling**, -e	butterfly
der **Stich**, -e	sting
der **Thunfisch**, -e	tuna fish
der **Tintenfisch**, -e	(small) octopus, squid
der **Weißfisch**, -e	whiting
der **Wurm**, -̈er	worm

ESSENTIAL + IMPORTANT WORDS *(neuter)*

das **Insekt**, -en	insect
das **Schalentier**, -e	shellfish
das **Wasser**	water

USEFUL PHRASES

im Wasser schwimmen to swim in the water
in der Luft fliegen to fly in the air
„Angeln verboten" "no fishing"

ESSENTIAL + IMPORTANT WORDS *(feminine)*

die **Biene**, -n	bee
die **Fliege**, -n	fly
die **Forelle**, -n	trout
die **Luft**	air
die **Sardine**, -n	sardine
die **Wespe**, -n	wasp

USEFUL WORDS *(feminine)*

die **Ameise**, -n	ant
die **Auster**, -n	oyster
die **Flosse**, -n	fin
die **Garnele**, -n	shrimp; prawn
die **Grille**, -n	cricket
die **Heuschrecke**, -n	grasshopper
die **Hornisse**, -n	hornet
die **Kaulquappe**, -n	tadpole
die **Kiemen** *(pl)*	gills
die **Krabbe**, -n	shrimp; prawn
die **Languste**, -n	crayfish
die **Libelle**, -n	dragonfly
die **(Mies)muschel**, -n	mussel
die **Motte**, -n	moth
die **Mücke**, -n	midge
die **Qualle**, -n	jellyfish
die **Raupe**, -n	caterpillar
die **Schmeißfliege**, -n	bluebottle
die **Schuppe**, -n	scale
die **Seezunge**, -n	sole
die **Seidenraupe**, -n	silkworm
die **Spinne**, -n	spider
die **Stechmücke**, -n	mosquito
die **Wanze**, -n	bug

USEFUL PHRASES

stechen **to sting**
die Biene/die Wespe sticht **the bee/the wasp stings**
die Mücke sticht **the midge bites**

ESSENTIAL WORDS *(masculine)*

der	Alkohol	alcohol
der	(Apfel)saft, ˝e	(apple) juice
der	Apfelstrudel	apple strudel
der	Apfelwein, -e	cider
der	Appetit, -e	appetite
der	Aufschnitt, -e	cold meats
der	Becher	mug; tumbler
die	Chips *(pl)*	crisps
der	Durst	thirst
der	Eintopf, ˝e	stew
der	Essig	vinegar
der	Fisch, -e	fish
der	Honig	honey
der	Hunger	hunger
der	Imbiss, -e	snack
der	Joghurt, -s	yoghurt
der	Kaffee	coffee
der	Kakao, -s	cocoa
der	Käse	cheese
der	Keks, -e	biscuit
der	Kellner	waiter
der	Kuchen	cake
der	Löffel	spoon
der	Nachtisch, -e	dessert, sweet
der	Orangensaft	orange juice
der	Pfeffer	pepper
der	Reis	rice
der	Salat, -e	salad
der	Schinken	ham
der	Schnellimbiss, -e	snack bar
der	Senf, -e	mustard
der	Sprudel	sparkling mineral water
der	Tee, -s	tea
der	Teller	plate
der	Tisch, -e	table
der	Wein, -e	wine
der	Zucker	sugar

USEFUL PHRASES

essen **to eat**; trinken **to drink**
könnte ich bitte eine Cola haben? **could I have a Coke please?**
wie wär's mit einem Apfelsaft? **do you fancy an apple juice?**
bezahlen bitte! **the bill please!**
schlucken **to swallow**; schmecken **to taste (good)**
probieren **to try**
das schmeckt ihm **he likes it**
schmeckt Ihnen der Wein? **do you like the wine?**
das schmeckt scheußlich! **that tastes dreadful!**
ich esse gern Käse **I like (eating) cheese**
ich trinke gern Tee **I like (drinking) tea**
ich mag Käse/Tee nicht, ich mag keinen Käse/Tee **I don't like cheese/tea**
ich esse lieber Brot/trinke lieber Bier **I prefer bread/beer**
hungrig sein, Hunger haben **to be hungry**
durstig sein, Durst haben **to be thirsty**
ich sterbe vor Hunger! **I'm starving!**
hast du schon gegessen? **have you eaten yet?**
frühstücken **to have breakfast**
vorbereiten **to prepare**; kochen **to cook**; backen **to bake**; braten **to fry**;
   grillen **to grill**; würzen **to season**
paniert **in breadcrumbs**
schneiden **to cut**; streichen **to spread**
einschenken **to pour** (*tea etc*)
bitten um **to ask for**; reichen **to pass, hand on**
Mahlzeit!, guten Appetit! **enjoy your meal!**
bedienen Sie sich!, nehmen Sie sich! **help yourselves!**
alkoholisch **alcoholic**; alkoholfrei **non-alcoholic**
den Tisch decken/abräumen **to lay** *or* **set/clear the table**
abwaschen, (das Geschirr) spülen **to wash up, do the dishes**
abtrocknen **to dry the dishes**

ESSENTIAL WORDS *(feminine)*

die	**Bedienung**	service; service charge
die	**Bestellung, -en**	order
die	**Bockwurst, -würste**	*type of pork sausage*
die	**(Braten)soße, -n**	gravy
die	**Bratwurst, -würste**	grilled *or* fried sausage
die	**Butter**	butter
die	**Cola**	Coke®
die	**Currywurst, -würste**	curried sausage
die	**Dose, -n**	box; tin, can
die	**Erfrischung, -en**	refreshment
die	**Flasche, -n**	bottle
die	**Frucht, -̈e**	(piece of) fruit
die	**Gabel, -n**	fork
die	**Imbissstube, -n**	snack bar
die	**Kaffeekanne, -n**	coffee pot
die	**Kartoffel, -n**	potato
die	**Kellnerin**	waitress
die	**Leberwurst**	liver sausage
die	**Limonade, -n, die Limo**	lemonade
die	**Mahlzeit, -en**	meal
die	**Margarine, -n**	margarine
die	**Milch**	milk
die	**Nachspeise, -n**	dessert, sweet
die	**Pizza, -s**	pizza
die	**kalte Platte, -n -n**	cold meal
die	**Portion, -en**	portion, helping
die	**Praline, -n**	*(individual)* chocolate
die	**Rechnung, -en**	bill
die	**Sahne**	cream
die	**Salzkartoffeln** *(pl)*	boiled potatoes
die	**Schlagsahne**	whipped cream
die	**Schokolade, -n**	chocolate
die	**Soße, -n**	sauce
die	**Speisekarte, -n**	menu
die	**Suppe, -n**	soup
die	**Tageskarte, -n**	today's menu
die	**Tasse, -n**	cup

ESSENTIAL WORDS (neuter)

das	Abendbrot	supper
das	Abendessen	evening meal
das	Bier, -e	beer
das	Bonbon, -s	sweet, sweetie
das	(Brat)hähnchen	(roast) chicken
das	Brot, -e	bread; loaf
ein	belegtes Brot, -n -e	open sandwich
das	Brötchen	(bread) roll
das	Butterbrot, -e	piece of bread and butter
das	Café, -s	café
das	Ei, -er	egg
das	Eis	ice cream
das	Essen	meal
das	Feuerzeug, -e	lighter
das	Fleisch	meat
das	Frühstück, -e	breakfast
das	Gemüse	vegetables
das	Getränk, -e	drink
das	Glas, ¨-er	glass
das	Graubrot, -e	brown bread
das	Gulasch	goulash
das	Kalbfleisch	veal
das	Kotelett, -e	chop
das	Menü, -s	menu
das	Messer	knife
das	Mineralwasser	mineral water
das	Mittagessen	lunch; dinner
das	Obst	fruit
das	Öl	oil
das	Omelett, -s	omelette
das	Picknick, -s or -e	picnic
das	Pils	lager
die	Pommes frites (pl)	chips, French fries
das	Restaurant, -s	restaurant
das	Rindfleisch	beef
das	Rührei	scrambled egg

ESSENTIAL WORDS *(feminine continued)*

die	**Teekanne, -n**	teapot
die	**Torte, -n**	flan, tart, cake
die	**Untertasse, -n**	saucer
die	**Wurst, -̈e**	sausage
die	**Zigarette, -n**	cigarette
die	**Zigarre, -n**	cigar

ESSENTIAL WORDS *(neuter continued)*

das	**Salz**	salt
das	**Schnitzel**	(veal) cutlet
das	**Schwarzbrot**	rye bread
das	**Schweinefleisch**	pork
das	**Spiegelei, -er**	fried egg
das	**Steak, -s**	steak
das	**Wasser**	water
das	**Weißbrot, -e**	white bread
das	**Wiener Schnitzel**	Wiener schnitzel
das	**Wirtshaus, -häuser**	inn
das	**Würstchen**	frankfurter

USEFUL PHRASES

das schmeckt sehr gut **this tastes very nice**
prost! **cheers!**
mit jdm anstoßen **to clink glasses with sb**
süß **sweet**; salzig **salty**; sauer **sour**

IMPORTANT WORDS *(masculine)*

der	**Aschenbecher**	ashtray
der	**Champagner**	champagne
der	**Dessertlöffel**	dessert spoon
der	**Döner**	kebab
der	**Einkaufswagen**	shopping trolley
der	**Esslöffel**	tablespoon
der	**Geschmack, ̈e**	taste
der	**Hamburger**	hamburger
der	**Kaugummi, -s**	chewing gum
der	**Knoblauch**	garlic
der	**Knödel**	dumpling
der	**Kognak, -s**	brandy
der	**Korken**	cork
der	**Rindsbraten**	roast beef
der	**Schnaps, ̈e**	schnapps; spirits
der	**Sekt, -e**	champagne
der	**Stammtisch, -e**	*table for the regulars*
der	**Strohhalm, -e**	(drinking) straw
der	**Tabak**	tobacco
der	**Teelöffel**	teaspoon
der	**Toast, -s**	toast
der	**Whisky, -s**	whisky

USEFUL PHRASES

rauchen **to smoke**
danke, ich rauche nicht **no thanks, I don't smoke**
„Rauchen verboten" **"no smoking"**
um Feuer bitten **to ask for a light**
anzünden **to light up**
ich versuche, das Rauchen aufzugeben **I'm trying to give up smoking**

IMPORTANT WORDS (feminine)

die	Auswahl (an + *dat*)	choice (of)
die	Gaststätte, -n	restaurant; pub
die	Getränkekarte, -n	wine list
die	Kneipe, -n	pub
die	Krabben (*pl*)	shrimps; prawns
die	Marmelade, -n	jam
die	Majonäse, -n	mayonnaise
die	Meeresfrüchte (*pl*)	seafood, shellfish
die	Nudeln (*pl*)	pasta, noodles
die	Orangenmarmelade, -n	marmalade
die	Salami, -s	salami
die	Salatsoße, -n	salad dressing
die	Schale, -n	bowl
die	Scheibe, -n	slice
die	Schüssel, -n	bowl, dish
die	Theke, -n	bar; counter
die	Vanillesoße, -n	custard
die	Vorspeise, -n	hors d'œuvre, starter
die	Weinkarte, -n	wine list
die	Wirtschaft, -en	pub

IMPORTANT WORDS (neuter)

das	Geflügel	poultry
das	Gericht, -e	dish, course
das	Geschirr	dishes, crockery
das	Hauptgericht, -e	main course
das	Lammfleisch	lamb
das	Mus	purée
das	Rezept, -e	recipe
das	Sandwich, -es	sandwich
das	Tablett, -e	tray
das	Trinkgeld, -er	tip

USEFUL PHRASES

bestellen **to order**
was können Sie mir empfehlen? **what do you recommend?**

USEFUL WORDS *(masculine)*

der	**Eiswürfel**	ice cube
der	**Kaffeefilter**	coffee-maker
der	**Kamillentee**	camomile tea
der	**Kartoffelbrei**	mashed potatoes *(pl)*
der	**Kartoffelsalat**	potato salad
der	**Krug (¨e) Wasser**	jug of water
der	**Pfannkuchen**	pancake
der	**Pudding**	blancmange
der	**Rahm**	cream
der	**Rotwein**	red wine
der	**(Schinken)speck**	bacon
der	**Teebeutel**	tea bag
der	**Wackelpeter**	jelly
der	**Weinbrand, ¨e**	brandy
der	**Weißwein**	white wine
der	**Zwieback**	toast *(in packets)*

USEFUL WORDS *(feminine)*

die	**Büchse, -n**	tin, can
die	**Eisdiele, -n**	ice cream parlour
die	**Frikadelle, -n**	rissole
die	**Konserven** *(pl)*	preserved foods
die	**Niere, -n**	kidney
die	**Pfeife, -n**	pipe
die	**Serviette, -n**	napkin, serviette
die	**Thermosflasche, -n**	flask

USEFUL WORDS *(neuter)*

das	**Besteck**	cutlery
das	**Geflügel**	poultry
das	**Kartoffelpüree**	mashed potatoes
das	**Mehl, -e**	flour
das	**Streichholz, ¨er**	match
das	**Tischtuch, ¨er**	tablecloth
das	**Wild**	game *(meat)*

ESSENTIAL WORDS *(masculine)*

der	Ausflug, ̈-e	outing, trip
der	Besuch, -e	visit; visitor
der	Brieffreund, -e	penfriend
der	Computer	computer
der	Fan, -s	fan
der	Film, -e	film
der	(Foto)apparat, -e	camera
der	Freund, -e	friend; boyfriend
der	Jugendklub, -s	youth club
der	MP3-Spieler	MP3 player
der	Plattenspieler	record player
der	Sänger	singer
der	Schlager	hit (record)
der	Spaziergang, ̈-e	walk
der	Sport	sport
der	Tanz, ̈-e	dance
der	Verein, -e	club

ESSENTIAL WORDS *(feminine)*

die	Brieffreundin	penfriend
die	CD, -s	CD
die	Diskothek, -en	disco
die	DVD, -s	DVD
die	Einladung, -en	invitation
die	Eintrittskarte, -n	(admission) ticket
die	Fotografie, -n	photograph; photography
die	Freizeit	free time, spare time
die	Freundin	friend; girlfriend
die	Musik	music
die	Sängerin	singer
die	Spielekonsole, -n	games console
die	(Spiel)karte, -n	(playing) card
die	Stereoanlage, -en	stereo (system)
die	Zeitschrift, -en	magazine
die	Zeitung, -en	newspaper

ESSENTIAL WORDS *(neuter)*

das	**Fernsehen**	watching television
das	**Fitnessstudio, -s**	fitness centre
das	**Foto, -s**	photograph
das	**Hobby, -s**	hobby
das	**Interesse, -n**	interest
das	**Kartenspiel, -e**	game of cards; pack of cards
das	**Kino, -s**	cinema
das	**Kofferradio, -s**	transistor (radio)
das	**Konzert, -e**	concert
das	**Lesen**	reading
das	**Magazin, -e**	magazine
das	**Museum, Museen**	museum
das	**Programm, -e**	(TV) programme
das	**Radio, -s**	radio
das	**Singen**	singing
das	**Spiel, -e**	game
das	**Taschengeld**	pocket money
das	**Theater**	theatre
das	**Wandern**	hiking, rambling
das	**Wochenende, -n**	weekend

USEFUL PHRASES

in meiner Freizeit **in my free *or* spare time**
die Zeit damit verbringen, etw zu tun **to spend time doing sth**
am Wochenende **at the weekend(s)**
sich ausruhen **to rest;** beschließen **to decide;** treffen **to meet**
viel Spaß! **enjoy yourself!, have fun!**
es hat mir wirklich gut gefallen **I really liked it**
ausgezeichnet! **excellent!;** toll! **terrific!**
einen Spaziergang machen **to go for a walk**
fernsehen **to watch television**
Radio hören **to listen to the radio**
umschalten **to turn over, change channels**
CDs hören **to play CDs;** aufnehmen **to record**
fotografieren **to take photos (of);** knipsen **to snap**
lesen **to read;** schreiben **to write;** sammeln **to collect**
malen **to paint;** zeichnen **to draw**

IMPORTANT WORDS *(masculine)*

der	**Drachen**	kite; hang-glider
der	**Karneval, -e** *or* **-s**	carnival
der	**Krimi, -s**	thriller, detective story
der	**Pfadfinder**	boy scout
der	**Roman, -e**	novel
der	**Shoppingsender**	shopping channel
der	**Treffpunkt, -e**	meeting place
der	**Videorekorder**	video (recorder)
der	**Walkman**®	personal stereo, Walkman®
der	**Zoo, -s**	zoo

IMPORTANT WORDS *(feminine)*

die	**Aufnahme, -n**	shot *(photo)*; recording
die	**Ausstellung, -en**	exhibition
die	**Besichtigung, -en**	visit
die	**(Briefmarken)sammlung, -en**	(stamp) collection
die	**Disko, -s**	disco
die	**Freizeitbeschäftigung, -en**	hobby, spare-time activity
die	**Illustrierte, -n**	magazine
die	**Musikkassette, -n**	music cassette
die	**Nachrichten** *(pl)*	news, newscast
die	**Pfadfinderin**	girl scout
die	**Sendung, -en**	transmission, programme
die	**Spielshow, -s**	game show
die	**Unterhaltung, -en**	entertainment; talk
die	**Verabredung, -en**	date, appointment
die	**Videokassette, -n**	video (cassette)
die	**Wanderung, -en**	walk, hike

IMPORTANT WORDS *(neuter)*

das	**Dia, -s**	slide, transparency
das	**Mitglied, -er**	member
das	**Schach**	chess
das	**Taschenbuch, ¨-er**	paperback

USEFUL WORDS (masculine)

der	**CD-Spieler**	CD player
das	**Chatraum, -räume**	chatroom
die	**Comics** (pl)	cartoons, comic strips
der	**Feierabend, -e**	end of work, evening
der	**Ohrstöpsel**	earplug
der	**Spielautomat, -en**	slot machine
der	**Zeitvertreib, -e**	pastime

USEFUL WORDS (feminine)

die	**CD, -s**, die **Compactdisc, -s**	compact disc, CD
die	**Fernsehsendung, -en**	TV programme
die	**Filmkamera, -s**	cine camera
die	**Freizeitdroge, -n**	recreational drug
die	**Hitliste, -n**	charts, top twenty
die	**Hitparade, -en**	charts, hit parade
die	**Party, -s**	party
die	**Versammlung, -en**	meeting, gathering

USEFUL WORDS (neuter)

das	**Album, Alben**	album
das	**Damespiel**	draughts
das	**Feriendorf, ̈-er**	holiday camp
das	**Ferienlager**	school camp
das	**Freizeitzentrum, -zentren**	leisure centre
das	**Gleitschirmfliegen**	paragliding
das	**Jugendzentrum, -zentren**	youth centre
das	**Kegeln**	bowling
das	**Kreuzworträtsel**	crossword (puzzle)
das	**Lied, -er**	song
das	**Skateboard, -s**	skateboard
das	**Snowboard, -s**	snowboard
das	**Surfen**	surfing

USEFUL PHRASES

ich interessiere mich für (+ acc) I am interested in …

eine Party geben to have a party

hast du Lust, zu meiner Party zu kommen? do you fancy coming to my party?

568 fruit

ESSENTIAL + IMPORTANT WORDS (masculine)

der	**Apfel, ⸚**	apple
der	**Apfelbaum, -bäume**	apple tree
der	**Birnbaum, -bäume**	pear tree
der	**Obstbaum, -bäume**	fruit tree
der	**Obstgarten, ⸚**	orchard
der	**Pfirsich, -e**	peach
der	**Pfirsichbaum, -bäume**	peach tree
der	**Weinstock, ⸚e**	vine

ESSENTIAL + IMPORTANT WORDS (feminine)

die	**Apfelsine, -n**	orange
die	**Banane, -n**	banana; banana tree
die	**Birne, -n**	pear
die	**Erdbeere, -n**	strawberry
eine	**Frucht, ⸚e**	a (piece of) fruit
die	**Himbeere, -n**	raspberry
die	**Kirsche, -n**	cherry
die	**Melone, -n**	melon
die	**Olive, -n**	olive
die	**Orange, -n**	orange; orange tree
die	**Pflaume, -n**	plum
die	**Schale, -n**	skin; peel; shell
die	**(Wein)traube, -n**	grape; bunch of grapes
die	**Zitrone, -n**	lemon

ESSENTIAL WORDS (neuter)

das	**Kompott, -e**	stewed fruit
das	**Obst**	fruit
das	**Stück Obst**	piece of fruit

USEFUL PHRASES
reif ripe; unreif not ripe; süß sweet; bitter sour, bitter
hart hard; weich soft; saftig juicy
pflücken to pick; sammeln to gather
essen to eat; beißen to bite
blaue/grüne Trauben black/green grapes

USEFUL WORDS *(masculine)*

der	Granatapfel, ⸚	pomegranate
der	Kern, -e	pip, stone *(in fruit)*
der	Nussbaum, -bäume	walnut tree
der	Rhabarber	rhubarb
der	Walnussbaum, -bäume	walnut tree
der	Weinberg, -e	vineyard
der	Weinstock, ⸚e	vine

USEFUL WORDS *(feminine)*

die	Ananas, - *or* -se	pineapple
die	Aprikose, -n	apricot; apricot tree
die	Backpflaume, -n	prune
die	Beere, -n	berry
die	Brombeere, -n	blackberry, bramble
die	Dattel, -n	date
die	Erdnuss, ⸚e	peanut
die	Feige, -n	fig
die	Grapefruit	grapefruit
die	Haselnuss, ⸚e	hazelnut
die	Heidelbeere, -n	bilberry
die	Johannisbeere, -n	redcurrant
die	Schwarze Johannisbeere, -n -n	blackcurrant
die	Kastanie, -n	chestnut; chestnut tree
die	Kiwi, -s	kiwi (fruit)
die	Kokosnuss, ⸚e	coconut
die	Mandarine, -n	tangerine
die	Nuss, ⸚e	nut
die	Pampelmuse, -n	grapefruit
die	Passionsfrucht, ⸚e	passion fruit
die	Stachelbeere, -n	gooseberry
die	Traube, -n	grape; bunch of grapes
die	Traubenlese	grape harvest, vintage
die	Walnuss, ⸚e	walnut
die	(Wein)rebe, -n	vine
die	Zwetsch(g)e, -n	plum

ESSENTIAL WORDS (masculine)

der	**Fernsehapparat, -e** or	television set
	der **Fernseher**	
der	**Herd, -e**	cooker
der	**Kleiderschrank, ⸚e**	wardrobe
der	**Kühlschrank, ⸚e**	fridge, refrigerator
der	**Plattenspieler**	record player
der	**Raum, Räume**	room
der	**Satellitenempfänger**	satellite receiver
der	**Schrank, ⸚e**	cupboard
der	**Sessel**	armchair
der	**Stuhl, ⸚e**	chair
der	**Tisch, -e**	table
der	**Wecker**	alarm clock

ESSENTIAL WORDS (feminine)

die	**Lampe, -n**	lamp
die	**Stehlampe, -n**	standard lamp, floor lamp
die	**Stereoanlage, -n**	stereo system
die	**Uhr, -en**	clock
die	**Waschmaschine, -n**	washing machine

ESSENTIAL WORDS (neuter)

das	**Bett, -en**	bed
das	**Bild, -er**	picture, painting
das	**Haus, Häuser**	house
das	**Sofa, -s**	settee, couch
das	**Telefon, -e**	telephone
das	**Zimmer**	room

USEFUL PHRASES

fernsehen to watch television; **im Fernsehen** on television
telefonieren to telephone; **anrufen** to phone, call
Musik hören to listen to music
programmieren to program

IMPORTANT WORDS (masculine)

der	CD-Brenner	CD burner
der	CD-Spieler	CD player
der	DVD-Brenner	DVD burner
der	DVD-Spieler	DVD player
der	Elektroherd, -e	electric cooker
der	Gasherd, -e	gas cooker
der	Nachttisch, -e	bedside table
der	Ofen, ⁝	oven
der	Spiegel	mirror
der	Videorekorder	video recorder

IMPORTANT WORDS (feminine)

die	Digicam, -s	digicam
die	Schreibmaschine, -n	typewriter
die	Spülmaschine, -n	dishwasher
die	Steckdose, -n	(wall) socket

IMPORTANT WORDS (neuter)

das	(Bücher)regal, -e	bookcase, bookshelves
ein	digitales Radio, -n -s	digital radio
das	Fax, -e	fax
das	Handy, -s	mobile phone
die	Möbel (pl)	furniture
das	Möbel(stück)	piece of furniture
das	Regal, -e	(set of) shelves
das	Videogerät, -e	video (recorder)
das	Walkman®	personal stereo, Walkman®

USEFUL PHRASES

ein Zimmer möblieren to furnish a room
ein möbliertes Zimmer a furnished room
bequem comfortable; unbequem uncomfortable
in dem Zimmer ist es sehr eng the room is very cramped
den Tisch decken/abräumen to lay or set/to clear the table
das Bett machen to make the bed
ins Bett gehen, zu Bett gehen to go to bed

USEFUL WORDS *(masculine)*

der	Anrufbeantworter	answering machine
der	Backofen, ⸚	oven
der	Beamer	data projector
der	Bücherschrank, ⸚e	bookcase
der	Couchtisch, -e	coffee table
der	Esstisch, -e	dining table
der	Frisiertisch, -e	dressing table
der	Heizofen, ⸚	fire, heater
der	Hocker	stool
der	Kabelanschluss, ⸚e	cable connection
der	Lehnsessel *or* der Lehnstuhl, ⸚e	armchair
der	Mikrowellenherd, -e	microwave oven
der	Möbelwagen	furniture van, removal van
der	Nachtspeicherofen	(night-)storage heater
der	Radiowecker	radio alarm clock
der	Satz (⸚e) Tische	nest of tables
der	Schaukelstuhl, ⸚e	rocking chair
der	Schirmständer	umbrella stand
der	Schnellkochtopf, ⸚e	pressure cooker
der	Schreibtisch, -e	writing desk
der	Sekretär, -e	bureau, writing desk
der	Staubsauger	vacuum cleaner, Hoover®
der	Teewagen	trolley
der	Umluftherd, -e	fan-assisted oven
der	Umzug, ⸚e	removal
der	Wäschetrockner	tumble dryer

USEFUL PHRASES

sitzen to sit, be sitting; sich setzen to sit down
sich hinlegen to lie down; sich ausruhen to rest
ein Zimmer ausräumen to clear out a room
ein Zimmer aufräumen *or* in Ordnung bringen to tidy up a room
putzen to clean; abstauben to dust; staubsaugen to hoover

USEFUL WORDS *(feminine)*

die	**Anrichte, -n**	dresser; sideboard
die	**Antenne, -n**	aerial
die	**Einrichtung**	furnishings *(pl)*
die	**Fernbedienung, -en**	remote control
die	**Gefriertruhe, -n**	freezer
die	**Kommode, -n**	chest of drawers
die	**Matratze, -n**	mattress
die	**Nähmaschine, -n**	sewing machine
die	**Satellitenantenne, -n**	satellite dish
die	**Schublade, -n**	drawer
die	**Spedition, -en**	removal firm
die	**Standuhr, -en**	grandfather clock
die	**Tiefkühltruhe, -n**	freezer, deep freeze
die	**Truhe, -n**	chest, trunk
die	**Videokamera, -s**	video camera
die	**Wäscheschleuder, -n**	spin dryer
die	**Waage, -n**	(bathroom) scales
die	**Wiege, -n**	cradle

USEFUL WORDS *(neuter)*

das	**Bord, -e**	shelf
das	**Etagenbett, -en**	bunk bed
das	**Gemälde**	painting, picture
das	**Gerät, -e**	appliance
das	**Kinderbettchen**	cot
das	**Rollo, -s** *or* das **Rouleau, -s**	blind
das	**Schubfach, ̈er**	drawer
ein	**schnurlose Telefon, -n -e**	cordless telephone
das	**Tonbandgerät, -e**	tape recorder

USEFUL PHRASES

elektrisch **electric**; anmachen, einschalten **to turn** *or* **switch on**
ausmachen, ausschalten **to turn** *or* **switch off**
es funktioniert nicht **it's not working**
heizen **to heat**; gemütlich **comfortable, cosy**

die	**Alpen** (pl)	the Alps
	Antwerpen (nt)	Antwerp
der	**Ärmelkanal**	the English Channel
der	**Atlantik,**	the Atlantic (Ocean)
der	**Atlantische Ozean**	
	Basel (nt)	Basle
	Bayern (nt)	Bavaria
	Berlin (nt)	Berlin
der	**Bodensee**	Lake Constance
die	**Britischen Inseln** (fpl)	the British Isles
	Brüssel (nt)	Brussels
die	**Donau**	the Danube
	Edinburg (nt)	Edinburgh
die	**Elbe**	the (river) Elbe
das	**Elsass** (nt)	Alsace
der	**Ferne Osten**	the Far East
	Genf (nt)	Geneva
der	**Genfer See**	Lake Geneva
	Gent (nt)	Ghent
Den	**Haag** (nt)	The Hague
	Hannover (nt)	Hanover
	Kairo (nt)	Cairo
die	**Kanalinseln** (fpl)	the Channel Islands
	Köln (nt)	Cologne
	Korsika (nt)	Corsica
	Lissabon (nt)	Lisbon
	Lothringen (nt)	Lorraine
	Mailand (nt)	Milan
	Mallorca (nt)	Majorca
das	**Mittelmeer**	the Mediterranean
die	**Mosel**	Moselle
	Moskau (nt)	Moscow
	München (nt)	Munich
der	**Nahe Osten**	the Middle East
die	**Nordsee**	the North Sea
die	**Ostsee**	the Baltic Sea
der	**Pazifik,**	the Pacific (Ocean)
der	**Pazifische Ozean**	
	Peking (nt)	Beijing
die	**Pyrenäen** (pl)	the Pyrenees

der	**Rhein**	the Rhine
	Rom (*nt*)	Rome
der	**Schwarzwald**	the Black Forest
die	**Seine**	the Seine
der	**Stille Ozean**	the Pacific Ocean
die	**Themse**	the Thames
	Venedig (*nt*)	Venice
der	**Vesuv**	Mount Vesuvius
	Warschau (*nt*)	Warsaw
	Wien (*nt*)	Vienna
die	**Wolga**	the Volga

USEFUL PHRASES

Athener, -in an Athenian

Bas(e)ler, -in a person from Basle

Bayer, -in a Bavarian

Böhme, Böhmin a person from Bohemia

Elsässer, -in a person from Alsace, an Alsatian

Flame, Flamin or Flämin a person from Flanders, a Fleming

Friese, Friesin a person from Frisia, a Frisian

Hamburger, -in a person from Hamburg

Hannoveraner, -in a person from Hanover, a Hanoverian

Hesse, Hessin a person from Hesse

Indianer, -in an (American) Indian

Londoner, -in a Londoner

Moskauer, -in a person from Moscow, a Muscovite

Münch(e)ner, -in a person from Munich

Neapolitaner, -in a Neapolitan

Pariser, -in a Parisian

Preuße, Preußin a Prussian

Rheinländer, -in a Rheinlander

Römer, -in a person from Rome, a Roman

Sachse, Sächsin a person from Saxony

Schwabe, Schwäbin a person from Swabia

Tiroler, -in a person from the Tyrol

Venezianer, -in a Venetian

Westfale, Westfälin a Westphalian

Wiener, -in a person from Vienna, a Viennese

GREETINGS AND FAREWELLS

guten Tag! good day, hello; good afternoon
guten Morgen! good morning
guten Abend! good evening
gute Nacht! good night (*when going to bed*)
auf Wiedersehen! goodbye
auf Wiederhören! goodbye (*on phone*)
hallo! hi!; **tschüss!** bye!; **servus** hello; goodbye
grüß Gott! hello
wie geht's?; wie geht es Ihnen? how are things?
gut, danke; es geht mir gut, danke very well, thank you
sehr angenehm pleased to meet you
bis später see you later
bis morgen see you tomorrow

BEST WISHES

ich gratuliere! congratulations!
alles Gute all the best, best wishes
herzlichen Glückwunsch congratulations, best wishes
alles Gute zum Geburtstag happy birthday
alles Gute zum Hochzeitstag congratulations on your wedding day
viel Glück all the best; the best of luck
machs gut! take care
fröhliche Weihnachten merry Christmas
gutes neues Jahr happy New Year
guten Appetit! have a good meal, enjoy your meal
prost! cheers; **zum Wohl!** good health!
Gesundheit! bless you! (*after a sneeze*)
viel Spaß! have a good time, enjoy yourself *etc*
schlaf gut! sleep well
gut geschlafen? did you sleep well?

grüßen, begrüßen to greet, welcome
sich verabschieden to say goodbye, take one's leave
(sich) vorstellen to introduce (oneself)

SURPRISE

ach du meine Güte oh my goodness, oh dear
so?, wirklich? really?
so, so! well, well!; **ach so!** oh I see!
na, so etwas! you don't say!
wie? what?
was für ein Glück! what a piece of luck!

POLITENESS

bitte please, excuse me
danke thank you; **nein danke** no thank you
ja bitte, bitte ja yes please
tu das ja nicht don't do that
danke schön, danke sehr, vielen Dank thank you very much, many thanks
nichts zu danken don't mention it
bitte schön, bitte sehr don't mention it
gern geschehen my pleasure, don't mention it
entschuldigen Sie, Entschuldigung excuse me, I'm sorry
verzeihen Sie, Verzeihung I'm sorry, I beg your pardon
pardon excuse me, I'm sorry
das macht nichts it doesn't matter
(wie) bitte? (I beg your) pardon?
hier bitte, bitte schön, bitte sehr there you are
mit Vergnügen with pleasure
machen Sie keine Umstände don't go to any trouble

WARNINGS

Achtung! watch out!; **Vorsicht!** be careful!
pass auf! look out!, watch out!
halten Sie! stop!
Feuer! fire!; **haltet den Dieb!** stop thief!
Ruhe!, ruhig! be quiet!; **halt den Mund!** shut up!
herein! come in!; **hinaus!** get out!
beeile dich! hurry up!; **hau ab!** clear off!
geh mir aus dem Weg! get out of my way!

AGREEMENT AND DISAGREEMENT

ja yes; **doch** yes (*when contradictory*)
nein no
jawohl yes indeed
natürlich of course
natürlich nicht, aber nein of course not
nicht wahr? isn't that right?
in Ordnung O.K., all right
gut good, O.K.
na gut, also gut O.K. then, all right then
schön fine
einverstanden! agreed!
genau, ganz recht exactly
desto besser so much the better
ich habe nichts dagegen I don't mind *or* object
das ist mir gleich *or* **einerlei** *or* **egal** I don't mind, it's all the same to me, it's
   all one to me
das stimmt that's right
das stimmt nicht that doesn't make sense
im Gegenteil on the contrary
nie!, um nichts in der Welt! never!, not on your life!
kümmern Sie sich um Ihre eigenen Dinge! mind your own business!
nieder mit ... down with ...

DISTRESS

Hilfe! help!
ach je! oh dear!
ach!, o weh! alas!
was ist los (mit dir)? what's the matter (with you)?, what's wrong (with you)?
leider (nicht) unfortunately (not)
es tut mir Leid I'm sorry
es tut mir wirklich Leid I'm really sorry
wie schade what a pity
das ist Pech it's a shame, that's bad luck
verflixt (noch mal)! blow!, drat!, dash it!
verflucht!, verdammt! damn!
ich habe es satt I'm fed up with it
ich kann ihn nicht ausstehen I can't stand him
was soll ich tun? what shall I do?
wie ärgerlich! what a nuisance!, how annoying!

OTHER EXPRESSIONS

vielleicht perhaps, maybe
ich weiß nicht I don't know
(ich habe) keine Ahnung (I've) no idea
ich weiß da nicht Bescheid I don't know (anything about it)
ich weiß nicht genau I don't know exactly
das kann ich mir vorstellen I can believe that
schade! shame!
mein Gott! good Lord!
(ach) du lieber Himmel! (good) heavens!, goodness gracious!
prima! great!
klasse! terrific!, marvellous!
machen Sie sich keine Sorgen don't worry
aber wirklich! well really!
du machst wohl Witze you must be joking *or* kidding!
so eine Frechheit! what a nerve *or* cheek!
armes Ding! poor thing!

ESSENTIAL WORDS *(masculine)*

der	Arzt, ̈e	doctor, G.P.
der	Durchfall	diarrhoea
die	Kopfschmerzen *(pl)*	a headache
	Kranke(r), -n	patient
der	Krankenwagen	ambulance
der	Zahnarzt, ̈e	dentist

ESSENTIAL WORDS *(feminine)*

die	Allergie, -n	allergy
die	Ärztin	doctor, G.P.
die	Erkältung, -en	cold; chill
die	erste Hilfe	first aid
die	Gesundheit	health
die	Grippe	flu, influenza
die	Klinik, -en	hospital, clinic
die	Krankenschwester, -n	nurse
die	Krankheit, -en	illness
die	Lebensgefahr	danger (to life)
die	Medizin	(science of) medicine
die	Pille, -n	pill
die	Tablette, -n	tablet, pill
die	Temperatur, -en	temperature
die	Verstopfung, -en	constipation

ESSENTIAL WORDS *(neuter)*

das	Fieber	fever, (high) temperature
das	Heimweh	homesickness
das	Kopfweh	headache
das	Krankenhaus, -häuser	hospital

USEFUL PHRASES

krank ill; gesund healthy; wohl well
schwach weak; atemlos breathless
müde tired; schwindlig dizzy; blass pale
sich erkälten to catch cold; erkältet sein to have a cold
husten to cough; niesen to sneeze; schwitzen to sweat

IMPORTANT WORDS *(masculine)*

der	**Apotheker**	(dispensing) chemist
der	**Atem**	breath
der	**Auslandskrankenschein, -e**	(European) health insurance card
die	**Bauchschmerzen** *(pl)*	stomach-ache
der	**Gips**	plaster; plaster of Paris
die	**Halsschmerzen** *(pl)*	a sore throat
der	**Husten**	cough
der	**Krankenpfleger**	(male) nurse
der	**Krankenschein, -e**	health insurance card
der	**Krebs**	cancer
die	**Magenschmerzen** *(pl)*	stomach-ache
der	**Operationssaal, -säle**	operating theatre
der	**Patient, -en**	patient
der	**Schmerz, -en**	pain, ache
der	**Schnupfen**	cold (*in the head*)
der	**Schweiß**	sweat
der	**Sonnenbrand, ̈e**	sunburn
der	**Tod, -e**	death
der	**Tropfen**	drop
der	**Verband, ̈e**	bandage, dressing
die	**Zahnschmerzen** *(pl)*	toothache

IMPORTANT WORDS *(feminine)*

die	**Behandlung**	treatment
die	**Feuerwehr, -en**	fire brigade
die	**Krankenkasse, -n**	health insurance
die	**Kur, -en**	health cure
die	**Operation, -en**	operation
die	**Patientin**	patient
die	**Ruhe**	rest
die	**Sorge, -n**	care, worry
die	**Spritze, -n**	syringe; injection
die	**Untersuchung, -en**	medical examination
die	**Verletzung, -en**	injury
die	**Versichertenkarte, -n**	health insurance card
die	**Wunde, -n**	wound

IMPORTANT WORDS *(neuter)*

das	**Aids**	AIDS, aids
das	**Aspirin**	aspirin
das	**Blut**	blood
das	**Heftpflaster**	sticking plaster
das	**Kondom, -e**	condom
das	**Medikament, -e**	medicine
das	**Rezept, -e**	prescription
das	**Thermometer**	thermometer
das	**Verhütungsmittel**	contraceptive

USEFUL WORDS *(feminine)*

die	**Abmagerungskur, -en**	(slimming) diet
die	**Akne**	acne
die	**Blase, -n**	blister; bladder
die	**Blinddarmentzündung, -en**	appendicitis
die	**Blutübertragung, -en**	blood transfusion
die	**Chemotherapie, -n**	chemotherapy
die	**Diät, -en**	(special) diet
die	**Droge, -n**	drug
die	**Epidemie, -n**	epidemic
die	**Genesung**	recovery
die	**Kraft, ̈e**	strength, power
die	**Magenverstimmung**	stomach upset
die	**Mandelentzündung**	tonsillitis
die	**Masern** *(pl)*	measles
die	**Migräne**	migraine
die	**Narbe, -n**	scar
die	**Poliklinik, -en**	health centre
die	**Röntgenaufnahme, -n**	X-ray
die	**Röteln** *(pl)*	German measles
die	**Salbe, -n**	ointment, cream
die	**Schwangerschaft, -en**	pregnancy
die	**Station, -en**	ward
die	**Übelkeit**	sickness, vomiting
die	**Watte**	cotton wool
die	**Windpocken** *(pl)*	chickenpox

USEFUL WORDS *(masculine)*

der	**Bazillus, Bazillen**	germ
der	**blaue Fleck, -n -en**	bruise
der	**Blutdruck**	blood pressure
der	**Drogenmissbrauch**	drug abuse
der	**Fußpilz**	athlete's foot
der	**Heuschnupfen**	hayfever
	HIV-Infizierte(r), -n	person who is HIV-positive
der	**Kratzer**	scratch
der	**Mumps**	mumps
der	**Puls**	pulse
der	**Rollstuhl, ⸚e**	wheelchair
der	**Schlaganfall, ⸚e**	stroke
der	**Schock, -s**	shock
der	**Sonnenstich, -e**	sunstroke
der	**Stress**	stress
der	**Stich, -e**	sting

USEFUL WORDS *(neuter)*

das	**Altersheim, -e**	old people's home
das	**Antibiotikum, -ka**	antibiotic
das	**Gift, -e**	poison
das	**Rauschgift, -e**	drug, narcotic
das	**Sprechzimmer**	surgery, consulting room
das	**Wartezimmer**	waiting room

USEFUL PHRASES

fallen, stürzen **to fall**; brechen **to break**
ich bin mit dem Auto verunglückt **I've had an accident with the car**
was fehlt Ihnen? **what's the matter with you?**
es blutet **it's bleeding**; es tut weh **it hurts**
verletzt **injured, hurt**; verwundet **wounded**
sich übergeben **to vomit, be sick**
untersuchen **to examine**; verbinden **to bandage**
pflegen **to look after, nurse**; behandeln **to treat**
verschreiben **to prescribe**; gute Besserung! **get well soon!**
sich erholen **to recover**; sterben **to die**; tot **dead**

ESSENTIAL WORDS *(masculine)*

der	**(Farb)fernseher**	(colour) television set
der	**Gast, ⸚e**	guest
der	**Gasthof, ⸚e**	hotel, inn
der	**Kellner**	waiter
der	**Koch, ⸚e**	cook
der	**Koffer**	case, suitcase
der	**Lift, -e** *or* **-s**	lift
der	**Notausgang, ⸚e**	emergency exit
der	**Reisepass, ⸚e**	passport
der	**Schalter**	switch
der	**Scheck, -s**	cheque
der	**Schlüssel**	key
der	**Stock, Stockwerke**	floor, storey
der	**Tag, -e**	day
der	**Weinkellner**	wine waiter
der	**Zuschlag, ⸚e**	extra charge

ESSENTIAL WORDS *(feminine)*

die	**Anmeldung**	registration
die	**Antwort, -en**	answer
die	**Bar, -s**	bar
die	**Bedienung**	service; service charge
die	**Dusche, -n**	shower
die	**Halbpension**	half board
die	**Kellnerin**	waitress
die	**Köchin**	cook
die	**Mahlzeit, -en**	meal
die	**Nacht, ⸚e**	night
die	**Pension, -en**	guest-house, boarding house
die	**Rechnung, -en**	bill
die	**Tasche, -n**	bag
die	**Toilette, -n**	toilet
die	**Übernachtung mit Frühstück**	bed and breakfast
die	**Vollpension**	full board
die	**Woche, -n**	week

ESSENTIAL + IMPORTANT WORDS *(neuter)*

das	**Badezimmer**	bathroom
das	**Café, -s**	café
das	**Doppelbett, -en**	double bed
das	**Doppelzimmer**	double room
das	**Einzelzimmer**	single room
das	**Erdgeschoss, -e**	ground floor, ground level
das	**(Farb)fernsehen**	(colour) television
das	**Formular, -e**	form
das	**Freibad, -̈er**	open-air swimming pool
das	**Fremdenzimmer**	guest room
das	**Frühstück, -e**	breakfast
das	**Gasthaus, -häuser**	inn, hotel
das	**Gepäck**	luggage
das	**Hotel, -s**	hotel
das	**Kleingeld**	small change
das	**Mittagessen**	lunch
das	**Restaurant, -s**	restaurant
das	**Speisezimmer**	dining room
das	**(Tele)fax, -e**	fax
das	**Telefon, -e**	telephone
das	**Treppenhaus, -häuser**	staircase
das	**Wirtshaus, -häuser**	inn
das	**Zimmer**	room
das	**Zimmermädchen**	chambermaid

USEFUL PHRASES

einpacken to get packed; auspacken to get unpacked
ich habe schon gebucht I have already booked
eine Reservierung bestätigen to confirm a reservation
sich in einem Hotel anmelden to book in at a hotel
ich möchte hier übernachten I'd like a room for the night here
ein Formular ausfüllen to fill in a form
3 Tage bleiben to stay for 3 days

IMPORTANT WORDS *(masculine)*

der	**Aufenthalt, -e**	stay
der	**Aufzug, -̈e**	lift
der	**Balkon, -s** *or* **-e**	balcony
der	**Blick, -e**	view
der	**Empfangschef, -s**	receptionist, reception clerk
der	**Feuerlöscher**	fire extinguisher
der	**Gepäckträger**	porter
der	**Hotelier, -s**	hotelier, hotel-keeper
der	**Mehrwertsteuer**	value added tax
der	**Prospekt, -e**	leaflet, brochure
der	**Reiseführer**	guide-book; travel guide *(person)*
der	**Reiseleiter**	travel courier
der	**Stern, -e**	star

IMPORTANT WORDS *(feminine)*

die	**Aussicht, -en**	view
die	**Empfangsdame, -n**	receptionist
die	**Garderobe, -n**	cloakroom
die	**Gaststätte, -n**	restaurant; pub
die	**Kneipe, -n**	pub
die	**Nummer, -n**	number
die	**Rezeption, -en**	reception, reception desk
die	**Terrasse, -n**	terrace
die	**Unterkunft, -künfte**	accommodation
die	**Veranstaltung, -en**	organization

USEFUL WORDS (*masculine*)

der	**Brand, -̈e**	fire
der	**(Gast)wirt, -e**	owner, innkeeper, landlord
der	**Ober**	waiter
der	**Oberkellner**	head waiter

USEFUL WORDS (*feminine*)

| die | **(Gast)wirtin** | owner, innkeeper, landlady |
| die | **Vorhalle, -n** | foyer |

USEFUL WORDS (*neuter*)

das	**Foyer**	foyer
das	**Kellergeschoss, -e**	basement
das	**Schwimmbecken**	swimming pool
das	**Stockwerk, -e**	floor, storey
das	**Trinkgeld, -er**	tip
das	**Wechselgeld**	change
das	**Zweibettzimmer**	twin-bedded room

USEFUL PHRASES

ich möchte ein Zimmer mit Dusche/mit Bad I'd like a room with a shower/with a bath

was kostet es?, wie teuer ist es? how much is it?

das ist ziemlich teuer that is rather expensive

das Zimmer hat Aussicht *or* Blick auf den Strand the room overlooks the beach

im ersten/zehnten Stock on the first/tenth floor

im Erdgeschoss on the ground floor, on ground level

Herr Ober! waiter!

Fräulein! excuse me, miss!

„Bedienung inbegriffen" "service included"

„inklusive Bedienung" "inclusive of service"

„Sie brauchen nur zu klingeln" "just ring"

„Zimmer frei" "vacancies"

ESSENTIAL WORDS *(masculine)*

der	Bungalow, -s	bungalow
der	Flur, -e	(entrance) hall
der	(Fuß)boden, ̈	floor
der	Garten, ̈	garden
der	Haushalt	household
der	Hof, ̈e	yard
der	Keller	cellar
der	Mieter	tenant
der	Park, -s	public park
der	Parkplatz, ̈e	parking space
der	Raum, Räume	room; space
der	Schlüssel	key
der	Speisesaal, -säle	dining room
der	Stein, -e	stone
der	Stock, Stockwerke	floor, storey

ESSENTIAL WORDS *(feminine)*

die	Adresse, -n	address
die	Dusche, -n	shower
die	Familie, -n	family
die	Garage, -n	garage
die	Hausfrau, -en	housewife
die	Haustür, -en	front door
die	Küche, -n	kitchen; cooking
die	Miete, -n	rent
die	Stadt, ̈e	town
die	Straße, -n	street, road
die	Toilette, -n	toilet
die	Treppe, -n	stairs, staircase
die	Tür, -en	door
die	Wand, ̈e	*(inside)* wall
die	Wohnung, -en	flat

USEFUL PHRASES

in der Stadt/auf dem Lande wohnen to live in the town/in the country
mieten to rent; bauen to build; besitzen to own

ESSENTIAL WORDS (neuter)

das	Bad, ̈-er; das Badezimmer	bathroom
das	Doppelhaus, -häuser	semi-detached (house)
das	Dorf, ̈-er	village
das	Einfamilienhaus, -häuser	detached house
das	Erdgeschoss, -e	ground floor, ground level
das	Esszimmer	dining room
das	Fenster	window
das	Haus, Häuser	house
das	Klo, das Klosett	toilet, loo
das	Reihenhaus, -häuser	terraced house
das	Schlafzimmer	bedroom
das	Schloss, ̈-er	lock
das	Treppenhaus	staircase
das	Wohnzimmer	lounge, living room
das	Zentrum, Zentren	centre
das	Zimmer	room

IMPORTANT WORDS (neuter)

das	Dach, ̈-er	roof
das	Gebäude	building
das	Gebiet, -e	area
das	Hochhaus, -häuser	high-rise (building)
die	Möbel (pl)	furniture
das	Möbel(stück)	piece of furniture
das	Parkett, -e	wooden or parquet floor
das	Tor, -e	gate

USEFUL WORDS (neuter)

das	Arbeitszimmer	study
das	Dachfenster	skylight
das	Gästezimmer	spare room, guest room
das	Kellergeschoss, -e	basement
das	Oberlicht, -er	skylight
das	Stockwerk, -e	floor, storey

IMPORTANT WORDS *(masculine)*

der **Aufzug, -̈e**	lift
der **Balkon, -s** *or* **-e**	balcony
der **Bezirk, -e**	district
der **Dachboden, -̈**	attic, loft
der **Einwohner**	inhabitant
der **Gang, -̈e**	corridor
der **Kamin, -e**	chimney; fireplace
der **Landkreis, -e**	region
der **Nachbar, -n**	neighbour
der **Rasen**	lawn; grass
der **Vorort, -e**	suburb

IMPORTANT WORDS *(feminine)*

die **Anlage, -n**	layout
die **Aussicht, -en**	view
die **Decke, -n**	ceiling
die **Gegend, -en**	district, area
die **Kohle, -n**	coal
die **Lage, -n**	position, situation
die **Mauer, -n**	*(outside)* wall
die **Nachbarin**	neighbour
die **Telefonnummer, -n**	phone number
die **Terrasse, -n**	patio
die **Türklingel, -n**	doorbell
die **Umgebung, -en**	surroundings *(pl)*
die **Zentralheizung, -en**	central heating

USEFUL PHRASES

es klopft somebody's knocking at the door
es klingelt somebody's ringing the doorbell
im ersten/dritten Stock on the first/third floor
im Erdgeschoss on the ground floor, on ground level
oben upstairs; unten downstairs
zu Hause, daheim at home
umziehen to move (house); einziehen to move in
sich einleben to settle down, settle in

USEFUL WORDS (masculine)

der	Besitzer	owner
der	(Fenster)laden, ⸚e	shutter
der or das	(Fenster)sims, -e	window sill or ledge
der	Hausmeister	caretaker
der	Hauswirt, -e	landlord
der or das	Kaminsims, -e	mantelpiece
der	Korridor, -e	corridor
der	Rauch	smoke
der	Schornstein, -e	chimney
der	(Treppen)absatz, ⸚e	landing
der	Umzug, ⸚e	removal
der	Wintergarten, ⸚	conservatory
der	Wohnblock, -s	block of flats
der	Zaun, Zäune	fence

USEFUL WORDS (feminine)

die	Allee, -n	avenue
die	Antenne, -n	aerial
die	Einrichtung, -en	furnishings (pl)
die	Etagenwohnung, -en	flat
die	Fensterscheibe, -n	window pane
die	Fliese, -n	tile
die	Gasse, -n	lane (in town)
die	Hecke, -n	hedge
die	Jalousie, -n	venetian blind
die	Kachel, -n	(wall) tile
die	Kellerwohnung, -en	basement flat
die	Mansarde, -n	attic
die	Putzfrau, -en	cleaner
die	Rumpelkammer, -n	box room, junk room
die	Stube, -n	room
die	(Tür)stufe, -n	(door)step
die	Verandatür, -en	French window
die	(Wohn)siedlung, -en	housing estate

ESSENTIAL WORDS *(masculine)*

der	**Briefkasten, ⸚**	letterbox
der	**Fernsehapparat, -e** *or*	television set
	der **Fernseher**	
der	**Föhn, -e**	hair-drier
der	**Knopf, ⸚e**	knob, button
der	**Kühlschrank, ⸚e**	fridge
der	**Schalter**	switch
der	**Schrank, ⸚e**	cupboard
der	**Topf, ⸚e**	pot
der	**Wecker**	alarm clock

ESSENTIAL WORDS *(feminine)*

die	**Bürste, -n**	brush
die	**Dusche, -n**	shower
die	**Farbe, -n**	paint; colour
die	**Gardine, -n**	curtain
die	**Hausarbeit**	housework
die	**Kanne, -n**	jug; pot
die	**Lampe, -n**	lamp
die	**Sachen** *(pl)*	things
die	**Seife**	soap
die	**Zahnbürste, -n**	toothbrush
die	**Zahncreme, -s** *or*	toothpaste
	die **Zahnpasta, -pasten**	

ESSENTIAL WORDS *(neuter)*

das	**Bild, -er**	picture, painting
das	**Handtuch, ⸚er**	towel
das	**Licht, -er**	light
das	**Poster**	poster
das	**Wasser**	water

USEFUL PHRASES

die Hausarbeit machen to do the housework
duschen to have a shower; baden to have a bath

IMPORTANT WORDS (masculine)

der	Abfall, ⸚e	rubbish, refuse
der	Abfalleimer	rubbish bin
der	Aschenbecher	ashtray
der	Haartrockner	hair-drier
der	Kamm, ⸚e	comb
der	Rasierapparat, -e	razor
der	Spiegel	mirror
der	Teppich, -e	carpet
der	Vorhang, ⸚e	curtain
der	(Wasser)hahn, ⸚e	tap

IMPORTANT WORDS (feminine)

die	(Bade)wanne, -n	bath
die	(Bett)decke, -n	blanket, cover
die	Bettwäsche	bed linen
die	Birne, -n	(light) bulb
die	Bratpfanne, -n	frying pan
die	Elektrizität	electricity
die	Kerze, -n	candle

IMPORTANT WORDS (neuter)

das	Federbett, -en	continental quilt
das	Feuer	fire
das	Gas	gas
das	Geschirr	crockery; pots and pans
das	Kissen	cushion; pillow
das	Kopfkissen	pillow
das	Putzen	cleaning
das	Rezept, -e	recipe
das	Shampoo, -s	shampoo
das	Spülbecken	sink
das	Tablett, -e	tray
das	Waschbecken	washbasin

USEFUL WORDS (*masculine*)

der **Besen**	broom
der **Bettvorleger**	bedside rug
der **Dampfkochtopf, ⁻e**	pressure cooker
der **Deckel**	lid
der **Eimer**	bucket
der **Griff, -e**	handle (*of door etc*)
der **Handbesen** or der **Handfeger**	brush
der **Heizkörper**	radiator
der **Henkel**	handle (*of jug etc*)
der **Kachelofen, ⁻**	tiled stove
der **Kessel**	kettle
der **Kleiderbügel**	coat hanger
der **Krug, ⁻e**	jug
der **Mixer**	(electric) blender
der **Müll**	rubbish, refuse
der **Mülleimer**	dustbin
der **Papierkorb, ⁻e**	waste paper basket
der **Pinsel**	paintbrush; brush
der **Rasierpinsel**	shaving brush
der **Schmutz**	dirt
der **Schneebesen**	whisk, egg beater
der **Schwamm, ⁻e**	sponge
der **Staub**	dust
der **Staubsauger**	vacuum cleaner, Hoover®
der **Teppichboden, ⁻**	fitted carpet
der **Toaster**	toaster
der **Ziergegenstand, ⁻e**	ornament

USEFUL PHRASES

sein eigenes Zimmer haben to have a room of one's own
die Tür aufmachen/zumachen, die Tür öffnen/schließen to open/
   close the door
das Zimmer betreten to go into the room
putzen to clean; abstauben to dust; staubsaugen to hoover
bürsten to brush; waschen to wash; bügeln to iron

USEFUL WORDS (feminine)

die	Brücke, -n	(narrow) rug
die	Daunendecke, -n	eiderdown
die	Fußmatte, -n	doormat
die	Heizdecke, -n	electric blanket
die	Kaffeemühle, -n	coffee grinder
die	Leiter, -n	ladder
die	Matte, -n	mat
die	Nackenrolle, -n	bolster
die	Rasierklinge, -n	razor blade
die	Röhre, -n	pipe
die	Rührmaschine, -n	(electric) mixer
die	Satellitenantenne, -n	satellite dish
die	Steppdecke, -n	(continental) quilt
die	Tapete, -n	wallpaper
die	Vase, -n	vase
die	Waage, -n	(set of) scales
die	Wäscheschleuder, -n	spin dryer

USEFUL WORDS (neuter)

das	Abwaschtuch, ̈-er	dish cloth
das	Bügelbrett, -er	ironing board or table
das	Bügeleisen	iron
das	Dampfbügeleisen	steam iron
das	Gemälde	painting, picture
das	Geschirrtuch, ̈-er	dish cloth; tea towel
das	Polster	cushion; pillow
das	Rohr, -e	pipe
das	Seifenpulver	soap powder
das	Staubtuch, ̈-er	duster

ESSENTIAL WORDS *(masculine)*

der	Absender (Abs.)	sender
der	Anruf, -e	telephone call
der	Bescheid, -e	information
der	Brief, -e	letter
der	Briefkasten, ˸	postbox, pillar box
der	Briefträger	postman
der	Cent, -s	cent
der	Euro, -s	euro
der	Fernsprecher	telephone
der	Geldbeutel	purse
der	Kugelschreiber; der **Kuli**, -s	ballpoint pen, Biro®
der	Kurs, -e	rate
der	Name, -n	name
der	Polizist, -en	policeman
der	Preis, -e	price, cost
der	(Reise)scheck, -s	(traveller's) cheque
der	Schalter	counter
der	(Telefon)hörer	(telephone) receiver
der	Umschlag, ˸e	envelope
der	Vorname, -n	first name, Christian name

USEFUL PHRASES

entschuldigen Sie bitte – wo ist der nächste Briefkasten? **excuse me – where is the nearest postbox?**

kennst du dich hier aus? **do you know this place (well)?**

wo bekomme ich Auskunft? **where can I get some information?**

ist es (nach Bremen) noch weit? **do we have far to go (to Bremen)?**

wie komme ich zum Bahnhof? **how do I get to the station?**

geradeaus **straight on**

die erste Straße links **the first street on the left**

die dritte Straße rechts **the third street on the right**

links/rechts abbiegen **to turn left/right**

2 Kilometer nördlich der Stadtmitte **2 kilometres north of the town centre**

ESSENTIAL WORDS *(feminine)*

die	Adresse, -n *or* die Anschrift, -en	address
die	Ansichtskarte, -n	picture postcard
die	Auskunft, -̈e	information; directory enquiries
die	Bank, -en	bank
die	Bezahlung, -en	payment
die	Briefkarte, -n	letter card
die	Briefmarke, -n	(postage) stamp
die	Einladung, -en	invitation
die	E-Mail, -s	e-mail
die	(Hand)tasche, -n	(hand)bag
die	Kasse, -n	cash desk; check-out; till
die	Münze, -n	coin
die	Polizei	police
die	Polizeiwache, -n	police station
die	Polizistin	policewoman
die	Post	post, mail
die	Postkarte, -n	postcard
die	Reparatur, -en	repair, repairing
die	Rückgabe, -n	return
die	SIM-Karte, -n	SIM card
die	SMS	text message
die	Sparkasse, -n	savings bank
die	Taste, -n	(push-)button
die	Telefonzelle, -n	callbox, telephone box
die	Unterschrift, -en	signature
die	Vorwahlnummer, -n	dialling code
die	Wechselstube, -n	bureau de change

USEFUL PHRASES

ich habe meine Tasche verloren – hat jemand sie gefunden? **I've lost my bag
  – has anyone found it?**
beschreiben **to describe**
liegen lassen **to leave behind**; klauen **to pinch**
ein Formular ausfüllen **to fill in a form**
der Bank *(dat)* Bescheid sagen **to inform the bank**

ESSENTIAL WORDS (neuter)

das	**Briefpapier, -e**	writing paper
das	**Fax(gerät), -e**	fax
das	**Formular, -e**	form
das	**Fundbüro, -s**	lost property office
das	**Handy, -s**	mobile phone
das	**Kleingeld**	small change
das	**Mobiltelefon, -e**	mobile phone
das	**Päckchen**	package, (*small*) parcel
das	**Paket, -e**	parcel, package
das	**Portemonnaie, -s**	purse
das	**Postamt, ̈er**	post office
das	**Postwertzeichen**	postage stamp
das	**Problem, -e**	problem
das	**Scheckheft, -e**	cheque book
das	**Telefon, -e**	telephone
das	**Telefonbuch, ̈er**	telephone directory
das	**Verkehrsamt, ̈er**	tourist information office

USEFUL PHRASES

einen Brief schreiben to write a letter
aufgeben to send, post; senden, schicken to send
zur Post gehen to go to the post office
den Brief einwerfen to post the letter (in postbox)
ein Paket aufgeben to hand in a parcel
faxen to fax
einige Briefmarken kaufen to buy some stamps
was ist das Porto für einen Brief nach Schottland? how much is a letter
   to Scotland?
3 Briefmarken zu 80 Cent 3 80-cent stamps
ist Post für mich da? is there any mail for me?
erwarten to expect
bekommen, erhalten to get, receive
zurückschicken to send back
mit Luftpost by airmail
portofrei freepost; postlagernd poste restante

IMPORTANT WORDS (*masculine*)

der	Anschluss, ¨-e	(telephone) extension
der	Fehler	fault; mistake, error
der	ISDN-Anschluss, ¨-e	ISDN connection
der	Luftpostbrief, -e	airmail letter
der	Personalausweis, -e	identity card
der	Postbeamte, -n	counter clerk
der	Zeuge, -n	witness

IMPORTANT WORDS (*feminine*)

die	(Bank)note, -n	(bank)note
die	Beschreibung, -en	description
die	Brieftasche, -n	wallet
die	Faxnummer, -n	fax number
die	Geldstrafe, -n	fine
die	Heimat, -en	home (town/country *etc*)
die	Leerung, -en	collection (*of mail*)
die	Luftpost	airmail
die	Nummer, -n	number
die	Postbeamtin	counter clerk
die	Postgebühr, -en	postage
die	Prepaidkarte, -n	prepaid card
die	Scheckkarte, -n	cheque card
die	Telefonnummer, -n	phone number
die	Verabredung, -en	date, appointment
die	Verbindung, -en	line, connection
die	Währung, -en	currency

USEFUL PHRASES

ich möchte einen Scheck einlösen I'd like to cash a cheque
unterschreiben to sign
ich möchte Pfunde (in Euro) umtauschen I'd like to change some pounds
  (into euros)
können Sie mir ein Euro wechseln? can you give me change of a euro?
wie viel Geld willst du wechseln? how much money do you want to change?
ich habe kein Kleingeld I don't have any (small) change
bar bezahlen to pay in cash
ein Scheck über 100 Pfund a cheque for £100

IMPORTANT WORDS *(neuter)*

das	**Bargeld**	cash
das	**Ferngespräch, -e**	trunk call
das	**Geschlecht, -er**	sex
das	**Missverständnis, -se**	misunderstanding
das	**Ortsgespräch, -e**	local call
das	**Pfund Sterling**	pound sterling
das	**R-Gespräch, -e**	reverse-charge call
das	**Telefongespräch, -e**	phone call
das	**Telegramm, -e**	telegram, cable
das	**Termin, -e**	*(doctor's etc)* appointment

USEFUL PHRASES

jdn anrufen, mit jdm telefonieren to phone *or* call sb
den Hörer abheben to lift the receiver
ein R-Gespräch führen to make a reverse-charge call
die Nummer suchen/wählen to look up/dial the number
können Sie mir die Vorwahlnummer sagen? can you tell me the dialling code?
drücken to press
das Telefon läutet the phone rings
wer ist am Apparat? who's speaking?
hallo, hier ist ... hello, this is ...
kann ich Peter sprechen? could I speak to Peter?
bleiben Sie am Apparat hold on, please
eine Nachricht hinterlassen to leave a message
besetzt engaged; außer Betrieb out of order
Sie sind falsch verbunden you have the wrong number
ich habe mich verwählt I dialled the wrong number
danke für den Anruf thank you for calling
ich rufe Sie zurück I'll call you back
die Verbindung ist sehr schlecht it's a bad line
den Hörer auflegen *or* einhängen to replace the receiver
mailen to e-mail; simsen to text
eine SMS-Nachricht schicken to send a text message

USEFUL WORDS *(masculine)*

der	**Einschreibebrief, -e**	registered letter
der	**Empfänger**	addressee
der	**Stempel**	postmark

USEFUL WORDS *(feminine)*

die	**Blockschrift**	block capitals *(pl)*
die	**Drucksache, -n**	printed matter
die	**Kaution, -en**	deposit
die	**Postanweisung, -en**	postal order
die	**Postleitzahl, -en**	postcode
die	**Steuer, -n**	tax

USEFUL WORDS *(neuter)*

das	**Branchenverzeichnis, -se**	Yellow Pages® *(pl)*
das	**Einschreiben**	registered letter
das	**Einwickelpapier**	wrapping paper
das	**Konto, Konten**	account
das	**Packpapier**	brown paper, wrapping paper
das	**Porto**	postage

USEFUL PHRASES

sprechen Sie Englisch? **do you speak English?**
was heißt das auf Deutsch? **what's that in German?**
könnten Sie das bitte wiederholen? **could you repeat that please?**
verstehen, kapieren **to understand**
wie schreibt man das? **how do you spell that?**
soll ich das buchstabieren? **shall I spell that for you?**
Lieber Franz **Dear Franz;** Liebe Bettina **Dear Bettina**
Sehr geehrter Herr Müller **Dear Mr Müller;** Sehr geehrte Frau Brown
  Dear Mrs Brown
Sehr geehrte Damen und Herren **Dear Sir** *or* **Madam**
Mit freundlichen Grüßen **Yours sincerely**
Viele Grüße **Love, Best wishes**
Hochachtungsvoll **Yours faithfully**

ESSENTIAL WORDS (*masculine*)

der **Ausweis, -e**	identity card
der **Polizist, -en**	policeman
der **Reisescheck, -s**	traveller's cheque
der **Scheck, -s**	cheque
der **Terrorismus**	terrorism

ESSENTIAL WORDS (*feminine*)

die **Auskunft, ⸚e**	information; particulars (*pl*)
die **Ausweiskarte, -n**	identity card
die **Bank, -en**	bank
die **Polizei**	police
die **Polizistin**	policewoman
die **Tasche, -n**	bag

ESSENTIAL WORDS (*neuter*)

das **Fundbüro, -s**	lost property office
das **Geld, -er**	money
das **Portemonnaie, -s**	purse

USEFUL PHRASES

verunglücken to have an accident
jdn überfahren to run sb over
verletzt injured; verwundet wounded
betrunken drunk
Notruf (110) emergency phone number
versichert sein to be insured
Hilfe! help!; haltet den Dieb! stop thief!
Feuer! fire!; Hände hoch! hands up!
Angst haben to be afraid
stehlen to steal; klauen to pinch; rauben to rob
eine Bank überfallen to rob a bank
entführen to kidnap; to hijack
verschwinden to disappear
die Polizei rufen to send for the police
retten to rescue; entkommen to escape; strafen to punish

IMPORTANT WORDS *(masculine)*

der	**Bandit, -en**	bandit
der	**Demonstrant, -en**	demonstrator
der	**Detektiv, -e**	detective
der	**Dieb, -e**	thief
der	**Diebstahl, ̈-e**	theft
der	**Entführer**	kidnapper; hijacker
der	**Gangster, -s**	gangster
die	**Geschworenen** *(pl)*	jury
der	**Privatdetektiv, -e**	private detective
der	**Retter**	rescuer
der	**Revolver**	gun, revolver
der	**Rowdy, -s**	hooligan
der	**Sicherheitsbeamte, -n**	security guard
der	**Streit, -e**	argument, dispute
der	**Taschendieb, -e**	pickpocket
der	**Terrorist, -en**	terrorist
	Tote(r), -n	dead man/woman
der	**Überfall, ̈-e**	raid; attack
der	**Unfall, ̈-e**	accident
der	**Zeuge, -n**	witness

IMPORTANT WORDS *(neuter)*

das	**Bargeld**	cash, ready money
das	**Gefängnis, -se**	prison
das	**Gericht, -e**	court
das	**Gesetz, -e**	law
das	**Recht, -e**	right

USEFUL PHRASES

demonstrieren to demonstrate
ein Gebäude (in die Luft) sprengen to blow up a building
erschießen to shoot (dead)
töten to kill; ermorden to murder
verhaften to arrest; ins Gefängnis kommen to go to jail
schuldig guilty; unschuldig innocent

IMPORTANT WORDS (feminine)

die	**Armee, -n**	army
die	**Atomwaffe, -n**	atomic weapon
die	**Bande, -n**	band, gang
die	**Beschreibung, -en**	description
die	**Bombe, -n**	bomb
die	**Brieftasche, -n**	wallet
die	**Demonstrantin**	demonstrator
die	**Demonstration, -en**	demonstration
die	**Diebin**	thief
die	**Droge, -n**	drug
die	**Erlaubnis, -se**	permission; permit
die	**Gefahr, -en**	danger, risk
die	**Geldstrafe, -n**	fine
die	**Notdienste** (pl)	emergency services
die	**Pflicht, -en**	duty
die	**Pistole, -n**	gun, pistol
die	**Rettung, -en**	rescue
die	**Terroristin**	terrorist
die	**Todesstrafe, -n**	death penalty
die	**Untersuchung, -en**	inquiry, investigation
die	**Zeugin**	witness

USEFUL WORDS (neuter)

das	**Gewehr, -e**	gun, rifle
das	**Heer, -e**	army
das	**Rauschgift, -e**	drug
das	**(Todes)urteil, -e**	(death) sentence
das	**Verbrechen**	crime
das	**Zuchthaus, -häuser**	(top-security) prison

USEFUL WORDS *(masculine)*

der	Beweis, -e	evidence, proof
der	Brand, ̈e	fire
der	Einbrecher	burglar
der	Einbruch, ̈e	burglary, break-in
der	Feind, -e	enemy
	Gefangene(r), -n	prisoner
der	Gefängniswärter	prison guard
der	Gerichtshof, ̈e	law court
der	Identitätsdiebstahl, ̈e	identity theft
der	Mord, -e	murder
der	Mörder	murderer, killer
der	Prozess, -e	trial, lawsuit
der	Raub	robbery
der	Räuber	robber
der	Raubüberfall, ̈e	robbery with violence
der	(Rechts)anwalt, ̈e	lawyer, barrister
der	Spion, -e	spy
der	Verbrecher	criminal
	Verdächtige(r), -n	suspect

USEFUL WORDS *(feminine)*

die	Alarmanlage, -n	burglar alarm
die	Belohnung, -en	reward
die	Fahrerflucht	hit-and-run driving
die	Festnahme, -n	arrest
die	Flucht, -en	escape
die	Haft	custody
die	Handschellen *(pl)*	handcuffs
die	Justiz	justice
die	Leiche, -n	corpse, body
die	(Polizei)wache, -n	police station
die	Regierung, -en	government
die	Schuld	guilt; fault
die	Unschuld	innocence
die	Verhaftung, -en	arrest
die	Versicherungspolice, -n	insurance policy

ESSENTIAL WORDS *(masculine)*

der	**Kaugummi**	chewing gum
der	**Stein, -e**	stone, rock

ESSENTIAL WORDS *(neuter)*

das	**Aluminium**	aluminium
das	**Benzin**	petrol
das	**Dieselöl**	diesel oil
das	**Gas**	gas
das	**Glas**	glass
das	**Gummiband, ̈-er**	rubber band; elastic
das	**Leder**	leather
das	**Öl, -e**	oil
das	**Papier, -e**	paper

USEFUL PHRASES

eine Baumwollbluse a cotton blouse

ein Seidenschal *(m)* a silk scarf

ein Holzstuhl *(m)* a wooden chair

ein Strohhut *(m)* a straw hat

ein Pelzmantel *(m)* a fur coat

ein Wollpullover *(m)* a woollen jumper

ein Pappkarton *(m)* a cardboard box

ein Lammfellmantel *(m)* a sheepskin coat

eine Tasche aus Leder a leather bag

die Tasche ist aus Leder the bag is made of leather

eine Vase aus Ton an earthenware vase

die Vase ist aus Ton the vase is made of earthenware

eisern, Eisen- iron

golden, Gold- gold, golden

hölzern, Holz- wooden

marmorn, Marmor- marble

silbern, Silber- silver

echt real, genuine

kostbar precious; teuer costly, expensive

IMPORTANT WORDS *(masculine)*

der	**Aufkleber**	sticker, label
der	**Denim**	denim
der	**Fleck, -e**	mark, spot
der	**Gips**	plaster; plaster of Paris
der	**Jeansstoff, -e**	denim
der	**Klebstoff, -e**	glue
der	**Kord**	cord, corduroy
der	**Kunststoff, -e**	synthetic
der	**Polyester**	polyester
der	**Stahl**	steel
der	**Stoff, -e**	cloth, material

IMPORTANT WORDS *(feminine)*

die	**Baumwolle**	cotton
die	**Bronze**	bronze
die	**Gebrauchsanweisung, -en**	directions for use *(pl)*
die	**Seide**	silk

IMPORTANT WORDS *(neuter)*

das	**Blei**	lead
das	**Gold**	gold
das	*or der* **Gummi**	rubber; gum
das	**Holz, -̈er**	wood
das	**Material, -ien**	material(s)
das	**Metall, -e**	metal
das	**Nylon**	nylon
das	**Petroleum**	paraffin
das	**Plastik**	plastic
das	**Seidenpapier**	tissue paper
das	**Silber**	silver
das	**Silberpapier**	silver paper
das	**Stroh**	straw
das	**Vinyl**	vinyl
das	**Wildleder**	suede

USEFUL WORDS (*masculine*)

der	**Backstein, -e**	brick
der	**Beton**	concrete
der	**Bindfaden, ⸚**	string
der	**Draht, ⸚e**	wire
der	**Faden, ⸚**	thread
der	**Kalk**	lime
der	**Karton, -s**	cardboard; cardboard box
der	**Kautschuk**	rubber (*substance*)
der	**Kleb(e)streifen**	adhesive tape
der	**Marmor**	marble
der	**Pelz, -e**	fur
der	**Samt**	velvet
der	**Satin**	satin
der	**Schaumgummi**	foam rubber
der	**Tesafilm**®	Sellotape®
der	**Ton**	clay
der	**Tweed**	tweed
der	**Zement**	cement
der	**Ziegelstein, -e** *or* der **Ziegel**	brick
der	**Zustand, ⸚e**	condition

USEFUL PHRASES

in gutem/schlechtem Zustand **in good/bad condition**
„trocken aufbewahren *or* lagern" **"keep dry"**
etw chemisch reinigen **to dry-clean sth**

USEFUL WORDS *(feminine)*

die	**Flüssigkeit, -en**	liquid
die	**Kohle**	coal
die	**Leinwand**	canvas
die	**Pappe, -n**	cardboard
die	**Plastikfolie, -n**	clingfilm
die	**Schnur, ̈e**	cord, string
die	**Spitze, -n**	lace
die	**Strickwaren** *(pl)*	knitwear
die	**Watte**	cotton wool
die	**Wolle**	wool

USEFUL WORDS *(neuter)*

das	**Acryl**	acrylic
das	**Blech**	tin
das	**Eisen**	iron
das	**Fell, -e**	fur, coat
das	**Kristall**	crystal
das	**Kupfer**	copper
das	**Leinen**	linen
das	**Messing**	brass
das	**Porzellan**	porcelain, china
das	**Schaffell**	sheepskin
das	**Segeltuch**	sailcloth, canvas
das	**Seil, -e**	rope; cable
das	**Stanniolpapier**	tinfoil
das	**Steingut**	earthenware
das	**Styropor**	polystyrene
das	**Wachs**	wax
das	**Zinn**	pewter; tin

ESSENTIAL + IMPORTANT WORDS *(masculine)*

der **Jazz**	jazz
der **Musiker**	musician
der **Triangel**	triangle
der **Zuhörer**	listener; *(pl)* audience

ESSENTIAL + IMPORTANT WORDS *(feminine)*

die **Blaskapelle, -n**	brass band
die **Blockflöte, -n**	recorder
die **Flöte, -n**	flute
die **Geige, -n**	violin, fiddle
die **Gitarre, -n**	guitar
die **Gruppe, -n**	group
die **Kapelle, -n**	band, orchestra
die **Klarinette, -n**	clarinet
die **Musik**	music
die **Note, -n**	note; *(pl)* music
die **Oboe, -n**	oboe
die **Taste, -n**	(piano) key
die **Trompete, -n**	trumpet

IMPORTANT WORDS *(neuter)*

das **Akkordeon, -s**	accordion
das **Bügelhorn, ⸚er**	bugle
das **Cello, -s** *or* **Celli**	cello
das **Horn, ⸚er**	horn
das **Klavier, -e**	piano
das **Konzert, -e**	concert; concerto
das **(Musik)instrument, -e**	(musical) instrument
das **Orchester**	orchestra; band
das **Saxophon, -e**	saxophone
das **Schlagzeug, -e**	drums *(pl)*
das **Xylophon, -e**	xylophone

USEFUL PHRASES

Klavier/Gitarre spielen to play the piano/the guitar
die Schlagermusik pop music; die klassische Musik classical music;
  die Blasmusik brass band music

USEFUL WORDS (masculine)

der Akkord, -e	chord
der Chor, ⁀e	choir; chorus
der Dirigent, -en	conductor
der Dudelsack, ⁀e	bagpipes (pl)
der Flügel	grand piano
der Kontrabass, -bässe	double bass
der Solist, -en	soloist
der Taktstock, -stöcke	(conductor's) baton
der Ton, ⁀e	note

USEFUL WORDS (feminine)

die Harfe, -n	harp
die Konzerthalle, -n	concert hall
die Mundharmonika, -s or -ken	mouth organ, harmonica
die Musikkapelle, -n	band (circus, military etc)
die Oper, -n	opera; opera house
die Orgel, -n	organ
die Posaune, -n	trombone
die Querflöte, -n	flute
die Saite, -n	string
die Solistin	soloist
die Tastatur, -en	keyboard
die Tonart, -en	(musical) key
die (große) Trommel, (-n) -n	(big, bass) drum
die Violine, -n	violin
die Ziehharmonika, -s	concertina; accordion

USEFUL WORDS (neuter)

das Becken	cymbals (pl)
das Fagott, -s or -e	bassoon
das Jagdhorn, ⁀er	bugle; hunting horn
das Opernhaus, -häuser	opera house
das Streichorchester	string orchestra
das Tamburin, -e	tambourine
das Violoncello, -s or -celli	violoncello
das Waldhorn, ⁀er	French horn

CARDINAL NUMBERS

nought	0	null
one	1	eins
two	2	zwei
three	3	drei
four	4	vier
five	5	fünf
six	6	sechs
seven	7	sieben
eight	8	acht
nine	9	neun
ten	10	zehn
eleven	11	elf
twelve	12	zwölf
thirteen	13	dreizehn
fourteen	14	vierzehn
fifteen	15	fünfzehn
sixteen	16	sechzehn
seventeen	17	siebzehn
eighteen	18	achtzehn
nineteen	19	neunzehn
twenty	20	zwanzig
twenty-one	21	einundzwanzig
twenty-two	22	zweiundzwanzig
twenty-three	23	dreiundzwanzig
thirty	30	dreißig
thirty-one	31	einunddreißig
thirty-two	32	zweiunddreißig
forty	40	vierzig
fifty	50	fünfzig
sixty	60	sechzig
seventy	70	siebzig
eighty	80	achtzig
ninety	90	neunzig
ninety-nine	99	neunundneunzig
a (*or* one) hundred	100	hundert

CARDINAL NUMBERS (*continued*)

a hundred and one	101	hunderteins
a hundred and two	102	hundertzwei
a hundred and ten	110	hundertzehn
a hundred and eighty-two	182	hundertzweiundachtzig
two hundred	200	zweihundert
two hundred and one	201	zweihunderteins
two hundred and two	202	zweihundertzwei
three hundred	300	dreihundert
four hundred	400	vierhundert
five hundred	500	fünfhundert
six hundred	600	sechshundert
seven hundred	700	siebenhundert
eight hundred	800	achthundert
nine hundred	900	neunhundert
a (*or* one) thousand	1000	(ein)tausend
a thousand and one	1001	tausendundeins
a thousand and two	1002	tausendundzwei
two thousand	2000	zweitausend
ten thousand	10 000	zehntausend
a (*or* one) hundred thousand	100 000	hunderttausend
a (*or* one) million	1 000 000	eine Million
two million	2 000 000	zwei Millionen

USEFUL PHRASES

1979 neunzehnhundertneunundsiebzig
2001 zweitausendundeins

gerade/ungerade Zahlen even/odd numbers
50 Prozent 50 per cent

ORDINAL NUMBERS

These can be masculine, feminine or neuter, and take the appropriate endings.

first	der Erste
second	der Zweite
third	der Dritte
fourth	der Vierte
fifth	der Fünfte
sixth	der Sechste
seventh	der Siebte
eighth	der Achte
ninth	der Neunte
tenth	der Zehnte
eleventh	der Elfte
twelfth	der Zwölfte
thirteenth	der Dreizehnte
fourteenth	der Vierzehnte
fifteenth	der Fünfzehnte
sixteenth	der Sechzehnte
seventeenth	der Siebzehnte
eighteenth	der Achtzehnte
nineteenth	der Neunzehnte
twentieth	der Zwanzigste
twenty-first	der Einundzwanzigste
twenty-second	der Zweiundzwanzigste
thirtieth	der Dreißigste
thirty-first	der Einunddreißigste
fortieth	der Vierzigste
fiftieth	der Fünfzigste
sixtieth	der Sechzigste
seventieth	der Siebzigste
eightieth	der Achtzigste
ninetieth	der Neunzigste
hundredth	der Hundertste
hundred and first	der Hunderterste
hundred and tenth	der Hundertzehnte

ORDINAL NUMBERS *(continued)*

two hundredth	der Zweihundertste
three hundredth	der Dreihundertste
four hundredth	der Vierhundertste
five hundredth	der Fünfhundertste
six hundredth	der Sechshundertste
seven hundredth	der Siebenhundertste
eight hundredth	der Achthundertste
nine hundredth	der Neunhundertste
thousandth	der Tausendste
two thousandth	der Zweitausendste
millionth	der Millionste
two millionth	der Zweimillionste

FRACTIONS

a half	halb, die Hälfte
one and a half kilos	eineinhalb Kilos, anderthalb Kilos
two and a half kilos	zweieinhalb Kilos
a third	ein Drittel *(nt)*
two thirds	zwei Drittel
a quarter	ein Viertel *(nt)*
three quarters	drei Viertel
a sixth	ein Sechstel *(nt)*
five and five sixths	fünf und fünf Sechstel
an eighth	ein Achtel *(nt)*
a twelfth	ein Zwölftel *(nt)*
a twentieth	ein Zwanzigstel *(nt)*
a hundredth	ein Hundertstel *(nt)*
a thousandth	ein Tausendstel *(nt)*
a millionth	ein Millionstel *(nt)*

USEFUL PHRASES

zum x-ten Mal for the umpteenth time
ein Millionär a millionaire
(0, 4) null Komma vier (0.4) nought point four
die Flasche war drei viertel leer the bottle was three-quarters empty

NUMBERS AND QUANTITIES

der	Becher (Joghurt)	pot (of yogurt)
ein	bisschen	a little (bit of)
die	Büchse, -n	tin, can
der	or das Deziliter	decilitre
das	Dutzend	dozen
	Dutzende von	dozens of
	etwas	a little (bit of)
das	Fass, ¨er	barrel
die	Flasche, -n (Wein)	bottle (of wine)
das	Glas, ¨er (Milch)	glass (of milk)
das	Glas, ¨er Marmelade	jar or pot of jam
eine	Halbe	a half (litre of beer etc)
ein	halbes Dutzend/ Pfund	half-a-dozen/-pound, a half dozen/pound
ein	halbes Kilo	half a kilo
ein	halber Liter	half a litre
die	Handvoll (Münzen)	handful (of coins)
der	Haufen	heap, pile
ein	Haufen	heaps of
	Hunderte von	hundreds of
	hundert Gramm Käse	a hundred grammes of cheese
die	Kanne, -n (Kaffee)	pot (of coffee)
das	Kilo(gramm)	kilo(gramme)
ein	Kleines	a half pint (of beer etc)
das	Knäuel Wolle or das Wollknäuel	ball of wool
der	or das Liter	litre
die	Menge, -n	crowd; heaps of
der	or das Meter (Stoff)	metre (of cloth)
das	Paar (Schuhe)	pair (of shoes)
das	Päckchen	packet
die	Packung Keks/ Zigaretten	packet of biscuits/ cigarettes
das	Pfund (Kartoffeln)	pound (of potatoes)
die	Portion, -en (Eis)	portion or helping (of ice cream)

NUMBERS AND QUANTITIES (continued)

der	**Riegel Seife**	cake or bar of soap
der	**Riegel Schokolade**	bar of chocolate, chocolate bar
die	**Schachtel, -n**	box; packet (of cigarettes)
die	**Schar, -en**	group, band
die	**Scheibe, -n (Brot)**	slice (of bread)
die	**Schüssel, -n**	bowl, dish
der	**Stapel**	pile
das	**Stück Zucker**	lump of sugar
das	**Stück Kuchen**	piece or slice of cake
das	**Stück Papier**	bit or piece of paper
die	**Tafel (-n) Schokolade**	bar of chocolate
die	**Tasse (voll)**	cup(ful)
	Tausende von	thousands of
der	**Teller**	plate
das	**Viertel(pfund)**	quarter(-pound)
ein	**wenig**	a little (bit) of
der	**Würfel Zucker**	lump of sugar
der	**Würfel Margarine**	half a pound of margarine (in cube shape)

USEFUL PHRASES
für das Dutzend/das Hundert/das Tausend per dozen/hundred/thousand,
  (for) a dozen/a hundred/a thousand

ESSENTIAL WORDS (*masculine*)

der **Artikel**	article
der **Ohrring, -e**	earring
der **Rasierapparat, -e**	razor
der **Ring, -e**	ring
der **Schlüsselring, -e**	key-ring
der **Schmuck**	jewellery

ESSENTIAL WORDS (*feminine*)

die **Armbanduhr, -en**	(wrist) watch
die **Haarbürste, -n**	hairbrush
die **Halskette, -n**	necklace
die **Kette, -n**	chain
die **Rasiercreme, -s**	shaving cream
die **Sache, -n**	thing
die **Schönheit**	beauty
die **Seife, -n**	soap
die **Zahnbürste, -n**	toothbrush
die **Zahnpasta, -pasten**	toothpaste

ESSENTIAL + IMPORTANT WORDS (*neuter*)

das **Armband, ̈er**	bracelet
das **Deo, -s**	deodorant
das **Gold**	gold
das **Haarwaschmittel**	shampoo
das **Handtuch, ̈er**	towel
das **Juwel, -en**	jewel; (*pl*) jewels, jewellery
das **Make-up**	foundation; make-up
das **Parfüm, -s** *or* **-e**	perfume, scent
das **Rasierwasser**	after-shave
das **Shampoo, -s**	shampoo
das **Silber**	silver
das **Taschengeld**	pocket money
das **Toilettenwasser**	toilet water

USEFUL PHRASES

baden to have a bath; duschen to have a shower
sich die Zähne putzen to brush one's teeth

IMPORTANT WORDS (masculine)

der	Ehering, -e	wedding ring
der	Gesichtspuder	face powder
der	Kamm, ⁻e	comb
der	Schönheitssalon, -s	beauty salon
der	Spiegel	mirror
der	Tampon, -s	tampon

IMPORTANT WORDS (feminine)

die	(Damen)binde	sanitary towel
die	Gesichtscreme, -s	face cream
die	Kosmetik	cosmetics (pl), make-up
die	Perle, -n	pearl; bead
die	Perlenkette, -n	beads, string of beads

USEFUL WORDS (masculine)

der	Anhänger	pendant
der	Edelstein, -e	gem, precious stone
der	Lidschatten	eyeshadow
der	Lippenstift, -e	lipstick
der	Lockenwickler	curler, roller
der	Nagellack	nail varnish, nail polish
der	Nagellackentferner	nail varnish remover
der	Trauring, -e	wedding ring
der	Waschbeutel	toilet bag
der	Waschlappen	face flannel

USEFUL WORDS (feminine)

die	Brosche, -n	brooch
die	Frisur, -en	hairstyle
die	Krawattennadel, -n	tie-pin
die	Perücke, -n	wig
die	Puderdose, -n	(powder) compact
die	Schminke, -n	make-up
die	Wimperntusche	mascara

USEFUL PHRASES

sich rasieren to shave; kämmen to comb; bürsten to brush

ESSENTIAL WORDS *(masculine)*

der	**Baum, Bäume**	tree
der	**Blumentopf, ¨e**	flower pot
der	**Garten, ¨**	garden
der	**Gärtner**	gardener
der	**Gemüsegarten, ¨**	vegetable garden
der	**Grund**	ground
der	**Obstgarten, ¨**	orchard
der	**Regen**	rain
der	**Sonnenschein**	sunshine
der	**Stein, -e**	stone, rock

ESSENTIAL WORDS *(feminine)*

die	**Biene, -n**	bee
die	**Blume, -n**	flower
die	**Erde, -n**	earth, soil
die	**(Garten)bank, ¨e**	(garden) seat *or* bench
die	**Gartentür, -en**	garden gate
die	**Rose, -n**	rose
die	**Sonne**	sun
die	**Wespe, -n**	wasp

ESSENTIAL WORDS *(neuter)*

das	**Blatt, ¨er**	leaf
das	**Gärtnern**	gardening
das	**Gemüse**	vegetable(s)
das	**Gras**	grass

USEFUL PHRASES

Blumen pflanzen to plant flowers
die Pflanzen wachsen the plants grow
gießen to water
pflücken to pick
ein Strauß Rosen/Veilchen, ein Rosenstrauß/Veilchenstrauß
   a bunch of roses/violets

IMPORTANT WORDS *(masculine)*

der	Boden, ⁝	ground, soil
der	Busch, ⁝e	bush, shrub
der	Krokus, - *or* -se	crocus
der	Pfad, -e	path
der	Rasen	lawn; turf
der	Schatten	shadow; shade
der	Stamm, ⁝e	trunk
der	Steingarten, ⁝	rockery, rock garden
der	Weg, -e	path
der	Wurm, ⁝er	worm

IMPORTANT WORDS *(feminine)*

die	Chrysantheme, -n	chrysanthemum
die	Dahlie, -n	dahlia
die	Hütte, -n	hut, shed
die	Hyazinthe, -n	hyacinth
die	Lilie, -n	lily
die	Orchidee, -n	orchid
die	Pflanze, -n	plant
die	Sonnenblume, -n	sunflower
die	Tulpe, -n	tulip

IMPORTANT WORDS *(neuter)*

das	Gartenhaus, -häuser	summerhouse
das	Laub(werk)	leaves *(pl)*, foliage
das	Unkraut	weed(s)
das	Werkzeug, -e	tool

USEFUL PHRASES

den Garten umgraben to dig the garden
den Rasen mähen to mow the lawn
im Schatten eines Baumes in the shade of a tree
im Schatten bleiben to stay in the shade
allerlei Pflanzen all kinds of plants
hier duftet es (gut) what a nice smell there is here

USEFUL WORDS (*masculine*)

der	**Ast, ̈-e**	branch
der	**Baumstamm, ̈-e**	tree trunk
der	**Blumenstrauß, (-sträuße)**	bunch *or* bouquet of flowers
der	**Dorn, -en**	thorn
der	**Duft, ̈-e**	perfume, scent
der	**Efeu**	ivy
der	**Flieder**	lilac
der	**Goldlack**	wallflower
der	**Halm, -e**	stalk, blade
der	**Löwenzahn**	dandelion
der	**Mohn, -e**	poppy
der	**Rasenmäher**	lawnmower
der	**Rosenstock, ̈-e**	rose bush
der	**Samen**	seed(s)
der	**Schlauch, Schläuche**	garden hose
der	**Schmetterling, -e**	butterfly
der	**Schubkarren**	wheelbarrow
der	**Stachel, -n**	thorn
der	**Stängel; der Stiel, -e**	stalk, stem
der	**Strauch, Sträucher**	shrub
der	**Strauß, Sträuße**	bunch *or* bouquet (of flowers)
der	**Tau**	dew
der	**Weiher**	pond
der	**Wintergarten, ̈**	conservatory
der	**Zaun, Zäune**	fence
der	**Zweig, -e**	branch

USEFUL PHRASES

Unkraut jäten to do the weeding
die Hecke schneiden to cut the hedge
die Blätter zusammenharken to rake up the leaves
umzäunt fenced in
sonnig sunny; schattig shady

USEFUL WORDS (feminine)

die	Beere, -n	berry
die	Blüte, -n	blossom
die	Butterblume, -n	buttercup
die	Gartenwicke, -n	sweet pea
die	Gießkanne, -n	watering can
die	Hacke, -n	hoe
die	Harke, -n	rake
die	Hecke, -n	hedge
die	Heckenschere, -n	hedge-cutters, garden shears
die	Hortensie, -n	hydrangea
die	Knospe, -n	bud
die	Leiter, -n	ladder
die	Margerite, -n	daisy
die	Narzisse, -n	narcissus, daffodil
die	Nelke, -n	carnation
die	Osterglocke, -n	daffodil
die	Pforte, -n	(garden) gate
die	Primel, -n	primrose
die	Rabatte, -n	border, flower bed
die	Walze, -n	roller
die	Wurzel, -n	root

USEFUL WORDS (neuter)

das	Blumenbeet, -e	flowerbed
das	Gänseblümchen	daisy
das	Geißblatt	honeysuckle
das	Gewächshaus, -häuser	greenhouse
das	Maiglöckchen	lily of the valley
das	Schneeglöckchen	snowdrop
das	Stiefmütterchen	pansy
das	Veilchen	violet
das	Vergissmeinnicht, -e	forget-me-not

ESSENTIAL WORDS *(masculine)*

der	**Ausflug, ⸚e**	trip, outing
der	**Badeanzug, ⸚e**	swimming *or* bathing costume
der	**Bikini, -s**	bikini
der	**Dampfer**	steamer
der	**Fahrgast, ⸚e**	passenger
der	**Fisch, -e**	fish
der	**Fischer**	fisherman
der	**Hafen, ⸚**	port, harbour
der	**Passagier, -e**	passenger
der	**Schwimmer**	swimmer
der	**Seehafen, ⸚**	seaport
der	**Seemann, (-leute)**	sailor, seaman
der	**Sonnenschein**	sunshine
der	**Spaziergang, ⸚e**	walk
der	**Stein, -e**	stone
der	**Strand, ⸚e**	shore, beach
der	**Urlauber**	holiday-maker

ESSENTIAL WORDS *(feminine)*

die	**Ansichtskarte, -n**	postcard
die	**Badehose, -n**	swimming *or* bathing trunks
die	**Fähre, -n**	ferry
die	**Hafenstadt, ⸚e**	port
die	**Insel, -n**	island
die	**Mannschaft, -en**	crew
die	**Schwimmerin**	swimmer
die	**See, -n**	sea
die	**Seekrankheit**	seasickness
die	**Seeluft**	sea air
die	**Sonne**	sun
die	**Sonnenbrille, -n**	(pair of) sunglasses
die	**Sonnencreme, -s**	sun(tan) cream
die	**Überfahrt, -en**	crossing
die	**Urlauberin**	holiday-maker

ESSENTIAL WORDS (neuter)

das	Ausland	abroad
das	Bad, ⸚er	bathe (in sea), swim
das	Badetuch, ⸚er	(bath) towel
das	Boot, -e	boat
das	Fischerboot, -e	fishing boat
das	Meer, -e	ocean, sea
das	Picknick, -e or -s	picnic
das	Ruder	oar; rudder
das	Schiff, -e	ship, vessel
das	Schwimmen	swimming
das	Sonnenöl, -e	suntan oil
das	Wasser	water

IMPORTANT WORDS (masculine)

der	Anker	anchor
	Badende(r), -n	bather, swimmer
der	Bord, -e	board
der	Horizont	horizon
der	(Meeres)boden	bottom (of the sea)
der	Ozean, -e	ocean
der	Prospekt, -e	leaflet, brochure
der	Rettungsring, -e	lifebelt
der	Sand, -e	send
der	Segler	sailor, yachtsman
der	Sonnenbrand, ⸚e	sunburn

USEFUL PHRASES

zwei Wochen Urlaub two weeks' holiday
am Meer at the seaside
ans Meer or an die See fahren to go to the seaside
es ist Flut/Ebbe the tide is in/out
schwimmen gehen to go for a swim; sich ausruhen to have a rest
sich sonnen to sunbathe; am Strand on the beach
eine Sonnenbrille tragen to wear sunglasses
braun werden to get a tan
einen Sonnenbrand bekommen to get sunburnt

IMPORTANT WORDS *(feminine)*

die	**Flagge, -n**	flag
die	**Küste, -n**	coast, shore; seaside
die	**Luftmatratze, -n**	lilo®, airbed
die	**Seglerin**	sailor, yachtswoman
die	**Vergnügungsfahrt, -en**	pleasure cruise

IMPORTANT WORDS *(neuter)*

das	**Reisebüro, -s**	travel agent's
das	**Segel**	sail
das	**Segeln**	sailing
das	**Teleskop, -e**	telescope
das	**Ufer**	shore *(lake)*; bank *(river)*

USEFUL WORDS *(masculine)*

der	**Eimer**	bucket
der	**Jachthafen, ⁻**	marina
der	**Kahn, ⁻e**	*(small)* boat
der	**Kai, -e** *or* **-s**	quay, quayside
der	**Kieselstein, -e**	pebble
der	**Krebs, -e**	crab
der	**Leuchtturm, ⁻e**	lighthouse
der	**Liegestuhl, ⁻e**	deckchair
der	**Mast, -e(n)**	mast
der	**Matrose, -n**	sailor
der	**Pier, -e** *or* **-s**	pier
der	**Rettungsschwimmer**	lifeguard
der	**Schaum**	foam
der	**Schiffbruch, ⁻e**	shipwreck
der	**Schornstein, ⁻e**	funnel
der	**(See)tang, -e**	seaweed
der	**Sonnenstich, -e**	sunstroke
der	**Spaten**	spade

USEFUL WORDS (feminine)

die	Boje, -n	buoy
die	Bucht, -en	bay
die	Ebbe, -n	low tide
die	Fahne, -n	flag
die	Flotte, -n	navy, fleet
die	Flut, -en	high tide
die	Jacht, -en	yacht
die	Klippe, -n	cliff
die	Kreuzfahrt, -en	cruise
die	Last, -en	load, cargo
die	Möwe, -n	seagull
die	Muschel(schale), -n (-n)	shell
die	Pauschalreise, -n	package tour
die	Sandburg, -en	sandcastle
die	(Schiffs)ladung, -en	cargo
die	Schwimmweste, -n	life jacket
die	(Sonnen)bräune	(sun)tan
die	Strömung, -en	current
die	Welle, -n	wave

USEFUL WORDS (neuter)

das	Deck, -s or -e	deck (of ship)
das	Fahrgeld, -er	fare
das	Floß, ̈-e	raft
das	Steuer	helm, tiller
das	Surfbrett, -er	surfboard
das	Tretboot, -e	pedal-boat, pedalo

USEFUL PHRASES

eine Bootsfahrt machen to go on a boat trip
an Bord gehen to go on board
ruhig calm; stürmisch stormy; bewegt choppy
seekrank werden to get seasick
untergehen to go under
ertrinken to drown

ESSENTIAL WORDS *(masculine)*

der	**Artikel**	article
der	**Bäcker**	baker
der	**Cent, -s**	cent
der	**Einkauf, -käufe**	shopping; purchase
der	**Euro, -s**	euro
der	**Fahrstuhl, ̈-e**	lift
der	**Franken**	(Swiss) franc
der	**Geldbeutel**	purse
der	**Geschäftsmann, -leute**	businessman
der	**Groschen**	10-pfennig piece; groschen
der	**Kiosk, -e**	kiosk
der	**Kunde, -n**	customer, client
der	**Laden, ̈-**	shop
der	**Markt, ̈-e**	market
der	**Preis, -e**	price
der	**Rappen**	centime
der	**Schalter**	counter (*post office, bank etc*)
der	**Scheck, -s**	cheque
der	**Schein, -e**	(bank)note
der	**Schuhmacher**	shoemaker, shoe repairer
der	**Sommerschlussverkauf**	summer sale
der	**Supermarkt, ̈-e**	supermarket

USEFUL PHRASES

einkaufen gehen **to go shopping**
Einkäufe machen **to do the shopping**
Schlange stehen **to queue up**
kaufen **to buy;** verkaufen **to sell;** jdn bedienen **to serve sb**
kann ich Ihnen behilflich sein? **can I help you?**
was darf es sein, bitte? **what would you like?**
ich möchte ... **I'd like...;** ich brauche ... **I need ...**
etw bezahlen **to pay for sth**
etwas stimmt nicht **there's something wrong somewhere**
ich möchte mich nur mal umsehen **I'm just looking**

ESSENTIAL WORDS *(feminine)*

die	**Apotheke, -n**	chemist's, pharmacy
die	**Bäckerei, -en**	bakery, baker's (shop)
die	**Bank, -en**	bank
die	**Bibliothek, -en**	library
die	**Buchhandlung, -en**	bookshop, bookseller's
die	**Drogerie, -n**	(retail) chemist's
die	**Etage, -n**	floor
die	**Farbe, -n**	colour
die	**Geschäftszeit, -en**	business hours
die	**Größe, -n**	size
die	**Handlung, -en**	shop
die	**Kasse, -n**	till; cash desk, checkout
die	**Konditorei, -en**	cake shop
die	**Kreditkarte, -n**	credit card
die	**Kundin**	customer, client
die	**Liste, -n**	list
die	**Metzgerei, -en**	butcher's (shop)
die	**Öffnungszeit, -en**	opening time
die	**Post, Postämter**	post office
die	**Rechnung, -en**	bill
die	**Schachtel, -n**	box
die	**Schuhgröße, -n**	shoe size
die	**Selbstbedienung (SB)**	self-service
die	**Sparkasse, -n**	savings bank
die	**Tierhandlung, -en**	pet shop
die	**Tüte, -n**	bag

USEFUL PHRASES

erhältlich **available**; ausverkauft **sold out**

beim Bäcker/Fleischer **at the baker's/butcher's**

anbieten **to offer**; etw probieren **to try sth (taste, sample)**

etw anprobieren **to try sth on**

das gefällt mir **I like that**

wählen **to choose**; wiegen **to weigh**

ESSENTIAL WORDS *(neuter)*

das	**Andenken**	souvenir
das	**Büro, -s**	office
das	**Café, -s**	café
das	**Einkaufen**	shopping
das	**Erdgeschoss, -e**	ground level, ground floor
das	**Geld**	money
das	**Geschäft, -e**	shop; trade, business; deal
das	**Geschenk, -e**	present, gift
das	**Kaufhaus, -häuser**	department store
das	**Kleingeld**	small change
das	**Portemonnaie, -s**	purse
das	**Postamt, ̈-er**	post office
das	**Restaurant, -s**	restaurant
das	**Schuhgeschäft, -e**	shoe shop
das	**Sonderangebot, -e**	bargain (offer), special offer
das	**Souvenir, -s**	souvenir
das	**Warenhaus, -häuser**	department store
das	**Wirtshaus, -häuser**	pub, inn

USEFUL PHRASES

was kostet das? **what does it cost?**
was macht das? **what does that come to?**
ich habe 15 Euro dafür bezahlt **I paid 15 euros for it**
einen Scheck ausstellen **to write out a cheque**
bar bezahlen **to pay cash**
Geld für Pralinen ausgeben **to spend money on chocolates**
zu teuer **too dear;** ganz billig **quite cheap**
kostenlos **free, free of charge;** umsonst **for nothing**
preiswert **good value;** ein preiswertes Angebot **a bargain**
das habe ich günstig bekommen **I got it at a good price**
das ist aber günstig! **what a bargain!**
Montags Ruhetag **closed on Mondays**

IMPORTANT WORDS *(masculine)*

der	Apotheker	(dispensing) chemist
der	Aufzug, -̈e	lift
der	Ausverkauf, -käufe	sale
die	Betriebsferien *(pl)*	holidays *(of a business)*
der	Bioladen, -läden	organic food shop
der	Buchhändler	bookseller
der	Einkaufskorb, -körbe	shopping basket
der	Einkaufswagen	shopping trolley
der	Fischhändler	fishmonger
der	Fleischer	butcher
der	Friseur, -e	hairdresser
der	Händler	dealer
der	Herrenfriseur, -e	barber, men's hairdresser
der	Juwelier	jeweller
der	Kassenzettel	receipt
der	Kaufmann, -leute	merchant
der	Konditor, -en	confectioner
der	Metzger	butcher
der	Obst- und Gemüsehändler	greengrocer
der	Obsthändler	fruiterer
der	Ökoladen, -läden	wholefood shop
der	Schlussverkauf, -käufe	(end-of-season) sale
der	Sonderpreis, -e	special price
der	Tabakladen, -̈	tobacconist's (shop)
der	Umtausch	exchange *(of goods)*
der	Verkauf, -käufe	sale
der	Verkäufer	salesman, shop assistant
der	Waschsalon, -s	laundrette
der	Zeitungshändler	newsagent

USEFUL PHRASES

GmbH Ltd

AG plc

IMPORTANT WORDS *(feminine)*

die **Abteilung, -en**	department
die **Anprobe, -n**	trying on
die **Auswahl (an** + *dat*)	choice (of)
die **Brieftasche, -n**	wallet
die **Firma, Firmen**	firm, company
die **Fleischerei, -en**	butcher's (shop)
die **Friseuse, -n**	hairdresser
die **Gaststätte, -n**	restaurant; pub
die **Kneipe, -n**	pub
die **Kundenkarte, -n**	charge card
die **Packung, -en**	packet, box
die **Parfümerie, -n**	perfume counter *or* shop
die **Quittung, -en**	receipt
die **Schaufensterpuppe, -n**	dummy, model
die **Schlange, -n**	queue
die **Schreibwarenhandlung, -en**	stationer's
die **Theke, -n**	counter (*in café, bar etc*)
die **Verkäuferin**	salesgirl, shop assistant
die **Waren** *(pl)*	goods, wares

IMPORTANT WORDS *(neuter)*

das **Einkaufszentrum, -tren**	shopping centre
das **Internetcafé, -s**	Internet café
das **Juweliergeschäft, -e**	jeweller's (shop)
das **Mediencenter**	media centre
das **Milchgeschäft, -e**	dairy
das **Obergeschoss, -e**	upper floor
das **Produkt, -e**	product; *(pl)* produce
das **Reisebüro, -s**	travel agent's
das **Schaufenster**	shop window
das **Untergeschoss, -e**	basement

USEFUL PHRASES

einen Schaufensterbummel machen **to go window-shopping**

USEFUL WORDS *(masculine)*

der	**Buchmacher**	bookmaker, "bookie"
der	**Einkaufsbummel**	shopping spree
der	**Eisenwarenhändler**	ironmonger
der	**(Flick)schuster**	cobbler, shoe repairer
der	**Gelegenheitskauf, -käufe**	bargain
der	**Grundstücksmakler**	estate agent
der	**Gutschein, -e**	voucher
der	**Handel**	trade, business
der	**Ladentisch, -e**	counter *(in shop)*
der	**Lebensmittelhändler**	grocer
der	**Optiker**	optician
der	**Uhrmacher**	watchmaker
der	**Waschsalon, -s**	laundrette

USEFUL WORDS *(feminine)*

die	**Bausparkasse, -n**	building society
die	**Besorgung, -en**	errand; purchase
die	**Bücherei, -en**	library
die	**Bude, -n**	stall
die	**Eisenwarenhandlung, -en**	ironmonger's, hardware shop
die	**Filiale, -n**	branch
die	**Garantie, -n**	guarantee
die	**Kragenweite, -n**	collar size
die	**Reinigung, -en**	cleaner's
die	**Rolltreppe, -n**	escalator
die	**Versicherungsgesellschaft, -en**	insurance company
die	**Videothek, -en**	video shop
die	**Wäscherei, -en**	laundry, cleaner's

USEFUL WORDS *(neuter)*

das	**Erzeugnis, -se**	product; produce
das	**Lebensmittelgeschäft, -e**	grocer's, general food store
das	**Wechselgeld**	change

ESSENTIAL WORDS *(masculine)*

der	**Ball, ̈e**	ball
der	**Fußball, ̈e**	football
der	**Fußballfan, -s**	football supporter
der	**Fußballspieler**	footballer
der	**Läufer**	runner
der	**Pass, ̈e**	pass
der	**Radsport**	cycling
der	**Rollschuh, -e**	roller skate
der	**Schlittschuh, -e**	ice skate
der	**Spieler**	player
der	**Sport, -e**	sport, game
der	**Sportplatz, ̈e**	sports ground, playing field
der	**Wintersport**	winter sport(s)

ESSENTIAL WORDS *(neuter)*

das	**Angeln**	fishing, angling
das	**Endspiel, -e**	final(s)
das	**Fitnesszentrum, -tren**	health club
das	**Freibad, ̈er**	open-air swimming pool
das	**Hallenbad, ̈er**	indoor swimming pool
das	**Hockey**	hockey
das	**Kricket**	cricket
das	**Laufen**	running
das	**Radfahren**	cycling
das	**Reiten**	horse-riding
das	**Rudern**	rowing
das	**Rugby**	rugby
das	**Schlittschuhlaufen**	(ice) skating
das	**Schwimmbad, ̈er**	swimming baths
das	**Schwimmen**	swimming
das	**Spiel, -e**	play; game, match
das	**Squash**	squash
das	**Stadion, -ien**	stadium
das	**Tennis**	tennis
das	**Turnen**	gymnastics

IMPORTANT WORDS (masculine)

der	Basketball, ⸚e	basketball
der	Fußballplatz, ⸚e	football pitch
der	Golfplatz, ⸚e	golf course
der	Golfschläger	golf club (stick)
der	Netzball, ⸚e	netball
der	Platz, ⸚e	ground, playing field
der	Pokal, -e	cup
der	Profi, -s	pro
der	Schläger	racket/bat/club etc
der	Ski, -er	ski
der	Teilnehmer	participant
der	Tennisplatz, ⸚e	tennis court
der	Volleyball, ⸚e	volleyball
der	Zuschauer	spectator

ESSENTIAL + IMPORTANT WORDS (feminine)

die	Angelrute, -n	fishing rod
die	Bundesliga	football league
die	Fußballelf, -en	football team
die	Halbzeit, -en	half (of match); half-time
die	Leichtathletik	athletics
die	Mannschaft, -en	team
die	Rennbahn, -en	racecourse, track
die	Spielerin	player
die	Spielhälfte, -n	half (of match)
die	Turnhalle, -n	gym(nasium)
die	Weltmeisterschaft, -en	world championship(s)

USEFUL PHRASES

treibst du gern Sport? do you like sports?
spielen to play; laufen to run; werfen to throw;
springen to jump; trainieren to train; joggen to go jogging
üben to practise; trimmen to do exercises
gewinnen to win; verlieren to lose
unentschieden enden to end in a draw

IMPORTANT WORDS (neuter)

das	Billard	billiards
das	Boxen	boxing
das	Ergebnis, -se	result
das	Golf(spiel)	golf
das	Jogging	jogging
das	Netz, -e	net
das	Pferderennen	horse racing; horse-race
das	Rennen	racing, race meeting
das	Schießen	shooting
das	Segeln	sailing
das	Skateboard, -s	skateboard
das	Skifahren; das Skilaufen	skiing
das	Snowboard, -s	snowboard
das	Tauchen	(underwater) diving
das	Tischtennis	table tennis
das	Tor, -e	goal
das	Ziel, -e	goal, aim; finish, finishing post

USEFUL WORDS (neuter)

das	Bergsteigen	mountaineering
das	Bogenschießen	archery
das	gemischte Doppel	mixed doubles
das	Drachenfliegen	hang-gliding
das	Fechten	fencing
das	Gleitschirmfliegen	paragliding
das	Jagen	hunting; shooting
das	Klettern	climbing, mountaineering
die	Olympischen Spiele (pl)	Olympic Games
das	Ringen	wrestling
das	Surfbrett	surfboard
das	Tauziehen	tug-of-war
das	Training	training
das	Turnier, -e	tournament
das	Wasserski	water-skiing

USEFUL WORDS *(masculine)*

der	Bergsteiger	mountaineer
der	Federball, ¨e	badminton; shuttlecock
der	Gegner	opponent
der	Hochsprung, ¨e	high jump
der	Kampf, ¨e	fight; contest
der	Meister	champion
der	Rodel	toboggan
der	Satz, ¨e	set (*tennis*)
der	Schiedsrichter	referee; umpire
der	Schlitten	sledge, sleigh
der	Sieger	winner
der	Stoß, ¨e	kick; push, thrust
der	Titelverteidiger	title-holder
der	Torwart, -e	goalkeeper
der	Trainer	trainer, coach; manager
die	Turnschuhe (*pl*)	tennis *or* gym shoes
	Unparteiische(r), -n	umpire; referee
der	Weitsprung, ¨e	long jump
der	(Welt)rekord, -e	(world) record
der	Wettbewerb, -e	competition
der	Wettkampf, ¨e	match, contest

USEFUL WORDS *(feminine)*

die	(Aschen)bahn, -en	(cinder) track
die	Bundesliga	national league
die	Eisbahn, -en	ice rink, skating rink
die	Kegelbahn, -en	bowling alley; skittle alley
die	Meisterschaft, -en	championship
die	Partie, -n	game, match
die	Punktzahl, -en	score
die	Runde, -n	lap, round
die	Siegerin	winner
die	Stoppuhr, -en	stopwatch
die	(Tabellen)spitze, -n	lead (*in league etc*)
die	Tribüne, -n	stand

ESSENTIAL WORDS (masculine)

der Ausgang, ¨-e	exit, way out
der Eingang, ¨-e	entrance, way in
der Film, -e	film
der Kinobesucher	cinema-goer
der Quatsch	rubbish
der Theaterbesucher	theatre-goer
die Zuhörer (pl)	audience (listeners)

ESSENTIAL WORDS (feminine)

die Eintrittskarte, -n	ticket
die Freizeit	free or spare time
die Handlung, -en	plot, action
die Kasse, -n	box office, ticket office
die Musik	music
die Reservierung, -en	booking
die (Theater)karte, -n	(theatre) ticket
die (Theater)kasse, -n	box office
die Vorstellung, -en	performance, show

ESSENTIAL WORDS (neuter)

das Kino, -s	cinema
das Konzert, -e	concert
das Spiel	acting; play
das Theater	theatre
das (Theater)stück, -e	play

USEFUL PHRASES

ich gehe gern ins Kino/ins Theater I like going to the cinema/the theatre
an der Vorverkaufskasse at the booking office
„ausverkauft" "sold out"
mein Lieblingsfilmstar my favourite film star
ein Film mit Untertiteln a film with subtitles
spannend exciting; langweilig boring
(kaum) sehenswert (hardly) worth seeing

IMPORTANT WORDS *(masculine)*

der	Applaus, -e	applause
der	Balkon, -s *or* -e	(dress) circle
der	Bühneneingang, ⸚e	stage door
der	Dramatiker	dramatist, playwright
der	(Film)star, -s	(film) star
der	Komiker	comedian
der	Konzertsaal, -säle	concert hall
der	Krieg, -e	war
der	Krimi, -s	thriller
der	Kritiker	critic
der	Rang, ⸚e	circle (*in theatre*)
der	Saal, Säle	hall; room
der	Schauspieler	actor
der	(Sitz)platz, ⸚e	seat
der	Spaß	fun
der	Spielplan, ⸚e	programme
der	Text, -e	script
der	Titel	title
der	Untertitel	subtitle
der	Videoclip, -s	video clip
der	Vorhang, ⸚e	curtain
der	Western, -s	western
die	Zuschauer *(pl)*	audience (*viewers*)
der	erste Rang	dress circle
der	zweite Rang	upper circle

USEFUL PHRASES

die Bühne betreten to step onto the stage
meine Damen und Herren! ladies and gentlemen!
ein Stück geben to put on a play
mit X und Y in den Hauptrollen with X and Y in the main roles
klatschen to clap

IMPORTANT WORDS *(feminine)*

die	**Aufführung, -en**	performance
die	**Bühne, -n**	stage, platform
die	**Ermäßigung, -en**	reduction
die	**Figur, -en**	character
die	**Garderobe, -n**	cloakroom; wardrobe
die	**Hauptrolle, -n**	main role or part
die	**Komödie, -n**	comedy
die	**Oper, -n**	opera; opera house
die	**Reklame, -n**	advertisement
die	**Rolle, -n**	role, part
die	**Saison, -s**	season
die	**Schauspielerin**	actress
die	**Schlange, -n**	queue
die	**Seifenoper, -n**	soap opera
die	**Show, -s**	show
die	**Szene, -n**	scene
die	**Theatergruppe, -n**	dramatic society
die	**Tragödie, -n**	tragedy

IMPORTANT WORDS *(neuter)*

das	**Ballett, -e**	ballet
das	**Drama, Dramen**	drama
das	**Foyer, -s**	foyer
das	**Kostüm, -e**	costume
das	**Kriminalstück, -e**	thriller
das	**Make-up**	make-up
das	**Musical, -s**	musical
das	**Opernglas, ¨er**	(pair of) opera glasses
das	**Orchester**	orchestra; band
das	**Parkett, -e**	stalls (pl)
das	**Schauspiel, -e**	play
das	**Schauspielhaus, -häuser**	theatre

USEFUL WORDS (masculine)

der	Abgang, ¨-e	exit (of actor)
der	Auftritt, -e	entrance (of actor); scene (of play)
der	Beifall	applause
der	Intendant, -en	stage manager
der	Orchesterraum, -räume	orchestra pit
der	Produzent, -en	(film) producer
der	Regisseur, -e	producer; director
der	Souffleur, -e	prompter
der	Spielfilm, -e	feature film
der	Western	western

USEFUL WORDS (feminine)

die	Farce, -n	farce
die	Galerie, -n	the "gods", gallery
die	Generalprobe, -n	dress rehearsal
die	Inszenierung, -en	production
die	Kapelle, -n	band
die	Kritik, -en	review
die	Leinwand, ¨-e	screen
die	Loge, -n	box
die	Pause, -n	interval
die	Platzanweiserin	usherette, attendant
die	Probe, -n	rehearsal
die	Schauspielkunst	acting
die	Souffleuse, -n	prompter
die	Tribüne, -n	platform
die	Zugabe, -n	encore

USEFUL WORDS (neuter)

das	Lustspiel, -e	comedy
das	Plakat, -e	poster, notice
das	Rampenlicht	footlights (pl)
das	Scheinwerferlicht, -er	spotlight
das	Trauerspiel, -e	tragedy

ESSENTIAL WORDS (*masculine*)

der	Abend, -e	evening
der	Augenblick, -e	moment, instant
der	Beginn, -e	beginning
der	Mittag, -e	mid-day, noon
der	Moment, -e	moment
der	Monat, -e	month
der	Morgen	morning
der	Nachmittag, -e	afternoon
der	Tag, -e	day
der	Vormittag, -e	morning
der	Wecker	alarm clock

ESSENTIAL WORDS (*feminine*)

die	Armbanduhr, -en	(wrist) watch
die	Jahreszeit, -en	season
die	Minute, -n	minute
die	Mitte	middle
die	Mitternacht, ⁻e	midnight
die	Nacht, ⁻e	night; night-time
die	Sekunde, -n	second
die	halbe Stunde, -n -n	half-hour, half-an-hour
die	Stunde, -n	hour
die	Tageszeit, -en	daytime
die	Uhr, -en	clock; time
die	Viertelstunde, -n	quarter of an hour
die	Weile, -n	while, short time
die	Woche, -n	week
die	Zeit, -en	time

ESSENTIAL WORDS (*neuter*)

das	Datum, Daten	date
das	Ende, -n	end
das	Jahr, -e	year
das	Jahrhundert, -e	century
das	Mal, -e	time, occasion
das	Wochenende, -n	weekend

USEFUL PHRASES

um 7 Uhr aufstehen **to get up at 7 o'clock**
um 11 Uhr zu Bett gehen **to go to bed at 11 o'clock**
wie viel Uhr ist es?, wie spät ist es? **what time is it?**
den Wievielten haben wir heute? **what is today's date?**
früh **early**; spät **late**; bald **soon**; später **later**
fast **almost**; pünktlich **punctual**
es ist gerade *or* Punkt 2 Uhr **it is exactly 2 o'clock**
halb 3 **half past 2**; halb 9 **half past 8**
gegen 8 Uhr **round about 8 o'clock**
es ist Viertel nach 5/Viertel vor 5 **it is a quarter past 5/a quarter to 5**

vorgestern	the day before yesterday
gestern	yesterday
am vorigen *or* **vorhergehenden Tag**	the day before, the previous day
heute	today
heute Abend	tonight
morgen	tomorrow
am nächsten *or* **folgenden Tag**	the next *or* following day
übermorgen	the day after tomorrow
am übernächsten Tag	two days later
vierzehn Tage	a fortnight

USEFUL PHRASES

morgens **in the morning**; nachmittags **in the afternoon**
abends **in the evening**; nachts **at night, by night**
tagsüber, am Tage **during the day**; stündlich **hourly**
täglich **daily**; wöchentlich **weekly**
monatlich **monthly**; jährlich **annually**; heutzutage **nowadays**

IMPORTANT WORDS *(feminine)*

die **Essenszeit, -en**	mealtime
die **Gelegenheit, -en**	opportunity, occasion
die **Kuckucksuhr, -en**	cuckoo clock
die **Uhrzeit, -en**	time of day

USEFUL PHRASES

einen Augenblick! **just a minute!**
in diesem/dem Augenblick **at this/that moment**
im selben Augenblick **at that very moment**
ich habe keine Zeit (dazu) **I have no time (for it)**
(sich) die Zeit vertreiben **to pass the time**
es ist Zeit zum Essen **it is time for lunch (dinner etc)**
eine Zeit lang bleiben **to stay for a while**
anderthalb Stunden warten **to wait an hour and a half**
damals **at that time**
nie, niemals **never;** jemals **ever**
diesmal **this time;** ein anderes Mal **another time**
nächstes Mal **next time**
das erste/letzte Mal **the first/last time**
zum ersten/letzten Mal **for the first/last time**
am Wochenende **at the weekend**
über das Wochenende **for the weekend**
ich habe es eilig **I'm in a hurry**
ich habe keine Eile **I'm in no hurry**
es hat keine Eile **there's no hurry**

USEFUL WORDS (*masculine*)

der	Einbruch der Nacht	nightfall
der	Kalender	calendar
der	Tagesanbruch	daybreak
der	(Uhr)zeiger	hand (*of clock etc*)
der	Zeitabschnitt, -e	time, period

USEFUL WORDS (*feminine*)

die	Epoche, -n	epoch, period
die	Gegenwart	present (*time, tense*)
die	Mittagszeit, -en	lunch time
die	Pause, -n	interval; pause, break
die	Standuhr, -en	grandfather clock
die	Stoppuhr, -en	stopwatch
die	Vergangenheit	past (*time, tense*)
die	Verspätung, -en	delay (*of vehicle*)
die	Zukunft	future (*time, tense*)

USEFUL WORDS (*neuter*)

das	Futur(um)	future tense
das	Jahrtausend, -e	millennium
das	Jahrzehnt, -e	decade
das	Mittelalter	the Middle Ages
das	Präsens	present tense
das	Schaltjahr, -e	leap year
das	Zeitalter	age, time
das	Zifferblatt, ¨-er	(clock) face, dial

USEFUL PHRASES

vor einer Woche/einem Monat/2 Jahren **a week/a month/2 years ago**
gestern/heute vor einer Woche **a week ago yesterday/today**
gestern/heute vor 2 Jahren **2 years ago yesterday/today**
in einer Woche/einem Monat/2 Jahren **in a week('s time)/a month('s time)/
  2 years(' time)**
morgen/heute in einer Woche **a week tomorrow/today**

ESSENTIAL + IMPORTANT WORDS *(masculine)*

der	Bastler	handyman
der	Bohrer	drill
der	Dosenöffner	tin-opener
der	Hammer, ¨	hammer
der	Holzhammer, ¨	mallet
der	Klebstoff, -e	glue
der	Korkenzieher	corkscrew
der	Schlüssel	key

ESSENTIAL + IMPORTANT WORDS *(feminine)*

die	Batterie, -n	battery
die	Baustelle, -n	building site
die	Gabel, -n	fork
die	Maschine, -n	machine; engine
die	Werkstatt, ¨en	workshop

ESSENTIAL + IMPORTANT WORDS *(neuter)*

das	Ding, -e	thing, object
das	Do-it-yourself	do-it-yourself, D.I.Y.
das *or der*	Gummi	rubber; gum
das	Gummiband, ¨er	rubber band; elastic
das	Kabel	wire; cable
das	Schloss, ¨er	lock

USEFUL WORDS *(neuter)*

das	Brett, -er	plank, board; shelf
das	Gerüst, -e	scaffolding
das	Seil, -e	rope, cable
das	Tau, -e	rope
das	Werkzeug, -e	tool

USEFUL PHRASES

basteln: er kann gut basteln he is good with his hands
wozu benutzt man ...? what do you use ... for?
reparieren to repair; etw reparieren lassen to have sth repaired
nageln to nail; sägen to saw

USEFUL WORDS *(masculine)*

der **Bolzen**	bolt
der **Büchsenöffner**	tin-opener
der **Draht, ̈e**	wire
der **Flaschenöffner**	bottle-opener
der **Hobel**	plane
der **Kleb(e)streifen**	adhesive tape
der **Meißel**	chisel
der **Nagel, ̈**	nail
der **Pickel**	pick, pickaxe
der **Pinsel**	paintbrush
der **Pressluftbohrer**	pneumatic drill
der **Schraubenschlüssel**	spanner
der **Schraubenzieher**	screwdriver
der **Schraubstock, ̈e**	vice
der **Stacheldraht, ̈e**	barbed wire
der **Stift, -e**	peg
der **Tesafilm**®	Sellotape®
der **Werkzeugkasten, ̈**	toolbox

USEFUL WORDS *(feminine)*

die **Feder, -n**	spring, coil
die **Feile, -n**	file
die **Heftzwecke, -n**	drawing pin, thumbtack
die **Kelle, -n**	trowel
die **Leiter, -n**	ladder
die **Nadel, -n**	needle; pin
die **Planke, -n**	plank
die **Reißzwecke, -n**	drawing pin, thumbtack
die **Säge, -n**	saw
die **Schaufel**	shovel; scoop
die **Schere, -n**	(pair of) scissors
die **Schnur, ̈e**	string, cord; wire, flex
die **Schraube, -n**	screw
die **Wasserwaage, -n**	spirit level
die **Zange, -n**	(pair of) pliers

ESSENTIAL WORDS *(masculine)*

der **Bahnhof, ̈e**	railway station
der **Bürgersteig, -e**	pavement
der **Busbahnhof, ̈e**	bus *or* coach station
der **Dom, -e**	cathedral
der **Laden, ̈**	shop
der **Markt, ̈e**	market
der **Markttag, -e**	market day
der **Park, -s**	(public) park
der **Parkplatz, ̈e**	parking place; car park
der **Polizist, -en**	policeman
der **Turm, ̈e**	tower
der **Weg, -e**	way

ESSENTIAL WORDS *(feminine)*

die **Brücke, -n**	bridge
die **Burg, -en**	castle
die **Bushaltestelle, -n**	bus stop
die **Ecke, -n**	corner, turning
die **Einbahnstraße, -n**	one-way street
die **Fabrik, -en**	factory, works
die **Fahrt, -en**	journey
die **Haltestelle, -n**	(bus *or* tram) stop
die **Hauptstraße, -n**	main road; main street
die **Innenstadt, ̈e**	city centre, town centre
die **Kirche, -n**	church
die **Klinik, -en**	hospital, clinic
die **Polizei**	police
die **(Polizei)wache, -n**	police station
die **Post, Postämter**	post office
die **Reise, -n** *or* die **Rundfahrt, -en**	tour
die **Stadt, ̈e**	town; city
die **Straße, -n**	street, road
die **Straßenecke, -n**	street corner
die **Tankstelle, -n**	service station, garage
die **U-Bahn, -en**	underground (railway)

ESSENTIAL WORDS *(neuter)*

das **Büro, -s**	office
das **Geschäft, -e**	shop
das **Heft, -e**	book (*of tickets*)
das **Hotel, -s**	hotel
das **Kaufhaus, -häuser**	department store
das **Kino, -s**	cinema
das **Krankenhaus, -häuser**	hospital
das **Museum, Museen**	museum
das **Parken**	parking
das **Parkhaus, -häuser**	(covered) car park
das **Postamt, ̈-er**	post office
das **Rathaus, -häuser**	town hall
das **Restaurant, -s**	restaurant
das **Schloss, ̈-er**	castle
das **Stadtzentrum, -tren**	city centre, town centre
das **Straßenschild, -er**	roadsign
das **Taxi, -s**	taxi
das **Theater**	theatre
das **Verkehrsamt, ̈-er**	tourist information centre

USEFUL PHRASES

in die Stadt gehen *or* fahren to go into town
in der Stadtmitte in the centre of town
eine Stadtrundfahrt machen to go on a tour of the city
die Straße übergehen to cross the road
die Sehenswürdigkeiten besichtigen to have a look at the sights

IMPORTANT WORDS *(masculine)*

der	**Betrieb**	bustle
der	**Bezirk, -e**	district
der	**Biergarten, ⸚**	beer garden
der	**Bürgermeister**	mayor
der	**Einwohner**	inhabitant
der	**Fahrscheinautomat, -en**	ticket machine
der	**Fahrscheinentwerter**	automatic ticket stamping machine
der	**Friedhof, ⸚e**	cemetery, graveyard
der	**Fußgänger**	pedestrian
der	**Kreisverkehr**	roundabout
der	**Platz, ⸚e**	square
der	**Verkehr**	traffic
der	**Verkehrsstau, -e**	traffic jam
der	**Zebrastreifen**	zebra crossing

IMPORTANT WORDS *(feminine)*

die	**Aussicht, -en**	view
die	**Bürgermeisterin**	female mayor
die	**Feuerwehrwache, -n**	fire station
die	**Fußgängerzone, -n**	pedestrian precinct
die	**Menge, -n**	crowd
die	**Schlange, -n**	queue
die	**Sehenswürdigkeiten** *(pl)*	sights, places of interest
die	**Umgebung, -en**	the surroundings *(pl)*

IMPORTANT WORDS *(neuter)*

das	**Denkmal, ⸚er**	monument
das	**Fahrzeug, -e**	vehicle
das	**Gebäude**	building
das	**Tor, -e**	gate(way), arch

USEFUL WORDS *(masculine)*

der	Abwasserkanal, ̈e	sewer
der	Bürger	citizen
der	Fußgängerüberweg, -e	pedestrian crossing
der	Kinderwagen	pram
der	Landkreis, -e	(like British) county
der	Marktplatz, ̈e	market place
der	Ort, -e	place, spot
der	Passant, -en	passer-by
der	Pfad, -e	path
der	Pflasterstein, -e	paving stone
der	Rad(fahr)weg, -e	cycle path *or* track
der	Stadtbewohner *or* der **Städter**	town dweller
der	Stadtrand, ̈er	the outskirts *(pl)*
der	Straßenübergang, ̈e	pedestrian crossing
der	Taxistand, ̈e	taxi rank
der	Umzug, ̈e	parade
der	Wegweiser	roadsign
der	Wohnblock, -s	block of flats
der	Wolkenkratzer	skyscraper

USEFUL PHRASES

in der Stadt/am Stadtrand wohnen to live in the town/in the suburbs
auf dem Platz in *or* on the square
an der Ecke at *or* on the corner
zum Markt gehen, auf den Markt gehen to go to the market
Weihnachtsmarkt Christmas fair
zu Fuß gehen to walk
mit dem Bus/mit dem Zug fahren to go by bus/by train
ein Taxi anrufen to call a taxi
ins Theater/ins Kino gehen to go to the theatre/the cinema
modern modern; alt old
sauber clean; schmutzig dirty
typisch typical; ziemlich quite; sehr very

USEFUL WORDS *(feminine)*

die	Altstadt	old (part of) town
die	Baustelle, -n	building site; roadworks
die	Bevölkerung, -en	population
die	Gasse, -n	lane, back street
die	Großstadt, ̈e	city
die	Kreuzung, -en	crossroads
die	Kunstgalerie, -n	art gallery
die	Leuchtreklame, -n	neon sign
die	Meinungsumfrage, -n	opinion poll
die	Parkuhr, -en	parking meter
die	Prozession, -en	procession
die	Sackgasse, -n	dead end
die	Siedlung, -en	housing estate
die	Sozialwohnung, -en	council flat *or* house
die	Spitze, -n	spire
die	Stadtmitte, -n	town centre; city centre
die	Statue, -n	statue
die	Straßenbahn, -en	tram
die	Straßenlaterne, -n	street lamp
die	Tour, -en	tour
die	Umgehungsstraße, -n	by-pass
die	Umleitung, -en	diversion
die	Vorstadt, ̈e	suburbs *(pl)*

USEFUL WORDS *(neuter)*

das **Gedränge**	crowd
das **Industriegebiet, -e**	industrial area
das **Kopfsteinpflaster**	cobblestones
das **Plakat, -e**	poster, notice
das **Schild, -er**	sign
das **(Stadt)viertel**	district
das **Werk, -e**	factory, works
das **Wohngebiet, -e**	built-up area
das **Zentrum, -tren**	city centre

USEFUL PHRASES

„Betreten der Baustelle verboten" **"building site: keep out"**

„Anlieger frei" **"residents only"**

„Vorsicht, bissiger Hund!" **"beware of the dog"**

„Fußgängerzone" **"pedestrian precinct"**

„bitte freihalten" **"please keep clear"**

„Parken verboten" **"no parking"**

„Vorfahrt achten!" **"give way"**

ESSENTIAL WORDS *(masculine)*

der **Ausgang**, ¨e	exit
der **Ausstieg**, -e	exit *(from train)*
der **Bahnhof**, ¨e	station
der **Bahnsteig**, -e	platform
der **D-Zug**, ¨e *(Durchgangszug)*	through train
der **Eilzug**, ¨e	limited-stop train
der **Eingang**, ¨e	entrance
der **Einstieg**, -e	entrance *(onto train)*
der **Entwerter**	ticket punching machine
der **Fahrgast**, ¨e	passenger
der **Fahrkartenschalter**	ticket *or* booking office
der **Fahrschein**, -e	ticket
der **Fahrplan**, ¨e	timetable
der **Hauptbahnhof**, ¨e	main *or* central station
der **Intercity(zug)**, -s/(¨e)	inter-city train
der **Koffer**	case, suitcase
der **Kofferkuli**, -s	luggage trolley
der **Nahverkehrszug**, ¨e	local train
der **Passagier**, -e	passenger
Reisende(r), -n	traveller
der **Rucksack**, ¨e	rucksack, backpack
der **Schnellimbiss**, -e	snack bar
der **Schnellzug**, ¨e	fast train, express train
der **Speisewagen**	dining car
der **U-Bahnhof**, ¨e	underground station
der **Wagen**	carriage, coach
der **Zug**, ¨e	train
der **Zuschlag**, ¨e	supplement

ESSENTIAL WORDS *(neuter)*

das **Gepäck**	luggage
das **Gleis**, -e	platform; track, rails
das **Rad**, ¨er	bike
das **Schließfach**, ¨er	left luggage locker
das **Taxi**, -s	taxi

ESSENTIAL WORDS *(feminine)*

die **Abfahrt, -en**	departure
die **Ankunft, ¨-e**	arrival
die **Auskunft, ¨-e**	information; information desk *or* office
die **Bahn, -en**	railway
die **Bahnlinie, -n**	railway line
die **Brücke, -n**	bridge
Deutsche Bahn (DB)	German Railways
die **Einfahrt, -en**	entrance
die **(einfache) Fahrkarte, (-n) -n**	(single) ticket
die **Fahrt, -en**	journey
die **Haltestelle, -n**	stop, station
die **Klasse, -n**	class
die **Linie, -n**	line
die **Reise, -n**	journey
die **Richtung, -en**	direction
die **Rückfahrkarte, -n**	return ticket
die **S-Bahn, -en**	high-speed railway; suburban railway
die **Station, -en**	station
die **Tasche, -n**	bag
die **U-Bahn, -en** *(Untergrundbahn)*	underground (railway)
die **U-Bahnstation, -en**	underground station
die **Uhr, -en**	clock; time

USEFUL PHRASES

auf dem Bahnhof **at the station**
sich erkundigen **to make inquiries**
einen Platz reservieren **to book a seat**
nach Bonn einfach **a single to Bonn**
nach Bonn und zurück **a return to Bonn**
zweimal nach Bonn und zurück **two returns to Bonn**
für diese Züge muss man Zuschlag bezahlen **you have to pay a supplement on these trains**
„bitte einsteigen!" **"all aboard"**; „alles aussteigen!" **"all change"**
muss ich umsteigen? **do I have to change trains?**

IMPORTANT WORDS *(masculine)*

der	Anschluss, -̈e	connection
der	Dienst, -e	service
der	Dienstwagen	guard's van
der	Eisenbahner	railwayman
der	Fahrausweis, -e	ticket
der	Gepäckwagen	luggage van
der	ICE, -s *or* der Intercityexpress	high-speed inter-city (train)
der	Liegewagen	couchette
der	Lokomotivführer	train driver
der	Platz, -̈e	seat
der	Schaffner	guard; ticket collector
der	Schlafwagen	sleeping car, sleeper
der	Zollbeamte, -n	customs officer

IMPORTANT WORDS *(feminine)*

die	Bahnhofsgaststätte, -n	station buffet
die	Bremse, -n	brake
die	Eisenbahn, -en	railway
die	Gepäckaufbewahrung, -en	left luggage office
die	Grenze, -n	border, frontier
die	Mehrfahrtenkarte, -n	season ticket
die	Notbremse, -n	alarm, communication cord
die	Verbindung, -en	connection
die	Verspätung, -en	delay
die	Zollkontrolle, -n	customs control *or* check

IMPORTANT WORDS *(neuter)*

das	Abteil, -e	compartment
das	Fahrgeld, -er	fare
das	Gepäcknetz, -e	luggage rack
das	Nichtraucherabteil, -e	non-smoking compartment
das	Raucherabteil, -e	smoking compartment
das	(Reise)ziel, -e	destination

USEFUL WORDS (masculine)

der	Anhänger	label, tag
der	Bahnübergang, ¨e	level crossing
der	Bestimmungsort, -e	destination (of goods)
der	Fahrpreis, -e	fare
der	Gepäckträger	porter
der	Güterzug, ¨e	goods train
der	Personenzug, ¨e	slow train; passenger train
der	Pfiff, -e	whistle
der	Schrankkoffer	trunk
der	Taxistand, ¨e	taxi rank
der	Vorortzug, ¨e	commuter train
der	Wartesaal, -säle	waiting room

USEFUL WORDS (feminine)

die	Bahncard, -s	railcard
die	(Eisenbahn)schienen (pl)	rails
die	Endstation, -en	terminus
die	Entgleisung, -en	derailment
die	Lokomotive, -n	locomotive, engine
die	Monatskarte, -n	monthly season ticket
die	Nummer, -n	number
die	Reservierung, -en	reservation
die	Rolltreppe, -n	escalator
die	Schienen (pl)	rails
die	Schranke, -n	level crossing gate
die	Sperre, -n	barrier
die	Strecke, -n	(section of) railway line or track
die	Wochenkarte, -n	weekly ticket

USEFUL PHRASES

mit der Bahn by rail
den Zug erreichen/verpassen to catch/miss one's train
ist dieser Platz frei? is this seat free?
hier ist besetzt this seat is taken
„nicht hinauslehnen" "do not lean out of the window"
verspätet delayed

USEFUL WORDS *(feminine)*

die	Beere, -n	berry
die	Birke, -n	birch
die	Blutbuche, -n	copper beech
die	Buche, -n	beech tree
die	Eibe, -n	yew
die	Eiche, -n	oak
die	Esche, -n	ash
die	Fichte, -n	spruce, pine
die	Föhre, -n	Scots pine
die	Kastanie, -n	chestnut; chestnut tree
die	Kiefer, -n	pine
die	Knospe, -n	bud
die	Linde, -n	lime tree
die	Mistel, -n	mistletoe
die	Pappel, -n	poplar
die	Pinie, -n	pine
die	Platane, -n	plane tree
die	Rinde, -n	bark
die	Rosskastanie, -n	horse chestnut
die	Stechpalme, -n	holly
die	Tanne, -n	fir tree
die	Trauerweide, -n	weeping willow
die	Ulme, -n	elm
die	Weide, -n	willow
die	Wurzel, -n	root

IMPORTANT + USEFUL WORDS *(neuter)*

das	Blatt, ¨-er	leaf
das	Geäst *(sg)*	branches
das	Gebüsch *(sg)*	bushes; undergrowth
das	Holz, ¨-er	wood *(material)*

USEFUL PHRASES

auf einen Baum klettern **to climb a tree**
im Herbst werden die Blätter gelb **the leaves turn yellow in autumn**
im Schatten eines Baums **in the shade of a tree**

ESSENTIAL + IMPORTANT WORDS *(masculine)*

der Baum, Bäume	tree
der Christbaum, -bäume	Christmas tree
der Forst, -e	forest
der Obstbaum, -bäume	fruit tree
der Obstgarten, -̈	orchard
der Schatten	shade, shadow
der Wald, -̈er	wood(s), forest
der Weihnachtsbaum, -bäume	Christmas tree

USEFUL WORDS *(masculine)*

der Ahorn, -e	maple
der Ast, -̈e	branch
der Buchsbaum, -bäume	box tree
der Busch, -̈e	bush, shrub
der Eich(en)baum, -bäume	oak tree
der Kastanienbaum, -bäume	chestnut tree
der Kiefernzapfen	pine cone
der Mistelzweig, -e	(sprig of) mistletoe
der Rotdorn, -e	hawthorn
der Stamm, -̈e	trunk
der Strauch, Sträucher	bush, shrub
der Tannenbaum, -bäume	fir tree
der Tannenzapfen	fir cone
der Weidenbaum, -bäume	willow
der Weinberg, -e	vineyard
der Wipfel	tree-top
der Zweig, -e	branch

ESSENTIAL WORDS (*masculine*)

der **Champignon, -s**	(button) mushroom
der **Kohl, -e**	cabbage
der **Kopfsalat, -e**	lettuce
der **Salat, -e**	lettuce; salad

IMPORTANT WORDS (*masculine*)

der **Blumenkohl, -e**	cauliflower
der **Knoblauch**	garlic
der **Pilz, -e**	mushroom
der **Rosenkohl**	Brussels sprouts (*pl*)
der **Vegetarier**	vegetarian

USEFUL WORDS (*masculine*)

der **Gartenkürbis, -se**	marrow
der **Kürbis, -se**	pumpkin
der **Lauch, -e**	leek
der **Mais**	sweetcorn
der **Maiskolben**	corn on the cob
der **(rote/grüne) Paprika, (-n) -s**	(red/green) pepper
der **Porree, -s**	leek
der **Rettich, -e**	(*large*) radish
der **Rotkohl, -e**	red cabbage
der *or* die **Sellerie**	celeriac; celery
der **Spargel**	asparagus
der **Spinat**	spinach
der *or* die **Stangensellerie**	celery
der **Weißkohl, -e**	white cabbage

USEFUL PHRASES

Gemüse anbauen **to grow vegetables**; organisch **organic**
Salzkartoffeln (*pl*) **boiled potatoes**
Pellkartoffeln (*pl*) **potatoes boiled in their jackets**
Bratkartoffeln (*pl*) **fried** *or* **sauté potatoes**
Knoblauchwurst (*f*) **garlic sausage**
geraspelte Möhre **grated carrot**
rot wie eine Tomate **as red as a beetroot**
vegetarisch **vegetarian**

ESSENTIAL WORDS *(feminine)*

die	**Bohne, -n**	bean
die	**grüne Bohne, -n -n**	French bean
die	**Erbse, -n**	pea
die	**Kartoffel, -n**	potato
die	**Tomate, -n**	tomato
die	**Zwiebel, -n**	onion

IMPORTANT WORDS *(feminine)*

die	**Aubergine, -n**	aubergine
die	**Avocado, -s**	avocado (pear)
die	**Brokkoli** *(pl)*	broccoli
die	**Gurke, -n**	cucumber
die	**Karotte, -n**	carrot
die	**Vegetarierin**	vegetarian

USEFUL WORDS *(feminine)*

die	**Artischocke, -n**	artichoke
die	**Aubergine, -n**	aubergine
die	**Brunnenkresse**	watercress
die	**Endivie, -n**	endive
die	**Erdartischocke, -n**	Jerusalem artichoke
die	**Essiggurke, -n**	gherkin
die	**Kresse**	cress
die	**Möhre, -n; die Mohrrübe, -n**	carrot
die	**Paprikaschote, -n**	pepper, capsicum
die	**Pastinake, -n**	parsnip
die	**Petersilie**	parsley
die	**Rübe, -n**	turnip
die	**Rote Bete** *or* **Rübe, -n -n**	beetroot
die	**Zucchini**	courgette

ESSENTIAL + IMPORTANT WORDS *(neuter)*

das	**Gemüse**	vegetable(s)
das	**Kraut, Kräuter**	herb; cabbage
das	**Radieschen**	radish
das	**Sauerkraut**	pickled cabbage

ESSENTIAL WORDS *(masculine)*

der **Bus, -se**	bus
der **Dampfer**	steamer
der **Krankenwagen**	ambulance
der **Lastkraftwagen (LKW)**	lorry, truck; heavy goods vehicle
der **Personenkraftwagen (PKW)**	private car
der **Polizeiwagen**	police car
der **Straßenbahnwagen**	tramcar
der **Tanker**	tanker
der **Wagen**	car; cart; carriage
der **Wohnwagen**	caravan
der **Zug, ̈-e**	train

ESSENTIAL WORDS *(feminine)*

die **Fähre, -n**	ferry
die **Straßenbahn, -en**	tram
die **U-Bahn, -en**	underground

ESSENTIAL WORDS *(neuter)*

das **Auto, -s**	car
das **Boot, -e**	boat
das **Fährboot, -e**	ferry-boat
das **Fahrrad, ̈-er**	bicycle
das **Flugzeug, -e**	plane, aeroplane
das **Mofa, -s**	moped *(small)*
das **Motorboot, -e**	motorboat
das **Motorrad, ̈-er**	motorbike, motorcycle
das **Rad, ̈-er**	bike
das **Ruderboot, -e**	rowing boat
das **Schiff, -e**	ship, vessel
das **Taxi, -s**	taxi
das **Wohnmobil, -e**	camper, motor caravan

USEFUL PHRASES

reisen to travel
fahren to go
eine Reise machen to go on a journey
gute Reise! have a good trip!
mit der Bahn or dem Zug fahren to go by rail or by train
mit dem Auto fahren to drive, go by car
nach Frankfurt fliegen to fly to Frankfurt
zu Fuß gehen to walk, go on foot
trampen, per Anhalter fahren to hitch-hike
mit einer Höchstgeschwindigkeit von 100 Kilometern pro Stunde fahren to
   drive at a maximum speed of 100 kilometres per hour
seine Fahrkarte entwerten to cancel one's ticket (in machine)
Gebrauchtwagen second-hand cars
mieten to hire
ein Mietauto (nt) a hired car
öffentliche Verkehrsmittel (pl) public transport

IMPORTANT WORDS *(masculine)*

der	**Bulldozer**	bulldozer
der	**Fahrpreis, -e**	fare
der	**Feuerwehrwagen**	fire engine
der	**Flugzeugträger**	aircraft carrier
der	**Hubschrauber**	helicopter
der	**Jeep, -s**	jeep
der	**Kindersportwagen**	baby buggy, push-chair
der	**Lieferwagen**	van; delivery van
der	**Möbelwagen**	removal van, furniture van
der	**(Motor)roller**	(motor) scooter
der	**(Reise)bus, -se**	coach
der	**Rücksitz, -e**	back seat
der	**Transporter**	van; transporter
der	**Vordersitz, -e**	front seat

IMPORTANT WORDS *(feminine)*

die	**Autofähre, -n**	car ferry
die	**fliegende Untertasse, -n -n**	flying saucer
die	**Gefahr, -en**	danger, risk
die	**Lokomotive, -n**	locomotive, engine

IMPORTANT WORDS *(neuter)*

das	**Fahrgeld, -er**	fare
das	**Fahrzeug, -e**	vehicle
das	**Feuerwehrauto, -s**	fire engine
das	**Kanu, -s**	canoe
das	**Moped, -s**	moped
das	**Raumschiff, -e**	spaceship
das	**Rettungsboot, -e**	lifeboat
das	**Schnellboot, -e**	speedboat
das	**Segelboot, -e**	sailing boat
das	**UFO, -s**	UFO *(unidentified flying object)*

USEFUL WORDS (masculine)

der	Anhänger	trailer
der	Karren	cart
der	Kinderwagen	pram
der	Kombiwagen	estate car, station wagon
der	Lastkahn, -̈e	barge
der	(Luft)ballon, -s or -e	balloon
der	Omnibus, -se	bus
der	Panzer	tank
der	Sattelschlepper	articulated lorry
der	Schleppdampfer; der Schlepper	tug, tugboat
der	Sessellift, -e or -s	chairlift
der	Streifenwagen	(police) patrol car
der	Vergnügungsdampfer	pleasure steamer

USEFUL WORDS (feminine)

die	Dampfwalze, -n	steamroller
die	Drahtseilbahn, -en	cable railway, funicular
die	Düse, -n	jet (plane)
die	Jacht, -en	yacht
die	Planierraupe, -n	bulldozer
die	Rakete, -n	rocket
die	Schwebebahn, -en	cable or overhead railway

USEFUL WORDS (neuter)

das	Düsenflugzeug, -e	jet plane
das	Luftkissenboot, -e	hovercraft
das	Paddelboot, -e	canoe
das	Schlauchboot, -e	inflatable dinghy
das	Segelflugzeug, -e	glider
das	Tankschiff, -e	tanker
das	Transportmittel	means of transport (goods)
das	U-Boot, -e (Unterseeboot)	submarine
das	Verkehrsmittel	means of transport (passengers)

ESSENTIAL WORDS *(masculine)*

der	Abend, -e	evening
der	Berg, -e	mountain
der	Blitz, -e	(flash of) lightning
der	Donner	thunder
der	Frost, ¨-e	frost
der	Frühling, -e	spring
der	Grad, -e	degree
der	Herbst, -e	autumn
der	Himmel	sky; heaven
der	Monat, -e	month
der	Morgen	morning
der	Nachmittag, -e	afternoon
der	Nebel	fog, mist
der	Nord(en)	north
der	Ort, -e *or* ¨-er	place
der	Osten	east
der	Regen	rain
der	Schnee	snow
der	Schneesturm, ¨-e	snowstorm
der	Sommer	summer
der	Sonnenschein	sunshine
der	Sturm, ¨-e	storm, gale; tempest
der	Süden	south
der	Westen	west
der	Wind, -e	wind
der	Winter	winter

USEFUL PHRASES

blitzen **to flash** (es blitzt); donnern **to thunder** (es donnert)
frieren **to freeze** (es friert); gießen **to pour** (es gießt)
nieseln **to drizzle** (es nieselt); regnen **to rain** (es regnet)
scheinen **to shine** (die Sonne scheint)
schneien **to snow** (es schneit)
es fängt an zu schneien **it's beginning to snow**

ESSENTIAL WORDS *(feminine)*

die	Insel, -n	island
die	Jahreszeit, -en	season
die	Luft	air
die	Nacht, ̈-e	night
die	Natur	nature
die	Sonne	sun
die	Temperatur, -en	temperature
die	Welt	world
die	Wolke, -n	cloud

ESSENTIAL WORDS *(neuter)*

das	Eis	ice
das	Gewitter	thunderstorm
das	Glatteis	black ice
das	Jahr, -e	year
das	Land, ̈-er	country
das	Licht, -er	light
das	Wetter	weather

USEFUL PHRASES

wie ist das Wetter heute? what's the weather like today?
wie ist das Wetter bei euch? what's the weather like with you?
wie ist die Wettervorhersage? what's the weather forecast?
heiß hot; kalt cold
warm warm; kühl cool
herrlich marvellous; schön lovely; schrecklich terrible
sonnig sunny; windig windy
mild mild; rau harsh
schwül sultry, close; trüb dull
bedeckt overcast; bewölkt cloudy
stürmisch stormy; neblig misty
trocken dry; nass wet; feucht damp
heiter bright; regnerisch rainy

IMPORTANT WORDS *(masculine)*

der	**Donnerschlag, ⸚e**	thunderclap
der	**Hagel**	hail
der	**Mond**	moon
der	**Mondschein**	moonlight
der	**Niederschlag, ⸚e**	rainfall, precipitation
der	**Planet, -en**	planet
der	**Regenschauer**	shower of rain
der	**(Regen)schirm, -e**	umbrella
der	**Regentropfen**	raindrop
der	**Schatten**	shadow; shade
der	**Schauer**	shower
der	**Schneefall, ⸚e**	snowfall
der	**Schneeregen**	sleet
der	**Smog**	smog
der	**Sonnenschirm, -e**	parasol, sunshade
der	**Stern, -e**	star
der	**Wetterbericht, -e**	weather report

IMPORTANT WORDS *(feminine)*

die	**Front, -en**	front
die	**Hitze**	heat
die	**Kälte**	cold
die	**Verbesserung, -en**	improvement
die	**Wetterlage**	weather situation
die	**Wettervorhersage,-n**	weather forecast

IMPORTANT WORDS *(neuter)*

das	**Halbdunkel**	semi-darkness
das	**Klima, -s** *or* **-ta**	climate
das	**Mondlicht**	moonlight
das	**Sauwetter**	awful weather

USEFUL PHRASES
herrschen to prevail; zeitweise for a time
vereinzelt bewölkt with (occasional) cloudy patches
plus plus; minus minus
so ein Sauwetter! what awful weather!

USEFUL WORDS (masculine)

der	Blitzableiter	lightning conductor
der	Dunst	haze
der	Eiszapfen	icicle
der	Gefrierpunkt	freezing point
der	Hochdruck	high pressure
der	Orkan, ⸚e	hurricane
der	Platzregen	downpour
der	Regenbogen	rainbow
der	Sonnenaufgang, ⸚e	sunrise
der	Sonnenstrahl, -en	ray of sunshine
der	Sonnenuntergang, ⸚e	sunset
der	Tagesanbruch	dawn, break of day
der	Tau	dew
der	Tiefdruck	low pressure
der	Windstoß, ⸚e	gust of wind

USEFUL WORDS (feminine)

die	Atmosphäre	atmosphere
die	Aufheiterungen (pl)	bright periods
die	Bö, -en	squall, gust of wind
die	Brise, -n	breeze
die	Dürre, -n	(period of) drought
die	Flut, -en	flood
die	Hitzewelle, -n	heat wave
die	Kältewelle, -n	cold spell
die	(Morgen)dämmerung, -en	dawn
die	Schneeflocke, -n	snowflake
die	Schneewehe, -n	snowdrift
die	Überschwemmung, -en	flood, deluge

USEFUL WORDS (neuter)

das	Barometer	barometer
das	Schneegestöber	flurry of snow
das	Tauwetter	thaw
das	Unwetter	thunderstorm
das	Zwielicht	twilight

ESSENTIAL WORDS (*masculine*)

der Ausweis, -e	card
der Empfang, ¨e	reception
der Herbergsvater, ¨	warden
der Junge, -n	boy
der Rucksack, ¨e	backpack, rucksack
der Schlafsack, ¨e	sleeping bag
der Spaziergang, ¨e	walk
der Speisesaal, -säle	dining room
der Stadtplan, ¨e	street map
der Urlaub, -e	holiday(s)

ESSENTIAL WORDS (*feminine*)

die Anmeldung, -en	registration
die Dusche, -n	shower
die Herbergsmutter, ¨	(female) warden
die Jugendherberge, -n	youth hostel
die Küche, -n	kitchen
die Landkarte, -n	map
die Mahlzeit, -en	meal
die Toilette, -n	toilet
die Übernachtung, -en	overnight stay

ESSENTIAL WORDS (*neuter*)

das Abendessen	dinner, evening meal
das Badezimmer	bathroom
das Bett, -en	bed
das Büro, -s	office
das Essen	food; meal
das Frühstück, -e	breakfast
das Mädchen	girl

USEFUL PHRASES

bleiben to stay
übernachten to spend the night
sich anmelden to register
mieten to hire
„Hausordnung für Jugendherbergen" "youth hostel rules"

IMPORTANT WORDS *(masculine)*

der	**Aufenthalt, -e**	stay
	Erwachsene(r), -n	adult
der	**Feuerlöscher**	fire extinguisher
	Jugendliche(r), -n	young person
der	**Mülleimer**	dustbin
der	**Prospekt, -e**	leaflet, brochure
der	**Reiseführer**	guidebook
der	**Schlafsaal, -säle**	dormitory
der	**Waschraum, -räume**	washroom
der	**Waschsalon, -s**	laundrette
der	**Zimmernachweis, -e**	accommodation office

IMPORTANT WORDS *(feminine)*

die	**Bettwäsche**	bed linen, bedclothes *(pl)*
die	**Mitgliedskarte, -n**	membership card
die	**Nachtruhe**	lights-out
die	**Ruhe**	quiet
die	**Unterkunft, -künfte**	accommodation
die	**Veranstaltung, -en**	organization
die	**Wäsche**	washing *(things)*

IMPORTANT WORDS *(neuter)*

das	**Etagenbett, -en**	bunk bed
das	**schwarze Brett, -n -er**	notice board

The vocabulary items on pages 672 to 695 have been grouped under parts of speech rather than topics because they can apply in a wide range of circumstances. Use them just as freely as the vocabulary already given.

ADJECTIVES

> **What is an adjective?**
> An **adjective** is a 'describing' word that tells you more about a person or thing, such as their appearance, colour, size or other qualities, for example, *pretty*, *blue*, *big*.

abgenutzt worn out (*object*)
abscheulich hideous
ähnlich (*+ dat*) similar (to), like
aktuell topical
albern silly, foolish
allerlei all kinds of
allgemein general
alltäglich ordinary; daily
alt old
amüsant amusing
andere(r, s) other
anders different
angenehm pleasant
angrenzend neighbouring
arm poor
artig well-behaved, good
aufgeregt excited
aufgeweckt bright, lively
aufrichtig sincere
ausführlich detailed, elaborate
ausgestreckt stretched (out)
ausgezeichnet excellent
ausschließlich sole, exclusive
außerordentlich extra-ordinary
befriedigend satisfactory
begeistert keen, enthusiastic
belebt busy (*street*)

beleuchtet illuminated
beliebt popular
bemerkenswert remarkable
benachbart neighbouring
bereit ready
berühmt famous
beschäftigt (mit) busy (with)
  (*of person*)
besetzt engaged; taken
besondere(r, s) special
besorgt worried, anxious
besser better
betrunken drunk
beunruhigt worried, disturbed
blöd silly, stupid
brav well-behaved
breit wide, broad
bunt colourful
dankbar grateful
dauernd perpetual, constant
delikat delicate; delicious
deutlich clear; distinct
dicht thick, dense
dick thick
doof daft, stupid
dreckig dirty, filthy
dringend urgent

dumm silly, stupid; annoying
dunkel dark
dünn thin
dynamisch dynamic
echt real, genuine
ehemalig old, former
ehrlich sincere, honest
eifrig keen, enthusiastic
eigen own
einfach simple; single
einzeln single, individual
einzig only
elegant elegant, smart
elektrisch, Elektro- electric
elend poor, wretched
End- final
endgültig final, definite
endlos endless
eng narrow; tight
entschlossen firm, determined
entsetzlich dreadful
entzückend delightful
erfahren experienced
ernst serious, solemn
ernsthaft serious, earnest
erreichbar reachable, within reach
erschöpft exhausted, worn out
erste(r, s) first
erstaunlich amazing,
   extraordinary
erstaunt astonished
fähig (zu) capable (of)
falsch false; wrong
faul rotten; lazy
feierlich solemn
fein fine
fern far-off, distant
fertig prepared, ready
fest firm, hard

fett fat; greasy
finster dark
flach flat
fortgeschritten advanced
fortwährend continual, endless
frech cheeky
frei free, vacant
frisch fresh
furchtbar frightful
fürchterlich terrible, awful
ganz whole, complete
geduldig patient
geeignet suitable
gefährlich dangerous
gefroren frozen
geheim secret
geheimnisvoll mysterious
gemischt mixed
gemütlich comfortable
genau exact, precise
gerade straight; even
geringste(r, s) slightest, least
gesamt whole, entire
geschichtlich historical
gestattet allowed
gewaltig tremendous, huge
gewalttätig violent
gewiss certain
gewöhnlich usual; ordinary;
   common
glatt smooth
gleich same; equal
glücklich happy; fortunate
gnädig gracious
gnädige Frau Madam
graziös graceful
grob coarse, rude
groß big, great, large; tall
großartig magnificent

günstig suitable, convenient
gut good
hart hard
hässlich ugly
Haupt- main
heftig fierce, violent
heiß hot
hell pale; bright, light
herrlich marvellous
hervorragend excellent
historisch historical
hoch high
höflich polite, civil
hübsch pretty
intelligent intelligent
interessant interesting
jede(r, s) each, every
jung young
kalt cold
kein no, not any
klar clear, sharp
klatschnass soaking wet
klein small, little
klug wise, clever
komisch funny
kompliziert complicated
körperlich physical
kostbar expensive; precious
kostenlos free (of charge)
köstlich delicious
kräftig strong
kühl cool
kurz short
lächelnd smiling
lächerlich ridiculous
lahm lame
Landes- national
lang long; tall (of person)
langsam slow

langweilig boring
laut loud, noisy
lebendig alive; lively
lebhaft lively (of person)
lecker delicious, tasty
leer empty
leicht easy; light (weight)
leidenschaftlich passionate
leise quiet; soft
letzte(r, s) last, latest; final
lieb dear
Lieblings- favourite
linke(r, s) left
lustig amusing; cheerful
sich lustig machen über (+ acc)
    to make fun of
luxuriös luxurious
Luxus- luxury, luxurious
mächtig powerful, mighty
mager thin
mehrere several
merkwürdig strange, odd
Militär-, militärisch military
mindeste(r, s) least
mitleidig sympathetic
modern modern
möglich possible
müde tired
munter lively
mutig courageous
mysteriös mysterious
nächste(r, s) next; nearest
nah(e) near; close
natürlich natural
nett nice, kind
neu new
neugierig curious
niedrig low
nötig necessary

notwendig necessary
nützlich useful
nutzlos useless
obligatorisch compulsory,
  obligatory
offen open; frank, sincere
offenbar, offensichtlich obvious
öffentlich public
offiziell official
ordentlich (neat and) tidy
Orts- local
pädagogisch educational
passend suitable
persönlich personal
populär popular
prächtig magnificent
privat private; personal
privilegiert privileged
pünktlich punctual
Quadrat-, quadratisch square
rau rough; harsh
rechte(r, s) right
reich rich
reif ripe
rein clean
reizend charming
religiös religious
reserviert reserved
richtig right, correct
riesig huge, gigantic
romantisch romantic
ruhig quiet, peaceful
rund round
sanft gentle, soft
satt full (*person*)
ich habe es satt I'm fed up (with it)
sauber clean
scharf sharp; spicy
schattig shady

scheu shy
schick smart, chic
schläfrig sleepy
schlank slender, slim
schlau cunning, sly
schlecht bad
schlimm bad
schmal narrow; slender
schmutzig dirty
schnell fast, quick, rapid
schön beautiful
schrecklich terrible; frightful
schroff steep; jagged; brusque
schüchtern shy
schwach weak
schweigsam silent
schwer heavy; serious
schwierig difficult
seltsam strange, odd, curious
sicher sure; safe
sichtbar visible
solche(r, s) such
Sonder- special
sonderbar strange, odd
sorgenfrei carefree
sorgfältig careful
spannend exciting
Stadt-, städtisch municipal, urban
ständig perpetual
stark strong; heavy
steif stiff
steil steep
still quiet, still
stolz (auf + *acc*) proud (of)
streng severe, harsh; strict
stur stubborn
süß sweet
sympathisch likeable
tapfer brave

technisch technical
tief deep
toll mad; terrific
tot dead
tragbar portable
traurig sad
treu true (*friend etc*)
trocken dry
typisch typical
übel wicked, bad
übrig left-over
unartig naughty
unbekannt unknown
uneben uneven
unerträglich unbearable
ungeheuer huge
ungezogen rude
unglaublich incredible
unglücklich unhappy; unfortunate
unheimlich weird
unmöglich impossible
ursprünglich original
verantwortlich responsible
verboten prohibited, forbidden
verlegen embarrassed
verletzt injured
verliebt in love

vernünftig sensible, reasonable
verrückt mad, crazy
verschieden various; different
verständlich understandable
viereckig square
volkstümlich popular (*of the people*)
voll (+ *gen*) full (of)
vollkommen perfect, complete
vollständig complete
vorderste(r, s) front (*row etc*)
wach awake
wahr true
warm warm
weich soft
weise wise
weit wide
wert worth
wichtig important
wild fierce, wild
wohlhabend well-off
wunderbar wonderful, marvellous
zäh tough
zahlreich numerous
zart gentle, tender
zig umpteen
zufrieden satisfied, contented
zusätzlich extra

ADVERBS

> **What is an adverb?**
> An **adverb** is a word usually used with verbs, adjectives or other
> adverbs that gives more information about when, how, where, or in
> what circumstances something happens: *quickly, happily, now* are all
> adverbs.

Many other adverbs have the same form as the adjective.

absichtlich deliberately, on purpose
allein alone, on one's own some day
allerdings certainly; of course,
  to be sure
am besten best, best of all
am liebsten most (of all), best
  (of all)
am meisten (the) most
anders otherwise; differently
auf einmal all at once
äußerst extremely, most
bald soon; almost
besonders especially, particularly
bestimmt definitely, for sure
bloß only, merely
da there; here; then
daher from there; from that
dahin (to) there; then
damals at that time
danach after that; afterwards
dann then
darin in it, in there
deshalb therefore, for that reason
doch after all
dort there
dorthin (to) there
draußen out of doors; outside
drinnen inside; indoors
drüben over there, on the other side

durchaus thoroughly, absolutely
eben exactly; just
eher sooner; rather
eigentlich really, actually
einmal once; one day,
endlich at last, finally
erst first; only (*time*)
erstens first(ly), in the first place
etwa about; perhaps
fast almost, nearly
früh early
ganz quite; completely
gar nicht not at all
gegenwärtig at present, at the
  moment
genau exactly, precisely
genug enough
gerade just, exactly
geradeaus straight ahead
gern(e) willingly; gladly
gewöhnlich usually
glücklicherweise fortunately
gut well
häufig frequently
heutzutage nowadays
hier here
hierher this way, here
hin und her to and fro
hinten at the back, behind

höchst highly, extremely
hoffentlich I hope, hopefully
immer always
immer noch still
inzwischen meanwhile, in the
  meantime
irgendwo(hin) (to) somewhere
je ... desto: je mehr desto besser
  the more the better
je ever
jedenfalls in any case
jedesmal each time, everytime
jedesmal wenn whenever
jemals ever; at any time
jetzt now
kaum hardly, scarcely
keineswegs in no way; by no
  means
komischerweise funnily (enough),
  in a funny way
künftig in future
lange for a long time
langsam slowly
lauter *(with pl)* nothing but, only
leider unfortunately
lieber rather, preferably
links left; on *or* to the left
manchmal sometimes
mehr more
meinetwegen for my sake; on my
  account
meistens mostly, for the most part
mitten (in) in the middle *or* midst
  (of)
möglichst as ... as possible
nachher afterwards
natürlich naturally
neu füllen *etc* to refill *etc*
neu newly; afresh, anew

nicht not
nichtsdestoweniger nevertheless
nie, niemals never
noch einmal (once) again
noch still; yet
normalerweise normally
nun now
nur just, only
oben above; upstairs
oft often
plötzlich suddenly
rechts right; on *or* to the right
richtig correctly; really
rundherum round about, all
  (a)round
schlecht badly
schließlich finally
schnell quickly
schon already
sehr very, a lot, very much
selbst even
selten seldom, rarely
so so, thus, like this
sofort at once, immediately
sogar even
sogleich at once, straight away
sonst otherwise; or else
spät late
überall(hin) everywhere
übrigens besides, by the way
umher about, around
ungefähr about, approximately
unten below; downstairs; at the
  bottom
unterwegs on the way
viel much, a lot
vielleicht perhaps, maybe
völlig completely
vorbei by, past

vorher before, previously, beforehand
wahrscheinlich probably
wann(?) when(?)
warum(?) why(?)
weit far
wie(?), wie! how(?), how!
wieder again
wirklich really
wo/woher/wohin/wovon(?) where/from where/(to) where/from where(?)

ziemlich fairly, rather
zu to
zuerst first; at first
zufällig by chance; by any chance
zurück back
zweitens second(ly), in the second place

SOME MORE NOUNS

> **What is a noun?**
> A **noun** is a 'naming' word for a living being, thing or idea, for example, *woman, Andrew, desk, happiness.*

das **Abenteuer** adventure
der **Abhang,** ¨e slope
die **Abkürzung, -en** abbreviation; short-cut
der **Abschnitt, -e** section
die **Absicht, -en** intention
der **Abstieg, -e** descent
die **Abteilung, -en** department, section
die **Abwesenheit, -en** absence
die **Ahnung, -en** idea, suspicion
die **Änderung, -en** alteration, change
der **Anfang,** ¨e beginning
zu **Anfang** at the beginning
die **Angst,** ¨e fear
ich habe **Angst (vor +** *dat*) I am afraid *or* frightened (of)
die **Anmeldung, -en** announcement
die **Anstalten** (*fpl*) preparations
die **Anstrengung, -en** effort
die **Antwort, -en** answer, reply
die **Anweisungen** (*fpl*) orders, instructions
die **Anwesenheit** presence
das **Anzeichen** sign, indication
die **Anzeige, -n** advertisement
der **Apparat, -e** machine
das **Ärgernis, -se** annoyance
die **Art, -en** way, method; kind, sort
auf meine **Art** in my own way
aller **Art** of all kinds
der **Aufenthalt, -e** stay

die **Aufmerksamkeit** attention; attentiveness
die **Aufsicht** supervision
der **Aufstieg, -e** ascent
der **Ausdruck,** ¨e term, expression
die **Auseinandersetzung, -en** argument
der **Ausgangspunkt, -e** starting point
die **Ausnahme, -n** exception
die **Ausstellung, -en** exhibition
die **Auswahl, -en (an +** *dat*) selection (of)
der **Bau** construction
die **Beaufsichtigung** supervision
die **Bedeutung, -en** meaning; importance
die **Bedingung, -en** condition, stipulation
das **Bedürfnis, -se** need
der **Befehl, -e** order, command
die **Begabung, -en** talent
der **Begriff: im Begriff sein, etw zu tun** to be about to do sth
das **Beispiel, -e** example
zum **Beispiel** for example
die **Bemerkung, -en** remark
die **Bemühung, -en** trouble, effort
die **Berechnung, -en** calculation
der **Bescheid, -e** message, information
jdm **Bescheid sagen** to let sb know

sein Bestes tun to do one's best
der Betrag, ⁻e sum, amount
  (*of money*)
der Blödsinn nonsense
die Botschaft, -en message, news;
  embassy
die Breite, -n width
der Bursche, -n fellow
die Chance, -n chance, opportunity
der Dank thanks (*pl*)
die Darstellung, -en portrayal,
  representation
das Denken thinking, thought
das Diagramm, -e diagram
die Dicke, -n thickness; fatness
der Dienst, -e service
die Dimension -en dimension
das Ding, -e thing, object
der Duft, ⁻e smell, fragrance
die Dummheit, -en stupidity;
  stupid mistake
der Dummkopf, ⁻e idiot
der Dunst, ⁻e vapour
die Ecke, -n corner
die Ehre, -n honour
die Einbildung, -en imagination
der Eindruck, ⁻e impression
der Einfall, ⁻e thought, idea
die Einzelheit, -en detail
die Eleganz elegance
der Empfang, ⁻e reception
die Empfindung, -en feeling,
  emotion
das Ende, -n end
zu Ende gehen to end
die Entschlossenheit resolution,
  determination
das Ereignis, -se event
die Erfahrung, -en experience

der Erfolg, -e result; success
das Ergebnis, -se result
die Erinnerung, -en memory,
  remembrance
die Erklärung, -en explanation
die Erkundigung, -en inquiry
die Erlaubnis, -se permission; permit
das Erlebnis, -se experience
der Ernst seriousness
im Ernst in earnest
das Erstaunen astonishment
die Erwiderung, -en retort
das Exil, -e exile (*state*)
der Feind, -e enemy
die Flamme, -n flame
die Folge, -n order; series; result
die Form, -en form, shape
die Frage, -n question
Fremde(r), -n, die Fremde, -n
  stranger; foreigner
die Freude, -n joy, delight
die Freundlichkeit, -en kindness
die Freundschaft, -en friendship
der Frieden peace
die Frische freshness
der Führer guide; leader
die Gebühr, -en fee, charge
das Gedächtnis, -se memory
der Gedanke, -n thought
die Geduld patience
die Gefahr, -en danger
der Gegenstand, ⁻e object
das Gegenteil, -e opposite
im Gegenteil on the contrary
die Gegenwart present
das Geheimnis, -se mystery; secret
die Gelegenheit, -en opportunity,
  occasion
das Gerät, -e device, tool

das **Geräusch**, -e sound, noise
der **Geruch**, ⸚e smell
das **Geschick**, -e fate; skill
der **Geselle**, -n fellow
der **Gesichtspunkt**, -e point of view
das **Glück** luck; happiness
der **Gott**, ⸚er god
der **(liebe) Gott** God
der **Grund**, ⸚e reason
die **Gruppe**, -n group
die **Grüße** (mpl) wishes
die **Güte** kindness
die **Hauptsache**, -n the main thing
der **Heimweg**, -e way home
die **Herstellung**, -en manufacture
die **Hilfe** help
der **Hintergrund**, ⸚e background
die **Hoffnung**, -en hope
die **Höflichkeit**, -en politeness
die **Höhe**, -n height; level
die **Idee**, -n idea
das **Interesse**, -n interest
der **Kampf**, ⸚e fight, battle
die **Kapelle**, -n chapel
das **Kapitel** chapter
die **Katastrophe**, -n disaster, catastrophe
die **Kenntnis**, -se knowledge
der **Kerl**, -e fellow, chap
die **Kette**, -n chain
der **Klang**, ⸚e sound
die **Klimaanlage** air conditioning
der **Kollege**, -n, die **Kollegin** colleague
die **Konstruktion**, -en construction
die **Kontrolle**, -n control, supervision
die **Kopie**, -n copy

der **Korb**, ⸚e basket
die **Kosten** (pl) cost(s); expenses
der **Kreis**, -e circle; district
der **Krieg**, -e war
der **Kurort**, -e health resort
der **Kuss**, ⸚e kiss
das **Lächeln** smile
die **Lage**, -n situation
die **Länge**, -n length
die **Lang(e)weile** boredom
der **Lärm** noise
der **Laut**, -e sound
das **Leben** life
der **Lebenslauf**, ⸚e CV
das **Leid** sorrow, grief
der **Leiter** chief, leader
der **Leser**, die **Leserin** reader
das **Licht**, -er light
die **Liebe**, -n love
die **Linie**, -n line
die **Liste**, -n list
die **Literatur** literature
das **Loch**, ⸚er hole
die **Lösung**, -en solution
die **Lücke**, -n opening, gap
die **Lüge**, -n lie
die **Lust: ich habe Lust, es zu tun** I feel like doing it
die **Macht**, ⸚e power
das **Magazin**, -e magazine
der **Mangel**, ⸚e (an + dat) lack (of), shortage (of)
die **Maschine**, -n machine
das **Maximum**, -a maximum
die **Meinung**, -en opinion, view
meiner Meinung nach in my opinion
das **meiste; die meisten** most
die **Meldung**, -en announcement

die **Menge**, -n crowd; quantity, lot
das **Minimum**, -a minimum
die **Mischung**, -en mixture
das **Missgeschick**, -e misfortune
das **Mitleid** sympathy
die **Mitteilung**, -en
  communication
das **Mittel** means; method
das **Modell**, -e model, version
die **Möglichkeit**, -en means;
  possibility
sein **Möglichstes tun** to do one's
  best
die **Mühe**, -n pains, trouble
die **Münze**, -n coin
der **Mut** courage, spirit
die **Nachrichten** (fpl) news;
  information
der **Nachteil**, -e disadvantage
die **Nähe: in der Nähe** close by
das **Netz**, -e network
die **Not** need, distress
die **Notiz**, -en note, item
die **Nummer**, -n number
das **Objekt**, -e object
die **Öffentlichkeit** the general
  public
die **Öffnung**, -en opening
die **Ordnung**, -en order
in **Ordnung bringen** to arrange,
  tidy (up)
alles ist in **Ordnung** everything is
  all right
der **Ort**, -e place
das **Pech** misfortune, bad luck
der **Pfeil**, -e arrow
das **Pfund**, -e pound (sterling);
  pound (weight)
der **Plan**, ¨e plan; map

der **Platz**, ¨e place; seat; room,
  space; square
die **Politik** politics; policy
das **Porträt**, -s portrait
das **Problem**, -e problem
das **Produkt**, -e product; produce
der **Punkt**, -e point; dot; full stop
die **Puppe**, -n doll
die **Qualität**, -en quality
der **Radau** hullaballoo
der **Rand**, ¨er edge; rim
der **Rat**, -schläge (piece of) advice
das **Rätsel** puzzle, riddle
der **Rauch** smoke
der **Raum**, **Räume** space; room
das **Recht**, -e law; justice; right
Recht haben to be right
die **Rede**, -n speech
eine **Rede halten** to make a speech
die **Regierung**, -en government;
  reign
die **Reihe**, -n series; line
ich bin an der **Reihe** it's my turn now
der **Reiz**, -e attraction, charm
die **Reklame**, -n advertisement
der **Rest** remainder, rest
die **Reste** (mpl) remains
das **Resultat**, -e result
der **Revolutionär**, -e revolutionary
der **Rhythmus**, -men rhythm
die **Richtung**, -en direction
die **Rückseite**, -n back (of page etc)
der **Ruf**, -e call, cry; reputation
die **Ruhe** rest; peace; calm; silence
die **Sache**, -n thing; matter
der **Schein**, -e (bank) note
ein **20-Mark-Schein** a 20-mark note
das **Schicksal**, -e fate
das **Schild**, -er sign; label

der **Schlag**, ⁼e blow, knock
der **Schluss**, ⁼e end(ing)
am **Schluss** at the end
der **Schmutz**, die **Schmutzigkeit**
  dirt, dirtiness
der **Schrei**, -e cry, scream
der **Schritt**, -e footstep; step, pace
die **Schuld** fault
ich bin nicht **schuld daran** it's not
  my fault
die **Schwierigkeit**, -en difficulty
die **Sensation**, -en stir, sensation
die **Serie**, -n series
die **Sicherheit**, -en security; safety
die **Sicht** sight; view
der **Sieg**, -e victory
der **Sinn**, -e mind; sense; meaning
die **Situation**, -en situation
die **Sorge**, -n care, worry
sich (dat) **Sorgen machen** to be
  worried
die **Sorte**, -n sort, kind
das **Souvenir**, -s souvenir
der **Spalt** crack, opening; split
die **Spalte**, -n column (of page)
der **Spaß**, ⁼e fun; joke
der **Spektakel** hullaballo
das **Spielzeug**, -e toy
die **Spur**, -en sign, trace
der **Staat**, -en state
der **Standpunkt**, -e point of view,
  standpoint
die **Stärke**, -n power, strength
die **Stelle**, -n place
die **Steuer**, -n tax
der **Stil**, -e style
die **Stille** quietness
die **Stimmung**, ⁼en mood;
  atmosphere

die **Strecke**, -n stretch; distance
das **Stück**, -e piece, part
die **Summe**, -n sum
das **System**, -e system
das **Talent**, -e talent
in der **Tat** in (actual) fact, indeed
die **Tätigkeit**, -en activity
der **Teil**, -e, das **Teil**, -e part, section
der **Text**, -e text
der **Titel** title
die **Tiefe**, -n depth
der **Traum**, ⁼e dream
der **Treffpunkt**, -e meeting place
der **Trost** comfort
die **Trümmer** (pl) wreckage; ruins
der **Typ**, -en type
Überlebende(r), -n survivor
die **Überraschung**, -en surprise
die **Umgebung**, -en surroundings
  (pl)
das **Unglück**, -e misfortune;
  bad luck; disaster
das **Unheil** evil; disaster,
  misfortune
das **Unrecht: Unrecht haben** to be
  wrong, be mistaken
die **Unterbrechung**, -en
  interruption
die **Unterhaltung**, -en
  conversation, chat
das **Unternehmen** undertaking,
  enterprise
der **Unterschied**, -e difference
der **Urlaub**, -e holidays, leave
die **Ursache**, -n reason, cause
die **Verabredung**, -en appointment
die **Verbindung**, -en connection
der **Vergleich**, -e comparison
das **Vergnügen** pleasure

der Versuch, -e attempt
das Vertrauen confidence
die Vorbereitung, -en preparation
der Vorschlag, -̈e suggestion
die Vorsicht care, caution
die Vorstellung, -en introduction;
  idea, thought
der Vorteil, -e advantage
die Wahl, -en choice, selection;
  election
der Wähler voter
die Wahrheit, -en truth
der Wechselkurs, -e exchange rate
die Weile, -n while
die Weise, -n way, method, manner
auf diese Weise in this way or
  manner
die Weite, -n width; distance
die Werbung, -en advertising
der Wert, -e value
die Wette, -n bet

die Wichtigkeit importance
die Wirklichkeit, -en fact, reality
die Wirkung, -en effect
der Witz, -e joke
der Wohlstand prosperity
das Wort, -̈er or -e word
der Wunsch, -̈e wish
die Wut rage, fury
die Zahl, -en number, figure
das Zeichen sign
die Zeile, -n line (of text)
die Zeitschrift, -en magazine
die Zeitung, -en newspaper
das Zentrum, Zentren centre
das Zeug stuff; gear
das Ziel, -e aim, goal; destination
das Ziffer, -n number, figure
der Zorn anger
die Zutaten (pl) ingredients
der Zweck, -e purpose

PREPOSITIONS AND CONJUNCTIONS

What is a preposition?
A preposition is one word such as *at, for, with, into* or *from*, or words such as *in front of* or *near to*, which are usually followed by a noun or a pronoun or, in English, a word ending in *-ing*.

Prepositions show how people and things relate to the rest of the sentence, for example, *She's <u>at</u> home; It's <u>for</u> you; You'll get <u>into</u> trouble; It's <u>in front of</u> you.*

What is a conjunction?
A conjunction is a word such as *and, but, or, so, if* and *because*, that links two words or phrases of a similar type, or two parts of a sentence, for example, *Diane <u>and</u> I have been friends for years; I left <u>because</u> I was bored.*

aber but; however
als when; as; than
als ob, als wenn as if, as though
also therefore, so
anstatt (+ *gen*) instead of
außer (+ *dat*) out of; except
außerhalb (+ *gen*) outside
bei (+ *dat*) near, by; at the house of
bevor before (*time*)
bis until, till (*conj*); (+ *acc*) until; (up) to, as far as
da as, since, seeing (that)
damit so that, in order that
dass that
denn for
ehe before
entweder ... oder either... or
gegenüber (+ *dat*) opposite; to(wards)
gerade als just as
hinter (+ *dat or acc*) behind
indem es, while
innerhalb (+ *gen*) in(side), within

je ..., desto the more ... the more
nachdem after
nun (da) now (that)
ob if, whether
obwohl although
oder or
ohne dass without
seit (+ *dat*) since
sobald as soon as
sodass so that
solange as long as
sondern (*after neg*) but
nicht nur ... sondern auch not only ... but also
sowohl ... als (auch) both... and
statt (+ *gen*) instead of
stattdessen instead
teils ... teils partly ... partly
trotz (+ *gen*) despite, in spite of
und and
während while (*conj*); (+ *gen*) during (*prep*)
weder ... noch neither ... nor

wegen *(+ gen)* because of
weil because
wenn when; if

wenn … auch although; even if
wie as, like

VERBS

What is a verb?
A **verb** is a 'doing' word which describes what somebody or something does, what they are, or what happens to them, for example, *play, be, disappear.*

abhängen von to depend on
abholen to fetch, go and meet (*somebody*)
ablehnen to refuse
abnehmen to lose weight
abschreiben to copy
akzeptieren to accept
anbeten to adore
anbieten to give, offer
anblicken to look (at)
ändern: seine Meinung ändern to change one's mind
anfangen to begin
angeben to state
angehören (+ *dat*) to belong to (*club etc*)
angreifen to attack; to touch
anhalten to stop; to continue
ankommen to arrive
ankündigen to announce
annehmen to accept; to assume
anschalten to switch on
antworten to answer, reply
anzeigen to announce
anziehen to attract; to put (on) (*clothes*)
sich ärgern to get angry
atmen to breathe
aufbewahren to keep, store
aufhängen to hang (up)
aufheben to raise, lift

aufhören to stop
aufkleben to stick on *or* onto
aufmachen to open
aufpassen (auf + *acc*) to watch; to be careful (of)
aufstehen to get up
aufwachen to wake up (*intransitive*)
aufwärmen to warm (up)
aufwecken to awaken, wake up (*transitive*)
ausdrücken to express
ausführen to carry out, execute
ausgeben to spend (*money*)
ausleihen to borrow
auslöschen to put out, extinguish
ausrufen to exclaim, cry (out)
sich ausruhen to rest
ausschalten to switch off
ausschlafen to have a good sleep
aussprechen to pronounce
ausstrecken to extend, hold out
sich ausstrecken to stretch out
auswählen to select
beabsichtigen to intend
beachten to observe, obey
sich (bei jdm) bedanken to say thank you (to sb)
bedauern to regret
bedecken to cover
bedeuten to mean
bedienen to serve; to operate

sich beeilen to hurry
beenden to finish
befehlen (+ *dat*) to order
sich befinden to be
begegnen (+ *dat*) to meet
beginnen to begin
begreifen to realize
behalten to keep, retain
behaupten to maintain
beherrschen to rule (over)
sich beklagen (über + *acc*) to
  complain (about)
bekommen to obtain
bemerken to notice
benachrichtigen to inform
benutzen to use
beobachten to watch
berichten to report
(sich) beruhigen to calm down
sich beschäftigen mit to attend to;
  to be concerned with
beschmutzen to dirty
beschreiben to describe
(be)schützen (vor + *dat*) to protect
  (from)
sich beschweren (über + *acc*)
  to complain (about)
besiegen to conquer
besitzen to own, possess
besprechen to discuss
bestehen (aus + *dat*) to consist (of),
  comprise
bestehen (auf + *dat*) to insist
  (upon)
bestellen to order
besuchen to attend, be present at,
  go to, visit
betreten to enter
beunruhigen to worry

(sich) bewegen to move
bewundern to admire
biegen to bend
bieten to offer
binden to tie
bitten to request
bitten um to ask for
bleiben to stay, remain
blicken (auf + *acc*) to glance (at),
  look (at)
borgen to borrow;
  jdm etw borgen to lend sb sth
brauchen to need
brechen to break
brennen to burn
bringen to bring, take
bummeln to wander; to skive
danken (+ *dat*) to thank
darstellen to represent
dauern to last
decken to cover
denken to think, believe
denken an (+ *acc*) to think of;
  to remember
denken über (+ *acc*) to think about;
  to reflect on
deuten (auf + *acc*) to point (to *or* at)
dienen to serve
diskutieren to discuss
drehen to turn; to shoot (*film*)
drucken to print
drücken to press, squeeze
durchführen to accomplish, carry
  out
durchqueren to cross, pass
  through
durchsuchen to search
dürfen to be allowed to
eilen to rush, dash

einfallen (+ *dat*) to occur (*to someone*)

einladen to invite

einrichten to establish, set up

einschalten to switch on

einschlafen to fall asleep

eintreten to come in

einwickeln to wrap (up)

empfangen to receive (*person*)

empfehlen to recommend

entdecken to discover

entführen to take away

enthalten to contain

(sich) entscheiden to decide

sich entschließen to make up one's mind

entschuldigen to excuse

sich entschuldigen (für) to apologize (for)

enttäuschen to disappoint

(sich) entwickeln to develop

sich ereignen to happen

erfahren to learn; to experience; **erfahren von** to hear about

erfolgreich successful

ergreifen to seize

erhalten to receive, get

sich erheben to rise

erinnern (an + acc) to remind (of)

sich erinnern (an + acc) to remember

erkennen to recognize

erklären to state; to explain

sich erkundigen (nach or über + acc) to inquire about

erlauben to allow, permit, let

erleben to experience

ermutigen to encourage

erobern to capture

erregen to disturb, excite

erreichen to reach; to catch (*train etc*)

errichten to erect

erschaffen to create

erscheinen to appear

erschrecken to frighten

erschüttern to shake, rock, stagger

erstaunen to astonish

erwachen to wake up (*intransitive*)

erwähnen to mention

erwarten to expect, await, wait for

erwidern to retort

erzählen to tell, explain

erziehen to bring up, educate

fallen to fall

fallen lassen to drop

falten to fold

fangen to catch

fassen to grasp; to comprehend

fehlen to be missing;

er fehlt mir I miss him

etw fertigmachen to bring sth about; to get sth ready

festbinden to tie, fasten

finden to find

fliehen (vor + dat, aus) to flee (from)

fließen (in + acc) to flow (into)

flüstern to whisper

folgen (+ *dat*) to follow

fordern to demand

fortgehen to go away

fortfahren to depart; to continue

fortsetzen to continue (*transitive*)

fragen to ask

sich fragen to wonder

sich freuen to be glad

führen to lead

füllen to fill
funkeln to sparkle
funktionieren to work (*of machine*)
sich fürchten (vor + *dat*) to
 be afraid *or* frightened (of)
geben to give
gebrauchen to use
gefallen (+ *dat*) to please;
 das gefällt mir I like that
gehen to go
gehorchen (+ *dat*) to obey
gehören (+ *dat*) to belong (to)
gelingen (+ *dat*) to succeed
gelten to be worth
genießen to enjoy
genügen to be sufficient
gern haben to like
geschehen to happen
gestatten to permit, allow
glauben (+ *dat*) to believe
glauben an (+ *acc*) to believe in
glühen to glow
gründen to establish
gucken to look
haben to have
halten to keep; to stop; to hold
 sich irren to be mistaken
halten für to consider (as)
handeln: es handelt sich um it is
 a question of
hängen to hang (up)
hassen to hate, loathe
hauen to cut, hew
heben to lift, raise
heimbringen to take home
helfen (+ *dat*) to help
herantreten an (+ *acc*) to approach
herausziehen to pull out
hereinkommen to enter, come in

hereinlassen to admit
herstellen to produce,
 manufacture
herunterlassen to lower
hineingehen (in + *acc*) to enter,
 go in (to)
hinlegen to put down
sich hinsetzen to sit down
hinstellen to put down
hinübergehen to go through;
 to go over
hinweisen to point out
hinweisen auf (+ *acc*) to refer to
hinzufügen to add
hoffen (auf + *acc*) to hope (for)
holen to fetch
horchen to listen
hören to hear
hüten to guard, watch over
interessieren to interest
sich für etw interessieren to be
 interested in sth
kämpfen to fight
kennen to know (*person, place*)
kennen lernen to meet, get to
 know
klagen to complain
klatschen to gossip
klettern to climb
klingeln to ring
klingen to sound
kochen to cook
kommen to come
können to be able (to)
kriegen to get, obtain
sich kümmern (um) to worry
 (about)
küssen to kiss
lassen to allow, let; to leave

laufen to run
leben to live
legen to lay
sich legen to lie down
Leid tun (+ *dat*) to feel sorry for
du tust mir Leid I feel sorry for you
es tut mir Leid I'm sorry
leiden to suffer; **ich kann ihn nicht leiden** I can't stand him
leihen to lend; **sich** (*dat*) **etw leihen** to borrow sth
leiten to guide, lead
lesen to read
lieben to love
liefern to deliver; to supply
liegen to be (situated)
loben to praise
löschen to put out
lösen to buy (*ticket*)
losmachen to unfasten undo, untie
loswerden to get rid of
lügen to lie, tell a lie
machen to do; to make
malen to paint
meinen to think, believe
mieten to hire, rent
mitbringen to bring
mitnehmen to take
mitteilen: jdm etw mitteilen to inform sb of sth
mögen to like
murmeln to murmur
müssen to have to (*must*), be obliged to
nachdenken (über + *acc*) to think (about)
nachsehen to check
nähen to sew

sich nähern (+ *dat*) to approach
nehmen to take
nennen to call, name
sich niederlegen to go to bed, lie down
notieren to note
öffnen to open
organisieren to organize
passen (+ *dat*) to suit, be suitable
passieren to happen
pflegen to take care of
plaudern to chat
pressen to press, squeeze
produzieren to produce
programmieren to program
protestieren to protest
prüfen to examine, check
rasieren to shave
raten (+ *dat*) to advise
räumen to clear away
reden to talk, speak
reinigen to clean, tidy up
reisen to go, travel
retten to save, rescue
riechen (nach) to smell (of)
rufen to call
sich rühren to stir
sagen (+ *dat*) to say (to), tell
säubern to clean
saugen to suck
schaden (+ *dat*) to harm
schallen to sound
schauen (auf + *acc*) to look (at)
scheinen to seem; to shine
schieben to push, shove
schießen to shoot
schlafen to sleep
schlafen gehen to go to bed
schlagen to hit, strike, knock, beat

sich schlagen to fight
(sich) schließen to close, shut
schneiden to cut
schnüren to tie
schreiben to write
schreien to shout, cry
schütteln to shake
schützen (vor + *dat*) to protect (from)
schweigen to be silent
schwören to swear
sehen to see
sein to be
senken to lower
setzen to put (down), place, set
sich setzen to settle, sit (down)
seufzen to sigh
singen to sing
sitzen to sit, be sitting
sollen ought (to)
sorgen für to take care of, look after
sich sorgen (um) to worry (about)
sparen to save
spaßen to joke
spazieren gehen to go for a walk
sprechen to speak
stattfinden to take place
stecken to put, stick
stehen to stand
stehen bleiben to stop (*still*)
steigen to come *or* go up, rise; to climb
stellen to put, place; to ask (*a question*)
sterben to die
stimmen to be right
stoppen to stop (*transitive*)
stören to disturb
stoßen to push, shove

strecken to stretch
streiten to argue, fight
sich streiten to quarrel
stürzen to fall, crash
sich stürzen (in *or* auf + *acc*) to rush *or* dash (into)
suchen to look for, search for
tanzen to dance
teilen to share, divide
teilnehmen (an + *dat*) to attend, be present at, go to, take part (in)
töten to kill
tragen to carry; to wear
träumen to dream
treffen to meet; to strike (*transitive*)
trennen to separate; to divide
treiben to drive; to go in for
trocknen to dry
tun to do
so tun, als ob to pretend (that)
überlegen to consider, reflect
überraschen to surprise
überreden to persuade
übersetzen to translate
(sich) umdrehen to turn round
umgeben sein von to be surrounded with *or* by
umgehen to avoid, bypass
umkehren to turn
umleiten to divert
umwerfen to overturn, knock over
unterbrechen to interrupt
unterhalten to support
(sich) unterhalten (über + *acc*) to converse *or* talk (about); to entertain
sich unterscheiden to differ, be different
unterschreiben to sign

untersuchen to examine
sich verabreden to make an appointment
verbessern to improve
verbieten to forbid, prohibit
verbinden to connect; to bandage
verbringen to pass *or* spend (*time*)
verdecken to hide, cover up
verderben to spoil, ruin
verdienen to deserve
vereinigen to unite
vergessen to forget
sich verhalten to act, behave
verhindern to prevent
verlangen to demand, order
verlassen to leave
verleihen (an + *acc*) to lend (to)
verletzen to harm
verlieren to lose
es vermeiden, etw zu tun to avoid doing sth
vermieten to let, rent
versäumen to miss
(ver)schließen to lock
verschwinden to disappear, vanish
versehen (mit) to provide
versichern (+ *dat*) to convince, assure
versprechen to promise
(sich) verstecken (vor + *dat*) to hide (from)
verstehen to understand;
was verstehen Sie darunter? what do you understand by that?
versuchen to try, taste, sample; to attempt to
verteidigen to defend
verteilen to distribute
verzeihen to pardon, forgive

vollenden to finish
vorbereiten to prepare
vorgeben to pretend
vorschlagen to suggest
(sich) vorstellen to introduce (oneself)
sich (*dat*) **etw vorstellen** to imagine sth
wachen to be awake
wachsen to grow
wagen to dare
wählen to elect; to choose
warten (auf + *acc*) to wait (for)
(sich) waschen to wash
wechseln to exchange; to change (*money*)
wecken to awaken, wake up (*transitive*)
wegnehmen to take off *or* away
sich weigern to refuse
weinen to cry
sich wenden an (+ *acc*) to apply to; to turn (to)
werden to become, grow, turn (out)
werfen to throw
wetten (auf + *acc*) to bet (on)
wiederholen to repeat
wiedersehen to see again
wischen to wipe
wissen to know
wohnen (in + *dat*) to live (in)
wohnen (bei + *dat*) to lodge (with), live (with)
wollen to want (to), wish (to)
sich wundern (über + *acc*) to wonder (at), be astonished (at *or* by)
es wundert mich I am surprised (at it)

das würde mich wundern!
  that would surprise me!
wünschen to wish
zählen to count
zeichnen to draw
zeigen to show, point
zelten to go camping
zerbrechen to break
zerreißen to tear up
zerstören to demolish, destroy
zerstreuen to scatter
ziehen to draw; to pull; to tug

zittern (vor + *dat*) to tremble (with)
zögern to hesitate
zugeben to confess, admit
zuhören (+ *dat*) to listen (to)
zumachen to close, shut (*transitive*)
zunehmen to put on weight
zurückkehren to come back, return
zurückkommen to go *or* come back
zurücksetzen, zurückstellen to
  replace
zweifeln to doubt
zwingen to force, oblige

Have you seen our full German range? Pick a title to fit your learning style.

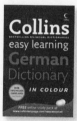

Dictionary
£8.99

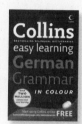

Grammar
£6.99

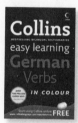

Verbs
£6.99

Words
£6.99

Collins Easy Learning Series

The bestselling language resources, perfect if you're learning German for the first time or brushing up on rusty skills.

Collins Easy Learning Audio Course

This exciting course allows learners to absorb the basics at home or on the move, without the need for thick textbooks and complex grammar.

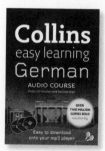